Lecture Notes in Artificial Intelligence   2225
Subseries of Lecture Notes in Computer Science
Edited by J. G. Carbonell and J. Siekmann

Lecture Notes in Computer Science
Edited by G. Goos, J. Hartmanis, and J. van Leeuwen

Springer
Berlin
Heidelberg
New York
Barcelona
Hong Kong
London
Milan
Paris
Tokyo

Naoki Abe Roni Khardon
Thomas Zeugmann (Eds.)

Algorithmic
Learning Theory

12th International Conference, ALT 2001
Washington, DC, USA, November 25-28, 2001
Proceedings

 Springer

Series Editors

Jaime G. Carbonell,Carnegie Mellon University, Pittsburgh, PA, USA
Jörg Siekmann, University of Saarland, Saarbrücken, Germany

Volume Editors

Naoki Abe
IBM, Thomas J. Watson Research Center, Room 33-237
P.O. Box 218, Yorktown, NY 10598, USA
E-mail: nabe@us.ibm.com

Roni Khardon
Tufts University, Dept.of Electrical Engineering and Computer Science
161 College Ave., Medford, MA 02155, USA
E-mail: roni@eecs.tufts.edu

Thomas Zeugmann
Medizinische Universität zu Lübeck, Inst. für Theoretische Informatik
Wallstr. 40, 23560 Lübeck, Germany
E-mail: thomas@tcs.mu-luebeck.de

Cataloging-in-Publication Data applied for

Die Deutsche Bibliothek - CIP-Einheitsaufnahme

Algorithmic learning theory : 12th international conference ; proceedings /
ALT 2001, Washington, DC, USA, November 25 - 28, 2001. Naoki Abe ... (ed.).
Berlin ; Heidelberg ; New York ; Barcelona ; Hong Kong ; London ; Milan ;
Paris ; Tokyo : Springer, 2001
    (Lecture notes in computer science ; Vol. 2225 : Lecture notes in
    artificial intelligence)
    ISBN 3-540-42875-5

CR Subject Classification (1998): I.2.6, I.2.3, F.1, F.2, F.4.1, I.7

ISBN 3-540-42875-5 Springer-Verlag Berlin Heidelberg New York

Springer-Verlag Berlin Heidelberg New York
a member of BertelsmannSpringer Science+Business Media GmbH

http://www.springer.de

© Springer-Verlag Berlin Heidelberg 2001
Printed in Germany

Typesetting: Camera-ready by author, data conversion by PTP Berlin, Stefan Sossna
Printed on acid-free paper   SPIN 10840965   06/3142   5 4 3 2 1 0

Additional Reviewers

Kazuyuki Amano
Jose Luis Balcázar
Asa Ben-Hur
Avrim Blum
Samir Chopra
Nello Cristianini
Philippe Ezequel
Paul Fischer
Ashutosh Garg
Ricard Gavalda
Gunter Grieser
Peter Grunwald
David Guijarro
Ralf Herbrich
Joerg Herrmann
Kouichi Hirata
Michael Houle
Don Hush
Jeff Jackson
Jean-Christophe Janodet
Jaz Kandola
Christopher Kermorvant
Efim Kinber
John Langford

Hugh Mallinson
Hiroshi Mamitsuka
Ron Meir
Tatsuya Motoki
Yasuhito Mukouchi
Jochen Nessel
Kazuhiko Ohno
José Oncina
Krishnan Pillaipakkamnatt
Lenny Pitt
Vasin Punyakanok
Yoshifumi Sakai
Arun Sharma
Frank Stephan
Noriko Sugimoto
Ichiro Tajika
Atsuhiro Takasu
Jun-ichi Takeuchi
Paul Vitanyi
Volodya Vovk
Chris Watkins
Dawn Wilkins
Bob Williamson
Dav Zimak

Table of Contents

New Learning Models

Online Learning

Inductive Inference

Refutable Inductive Inference

Learning Structures and Languages

Editors' Introduction

Learning theory is an active research area with contributions from various fields including artificial intelligence, theoretical computer science, and statistics. The main thrust is an attempt to model learning phenomena in precise ways and study the mathematical properties of these scenarios. In this way one hopes to get a better understanding of the learning scenarios and what is possible or as we call it learnable in each. Of course this goes with a study of algorithms that achieve the required performance. Learning theory aims to define reasonable models of phenomena and find provably successful algorithms within each such model. To complete the picture we also seek impossibility results showing that certain things are not learnable within a particular model, irrespective of the particular learning algorithms or methods being employed.

Unlike computability theory, where we have a single uniform notion of what is computable across multiple models of computation, not all learning models are equivalent. This should not come as a surprise, as the range of learning phenomena found in nature is wide, and the way in which leaning systems are applied in real world engineering problems is varied. Learning models cover this spectrum and vary along various aspects such as parameters characterizing the learning environment, the learning agent, and evaluation criteria. Some of these are: Is there a "teacher"? Is the teacher reliable or not? Is the learner passive or active? Is the learning function required to be computable or efficient (polynomial time)? Is learning done on-line, getting one example at a time, or in batch? Is the learner required to reproduce learned concepts exactly or is it merely required to produce a good approximation? Are the hypotheses output by the learner required to be in a certain representation class or are they free of syntactic constraints? Naturally such variations lead to dramatically different results. Learning theory has been extensively studying these aspects getting a deeper understanding of underlying phenomena and better algorithms for the various problems.

Over the last few years learning theory has had a direct impact on practice in machine learning and its various application areas, with some algorithms driving leading edge systems. To name a few techniques having roots in learning theory and that have been applied to real world problems, there are support vector machines, boosting techniques, on-line learning algorithms, and active learning methods. Each of these techniques has proven extremely effective in the respective application areas of relevance, such as pattern recognition, web and data mining, information extraction, and genomics. Such developments have recently inspired researchers in the field to investigate the relation between theory and practice, by combining theory with experimental validation or applications.

Thus the picture is not uniform, and the field is making progress by exploring new models to capture new problems and phenomena, and studying algorithmic questions within each of these models. It is with this light that the papers in the proceedings should be read. We have collected the papers in subgroups with

N. Abe, R. Khardon, and T. Zeugmann (Eds.): ALT 2001, LNAI 2225, pp. 1–7, 2001.

headings to highlight certain similar aspects either in topic or style but one should keep in mind that often a paper could be classified in more than one category.

The invited lecture for ALT 2001 and DS 2001 by Setsuo Arikawa describes the Discovery Science Project in Japan which aimed to develop new methods for knowledge discovery, to install network environments for knowledge discovery, and to establish Discovery Science as a new area of Computer Science and Artificial Intelligence. Though algorithmic learning theory and machine learning have been integrated into this project, the researchers involved took a much broader perspective. Their work shed new light on many problems studied in learning theory and machine learning and led to a fruitful interaction between the different research groups participating in the project.

In her invited lecture, Dana Angluin presents a comprehensive survey of the state of the art of learning via membership or equivalence queries or both, a field she has initiated (cf.[1]). Major emphasis is put on the number of queries needed to learn a class of concepts. This number is related to various combinatorial characterizations of concept classes such as the teaching dimension, the exclusion dimension, the extended teaching dimension, the fingerprint dimension, the sample exclusion dimension, the well-known Vapnik-Chervonenkis dimension, the abstract identification dimension, and the general dimension. Each of these dimensions emphasises a different view on the learning problem and leads to a better understanding of what facilitates or complicates query learning.

Robot Baby 2001 is presented by Paul R. Cohen *et al.* in his invited lecture. This paper provides strong evidence that meaningful representations are learnable by programs. Different notions of meaning are discussed, and special emphasis is put on a functional notion of meaning being appropriate for programs to learn. Several interesting algorithms are provided and experimental results of their application are surveyed. This work raises an interesting challenge of deriving theoretical results capturing aspects of practical relevance thus tightening the relation between theory and practice.

Papers in the first section deal with complexity aspects of learning. Yang studies learnability within the statistical query (SQ) model introduced by Kearns [10]. This model captures one natural way to obtain noise robustness when examples are drawn identically and independently distributed (i.i.d.) from a fixed but unknown distribution, as in the well known PAC model [15]. In this case, if the algorithm does not rely directly on specific examples but rather on measurable statistical properties of examples then it is guaranteed to be robust to classification noise [10]. Yang studies learnability when the class of concepts in question includes highly correlated concepts, showing a lower bound in terms of the desired performance accuracy. This yields non-learnability results in the SQ model for a certain class of concepts which are contrasted with the PAC learnability of the same class. This result provides an interesting example for separating these learning models, since except for classes of parity functions practically all known PAC learnable classes have been shown to be SQ learnable as well.

The name boosting captures a class of algorithms that use "weak" learners (which provide good but imperfect hypotheses) to build more accurate hypotheses [8]. The idea is to combine several runs of the weak learner in the process and techniques vary in the way this is done. It was recently observed [11,12] that the well known decision tree learning algorithms [14] can be viewed as boosting algorithms. Hatano improves these results by providing a tighter analysis of decision tree learning as boosting when the trees include splits with more than two branches.

It is well known [3,4] that an algorithm which uses hypotheses of bounded capacity and finds a hypothesis consistent with training data learns the concept class in question in the PAC learning model. Similar results hold for algorithms that minimize the number of inconsistencies with training data. Various negative results for neural networks showing that the above is infeasile have been derived. Šíma continues this line by showing that for the sigmoid activation function even approximating the minimum training error is intractable. This is important as the popular backpropagation algorithm uses a gradient method to try to optimize exactly this function.

Support vector machines (SVM) [5,6] use a neural model with a single neuron and threshold activation function but combine two aspects to overcome learning difficulties with neural models. First, the input domain is implicitly enhanced to include a large number of possibly useful features. Second, the algorithm uses optimization techniques to find a threshold function of "maximum margin" providing robustness, since examples are not close to the decision surface of the hyperplane. The first aspect is done using the so called kernel functions which are used directly in the optimization procedure so that the enhanced features are not produced explicitly. Sadohara presents a kernel appropriate for learning over Boolean domains. Using this kernel is equivalent to learning a threshold element where features are all conjunctions of the basic feature set. This is highly relevant to the problem of learning DNF expressions; a question which has received considerable attention in learning theory. The paper also present experiments demonstrating that SVM using this kernel performs well and compares favorably with other systems on Boolean data.

Balcázar *et al.* propose a sampling based algorithm for solving the quadratic optimization problem involved in SVM (albeit not to the kernel construction). The intention is to improve complexity in cases where the number of examples is large. The basic idea is to use random sub-samples from the data set where the distribution is carefully controlled to iteratively improve the solution so that convergence is guaranteed in a small number of rounds. Algorithms are proposed both for the separable case and the "noisy" non-separable case, and practical complexity aspects of the methods are developed.

The next section introduces models which try to capture new aspect of learning phenomena and study the complexity of learning within these. Garg and Roth introduce the notion of coherence constraint. The idea is that several concepts exist over the instance space and they are correlated. This correlation is captured by a coherency constraint which effectively implies that certain inputs (on which the constraint is violated) are not possible. The paper shows that the existence of such constraints implies reduced learning complexity in several scenarios. Experiments illustrate that this indeed happens in practice as well.

Kwek introduces a model where several concepts are learned simultaneously and where some concepts may depend on others. Since intermediate concepts are used as features in other concept descriptions the overall descriptional power is much higher. Nevertheless the paper shows that learnability of the representation class used for each concept implies learnability of all concepts in several models e.g. the PAC model. When the learner is active, that is when membership queries are allowed, this does not hold.

Dooly *et al.* study the so-called multiple instance learning problem. In this problem, motivated by molecular drug activity applications, each example is described as a set of configurations one of which is responsible for the observed activity or label (cf. [7]). The paper studies the case where the "label" is real valued giving a quantitative rather than binary measure of the activity. Negative results on learning from examples are presented and a new model of active learning, allowing membership or value queries is shown to allow learnability.

On-line prediction games provide a model for evaluating learners or prediction strategies under very general conditions [16]. In this framework an iterative game is played where in each step the learner makes a prediction, observes the true value and suffers a loss based on these two values and a fixed loss function. The prediction complexity of a sequence gives a lower bound on the loss of any prediction algorithm for the sequence and can thus be seen as another way to characterize the inherent complexity of strings. The paper by Kalnishkan *et al.* derives results on the average complexity when the sequence is i.i.d. Bernoulli and relates this to the information complexity of the sequence. As a result it is shown that the Kolmogorov complexity does not coincide with the prediction complexity for the binary game. The paper by Vyugin and V'yugin studies the relation between Kolmogorov and predictive complexity. In particular, a gap is established which depends logarithmically on the length of the strings.

Research in inductive inference follows seminal work by Gold [9] who introduced the model of learning in the limit. Here finite complexity rather than polynomial complexity defines the notion of feasibility. For concept learning, Gold defined two learning models, i.e., *Text* where the learner sees only positive examples of the underlying concept and *Informant* where both positive and negative examples are seen. Jain and Stephan study several intermediate models based on the strategy of information presentation where the learner switches from asking to see positive to negative examples or vice versa. A hierarchy between the notions is established, and a more refined hierarchy is shown in case that the number of times the learner switches example types is limited.

In a second paper Jain and Stephan study the problem of learning to separate pairs of disjoint sets which do not necessarily cover the instance space. Several restrictions on the learner are studied within this framework, for example: conservative learners who only abandon hypotheses which were contradicted by data, and set-driven learners whose hypotheses do exclusively depend on the range of the input. The effect of these restrictions and their interaction is extensively studied. The two notions mentioned here are not comparable if the learner converges on all data sequences.

Jain *et al.* study a related model of learning union of languages. Two main variants are discussed where the learner either needs to identify the union or is required to identify the element languages composed in the union. Several results relating the strength of the models are derived establishing hierarchies when the number of languages in the union is increased, as well as identifying complete problems under appropriate reductions for these classes.

Zilles studies a notion of meta-learning where a single learning algorithm can learn several concept classes by being given an index of the class as a parameter. Two scenarios are discussed where the learner either uses a single representation for hypotheses in all classes or can change the representation with the class. The paper studies the effect of restricting the learner, for example to be conservative as described above, on the learnable classes. Various separation results are given using finite concept classes to separate the models.

The next group of papers also deals with inductive inference. The common aspect studied by all these papers is the notion of refutation originally introduced in [13], which was in part motivated by the design of automatic discovery systems, in which the choice of the hypothesis class is a critical parameter. In their paper [13], the following scenario is considered. The learner is given a hypothesis space of uniformly recursive concepts in advance. Whenever the target concept can be correctly described by a member of this hypothesis space, then the learner has to identify it in the limit. If, however, the learner is fed data of a target concept that has no correct description within the hypothesis space given, then the learner has to refute the whole hypothesis space after a finite amount of time by outputting a special refutation symbol and stopping the learning process. Thus, within the model of learning refutably, the learner either identifies a target concept or itself indicates its inability to do so.

Mukouchi and Sato extend the original approach by relaxing the correctness criterion and by allowing noisy examples. In their new model, the learner must succeed to infer a target concept provided it has a (weak) k-neighbor in the hypothesis space; otherwise it has again to refute the hypothesis space. Here a (weak) k-neighbor is defined in terms of a distance over strings.

Jain *et al.* study several variations of learning refutably. Now, the target concepts are drawn from the set of all recursive functions and an acceptable programming system is given as hypothesis space. Thus, it is no longer appropriate to refute the whole hypothesis space, since it contains a correct description for every target. Nevertheless, the learner may not be able to solve its learning task. This can be indicated by either outputting the refuting symbol and stopping the learning process, or by converging to the refutation symbol, or by outputting the refutation symbol infinitely often. All these models of learning refutably are studied, related to one another as well as their combination with other, previously studied learning models within the setting of inductive inference.

Last but not least within this group of papers, Merkle and Stephan extend the original notion of learning with refutation from positive data by introducing the notion of refutation in the limit and by considerably extending the notion of *Text*. Now, the data-sequences are sequences of first-order sentences describing the target. Several new and interesting hierarchies are then established.

The papers in the last section study learnability of formal languages and structured data. Arimura *et al.* consider the problem of identifying tree patterns in marked data. The paper extends previous work by allowing gaps in the tree pattern, that is, internal sub-trees may be skipped when matching a tree pattern to an example tree. The paper shows that the task is solvable in polynomial time in an active learning setting where the learner can ask queries.

Elementary formal systems are similar to logic programs operating on strings and having a distinguished unary predicate. The true atoms for this predicate define a formal language. Lange *et al.* extend work on learnability [2] of such systems to allow negation in the logic program. The extension is done along the lines of stratified logic programs. Learnability is studied and compared to the case before the extension. In Gold's paradigm some positive results do not transfer to the extended systems, but in the PAC model the main known positive result is shown to hold for the extended systems.

The problem of learning regular languages has been extensively studied with several representation schemes. Dennis *et al.* study learnability of regular languages using a non-deterministic representation based on residuals — completion languages for prefixes of words in the language. While the representation is shown not to be polynomially learnable, parameters of the representation are studied empirically and these suggest a new learning algorithm with desirable properties. Experiments show that the algorithm compares favorably with other systems.

The class of Büchi automata defines languages over infinite strings. When modeling learnability of such languages one is faced with the question of examples of infinite size. The paper by de la Higuera and Janodet introduces a model of learning such languages from finite prefixes of examples. While the complete class is not learnable a sub-class is identified and shown learnable in the limit with polynomial update on each example.

As the above descriptions of papers demonstrate, the range of learning problems and issues addressed by the papers in this volume is rich and varied. While we have partitioned the papers mainly according to the techniques used, they could have been classified according to the classes of objects that are being learned. These include representations of formal languages, recursive functions, Boolean concepts over Boolean domains, real valued functions, neural networks, and kernel based SVM. Several of the papers also combine the theoretical study with an empirical investigation or validation of new ideas, and it would also be beneficial to classify them according to the types of relevant application areas.

While the papers in this volume will surely not give an exhaustive list of problems addressed and types of theory developed in learning theory in general, it is our hope that they will give an idea of where the field stands currently and where it may be going in the future.

References

1. Dana Angluin. Queries and concept learning. *Machine Learning*, 2(4):319–342, 1988.
2. S. Arikawa, T. Shinohara, A. Yamamoto. Elementary formal systems as a unifying framework for language learning. In *Proc. Second Annual Workshop on Computational Learning Theory*, pages 312–327, Morgan Kaufmann, San Mateo, CA, 1989.
3. A. Blumer, A. Ehrenfeucht, D. Haussler, and M. K. Warmuth. Occam's razor. *Inform. Proc. Lett.*, 24:377–380, 1987.
4. A. Blumer, A. Ehrenfeucht, D. Haussler, and M. K. Warmuth. Learnability and the Vapnik-Chervonenkis dimension. *Journal of the ACM*, 36(4):929–965, 1989.
5. C. Cortes and V. N. Vapnik. Support-vector Networks, *Machine Learning* 20:273–297, 1995.
6. Nello Cristianini and John Shawe-Taylor. *An Introduction to Support Vector Machines and Other Kernel-Based Learning Methods*. Cambridge University Press, Cambridge, U.K., 2000.
7. T. G. Dietterich, R. H. Lathrop, and T. Lozano-Pérez. Solving the multiple-instance problem with axis-parallel rectangles. *Artificial Intelligence*, 89(1-2):31–71, 1997.
8. Y. Freund and R. Schapire. A decision-theoretic generalization of on-line learning and an application to boosting. *Journal of Computer and System Sciences*, 55(1):119–139, 1997.
9. E Mark Gold. Language identification in the limit. *Information and Control*, 10:447–474, 1967.
10. Michael Kearns. *Efficient noise-tolerant learning from statistical queries.* In *Journal of the ACM*, 45(6):983–1006, 1998.
11. Michael Kearns and Yishay Mansour. On the boosting ability of top-down decision tree learning algorithms. *Journal of Computer and System Sciences*, 58(1):109–128, 1999.
12. Yishay Mansour and David McAllester. Boosting using branching programs. In *Proc. 13th Annual Conference on Computational Learning Theory*, pages 220–224. Morgan Kaufmann, San Francisco, 2000.
13. Yasuhito Mukouchi and Setsuo Arikawa. Towards a mathematical theory of machine discovery from facts. *Theoretical Computer Science*, 137(1):53–84, 1995.
14. J. R. Quinlan. Induction of decision trees. *Machine Learning*, 1:81–106, 1986.
15. Leslie G. Valiant. A theory of the learnable. *Communications of the ACM*, 27 (11):1134–1142, 1984.
16. V. Vovk. A game of prediction with expert advice. *Journal of Computer and System Sciences*, 36:153–173, 1998.

Yorktown
Medford
Lübeck
September 2001

Naoki Abe
Roni Khardon
Thomas Zeugmann

The Discovery Science Project in Japan

Setsuo Arikawa

Department of Informatics
Kyushu University
Fukuoka 812-8581, Japan
arikawa@i.kyushu-u.ac.jp

Abstract. The Discovery Science project in Japan in which more than sixty scientists participated was a three-year project sponsored by Grant-in-Aid for Scientific Research on Priority Area from the Ministry of Education, Culture, Sports, Science and Technology (MEXT) of Japan. This project mainly aimed to (1) develop new methods for knowledge discovery, (2) install network environments for knowledge discovery, and (3) establish Discovery Science as a new area of Computer Science / Artificial Intelligence Study.

In order to attain these aims we set up five groups for studying the following research areas:

(A) Logic for/of Knowledge Discovery
(B) Knowledge Discovery by Inference/Reasoning
(C) Knowledge Discovery Based on Computational Learning Theory
(D) Knowledge Discovery in Huge Database and Data Mining
(E) Knowledge Discovery in Network Environments

These research areas and related topics can be regarded as a preliminary definition of Discovery Science by enumeration. Thus Discovery Science ranges over philosophy, logic, reasoning, computational learning and system developments.

In addition to these five research groups we organized a steering group for planning, adjustment and evaluation of the project. The steering group, chaired by the principal investigator of the project, consists of leaders of the five research groups and their subgroups as well as advisors from the outside of the project. We invited three scientists to consider the Discovery Science overlooking the above five research areas from viewpoints of knowledge science, natural language processing, and image processing, respectively.

The group A studied discovery from a very broad perspective, taking into account of historical and social aspects of discovery, and computational and logical aspects of discovery. The group B focused on the role of inference/reasoning in knowledge discovery, and obtained many results on both theory and practice on statistical abduction, inductive logic programming and inductive inference. The group C aimed to propose and develop computational models and methodologies for knowledge discovery mainly based on computational learning theory. This group obtained some deep theoretical results on boosting of learning algorithms and the minimax strategy for Gaussian density estimation, and also

N. Abe, R. Khardon, and T. Zeugmann (Eds.): ALT 2001, LNAI 2225, pp. 9–11, 2001.

methodologies specialized to concrete problems such as algorithm for finding best subsequence patterns, biological sequence compression algorithm, text categorization, and MDL-based compression. The group D aimed to create computational strategy for speeding up the discovery process in total. For this purpose, the group D was organized with researchers working in scientific domains and researchers from computer science so that real issues in the discovery process can be exposed out and practical computational techniques can be devised and tested for solving these real issues. This group handled many kinds of data: data from national projects such as genomic data and satellite observations, data generated from laboratory experiments, data collected from personal interests such as literature and medical records, data collected in business and marketing areas, and data for proving the efficiency of algorithms such as UCI repository. So many theoretical and practical results were obtained on such a variety of data. The group E aimed to develop a unified media system for knowledge discovery and network agents for knowledge discovery. This group obtained practical results on a new virtual materialization of DB records and scientific computations that help scientists to make a scientific discovery, a convenient visualization interface that treats web data, and an efficient algorithm that extracts important information from semi-structured data in the web space.

This lecture describes an outline of our project and the main results as well as how the project was prepared. We have published and are publishing special issues on our project from several journals [5],[6],[7],[8],[9],[10]. As an activity of the project we organized and sponsored Discovery Science Conference for three years where many papers were presented by our members [2],[3],[4]. We also published annual progress reports [1], which were distributed at the DS conferences. We are publishing the final technical report as an LNAI [11].

References

1. S. Arikawa, M. Sato, T. Sato, A. Maruoka, S. Miyano, and Y. Kanada. Discovery Science Progress Report No.1 (1998), No.2 (1999), No.3 (2000). *Department of Informatics, Kyushu University.*
2. S. Arikawa, and H. Motoda. Discovery Science. *LNAI, Springer* 1532, 1998.
3. S. Arikawa, and K. Furukawa. Discovery Science. *LNAI, Springer* 1721, 1999.
4. S. Arikawa, and S. Morishita. Discovery Science. *LNAI, Springer* 1967, 2000.
5. H. Motoda, and S. Arikawa (Eds.) Special Feature on Discovery Science. *New Generation Computing,* 18(1): 13–86, 2000.
6. S. Miyano (Ed.) Special Issue on Surveys on Discovery Science. *IEICE Transactions on Information and Systems,* E83-D(1): 1–70, 2000.
7. H. Motoda (Ed.) Special Issue on Discovery Science. *Journal of Japanese Society for Artificial Intelligence,* 15(4):592–702, 2000.
8. S. Morishita, and S. Miyano (Eds.) Discovery Science and Data Mining (in Japanese). *bit special volume , Kyoritsu Shuppan,* 2000.
9. S. Arikawa, M. Sato, T. Sato, A. Maruoka, S. Miyano, and Y. Kanada. The Discovery Science Project. *Journal of Japanese Society for Artificial Intelligence,* 15(4) 595–607, 2000.

10. S. Arikawa, H. Motoda, K. Furukawa, and S. Morishita (Eds.) Theoretical Aspects of Discovery Science. *Theoretical Computer Science* (to appear)
11. S. Arikawa, and A. Shinohara (Eds.) Progresses in Discovery Science. *LNAI, Springer* (2001, to appear)

Queries Revisited

Dana Angluin

Computer Science Department
Yale University
P. O. Box 208285
New Haven, CT 06520-8285
angluin@cs.yale.edu

Abstract. We begin with a brief tutorial on the problem of learning a finite concept class over a finite domain using membership queries and/or equivalence queries. We then sketch general results on the number of queries needed to learn a class of concepts, focusing on the various notions of combinatorial dimension that have been employed, including the teaching dimension, the exclusion dimension, the extended teaching dimension, the fingerprint dimension, the sample exclusion dimension, the Vapnik-Chervonenkis dimension, the abstract identification dimension, and the general dimension.

1 Introduction

Formal models of learning reflect a variety of differences in tasks, sources of information, prior knowledge and capabilities of the learner, and criteria of successful performance. In the model of exact identification with queries [1], the task is to identify an unknown concept drawn from a known concept class using queries to gather information about the unknown concept. The two most studied types of queries are membership queries and equivalence queries. In a membership query, the learner asks if a particular domain element is included in the unknown concept or not. In an equivalence query, the learner proposes a particular concept, and is told either that the proposed concept is the same as the unknown concept, or is given a counterexample, that is, a domain element that is classified differently by the proposed concept and the unknown concept. If there are several possible counterexamples, the choice of which one to present is generally assumed to be made adversarially.

Researchers have invented a wonderful variety of ingenious and beautiful polynomial-time learning algorithms that use queries to achieve exact identification of different classes of concepts, as well as important modifications of the basic model to incorporate more realism, e.g., background knowledge and errors. However, this survey will focus on the question of how many queries are needed to learn different classes of concepts, ignoring other computational costs. The analogous question in the PAC model [19] is how many examples are needed to learn different classes of concepts. In the case of the PAC model, bounds in terms of a combinatorial property of the concept class called the Vapnik-Chervonenkis

N. Abe, R. Khardon, and T. Zeugmann (Eds.): ALT 2001, LNAI 2225, pp. 12–31, 2001.
© Springer-Verlag Berlin Heidelberg 2001

dimension early provided a satisfying answer [7,8]. In the case of learning with queries, the development has been both more gradual and more variegated.

2 Preliminaries

The *domain* X is a nonempty finite set. A *concept* is any subset of X, and a *concept class* is any nonempty set of concepts. We ignore the issues of how concepts and domain elements are represented. We distinguish certain useful concept classes: the class 2^X of all subsets of X, and the class $S(X)$ of singleton subsets of X. We also define $S^+(X)$, the class $S(X)$ together with the empty set.

One way to visualize a domain X and a concept class C is as a binary matrix whose rows are indexed by the concepts, say $c_1, c_2, \ldots, c_M$, and whose columns are indexed by the elements of X, say, $x_1, x_2, \ldots, x_N$, and whose (i, j) entry is 1 if $x_j \in c_i$ and 0 otherwise. An example is given in Figure 1.

	x_1	x_2	x_3
c_1	1	0	1
c_2	0	0	1
c_3	1	1	0
c_4	1	0	0

Fig. 1. Matrix representation of the concept class $C_0 = \{c_1, c_2, c_3, c_4\}$, where $c_1 = \{x_1, x_3\}$, $c_2 = \{x_3\}$, $c_3 = \{x_1, x_2\}$, $c_4 = \{x_1\}$

The rows (representing concepts) are all distinct, though the columns need not be. For our purposes the columns (representing domain elements) may also be assumed to be distinct, because there is no point in distinguishing between elements x and x' that are contained in exactly the same set of concepts. Thus, a domain and concept class can be represented simply as a finite binary relation whose rows are distinct and whose columns are distinct. This makes clear the symmetry of the roles of the domain and the concept class.

For any concept $c \subseteq X$ we define two basic types of queries with respect to c. In a *membership query*, the input is an element $x \in X$, and the output is 1 if $x \in c$ and 0 if $x \notin c$. In an *equivalence query*, the input is a concept $c' \subseteq X$, and the output is either "yes," if $c' = c$, or an element x in the symmetric difference of c and c', if $c' \neq c$. Such an element x is a *counterexample*. The choice of a counterexample is nondeterministic.

A learning problem is specified by giving the domain X, the class of concepts C, and the permitted types of queries. The task of a learning algorithm is to identify an unknown concept c drawn from C using the permitted types of queries. Because we ignore computational resources other than the number of queries, we use decision trees to model learning algorithms.

A *learning algorithm over* X is a finite rooted tree that may have two types of internal nodes. A *membership query node* is labelled by an element $x \in X$ and has two outgoing edges, labelled by 0 and 1. An *equivalence query node* is labelled by a concept $c \subseteq X$ and has $|X| + 1$ outgoing edges, labelled by "yes" and the elements of X. The leaf nodes are unlabelled. An example of a learning algorithm T_0 that uses only membership queries is given in Figure 2.

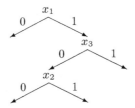

Fig. 2. MQ-algorithm T_0 over domain $X = \{x_1, x_2, x_3\}$

Given a learning algorithm T and a concept class C, we recursively define the *evaluation of T on C* as follows. Each node of T will be assigned the subset of C consistent with the answers to queries along the path from the root to that node.

The root node is assigned C itself. Suppose an internal node v has been assigned the subset C' of C. If v is a membership query labelled by x, then the 0-child of v is assigned the subset of C' consisting of concepts c such that $x \notin c$, and the 1-child of v is assigned the subset of C' consisting of concepts c such that $x \in c$. In this case, the set C' is partitioned between the two children of v. If v is an equivalence query labelled by c', then for each $x \in X$, the x-child of v is assigned the subset of C' consisting of concepts c such that x is in the symmetric difference of c' and c. The "yes"-child of v is assigned the singleton $\{c'\}$ if $c' \in C'$, otherwise it is assigned the empty set. In this case, we do not necessarily have a partition; a concept in C' may be assigned to several of the children of v. The assignment produced by evaluation of the tree T_0 on the concept class C_0 is shown in Figure 2.

A learning algorithm T is *successful* for a class of concepts C if in the evaluation of T on C, there is no leaf ℓ of T such that two distinct concepts $c, c' \in C$ are assigned to ℓ. This implies that T has at least $|C|$ leaves, because in the evaluation of T on C each element of C is assigned to at least one leaf, and no two elements of C are assigned to the same leaf of T. It also implies that the decision tree T may be used to identify an unknown concept $c \in C$ by asking queries starting with the root and following the edges corresponding to the answers,

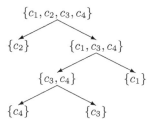

Fig. 3. Assignment produced by evaluation of T_0 from Figure 2 on C_0

until a leaf is reached, at which point exactly one concept $c \in C$ is consistent with the answers received.

Let T be a learning algorithm over X. The *depth of T*, denoted $d(T)$ is the maximum number of edges in any path from the root to a leaf of T. Let $c \subseteq X$ be any concept. The *depth of c in T*, denoted $d(c, T)$, is the maximum number of edges in a path from the root to any leaf assigned c in the evaluation of T on the class $\{c\}$. This is the worst-case number of queries used by the algorithm T in identifying c. Figure 2 shows that T_0 is successful for C_0, and $d(c_4, T_0) = 3$.

3   Membership Queries Only

A *MQ-algorithm* uses only membership queries. The partition property of membership queries implies that every concept is assigned to just one leaf of a MQ-algorithm. If a MQ-algorithm T is successful for a concept class C, then

$$\log |C| \leq d(T), \tag{1}$$

because T is a binary tree with at least $|C|$ leaves.

Let $T_{MQ}(C)$ denote the set of MQ-algorithms T that are successful for C, and have no leaf assigned $\emptyset$ in the evaluation of C. To see that $T_{MQ}(C)$ is nonempty, consider the *exhaustive MQ-algorithm* that systematically queries every element of X in turn. Certainly, no two concepts are assigned to the same leaf, although some leaves may be assigned $\emptyset$. If so, redundant queries may be pruned until every leaf is assigned exactly one concept from C. This MQ-algorithm is successful for every concept class over X. Its depth is at most $|X|$.

Define the *MQ-cost* of a class C of concepts over X, denoted $\#\mathrm{MQ}(C)$, as

$$\#\mathrm{MQ}(C) = \min_{T \in T_{MQ}(C)} \max_{c \in C} d(c, T). \tag{2}$$

Then

$$\log |C| \leq \#\mathrm{MQ}(C) \leq |X|, \tag{3}$$

because any MQ-algorithm successful on C has depth at least $\log |C|$, and the exhaustive MQ-algorithm has depth $|X|$. For the class 2^X, the upper and lower bounds are equal. MQ-algorithms are equivalent to the mistake trees of Littlestone [15].

4   Equivalence Queries Only

Consider the learning algorithm T_1, which uses only equivalence queries over X, presented in Figure 4. The evaluation of T_1 on the concept class C_0 is presented in Figure 5.

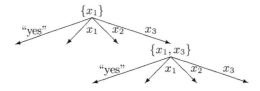

Fig. 4. Equivalence query algorithm T_1

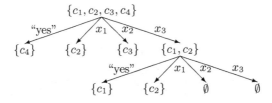

Fig. 5. Evaluation of T_1 on C_0

The algorithm T_1 is successful for C_0, because no two concepts from C_0 are assigned to the same leaf of T_1. The concept c_2 is assigned to two different leaves of T_1, illustrating the non-partition property of equivalence queries.

Given a concept class C, a *proper equivalence query* with respect to C is an equivalence query that uses an element $c \in C$. We use the notation EQ for equivalence queries proper with respect to a class C, and XEQ for *extended equivalence queries*, which are unrestricted. A useful generalization allows equivalence queries from a hypothesis class H containing C, but for simplicity we do not pursue that option. The equivalence queries in T_1 involve only concepts that are elements of C_0, namely $c_4 = \{x_3\}$ and $c_1 = \{x_1, x_3\}$. Consequently, we say that T_1 is an *EQ-algorithm for C_0*.

Given a concept class C, let $T_{EQ}(C)$ denote the set of EQ-algorithms successful for C, and let $T_{XEQ}(C)$ denote the set of XEQ-algorithms successful for C. Clearly, $T_{EQ}(C) \subseteq T_{XEQ}(C)$. To see that $T_{EQ}(C)$ is nonempty, consider the *exhaustive EQ-algorithm for C*, which consists of making an equivalence query with every element of C, except one, in some order. This gives an EQ-algorithm of depth $|C| - 1$ that is successful for C.

Define

$$\#\text{EQ}(C) = \min_{T \in T_{EQ}(C)} \max_{c \in C} d(c, T), \tag{4}$$

and

$$\#\text{XEQ}(C) = \min_{T \in T_{XEQ}(C)} \max_{c \in C} d(c, T). \tag{5}$$

For every concept class C,

$$\#\text{XEQ}(C) \leq \#\text{EQ}(C) \leq |C| - 1. \tag{6}$$

For the class of singletons, $S(X)$, a simple adversary argument shows that $\#\text{EQ}(S(X)) = |X| - 1$, attaining the upper bound above. For the same class, a single XEQ with the empty set discloses the identity of the target concept, therefore, $\#\text{XEQ}(S(X)) = 1$.

5   Membership and Equivalence Queries

Algorithms may involve both membership and equivalence queries. We distinguish MQ&EQ-algorithms, in which all the equivalence queries are proper for the concept class under consideration, from MQ&XEQ-algorithms, in which there is no restriction on the equivalence queries. Figure 6 shows T_2, a MQ&EQ-algorithm that is successful for the class C_0.

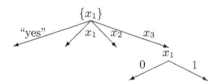

Fig. 6. MQ&EQ-algorithm T_2 for the concept class C_0

Let $T_{MQ\&EQ}(C)$ denote the set of MQ&EQ-algorithms successful for the concept class C. Define

$$\#\text{MQ\&EQ}(C) = \min_{T \in T_{MQ\&EQ}(C)} \max_{c \in C} d(c, T). \tag{7}$$

For any concept class C, because MQ&EQ-algorithms have both types of queries available, we have the following inequalities.

$$\#\text{MQ\&EQ}(C) \leq \#\text{MQ}(C), \tag{8}$$

and

$$\#\mathrm{MQ\&EQ}(C) \leq \#\mathrm{EQ}(C). \tag{9}$$

For the concept class C, let $T_{MQ\&XEQ}(C)$ denote the set of MQ&XEQ-algorithms successful for C. Define

$$\#\mathrm{MQ\&XEQ}(C) = \min_{T \in T_{MQ\&XEQ}(C)} \max_{c \in C} d(c, T). \tag{10}$$

Clearly,

$$\#\mathrm{MQ\&XEQ}(C) \leq \#\mathrm{MQ\&EQ}(C). \tag{11}$$

6   XEQ's, Majority Vote, and Halving

The first query in the algorithm T_1 is very productive, in the sense that no child of the root is assigned more than half the concepts in C_0. The existence of such a productive query is fortuitous in the case of EQ's, but is guaranteed in the case of XEQ's. In particular, for any class C of concepts over X, we define the *majority vote of* C, denoted $c_m(C)$, as follows.

$$(\forall x \in X)[x \in c_m(C) \leftrightarrow |\{c' \in C : x \in c'\}| > |C|/2]. \tag{12}$$

That is, an element x is placed in $c_m(C)$ if and only if more than half the concepts in C contain x. Thus, any counterexample to the majority vote concept eliminates at least half the possible concepts. The majority vote concept for C_0 is $\{x_1\} = c_4$.

The *halving algorithm for* C may be described as follows. Starting with the root, construct the tree of XEQ's and the evaluation of the tree on C concurrently. If there is a leaf assigned C' and C' has cardinality more than 1, then extend the tree and its evaluation on C by replacing the leaf with an XEQ labelled by the majority vote concept, $c_m(C')$. Because the set of concepts assigned to a node can be no more than half of the concepts assigned its parent, no path in the tree can contain more than $\lfloor \log |C| \rfloor$ XEQ's. Thus, for any concept class C,

$$\#\mathrm{XEQ}(C) \leq \lfloor \log |C| \rfloor. \tag{13}$$

The halving algorithm is good, but not necessarily optimal [15,16].

7   An Optimal XEQ-Algorithm

Littlestone [15] defines the *standard optimal algorithm*, which achieves an XEQ-algorithm of depth $\#\mathrm{XEQ}(C)$ for any concept class C. He proves the non-obvious result that

$$\#\mathrm{XEQ}(C) = \max_{T \in T_{MQ}(C)} \min_{c \in C} d(c, T). \tag{14}$$

That is, the optimal number of XEQ's to learn a class C is the largest d such that there is a MQ-algorithm successful for C in which the depth of each leaf is at least d.

Maass and Turán [16] use this result to show that

$$\#\mathrm{XEQ}(C)/\log(\#\mathrm{XEQ}(C)+1) \leq \#\mathrm{MQ\&XEQ}(C). \tag{15}$$

This shows that the addition of MQ's cannot produce too much of an improvement over XEQ's alone.

To prove this, let $d = \#\mathrm{XEQ}(C)$ and consider a MQ-algorithm T successful for C such that every leaf is at depth at least d. Let V denote the set of nodes v at depth d in T such that a concept $c \in C$ assigned to a descendant of v is consistent with the all the replies to queries so far. Initially, V contains 2^d nodes.

An adversary answers MQ's and XEQ's so as to preserve at least a fraction $1/(d+1)$ of V as follows. For a membership query with element x, if at least half the current elements would be preserved by the answer 1, then answer 1, else answer 0. For an equivalence query with the concept c' (not necessarily in C), consider the node v at depth d in T that c' is assigned to. If we consider the d nodes that are siblings of nodes along the path from the root to v, at least one of them, say v' must account for a fraction of at least $1/(d+1)$ of the current elements of V. If the label on the parent of v' is x, then answer the equivalence query with x. Thus, after j queries, there are at least $2^d/(d+1)^j$ elements left in V. Thus, the adversary forces at least $d/\log(d+1)$ queries.

8   Dimensions of Exact Learning

In this section we consider some of the dimensions introduced to bound the cost of learning a concept class with various combinations of queries. For some of these we have suggested different names, to try to bring out the relationships between these definitions.

8.1   The Teaching Dimension

Given a concept class C and a concept $c \in C$, a *teaching set* for c with respect to C is a set $S \subseteq X$ such that no other concept in C classifies all the examples in S the same way c does. For example, $\{x_1, x_3\}$ is a teaching set for the concept c_1 with respect to C_0 because no other concept in C_0 contains both elements. Also, $\{x_1\}$ is a teaching set for the concept c_2 with respect to C_0 because every other concept in C_0 contains x_1. If a learner is presented with an unknown concept from C, by making membership queries for each of the elements in a teaching set for c, the learner can verify whether or not the unknown concept is c.

The *teaching dimension* of a concept class C, denoted $\mathrm{TD}(C)$, is the maximum over all $c \in C$ of the minimum size of a teaching set for c with respect to C [10,18]. It is the worst case number of examples a teacher might have to present to a learner of a concept $c \in C$ to eliminate all other possible concepts in C.

Examples. The teaching dimension of C_0 is 2. The teaching dimension of $S(X)$, the set of singletons over X, is 1 because each set contains an element unique to that set. However, the teaching dimension of $S^+(X)$, the singletons together with the empty set, is $|X|$, because the only teaching set for the empty set in this situation is X itself.

In terms of MQ-algorithms, we have

$$\text{TD}(C) = \max_{c \in C} \min_{T \in T_{MQ}(C)} d(c, T). \tag{16}$$

This is true because the labels on any path from the root to a leaf assigned c in a MQ-algorithm successful for C constitute a teaching set for c with respect to C – any other concept in C must disagree with c on at least one of them, or it would have been assigned to the same leaf as c. Conversely, given a teaching set S for c with respect to C, we can construct a MQ-algorithm that asks queries for those elements first, stopping if the answers are those for c, and continuing exhaustively otherwise. This will produce a MQ-algorithm successful for C in which c is assigned to a leaf at depth $|S|$. Thus the minimization finds the size of the smallest teaching set for a given c, and this is maximized over $c \in C$.

Note that the max and min operations are exchanged in the two equations (2) and (16), and therefore by the properties of max and min,

$$\text{TD}(C) \leq \#\text{MQ}(C). \tag{17}$$

(Note that (2), (14) and (16) involve three out of the four possible combinations of max, min, $c \in C$, and $T \in T_{MQ}(C)$.)

8.2   The Exclusion Dimension

The teaching dimension puts a lower bound on the number of examples a teacher may need to convince a skeptical student of the identity of a concept in C. What about concepts not in C? For a concept $c' \notin C$, how many examples does it take to prove that the concept is not in C? For technical reasons, we consider a slightly different notion, namely, the number of examples to reduce to at most one the set of concepts in C that agree with c' on the examples.

If C is a class of concepts and c' an arbitrary concept, then a *specifying set* for c' with respect to C is a set S of examples such that at most one concept $c \in C$ agrees with the classification of c' for all the elements of S. If $c' \in C$, then a specifying set for c' with respect to C is just a teaching set for c' with respect to C.

Suppose $c' \notin C$ and suppose S is a specifying set for c' with respect to C. There are two possibilities: either there is no concept $c \in C$ that agrees with the classification of c' for every example in S, or there is exactly one such concept $c \in C$. If there is one such, say c, we can add to S a single example on which c' and c disagree to construct a set S' such that no concept in C agrees with the classification of c' on every example in S'. Thus, a specifying set may require at most one more example to become a "proof" that $c' \notin C$.

Define the *exclusion dimension*, denoted $\text{XD}(C)$, of a concept class C as the maximum over all concepts $c' \notin C$, of the minimum size of any specifying set for c' with respect to C. If $C = 2^X$, define the exclusion dimension of C to be 0.

This is the same as the unique specification dimension of Hegedüs [12] and the certificate size of Hellerstein *et al.* [13].

Examples. $\mathrm{XD}(S(X)) = |X| - 1$ because for the empty set we must specify $|X| - 1$ examples as not belonging to the empty set to reduce the possible concepts to at most one (the singleton containing the element not specified.) However, for $|X| \geq 2$, $\mathrm{XD}(S^+(X)) = 1$ because any concept not in $S^+(X)$ contains at least two elements, and specifying that one of them belongs to the concept is enough to rule out the empty set and all but one singleton subset of X. We have $\mathrm{XD}(C_0) = 1$, because each of the concepts not in C_0 has a specifying set of size 1. For example, the empty set has a specifying set $\{x_1\}$ with respect to C_0, because only c_2 also does not include x_1, and the set $\{x_1, x_2, x_3\}$ has a specifying set $\{x_2\}$ with respect to C_0, because only c_3 also includes x_2.

The argument for (16) generalizes to give

$$\mathrm{XD}(C) = \max_{c' \notin C} \min_{T \in T_{MQ}(C)} d(c', T). \tag{18}$$

Let T be any MQ-algorithm that is successful for C. Consider any concept $c' \notin C$, the leaf ℓ of T that c' is assigned to, and the set S of elements queried on the path from the root to ℓ. Because at most one element of C is assigned to ℓ, S is a specifying set for c'.

Conversely, if $c' \notin C$ and S is a specifying set for c', then we may construct a MQ-algorithm successful for C by querying the elements of S. If an answer disagrees with the classification by c', then continue with the exhaustive MQ algorithm. If the answers for all the elements of S agree with the classifications by c', then there is at most one concept in C consistent with those answers, and the algorithm may halt.

Hence, the smallest specifying set for c' has size equal to the minimum depth of c' in any MQ-tree successful for C, and (18) follows.

Also, for any concept class C,

$$\mathrm{XD}(C) \leq \#\mathrm{MQ}(C). \tag{19}$$

Consider any MQ-tree of depth $\#\mathrm{MQ}(C)$ that is successful for C. Every $c' \notin C$ has a specifying set consisting of the elements queried along the path in T that c' is assigned to, which is therefore of size at most $\#\mathrm{MQ}(C)$.

8.3   The Extended Teaching Dimension

The combination of the teaching dimension and the exclusion dimension yields the extended teaching dimension [12]. The *extended teaching dimension* of a concept class C, denoted $\mathrm{XTD}(C)$, is the maximum over all concepts $c' \subseteq X$, of the minimum size of any specifying set for c' with respect to C. Clearly, for any concept class C,

$$\mathrm{XTD}(C) = \max\{\mathrm{TD}(C), \mathrm{XD}(C)\}. \tag{20}$$

From (16) and (18) we have

$$\mathrm{XTD}(C) = \max_{c \in 2^X} \min_{T \in T_{MQ}(C)} d(c, T). \tag{21}$$

From (17) and (19), we have

$$\mathrm{XTD}(C) \leq \#\mathrm{MQ}(C). \tag{22}$$

Examples. $\mathrm{XTD}(C_0) = 2 = \max\{2, 1\}$. If $|X| \geq 2$, $\mathrm{XTD}(S(X)) = |X| - 1$ and $\mathrm{XTD}(S^+(X)) = |X|$.

9   The Testing Perspective

In the simplest testing framework there is an unknown item, for example, a disease, and a number of possible binary tests to perform to try to identify the unknown item. There is a finite binary relation between the possible items and the possible tests; performing a test on the unknown item is analogous to a membership query, and adaptive testing algorithms correspond to MQ-algorithms. Hence the applicability of Moshkov's results on testing to questions about MQ-algorithms. The frameworks are not completely parallel. Moshkov introduces the analog of equivalence queries for the testing framework [17].

We take a brief excursion to consider the computational difficulty of the problem of constructing an optimal testing algorithm (or, equivalently, MQ-algorithm.) There is a natural (and expensive) dynamic programming method for constructing an optimal MQ-algorithm. Hyafil and Rivest show that it is NP-complete to decide, given a binary relation and a depth bound, whether the relation has a MQ-algorithm with at most that depth [14]. Arkin *et al.* [3] consider this problem in the context of the number of probes needed to determine which one of a finite set of geometric figures is present in an image. They prove an approximation result for the natural (and efficient) greedy algorithm for this problem, which we now describe.

An MQ-algorithm and its evaluation on C are constructed top-down and simultaneously. For each leaf node assigned more than one concept from C, choose a membership query that partitions the set of concepts assigned to the node as evenly as possible, and extend the tree and its evaluation until every leaf node is assigned exactly one concept from C. Arkin *et al.* show that this method achieves a tree whose height is within a factor of $\lceil \log |C| \rceil$ of the optimal height. (This greedy tree-construction method is a standard one in the literature of constructing decision trees from given example classifications, although decision trees compute classifications rather than identifications.)

10   XTD and MQ-Algorithms

Using a specifying set S for a concept c', we can replace an equivalence query with c' by a sequence of membership queries with the elements of S as follows. If a membership query with x gives an answer different from the classification by c', we proceed as though the equivalence query received counterexample x in reply. If the answers for all the elements of S are the same as the classifications by c', then at most one element of C is consistent with all these answers, and the learning algorithm can safely halt.

If we apply this basic method to replace each XEQ of the halving algorithm by a sequence of at most $\text{XTD}(C)$ MQ's, we get the following for any concept class C.

$$\#\text{MQ}(C) \le (\text{XTD}(C)) \cdot (\lfloor \log |C| \rfloor). \tag{23}$$

We could instead replace each XEQ in the standard optimal algorithm by a sequence of at most $\text{XTD}(C)$ MQ's to obtain

$$\#\text{MQ}(C) \le (\text{XTD}(C)) \cdot (\#\text{XEQ}(C)). \tag{24}$$

Hegedüs [12] gives an improvement over (23), achieved by an algorithm with a greedy ordering of the MQ's used in the simulation of one XEQ.

$$\#\text{MQ}(C) \le (2\text{XTD}(C)/(\log \text{XTD}(C))) \cdot (\lfloor \log |C| \rfloor). \tag{25}$$

He also gives an example of a family of concept classes for which this improved bound is asymptotically tight.

These results give a reasonably satisfying characterization of the number of membership queries needed to learn a concept class C in terms of a combinatorial parameter of the class, the extended teaching dimension, $\text{XTD}(C)$. The factor of roughly $\log |C|$ difference between the lower bound and the upper bound may be thought of as tolerably small, being the number of bits needed to name all the concepts in C. Analogous results are achievable for algorithms that use MQ's and EQ's and for algorithms that use EQ's alone.

11   XD and MQ&EQ-Algorithms

Generalizing Moshkov's results, Hegedüs [12] bounds the number of MQ's and EQ's needed to learn a concept class in terms of the exclusion dimension. Independently, Hellerstein *et al.* [13], introduce the idea of polynomial certificates to characterize learnability with a polynomial number of MQ's and EQ's.

For any concept class C,

$$\text{XD}(C) \le \#\text{MQ\&EQ}(C) \le (\text{XD}(C)) \cdot (\lfloor \log |C| \rfloor). \tag{26}$$

An adversary argument establishes the lower bound. Let $c' \notin C$ be any concept such that the minimum specifying set for c' has size $d = \#\text{MQ\&EQ}(C)$. An adversary can answer any sequence of at most $(d-1)$ MQ's and EQ's as though the target concept were c'. (Note that because EQ's must use concepts in C, there cannot be an equivalence query with c' itself.) At this point, there must be at least two concepts in C consistent with the answers given, so a successful learning algorithm must ask at least one more query.

The upper bound is established by a simulation of the halving algorithm. If an XEQ is made with concept c', then if $c' \in C$, it is already an EQ and need not be replaced. If $c' \notin C$, then we take a minimum specifying set S for c' with respect to C and replace the XEQ by MQ's about the elements of S, as described in Section 10.

Using the standard optimal algorithm instead of the halving algorithm gives the following.

$$\#\mathrm{MQ\&EQ}(C) \leq (\mathrm{XD}(C)) \cdot (\#\mathrm{XEQ}(C)). \tag{27}$$

Again Hegedüs improves the upper bound of (26) by making a more careful choice of the ordering of MQ's, and gives an example of a family of classes for which the improved bound is asymptotically tight.

$$\#\mathrm{MQ\&EQ}(C) \leq (2\mathrm{XD}(C)/(\log \mathrm{XD}(C))) \cdot (\lfloor \log |C| \rfloor). \tag{28}$$

The key difference in the bounds for MQ-algorithms and MQ&EQ-algorithms is that with both MQ's and EQ's, we do not need to replace an XEQ with a concept $c \in C$, so only the specifying sets for concepts *not* in C matter, whereas with only MQ's we may need to simulate XEQ's for concepts in C, so specifying sets for *all* concepts may matter.

12   A Dimension for EQ-Algorithms?

Can we expect a similar characterization for learning a class C with proper equivalence queries only? The short answer is yes, but the story is a little more complicated.

We'll need samples as well as concepts. A *sample s* is a partial function from X to $\{0,1\}$. A sample may also be thought of as a subset of elements of X and their classifications, or a function from X to $\{0,1,*\}$, with $*$ standing for "undefined." If we identify a concept c with its characteristic function, mapping X to $\{0,1\}$, then a concept is a special case of a sample. Two samples are *consistent* if they take the same values on the elements common to both of their domains. A sample s' *extends* a sample s if they are consistent and the domain of s is a subset of the domain of s'.

It is interesting to note that the partial equivalence queries of Maass and Turán [16] can be characterized as equivalence queries with samples instead of just concepts.

12.1   The Fingerprint Dimension

Early work on lower bounds for equivalence queries introduced the property of *approximate fingerprints* [2], which is sufficient to guarantee that a family of classes of concepts cannot be learned with a polynomial number of EQ's. This technique was applied to show that there is no polynomial-time EQ-algorithm for finite automata, DNF formulas, and many other classes of concepts.

Gavaldà [9] proved that a suitable modification of the negation of the approximate fingerprint property is both necessary and sufficient for learnability with a polynomial number of proper equivalence queries. Hayashi *et al.* [11] generalized the definitions to cover combinations of various types of queries. Stripped of details not relevant to this development, the ideas may be formulated as follows.

If C is a concept class, $c \in C$, and d is a positive integer, then we define c to be $1/d$-*good* for C if for every $x \in X$, a fraction of at least $1/d$ of the concepts in C agree with the classification of x by c. This idea generalizes the majority vote concept for a class C, which is $1/2$-good for C. If we make an EQ with a concept c that is $1/d$-good for C, then any counterexample must eliminate a fraction of at least $1/d$ of the concepts in C.

Given a concept class C, we say that $C' \subseteq C$ is *reachable* from C if there exists a sample s such that C' consists of all those concepts in C that are consistent with s. Not every subclass of a concept class is necessarily reachable.

Examples. For $C = S^+(X)$, the subclasses $\{\{x\}\}$ are reachable (using the sample $s = \{(x,1)\}$), and subclasses consisting of $S^+(Y)$ for $Y \subseteq X$ are reachable (using a sample that maps the elements of $X - Y$ to 0), but the subclass $S(X)$, consisting of the singletons, is not reachable.

Given a concept class C, the *fingerprint dimension* of C, denoted $\mathrm{FD}(C)$, is the least positive integer d such that for every reachable subclass C' of C, there is a concept $c' \in C'$ that is $1/d$-good for C'.

To see that $\mathrm{FD}(C)$ is well-defined, note that for any concept class C and any concept $c \in C$, c is at least $1/|C|$-good for C, because c at least agrees with itself. A concept class C containing only one concept has $\mathrm{FD}(C) = 1$, but any concept class C containing at least two concepts has $\mathrm{FD}(C) \geq 2$.

We now show that the fingerprint dimension gives bounds on the number of EQ's necessary to learn a class of concepts for any class C of concepts, as follows.

$$\mathrm{FD}(C) - 1 \leq \#\mathrm{EQ}(C) \leq \lceil \mathrm{FD}(C) \ln |C| \rceil. \tag{29}$$

If C has only one concept, then $0 = \mathrm{FD}(C) - 1 = \#\mathrm{EQ}(C)$, so both inequalities hold in this case. Assume C has at least two concepts, and let $d = \mathrm{FD}(C)$. Clearly $d \geq 2$.

We describe a learning algorithm to achieve the upper bound. At any point, there is a class C' reachable from C that is consistent with the answers to all the queries made so far. If C' contains one element, then the algorithm halts. Otherwise, by the definition of $\mathrm{FD}(C)$ there is a concept $c' \in C'$ that is $1/d$-good for C', and the algorithm makes an EQ with this concept c'.

Either the answer is "yes," or a counterexample x eliminates a fraction of at least $1/d$ of the concepts in C'. This continues until exactly one concept $c \in C$ is consistent with all the answers to queries. Then i queries are sufficient if $(1 - 1/d)^i |C| \leq 1$. Hence, $\lceil d \ln |C| \rceil$ EQ's suffice.

For the lower bound, because d is a minimum, there is a reachable subclass C' of C that has no $1/(d-1)$-good concept. For this to be true, $|C'| \geq d$. Thus, for each concept $c' \in C'$, there exists an element $x \in X$ such that the fraction of concepts in C' that agree with the classification of x by c' is smaller than $1/(d-1)$. (This x could be termed a $1/(d-1)$-approximate fingerprint for c' with respect to C'.)

Let s be the sample that witnesses the reachability of C' from C. That is, C' consists of those elements of C that are consistent with s. We describe an adversary to answer EQ's for C that maintains a fraction of at least $(d - i - 1)/(d - 1)$ of the concepts in C' consistent with the answers to the first i EQ's.

This is clearly true when $i = 0$. For an EQ with $c \in C$, if $c \notin C'$, then c must not be consistent with s, and the adversary returns as a counterexample any element x such that s and c classify x differently. If $c \in C'$, then by our choice of C', there is an element x such that the fraction of elements of C' that classify x the same way as c is smaller than $1/(d-1)$. The adversary returns any such x as a counterexample. Queries of the first type do not eliminate any elements of C', and queries of the second type eliminate fewer than $(1/(d-1))|C'|$ elements of C', so after $d - 2$ EQ's, there are at least

$$|C'|/(d - 1) > 1$$

concepts in C' consistent with all the answers the adversary has given. Hence, any EQ-algorithm must use at least $d - 1$ EQ's, establishing the lower bound.

12.2   The Sample Exclusion Dimension

Balcázar *et al.* introduce the strong consistency dimension [6], which also yields bounds on the number of EQ's to learn a concept class. We give a slight variant of that definition, which generalizes the exclusion dimension from concepts to samples.

Let C be a concept class and s a sample. A *specifying set* for s with respect to C is a set S contained in the domain of s such that at most one concept $c \in C$ is consistent with the sample s' obtained by restricting s to the elements of S. Note that this coincides with our previous definition of a specifying set if s is itself a concept.

Define the *sample exclusion dimension* of a class C of concepts, denoted $\mathrm{SXD}(C)$, to be the maximum over all samples s such that s is not consistent with any $c \in C$, of the minimum size of any specifying set for s. This generalizes the exclusion dimension from concepts not in C to samples not consistent with any concept in C. For $C = 2^X$ we stipulate that $\mathrm{SXD}(C) = 0$.

Because the maximization is over samples and not just concepts, for any class of concepts C,

$$\mathrm{XD}(C) \leq \mathrm{SXD}(C). \tag{30}$$

This differs from the strong consistency dimension introduced by Balcázar *et al.* [6] by at most 1, and coincides, in the case of equivalence queries, with the abstract identification dimension, also introduced by Balcázar et al. [4].

Examples. To get a sense of the difference between the exclusion dimension and the sample exclusion dimension, consider the concept class C_1, presented in Figure 7. This is a version of *addressing*, described by Maass and Turán [16].

The empty set is not an element of C_1, but it has a specifying set $\{x_1, x_2\}$, because only c_1 also does not include either x_1 or x_2. However, the sample

$$s = \{(y_1, 0), (y_2, 0), (y_3, 0), (y_4, 0)\},$$

	x_1	x_2	y_1	y_2	y_3	y_4
c_1	0	0	1	0	0	0
c_2	0	1	0	1	0	0
c_3	1	0	0	0	1	0
c_4	1	1	0	0	0	1

Fig. 7. Concept class C_1, a version of *addressing*

which is not defined for x_1 and x_2, is not consistent with any element of C_1, but its smallest specifying sets have 3 elements, for example, $\{y_1, y_2, y_3\}$. Generalizing this example to 2^n concepts with n address bits gives an exponential disparity between the exclusion dimension and the sample exclusion dimension.

The sample exclusion dimension is a lower bound on the number of EQ's needed to learn a concept class C. For any concept class C,

$$\text{SXD}(C) \leq \#\text{EQ}(C). \tag{31}$$

If $C = 2^X$, then $\text{SXD}(C) = 0$ and the bound holds, so assume $C \neq 2^X$. We describe an adversary to enforce at least $d = \text{SXD}(C)$ EQ's. Let s be a sample that is not consistent with any $c \in C$ such that the size of the smallest specifying set for s with respect to C has size d. Any EQ with a concept $c \in C$ can be answered with an element x in the domain of s, because s is not consistent with any $c \in C$. Up to $(d-1)$ EQ's can be answered thus, and there will still be at least two concepts in C consistent with all the answers given, so any successful learning algorithm must make at least one more EQ.

Combining (29) and (31), we have

$$\text{SXD}(C) \leq \#\text{EQ}(C) \leq \lceil \text{FD}(C) \ln |C| \rceil. \tag{32}$$

The sample exclusion dimension also gives an upper bound on the fingerprint dimension.

$$\text{FD}(C) \leq \text{SXD}(C) + 1. \tag{33}$$

If C contains only one concept, then $\text{FD}(C) = 1$ and $\text{SXD}(C) = 0$, and the bound holds. Assume that C contains at least two concepts, and let $d = \text{SXD}(C)$. Clearly $d \geq 1$. Consider any subclass C' reachable from C, and let s be the sample that witnesses the reachability of C'. That is, C' is the set of concepts in C consistent with s. We show that C' contains a concept c' that is $1/(d+1)$-good for C'.

Define another sample s' as follows. Let $s'(x) = 1$ if a fraction of more than $d/(d+1)$ concepts in C' contain x, and let $s'(x) = 0$ if a fraction of more than $d/(d+1)$ concepts in C' do not contain x. Note that s' is not defined for elements x for which the majority vote of C' does not exceed a fraction $d/(d+1)$ of the total number of elements of C'. Note that s' extends s because all of the elements of C' agree on elements in the domain of s.

We claim that s' is consistent with some element of C. If not, then by the definition of $\mathrm{SXD}(C)$, there exists a specifying set S for s' with respect to C that contains at most d elements. Consider the set of elements of C' that are consistent with s' for all the elements of S. Agreement with s' on each element of S eliminates a fraction of less than $1/(d+1)$ of the elements of C', so agreement on all the elements of S eliminates a fraction smaller than $d/(d + 1)$ of the elements of C'. Thus, at least one element of C' is consistent with s' on all the elements of S, contradicting the assumption that s' is not consistent with any element in C.

Thus, there is some element $c \in C$ consistent with s', and since s' extends s, $c \in C'$. Thus, the concept c is a $1/(d+1)$-good element of C'. Because C' was an arbitrary reachable subclass of C, we have that $\mathrm{FD}(C) \leq (d + 1)$, establishing the bound.

As a corollary of (33) and the upper bound in (29), we have

$$\#\mathrm{EQ}(C) \leq \lceil (\mathrm{SXD}(C) + 1) \ln |C| \rceil. \tag{34}$$

12.3   Inequivalence of $\mathrm{FD}(C)$ and $\mathrm{SXD}(C)$

Despite their similar properties in bounding $\#\mathrm{EQ}(C)$, the two dimensions $\mathrm{FD}(C)$ and $\mathrm{SXD}(C)$ are different for some concept classes.

Let $X_{2k+1} = \{x_1, x_2, \ldots, x_{2k+1}\}$ and let C_k consist of all subsets of X_{2k+1} of cardinality at most k. Then $|C_k| = 2^{2k}$ and $\ln |C| = \Theta(k)$.

We have $\mathrm{SXD}(C_k) = k$ because the only samples inconsistent with every concept in C must take on the value 1 for at least $k + 1$ domain elements, and a minimum specifying set will contain k domain elements with the value 1. On the other hand, $\mathrm{FD}(C_k) = 2$, because every reachable subclass of C_k contains its majority vote concept. Of course, $\#\mathrm{EQ}(C_k) = k$, by a strategy that begins by conjecturing the empty set, and adds positive counterexamples to the conjecture until it is answered "yes."

Thus, for the family of classes C_k, the sample exclusion dimension gives a tight lower bound, k, and a loose upper bound, $O(k^2)$, while the fingerprint dimension gives a loose lower bound, 1, and an asymptotically tight upper bound, $O(k)$, on the number of EQ's required for learning. This is asymptotically as large as the discrepancy can be, as witnessed by (32), which is the combination that gives the strongest bounds on $\#\mathrm{EQ}(C)$ at present.

13   What about the VC-Dimension?

Because the Vapnik-Chervonenkis dimension is so useful in PAC learning, it is natural to ask what its relationship is to learning with queries. A set $S \subseteq X$ is *shattered* by a concept class C if all $2^{|S|}$ possible labellings of elements in S are achieved by concepts from C. The VC-dimension of a class C of concepts, denoted VCD(C), is the maximum cardinality of any set shattered by C. It is clear that for any concept class C,

$$VCD(C) \leq \log |C|. \tag{35}$$

This and (3) imply

$$VCD(C) \leq \#MQ(C). \tag{36}$$

As Littlestone [15] observed, an adversary giving counterexamples from a shattered set can enforce VCD(C) XEQ's, and therefore

$$VCD(C) \leq \#XEQ(C) \leq \#EQ(C). \tag{37}$$

Maass and Turán [16] show that for any concept class C,

$$\frac{1}{7}VCD(C) \leq \#MQ\&EQ(C). \tag{38}$$

They give an example of a family of concept classes that shows that the constant $1/7$ cannot be improved to be larger than 0.41, and also show that

$$\frac{1}{7}VCD(C) \leq \#MQ\&XEQ(C). \tag{39}$$

14   More General Dimensions

Balcázar *et al.* present generalizations of the dimensions XTD(C), XD(C) and SXD(C) to arbitrary kinds of example-based queries [4], and beyond [5]. It is outside the scope of this sketch to treat their results fully, but we briefly describe the settings. For convenience we identify a concept c with its characteristic function, and write $c(x) = 1$ if $x \in c$.

In [4], for an example-based query with a target concept c, the possible replies are identified with samples consistent with c, that is, with subfunctions of c. Thus, for a membership query about x, the reply is the singleton sample $\{(x, c(x))\}$. For an equivalence query with the concept c', the possible replies are either a counterexample x, which is represented by the sample $\{(x, c(x))\}$, or "yes," which is represented by the sample equal to c, completely specifying it. For a subset query with c', the possible replies are either a counterexample, which is a singleton sample $\{(x, 0)\}$ such that $c'(x) = 1$ and $c(x) = 0$, or "yes," which is represented by the sample consisting of all pairs $(x, 1)$ such that $c'(x) = 1$.

A protocol is a ternary relation on queries, target concepts, and possible answers. Two conditions are imposed on the relation. One is *completeness*, which requires that every possible query and target concept, there is at least one possible answer. The other is *fair play*, which requires that if an answer a is possible for a query q and a target concept c, then for any other target concept c' such that the answer a is a subfunction of c', a is a possible answer for q with target concept c'. The fair play condition ensures that an answer cannot "rule out" a candidate hypothesis unless it is inconsistent with it. For this setting, a very general dimension, the *abstract identification dimension*, is defined and shown to generalize the extended teaching dimension, the exclusion dimension, and the sample exclusion dimension.

In [5], Balcázar *et al.* define an even more general setting, covering many kinds of non-example-based queries. In this setting, the answer to a query is identified with a property that is true of the target concept, or equivalently, a subset of concepts that includes the target concept, or a Boolean function on all possible concepts that is true for the target concept. For example, if the target concept is c, a *restricted equivalence query* with the concept c' returns only the answers "yes" (if $c' = c$) and "no" (if $c' \neq c$), with no counterexample. The reply "yes" can be formalized as the singleton $\{c\}$, specifying c completely, while the reply "no" can be formalized as the set $2^X - \{c'\}$, which gives only the information that $c \neq c'$. In this setting, the authors define the *general dimension* for a target class and learning protocol and prove that the optimal number of queries for the class and the protocol is bounded between this dimension and this dimension times $\lceil \ln |C| \rceil$.

15   Remarks

The approach of bounding the number of queries required to learn concepts from a class C using combinatorial properties of C has made great progress. This sketch has omitted very many things, including the fascinating applications of these results to specific concept classes. One major open problem is whether DNF formulas can be learned using a polynomial number of MQ's and EQ's. The reader is strongly encouraged to consult the original works.

Acknowledgements. Preparation of this paper was supported in part by the National Science Foundation, grant CCR-9610295.

References

1. D. Angluin. Queries and concept learning. *Machine Learning*, 2:319–342, 1988.
2. D. Angluin. Negative results for equivalence queries. *Machine Learning*, 5:121–150, 1990.
3. E. M. Arkin, H. Meijer, J. S. B. Mitchell, D. Rappaport, and S. S. Skiena. Decision trees for geometric models. In *Proceedings of the Ninth Annual Symposium on Computational Geometry*, pages 369–378, San Diego, CA, 1993. ACM Press.
4. J. L. Balcázar, J. Castro, and D. Guijarro. Abstract combinatorial characterizations of exact learning via queries. In *Proceedings of the 13th Annual Conference on Computational Learning Theory*, pages 248–254. Morgan Kaufmann, San Francisco, 2000.
5. J. L. Balcázar, J. Castro, and D. Guijarro. A general dimension for exact learning. In *Proceedings of the 14th Annual Conference on Computational Learning Theory*, 2001.

6. J. L. Balcázar, J. Castro, D. Guijarro, and H.-U. Simon. The consistency dimension and distribution-dependent learning from queries. In *Proceedings of the 10th International Conference on Algorithic Learning Theory - ALT '99*, volume 1720 of *LNAI*, pages 77–92. Springer-Verlag, 1999.

7. A. Blumer, A. Ehrenfeucht, D. Haussler, and M. K. Warmuth. Learnability and the Vapnik-Chervonenkis dimension. *J. ACM*, 36:929–965, 1989.

8. A. Ehrenfeucht, D. Haussler, M. Kearns, and L. Valiant. A general lower bound on the number of examples needed for learning. *Inform. Comput.*, 82:247–261, 1989.

9. R. Gavaldà. On the power of equivalence queries. In *EUROCOLT: European Conference on Computational Learning Theory*, pages 193–203. Clarendon Press, 1993.

10. S. A. Goldman and M. J. Kearns. On the complexity of teaching. *J. of Comput. Syst. Sci.*, 50:20–31, 1995.

11. Y. Hayashi, S. Matsumoto, A. Shinohara, and M. Takeda. Uniform characterizations of polynomial-query learnabilities. In *Proceedings of the 1st International Conference on Discovery Science (DS-98)*, volume 1532 of *LNAI*, pages 84–92, 1998.

12. T. Hegedüs. Generalized teaching dimensions and the query complexity of learning. In *Proceedings of the 8th Annual Conference on Computational Learning Theory*, pages 108–117. ACM Press, New York, NY, 1995.

13. L. Hellerstein, K. Pillaipakkamnatt, V. Raghavan, and D. Wilkins. How many queries are needed to learn? In *Proceedings of the Twenty-Seventh Annual ACM Symposium on the Theory of Computing*, pages 190–199, 1995.

14. R. Hyafil and R. L. Rivest. Constructing optimal binary trees is NP-complete. *Information Processing Letters*, 5:15–17, 1976.

15. N. Littlestone. Learning quickly when irrelevant attributes abound: A new linear-threshold algorithm. *Machine Learning*, 2:285–318, 1988.

16. W. Maass and G. Turán. Lower bound methods and separation results for on-line learning models. *Machine Learning*, 9:107–145, 1992.

17. M. Moshkov. Test theory and problems of machine learning. In *Proceedings of the International School-Seminar on Discrete Mathematics and Mathematical Cybernetics*, pages 6–10. MAX Press, Moscow, 2001.

18. A. Shinohara and S. Miyano. Teachability in computational learning. *New Generation Computing*, 8(4):337–348, 1991.

19. L. G. Valiant. A theory of the learnable. *Commun. ACM*, 27:1134–1142, 1984.

Robot Baby 2001

Paul R. Cohen[1], Tim Oates[2], Niall Adams[3], and Carole R. Beal[4]

[1] Department of Computer Science, University of Massachusetts, Amherst
cohen@cs.umass.edu
[2] Department of Computer Science, University of Maryland, Baltimore County
oates@cs.umbc.edu
[3] Department of Mathematics, Imperial College, London
n.adams@ic.ac.uk
[4] Department of Psychology, University of Massachusetts, Amherst
cbeal@psych.umass.edu

Abstract. In this paper we claim that meaningful representations can be learned by programs, although today they are almost always designed by skilled engineers. We discuss several kinds of meaning that representations might have, and focus on a functional notion of meaning as appropriate for programs to learn. Specifically, a representation is meaningful if it incorporates an indicator of external conditions and if the indicator relation informs action. We survey methods for inducing kinds of representations we call structural abstractions. Prototypes of sensory time series are one kind of structural abstraction, and though they are not denoting or compositional, they do support planning. Deictic representations of objects and prototype representations of words enable a program to learn the denotational meanings of words. Finally, we discuss two algorithms designed to find the macroscopic structure of episodes in a domain-independent way.

1 Introduction

In artificial intelligence and other cognitive sciences it is taken for granted that mental states are representational. Researchers differ on whether representations must be *symbolic*, but most agree that mental states have *content* — they are *about* something and they *mean* something — irrespective of their form. Researchers differ too on whether the meanings of mental states have any causal relationship to how and what we think, but most agree that these meanings are (mostly) known to us as we think. Of formal representations in computer programs, however, we would say something different: Generally, the meanings of representations have no influence on the operations performed on them (e.g., a program concludes q because it knows $p \rightarrow q$ and p, irrespective of what p and q are about); yet the representations *have* meanings, known to us, the designers and end-users of the programs, and the representations are provided to the programs *because* of what they mean (e.g., if it was not relevant that the patient has a fever, then the proposition `febrile(patient)` would not be provided to the program — programs are designed to operate in domains where

N. Abe, R. Khardon, and T. Zeugmann (Eds.): ALT 2001, LNAI 2225, pp. 32–56, 2001.

meaning matters.). Thus, irrespective of whether the contents of mental states have any causal influence on what and how *we* think, these contents clearly are intended (by us) to influence what and how our programs think. The meanings of representations are not irrelevant but we have to provide them.

If programs could learn the meanings of representations it would save us a great deal of effort. Most of the intellectual work in AI is done not by programs but by their creators, and virtually *all* the work involved in specifying the meanings of representations is done by people, not programs (but see, e.g., [27,22, 14]). This paper discusses kinds of meaning that programs might learn and gives examples of such programs.

How do people and computers come to have contentful, i.e., meaningful, mental states? As Dennett [10] points out, there are only three serious answers to the question: Contents are learned, told, or innate. Lines cannot be drawn sharply between these, in either human or artificial intelligence. Culture, including our educational systems, blurs the distinction between learning and being told; and it is impossible methodologically to be sure that the meanings of mental states are innate, especially as some learning occurs in utero [9] and many studies of infant knowledge happen weeks or months after birth.

One might think the distinctions between learning, being told, and innate knowledge are clearer in artificial systems, but the role of engineers is rarely acknowledged [8,30,12]. Most AI systems manipulate representations that mean what engineers intend them to mean; the meanings of representations are exogenous to the systems. It is less clear where the meanings of *learned* representations reside, in the minds of engineers or the "minds of the machines" that run the learning algorithms. We would not say that a linear regression algorithm knows the meanings of data or of induced regression lines. Meanings are assigned by data analysts or their client domain experts. Moreover, these people select data for the algorithms with some prior idea of what they mean. Most work in machine learning, KDD, and AI and statistics are essentially data analysis, with humans, not machines, assigning meanings to regularities found in the data.

We have nothing against data analysis, indeed we think that learning the meanings of representations *is* data analysis, in particular, analysis of sensory and perceptual time series. Our goal, though, is to have the machine do *all* of it: select data, process it, and interpret the results; then iterate to resolve ambiguities, test new hypotheses, refine estimates, and so on [1]. The relationship between domain experts, statistical consultants, and statistical algorithms is essentially identical to the relationship between domain experts, AI researchers, and their programs: In both cases the intermediary translates meaningful domain concepts into representations that programs manipulate, and translates the results back to the domain experts. We want to do away with the domain expert and the en-

---

[1] An early effort in our laboratory to automate applied statistics was Rob St. Amant's dissertation [26,25]; while it succeeded in many respects, it had only weak notions of the meaning of representations, so its automated data analysis had a formal, syntactic feel (e.g., exploring high leverage points in regression analysis).

gineers/statistical consultants, and have programs learn representions and their meanings, autonomously.

One impediment to learning the meanings of representations is the fuzziness of commonsense notions of meaning. Suppose a regression algorithm induces a strong relationship between two random variables x and y and represents it in the conventional way: $y = 1.31x - .03$, $R^2 = .86$, $F = 108.3$, $p < .0001$. One meaning of this representation is provided by classical inferential statistics: x and y appear linearly related and the relationship between these random variables is very unlikely to be accidental. Note that this meaning is not accessible in any sense to the regression algorithm, though it could be known, as it is conventional and unambiguous. [2] Now, the statistician might know that x is daily temperature and y is ice-cream sales, and so he or his client domain expert might assign additional meaning to the representation, above. For instance, the statistician might warn the domain expert that the assumptions of linear regression are not well-satisfied by the data. Ignoring these and other cautions, the domain expert might even interpret the representation in causal terms (i.e., hot weather causes people to buy ice-cream). Should he submit the result to an academic journal, the reviews would probably criticize this semantic liberty and would in any case declare the result as meaningless in the sense of being utterly unimportant and unsurprising.

This little example illustrates at least five kinds of meaning for the representation $y = 1.31x - .03$, $R^2 = .86$, $F = 108.3$, $p < .0001$. There is the *formal* meaning, including the mathematical fact that 86 % of the variance in the random variable y is explained by x. Note that this meaning has nothing to do with the denotations of y and x, and it might be utter nonsense in the domain of weather and ice-cream, but, of course, the formal meaning of the representation is not about weather and ice cream, it is about random variables. Another kind of meaning has to do with the *model* that makes y and x denote ice cream and weather. When the statistician warns that the residuals of the regression have structure, he is saying that a linear model might not summarize the relationship between x and y as well as another kind of model. He makes no reference to the denotations of x and y, but he might, as when he warns that ice cream sales are not normally distributed. In both cases, the statistician is questioning whether the domain (ice cream sales and weather) is faithfully represented by the model (a linear function between random variables). He is questioning whether the "essential features" of the domain are represented, and whether they are somehow distorted by the regression procedure.

The domain expert will introduce a third kind of meaning: he will interpret $y = 1.31x - .03$, $R^2 = .86$, $F = 108.3$, $p < .0001$ as a statement about ice cream sales. This is not to say that every aspect of the representation has an interpretation in the domain—the expert might not assign a meaning to the coefficient $-.03$—only that, to the expert, the representation is not a formal object but

---

[2] Indeed, there is a sense in which stepwise regression algorithms know what F statistics mean, as the values of these statistics directly affect the behavior of the algorithms.

a statement about his domain. We could call this kind of meaning the *domain* semantics, or the *functional* semantics, to emphasize that the interpretation of a representation has some effect on what the domain expert *does* or thinks about.

Having found a relationship between ice cream sales and the weather, the expert will feel elated, ambitious, or greedy, and this is a fourth, *affective* kind of meaning. Let us suppose, however, that the relationship is not real, it is entirely spurious (an artifact of a poor sampling procedure, say) and is contradicted by solid results in the literature. In this case the representation is meaningless in the sense that it does not *inform* anyone about how the world really works.

To which of these notions of meaning should a program that learns meanings be held responsible? The semantics of classical statistics and regression analysis in particular are sophisticated, and many humans perform adequate analyses without really understanding either. More to the point, what good is an agent that learns *formal* semantics in lieu of *domain* or *functional* semantics? The relationship between x and y can be learned (even without a statistician specifying the form of the relationship), but so long as it is a *formal* relationship between random variables, and the denotations of x and y are unknown to the learner, a more knowledgeable agent will be required to translate the formal relationship into a domain or functional one. The denotations of x and y might be learned, though generally one needs some knowledge to bootstrap the process; for example, when we say, "x denotes daily temperature," we call up considerable amounts of common-sense knowledge to assign this statement meaning. [3] As to affective meanings, we believe artificial agents will benefit from them, but we do not know how to provide them.

This leaves two notions of meaning, one based in the functional roles of representations, the other related to the informativeness of representations. The philosopher Fred Dretske wrestled these notions of meaning into a theory of how meaning can have causal effects on behavior [11,12]. Dretske's criteria for a state being a meaningful representational state are: the state must *indicate* some condition, have the *function* of indicating that condition, and have this function assigned as the result of a *learning* process. The latter condition is contentious [10,8], but it will not concern us here as this paper is about learning meaningful representations. The other conditions say that a reliable indicator relationship must exist and be exploited by an agent for some purpose. Thus, the relationship between mean daily temperature (the indicator) and ice-cream sales (the indicated) is apt to be meaningful to ice-cream companies, just as the relationship between sonar readings and imminent collisions is meaningful to mobile robots, because in each case an agent can do something with the relationship. Learning meaningful representations, then, is tantamount to learning reliable relationships between denoting tokens (e.g., random variables) and learning what to do when the tokens take on particular values.

---

[3] Projects such as Cyc emphasize the denotational meanings of representations [17, 16]. Terms in Cyc are associated with axioms that say what the terms mean. It took a collosal effort to get enough terms and axioms into Cyc to support the easy acquisition of new terms and axioms.

The minimum required of a representation by Dretske's theory is an indicator relationship $s \leftarrow I(S)$ between the external world state S and an internal state s, and a function that exploits the indicator relationship through some kind of action a, presumably changing the world state: $f(s, a) \rightarrow S$. The problems are to learn representations $s \sim S$ and the functions f (the relationship $\sim$ is discussed below, but here means "abstraction").

These are familiar problems to researchers in the reinforcement learning community, and we think reinforcement learning is a way to learn meaningful representations (with the reservations we discuss in [30]). We want to up the ante, however, in two ways. First, the world is a dynamic place and we think it is necessary and advantageous for s to represent how the world changes. Indeed, most of our work is concerned with learning representations of dynamics.

Second, a *policy* of the form $f(s, a) \rightarrow s$ manifests an intimate relationship between representations s and the actions a conditioned on them: s contains the "right" information to condition a. The right information is almost always an abstraction of raw state information; indeed, two kinds of abstraction are immediately apparent. Not all state information is causally relevant to action, so one kind of abstraction involves selecting information in S to include in s (e.g., subsets or weighted combinations or projections of the information in S). The other kind of abstraction involves the *structure* of states. Consider the sequence AABACAABACAABACAABADAABAC. Its structure can be described many ways, perhaps most simply by saying, "the sequence AABAx repeats five times, and $x =$C in all but the fourth replication, when $x =$D." This might be the abstraction an agent needs to act; for example, it might condition action on the distinction between AABAC and AABAD, in which case the "right" representation of the sequence above is something like this $p_1 s_1 p_1 s_1 p_1 s_1 p_1 s_2 p_1 s_1$, where p and s denote *structural* features of the original sequence, such as "prefix" and "suffix'. We call representations that include such structural features *structural abstractions*.

To recap, representations s are meaningful if they are related to action by a function $f(s, a) \rightarrow S$, but f can be stated more or less simply depending on the abstraction $s \sim S$. One kind of abstraction involves selecting from the information in S, the other is structural abstraction. The remainder of this paper is concerned with learning structural abstractions.[4] Note that, in Dretske's terms, structural abstractions can be indicator functions but not all indicator functions are structural abstractions. Because the world is dynamic, we are particularly concerned with learning structural abstractions of time series.

2   Approach

In the spirit of dividing problems to conquer them we can view the problem of learning meaningful representations as having two parts:

---

[4] Readers familiar with Artificial Intelligence will recognize the problem of learning structural abstractions as what we call "getting the representation right," a creative process that we reserve unto ourselves and to which, if we are honest, we must attribute most of the performance of our programs.

1. Learn representations $s \sim S$
2. Learn functions $f(s, a) \to S$

This strategy is almost certainly wrong because, as we said, s is supposed to inform actions a, so should be learned while trying to act. Researchers do not always follow the best strategy (we don't, anyway) and the divide and conquer strategy we did follow has produced an unexpected dividend: We now think it is possible that some kinds of structural abstraction are *generally* useful, that is, they inform large classes of actions. (Had we developed algorithms to learn s to inform particular actions a we might have missed this possibility.) Also, some kinds of actions, particularly those involving deictic acts like pointing or saying the name of a referent, provide few constraints on representations.

Our approach, then, is to learn structural abstractions first and functions relating representations and actions to future representations, second.

3 Structural Abstractions of Time Series and Sequences

As a robot wanders around its environment, it generates a sequence of values of state variables. At each instant t we get a vector of values x_t (our robot samples its sensors at 10Hz, so we get ten such vectors each second). Suppose we have a long sequence of such vectors $X = x_0, x_1, \ldots$. Within X are subsequences x_{ij} that, when subjected to processes of structural abstraction, give rise to *episode structures* that are meaningful in the sense of informing action [5]. The trick is to find the subsequences x_{ij} and design the abstraction processes that produce episode structures. We have developed numerous methods of this sort and survey them briefly, here.

3.1 Structural Abstraction for Continuous Multivariate Series

State variables such as translational velocity and sonar readings take continuous values, in contrast to categorical variables such as "object present in the visual field." Figure 1 shows four seconds of data from a Pioneer 1 robot as it moves past an object. Prior to moving, the robot establishes a coordinate frame with an x axis perpendicular to its heading and a y axis parallel to its heading. As it begins to move, the robot measures its location in this coordinate frame. Note that the ROBOT-X line is almost constant. This means that the robot did not change its heading as it moved. In contrast, the ROBOT-Y line increases, indicating that the robot does increase its distance along a line parallel to its original heading. Note especially the VIS-A-X and VIS-A-Y lines, which represent the horizontal and vertical locations, respectively, of the centroid of a patch of light on the robotUs "retina," a CCD camera. VIS-A-X decreases, meaning that the object drifts to the left on the retina, while VIS-A-Y increases, meaning the

---

[5] Ideally, structural abstraction should be an on-line process that influences action continuously. In practice, most of our algorithms gather data in batches, form abstractions, and use these to inform action in later episodes.

object moves toward the top of the retina. Simultaneously, both series jump to constant values. These values are returned by the vision system when nothing is in the field of view.

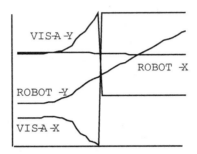

Fig. 1. As the robot moves, an object approaches the periphery of its field of view then passes out of sight.

Every time series that corresponds to moving past an object has qualitatively the same structure as the one in Figure 1. It follows that if we had a statistical technique to group the robotUs experiences by the characteristic patterns in multivariate time series (where the variables represent sensor readings), then this technique would in effect learn a taxonomy of the robotUs experiences. *Clustering by dynamics* [28] is such a technique:

1. A long multivariate time series is divided into segments, each of which represents an episode such as moving toward an object, avoiding an object, crashing into an object, and so on. (Humans divide the series into episodes by hand; more on this in section 5.) The episodes are not labeled in any way.
2. A dynamic time warping algorithm compares every pair of episodes and returns a number that represents the degree of similarity between the time series in the pair. Dynamic time warping is a technique for "morphing" one multivariate time series into another by stretching and compressing the horizontal (temporal) axis of one series relative to the other [13]. The algorithm returns a degree of mismatch (conversely, similarity) between the series after the best fit between them has been found.
3. Given similarity numbers for every pair of episodes, it is straightforward to cluster episodes by their similarity.
4. Another algorithm finds the "central member" of each cluster, which we call the *cluster prototype* following Rosch [24].

Clustering by dynamics produces structural abstractions (prototypes) of time series, the question is whether these abstractions can be meaningful in the sense of informing action. In his PhD dissertation, Matt Schmill shows how to use prototypes as planning operators. The first step is to learn rules of the form, "in state i, action a leads to state j with probability p." These rules are learned by a classical decision-tree induction algorithm, where features of states are decision variables. Given such rules, the robot can plan by means-ends analysis. It plans not to achieve world states specified by exogenous engineers, as in conventional generative planning, but to achieve world states which are preconditions for its actions. Schmill calls this "planning to act," and it has the effect of gradually increasing the size of the corpus of prototypes and things the robot can do. The neat thing about this approach is that every action produces new data, i.e., revises the set of prototypes. It follows that the robot should plan more frequently and more reliably as it gains more experiences, and in recent experiments, Schmill demonstrates this. Thus, Schmill's work shows that clustering by dynamics yields structural abstractions of time series that are meaningful in the sense of informing action.

There is also a strong possibility that prototypes of this kind are meaningful in the sense of informing communicative actions. Oates, Schmill and Cohen [29] report a very high degree of concordance between the clusters of episodes generated by the dynamic time warping method, above, and clusters generated by a human judge. The prototypes produced by dynamic time warping are not weird and unfamiliar to people, but seem to correspond to how humans themselves categorize episodes. Were this not the case, communication would be hard, because the robot would have an ontology of episodes unfamiliar to people. Oates, in particular, has been concerned with communication and language, and has developed several methods for learning structural abstractions of time series that correspond to words in speech and denotations of words in time series of other sensors, as we shall see, shortly.

3.2   Structural Abstraction for Categorical Sequences

Ramoni, Sebastiani and we have developed Bayesian algorithms for clustering activities by their dynamics [18]. In this work, dynamics are captured in first-order markov chains, and so the method is best-suited to clustering sequences of discrete symbols. The Bayesian Clustering by Dynamics (BCD) algorithm is easily sketched: Given time series of tokens that represent states, construct a transition probability table (i.e., a markov chain model) for each series, then measure the similarity between each pair of tables using the Kullback-Liebler (KL) distance, and finally group similar tables into clusters. The BCD algorithm is *agglomerative*, which means that initially, there is one cluster for each markov chain, then markov chains are merged, iteratively, until a stopping criterion is met. Merging two markov chains yields another markov chain. The stopping criterion in BCD is that the posterior probability of the clustering is maximum. Said in another way, BCD solves a Bayesian model selection problem where the model it seeks is the most probable *partition* of the original markov chains given the data and the priors (a partition is a division of a set into mutually exclusive and exhaustive subsets). As the space of partitions is exponential, BCD uses the KL distance as a heuristic to propose which markov chains to merge, but only merges them if doing so improves the marginal likelihood of the resulting partition. We have developed versions of BCD for series of a single state variable and for series of vectors of state variables [18,23].

The clusters found by BCD have never been used by the robot to inform its actions, as in Schmill's experiments, so we cannot say they are meaningful to the robot. It is worth mentioning that they have high concordance with the clustering produced by dynamic time warping and with human clustering, when applied to the series in the Oates et al. experiment, cited above.

3.3   A Critique of Sensory Prototypes

Clustering by dynamics, whether by dynamic time warping or Bayesian model selection, takes a set of time series or sequences and returns a partition of the set. Prototypes, or "average members," may then be extracted from the resulting subsets. While the general idea of clustering by dynamics is attractive (it does produce meaningful structural abstractions), the methods described above have two limitations. First, they require someone (or some algorithm) to divide a time series into shorter series that contain instances of the structures we want to find. For example, if we want to find classes of interactions with objects, we must provide a set of series each of which contains one interaction with objects. Neither technique can accept time series of numerous undifferentiated activities (e.g., produced by a robot roaming the lab for an hour).

A more serious problem concerns the kinds of structural abstraction produced by the methods. The dynamic time warping method produces "average episodes," of which Figure 1 is an example, and BCD produces "average markov chains," which are just probability transition matrices. Suppose we examine an instance of each representation that corresponds to the robot rolling past a cup. Can we find anything in either representation that denotes the cup? We cannot. Consequently, these representations cannot inform actions that depend on individuating the cup; for example, the robot could not respond correctly to the directive, "Turn toward the cup." The abstractions produced by the algorithms contain sufficient structure to cluster the episodes, but still lack much of the structure of the episodes. This is particularly true of the markov chain models, in which the series is chopped up into one-step transitions and all global information about the "shape" of the series is lost, but even the representation in Fig. 1 does not individuate the objects in an episode.

If one is comfortable with a crude distinction between sensations and concepts, then the structural abstractions produced by the methods described above are entirely sensory [21]. They are abstractions of the dynamics of sensor values— of how an episode "feels"—they do not represent concepts such as objects, actors, actions, spatial relationships, and the like. Fig. 1 represents the *sensations* of moving past an object, so it is meaningful if the robot conditions actions on its sensations (as it does in Matt Schmill's work) but it is not a representation of an object, the act of moving, the distance to the object, or any other individuated entity.

Nor for that matter do these abstractions make explicit other structural features of episodes, such as the boundaries between sub-episodes or cycles among states.

Oates has developed methods for learning structural abstractions of time series that individuate words in speech and objects in a scene. Oates' methods are described in the following section. We also have implemented algorithms for finding the boundaries in episodes and the hierarchical structure of episodes; these are described in section 5.

4   Learning Word Meanings

Learning the meanings of words in speech clearly requires individuation of elements in episodes. Suppose we wanted to talk to the robot about cups: We would say, "there's a cup" when we see it looking at a cup; or, "a cup is on your left," when a cup is outside its field of view; or, "point to the cup," when there are several objects in view, and so on. To learn the meaning of the word "cup" the robot must first individuate the word in the speech signal, then individuate the object "cup" in other sensory series, associate the representations; and perhaps estimate some properties of the object corresponding to the cup, such as its color, or the fact that it participates as a target in a "turn toward" activity. In his PhD dissertation, Oates discusses an algorithm called PERUSE that does all these things [20].

To individuate objects in time series Oates relies on *deictic markers* — functions that map from raw sensory data to representations of objects [4,3,1]. A simple deictic marker might construct a representation whenever the area of colored region of the visual field exceeds a threshold. The representation might include attributes such as the color, shape, and area, of the object, as well as the intervals during which it is in view, and so on.

To individuate words in speech, Oates requires a corpus of speech in which words occur multiple times (e.g., multiple sentences contain the word "cup"). Spoken words produce similar (but certainly not identical) patterns in the speech signal, as one can see in Figure 2. (In fact, Oates' representation of the speech signal is multivariate but the univariate series in Fig. 2 will serve to describe his approach.) If one knew that a segment in Figure 2 corresponded to a word, then one could find other segments like it, and construct a prototype or average representation of these. For instance, if one knew that the segment labeled A in Figure 2 corresponds to a word, then one could search for similar segments in the other sentences, find A', and construct a prototype from them. These problems are by no means trivial, as the boundaries of words are not helpfully marked in speech. Oates treats the boundaries as hidden variables and invokes the Expectation Maximization algorithm to learn a model of each word that optimizes the placement of the boundaries. However, it is still necessary to begin with a segment that probably corresponds to a word. To solve this problem, Oates relies on versions of the boundary entropy heuristic and frequency heuristics, discussed below. In brief, the entropy of the distribution of the "next tick" spikes at episode (e.g., word) boundaries; and the patterns in windows that contain boundaries tend to be less frequent than patterns in windows that do not. These heuristics, combined with some methods for growing hypothesized word segments, suffice to bootstrap the process of individuating words in speech.

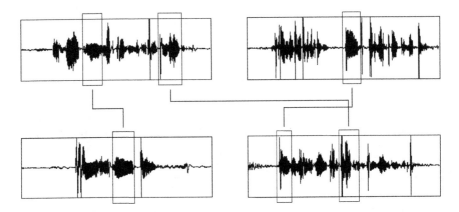

Fig. 2. Corresponding words in four sentences. Word boundaries are shown as boxes around segments of the speech signal. Segments that correspond to the same word are linked by connecting lines.

Given prototypical representations of words in speech, and representations of objects and relations, Oates' algorithm learns associatively the *denotations* of the words. Denotation is a common notion of meaning: The meaning of a symbol is what it points to, refers to, selects from a set, etc. However, naive implementations of denotation run into numerous difficulties, especially when one tries to learn denotations. One difficulty is that the denotations of many (perhaps most) words cannot be specified as boolean combinations of properties (this is sometimes called the problem of necessary and sufficient conditions). Consider the word "cup". With repeated exposure, one might learn that the word denotes prismatic objects less than five inches tall. This is wrong because it is a bad description of cups, and it is more seriously wrong because no such description of cups can reliably divide the world into cups and non-cups (see, e.g., [15,5]).

Another difficulty with naive notions of denotation is referential ambiguity. Does the word "cup" refer to an object, the shape of the object, its color, the actions one performs on it, the spatial relationship between it and another object, or some other feature of the episode in which the word is uttered? How can an algorithm learn the denotation of a word when so many denotations are logically possible?

Let us illustrate Oates' approach to these problems with the word "square," which has a relatively easy denotation. Suppose one's representation of an object includes its apparent height and width, and the ratio of these. An object will appear square if the ratio is near 1.0. Said differently, the word "square" is more likely to be uttered when the ratio is around 1.0 than otherwise. Let ϕ be the group of sensors that measures height, width and their ratio, and let x be the value of the ratio. Let U be an utterance and W be a word in the utterance. Oates defines the denotation of W as follows:

$$denote(W, \phi, x) = Pr(contains(U, W)|about(U, \phi), x) \qquad (1)$$

The denotation of the word "square" is the probability that it is uttered given that the utterance is about the ratio of height to width and the value of the ratio. More plainly, when we say "square" we are talking about the ratio of height to width and we are more likely to use the word when the value of the ratio is close to 1.0. This formulation of denotation effectively dismisses the problem of necessary and sufficient conditions, and it brings the problem of referential ambiguity into sharp focus, for when an algorithm tries to *learn* denotations it does not have access to the quantities on the right hand side of Eq. 1, it has access only to the words it hears:

$$hear(W, \phi, x) = Pr(contains(U, W)|x) \qquad (2)$$

The problem (for which Oates provides an algorithm) is to get $denote(W, \phi, x)$ from $hear(W, \phi, x)$.

At this juncture, however, we have said enough to make the case that word meanings can be learned from time series of sensor and speech data. We claim that Oates' PERUSE algorithm constructs representations and learns their meanings by itself. Although the deictic representations of objects are not learned, the representations of words *are* learned and so are the associations between features of the deictic representations and words. PERUSE learns "above" and learns to associate the word with a spatial relationship. At no point does an engineer implant representations in the system and provide them with interpretations. Although PERUSE is a suite of statistical methods, it is about as far from the data analysis paradigm with which we began this paper as one can imagine. In that example, an analyst and his client domain expert select and provide data to a linear regression algorithm because it means something to them, and the algorithm computes a regression model that (presumably) means something to them. Neither data nor model mean anything to the algorithm. In contrast, PERUSE selects and processes speech data in such a way that the resulting prototypes are likely to be individuated entities (more on this, below), and it assigns meaning to these entities by finding their denotations as described earlier. Structural abstraction of representations and assignment of meaning are all done by PERUSE.

The algorithm clearly learns meaningful representations, but are they meaningful in the sense of informing action? As it happens, PERUSE builds word representations sufficient for a robot to respond to spoken commands and to translate words between English, German and Mandarin Chinese. The denotational meanings of the representations are therefore sufficient to inform some communicative acts.

5   Elucidating Episode Structure

Earlier we described our problem as learning structural abstractions of state information, particularly abstractions of the dynamics of state variables, which inform action. Section 3 introduced clustering by dynamics and sensory abstractions which did not individuate objects or the structure of a robot's activities. The previous section showed how to individuate words and objects and learn denotations. This section is concerned with the structure of activities.

Time series data are sampled at some frequency (10 Hz for our robots) but the robot changes what it is doing more slowly. Of course, one can describe what a robot is doing at any time scale (up to 10 Hz), but some descriptions are better than others in ways we will describe shortly. First, an example. Figure 3 shows three variables from a multivariate time series, each running for 1500 ticks, or 150 seconds. These series together tell a story: the robot approaches an object and starts to orbit it; at two points (around tick 500 and again around tick 800) the object disappears from view, and the robot's movement pattern changes in response. At this relatively macroscopic scale, then, the robot changes its activity half a dozen times, although, as one can see, its sensor values change with much higher frequency.

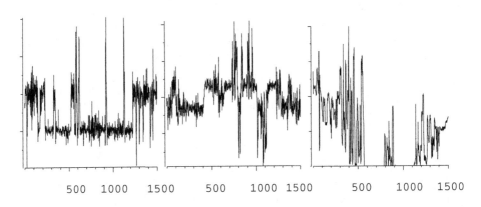

500   1000   1500   500   1000 1500   500   1000   1500

Fig. 3. Time series of translational velocity, rotational velocity, and area of a region in the visual field.

By *episodic structure* we mean relatively macroscopic patterns in time series that are meaningful in the sense of informing action. If Oates showed how to individuate things we might denote with nouns, prepositions, and adjectives, episodic structure individuates things we might denote with verbs.

As noted earlier, the right way to proceed might be to couple the problem of learning episodic structure with the problem of learning how to act, but we have approached the problems as if they were independent. This means we need a way to assess whether a segment of a time series is apt to be meaningful—capable of informing action—which is independent of the actions an agent might perform.

Said differently, we are looking for a particular kind of marker in time series, one that says, "If you divide the series at these markers, then there is a good chance that the segments between the markers will be meaningful in the sense of informing action."

We have identified four kinds of markers of episode structures.

Coincidences. Random coincidences are rare, so coincidences often mark the boundaries of episode structures. Figure 4 shows the same time series as in Figure 3, though the series have been smoothed and shifted vertically away from each other on the vertical axis. Vertical lines have been added at some of the points where two or more of the series change slope sharply. Now, if the series were unrelated, then such an inflection in one would be very unlikely to coincide with an inflection in another, for inflections are rare. If rare events in two or more series coincide, then the series are probably not unrelated. Moreover, the points of coincidence are good markers of episode structures, as they are points at which something causes changes in the series to coincide.

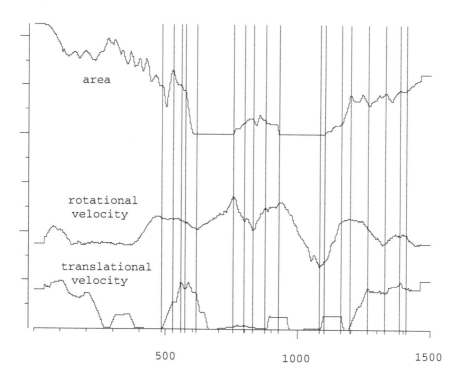

Fig. 4. The series from Figure 3, smoothed and shifted apart on the vertical axis. Vertical lines show points at which two or more of the series experience a significant change in slope.

Boundary entropy. Every unique subsequence in a series is characterized by the distribution of subsequences that follow it; for example, the subsequence

"en" in this sentence repeats five times and is followed by tokens c, ", t and s. This distribution has an entropy value. In general, every subsequence of length has a *boundary entropy*, which is the entropy of the distribution of subsequences that follow it. If a subsequence S is an episode, then the boundary entropies of subsequences of S will have an interesting profile: They will start relatively high, then sometimes drop, then peak at the last element of S. The reasons for this are, first, that the predictability of elements within an episode increases as the episode extends over time; and, second, that the element that immediately follows an episode is relatively uncertain. Said differently, within episodes, we know roughly what will happen, but at episode boundaries we become uncertain.
Frequency. Episode structures are meaningful if they inform action. Rare structures might be informative in the information theoretic sense, have few opportunities to inform action because they arise infrequently. Consequently, all human and animal learning places a premium on frequency (and, by the way, learning curves have their characteristic shape). In general, episode structures are common structures. However, not all common structures are episode structures. Very often, the most frequent structures in a domain are the smallest or shortest, while the meaningful structures—those that inform action—are longer. A useful example of this phenomenon comes from word morphology. The following subsequences are the 100 most frequently-occurring patterns in the first 10,000 characters of Orwell's book *1984*, but many are not morphemes, that is, meaningful units:

> th in the re an en as ed to ou it er of at ing was or st on ar and es ic el al om
> ad ac is wh le ow ld ly ere he wi ab im ver be for had ent itwas with ir win gh
> po se id ch ot ton ap str his ro li all et fr andthe ould min il ay un ut ur ve
> whic dow which si pl am ul res that were ethe wins not winston sh oo up ack
> ter ough from ce ag pos bl by tel ain

Even so, frequency provides a good marker for the boundaries of episode structures. Suppose that the subsequences wx and yz are both both very common and subsequence xy is rare; where would you place a boundary in the sequence $wxyz$?
Changes in Probability Distributions. Sequences can be viewed as the outputs of finite state machines, and many researchers are interested in inducing the machines that generate sequences. Our interest is slightly different; we want to know the boundaries of sequences. Another way to say this is we want to place boundaries in such a way that the probability distributions to the left and right of the boundaries are different.

5.1   Algorithms

This section presents two algorithms for learning episode structures. The first is based on the coincidence heuristic, above; the second relies on boundary entropy and frequency. These algorithms are described in detail in [6,7], respectively, and some of the material in the following sections is excerpted from these papers. We are working on an online version of BCD that implements the "change in probability distribution" heuristic but the work is preliminary.

Fluents and Temporal Relationships. The fluent learning algorithm induces episode structures from time series of binary vectors. A binary vector $\boldsymbol{b}_t$ is a simple representation of a set of logical propositions at time t: $\boldsymbol{b}[i]_t = 1$ means proposition p_i is true. If a proposition is true for all the discrete times in the range m, n (i.e., $\boldsymbol{b}[i]_{m,n} = 1$) then the proposition is called a *base fluent*. (States with persistence are called fluents by McCarthy [19].) In an experiment with a Pioneer 1 mobile robot, we collected a dataset of 22535 binary vectors of length 9. Sensor readings such as translational and rotational velocity, the output of a "blob vision" system, sonar values, and the states of gripper and bump sensors, were inputs to a simple perceptual system that produced the following nine propositions: STOP, ROTATE-RIGHT, ROTATE-LEFT, MOVE-FORWARD, NEAR-OBJECT, PUSH, TOUCH, MOVE-BACKWARD, STALL.

Allen [2] gave a logic for relationships between the beginnings and ends of fluents. We use a nearly identical set of relationships:

SBEB   X starts before Y, ends before Y; Allen's "overlap"
SWEB   Y starts with X, ends before X; Allen's "starts"
SAEW   Y starts after X, ends with X; Allen's "finishes"
SAEB   Y starts after X, ends before X; Allen's "during"
SWEW   Y starts with X, ends with X; Allen's "equal"
SE   Y starts after X ends; amalgamating Allen's "meets" and "before"

In Allen's calculus, "meets" means the end of X coincides exactly with the beginning of Y, while "before" means the former event precedes the latter by some interval. In our work, the truth of a predicate such as SE or SBEB depends on whether start and end events happen within a window of brief duration. Said differently, "starts with" means "starts within a few ticks off" and "starts before" means "starts more than a few ticks before." The reason for this window is that on a robot, it takes time for events to show up in sensor data and be processed perceptually into propositions, so coinciding events will not necessarily produce propositional representations at exactly the same time.

Let $\rho \in$ [SBEB,SWEB,SAEW,SAEB,SWEW,SE], and let f be a proposition (e.g., MOVING-FORWARD). Composite fluents have the form:

$$F \leftarrow f \mid \rho(f, f)$$
$$CF \leftarrow \rho(F, F)$$

That is, a fluent F may be a proposition or a temporal relationship between propositions, and a composite fluent is a temporal relationship between fluents. A situation has many alternative fluent representations, we want a method for choosing some over others. The method will be statistical: We will only accept $\rho(F, F)$ as a representation if the constituent fluents are statistically associated, if they "go together."

Consider a composite fluent like SBEB(brake,clutch): When I approach a stop light in my standard transmission car, I start to brake, then depress the clutch to stop the car stalling; later I release the brake to start accelerating, and then I release the clutch. To see whether this fluent— SBEB(brake,clutch)—is statistically significant, we need two contingency tables, one for the relationship "start braking then start to depress the clutch" and one for "end braking and then end depressing the clutch":

	$s(x=clutch)$	$s(x!=clutch)$			$e(x=clutch)$	$e(x!=clutch)$
$s(x=brake)$	$a1$	$b1$		$e(x=brake)$	$a2$	$b2$
$s(x!=brake)$	$c1$	$d1$		$e(x!=brake)$	$c2$	$d2$

Imagine some representative numbers in these tables: Only rarely do I start something other than braking and then depress the clutch, so $c1$ is small. Only rarely do I start braking and then start something other than depressing the clutch (otherwise the car would stall), so $b1$ is also small. Clearly, $a1$ is relatively large, and $d1$ bigger, still, so the first table has most of its frequencies on a diagonal, and will produce a significant χ^2 statistic. Similar arguments hold for the second table. When both tables are significant, we say SBEB(brake,clutch) is a significant composite fluent.

Fluent learning algorithm. The fluent learning algorithm incrementally processes a time series of binary vectors. At each tick, a bit in the vector $\boldsymbol{b_t}$ is in one of four states:

$$\text{Still off: } b_{t-1} = 0 \wedge b_t = 0$$
$$\text{Still on: } b_{t-1} = 1 \wedge b_t = 1$$
$$\text{Just off: } b_{t-1} = 1 \wedge b_t = 0$$
$$\text{Just on: } b_{t-1} = 0 \wedge b_t = 1$$

The fourth case is called *opening*; the third case *closing*. It is easy to test when base fluents (those corresponding to propositions) open and close, slightly more complicated for composite fluents such as SBEB(f_1,f_2), because of the ambiguity about which fluent opened. Suppose we see open(f_1) and then open(f_2). It's unclear whether we have just observed open(SBEB(f_1,f_2)), open(SAEB(f_1,f_2)), or open(SAEW(f_1,f_2)). Only when we see whether f_2 closes after, before, or with f_1 will we know which of the three composite fluents opened with the opening of f_2.

The fluent learning algorithm maintains contingency tables that count co-occurrences of open and close events. We restrict the number of ticks, m, by which one opening must happen after another: m must be bigger than a few ticks, otherwise we treat the openings as simultaneous; and it must be smaller than the length of a short-term memory.[6] At each tick, the algorithm first decides which simple and composite fluents have closed. With this information, it can

---

[6] The short term memory has two kinds of justification. First, animals do not learn associations between events that occur far apart in time. Second, if every open event could be paired with every other (and every close event) over a long duration, then the fluent learning system would have to maintain an enormous number of contingency tables.

disambiguate which composite fluents opened at an earlier time (within the bounds of short term memory). Then, it finds out which simple and composite fluents have just opened, or might have opened. This done, it updates the open and close contingency tables for all fluents that have just closed. Next, it updates the χ_2 statistic for each table and it adds the newly significant composite fluents to the list of accepted fluents.

Two fluents learned by the algorithm are shown in Figure 5 (others are discussed in [6]). These fluents were never used by the robot for anything (besides learning other fluents) so they are not meaningful representations in the sense of Section 1, but they illustrate the kind of structural abstractions produced by the fluent learning process. The first captures a strong regularity in how the robot approaches an obstacle. Once the robot detects an object visually, it moves toward it quite quickly, until the sonars detect the object. At that point, the robot immediately stops, and then moves forward more slowly. Thus, we expect to see SAEB(NEAR-OBJECT,STOP), and we expect this fluent to start before MOVE-FORWARD, as shown in the first fluent. The second fluent shows that the robot stops when it touches an object but remains touching the object after the STOP fluent closes (SWEB(TOUCH,STOP)) and this composite fluent starts before and ends before another composite fluent in which the robot is simultaneously moving forward and pushing the object. This fluent describes exactly how the robot pushes an object.

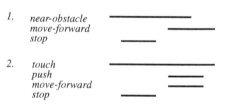

Fig. 5. Two composite fluents. These were learned without supervision from a time series of 22535 binary vectors of robot data.

Fluent learning works for multivariate time series in which all the variables are binary. It does not attend to the durations of fluents, only the temporal relationships between open and close events. This is an advantage in domains where the same episode can take different amounts of time, and a disadvantage in domains where duration matters. Because it is a statistical technique, fluent learning finds common patterns, not all patterns; it is easily biased to find more or fewer patterns by adjusting the threshold value of the statistic and varying the size of the fluent short term memory. Fluent learning elucidates the hierarchical structure of episodes (i.e., episodes contain episodes) because fluents are themselves nested. We are not aware of any other algorithm that is unsupervised, incremental, multivariate, and elucidates the hierarchical structure of episodes.

The Voting Experts Algorithm. The voting experts algorithm is designed to find boundaries of substructures within episodes, places where one macroscopic part of an episode gives way to another. It incorporates "experts" that attend to boundary entropy and frequency, and is easily extensible to include experts that attend to other characteristics of episode structures. Currently the algorithm works with univariate sequences of categorical data. The algorithm simply moves a window across a time series and asks, for each location in the window, whether to "cut" the series at that location. Each expert casts a vote. Each location takes n steps to traverse a window of size n, and is seen by the experts in n different contexts, and may accrue up to n votes from each expert. Given the results of voting, it is a simple matter to cut the series at locations with high vote counts. The algorithm has been tested extensively with sequences of letters in text: Spaces, punctuation and capitalization are removed, and the algorithm is able to recover word boundaries. It also performs adequately, though not brilliantly, on sequences of robot states. Research in that domain continues.

Here are the steps of the algorithm:

Build a prefix tree of depth $n+1$. Nodes at level i of an prefix tree represent ngrams of length i. The children of a node are the extensions of the ngram represented by the node. For example, $a\ b\ c\ a\ b\ d$ produces the following prefix tree of depth 2:

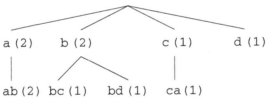

Every ngram of length 2 or less in the sequence $a\ b\ c\ a\ b\ d$ is represented by a node in this tree. The numbers in parentheses represent the frequencies of the subsequences. For example, the subsequence $a\ b$ occurs twice, and every occurrence of a is followed by b.

For the first 10,000 characters in George Orwell's book *1984*, a prefix tree of depth 7 includes 33774 nodes, of which 9109 are leaf nodes. That is, there are over nine thousand unique subsequences of length 7 in this sample of text, although the average frequency of these subsequences is 1.1; most occur exactly once. The average frequencies of subsequences of length 1 to 7 are 384.4, 23.1, 3.9, 1.8, 1.3, 1.2, and 1.1.

Calculate boundary entropy. The boundary entropy of an ngram is the entropy of the distribution of tokens that can extend the ngram. The entropy of a distribution of a random variable x is just $-\sum Pr(x)\log Pr(x)$. Boundary entropy is easily calculated from the prefix tree. For example, the node a has entropy equal to zero because it has only one child whereas the entropy of node b is 1.0 because it has two equiprobable children.

Standardize frequencies and boundary entropies. In most domains, there is a systematic relationship between the length and frequency of patterns; in general, short patterns are more common than long ones (e.g., on average, for subsets of 10,000 characters from Orwell's text, 64 of the 100 most frequent patterns are of length 2; 23 are of length 3, and so on). Our algorithm will compare the frequencies and boundary entropies of ngrams of different lengths, but in all cases we will be comparing how *unusual* these frequencies and entropies are, relative to other ngrams of the same length. To illustrate, consider the words "a" and "an". In the first 10000 characters of Orwell's text, "a" occurs 743 times, "an" 124 times, but "a" occurs only a little more frequently than other one-letter ngrams, whereas "an" occurs much more often than other two-letter ngrams. In this sense, "a" is ordinary, "an" is unusual. Although "a" is much more common than "an" it is much less unusual relative to other ngrams of the same length. To capture this notion, we standardize the frequencies and boundary entropies of the ngrams. Standardized, the frequency of "a" is 1.1, whereas the frequency of "an" is 20.4. We standardize boundary entropies in the same way, and for the same reason.

Score potential segment boundaries. In a sequence of length k there are $k - 1$ places to draw boundaries between segments, and, thus, there are 2^{k-1} ways to divide the sequence into segments. Our algorithm is greedy in the sense that it considers just $k - 1$, not 2^{k-1}, ways to divide the sequence. It considers each possible boundary in order, starting at the beginning of the sequence. The algorithm passes a window of length n over the sequence, halting at each possible boundary. All of the locations within the window are considered, and each garners zero or one vote from each expert. Because we have two experts, for boundary-entropy and frequency, respectively, each possible boundary may garner up to $2n$ votes. This is illustrated in Figure 6. A window of length 3 is passed along the sequence itwasacold.

Initially, the window covers itw. The entropy and frequency experts each decide where they could best insert a boundary within the window. The boundary entropy expert votes for the location that produces the ngram with the highest standardized boundary entropy, and the frequency expert places a boundary so as to maximize the sum of the standardized frequencies of the ngrams to the left and the right of the boundary. In this example, the entropy expert favors the boundary between t and w, while the frequency expert favors the boundary between w and whatever comes next. Then the window moves one location to the right and the process repeats. This time, both experts decide to place the boundary between t and w. The window moves again and both experts decide to place the boundary after s, the last token in the window. Note that each potential boundary location (e.g., between t and w) is seen n times for a window of size n, but it is considered in a slightly different context each time the window moves. The first time the experts consider the boundary between w and a, they are looking at the window itw, and the last time, they are looking at was.

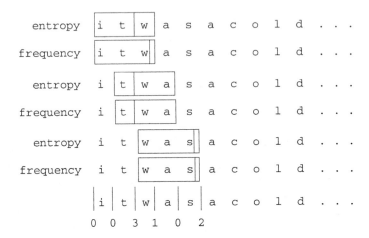

Fig. 6. The operation of the voting experts algorithm.

In this way, each boundary gets up to $2n$ votes, or $n = 3$ votes from each of two experts. The wa boundary gets one vote, the tw boundary, three votes, and the sa boundary, two votes.

Segment the sequence. Each potential boundary in a sequence accrues votes, as described above, and now we must evaluate the boundaries in terms of the votes and decide where to segment the sequence. Our method is a familiar "zero crossing" rule: If a potential boundary has a locally maximum number of votes, split the sequence at that boundary. In the example above, this rule causes the sequence itwasacold to be split after it and was. We confess to one embellishment on the rule: The number of votes for a boundary must exceed a threshold, as well as be a local maximum. We found that the algorithm splits too often without this qualification. In the experiments reported below, the threshold was always set to n, the window size. This means that a location must garner half the available votes (for two voting experts) and be a local maximum to qualify for splitting the sequence.

The algorithm performs well at a challenging task, illustrated below. In this block of text—the first 200 characters in Orwell's *1984*—all spaces and punctuation have been excised, and all letters made capital; and to foil your ability to recognize words, the letters have been recoded in a simple way (each letter is replaced by its neighbor to the right in the alphabet, and Z by A):

H S V Z R Z A Q H F G S B N K C C Z X H M Z O Q H K Z M C S G D B K N B J R V D Q D R S Q
H J H M F S G H Q S D D M V H M R S N M R L H S G G H R B G H M M T Y Y K D C H M S N G
H R A Q D Z R S H M Z M D E E N Q S S N D R B Z O D S G D U H K D V H M C R K H O O D C
P T H B J K X S G Q N T F G S G D F K Z R R C N N Q R N E U H B S N Q X L Z M R H N M R S
G N T F G M N S P T H B J K X D M N T F G S

Suppose you had a block of text several thousand characters long to study at leisure. Could you place boundaries where they should go, that is, in locations that correspond to words in the original text? (You will agree that the original text is no more meaningful to the voting experts algorithm than the text above is to you, so the problem we pose to you is no different than the one solved by the algorithm.)

To evaluate the algorithm we designed several performance measures. The *hit rate* is the number of boundaries in the text that were indicated by the algorithm, and the *false positive rate* is the number of boundaries indicated by the algorithm that were not boundaries in the text. The *exact word* rate is the proportion of words for which the algorithm found both boundaries; the *dangling* and *lost* rates are the proportions of words for which the algorithm identifies only one, or neither, boundary, respectively. We ran the algorithm on corpora of Roma-ji text and a segment of Franz Kafka's *The Castle* in the original German. Roma-ji is a transliteration of Japanese into roman characters. The corpus was a set of Anime lyrics, comprising 19163 roman characters. For comparison purposes we selected the first 19163 characters of Kafka's text and the same number of characters from Orwell's text. We stripped away spaces, puncuation and capitalization and the algorithm induced word boundaries. Here are the results:

	Hit rate	F. P. rate	Exact	Dangling	Lost
English	.71	.28	.49	.44	.07
German	.79	.31	.61	.35	.04
Roma-ji	.64	.34	.37	.53	.10

Clearly, the algorithm is not biased to do well on English, in particular, as it actually performs best on Kafka's text, losing only 4% of the words and identifying 61% exactly. The algorithm performs less well with the Roma-ji text; it identifies fewer boundaries accurately (i.e., places 34% of its boundaries within words) and identifies fewer words exactly. The explanation for these results has to do with the lengths of words in the corpora. We know that the algorithm loses disproportionately many short words. Words of length 2 make up 32% of the Roma-ji corpus, 17% of the Orwell corpus, and 10% of the Kafka corpus, so it is not surprising that the algorithm performs worst on the Roma-ji corpus and best on the Kafka corpus.

As noted earlier, the algorithm performs less well with time series of robot states. The problem seems to be that episode substructures are quite long (over six seconds or 60 discrete ticks of data, on average, compared with Orwell's average word length, around 5.) The voting experts algorithm can find episode structures that are longer than the depth of its prefix tree, but recall that the frequency of ngrams drops with their length, so most long ngrams occur only once. This means the frequency and boundary entropy experts have no distributions to work with, and even if they did, they would have difficulty estimating the distributions with any accuracy from such small numbers.

Still, it is remarkable that two very general heuristic methods can segment text into words with such accuracy. Our results lead us to speculate that frequency and boundary entropy are general markers of episode substructures, a claim we are in the process of testing in other domains. Recall that Oates used these heuristics to bootstrap the process of finding words in the speech signal.

6 Conclusion

The central claim of this paper is that programs can learn representations and their meanings. We adopted Dretske's definition that a representation is meaningful if it reliably indicates something about the external world and the indicator relationship is exploited to inform action. These criteria place few constraints on what is represented, how it is represented, and how representations inform action, yet these questions lie at the heart of AI engineering design, and answering them well requires considerable engineering skill. Moreover, these criteria admit representations that are meaningful in the given sense *to an engineer* but not to a program. This is one reason Dretske [12] required that the function of the indicator relationship be *learned*, to ensure that meaning is endogenous in the learning agent. Dretske's requirement leads to some philosophical problems [10] and we do not think it can survive as a *criterion* for contentful mental states [8]. However, we want programs to learn the meanings of representations not as a condition in a philosophical account of representation, meaning and belief, but as a practical move beyond current AI engineering practice, in which all meanings are exogenous; and as a demonstration of how symbolic representations might develop in infant humans.

What is the status of our claim that programs can learn representations and their meanings? As our adopted notion of meaning does not constrain what is represented, how it is represented, and how representations inform action, we have considerable freedom in how we gather evidence relevant to the claim. In fact, we imposed additional constraints on learned representations in our empirical work: They should be grounded in sensor data from a robot; the data should have a temporal aspect and time or the ordinal sequence of things should be an explicit part of the learned representations; and the representations should not merely inform action, but should inform two essentially human intellectual accomplishments, language and planning. We have demonstrated that a robot can learn the meanings of words, and construct simple plans, and that both these abilities depend on representations and meanings learned by the robot. In general, we have specified *how* things are to be represented (e.g., as transition probability matrices, sequences of means and variances, multivariate time series, fluents, etc.) but the contents of the representations (i.e., what is represented) and the relationship between the contents and actions have been learned.

Acknowledgments. The authors wish to thank the many graduate students who have worked on the Robot Baby project, particularly Marc Atkin, Brendan Burns, Anyuan Guo, Brent Heeringa, Gary King, Laura Firiou, and Matt Schmill. We thank Mary Litch, Clayton Morrison, Marco Ramoni and Paola Sebastiani for their lively contributions to the ideas herein. David Westbrook deserves special thanks from all the members of the Experimental Knowledge Systems Laboratory for his many contributions.

This work was supported by DARPA under contract(s) DARPA / USAS-MDCDASG60 - 99 - C -0074 and DARPA / AFRLF30602-00-1-0529, and by a Visiting Fellowship Research Grant number GR/N24193 to support Paul Cohen from the Engineering and Physical Sciences Research Council (UK).

References

1. Philip E. Agre and David Chapman. Pengi: An implementation of a theory of activity. In *Proceedings of the Sixth National Conference on Artificial Intelligence*, pages 268–272, Seattle, Washington, 1987. American Association for Artificial Intelligence.
2. James F. Allen. An interval based representation of temporal knowledge. In *Proceedings of the Seventh International Joint Conference on Artificial Intelligence*, pages 221–226, San Mateo, CA, 1981. Morgan Kaufmann Publishers, Inc.
3. Dana H. Ballard, Mary M. Hayhoe, and Polly K. Pook. Deictic codes for the embodiment of cognition. Computer Science Department, University of Rochester.
4. D.H. Ballard. Reference frames for animate vision. In *Proceedings of the Eleventh International Joint Conference on Artificial Intelligenc*. Morgan Kaufmann Publishers, Inc., 1989.
5. Paul Bloom. *How Children Learn the Meanings of Words*. MIT Press, 2000.
6. Paul Cohen. Fluent learning: Elucidating the structure of episodes. In *Proceedings of Fourth Symposium on Intelligent Data Analysis*. Springer, 2001.
7. Paul Cohen and Niall Adams. An algorithm for segmenting categorical time series into meaningful episodes. In *Proceedings of Fourth Symposium on Intelligent Data Analysis*. Springer, 2001.
8. Paul R. Cohen and Mary Litch. What are contentful mental states? dretske's theory of mental content viewed in the light of robot learning and planning algorithms. In *Proceedings of the Sixteenth National Conference on Artificial Intelligence*, 1999.
9. Bénédicte de Boysson-Bardies. *How Language Comes to Children*. MIT Press, 2001.
10. Daniel Dennett. Do it yourself understanding. In Daniel Dennett, editor, *Brainchildren, Essays on Designing Minds*. MIT Press and Penguin, 1998.
11. Fred Dretske. *Knowledge and the Flow of Information*. Cambridge University Press, 1981. Reprinted by CSLI Publications, Stanford University.
12. Fred Dretske. *Explaining Behavior: Reasons in a World of Causes*. MIT Press, 1988.
13. Joseph B. Kruskall and Mark Liberman. The symmetric time warping problem: From continuous to discrete. In *Time Warps, String Edits and Macromolecules: The Theory and Practice of Sequence Comparison*. Addison-Wesley, 1983.
14. B. Kuipers. The spatial semantic hierarchy. *Artificial Intelligence*, 119:191–233, 2000.
15. George Lakoff. *Women, Fire, and Dangerous Things*. University of Chicago Press, 1984.
16. D. B. Lenat. Cyc: Towards programs with common sense. *Communications of the ACM*, 33(8), 1990.
17. D. B. Lenat and R. V. Guha. *Building large knowledge-based systems: Representation and inference in the Cyc project*. Addison Wesley, 1990.

18. Paola Sebastiani, Marco Ramoni and Paul Cohen. Bayesian clustering by dynamics. *Machine Learning*, to appear(to appear):to appear, 2001.
19. John McCarthy. Situations, actions and causal laws. Stanford Artificial Intelligence Project: Memo 2, also, http://wwwformal.stanford.edu/jmc/mcchay69/ mcchay69.htm, 1963.
20. J. T. Oates. *Grounding Knowledge in Sensors: Unsupervised Learning for Language and Planning*. PhD thesis, Department of Computer Science, University of Massachusetts, 2001.
21. Tim Oates, Paul R. Cohen, Marc S. Atkin and Carole R. Beal. NEO: Learning conceptual knowledge by sensorimotor interaction with an environment. In *Proceedings of the First International Conference on Autonomous Agents*, pages 170–177, 1997.
22. David Pierce and Benjamin Kuipers. Map learning with uninterpreted sensors and effectors. *Artificial Intelligence Journal*, 92:169–229, 1997.
23. Marco Ramoni, Paola Sebastiani, and Paul Cohen. Multivariate clustering by dynamics. In *Proceedings of the Seventeenth National Conference on AI*, pages 633–638. AAAI Press/The MIT Press, 2000.
24. E. Rosch and C. B. Mervis. Family resemblances: Studies in the internal structure of categories. *Cognitive Psychology*, 7:573–605, 1975.
25. Robert St. Amant and Paul R. Cohen. Intelligent Support for Exploratory Data Analysis. *The Journal of Computational and Graphical Statistics*, 1998.
26. Robert St. Amant and Paul R. Cohen. Interaction With a Mixed-Initiative System for Exploratory Data Analysis. *Knowledge-Based Systems*, 10(5):265–273, 1998.
27. Luc Steels. *The Talking Heads Experiment: Volume I. Words and Meanings*. Laboratorium, Antwerpen, 1999. This is a museum catalog but is in preparation as a book.
28. Paul Cohen, Tim Oates, Matthew Schmill. Identifying qualitatively different outcomes of actions: Gaining autonomy through learning. In *Proceedings Fourth International Conference on Autonomous Agents, pp 110-111*. ACM, 2000.
29. Paul Cohen, Tim Oates, Matthew Schmill. A method for clustering the experience of a mobile robot that accords with human judgments. In *Proceedings of Seventeenth National Conference, pp. 846-851*. AAAI Press/The MIT Press, 2000.
30. Paul Utgoff and Paul R. Cohen. Applicability of reinforcement learning. In *The Methodology of Applying Machine leraning Problem Definition, Task Decompostion and Technique Selection Workshop, ICML-98*, pages 37–43, 1998.

Discovering Mechanisms: A Computational Philosophy of Science Perspective*

Lindley Darden

Department of Philosophy
University of Maryland
College Park, MD 20742
darden@carnap.umd.edu
http://www.inform.umd.edu/PHIL/faculty/LDarden/

Abstract. A task in the philosophy of discovery is to find reasoning strategies for discovery, which fall into three categories: strategies for generation, evaluation and revision. Because mechanisms are often what is discovered in biology, a new characterization of mechanism aids in their discovery. A computational system for discovering mechanisms is sketched, consisting of a simulator, a library of mechanism schemas and components, and a discoverer for generating, evaluating and revising proposed mechanism schemas. Revisions go through stages from how possibly to how plausibly to how actually.

* The full version of this paper is published in the Proceedings of the 4th International Conference on Discovery Science, Lecture Notes in Artificial Intelligence Vol. 2226

N. Abe, R. Khardon, and T. Zeugmann (Eds.): ALT 2001, LNAI 2225, p. 57, 2001.

Inventing Discovery Tools: Combining Information Visualization with Data Mining*

Ben Shneiderman

Department of Computer Science, Human-Computer Interaction Laboratory,
Institute for Advanced Computer Studies, and Institute for Systems Research
University of Maryland, College Park, MD 20742 USA
ben@cs.umd.edu

Abstract. The growing use of information visualization tools and data mining algorithms stems from two separate lines of research. Information visualization researchers believe in the importance of giving users an overview and insight into the data distributions, while data mining researchers believe that statistical algorithms and machine learning can be relied on to find the interesting patterns. This paper discusses two issues that influence design of discovery tools: statistical algorithms vs. visual data presentation, and hypothesis testing vs. exploratory data analysis. I claim that a combined approach could lead to novel discovery tools that preserve user control, enable more effective exploration, and promote responsibility.

---

* The full version of this paper is published in the Proceedings of the 4th International Conference on Discovery Science, Lecture Notes in Artificial Intelligence Vol. 2226

N. Abe, R. Khardon, and T. Zeugmann (Eds.): ALT 2001, LNAI 2225, p. 58, 2001.

On Learning Correlated Boolean Functions
Using Statistical Queries (Extended Abstract)

Ke Yang

Computer Science Department, Carnegie Mellon University, 5000 Forbes Ave.,
Pittsburgh, PA 15213, USA.
yangke@cs.cmu.edu,
http://www.cs.cmu.edu/~yangke

Abstract. In this paper, we study the problem of using statistical query (SQ) to learn a class of highly correlated boolean functions, namely, a class of functions where any pair agree on significantly more than $1/2$ fraction of the inputs. We give an almost-tight bound on how well one can approximate all the functions without making any query, and then we show that beyond this bound, the number of statistical queries the algorithm has to make increases with the "extra" advantage the algorithm gains in learning the functions. Here the advantage is defined to be the probability the algorithm agrees with the target function minus the probability the algorithm doesn't agree.

An interesting consequence of our results is that the class of booleanized linear functions over a finite field $(f_{(a}(x) = 1$ iff $\phi(a \cdot x) = 1$, where ϕ is an arbitrary boolean function that maps any elements in GF_p to ± 1) is not efficiently learnable. This result is useful since the hardness of learning booleanized linear functions over a finite field is related to the security of certain cryptosystems ([B01]). In particular, we prove that the class of linear threshold functions over a finite field $(f_{(a,b}(x) = 1$ iff $a \cdot x \geq b)$ cannot be learned efficiently using statistical query. This contrasts with Blum et. al.'s result [BFK+96] that linear threshold functions over reals (perceptions) are learnable using the SQ model.

Finally, we describe a PAC-learning algorithm that learns a class of linear threshold functions in time that is provably impossible for statistical query algorithms. With properly chosen parameters, this class of linear threshold functions become an example of PAC-learnable, but not SQ-learnable functions that are not parity functions.

1   Introduction

Pioneered by Valiant [V84], machine learning theory is concerned with problems like "What class of functions can be efficiently learned under this learning model?". Among different learning models there are the Probably Approximately Correct model (PAC) by Valiant [V84] and the Statistical Query model (SQ) by Kearns [K98].

The SQ model is a restriction to the PAC model, where the learning algorithm doesn't see the samples with their labels, but only get the probabilities that a

N. Abe, R. Khardon, and T. Zeugmann (Eds.): ALT 2001, LNAI 2225, pp. 59–76, 2001.

predicate is true: to be more precise, the learning algorithm provides a predicate
· $g(x, y)$ and a tolerance ϵ, and an SQ oracle returns a real number v that is ϵ-close
to the expected value of $g(x, f(x))$ according a distribution of x, where f is the
target functions. While seemingly a lot weaker than the PAC model, SQ model
turns out to be very useful: in fact, a lot of known PAC learning algorithms are
actually SQ model algorithms, or can be converted to SQ model algorithms. The
readers are referred to [K98] for a more comprehensive description.

One interesting feature for SQ model is that there are information-theoretical
lower-bounds on the learnability of certain classes of functions. Kearns [K98]
proved that parity functions cannot be efficiently learned in the SQ model. Blum
et. al. [BFJ+94] extended his result by showing that if a class of functions has
"SQ-dimension" (informally, the maximum number of "almost un-correlated"
functions in the class, where the "correlation" between two functions is the
probability these two functions agree minus the probability they disagree) d,
then a SQ learning algorithm has to make $\Omega(d^{1/3})$ queries, each of tolerance
$O(d^{-1/3})$ in order to weakly learn $\mathcal{F}$. In [J00], Jackson further strengthened
this lower bound by proving that $\Omega(2^n)$ queries are needed for an SQ-based
algorithm to learn the class of parity functions over n bits. This result can
be extended to any class of completely uncorrelated functions: $\Omega(d)$ queries
are needed for an SQ-based algorithm to learn a class of functions if this class
contains d functions that are completely uncorrelated. Notice that this upper
bound is optimal: [BFJ+94] proved that there are weak-learning algorithms for
the class of functions using $O(d)$ queries.

In this paper, we study the problem of learning *correlated* functions. Suppose
there is a class of boolean functions $\mathcal{F} = \{f_1, f_2, ..., f_d\}$, where any pair functions f_i, f_j are highly correlated, namely f_i and f_j agree on $(1 + \lambda)/2$ fraction
of the inputs, where λ can be significantly larger than 0 (say, $\lambda = 1/3$). There
are natural classes of correlated functions: for example, the "booleanized linear
functions" in a finite field GF_p defined in this paper. Informally, these functions
are of the form $f_a(x) = \phi(a \cdot x)$, where ϕ (called a "booleanizer") is an arbitrary
function that maps any element in GF_p to a boolean value ($+1$ or -1), and both
a and x are vectors over GF_p. Booleanized linear functions can be viewed as
natural extensions to parity functions (which are linear functions in GF_2), and
intuitively, should be hard to learn by statistical query (since parity functions
cannot be efficiently learned by statistical query). Actually they are (implicitly)
conjectured to be hard to learn in general, and there are cryptosystems whose
security is based on the assumption that booleanized linear functions are hard to
learn. One example is the "blind encryption scheme" proposed by Baird [B01]:
Roughly speaking, this private-key crypto-scheme picks a random f_a as the secret key, and encrypts a '0' bit by a random x such that $f_a(x) = +1$, and a '1'
bit by a random x such that $f_a(x) = -1$ Knowing the secret key, decryption is
just an invocation of the f_a, which can be done very efficiently. Furthermore, it
is (implicitly in [B01]) conjectured, that, by only inspecting random plaintext-
ciphertext pairs $\langle x, f_a(x) \rangle$, it is hard to learn the function f_a[1]. However, the

---

[1] This is not exactly what the "blind encryption scheme" does, but is similar.

results from [K98], [BFJ+94], [J00] don't immediately apply here since these booleanized linear functions are indeed correlated, and the correlation can be very large (for example, [BFJ+94] requires the the correlation between any two functions to be $O(1/d^3)$, where for the booleanized linear functions, the correlation is of order $\Omega(1/d)$, and can even be constants).

Notice that in the case of correlated functions, the notion of "weak learning" can become trivial: if any pair of functions have correlation λ, i.e., they agree on $(1+\lambda)/2$ fraction of the inputs, then by always outputing $f_1(x)$ on every input x, an algorithm can approximate any function f_i with advantage at least λ, (the advantage of an algorithm is defined as the probability the algorithm predicts a function correctly minus the probability the algorithm predicts incorrectly). So if λ is non-negligibly larger than 0, this algorithm "weakly learns" the function class without even making any query to the target function.

In the first part of this paper, we prove that without making any query, an algorithm can have maximally $\sqrt{\frac{1+(d-1)\lambda}{d}}$ advantage in approximating all the target functions $f_1, f_2, ..., f_d$, if any pair has almost the same correlation λ. We show this bound is almost tight by demonstrating an example where $\sqrt{\frac{1+(d-1)\lambda}{d}}$ advantage can be almost achieved for a specific class of functuions. Also we prove that in order to have an "extra" advantage S, about $\sqrt{d} \cdot S/2$ queries are needed. This shows a advantage-query complexity trade-off: the more advantage one wants, the more queries one has to make. One consequence of our result is that booleanized linear functions cannot be learned efficiently using statistical query, and if the booleanizer is "almost unbiased" and the finite field GF_p is large, one cannot even weakly learn this class of functions. Our result provides some positive evidence towards the security of the blind encryption scheme by Baird [B01].

The technique we used in the proof, which could be of interest by itself, is to keep track of the "all-pair statistical distance" between scenarios when the algorithm is given different target functions — we denote this quantity by Δ. We prove that:

1. Before the algorithm makes any query, $\Delta = 0$.
2. After the algorithm finishes all the queries, Δ is "large".
3. Each query only increases Δ by a "small" amount.

And then we conclude that a lot of queries are needed in order to learn $\mathcal{F}$ well.

One interesting consequence from our result is that the class of linear threshold functions are not efficiently learnable. A linear threshold function in a finite field is defined as $f_{a,b}(x) = 1$ if $a \cdot x \geq b$, and -1 otherwise, where $a \in GF_p^n$ and $b \in GF_p$. These linear threshold functions over GF_p are interesting, since their counterparts over reals are well-known as "perceptions" and they learnability are well studied. Blum et. al. [BFK+96] proved that there are statistical query algorithms that learn linear threshold function over reals in polynomial time, even in the presence of noise — that contrasts sharply with our result.

In the second part of this paper, We present a learning algorithm, BUILD-TREE , that learns a class of linear threshold functions over a finite field GF_p

where the threshold b is fixed to be $(p+1)/2$. Our algorithm uses a random example oracle, which produces a random pair $\langle \boldsymbol{x}, f_{\boldsymbol{a}}(\boldsymbol{x}) \rangle$ upon each invocation. The algorithm's running time is $p^{O(n/\log n)}$ while the brutal-force search algorithm takes time $p^{\Omega(n)}$, and any statistical query learning algorithm also has to take time $p^{\Omega(n)}$ to even weakly learn the functions. If we "pad" the input properly, we can make BUILD-TREE 's running time polynomial in the input size, while still no SQ learning algorithms can learn the class efficiently. This gives an example of PAC-learnable, but not SQ-learnable class of functions. Previously, both [K98] and [BFJ+94] proved that the class of parity functions fits into this category, and later [BKW00] proved that a class of noisy parity functions also fits. Our example is the first class of functions in this category that are correlated and not parity functions. This result provides some insights towards better understanding of SQ-learning algorithms.

The rest of the paper is organized as follows: section 2 gives some notations and definitions to be used in this paper; section 3 proves a lower bound for SQ-learning algorithms; section 4 discusses the algorithm BUILD-TREE and its analysis.

Due to space constraint, most proofs to the lemmas and theorems in this paper are omitted.

2   Notations and Definitions

We give the notations and definitions to be used in the paper.

2.1   Functions and Oracles

Throughout this paper we are interested in functions whose input domain is a finite set Ω, where $|\Omega| = M$, and whose outputs domain is $\{-1, +1\}$. An input x to a function f is called a *positive example* if $f(x) = +1$, and a *negative example* if $f(x) = -1$. Sometimes when the function f is clear from the context, we call the value of $f(x)$ the *label* of x. In a lot of cases, Ω takes a special form: $\Omega = GF_p^n$, where p is a prime number and n is a positive integer. In this case, we write an input in the vector form: $\boldsymbol{x}$, we use x^i to denote its i-th entry, an element in GF_p.

We now define the notion of learning a functions. The overall model is an algorithm A with oracle access to a function f that A tries to learn (we call f the *target function*). A is given an input X and makes queries to the oracle. Finally A outputs a bit as its prediction of $A(X)$.

We use an "honest SQ-oracle" model, which is similar to the definition of "SQ-based algorithm" in [J00]:

Definition 2.1. *An* honest SQ-oracle *for function f takes two parameters g and N as inputs, where $g : GF_p^n \times \{-1, +1\} \rightarrow \{-1, +1\}$ is a function that takes an input in GF_p^n and a boolean input and outputs a binary value, and N is a positive integer written in* unary, *called the* sample count. *The oracle returns*

$\frac{1}{N} \sum_{i=1}^{N} g(\boldsymbol{X}_i, f(\boldsymbol{X}_i))$ *where each $\boldsymbol{X}_i$ is a random variable independently chosen according to a pre-determined distribution D. We denote this oracle by HSQ_f*

Notice that this definition of an honest SQ-oracle is different from the mostly-used definition of a "normal" SQ-oracle (sometimes denoted as $STAT_f$) as in [AD98], [BFJ+94], [BFK+96], [BKW00], [K98]. Kearns [K98] proved that one can simulate a $STAT_f$ oracle efficiently in PAC learning model, and Decatur [D95] extensively studied the problem of efficiently simulating a $STAT_f$ oracle. Both their results can be easily extended to show that an honest SQ-oracle can be used to efficiently simulate a "normal" SQ-oracle. Therefore a lower bound with respect to an honest SQ-oracle automatically translates to a lower bound with respect to a "normal" SQ-oracle up to a polynomial factor.

2.2 Bias and Inner Products of Functions

We define the *bias* of a real function f over Ω to be the *expected value* of f under a distribution D, and we denote that by $\langle f \rangle_D$:

$$\langle f \rangle_D = E_D[f(x)] = \sum_{x \in \Omega} D(x) f(x)$$

We define the *inner product* of two real functions over Ω to be the *expected value of $f \cdot g$*, denoted by $\langle f, g \rangle_D$:

$$\langle f, g \rangle_D = E_D[f(x)g(x)] = \sum_{x \in \Omega} D(x) \cdot f(x) g(x)$$

In the rest of the paper, we often omit the letter D if the distribution is clear from the context.

We can also view the inner product as the "correlation" between f and g. It is easy to verify that the definition of inner product is a proper one. Also it is important to observe that if f is a boolean functions, i.e., $\forall x, f(x) \in \{-1, +1\}$, then $\langle f, f \rangle = 1$.

2.3 Approximating and Learning Functions

Given a function $f : \Omega \to \{-1, +1\}$ and an algorithm A which take elements in Ω and outputs ± 1, we can measure how well A approximates f. The algorithm could be a randomized one and thus the output of A on any input is a random variable. We define the *characteristic function* of algorithm A to be a real-valued function over the same domain Ω: $\psi_A : \Omega \to [-1, +1]$, such that

$$\psi_A(x) = 2 \cdot \Pr[A \text{ outputs 1 on } x] - 1$$

where the probability is taken over the randomness A uses and, if A make oracle queries, the randomness from the oracles.

It is easy to verify that $\psi_A(x)$ is always within the range $[-1, 1]$. Given a probabilistic distribution D over Ω, we define the *advantage* of algorithm A in approximating function f to be

$$\langle f, \psi_A \rangle = \Pr_{A,D}[A \text{ agrees with } f \text{ on input } x] - \Pr_{A,D}[A \text{ disagrees with } f \text{ on input } x]$$

where the probability is taken over the randomness from A and the x that is randomly chosen from Ω according to D.

It is not hard to see that if A always agrees with f, then $\psi_A = f$, and the advantage of A in approximating f is 1; if A randomly guesses a value for each input, then $\psi_A \equiv 0$, and the advantage of A is 0.

For a class of functions $\mathcal{F}$, and an oracle algorithm A, we say A *approximates* $\mathcal{F}$ *with advantage* α if for every function $f \in \mathcal{F}$, the advantage of A in approximating f is at least α. In the case A queries an honest SQ-oracle HSQ_f in order to approximate the target function f, we say A *learns* $\mathcal{F}$ with advantage α with respect to an honest SQ-oracle.

We note that the "advantage" measure for learning a function isn't very different from the more commonly used "accuracy/confidence" measure in PAC learning. Recall that an algorithm learns $\mathcal{F}$ with accuracy ϵ and confidence δ, if for any $f \in \mathcal{F}$, the algorithm A, using an oracle about f, with probability at least $1 - \delta$, agrees with f with probability at least $1 - \epsilon$. It is easy to prove the following facts:

Lemma 2.1. *Let $\mathcal{F}$ be a class of boolean functions over Ω, and let A be an oracle algorithm. If A learns $\mathcal{F}$ with accuracy ϵ and confidence δ, then A learns $\mathcal{F}$ with advantage at least $1 - 2\epsilon - 2\delta$. On the other hand, if A learns $\mathcal{F}$ with advantage at least α, then A learns $\mathcal{F}$ with accuracy ϵ and confidence δ for any (ϵ, δ) pair satisfying*

$$\alpha \geq 1 - 2\epsilon\delta$$

$\square$

The proof is a simple application of the Markov Inequality.

Therefore, roughly speaking: if an algorithm A learns $\mathcal{F}$ with high confidence and high accuracy (A "strongly" learns $\mathcal{F}$), then the advantage of A in learning $\mathcal{F}$ is close to 1; if A learns $\mathcal{F}$ weakly, then the advantage of A is non-negligibly higher than 0. On the other hand, if the advantage A has in learning $\mathcal{F}$ is close to 1, then A (strongly) learns $\mathcal{F}$.

The reason that we use the advantage measure in this paper is that we want to show a continuous "trade-off" result between how many queries are needed and how "well" an algorithm learns $\mathcal{F}$, and using one single parameter makes the discussion more convenient.

2.4 Booleanized Linear Functions and Linear Threshold Functions in Finite Fields

Suppose p is a prime number and n a positive integer. Given an arbitrary function that maps inputs from GF_p to boolean values,

$$\phi : GF_p \to \{-1, +1\}$$

we define a class $\mathcal{F}_\phi$ of *booleanized linear functions* as a collections of boolean functions:

$$\mathcal{F}_\phi = \{f_{a,\phi}(x) := \phi(a \cdot x) \mid a \in GF_p^n\},$$

and we call function ϕ the *booleanizer*.

Booleanized linear functions can be viewed as natural extensions of parity functions (which are linear functions over GF_2^n).

If the booleanizer function, ϕ, is a *threshold* function:

$$\phi_b(x) = \begin{cases} 1 & \text{, if } x \geq b \\ -1 & \text{, if } x < b \end{cases}$$

we call the corresponding class of booleanized linear functions *linear threshold functions*, and denote the functions by $f_{a,b}$.

2.5 The Tensor Product and Statistical Distance

Given two probabilistic distributions D and D' over spaces Λ and Λ', we define their *tensor product* $D \otimes D'$ to be a new distribution over $\Lambda \times \Lambda'$:

$$\Pr_{D \otimes D'}[(X, X') = (x, x')] = \Pr_D[X = x] \cdot \Pr_{D'}[X' = x']$$

Given a finite space Λ and distributions $D_1, D_2, ..., D_m$ over Λ, we define the *all-pair L_2 statistical distance* (abbreviated as SD) among $D_1, D_2, ..., D_m$ to be

$$\mathsf{SD}_2(D_1, D_2, ..., D_m) = \left[\sum_{i=1}^m \sum_{j=1}^m \sum_{x \in \Lambda} \left(\Pr_{D_i}[X = x] - \Pr_{D_j}[X = x] \right)^2 \right]^{\frac{1}{2}}$$

Under this definition, it is easy to see that

$$\mathsf{SD}_2(D, D) = 0$$

and

$$\mathsf{SD}_2(D_1, D_2, ..., D_m) = \left[\frac{1}{2} \sum_{i=1}^m \sum_{j=1}^m \mathsf{SD}_2(D_i, D_j)^2 \right]^{\frac{1}{2}}$$

for $m > 2$.

One useful property of the all-pair L_2 statistical distance is the sub-additivity:

Lemma 2.2. *Let $D_1, D_2, ..., D_m$ be distributions over Λ and $D'_1, D'_2, ..., D'_m$ be distributions over Λ'. Then we have*

$$\mathsf{SD}_2(D_1 \otimes D'_1, D_2 \otimes D'_2, ..., D_m \otimes D'_m) \leq \mathsf{SD}_2(D_1, D_2, ..., D_m) + \mathsf{SD}_2(D'_1, D'_2, ..., D'_m)$$

$\square$

Since each random variable naturally induces a distribution, we can also define all-pair L_2 statistical distance among random variables: For random variables $X_1, X_2, ..., X_m$, their all-pair L_2 statistical distance is defined to be the all-pair L_2 statistical distance among the the distributions induced by them. The sub-additivity property remains true: suppose we have random variables $X_1, X_2, ..., X_m$ and $Y_1, Y_2, ..., Y_m$, such that X_i is independent to Y_j for any pair of $i, j \in \{1, 2, ..., m\}$, we have

$$\mathsf{SD}_2(X_1Y_1, X_2Y_2, ..., X_mY_m) \leq \mathsf{SD}_2(X_1, X_2, ..., X_m) + \mathsf{SD}_2(Y_1, Y_2, ..., Y_m)$$

2.6   Chernoff Bounds

We will be using Chernoff bounds in our paper, and our version is from [MR95].

Theorem 2.1. *Let $X_1, X_2, ..., X_n$ be a sequence of n independent $\{0, 1\}$ random variables. Let S be the sum of the random variables and $\mu = E[S]$. Then, for $0 \leq \delta \leq 1$, the following inequalities hold:*

$$\Pr[S > (1 + \delta)\mu] \leq e^{-\delta^2\mu/3}$$

and

$$\Pr[S < (1 - \delta)\mu] \leq e^{-\delta^2\mu/2}$$

$\square$

3   Statistical Query Model: Negative Results

In this section we present a negative result characterizing the Statistical Query Model.

Throughout this section, we use Ω to denote a finite set of size M and we are interested in functions mapping elements in Ω to $+1$ or -1.

3.1   Statistical Dimension and Fourier Analysis

Definition 3.1. *Let Ω be a finite set of size M and let $\mathcal{F}$ be a class of boolean functions whose input domain is Ω, and D a distribution over Ω, we define* $\mathsf{SQ\text{-}DIM}(\mathcal{F}, D)$, *the statistical query dimension of $\mathcal{F}$ with respect to D, to be the largest natural number d such that there exists a real number λ, satisfying $0 \leq \lambda \leq 1/2$, and that $\mathcal{F}$ contains d functions $f_1, f_2, ..., f_d$ with the property that for all $i \neq j$, we have*

$$|\langle f_i, f_j \rangle - \lambda| \leq \frac{1}{d^3}$$

Notice the definition of $\mathsf{SQ\text{-}DIM}$ in [BFJ+94] can be regarded as the special case where $\Omega = \{-1, +1\}^n$ with the restriction that $\lambda = 0$.

Notice though each of the functions $f_1, f_2, ..., f_d$ can be highly correlated to others, we view this correlated a "false correlation": as we will prove in the next lemma, we can "extract" d new functions $\tilde{f}_1, \tilde{f}_2, ..., \tilde{f}_d$ from $f_1, f_2, ..., f_d$, such that the new functions are almost totally uncorrelated to each other.

Lemma 3.1. *Let Ω, D, d, λ, and $f_1, f_2, ..., f_d$ be as defined in definition 3.1, and $\lambda > 0$. We define d real-valued functions $\tilde{f}_1, \tilde{f}_2, ..., \tilde{f}_d$:*

$$\tilde{f}_i(x) = \frac{1}{\sqrt{1-\lambda}} f_i(x) - \frac{1}{d} \cdot \left(\frac{1}{\sqrt{1-\lambda}} - \frac{1}{\sqrt{1+(d-1)\lambda}} \right) \cdot \sum_{j=1}^{d} f_j(x) \quad (1)$$

Then we have

$$|\langle \tilde{f}_i, \tilde{f}_i \rangle - 1| \le \frac{8}{d^3} \ , \ \forall i \quad (2)$$

and

$$|\langle \tilde{f}_i, \tilde{f}_j \rangle| \le \frac{8}{d^3} \ , \ \forall i \ne j \quad (3)$$

$\square$

So we now get a group of functions $\tilde{f}_1, \tilde{f}_2, ..., \tilde{f}_d$ that are "almost" orthogonal. However, these d new functions are nor necessarily boolean functions.

Next, we can extend this group of functions to a basis and perform Fourier analysis on the basis. The part of analysis are very similar to the proofs in [BFJ+94], but with different parameters and (sometimes) improved bounds. The detailed analysis are in the appendix.

3.2   Approximating a Function without a Query

We give an upper bound on the advantage an algorithm A can have to approximating a class of functions, if A doesn't make any queries.

Theorem 3.1. *Let Ω be a finite set of size M, let D be a probabilistic distribution over Ω. Let $\mathcal{F}$ be a class of boolean functions $\mathcal{F} = \{f_1, f_2, ..., f_d\}$, such that $|\langle f_i, f_j \rangle - \lambda| \le 1/d^3$ for all pairs $i \ne j$, where $\lambda > 0$. Let $g : \Omega \to [-1, +1]$ be the characteristic function of an algorithm A such that $\langle g, f_i \rangle \ge T$ for $i = 1, 2, ..., d$. Then we have*

$$T \le \sqrt{\frac{1 + (d-1)\lambda}{d}} + \frac{70}{d}$$

for $d > 100$.

$\square$

We next show that this bound is "almost tight", i.e., we give an example where $T = \sqrt{\frac{1+(d-1)\lambda}{d}}$.

Theorem 3.2. *For any odd prime p and any integer $n \ge 2$, there exists a class of $d = p^{n-1}$ boolean functions over GF_p^n: $\mathcal{F} = \{f_1, f_2, ..., f_d\}$, and a distribution D, such that: any pair of the functions has identical inner product λ and the inner product of constant function $g(x) \equiv 1$ and any f_i is $\langle g, f_i \rangle_D = \sqrt{\frac{1+(d-1)\lambda}{d}}$.*

3.3   A Lower Bound for Statistical Query Learning

We have proved that without making any queries, a learning algorithm cannot learn a function family with advantage more than $\sqrt{\frac{1+(d-1)\lambda}{d}}$. Next we show that in order to improve the advantage, a lot of (normally exponentially many) queries have to be made. More precisely, we have the following theorem:

Theorem 3.3. *Let Ω be a finite set of size M, let D be a probabilistic distribution over Ω. Let $\mathcal{F}$ be a class of boolean functions $\mathcal{F} = \{f_1, f_2, ..., f_d\}$, such that $|\langle f_i, f_j \rangle - \lambda| \leq 1/d^3$ for all pairs $i \neq j$, where $1/2 \geq \lambda > 0$ and $d > 100$. Let A be an algorithm that makes Q queries to an honest SQ-oracle , each of which has sample count at most N, and learns $\mathcal{F}$ with advantage $S + \sqrt{\frac{1+(d-1)\lambda}{d}}$, where $S \geq d^{-1/4}$, then we have*

$$NQ \geq \frac{\sqrt{d} \cdot S}{2}$$

$\square$

We comment that the total running time of A is bounded by NQ, since N is written in unary. Therefore thus the running time of A is also bounded from below by $\sqrt{d} \cdot S/2$. This theorem gives a tradeoff between the running time of A and the "extra" advantage it can have in learning $\mathcal{F}$: the running time goes up linearly with the advantage, and especially, to get a constant advantage, a running time of $\Omega(d^{1/2})$ is needed.

Proof. We assume A is a Turing Machine. Suppose the target function is f_j. We define the *state* of A after the k-th query to be the binary string S_k^j that describes the contents on A's tapes, the position of the heads, the current internal state of A. We define S_0^j to be the state of A before A starts. Notice each S_k^j is a random variable: the randomness comes from both the honest SQ-oracle and the random coins A tosses.

In the rest of the proof, we will omit the subscript A if there is no danger of confusion.

We define Δ_k to be the all-pair L_2 statistical distance among $S_k^1, S_k^2, ..., S_k^d$:

$$\Delta_k = \mathsf{SD}_2(S_k^1, S_k^2, ..., S_k^d)$$

Intuitively, Δ_k measures how "differently" A behaves when it has different target functions as inputs from the oracle.

We shall prove the following lemmas (in the appendix) considering the Δ_k's:

Lemma 3.2. $\Delta_0 = 0$.

This is obvious since A hasn't made any queries yet, and the state of A is independent of the target function.

Lemma 3.3. $\Delta_{k+1} - \Delta_k \leq N \cdot \sqrt{d}$ $\square$

Next we show the that in order to learn $\mathcal{F}$ with large advantage, the all-pair statistical distance has to be large.

Lemma 3.4. *If A learns* $\mathcal{F}$ *with advantage* $S + \sqrt{\frac{1+(d-1)\lambda}{d}}$ *where* $S \geq d^{-1/4}$. *Then* $\Delta_Q \geq \frac{dS}{2}$. $\qquad\qquad\qquad\qquad\qquad\qquad\qquad\qquad\qquad\Box$

Now putting lemma 3.2, 3.2, and lemma 3.4 together, we have $NQ\sqrt{d} \geq \frac{dS}{2}$, or

$$NQ \geq \frac{\sqrt{d} \cdot S}{2}$$

As a comparison, implicit in [J00] is the following theorem:

Theorem 3.4 (Implicit in [J00]). *Let* Ω *be a finite set of size* M, *let* D *be a probabilistic distribution over* Ω. *Let* F *be a class of boolean functions* $\mathcal{F} = \{f_1, f_2, ..., f_d\}$, *such that* $\langle f_i, f_j \rangle = 0$ *for all pairs* $i \neq j$. *Let* A *be an algorithm that makes* Q *queries to an honest SQ-oracle, each of which has sample count at most* N, *and learns* $\mathcal{F}$ *with advantage* S, *then we have*

$$NQ = \Omega(d) - \frac{1}{S^2}$$

Proof's sketch: Notice this is the case that all target functions are completely orthogonal and Fourier Analysis works perfectly: one can extend $\mathcal{F}$ to an orthonormal basis directly. Suppose A has an advantage of S. Then the characteristic function ψ_A has a coefficient at least S for the target function. However ψ_A can have at most $1/S^2$ coefficients that are larger than or equal to S, by Parseval's equality. One can simply query $1/S^2$ more times to completely determine the target functions and have an advantage of 1. But as proved in [J00], $\Omega(d)$ queries are needed to learn $\mathcal{F}$ with advantage 1. Therefore we have $NQ = \Omega(d - 1/S^2)$. $\qquad\qquad\qquad\qquad\qquad\qquad\qquad\qquad\qquad\qquad\Box$

The bound in [J00] is a bound for the specific case that all functions are orthogonal to each other, and in this case, it is better than the bound given in this paper. Our bound is weaker, but it works for a more general class of functions.

3.4 Hardness for Learning Booleanized Linear Functions over a Finite Field

Next we show that the class of booleanized linear functions cannot be learned efficiently using statistical query:

Theorem 3.5. *Let* p *be an odd prime and* $n > 1$ *an integer. Let* $\phi : GF_p \rightarrow \{-1, +1\}$ *be a booleanizer such that* $-\frac{1}{\sqrt{2}} \leq \langle \phi \rangle \leq \frac{1}{\sqrt{2}}$. *and let* $\mathcal{F}$ *be a class of booleanized linear functions:*

$$\mathcal{F} = \{f_{a,\phi} \mid a^n = 1\}$$

Let D be the uniform distribution over GF_p^n. Then any algorithm with an access to an honest SQ-oracle that learns $\mathcal{F}$ with advantage $|\langle\phi\rangle|+S+1/p^{n-1}$, where $S \geq p^{-(n-1)/4}$, with respect to distribution D, has a running time at least $p^{(n-1)/2} \cdot S/2$.   □

Notice that it is not hard to prove that each function $f_{a,\phi}$ has bias $\langle\phi\rangle$. If $\langle\phi\rangle \geq 0$, then the constant function $g(x) = +1$ already has an advantage $\langle\phi\rangle$ in approximating $\mathcal{F}$, otherwise $g(x) = -1$ has an advantage $\langle\phi\rangle$ in approximating $\mathcal{F}$.

This result gives some positive evidence towards the security of the private-key cryptosystem proposed by Baird [B01].

Since linear threshold functions are special cases for booleanized linear functions, we have the following theorem:

Theorem 3.6. *Let p be an odd prime and $n > 1$ an integer. Let b be a non-zero element in GF_p such that $(p-1)/4 \leq b \leq 3(p-1)/4$, and let $\mathcal{F}$ be a class of linear threshold functions:*

$$\mathcal{F} = \{f_{a,b} \mid a^n = 1\}$$

Let D be the uniform distribution over GF_p^n. Then any algorithm with an access to an honest SQ-oracle that learns $\mathcal{F}$ with advantage $|(p-2b)/p| + S + 1/p^{n-1}$, where $S \geq p^{-(n-1)/4}$, with respect to distribution D, has a running time at least $p^{(n-1)/2} \cdot S/2$.

Furthermore, we have:

Corollary 3.1. *For the class of linear threshold functions, in the case that p is exponentially large in n and $b = (p+1)/2$, no statistical query algorithm can weakly learn $\mathcal{F}$.*

Proof. When $b = (p+1)/2$, we have $(p-2b)/p = -1/p$, which is exponentially small in n. If an algorithm A weakly learns $\mathcal{F}$, it has to have an advantage $\epsilon > \frac{1}{n^c}$ for some constant c. Then by theorem 3.6 the running time of A has to be at least $p^{(n-1)/2} \cdot (\epsilon - 1/p - 1/p^{n-1})$, which is exponentially large in n.

4   Algorithm for Linear Threshold Functions

In this section we present an algorithm BUILD-TREE that learns a special class of linear threshold functions as shown in corollary 3.1, using a random example oracle. The running time of BUILD-TREE is slightly better than the brutal-force algorithm, and also slightly better than the lower bound for the statistical query model.

We first state the problem: pick an integer $n > 1$ and an odd prime p such that p is exponentially large in n. Let $b = (p+1)/2$, and the class of functions is the class of linear threshold functions with the fixed b and with the constraint that the n-th entry of $\boldsymbol{a}$ is 1:

$$\mathcal{F} = \{f_{\boldsymbol{a}} \mid a^n = 1\}^2$$

The distribution over the inputs is the uniform distribution. We show an algorithm that learns any function $f \in \mathcal{F}$ in time $p^{O(n/\log n)}$, with advantage 0.5, with respect to a random example oracle. Notice the brutal-force algorithm that examines all possible functions has running time $p^{\Omega(n)}$ and any SQ-algorithm much also have a running time $p^{\Omega(n)}$ to have a constant advantage in learning $\mathcal{F}$.

4.1 Description of the Algorithm

The idea for BUILD-TREE is pretty intuitive: given a target function $f_{\boldsymbol{a}}$, we know there is a "secret vector" $\boldsymbol{a}$ associated with the function. If one picks a *random* negative example $\boldsymbol{x}$, then the *expected* value of $\boldsymbol{a} \cdot \boldsymbol{x}$ is $(p-1)/4$. If we draw $(4q+1)$ independent random negative samples, the expected sum of the inner products is about $(4q+1)(p-1)/4$, which is about $(p-1)/4$ modulo p, if $q \ll p$ (in our algorithm, we have $q = O(\log n) = O(\log \log p)$). So it is more likely that the sum of $(4q+1)$ random negative examples is still a negative example than is a positive one. The algorithm exploits this "marginal difference", boosts it by Chernoff bound, and gains a constant advantage in learning $\mathcal{F}$. What BUILD-TREE does is: it first draws $p^{O(n/\log n)}$ negative examples, and when getting an input $\boldsymbol{X}$, it tries to write $\boldsymbol{X}$ as the sum of $(4q+1)$ negative examples it drew, and estimates the success probability. If the success probability is high, it outputs "$f(\boldsymbol{X}) = -1$", otherwise it outputs "$f(\boldsymbol{X}) = +1$". The name of the algorithm comes from the fact that the algorithm estimates the probability by building a complete binary tree from the samples it draws.

Our algorithm is inspired by the algorithm Blum et. al. used in [BKW00] to learn noisy parity functions, where the main idea is also trying to write an input as the sum of logarithmically many samples.

Now we describe BUILD-TREE in more detail:

The algorithm BUILD-TREE has a random example oracle EX_f, which, at each invocation, produces a random pair $(\boldsymbol{x}, f_{\boldsymbol{a}}(\boldsymbol{x}))$, where $\boldsymbol{x}$ is uniformly chosen from GF_p^n. The algorithm also has an input $\boldsymbol{X}$ on which it tried to predict $f_{\boldsymbol{a}}(\boldsymbol{X})$.

The algorithm consists of 2 phases. In Phase I, it draws about $p^{O(n/\log n)}$ samples and processes them; in Phase II, it reads the input $\boldsymbol{X}$ and tries to build a complete binary tree from the samples it drew in Phase I, where each node is a multi-set of elements in GF_p^n; finally, BUILD-TREE counts the number of elements in the root node and use this number to predict $f_{\boldsymbol{a}}(\boldsymbol{X})$. In the description thet follows, we identify "groups" with "multisets".

---

[2] In the rest of this section, we omit b in the description of $f_{a,b}$ since b is fixed to be $(p+1)/2$.

- **Phase I:** We define $a = \log n/2$ and $b = 2n/\log n$, and think of each vector in GF_p^n as divided into a blocks, each block containing b elements in GF_p. We define

$$K = p^b \cdot 2^{2^{a+1}} \cdot n$$

BUILD-TREE draws $2^{a-1}(2^a + 1)K$ negative samples. Notice each f_a is "reasonably balanced" and thus there would be no trouble getting enough negative samples. We use N to denote $2^{a-1}K$. BUILD-TREE groups these samples into $2^a + 1$ groups of N elements each, and denotes these groups by $G_0, G_1, ..., G_{2^a}$. Then it add the last 2 groups G_{2^a-1} and G_{2^a} entry-wise to form a new group, G'_{2^a-1}. More precisely, suppose $G_{2^a-1} = \{a_1, a_2, ..., a_N\}$ and $G_{2^a} = \{b_1, b_2, ..., b_N\}$, then

$$G'_{2^a-1} = \{a_1 + b_1, a_2 + b_2, ..., a_N + b_N\}$$

is also a group of N numbers. Now define $G'_i = G_i$, for $i = 0, 1, ..., 2^a - 2$, and now we have 2^a groups $G'_1, ..., G'_{2^a-1}$ of N elements.
- **Phase II:** In this phase BUILD-TREE gets a new sample $\boldsymbol{X}$ and it tries to learn $f_a(\boldsymbol{X})$. The approach is to try to write $\boldsymbol{X}$ as the sum of $2^a + 1$ negative samples drawn from phase I. More precisely BUILD-TREE tries to find 2^a elements $\boldsymbol{x}_0, \boldsymbol{x}_1, ..., \boldsymbol{x}_{2^a-1}$, such that $\boldsymbol{x}_i \in G'_i$ for $i = 0, 1, ..., 2^a - 1$ and

$$\boldsymbol{X} = \boldsymbol{x}_0 + \boldsymbol{x}_1 + \cdots + \boldsymbol{x}_{2^a-1}.$$

Notice $\boldsymbol{x}_{2^a-1} \in G'_{2^a-1}$ is already a sum of 2 negative samples, and thus if one can find such 2^a elements, $\boldsymbol{X}$ is the sum of $2^a + 1$ negative samples. Since BUILD-TREE is working in GF_p, it can compute $\boldsymbol{Y} = \frac{1}{2^a}\boldsymbol{X}$, and subtract $\boldsymbol{Y}$ from each element in each group G'_i. More precisely, we define

$$A_i = \{\boldsymbol{x} - \boldsymbol{Y} \mid \boldsymbol{x} \in G'_i\}$$

for $i = 0, 1, ..., 2^a - 1$. Then the task for BUILD-TREE becomes finding 2^a elements, one from each A_i such that they add up to $\boldsymbol{0}$.

To do so, BUILD-TREE will build a complete binary tree of multi-sets. First some notations: We define the *height* of a node in a binary tree as the shortest distance from this node to a leaf node, and a leaf node has height 0. The height of a binary tree is the height of its root. A node that is neither a leaf node nor the root node is called an *internal node*. There are $(2^a - 2)$ internal nodes for a complete binary tree of height a.

Here is the actual construction:

BUILD-TREE will build a complete binary tree of height a, and there are 2^{a-k} nodes of height k: we will denote these nodes by $G_0^k, G_1^k, ..., G_{2^{a-k}-1}^k$. The construction is from bottom-up: one builds the nodes of height 0, or the leaf nodes first, and then the node of height $1, 2, ..., a - 1$, and finally the root node. An invariant that BUILD-TREE maintains is: all non-root nodes of height l contain $2^{a-l-1}K$ elements, all of which have 0's at the first l blocks.

- **LEAF NODES:**
  The leaf nodes are just the sets $A_0, A_1, ..., A_{2^a-1}$. In other words, let $G_i^0 = A_i$ for $i = 0, 1, ..., 2^a - 1$.
- **INTERNAL NODES:**
  After all the nodes of height $(l - 1)$ are built, BUILD-TREE constructs the nodes of height l.

  To construct node G_i^l, BUILD-TREE needs nodes G_{2i}^{l-1} and G_{2i+1}^{l-1}, namely, the two children nodes of G_i^l. The BUILD-TREE does the following:

  It starts by setting G_i^l to be the empty set and label all elements in G_{2i}^{l-1} and G_{2i+1}^{l-1} as "unmarked".

  It repeats the following "SELECT-AND-MARK" process for $2^{a-l-1}K$ times:

  BEGIN OF SELECT-AND-MARK
  * BUILD-TREE (arbitrarily) picks an unmarked element $u \in G_{2i}^{l-1}$, and scans G_{2i+1}^{l-1} to check if there is an unmarked element $v \in G_{2i+1}^{l-1}$, such that $u + v$ has the first l blocks all-zero. Notice that both u and v has the first $l - 1$ blocks all-zero already, and thus BUILD-TREE is actually looking for a v whose l-th block is the complement of that of u.
  * If BUILD-TREE finds such a v, it puts $u + v$ into G_i^l and labels both u and v as "marked".
  * If BUILD-TREE can't find such a v, it aborts: the algorithm fails.

  END OF SELECT-AND-MARK
  If BUILD-TREE doesn't abort in the $2^{a-l-1}K$ SELECT-AND-MARK processes, it constructs a set G_i^l of size $2^{a-l-1}K$.
- **ROOT NODE:**
  If BUILD-TREE doesn't abort in constructing the $(2^a - 2)$ internal nodes, it proceeds to build the root node, G_0^a. Notice the children of node G_0^a are nodes G_0^{a-1} and G_1^{a-1}, each of which contains K elements: suppose that

  $$G_0^{a-1} = \{u_1, u_2, ..., u_K\}$$

  and

  $$G_1^{a-1} = \{v_1, v_2, ..., v_K\}$$

  Then the root node G_0^a is

  $$G_0^a = \{u_i + v_i \mid u_i + v_i = \mathbf{0}, \ i = 1, 2, ..., K\}$$

  In other words, G_0^a is a multi-set of $\mathbf{0}$'s, and the size of G_0^a depends on the number of corresponding pairs of vectors in G_0^{a-1} and G_1^{a-1} that are complement to each other.

In this way BUILD-TREE builds a complete binary tree all the way up the the root. If the size of the root node is greater than $2^{2^{a+1}} \cdot n$, BUILD-TREE outputs "$f(X) = -1$"; otherwise is outputs "$f(X) = +1$".

4.2 Analysis of the BUILD-TREE Algorithm

The detailed analysis is in the appendix, and we state the theorem here:

Theorem 4.1. *With probability at least* 0.8, *the* BUILD-TREE *algorithm learns* $\mathcal{F}$ *with accuracy* $1 - e^{-0.03n}$. *In other words, the* BUILD-TREE *algorithm learns* $\mathcal{F}$ *with advantage* 0.5, *and has a running time* $p^{O(n/\log n)}$. $\qquad\square$

It is interesting to compare BUILD-TREE with the algorithm used in [BKW00], to learn parity functions in the presence of noise, which also draws many samples, view each sample as blocks, and tries to write an input as the sum of $O(\log n)$ samples, and both algorithms have a similar sub-exponential bound. However, there are differences: in [BKW00], the algorithm draws samples with labels, and it writes an input as the sum of $O(\log n)$ samples to fight the noise — if there were no noise, it is easy to learn the function by Gauss elimination; in this paper, BUILD-TREE only draws negative examples, and it writes an input as the sum of $O(\log n)$ negative sample to create a probabilistic gap — there is no noise in the problem. Furthermore, the algorithm in [BKW00] is satisfied with justing finding a way to write an input as a sum of $O(\log n)$ samples, while BUILD-TREE has to estimate the probability that an input can be written as a sum of $O(\log n)$ samples, and thus is more complicated in this sense.

Notice that, using the same "padding" technique as in [BKW00], we can make the BUILD-TREE is polynomial-time algorithm: one simply pad $p^{n/\log n}$ zeros to the input of BUILD-TREE , and then BUILD-TREE 's running time becomes polynomial in the input length. However, still no polynomial-time algorithms can learn this class of linear threshold functions in statistical query model. This gives an example of PAC-learnable, but not SQ-learnable class of functions. Previously, both [K98] and [BFJ+94] proved that the class of parity functions fits into this category, and later [BKW00] proved that a class of noisy parity functions also fits. The linear threshold functions over a finite field is the first class of functions in this category that are not parity functions. We hope this result can provide further insights into SQ-learning algorithms.

5 Conclusions and Open Problems

In this paper, we discussed the problem of learning (highly) correlated functions in the statistical query model. We showed an almost-tight upper bound of the advantage an algorithm can have in approximating a class of functions simultaneously. We also showed that any SQ algorithm trying to get a better advantage in learning the class of functions has to make a lot of queries. A consequence of our result is that the class of booleanized linear functions over finite fields are not SQ-learnable, which include linear threshold functions. Finally we demonstrated a PAC learning algorithm that learns a class of linear threshold functions with constant advantage and running time that is provably impossible for SQ-algorithms. With proper padding, our algorithm can be made in polynomial-time, and thus putting linear threshold functions into the category of

PAC-learnable, but not SQ-learnable functions, and they are the first class in this category that are not parity functions.

The technique we used in this paper to prove the lower bound is to keep track of the "all-pair statistical distance" between scenarios when the algorithm is given different target functions Appaently, our technique is similar to the one used in [A00], where the author proved a lower bound of quantum queries a quantum search algorithm has to make, but in a different setting. Their technique is to keep track of the sum of the absolute values of the off-diagonal entries in in the system's density matrix — we denote this quantity by S. Roughly speaking, the author in [A00] proved that:

1. Before the algorithm makes any quantum queries, S is large.
2. After the algorithm finishes all the queries, S is small.
3. Each quantum query only decreases S by a small amount.

And then they conclude that lot of quantum queries are needed. It would be interesting to investigate if there is a deeper relationship between the 2 techniques.

People already understand SQ-learning un-correlated functions: both lower bounds and upper bounds on the number of queries are shown, and the two bounds match. Our paper gives a lower bound for SQ-learing a class of functions that are correlated the same way, but no matching upper bound is known. Even less is known for the case that all the functions are correlated, but not in the same way. In general, given d functions $f_1, f_2, ..., f_d$ and their pair-wise correlation $\langle f_i, f_j \rangle$ for all $i \neq j$, can we find a good lower bound for the number of queries needed to learning these d functions well? Is there an (even non-uniform) matching upper bound?

Another interesting problem is: do there exist efficient algorithms to learn booleanized linear functions over finite fields? For parity functions over GF_2, they are easy to learn when there is no noise, and hard if there is noise — the state of art are Blum et. al.'s algorithm [BKW00], which takes time $O(2^{n/\log n})$ for n-bit parity functions with respect to uniform noise of constant rate, and Goldreich-Levin-Jackson's algorithm [GL89], [J00], which takes time $O(2^{n/2})$ for n-bit parity functions, with respect to uniform noise of rate $(1/2 - 1/\mathsf{poly}(n))$ and some classes of malicious noise. However, in the case of finite fields of large characteristics, it seems it is hard to learn the booleanized linear functions even without noise. Notice an efficient learning algorithm will break Baird's "blind computation" cryptosystem, and an hardness result will automatically translate to a security proof for Baird's system.

Another interesting topic is learning functions in finite fields in general: instead of limiting the outputs of functions to be boolean, we can allow functions to output elements in a finite field, or some other large domains. What kind of functions are learnable?

Acknowledgement. Leemon Baird gave the initial motivation of this paper by mentioning his cryptosystem, which lead us into studying the problem of learning booleanized linear functions. Avrim Blum gave a lot of invaluable advice on what problems are interesting and helped formulate ideas into a paper. Adam Kalai and Steven Rudich helped clarify many concepts and especially helped me understand what the right problems should be asked. Salil Vadhan showed me the idea of proving the sub-additivity of all-pair statistical distance, which is one of the essential tools used in the paper. Finally the author wishes to thank the anonymous referees for pointing out numerous typos and mistakes in the original verison of the paper.

References

[A00]   Andris Ambainis. *Quantum lower bounds by quantum arguments*, In *Proceedings of the 32nd ACM Symposium on Theory of Computing*, pages 636-643, 2000.

[AD98]   Javed Aslam and Scott Decatur. *General Bounds on Statistical Query Learning and PAC learning with Noise via Hypothesis Boosting*, In *Information and Computation*, 141, pages 85-118 (1998).

[B01]   Leemon Baird. *Blind Computation*. Manuscript, 2001.

[BFJ+94] Avrim Blum, Merrick Furst, Jeffrey Jackson, Michael Kearns, Yishay Mansour, and Steven Rudich. *Weakly Learning DNF and Characterizing Statistical Query Learning Using Fourier Analysis*. In *Proceedings of the 26th Annual ACM Symposium on Theory of Computing*, pages 253–262, 1994.

[BFK+96] Avrim Blum, Alan Frieze, Ravi Kannan, and Santosh Vempala, *A Polynomial-time Algorithm for Learning Noisy Linear Threshold Functions*, In *Algorithmica, 22:35-52, 1998*. An extended abstract appears in *Proceedings of the 37th Annual Symposium on Foundations of Computer Science (FOCS'96)*, pages 330–338.

[BKW00]   Avrim Blum, Adam Kalai and Hal Wasserman, *Noise-tolerant Learning, the Parity problem, and the Statistical Query model.* In *Proceedings of the 32nd Annual ACM Symposium on Theory of Computing*, pp. 435–440, 2000.

[D95]   Scott Decatur, *Efficient Learning from Faulty Data*. Ph.D. Thesis, Harvard University, TR-30-95, 1995.

[GL89]   Oded Goldreich and Leonid Levin, *A hard-core predicate for all one-way functions.* In *Proceedings of the 21st Annual ACM Symposium on Theory of Computing*, pp. 25-32, 1989.

[J00]   Jeff Jackson *On the Efficiency of Noise-Tolerant PAC Algorithms Derived from Statistical Queries.* In *Proceedings of the 13th Annual Workshop on Computational Learning Theory*, 2000.

[K98]   Michael Kearns. *Efficient noise-tolerant learning from statistical queries.* In *Journal of the ACM*, 45(6), pp. 983 — 1006, 1998. Preliminary version in *Proceedings of the 25th Annual ACM Symposium on Theory of Computing*, pp. 392–401, 1993.

[MR95]   Rajeev Motwani and Prabhakar Raghavan, *Randomized Algorithms*, Cambridge University Press, 1995.

[SS96]   Robert Schapire and Linda Selle, *Learning Sparse Multivariate Polynomials over a Field with Queries and Counterexamples*. In *Journal of Computer and System Sciences*, 52, 201-213, 1996.

[V01]   Salil Vadhan, *Private Communication*.

[V84]   Leslie Valiant, *A theory of the Leanable*. In *Communications of the ACM*, 27(11): 1134–1142, November 1984.

A Simpler Analysis of the Multi-way Branching Decision Tree Boosting Algorithm

Kohei Hatano

Department of Mathematical and Computing Sciences,
Tokyo Institute of Technology,
Ookayama 2-12-1, Meguro-ku, Tokyo, 152-8552, Japan
hatano@is.titech.ac.jp

Abstract. We improve the analysis of the decision tree boosting algorithm proposed by Mansour and McAllester. For binary classification problems, the algorithm of Mansour and McAllester constructs a multiway branching decision tree using a set of multi-class hypotheses. Mansour and McAllester proved that it works under certain conditions. We give a much simpler analysis of the algorithm and simplify the conditions. From this simplification, we can provide a simpler algorithm, for which no prior knowledge on the quality of weak hypotheses is necessary.

1 Introduction

Boosting is a technique to construct a "strong" hypothesis combining many "weak" hypotheses. This technique was first proposed by Schapire [9] originally to prove the equivalence between strong and weak learnability in PAC-learning. Many researchers have improved boosting techniques such as AdaBoost [5] and so on. (See for example, [4,3,10,11].) Among them, Kearns and Mansour [6] showed that the learning process of well-known decision tree learning algorithms such as CART [2] and C4.5 [8] can be regarded as boosting, thereby giving some theoretical justification to those popular decision tree learning tools.

More precisely, Kearns and Mansour formalized the process of constructing a decision tree as the following boosting algorithm. For any binary classification problem, let H_2 be a set of binary hypotheses for this classification problem. Starting from the trivial single-leaf decision tree, the learning algorithm improves the tree by replacing some leaf of the tree (chosen according to a certain rule) with an internal node that corresponds to a hypothesis $h \in H_2$ (again chosen according to a certain rule). It is shown that the algorithm outputs a tree T with its training error below $s^{-\gamma}$, where s is the number of leaves of T, provided that for any distribution, there always exists some hypothesis in H_2 whose "advantage" is larger than γ $(0 < \gamma \le 1)$ for the classification problem. This implies that $(1/\varepsilon)^{(1/\gamma)}$ steps are sufficient for the desired training error ε. (See the next section for the detail; in particular, the definition of "advantage".)

There are two extensions of the result of Kearns and Mansour. Takimoto and Maruoka generalized the algorithm for multi-class learning [12]. Their algorithm uses, for any fixed $K \ge 2$, K-class hypotheses, i.e., hypotheses providing

N. Abe, R. Khardon, and T. Zeugmann (Eds.): ALT 2001, LNAI 2225, pp. 77–92, 2001.

K branches. On the other hand, Mansour and McAllester gave a generalized algorithm that constructs a decision tree (for binary classification) by using multi-class hypotheses that provide *at most* K branches [7]. That is, their algorithm may construct a decision tree having nodes with different number of branches.

In this paper, we improve the analysis of Mansour and McAllester's algorithm.

Consider the situation of constructing a decision tree of size s for a given s by using multi-class hypotheses such that the size of the ranges are bounded by some constant $K \geq 2$. Mansour and McAllester showed that their algorithm produces a size s decision tree with training error bound $s^{-\gamma}$ under the following condition.

The condition of Mansour and McAllester
    At each boosting step, there always exists a hypothesis h satisfying the
    following:
    (1) h is either binary (in which case $k = 2$) or k-class with some k, $2 <
        k \leq K$, such that $k \leq (s/s')(\gamma e_\gamma(k)/2)$, where s' is the current decision
        tree size, and
    (2) h has advantage larger than $\gamma g_\gamma(k)$.
    Here g_γ and e_γ are defined by

$$g_\gamma(k) = \frac{1 - e_\gamma(k)}{\gamma} \approx \ln k, \quad \text{and} \quad e_\gamma(k) = \prod_{i=1}^{k-1}\left(1 - \frac{\gamma}{i}\right).$$

This result intuitively means that if we can assume, at each boosting step, some hypothesis that is better than a binary hypothesis with advantage γ, then the algorithm produces a tree that is as good as the one produced by the original boosting algorithm using only binary hypotheses with advantage γ. (Note that $g_\gamma(2) = 1$ by definition.)

We simplify their analysis, thereby obtaining the following improved condition, which also makes the algorithm simpler. (Here we consider the same situation and the goal as above.)

Our condition
    At each boosting step, there always exists a hypothesis h satisfying the
    following:
    (1) h is either binary (in which case $k = 2$) or k-class with some k, $2 <
        k \leq K$, such that $k \leq s/s'$, and
    (2) h has advantage larger than $\gamma \lceil \log k \rceil$.

This condition is simpler, and the above explained intuition becomes clearer under this condition. The item (2) of this new condition means that k-class hypothesis h is better than an "equivalent" depth $\lceil \log k \rceil$ decision tree consisting of binary hypotheses with advantage γ. That is, if we can always find such a hypothesis at each boosting step, then the algorithm produces a tree that is as good as the one produced by the original boosting algorithm using only binary hypotheses with advantage γ.

In fact, based on this new interpretation, we propose to compare the quality of weak k-class hypotheses for different k based on the quantity computed as the information gain over $\lceil \log k \rceil$. This simplifies the original algorithm of Mansour and McAllester, and moreover, by this modification, we no longer need to know a lower bound γ for the advantage of binary weak hypotheses.

Technically, the item (2) of our condition is stronger (i.e., worse) than the original one; this is because $\lceil \log k \rceil \geq g_\gamma(k)$. But the item (1) of our condition is weaker (i.e., better) than the original one.

In our argument, we introduce *Weight Distribution Game* for analyzing the worst-case error bound.

2 Preliminaries

We introduce our learning model briefly. Our model is based on PAC learning model proposed by Valiant[13]. Let X denote an instance space. We assume the unknown target function $f : X \to \{0, 1\}$. The learner is given a *sample S* of m labeled examples, $S = (\langle x_1, f(x_1) \rangle, \ldots, \langle x_1, f(x_m) \rangle)$, where each x_i is drawn independently randomly with respect to an unknown distribution P over X. The goal of the learner is, for any given constants ε and δ ($0 < \varepsilon, \delta < 1$), to output a hypothesis $h_f : X \to \{0, 1\}$ such that its *generalization error* $\epsilon(h_f) \overset{\text{def}}{=} \Pr_P[f(x) \neq h_f(x)]$ is below ε, with probability at least $1 - \delta$.

In order to accomplish the goal, it is sufficient to design learning algorithms based on "Occam Razor."[1]. Namely, it is sufficient to construct a learning algorithm that outputs a hypothesis h_f satisfying the following conditions: For sufficiently large sample, (1) h_f's *training error* $\hat{\epsilon}(h_f) \overset{\text{def}}{=} \Pr_D[f(x) \neq h_f(x)]$ is small, where D is the uniform distribution over S, and (2) $size(h_f) = o(m)$, where $size(\cdot)$ represents the length of the bit string for h_f under some fixed encoding scheme.

In this paper we consider decision tree learning, i.e., the problem of constructing a decision tree satisfying the above PAC learning criteria. More precisely, for a given target f, we would like to obtain some decision tree T representing a hypothesis h_T whose generalization error is bounded by a given ε (with high probability). Note that if a hypothesis is represented as a decision tree, the second condition of Occam learning criterion can be interpreted as the number of leaves of the tree being sufficiently small with respect to the size of the sample. By the Occam Razor approach mentioned above, we can construct a decision tree learning algorithm that meets the criteria.

Here we recall some basic notations about decision trees. We assume a set H of hypothesis $h : X \to R_h$, where $2 \leq |R_h| \leq K$ for any fixed integer K. We allow each $h \in H$ to have different range. We denote the set of decision trees determined by H as $\mathcal{T}(H)$. A decision tree consists of internal nodes and leaves. Let T be any decision tree in $\mathcal{T}(H)$. Each internal node is labeled a hypothesis

$h \in H$ and it has $|R_h|$ child nodes corresponding to the value of h, where child nodes are either internal nodes or leaves. Each leaf is labeled 0 or 1.

When the number of branches of each node in T is some fixed $k \geq 2$, we call T a *k-way branching decision tree*. In general cases, including cases when the number of branches of each node in T is different, we call T a *multi-way branching decision tree*.

Finally let us clarify here how a decision tree is used to classify a given instance. Suppose that an instance $x \in X$ is given to a decision tree T. First the root node of T is visited. Then the child node corresponding to the values of $h(x)$ is visited next, and so on. Finally, x reaches to some leaf. T answers the label of the leaf.

Now we introduce the notion of boosting. In the classical definition, boosting is to construct a hypothesis h_f such that $\Pr_D[f(x) \neq h_f(x)] \leq \varepsilon$ for any given ε combining hypotheses $h_1, \ldots, h_t$, where each h_i satisfies that $\Pr_{D_i}[f(x) \neq h_i(x)] \leq 1/2 - \gamma$ for some distribution D_i over X ($i = 1, \ldots, t$, for some $t \geq 1$). However, in this paper, we measure the goodness of hypotheses from an information-theoretic point of view. For this we use the pseudo entropy proposed by Takimoto and Maruoka [12].

Definition 1 A function $G : [0,1]^2 \to [0,1]$ is a *pseudo-entropy function* if, for any $q_0, q_1 \in [0,1]$ such that $q_0 + q_1 = 1$,

1. $\min\{q_0, q_1\} \leq G(q_0, q_1)$,
2. $G(q_0, q_1) = 0 \iff q_0 = 1$ or $q_1 = 1$, and
3. G is concave and symmetric about $(1/2, 1/2)$.

For example, Shannon entropy function $q_0 \log(1/q_0) + q_1 \log(1/q_1)$ and $\sqrt{q_0 q_1}$ (proposed by Kearns and Mansour [6]) are pseudo-entropy functions. Next we define the entropy of function f using a pseudo-entropy function G.

Definition 2 The *G-entropy* of f with respect to D, denoted by $H_G^D(f)$, is defined as

$$H_D^G(f) \overset{\text{def}}{=} G(q_0, q_1),$$

where $q_i = \Pr_D[f(x) = i]$ ($i = 0, 1$).

We can interpret G-entropy as "impurity" of the values of f under the distribution D. For example, if f takes only one value, G-entropy becomes the minimum. If the value of f is random, G-entropy becomes the maximum.

We also define the conditional G-entropy given a hypothesis $h : X \to R_h$, where R_h is a finite set but possibly different from $\{0, 1\}$.

Definition 3 The *Conditional G-entropy* of f given h with respect to D, denoted by $H_D^G(f|h)$, is defined as $H_D^G(f|h) \overset{\text{def}}{=} \sum_{j \in R_h} \Pr_D[h(x) = j] G(q_{0|j}, q_{1|j})$, where $q_{i|j} = \Pr_D[f(x) = i|h(x) = j]$ ($i = 0, 1, j \in R_h$).

Since the range of h may be different from that of f, we have to give a way to interpret values of h. More precisely, we define a mapping $M : R_h \to \{0,1\}$: $M(j) \overset{\text{def}}{=} \arg_{i=0,1} \max q_{i|j}$. We show the following relationship between the classification error and the G-entropy.

Proposition 1 $\Pr_D[f(x) \neq M(h(x))] \leq H_D^G(f|h)$.

Proof. We denote $w_j = \Pr_D[h(x) = j]$ for $j \in R_h$. Then, we have

$$
\Pr_D[f(x) \neq M(h(x))] = \sum_{j \in R_h} w_j \Pr_D[f(x) \neq M(h(x))|h(x) = j]
$$
$$
= \sum_{j \in R_h} w_j \min\{q_{0|j}, q_{1|j}\}
$$
$$
\leq \sum_{j \in R_h} w_j G(q_{0|j}, q_{1|j}) = H_D^G(f|h).
$$

$\square$

We note that if $H_D^G(f|h) = 0$, then the error probability $\Pr_D[f(x) \neq M(h(x))]$ also becomes 0.

Following relationship between "error-based" and "information-based" hypotheses was first proved by Kearns and Mansour [6].

Lemma 2 (Kearns and Mansour [6]) Suppose $G(q_0, q_1) = \sqrt{q_0 q_1}$. For any distribution D over X, if there exists a hypothesis $h : X \to \{0,1\}$ such that $\Pr_D[f(x) \neq h(x)] \leq 1/2 - \delta$, then there exists a hypothesis $h' : X \to \{0,1\}$ such that $H_D^G(f) - H_D^G(f|h') \geq \frac{\delta^2}{16} H_D^G(f)$.

Motivated from the above lemma, we state our assumption. We assume a set of "information-based weak hypotheses" of the target function f.

Definition 4 Let f be any boolean function over X. Let $G : [0,1]^2 \to [0,1]$ be any pseudo-entropy function. Let H be any set of hypotheses. H and G satisfy the γ-*weak hypothesis assumption* for f if for any distribution D over X, there exists a hypothesis $h \in H$ satisfying

$$
H_D^G(f) - H_D^G(f|h) \geq \gamma H_D^G(f),
$$

where $0 < \gamma \leq 1$. We call this constant γ *advantage* and refer to the reduction $H_D^G(f) - H_D^G(f|h)$ as *gain*.

3   Learning Binary Decision Trees

Before studying the multi-way branching decision tree learning algorithm, we review a binary decision tree learning algorithm proposed by Kearns and Mansour [6].

For the binary target function f, this algorithm constructs binary decision trees. We assume that the algorithm is given some pseudo-entropy function G and a set H_2 of binary hypotheses $h : X \to R_h, |R_h| = 2$ in advance. We call the algorithm $\textbf{TOPDOWN}_{\textbf{G},\textbf{H}_2}$. The description of $\textbf{TOPDOWN}_{\textbf{G},\textbf{H}_2}$ is given in Figure 1.

In what follows, we explain the idea and the outline of this algorithm. $\textbf{TOPDOWN}_{\textbf{G},\textbf{H}_2}$, given a sample S and an integer $s \geq 2$ as input, outputs a decision tree with s leaves, where internal nodes are labeled with functions in H_2. The algorithm's goal is to obtain a decision tree that has small training error on S under the uniform distribution D over S. For this, the algorithm tries to reduce the conditional G-entropy of f, given a constructed decision tree.

Let T be a decision tree that the algorithm has constructed so far. (Initially, T is a tree with a single leaf.) Let $L(T)$ denote the set of leaves of T. (We denote $|T| = |L(T)|$.) Then T can be regarded as a mapping from X to $L(T)$. For each $\ell \in L(T)$, we define $w_\ell \overset{\text{def}}{=} \Pr_D[T(x) = \ell]$ and $q_{i|\ell} \overset{\text{def}}{=} \Pr_D[f(x) = i|T(x) = \ell]$ (where $i = 0, 1$).

Then the training error of T, which we denote as $\hat{\epsilon}(T)$, is computed as follows: $\hat{\epsilon}(T) = \Pr_D[f(x) \neq M(T(x))]$, where $M(\ell) \overset{\text{def}}{=} \arg_{i=0,1} \max q_{i|\ell}$ for any $\ell \in L(T)$. We denote the conditional G-entropy of f given T as

$$H_D^G(f|T) \overset{\text{def}}{=} \sum_{\ell \in L(T)} w_\ell G(q_{0|\ell}, q_{1|\ell}).$$

From Proposition 1, we have $\hat{\epsilon}(T) \leq H_D^G(f|T)$. In order for reducing this entropy, the algorithm makes a local change to the tree T. At each local change, the algorithm chooses a leaf $\ell \in L(T)$ and $h \in H_2$ and replaces ℓ with a new internal node labeled h (and its two new child leaves). The tree obtained in this way is denoted $T_{\ell,h}$. Compared with T, $T_{\ell,h}$ has one more leaf.

We explain the way to choose ℓ and h at each local change. The algorithm chooses ℓ that maximizes $w_\ell G(q_{0|\ell}, q_{1|\ell})$; it calculates a sample S_ℓ that is a subset of S reaching ℓ. Finally the algorithm chooses $h \in H_2$ that maximizes the gain $H_{D_\ell}^G(f) - H_{D_\ell}^G(f|h)$, where D_ℓ is the uniform distribution over S_ℓ. Note that $H_D^G(f|T) - H_D^G(f|T_{\ell,h}) = w_\ell(H_{D_\ell}^G(f) - H_{D_\ell}^G(f|h))$. Thus, if the gain is positive, then we reduce the conditional G-entropy.

For the efficiency of this boosting algorithm, Kearns and Mansour showed the following result.

Theorem 3 (Kearns and Mansour [6]) Assume that H_2 and G satisfy the γ-weak hypothesis assumption. Then, $\textbf{TOPDOWN}_{\textbf{G},\textbf{H}_2}(S, s)$ outputs T with $\hat{\epsilon}(T) \leq H_G^D(f|T) \leq s^{-\gamma}$.

4   Learning Multi-way Branching Decision Trees

We propose a simpler version of Mansour and McAllester's algorithm, which constructs multi-way branching decision trees. We weaken and simplify some technical conditions of their algorithm.

TOPDOWN$_{\mathbf{G,H_2}}$ (S, s)
___
begin
   $T \leftarrow$ the single leaf tree;
   While $|T| < s$ **times do**
      $\ell \leftarrow \arg\max_{\ell \in L(T)} w_\ell G(q_{0|\ell}, q_{1|\ell})$;
      $S_\ell \leftarrow \{\langle x, f(x)\rangle \in S | T(x) = \ell\}$;
      $D_\ell \leftarrow$ the uniform distribution over S_ℓ;
      $h \leftarrow \arg\max_{h \in H_2}(H^G_{D_\ell}(f) - H^G_{D_\ell}(f|h))$;
      $T \leftarrow T_{\ell,h}$;
   end-while
   Output T ;
end.

Fig. 1. Algorithm **TOPDOWN$_{\mathbf{G,H_2}}$**

Let H be a set of hypotheses where each $h \in H$ is a function from X to R_h $(2 \leq |R_h| \leq K)$. We assume that H contains a set of binary hypotheses H_2. The algorithm is given H and some pseudo-entropy function $G : [0,1]^2 \to [0,1]$ beforehand. We call the algorithm **TOPDOWN-M$_{\mathbf{G,H}}$**. **TOPDOWN-M$_{\mathbf{G,H}}$**, given a sample S and an integer $s \geq 2$ as input, outputs a multi-way branching decision tree T with $|T| = s$.

The algorithm is a generalization of **TOPDOWN$_{\mathbf{G,H_2}}$**. One of the main modification is the criterion to choose hypotheses. **TOPDOWN-M$_{\mathbf{G,H}}$** chooses the hypothesis $h : X \to R_h$ such that maximizes the gain over $\lceil \log |R_h| \rceil$, not merely comparing the gain. Because the given size of the tree is limited, in order to reduce the conditional G-entropy as much as possible, it is natural to choose a hypothesis with smaller range among hypotheses that have the same amount of gain. On the other hand, the criterion that Mansour and McAllester's algorithm uses is the gain over $g_\gamma(|R_h|)$. Note that it is necessary to know γ to compute g_γ.

The other modification is a constraint of hypotheses with respect to the size of the tree. We say that a hypothesis h is *acceptable* for tree T and target size s if either $|R_h| = 2$ or $2 < |R_h| \leq s/|T|$.

Note that if $|T| \geq s/2$, then only binary hypotheses are acceptable. However H contains H_2 thus the algorithm can always select a hypothesis that is acceptable for any T and s. We show the details of the algorithm in Figure 2. Note that if $H_2 \subset H$ satisfies the γ-weak hypothesis assumption and hypothesis $h : X \to R_h$ is selected for ℓ, then

$$H^G_{D_\ell}(f) - H^G_{D_\ell}(f|h) \geq \gamma \lceil \log |R_h| \rceil H^G_{D_\ell}(f).$$

4.1 Our Analysis

We give an analysis for the algorithm **TOPDOWN-M$_{\mathbf{G,H}}$**.

TOPDOWN-M$_{\mathbf{G,H}}(S, s)$

begin

$T \leftarrow$ the single-leaf tree;

While $(|T| < s)$ **do**

$\ell \leftarrow \arg\max_{\ell \in L(T)} w_\ell G(q_{0|\ell}, q_{1|\ell})$;

$S_\ell \leftarrow \{\langle x, f(x) \rangle \in S | T(x) = \ell\}$;

$D_\ell \leftarrow$ the uniform distribution over S_ℓ ;

$h \leftarrow \arg\max_{\substack{h \in H, \\ \text{acceptable for } T \text{ and } s}} \dfrac{H^G_{D_\ell}(f) - H^G_{D_\ell}(f|h)}{\lceil \log |R_h| \rceil}$

$T \leftarrow T_{\ell,h}$;

end-while

Output T ;

end.

Fig. 2. Algorithm **TOPDOWN-M$_{\mathbf{G,H}}$**

First we define some notations. For any leaf ℓ, we define *weight* W_ℓ as

$$W_\ell \stackrel{\text{def}}{=} w_\ell G(q_{0|\ell}, q_{1|\ell}).$$

The weight of a tree is just the total weight of all its leaves. Then by definition, we immediately have the following relations.

Fact 1 1. $\hat{\epsilon}(T) \leq \sum_{\ell \in L(T)} W_\ell$.
2. If H_2 and G satisfy γ-weak hypothesis assumption, then for any leaf ℓ and weights of ℓ's child leaves $W_1, \ldots, W_k$ $(2 \leq k \leq K)$, we have $W_1 + \cdots + W_k \leq (1 - \gamma\lceil \log k \rceil)W_\ell$.

From Fact 1 (1), in order to bound the training error of the tree, it suffices for us to consider the weight of the tree. On the other hand, it follows from Fact 1 (2) that at each boosting step, the weight of the tree gets decreased by at least $\gamma\lceil \log k \rceil W_\ell$, provided that a leaf ℓ is "expanded" by this boosting step and a k-class hypothesis is chosen for ℓ. Thus, we need to analyze how the weight of the tree gets decreased under the situation that, at each boosting step, (i) the leaf ℓ of the largest weight is selected and expanded, and (ii) the weight gets decreased *exactly* by $\gamma\lceil \log k \rceil W_\ell$, when a k-class hypothesis is chosen for ℓ. That is, we consider the worst-case under the situation and discuss how the tree's weight gets decreased in the worst-case. Notice that the only freedom left here is (i) the number of child nodes k under the constraint $k = 2$ or $2 < k \leq s/|T|$, and (ii) the distribution of the weights $W_1, \ldots, W_k$ of child leaves of ℓ under the constraint $W_1 + \cdots + W_k = (1 - \gamma\lceil \log k \rceil)W_\ell$. Therefore, for analyzing the worst-case, we would like to know the way to determine the number of child nodes and the way to distribute the weight W_ℓ to its child nodes in order to minimize the decrease of the total tree weight. This fact motivates us to define the following combinatorial game.

Weight Distribution Game

1. Initially, the player is given a single-leaf tree T where weight of the leaf is W, $(0 \leq W \leq 1)$, and an integer s $(s \geq 2)$.
2. While $|T| < s$, the player repeat the following procedures:
   a) Choose the leaf ℓ that has the maximum weight.
   b) Choose any integer k (≥ 2) satisfying either $k = 2$ or $2 < k \leq s/|T|$.
   c) Expand the leaf ℓ; replace the leaf with an internal node with k child leaves and assign weights $W_1, \ldots, W_k$ of child nodes so that the following equation holds: $W_1 + \cdots + W_k = (1 - \gamma \lceil \log k \rceil) W_\ell$.

Player's goal: Maximize the weight of the final tree T with s leaves.

The best strategy for the player in this game is given by the following result. (The proof is given in the next subsection.)

Theorem 4 In the Weight Distribution Game, the tree weight is maximized if the player always chooses the number of child leaves k equals to 2 and distributes the weight of expanded leaf *equally* to all its child nodes.

Now the worst-case situation for our boosting algorithm is clear from this result and our discussion above. That is, the G-entropy of f, given the tree, gets decreased *slowest* when every chosen hypothesis is binary and divides the leaf's entropy equally to its all child nodes. Thus, by analyzing this case, we would be able to derive an upper bound of the training error.

Theorem 5 Assume that $H_2 \subset H$ satisfies the γ-weak hypothesis assumption for f. Then, **TOPDOWN-M$_{\mathbf{G,H}}$**(S, s) outputs T with $\hat{\epsilon}(T) \leq H_G^D(f|T) \leq s^{-\gamma}$.

Proof. In the Weight Distribution Game, suppose that the player chooses the number of child nodes $k = 2$ and distributes the weight of each leaf equally among its new child leaves. Then the player always chooses a leaf in the oldest generation that is not expanded yet. Note that after $s-1$ expansions, the number of the leaves of the tree becomes s. Let $t = s - 1$. Suppose that after the t th expansion, all leaves in the i th generation are expanded (we assume the initial leaf is in the first generation) and there are t' leaves expanded in the $i + 1$ th generation $(0 \leq t' \leq 2^i)$. Then the number of all expansions t is given by $t = \sum_{j=1}^{i} 2^{j-1} + t' = 2^i - 1 + t'$.

One can observe that just after all leaves in each generation are expanded, the weight of the tree is multiplied by $(1 - \gamma)$. Thus after all expansions in the i th generation, the weight of the tree is $W(1 - \gamma)^i$. Because the weight of each leaf in the $i + 1$ generation is $W(1 - \gamma)^i/2^i$, the weight of the tree after the t th expansion is $W(1 - \gamma)^i(1 - t'\gamma/2^i)$. Note that $1 - x \leq e^{-x}$ for any $0 \leq x \leq 1$ and $W \leq 1$. Then we have

$$W(1 - \gamma)^i \left(1 - \frac{t'\gamma}{2^i}\right) \leq \exp[-\gamma(i + t'/2^i)].$$

From the fact that $i + t'/2^i \geq \ln(2^i + t')$, we have

$$\exp[-\gamma(i + t'/2^i)] \leq \exp[-\gamma \ln(2^i + t')]$$
$$= s^{-\gamma}.$$

$\square$

4.2 Weight Distribution Game

We are proving here Theorem 4. First we prepare some notations. Let $\mathcal{D}_k$ denote the set of all possible distributions over $\{1, \ldots, k\}$ $(2 \leq k \leq K)$. In particular, let d_k^* be the uniform one, i.e., $d_k^* = (1/k, \ldots, 1/k)$. We also define $\mathcal{D} = \bigcup_{k \geq 2} \mathcal{D}_k$. Note that for any distribution $d_k \in \mathcal{D}$, the subscript k is the size of the domain of d_k.

For any sequences of distributions $d_{k_1}^{(1)}, \ldots, d_{k_t}^{(t)} \in \mathcal{D}^t$ $(t \geq 1)$, we denote $\mathrm{sum}(W, d_{k_1}^{(1)}, \ldots, d_{k_t}^{(t)})$ as the weight of the tree obtained by the following way:

1. the initial weight is W; and,
2. at the i th step, the number of child nodes is k_i and the way to distribute weights is specified by $d_{k_i}^{(i)}$ $(1 \leq i \leq t)$.

Then we consider a sequence of distributions corresponding to a sequence of hypotheses that are acceptable for s. We say that such a sequence is acceptable. More precisely, a sequence of distributions $d_{k_1}, \ldots, d_{k_t}$ with length t is *acceptable* for s if $s = (k_1 - 1) + \cdots + (k_t - 1) + 1$ and for any integer i $(1 \leq i \leq t)$, $k_i = 2$, or $2 < k_i \leq s/\{(k_1 - 1) + \cdots + (k_{i-1} - 1) + 1\}$. By using this notation, Theorem 4 can be re-written as follows.

Theorem 6 For any weight W, any integer $s \geq 2$ and any sequence of distributions $d_{k_1}^{(1)}, \ldots, d_{k_t}^{(t)} \in \mathcal{D}^t$ that is acceptable for s,

$$\mathrm{sum}(W, d_{k_1}^{(1)}, \ldots, d_{k_t}^{(t)}) \leq \mathrm{sum}(W, \underbrace{d_2^*, \ldots, d_2^*}_{s-1}).$$

To prove the theorem, we show that the following relation holds for any integer u $(1 \leq u \leq s - 1)$ and any sequence of distributions $d_{k_1}^{(1)}, \ldots, d_{k_u}^{(u)} \in \mathcal{D}^u$,

$$\mathrm{sum}(W, d_{k_1}^{(1)}, \ldots, d_{k_u}^{(u)} \underbrace{d_2^*, \ldots, d_2^*}_{t}) \leq \mathrm{sum}(W, d_{k_1}^{(1)}, \ldots, d_{k_{u-1}}^{(u-1)} \underbrace{d_2^*, \ldots, d_2^*}_{t+k_{u-1}-1}),$$

where t is the integer such that the sequence $d_{k_1}^{(1)}, \ldots, d_{k_u}^{(u)}, d_2^*, \ldots, d_2^* \in \mathcal{D}^{u+t}$ is acceptable for s. We prove this relation in Lemma 8. Before doing this, we begin with a rather simple lemma.

Lemma 7 For any weight $W \in [0, 1]$, any integer $s \geq 2$, any distribution $d_k \in \mathcal{D}$, and the sequence of distributions $d_k, d_2^*, \ldots, d_2^* \in \mathcal{D}^t$, that is acceptable for s and has length t,

$$\text{sum}(W, \underbrace{d_k, d_2^*, \ldots, d_2^*}_{t}) \leq \text{sum}(W, \underbrace{d_2^*, \ldots, d_2^*}_{s-1}).$$

Proof. Suppose that the player does not choose a leaf whose weight is the maximum. Instead, suppose the player always select a leaf in the oldest generation, that is not expanded yet, whose weight is the maximum among weights of all leaves in the same generation. We denote the sum under the situation above as sum'. In this situation, the player may not choose the leaf with the maximum weight at each step. That makes the sum less than that in the original setting. Thus, we have

$$\text{sum}(W, \underbrace{d_k, d_2^*, \ldots, d_2^*}_{t}) \leq \text{sum}'(W, \underbrace{d_k, d_2^*, \ldots, d_2^*}_{t}).$$

Now we prove that the following inequality holds.

$$\text{sum}'(W, \underbrace{d_k, d_2^*, \ldots, d_2^*}_{t}) \leq \text{sum}(W, \underbrace{d_k^*, d_2^*, \ldots, d_2^*}_{t}). \tag{1}$$

Let T' and T^* be the trees corresponding to left and right side of the above inequality respectively.

First, consider the case when T' and T^* are completely balanced, i.e., the case just after all leaves of the trees in the $i + 1$ th generation are expanded for some i. Then the weights of both T' and T^* are $W(1 - \gamma\lceil \log k \rceil)(1 - \gamma)^i$ thus inequality (1) holds.

Second, we consider the other case, that is, T' and T^* are not completely balanced. Suppose that T' and T^* are trees such that all leaves in the $i + 1$ th generation and l' leaves in the $i + 2$ th generation are expanded ($1 \leq t' \leq k2^i$). We denote the numbers of child nodes in the $i + 2$ th generation of both trees as $J = k2^i$. We also denote the weights of nodes in the $i + 2$ th generation of T' as $W_1, \ldots, W_J$. (W.l.o.g., we assume that $W_1 \geq \cdots \geq W_J$.) Then it holds that $\sum_{j=1}^{J} W_j = W(1 - \gamma\lceil \log k \rceil)(1 - \gamma)^i$. On the other hand, the weight of each node in the $i + 2$ th generation of T^* are the same. We denote the weights as $\widehat{W} = W(1 - \gamma\lceil \log k \rceil)(1 - \gamma)^i / J$. Now we claim that for any t', $1 \leq t' \leq J$,

$$\sum_{j=1}^{t'} W_j \geq t'\widehat{W}.$$

Suppose not, namely, $\sum_{j=1}^{t'} W_j < t'\widehat{W}$ for some t'. Then we have $W_{t'} < \widehat{W}$. Because the sequence $\{W_j\}$ is monotone decreasing, it holds that $\sum_{j=1}^{J} W_j < J\widehat{W}$. But this contradicts that $\sum_{j=1}^{J} W_j = J\widehat{W} = W(1 - \gamma\lceil \log k \rceil)(1 - \gamma)^i$. This completes the proof of the claim. Then, we have

$$\text{sum}'(W, \underbrace{d_k, d_2^*, \ldots, d_2^*}_{t}) = W(1 - \gamma\lceil\log k\rceil)(1 - \gamma)^i - \gamma\sum_{j=1}^{t'} W_j$$

$$\leq W(1 - \gamma\lceil\log k\rceil)(1 - \gamma)^i - \gamma t'\widehat{W}$$

$$= \text{sum}(W, \underbrace{d_k^*, d_2^*, \ldots, d_2^*}_{t}).$$

Now we have proved the inequality (1). Next we prove the following inequality.

$$\text{sum}(W, \underbrace{d_k^*, d_2^*, \ldots, d_2^*}_{t}) \leq \text{sum}(W, \underbrace{d_2^*, \ldots, d_2^*}_{s-1}).$$

Suppose s is given as follows: $s = 2^i + s'$ ($2^i \leq s \leq 2^{i+1}$, $s' \geq 0$). Then, we have

$$\text{sum}(W, \underbrace{d_2^*, \ldots, d_2^*}_{s-1}) = (1 - \gamma)^i W - s'\gamma\frac{(1 - \gamma)^i}{2^i} W$$

$$= (1 - \gamma)^i \left(1 - \frac{s'\gamma}{2^i}\right) W$$

$$\overset{\text{def}}{=} \phi_\gamma(s)W.$$

On the other hand, suppose s is given as follows: $s = k2^{i'} + s''$ ($k2^{i'} \leq s \leq k2^{i'+1}$, $s'' \geq 0$). Then, we have

$$\text{sum}(W, \underbrace{d_k^*, d_2^*, \ldots, d_2^*}_{t}) = (1 - \gamma\lceil\log k\rceil)(1 - \gamma)^{i'} W$$

$$- s''\gamma\frac{(1 - \gamma\lceil\log k\rceil)(1 - \gamma)^{i'}}{k2^{i'}} W$$

$$= (1 - \gamma\lceil\log k\rceil)(1 - \gamma)^{i'} \left(1 - \frac{s''\gamma}{k2^{i'}}\right) W$$

$$= (1 - \gamma\lceil\log k\rceil)\phi_\gamma(s/k)W$$

We note that $\phi_\gamma(2s) = (1-\gamma)\phi_\gamma(s)$ and ϕ_γ is monotone non-increasing function. That implies,

$$\frac{\phi_\gamma(s)}{(1 - \gamma)^{\lfloor\log k\rfloor}} \leq \phi_\gamma\left(\frac{s}{k}\right) \leq \frac{\phi_\gamma(s)}{(1 - \gamma)^{\lceil\log k\rceil}}.$$

Now the following inequality holds:

$$\text{sum}(W, \underbrace{d_k^*, d_2^*, \ldots, d_2^*}_{t}) \leq (1 - \gamma\lceil\log k\rceil)\frac{\phi_\gamma(s)}{(1 - \gamma)^{\lceil\log k\rceil}}$$

$$\leq \phi_\gamma(s)$$

$$= \text{sum}(W, \underbrace{d_2^*, \ldots, d_2^*}_{s-1}).$$

This completes the proof. $\qquad\qquad\qquad\qquad\qquad\qquad\qquad\qquad\qquad\square$

Next we prove our main lemma.

Lemma 8 For any weight $W \in [0,1]$, any integer $s \geq 2$, any sequence of distributions $d_{k_1}^{(1)}, \ldots, d_{k_u}^{(u)}, d_2^*, \ldots, d_2^* \in \mathcal{D}^{u+t}$,that is acceptable for s, having length $u + t$, and the sequence of distributions $d_{k_1}^{(1)}, \ldots, d_{k_{u-1}}^{(u-1)}, d_2^*, \ldots, d_2^* \in \mathcal{D}^{u+t+k_u-2}$ having length $u + t + k_u - 2$,

$$\text{sum}(W, d_{k_1}^{(1)}, \ldots, d_{k_u}^{(u)}, \underbrace{d_2^*, \ldots, d_2^*}_{t}) \leq \text{sum}(W, d_{k_1}^{(1)}, \ldots, d_{k_{u-1}}^{(u-1)}, \underbrace{d_2^*, \ldots, d_2^*}_{t+k_u-1})$$

Proof. We prove this inequality starting from the right side. Note that if the sequence $d_{k_1}^{(1)}, \ldots, d_{k_u}^{(u)}, d_2^*, \ldots, d_2^*$ of length $u + t$ is acceptable for s, then the sequence $d_{k_1}^{(1)}, \ldots, d_{k_{u-1}}^{(u-1)}, d_2^*, \ldots, d_2^*$ with length $u + t + k_u - 2$ is also acceptable for s.

Let T be the tree corresponding to the sum $\text{sum}(W, d_{k_1}^{(1)}, \ldots, d_{k_{u-1}}^{(u-1)}, \underbrace{d_2^*, \ldots, d_2^*}_{t+k_u-1})$.

Let L_{u-1} be the set of leaves of T after the $u - 1$ th expansion. Then, we have

$$\text{sum}(W, d_{k_1}^{(1)}, \ldots, d_{k_{u-1}}^{(u-1)}, \underbrace{d_2^*, \ldots, d_2^*}_{t+k_u-1}) = \sum_{\ell \in L_{u-1}} \text{sum}(W_\ell, \underbrace{d_2^*, \ldots, d_2^*}_{t_\ell}),$$

where t_ℓ is the number of expansions for leaf ℓ and its descendant leaves. Note that $t = \sum_{\ell \in L_{u-1}} t_\ell$. Let ℓ^* be the leaf in L_{u-1} that has the maximum weight. (So ℓ^* is the u th leaf to be expanded.) Let T_{ℓ^*} be the subtree of T rooted at ℓ^*. Let $\widehat{T}_{\ell^*}$ be a tree that has the following properties: (i) $|T_{\ell^*}| = |\widehat{T}_{\ell^*}|$, and (ii) $\widehat{T}_{\ell^*}$ is generated according to $d_{k_u}, \underbrace{d_2^*, \ldots, d_2^*}_{t_{\ell^*} - k_u + 1}$, whereas T_{ℓ^*} is generated according to $\underbrace{d_2^*, \ldots, d_2^*}_{t_{\ell^*}}$. Now we consider replacing T_{ℓ^*} with $\widehat{T}_{\ell^*}$. To do this, we need to guarantee that $k_u \leq |T_{\ell^*}|$. This is clear when $k_u = 2$. Then we consider the other case. Because the sequence $d_{k_1}^{(1)}, \ldots, d_{k_u}^{(u)}, d_2^*, \ldots, d_2^*$ is acceptable for s, by definition, we have $k_u \leq s/|L_{u-1}|$. On the other hand, T_{ℓ^*} is the biggest subtree among all subtrees rooted at leaves in L_{u-1}. This implies $s/|L_{u-1}| \leq |T_{\ell^*}|$. Now we guarantee that $k_u \leq |T_{\ell^*}|$. From Lemma 7, we have

$$\text{sum}(W_{\ell^*}, \underbrace{d_2^*, \ldots, d_2^*}_{t_\ell}) \geq \text{sum}(W_{\ell^*}, d_{k_u}^{(u)} \underbrace{d_2^*, \ldots, d_2^*}_{t_\ell - k_u + 1}).$$

Thus we conclude that by replacing subtree T_{ℓ^*} with $\widehat{T}_{\ell^*}$, the weight of T becomes small. We denote the replaced tree as $\widehat{T}$, and denote its weight as $\widehat{\text{sum}}$. Then, we have

$$\sum_{\ell \in L_{u-1}} \text{sum}(W_\ell, \underbrace{d_2^*, \ldots, d_2^*}_{t_\ell}) \geq \widehat{\text{sum}}(W, d_{k_1}^{(1)}, \ldots, d_{k_u}^{(u)}, \underbrace{d_2^*, \ldots, d_2^*}_{t}).$$

The tree $\widehat{T}$ may not be produced according to the rule that the leaf that has the maximum weight is to be expanded first. Thus, the sum of weights of $\widehat{T}$ may be larger than the tree produced according to the rule. Now we have

$$\widehat{\mathrm{sum}}(W, d_{k_1}^{(1)}, \ldots, d_{k_u}^{(u)}, \underbrace{d_2^*, \ldots, d_2^*}_{t}) \geq \mathrm{sum}(W, d_{k_1}^{(1)}, \ldots, d_{k_u}^{(u)}, \underbrace{d_2^*, \ldots, d_2^*}_{t}).$$

This completes the proof.   □

Now the proof of our theorem is easy.

Proof for Theorem 6 From Lemma 8, for any sequence of distribution $d_{k_1}, \ldots, d_{k_t} \in \mathcal{D}^t$ that is acceptable for s, we have

$$\begin{aligned}
\mathrm{sum}(W, d_{k_1}^{(1)}, \ldots, d_{k_t}^{(t)}) \leq & \mathrm{sum}(W, d_{k_1}^{(1)}, \ldots, d_{k_t-1}^{(t-1)}, \underbrace{d_2^*, \ldots, d_2^*}_{k_t-1}) \\
\leq & \mathrm{sum}(W, d_{k_1}^{(1)}, \ldots, d_{k_t-2}^{(t-2)}, \underbrace{d_2^*, \ldots, d_2^*}_{k_{t-1}+k_t-2}) \\
\leq & \ldots \\
\leq & \mathrm{sum}(W, \underbrace{d_2^*, \ldots, d_2^*}_{s-1}).
\end{aligned}$$

□

Acknowledgements. I am grateful to Prof. Osamu Watanabe for his constant support during this research, and to Tadashi Yamazaki for important hints and comments. I also thank members of Watanabe research group for helpful discussions and the anonymous referees for valuable comments.

References

1. A. Blumer, A. Ehrenfeucht, D. Haussler, and M. K. Warmuth. Occam's razor. *Information Processing Letters*, 24:377–380, April 1987.
2. L. Breiman, J. H. Friedman, R. A. Olshen, and C. J. Stone. *Classification and Regression Trees*. Wadsworth International Group, 1984.
3. Carlos Domingo and Osamu Watanabe. MadaBoost: A modification of AdaBoost. In *Proceedings of 13th Annual Conference on Computational Learning Theory*, pages 180–189. Morgan Kaufmann, San Francisco, 2000.
4. Y. Freund. Boosting a weak learning algorithm by majority. *Information and Computation*, 121(2):256–285, September 1995.
5. Yoav Freund and Robert E. Schapire:. A decision-theoretic generalization of on-line learning and an application to boosting. *Journal of Computer and System Sciences*, 55(1):119–139, 1997.
6. M. Kearns and Y. Mansour. On the boosting ability of top-down decision tree learning algorithms. *Journal of Computer and System Sciences*, 58(1):109–128, 1999.

7. Y. Mansour and D. McAllester. Boosting with multi-way branching in decision trees. In *Advances in Neural Information Processing Systems*, volume 12, pages 300–306. The MIT Press, 2000.
8. J. Ross Quinlan. *C4.5: Programs for Machine Learning*. Morgan Kaufmann, 1993.
9. Robert E. Schapire. The strength of weak learnability. *Machine Learning*, 5(2):197–227, 1990.
10. Robert E. Schapire. Using output codes to boost multiclass learning problems. In *Proc. 14th International Conference on Machine Learning*, pages 313–321. Morgan Kaufmann, 1997.
11. Robert E. Schapire and Yoram Singer. Improved boosting algorithms using confidence-rated predictions. *Machine Learning*, 37(3):297–336, 1999.
12. Eiji Takimoto and Akira Maruoka. On the boosting algorithm for multiclass functions based on information-theoretic criterion for approximation. In *Proceedings of the 1st International Conference on Discovery Science*, volume 1532 of *Lecture Notes in Artificial Intelligence*, pages 256–267. Springer-Verlag, 1998.
13. L. G. Valiant. A theory of the learnable. *Communications of the ACM*, 27(11):1134–1142, November 1984.

Minimizing the Quadratic Training Error of a Sigmoid Neuron Is Hard

Jiří Šíma*

Department of Theoretical Computer Science,
Institute of Computer Science, Academy of Sciences of the Czech Republic,
P. O. Box 5, 182 07 Prague 8, Czech Republic, sima@cs.cas.cz

Abstract. We first present a brief survey of hardness results for training feedforward neural networks. These results are then completed by the proof that the simplest architecture containing only a single neuron that applies the standard (logistic) activation function to the weighted sum of n inputs is hard to train. In particular, the problem of finding the weights of such a unit that minimize the relative quadratic training error within 1 or its average (over a training set) within $13/(31n)$ of its infimum proves to be NP-hard. Hence, the well-known back-propagation learning algorithm appears to be not efficient even for one neuron which has negative consequences in constructive learning.

1 The Complexity of Neural Network Loading

Neural networks establish an important class of learning models that are widely applied in practical applications to solving artificial intelligence tasks [13]. The most prominent position among successful neural learning heuristics is occupied by the *back-propagation* algorithm [31] which is often used for training feedforward networks. This algorithm is based on the gradient descent method that minimizes the quadratic regression error of a network with respect to a training data. For this purpose, each unit (neuron) in the network applies a differentiable activation function (e.g. the *standard logistic sigmoid*) to the weighted sum of its local inputs rather than the discrete *Heaviside (threshold) function* with binary outputs. However, the underlying optimization process appears very time consuming even for small networks and training tasks. This was confirmed by an empirical study of the learning time required by the back-propagation algorithm which suggested its exponential scaling with the size of training sets [35] and networks [36]. Its slow convergence is probably caused by the inherent complexity of training feedforward networks.

The first attempt to theoretically analyze the time complexity of learning by feedforward networks is due to Judd [21] who introduced the so-called *loading problem* which is the problem of finding the weight parameters for a given fixed network architecture and a training task so that the network responses are perfectly consistent with all training data. For example, an efficient loading

* Research supported by grants GA AS CR B2030007 and GA ČR No. 201/00/1489.

N. Abe, R. Khardon, and T. Zeugmann (Eds.): ALT 2001, LNAI 2225, pp. 92–105, 2001.

algorithm is required for the proper PAC learnability [6] (besides the polynomial VC-dimension that the most common neural network models possess [30,38]). However, Judd proved the loading problem for feedforward networks to be NP-complete even if very strong restrictions are imposed on their architectures and training tasks [21]. The drawback of Judd's proofs is in using quite unnatural network architectures with irregular interconnection patterns and a fixed input dimension while the number of outputs grows which do not appear in practice. On the other hand, his arguments are valid for practically all the common unit types including the sigmoid neurons. Eventually, Judd provided a polynomial-time loading algorithm for restricted shallow architectures [20] whose practical applicability was probably ruled out by the hardness result for loading deep networks [32]. Further, Parberry proved a similar NP-completeness result for loading feedforward networks with irregular interconnections and only a small constant number of units [27]. In addition, Wiklicky showed that the loading problem for higher-order networks with integer weights is even algorithmically not solvable [39].

In order to achieve the hardness results for common layered architectures with complete connectivity between neighbor layers, Blum and Rivest in their seminal work [5] considered the smallest conceivable two-layer network with only 3 binary neurons (two hidden and one output units) employing the Heaviside activation function. They proved the loading problem for such a 3-node network with n inputs to be NP-complete and generalized the proof for a polynomial number of hidden units (in terms of n) when the output neuron computes logical AND [5]. Hammer further replaced the output AND gate by a threshold unit [11] while Kuhlmann achieved the proof for the output unit implementing any subclass of Boolean functions depending on all the outputs from hidden nodes [23]. Lin and Vitter extended the NP-completeness result even for a 2-node cascade architecture with one hidden unit connected to the output neuron that also receives the inputs [24]. Megiddo, on the other hand, showed that the loading problem for two-layer networks with a *fixed* number of real inputs and the Heaviside hidden nodes, and the output unit implementing an arbitrary Boolean function is solvable in polynomial time [26].

Much effort has been spent to generalize the hardness results also for continuous activation functions, especially for the standard sigmoid used in the back-propagation heuristics for which the loading problem is probably at least algorithmically solvable [25]. DasGupta et al. proved that loading a 3-node network whose two hidden units employ the continuous saturated-linear activation function while the output neuron applies the threshold function for dichotomic *classification* purposes is NP-complete [8]. Further, Höffgen showed the NP-completeness of loading a 3-node network employing the standard activation function for *exact interpolation* but with the severe restriction to binary weights [15]. A more realistic setting as concerns the back-propagation learning was first considered in [33] where loading a 3-node network with two standard sigmoid hidden neurons was proved to be NP-hard although an additional constraint on the weights of the output threshold unit used for binary classification was assumed which is satisfied e.g. when the output bias is zero. Hammer replaced this constraint by requiring the output unit with bounded weights to respond with outputs that are in absolute value greater than a given *accuracy* which excludes a small output interval around zero from the binary classification [12]. This approach also allows to generalize the hardness result for a more general class of activation functions than just the standard sigmoid. On the other hand, there exist activation functions that have still appropriate mathematical properties and for which the feedforward networks are always loadable [34].

Furthermore, the loading problem assumes the correct classification of all training data while in practice one is typically satisfied by the weights yielding a small training error. Therefore, the complexity of *approximately interpolating* a training set with in general *real outputs* by feedforward neural networks has further been studied. Jones considered a 3-node network with n inputs, two hidden neurons employing any monotone Lipschitzian sigmoidal activation function (e.g. the standard sigmoid) and one linear output unit with bounded weights [19]. For such a 3-node network he proved that learning the patterns with real outputs from $[0, 1]$ each within a small absolute error $0 < \varepsilon < 1/10$ is NP-hard implying that the problem of finding the weights that minimize the quadratic regression error within a fixed ε of its infimum (or absolutely) is also NP-hard. This NP-hardness proof was generalized for polynomial number k of hidden neurons and a *convex* linear output unit (with zero bias and nonnegative weights whose sum is 1) when the *total* quadratic error is required to be within $1/(16k^5)$ of its infimum (or within $1/(4k^3)$ for the Heaviside hidden units) [19].

In addition, Vu found the *relative* error bounds (with respect to the error infimum) for hard approximate interpolation which are independent on the training set size p by considering the *average* quadratic error that is defined as the total error divided by p. In particular, he proved that it is NP-hard to find weights of a two-layer network with n inputs, k hidden sigmoid neurons (satisfying some Lipschitzian conditions) and one linear output unit with zero bias and positive weights such that for a given training data the relative average quadratic error is within a fixed bound of order $O(1/(nk^5))$ of its infimum [37]. Moreover, for two-layer networks with k hidden neurons employing the Heaviside activations and one sigmoid (or threshold) output unit, Bartlett and Ben-David improved this bound to $O(1/k^3)$ which is even independent on the input dimension [4]. In the case of the threshold output unit used for classification, DasGupta and Hammer proved the same relative error bound $O(1/k^3)$ on the fraction of correctly classified training patterns which is NP-hard to achieve for training sets of size $k^{3.5} \leq p \leq k^4$ related to the number k of hidden units [7]. They also showed that it is NP-hard to approximate this success ratio within a relative error smaller than $1/2244$ for two-layer networks with n inputs, two hidden sigmoid neurons and one output threshold unit (with bounded weights) exploited for the classification with an accuracy $0 < \varepsilon < 0.5$. On the other hand, minimizing the ratio of the number of *misclassified* training patterns within every constant larger than 1 for feedforward threshold networks with zero biases in the first hidden layer is NP-hard [7].

The preceding results suggest that training feedforward networks with *fixed* architectures is hard indeed. However, the possible way out of this situation might be the *constructive learning algorithms* that adapt the network architecture to a particular training task. It is conjectured that for a successful generalization the network size should be kept small, otherwise a training set can easily be wired into the network implementing a look-up table [34]. A constructive learning algorithm usually requires an efficient procedure for minimizing the training error by adapting the weights of only a *single* unit that is being added to the architecture while the weights of remaining units in the network are already fixed (e.g. [9]). Clearly, for a single binary neuron employing the Heaviside activation function the weights that are consistent with a given training data can be found in polynomial time by linear programming provided that they exist (although this problem restricted to binary weights is NP-complete [28] and also to decide whether the Heaviside unit can implement a Boolean function given in a disjunctive or conjunctive normal form is co-NP-complete [14]). Such weights do not often exist but a good approximate solution would be sufficient for constructive learning. However, several authors provided NP-completeness proofs for the problem of finding the weights for a single Heaviside unit so that the number of misclassified training patterns is at most a given constant [16,29] which remains NP-complete even if the bias is assumed to be zero [1,18]. In addition, this issue is also NP-hard for a fixed error that is a constant multiple of the optimum [3].

Hush further generalized these results for a single *sigmoid* neuron by showing that it is NP-hard to minimize the training error under the L_1 norm strictly within 1 of its infimum [17]. He conjectured that a similar result holds for the quadratic error corresponding to the L_2 norm which is used in the back-propagation learning. In the present paper this conjecture is proved. In particular, it will be shown that the issue of deciding whether there exist weights of a single neuron employing the standard activation function so that the total quadratic error with respect to a training data is at most a given constant is NP-hard. The presented proof also provides an argument that the problem of finding the weights that minimize the relative quadratic training error within 1 or its average within $13/(31n)$ of its infimum is NP-hard. This implies that the popular back-propagation learning algorithm may be not efficient even for a single neuron and thus has negative consequences in constructive learning. For the simplicity, we will consider only the standard sigmoid in this paper while in the full version we plan to reformulate the theorem for a more general class of sigmoid activation functions.

2   Training a Standard Sigmoid Neuron

In this section the basic definitions regarding a sigmoid neuron and its training will be reviewed. A single (perceptron) *unit (neuron)* with n real inputs $x_1, \ldots, x_n \in \mathbb{R}$ first computes its real *excitation*

$$\xi = w_0 + \sum_{i=1}^{n} w_i x_i \tag{1}$$

where $\boldsymbol{w} = (w_0, \ldots, w_n) \in \mathbb{R}^{n+1}$ is the corresponding real *weight* vector including a *bias* w_0. The *output* y is then determined by applying a nonlinear activation function σ to its excitation:

$$y = \sigma(\xi). \tag{2}$$

We fix σ to be the *standard (logistic) sigmoid*:

$$\sigma(\xi) = \frac{1}{1 + e^{-\xi}} \tag{3}$$

which is employed in the widely used *back-propagation* learning heuristics. Correspondingly, we call such a neuron the *standard sigmoid unit*.

Furthermore, a *training set*

$$T = \{(\boldsymbol{x}_k, d_k); \, \boldsymbol{x}_k = (x_{k1}, \ldots, x_{kn}) \in \mathbb{R}^n, \, d_k \in [0,1], \, k = 1, \ldots, p\} \tag{4}$$

is introduced containing p pairs—*training patterns*, each composed of an n-dimensional real input $\boldsymbol{x}_k$ and the corresponding desired scalar output value d_k from $[0,1]$ to be consistent with the range of activation function (3). Given a weight vector $\boldsymbol{w}$, the *quadratic training error*

$$E_T(\boldsymbol{w}) = \sum_{k=1}^{p} (y(\boldsymbol{w}, \boldsymbol{x}_k) - d_k)^2 = \sum_{k=1}^{p} \left(\sigma \left(w_0 + \sum_{i=1}^{n} w_i x_{ki} \right) - d_k \right)^2 \tag{5}$$

of a neuron with respect to the training set T is defined as the difference between the actual outputs $y(\boldsymbol{w}, \boldsymbol{x}_k)$ depending on the current weights $\boldsymbol{w}$ and the desired outputs d_k over all training patterns $k = 1, \ldots, p$ measured by the L_2 regression norm. The main goal of learning is to minimize the training error (5) in the weight space. The decision version for the problem of minimizing the error of a neuron employing the standard sigmoid activation function with respect to a given training set is formulated as follows:

Minimum Sigmoid-Unit Error (MSUE)
Instance: A training set T and a positive real number $\varepsilon > 0$.
Question: Is there a weight vector $\boldsymbol{w} \in \mathbb{R}^{n+1}$ such that $E_T(\boldsymbol{w}) \leq \varepsilon$?

3   Minimizing the Training Error Is Hard

In this section the main result that training even a single standard sigmoid neuron is hard will be proved:

Theorem 1. *The problem MSUE is NP-hard.*

Proof. In order to achieve the NP-hardness result, a known NP-complete problem will be reduced to the MSUE problem in polynomial time. In particular, the following *Feedback Arc Set* problem is employed which is known to be NP-complete [22]:

Feedback Arc Set (FAS)

Instance: A directed graph $G = (V, A)$ and a positive integer $a \leq |A|$.
Question: Is there a subset $A' \subseteq A$ containing at most $a \geq |A'|$ directed edges
such that the graph $G' = (V, A \setminus A')$ is acyclic?

The FAS problem was also exploited for a corresponding result concerning the
Heaviside unit [29]. However, the reduction is adapted here for the standard
sigmoid activation function and its verification substantially differs.

Given a FAS instance $G = (V, A)$, a, a corresponding graph $G_r = (V_r, A_r)$ is
first constructed so that every directed edge $(u, v) \in A$ in G is replaced by five
parallel oriented paths

$$P_{(u,v),h} = \{(u, u_v), (u_v, u_{vh1}), (u_{vh1}, u_{vh2}), \ldots, (u_{vh,r-1}, v)\} \tag{6}$$

for $h = 1, \ldots, 5$ in G_r sharing *only* their first edge (u, u_v) and vertices u, u_v, v.
Each path $P_{(u,v),h}$ includes

$$r = 8a + 6 \tag{7}$$

additional vertices $u_v, u_{vh1}, u_{vh2}, \ldots, u_{vh,r-1}$ unique to $(u, v) \in A$, i.e. the subsets of edges

$$A_{(u,v)} = \bigcup_{h=1}^{5} P_{(u,v),h} \tag{8}$$

corresponding to different $(u, v) \in A$ are pairwise disjoint. Thus,

$$V_r = V \cup \{u_v; (u, v) \in A\}$$
$$\cup \{u_{vh1}, u_{vh2}, \ldots, u_{vh,r-1}; (u, v) \in A, h = 1, \ldots, 5\} \tag{9}$$
$$A_r = \bigcup_{(u,v) \in A} A_{(u,v)} . \tag{10}$$

It follows that $n = |V_r| = |V| + (5r - 4)|A|$ and $s = |A_r| = (5r + 1)|A|$. Obviously,
the FAS instance G, a has a solution iff the FAS problem is solvable for G_r, a. The
graph G_r is then exploited for constructing the corresponding MSUE instance
with a training set $T(G)$ for the standard sigmoid unit with $n = (40a + 26)|A| +
|V| = O(|A|^2 + |V|)$ inputs:

$$T(G) = \{(\boldsymbol{x}_{(i,j)}, 1), (-\boldsymbol{x}_{(i,j)}, 0); (i, j) \in A_r,$$
$$\boldsymbol{x}_{(i,j)} = (x_{(i,j),1}, \ldots, x_{(i,j),n}) \in \{-1, 0, 1\}^n\} \tag{11}$$

that contains $p = 2s = (80a + 62)|A| = O(|A|^2)$ training patterns, for each edge
$(i, j) \in A_r$ one pair $(\boldsymbol{x}_{(i,j)}, 1), (-\boldsymbol{x}_{(i,j)}, 0)$ such that

$$x_{(i,j),\ell} = \begin{cases} -1 & \text{for } \ell = i \\ 1 & \text{for } \ell = j \\ 0 & \text{for } \ell \neq i, j \end{cases} \quad \ell = 1, \ldots, n, \quad (i, j) \in A_r . \tag{12}$$

In addition, the error in the MSUE instance is required to be at most

$$\varepsilon = 2a + 1 . \tag{13}$$

Clearly, the present construction of the corresponding MSUE instance can be achieved in a polynomial time in terms of the size of the original FAS instance.

Now, the correctness of the reduction will be verified, i.e. it will be shown that the MSUE instance has a solution iff the corresponding FAS instance is solvable. So first assume that there exists a weight vector $\boldsymbol{w} \in \mathbb{R}^{n+1}$ such that

$$E_{T(G)}(\boldsymbol{w}) \leq \varepsilon. \tag{14}$$

Define a subset of edges

$$A' = \{(u, v) \in A; w_u \geq w_v\} \subseteq A \tag{15}$$

in G. First observe that graph $G' = (V, A \setminus A')$ is acyclic since each vertex $u \in V \subseteq V_r$ is evaluated by a real weight $w_u \in \mathbb{R}$ so that any directed edge $(u, v) \in A \setminus A'$ in G' satisfies $w_u < w_v$.

Moreover, it must be checked that $|A'| \leq a$. For this purpose, the error $E_{T(G)}(\boldsymbol{w})$ introduced in (5) is expressed for the training set $T(G)$ by using (12) and (10) as follows:

$$\begin{aligned}
E_{T(G)}(\boldsymbol{w}) &= \sum_{(i,j) \in A_r} (\sigma(w_0 - w_i + w_j) - 1)^2 + \sum_{(i,j) \in A_r} \sigma^2(w_0 + w_i - w_j) \\
&= \sum_{(u,v) \in A} \sum_{(i,j) \in A_{(u,v)}} \left(\sigma^2(-w_0 + w_i - w_j) + \sigma^2(w_0 + w_i - w_j) \right)
\end{aligned} \tag{16}$$

where the property $\sigma(-\xi) = 1 - \sigma(\xi)$ of the standard sigmoid (3) is employed. This error is lower bounded by considering only the edges from $A' \subseteq A$:

$$E_{T(G)}(\boldsymbol{w}) \geq \sum_{(u,v) \in A'} EA_{(u,v)} \tag{17}$$

where each term $EA_{(u,v)}$ for $(u, v) \in A'$ will below be proved to satisfy

$$EA_{(u,v)} = \sum_{(i,j) \in A_{(u,v)}} \left(\sigma^2(-w_0 + w_i - w_j) + \sigma^2(w_0 + w_i - w_j) \right) > \frac{\varepsilon}{a+1}. \tag{18}$$

Clearly, e.g. $w_0 \geq 0$ can here be assumed without loss of generality. For each $(u, v) \in A'$ let $P_{(u,v)}$ be a path with the minimum error

$$EP_{(u,v)} = \sum_{(i,j) \in P_{(u,v)}} \left(\sigma^2(-w_0 + w_i - w_j) + \sigma^2(w_0 + w_i - w_j) \right) \tag{19}$$

among paths $P_{(u,v),h}$ for $h = 1, \ldots, 5$. Furthermore, sort the edges $(i,j) \in P_{(u,v)}$ with respect to associated *decrements* $w_i - w_j$ in nonincreasing order and denote by $(c, d), (e, f) \in P_{(u,v)}$ the first two edges, respectively, in the underlying sorted sequence, i.e. $w_c - w_d \geq w_e - w_f \geq w_i - w_j$ for all $(i, j) \in P_{(u,v)} \setminus \{(c, d), (e, f)\}$.

First consider the case when $w_0 + w_e - w_f \geq \ln 2$, i.e. $\sigma^2(w_0 + w_e - w_f) \geq 4/9$ according to (3). It follows from definition of $P_{(u,v)}$ and (8) that

$$
\begin{aligned}
EA_{(u,v)} &\geq \sum_{(i,j) \in A_{(u,v)} \backslash \{(u,u_v)\}} \left(\sigma^2(-w_0 + w_i - w_j) + \sigma^2(w_0 + w_i - w_j) \right) \\
&\geq 5 \cdot \sum_{(i,j) \in P_{(u,v)} \backslash \{(u,u_v)\}} \left(\sigma^2(-w_0 + w_i - w_j) + \sigma^2(w_0 + w_i - w_j) \right) \\
&\geq 5 \cdot \sigma^2(w_0 + w_e - w_f) \geq \frac{20}{9} > \frac{\varepsilon}{a+1}
\end{aligned}
\tag{20}
$$

since $P_{(u,v)} \backslash \{(u, u_v)\}$ contains an edge $(i, j) \in \{(c, d), (e, f)\}$ with $\sigma^2(w_0 + w_i - w_j) \geq \sigma^2(w_0 + w_e - w_f)$ by definition of (e, f) due to σ^2 is increasing. This proves inequality (18) for $w_0 + w_e - w_f \geq \ln 2$.

On the other hand suppose that $w_0 + w_e - w_f < \ln 2$. In this case vertices $i \in V_r$ on path $P_{(u,v)}$ ($(u, v) \in A'$) will possibly be re-labeled with new weights $w'_i \in \mathbb{R}$ except for fixed w_u, w_v so that there is at most one edge $(c, d) \in P_{(u,v)}$ with a positive decrement $w_c - w_d > 0$ or all the edges $(i, j) \in P_{(u,v)}$ are associated with nonnegative decrements $w_i - w_j \geq 0$ while the error $EP_{(u,v)}$ introduced in (19) is not increased. Note that error $EP_{(u,v)}$ depends only on decrements $w_i - w_j$ rather than on the actual weights w_i, w_j. For example, these decrements can arbitrarily be permuted along path $P_{(u,v)}$ producing new weights whereas $EP_{(u,v)}$ and w_u, w_v do not change. Recall from definition of $(c, d), (e, f)$ that for all $(i, j) \in P_{(u,v)} \backslash \{(c, d)\}$ it holds

$$
- w_0 + w_i - w_j \leq w_0 + w_i - w_j \leq w_0 + w_e - w_f < \ln 2 \, .
\tag{21}
$$

Now, suppose that there exists an edge $(i, j) \in P_{(u,v)} \backslash \{(c, d)\}$ with a positive decrement $0 < w_i - w_j \leq w_c - w_d$ together with an edge $(\ell, m) \in P_{(u,v)}$ associated with a negative decrement $w_\ell - w_m < 0$. Then these decrements are updated as follows:

$$
w'_i - w'_j = w_i - w_j - \Delta
\tag{22}
$$
$$
w'_\ell - w'_m = w_\ell - w_m + \Delta
\tag{23}
$$

where $\Delta = \min(w_i - w_j, w_m - w_\ell) > 0$. This can be achieved e.g. by permuting the decrements along path $P_{(u,v)}$ so that $w_i - w_j$ follows immediately after $w_\ell - w_m$ (this produces new weights but preserves $EP_{(u,v)}$) and by decreasing the weight of the middle vertex that is common to both decrements by Δ which clearly influences error $EP_{(u,v)}$. However, for $\xi < \ln 2$ the first derivative $(\sigma^2)'$ is increasing because

$$
(\sigma^2(\xi))'' = \frac{2e^{-\xi} (2e^{-\xi} - 1)}{(1 + e^{-\xi})^4} > 0
\tag{24}
$$

for $\xi < \ln 2$ according to (3). Hence,

$$\sigma^2(-w_0 + w_i - w_j) + \sigma^2(-w_0 + w_\ell - w_m) > \sigma^2(-w_0 + w_i - w_j - \Delta)$$
$$+\sigma^2(-w_0 + w_\ell - w_m + \Delta) \quad (25)$$

$$\sigma^2(w_0 + w_i - w_j) + \sigma^2(w_0 + w_\ell - w_m) > \sigma^2(w_0 + w_i - w_j - \Delta)$$
$$+\sigma^2(w_0 + w_\ell - w_m + \Delta) \quad (26)$$

according to (21). This implies that error $EP_{(u,v)}$ only decreases while $w_i' - w_j' = 0$ or $w_\ell' - w_m' = 0$. By repeating this re-labeling procedure eventually at most one positive decrement $w_c - w_d > 0$ remains or all the negative decrements are eliminated.

Furthermore,

$$w_c - w_d + \sum_{(i,j)\in P_{(u,v)}\setminus\{(c,d)\}} (w_i - w_j) = w_u - w_v \geq 0 \quad (27)$$

due to $(u,v) \in A'$ which implies

$$w_d - w_c \leq \sum_{(i,j)\in P_{(u,v)}\setminus\{(c,d)\}} (w_i - w_j). \quad (28)$$

Thus,

$$w_d - w_c \leq w_i - w_j \quad (29)$$

can be assumed for all $(i,j) \in P_{(u,v)}$ since the decrements $w_i - w_j$ for $(i,j) \in P_{(u,v)} \setminus \{(c,d)\}$ in sum (28) can be made all nonpositive or all nonnegative. According to (29) inequality (18) would follow from

$$EA_{(u,v)} \geq EP_{(u,v)} \geq \sigma^2(-w_0 + w_c - w_d) + r \cdot \sigma^2(-w_0 + w_d - w_c)$$
$$+\sigma^2(w_0 + w_c - w_d) + r \cdot \sigma^2(w_0 + w_d - w_c) > \frac{\varepsilon}{a+1} \quad (30)$$

because there are r edges (i,j) on path $P_{(u,v)}$ except for (c,d) and σ^2 is increasing. The particular terms of addition (30) can suitably be coupled so that it suffices to show

$$\sigma^2(\xi) + r \cdot \sigma^2(-\xi) > \frac{\varepsilon}{2(a+1)} \quad (31)$$

for any excitation $\xi \in \mathbb{R}$. For this purpose, a boundary excitation

$$\xi_b = \ln\left(\frac{\varepsilon + \sqrt{2\varepsilon(a+1)}}{2(a+1) - \varepsilon}\right) = \ln\left(2a + 1 + \sqrt{4a^2 + 6a + 2}\right) \quad (32)$$

is derived from (3), (13) such that

$$\sigma^2(\xi_b) = \frac{\varepsilon}{2(a+1)}. \quad (33)$$

Thus, $\sigma^2(\xi) > \sigma^2(\xi_b)$ for $\xi > \xi_b$ due to σ^2 is increasing which clearly implies (31) for $\xi > \xi_b$ according to (33). For $\xi \leq \xi_b$, on the other hand, it will even be proved that

$$\sigma^2(\xi) + r \cdot \sigma^2(-\xi) \geq 1 > \frac{\varepsilon}{2(a+1)} \quad (34)$$

which reduces to

$$r \geq \frac{1 - \sigma^2(\xi)}{\sigma^2(-\xi)} = 2e^{\xi} + 1 \tag{35}$$

by using (3). Moreover, it is sufficient to verify (35) only for $\xi = \xi_b$, i.e.

$$r \geq 2e^{\xi_b} + 1 \tag{36}$$

since $2e^{\xi} + 1$ is increasing. Inequality (36) can be checked by substituting (7) for r and (32) for ξ_b which completes the argument for (30) and consequently for (18).

Finally, by introducing (14) and (18) into inequality (17) it follows that

$$\varepsilon \geq E_{T(G)}(\boldsymbol{w}) > |A'| \cdot \frac{\varepsilon}{a+1} \tag{37}$$

which gives $|A'| < a + 1$ or equivalently $|A'| \leq a$. This completes the proof that A' is a solution of the FAS problem.

On the other hand, assume that there exists a solution $A' \subseteq A$ of the FAS instance containing at most $a \geq |A'|$ directed edges making graph $G' = (V, A \backslash A')$ acyclic. Define a subset

$$A'_r = \{(u, u_v); (u, v) \in A'\} \tag{38}$$

containing $|A'_r| = |A'| \leq a$ edges from A_r. Clearly, graph $G'_r = (V_r, A_r \setminus A'_r)$ is also acyclic and hence its vertices $i \in V_r$ can be evaluated by *integers* w'_i so that any directed edge $(i, j) \in A_r \setminus A'_r$ satisfies $w'_i < w'_j$. Now, the corresponding weight vector $\boldsymbol{w}$ is defined as

$$w_i = K \cdot w'_i \tag{39}$$

for $i \in V_r$ where $K > 0$ is a sufficiently large positive constant, e.g.

$$K = \ln\left(\sqrt{p} - 1\right) = \ln\left(\sqrt{2s} - 1\right) \tag{40}$$

(recall $p = |T(G)| = 2s$ where $s = |A_r|$) while $w_0 = 0$ which will be proved to be a solution for the MSUE instance. The error (16) can be rewritten for $\boldsymbol{w}$:

$$E_{T(G)}(\boldsymbol{w}) = \sum_{(i,j) \in A_r} 2\sigma^2(w_i - w_j)$$

$$= 2 \sum_{(i,j) \in A'_r} \sigma^2(w_i - w_j) + 2 \sum_{(i,j) \in A_r \setminus A'_r} \sigma^2(w_i - w_j). \tag{41}$$

For $(i, j) \in A_r \setminus A'_r$ it holds

$$w_i - w_j = K(w'_i - w'_j) \leq -K < 0 \tag{42}$$

according to (39) where $w'_i - w'_j \leq -1$ due to w'_i, w'_j are integers. This implies

$$\sigma^2(w_i - w_j) \leq \sigma^2(-K) = \frac{1}{2s} \tag{43}$$

for $(i, j) \in A_r \setminus A'_r$ by formulas (3), (40) due to σ^2 is increasing. Hence, the error (41) can be upper bounded as

$$E_{T(G)}(\boldsymbol{w}) \leq 2\,|A'_r| + 2s\,\sigma^2(-K) \leq 2a + 1 = \varepsilon \qquad (44)$$

by using $|A'_r| \leq a$, $\sigma^2(\xi) < 1$, and $|A_r \setminus A'_r| \leq s$. Therefore $\boldsymbol{w}$ is a solution of the MSUE problem. This completes the proof of the theorem.   □

The proof of Theorem 1 also provides the NP-hardness result regarding the relative (average) error bounds:

Corollary 1. *Given a training set T containing $p = |T|$ training patterns, it is NP-hard to find a weight vector $\boldsymbol{w} \in \mathbb{R}^{n+1}$ of the standard sigmoid neuron with n inputs for which the quadratic error $E_T(\boldsymbol{w})$ with respect to T is within 1 of its infimum, or the average quadratic error $E_T(\boldsymbol{w})/p$ is within $13/(31n)$ of its infimum.*

Proof. Given a FAS instance $G = (V, A)$, a, a corresponding MSUE instance $T(G)$, ε is constructed according to (11), (13) in polynomial time. Assume that a weight vector $\boldsymbol{w}^* \in \mathbb{R}^{n+1}$ could be found such that

$$E_{T(G)}(\boldsymbol{w}^*) \leq \inf_{\boldsymbol{w} \in \mathbb{R}^{n+1}} E_{T(G)}(\boldsymbol{w}) + 1\,. \qquad (45)$$

The corresponding subset of edges $A^* \subseteq A$ making graph $G^* = (V, A \setminus A^*)$ acyclic can be then read from $\boldsymbol{w}^*$ according to (15). It will be proved in the following that $|A^*| \leq a$ iff the original FAS instance has a solution. This means that finding the weight vector $\boldsymbol{w}^*$ that satisfies (45) is NP-hard.

It suffices to show that for $|A^*| \geq a + 1$ there is no subset $A' \subseteq A$ such that $|A'| \leq a$ and $G' = (V, A \setminus A')$ is acyclic since the opposite implication is trivial. On the contrary suppose that such a subset A' exists. It follows from (45), (37), and (13) that

$$\inf_{\boldsymbol{w} \in \mathbb{R}^{n+1}} E_{T(G)}(\boldsymbol{w}) \geq E_{T(G)}(\boldsymbol{w}^*) - 1 > |A^*| \cdot \frac{2a+1}{a+1} - 1 \geq 2a\,. \qquad (46)$$

On the other hand, a weight vector $\boldsymbol{w}' \in \mathbb{R}^{n+1}$ corresponding to subset $A' \subseteq A$ could be defined by (39) that would lead to an error

$$E_{T(G)}(\boldsymbol{w}') \leq 2a + 2s\,\sigma^2(-K) \qquad (47)$$

according to (44). However, from (3), (5), and (46) there exists $K > 0$ such that

$$2s\,\sigma^2(-K) < -2a + \inf_{\boldsymbol{w} \in \mathbb{R}^{n+1}} E_{T(G)}(\boldsymbol{w}) < p = 2s \qquad (48)$$

which provides a contradiction $E_{T(G)}(\boldsymbol{w}') < \inf_{\boldsymbol{w} \in \mathbb{R}^{n+1}} E_{T(G)}(\boldsymbol{w})$ by using (47).

Finally, it follows from the underlying reduction that approximating the average quadratic error $E_T(\boldsymbol{w})/p$ within $13/(31n)$ of its infimum is also NP-hard due to $p < 31n/13$.   □

4   Conclusions

The hardness results for loading feedforward networks are completed by the proof that the approximate training of only a single sigmoid neuron, e.g. by using the popular back-propagation heuristics, is hard. This suggests that the constructive learning algorithms that minimize the training error gradually by adapting unit by unit may also be not efficient. In the full version of the paper we plan to formulate the conditions for a more general class of sigmoid activation functions under which the proof still works.

References

1. E. Amaldi: On the complexity of training perceptrons. In T. Kohonen, K. Mäkisara, O. Simula, and J. Kangas (eds.), *Proceedings of the ICANN'91 First International Conference on Artificial Neural Networks*, 55–60, North-Holland, Amsterdam: Elsevier Science Publisher, 1991.
2. M. Anthony and P. L. Bartlett: *Neural Network Learning: Theoretical Foundations.* Cambridge, UK: Cambridge University Press, 1999.
3. S. Arora, L. Babai, J. Stern, and Z. Sweedyk: The hardness of approximate optima in lattices, codes, and systems of linear equations. *Journal of Computer and System Sciences* **54**(2):317–331, 1997.
4. P. L. Bartlett and S. Ben-David: Hardness results for neural network approximation problems. In P. Fischer and H.-U. Simon (eds.), *Proceedings of the EuroCOLT'99 Fourth European Conference on Computational Learning Theory*, LNAI **1572**, 50–62, Berlin: Springer-Verlag, 1999.
5. A. L. Blum and R. L. Rivest: Training a 3-node neural network is NP-complete. *Neural Networks* **5**(1):117–127, 1992.
6. A. Blumer, A. Ehrenfeucht, D. Haussler, and M. K. Warmuth: Learnability and the Vapnik-Chervonenkis dimension. *Journal of the ACM* **36**(4):929–965, 1989.
7. B. DasGupta and B. Hammer: On approximate learning by multi-layered feedforward circuits. In H. Arimura, S. Jain, and A. Sharma (eds.), *Proceedings of the ALT'2000 Eleventh International Conference on Algorithmic Learning Theory*, LNAI **1968**, 264–278, Berlin: Springer-Verlag, 2000.
8. B. DasGupta, H. T. Siegelmann, and E. D. Sontag: On the complexity of training neural networks with continuous activation functions. *IEEE Transactions on Neural Networks* **6**(6):1490–1504, 1995.
9. S. E. Fahlman and C. Lebiere: The cascade-correlation learning architecture. In D. S. Touretzky (ed.), *Advances in Neural Information Processing Systems (NIPS'89)*, Vol. **2**, 524–532, San Mateo: Morgan Kaufmann, 1990.
10. M. R. Garey and D. S. Johnson: *Computers and Intractability: A Guide to the Theory of NP-Completeness.* San Francisco: W. H. Freeman, 1979.
11. B. Hammer: Some complexity results for perceptron networks. In L. Niklasson, M. Boden, and T. Ziemke (eds.), *Proceedings of the ICANN'98 Eight International Conference on Artificial Neural Networks*, 639–644, Berlin: Springer-Verlag, 1998.
12. B. Hammer: Training a sigmoidal network is difficult. In M. Verleysen (ed.) *Proceedings of the ESANN'98 Sixth European Symposium on Artificial Neural Networks*, 255–260, D-Facto Publications, 1998.
13. S. Haykin: *Neural Networks: A Comprehensive Foundation.* Upper Saddle River, NJ: Prentice-Hall, 2nd edition, 1999.

14. T. Hegedüs and N. Megiddo: On the geometric separability of Boolean functions, *Discrete Applied Mathematics* **66**(3):205–218, 1996.
15. K.-U. Höffgen: Computational limitations on training sigmoid neural networks. *Information Processing Letters* **46**(6):269–274, 1993.
16. K.-U. Höffgen, H.-U. Simon, and K. S. Van Horn: Robust trainability of single neurons. *Journal of Computer and System Sciences* **50**(1):114–125, 1995.
17. D. R. Hush: Training a sigmoidal node is hard. *Neural Computation* **11**(5):1249–1260, 1999.
18. D. S. Johnson and F. P. Preparata: The densest hemisphere problem. *Theoretical Computer Science* **6**(1):93–107, 1978.
19. L. K. Jones: The computational intractability of training sigmoidal neural networks. *IEEE Transactions on Information Theory* **43**(1):167–173, 1997.
20. J. S. Judd: On the complexity of loading shallow networks. *Journal of Complexity* **4**(3):177–192, 1988.
21. J. S. Judd: *Neural Network Design and the Complexity of Learning.* Cambridge, MA: The MIT Press, 1990.
22. R. M. Karp: Reducibility among combinatorial problems. In R. E. Miller and J. W. Thatcher (eds.), *Complexity of Computer Computations*, 85–103, New York: Plenum Press, 1972.
23. Ch. Kuhlmann: Hardness results for general two-layer neural networks. In N. Cesa-Bianchi and S. A. Goldman (eds.), *Proceedings of the COLT 2000 Thirteenth Annual Conference on Computational Learning Theory*, 275–285, 2000.
24. J.-H. Lin and J. S. Vitter: Complexity results on learning by neural nets. *Machine Learning* **6**:211–230, 1991.
25. A. Macintyre and E. D. Sontag: Finiteness results for sigmoidal "neural" networks. In *Proceedings of the STOC'93 Twenty-Fifth Annual ACM Symposium on the Theory of Computing*, 325–334, New York: ACM Press, 1993.
26. N. Megiddo: On the complexity of polyhedral separability. *Discrete Computational Geometry* **3**:325–337, 1988.
27. I. Parberry: On the complexity of learning with a small number of nodes. In *Proceedings of the International Joint Conference on Neural Networks*, Vol. **3**, 893–898, 1992.
28. L. Pitt and L. G. Valiant: Computational limitations on learning from examples. *Journal of the ACM* **35**(4):965–984, 1988.
29. V. P. Roychowdhury, K.-Y. Siu, and T. Kailath: Classification of linearly non-separable patterns by linear threshold elements. *IEEE Transactions on Neural Networks* **6**(2):318–331, 1995.
30. V. P. Roychowdhury, K.-Y. Siu, and A. Orlitsky (eds.): *Theoretical Advances in Neural Computation and Learning.* Boston: Kluwer Academic Publishers, 1994.
31. D. E. Rumelhart, G. E. Hinton, and R. J. Williams: Learning representations by back-propagating errors. *Nature* **323**:533–536, 1986.
32. J. Šíma: Loading deep networks is hard. *Neural Computation* **6**(5):842–850, 1994.
33. J. Šíma: Back-propagation is not efficient. *Neural Networks* **9**(6):1017–1023, 1996.
34. E. D. Sontag: Feedforward networks for interpolation and classification. *Journal of Computer and System Sciences* **45**(1):20–48, 1992.
35. G. Tesauro: Scaling relationships in back-propagation learning: dependence on training set size. *Complex Systems* **1**(2):367–372, 1987.
36. G. Tesauro and B. Janssens: Scaling relationships in back-propagation learning. *Complex Systems* **2**(1):39–44, 1988.

37. V. H. Vu: On the infeasibility of training neural networks with small squared errors. In M. I. Jordan, M. J. Kearns, and S. A. Solla (eds.), *Advances in Neural Information Processing Systems (NIPS'97)*, Vol. **10**, 371–377, The MIT Press, 1998.
38. M. Vidyasagar: *A Theory of Learning and Generalization.* London: Springer-Verlag, 1997.
39. H. Wiklicky: The neural network loading problem is undecidable. In J. Shawe-Taylor and M. Anthony (eds.), *Proceedings of the EuroCOLT'93 First Conference on Computational Learning Theory*, 183–192, Oxford: Clarendon Press, 1994.

Learning of Boolean Functions Using Support Vector Machines

Ken Sadohara

National Institute of Advanced Industrial Science and Technology (AIST)
AIST Tsukuba Central 2, 1-1-1 Umezono, Tsukuba-shi, Ibaraki, Japan
ken.sadohara@aist.go.jp

Abstract. This paper concerns the design of a Support Vector Machine
(SVM) appropriate for the learning of Boolean functions. This is motivated by the need of a more sophisticated algorithm for classification in
discrete attribute spaces. Classification in discrete attribute spaces is reduced to the problem of learning Boolean functions from examples of its
input/output behavior. Since any Boolean function can be written in Disjunctive Normal Form (DNF), it can be represented as a weighted linear
sum of all possible conjunctions of Boolean literals. This paper presents a
particular kernel function called the DNF kernel which enables SVMs to
efficiently learn such linear functions in the high-dimensional space whose
coordinates correspond to all possible conjunctions. For a limited form of
DNF consisting of positive Boolean literals, the monotone DNF kernel
is also presented. SVMs employing these kernel functions can perform
the learning in a high-dimensional feature space whose features are derived from given basic attributes. In addition, it is expected that SVMs'
well-founded capacity control alleviates overfitting. In fact, an empirical
study on learning of randomly generated Boolean functions shows that
the resulting algorithm outperforms C4.5. Furthermore, in comparison
with SVMs employing the Gaussian kernel, it is shown that DNF kernel
produces accuracy comparable to best adjusted Gaussian kernels.

1 Introduction

In this paper, Support Vector Machines (SVMs) [15,4] is applied to classification in discrete attribute spaces with the aim of overcoming difficulties involved
in existing algorithms. Classification, which is a primary data mining task, is
learning a function that maps data into one of several predefined classes. Especially, numerous studies have been made in a specific framework where data are
described by a fixed set of attributes and their discrete values. Since the framework can be reduced to the learning of Boolean functions, this paper concerns
the design of SVMs appropriate for the learning of Boolean functions.

For classification in discrete attribute spaces, C4.5 [13] is one of the most
widely used learning algorithms. However, several problems causing a decrease
in accuracy have been pointed out.

One problem is that its way of overfitting avoidance is not always effective.
In order to prevent decision trees from overly fitting to a given training data and

N. Abe, R. Khardon, and T. Zeugmann (Eds.): ALT 2001, LNAI 2225, pp. 106–118, 2001.

decreasing accuracy for unseen data, C4.5 prunes overly complex decision trees. However, as discussed in the literature [6], this way of overfitting avoidance is not supported theoretically, and is shown not to be always effective as a practical heuristic.

Another problem stems from its univariate node-splits strategy: constructing a decision tree whose nodes are split by a single attribute most relevant to class membership at each node. This strategy is based on the assumption that every attribute constituting decision rules are relevant to class membership and thus the rules can be obtained by collecting such attributes one by one. However, the assumption is not always true under the information theoretical relevancy measure employed in C4.5. There is a case that an attribute is not relevant to class membership by itself though it has high relevancy when other attributes' values are known. The literature [12] illustrates that, in the multiplexer family of tasks, address bits, which are important attributes for class decision, show no relevancy to class membership, and this phenomenon leads to inaccurate decision trees. One way to overcome this problem is to use feature construction [9]: creating new features by combining some attributes and splitting nodes by the newly created features. However, due to a large number of combinations of attributes, it is infeasible to select a feature most relevant at each node.

To cope with these problems, this paper applies SVMs to classification in discrete attribute spaces. SVMs adopt a well-founded approach to overfitting avoidance: minimizing a statistical bound of the error rate for unseen data. Furthermore, SVMs provide a method of efficient learning in a feature space consisting of a large number of features derived from basic attributes. It is expected that these capabilities of SVMs deliver a good performance on classification in discrete attribute spaces.

A characteristic of SVMs is that target functions are not learned directly in an input space but in a feature space whose features are derived from basic attributes. For the learning of Boolean functions, it is reasonable to use the feature space whose features are all possible conjunctions of negated or non-negated Boolean variables. This is because any Boolean function can be written in Disjunctive Normal Form (DNF) and thus the function can be represented as a weighted linear sum of the features as described in Section 4. The linear function in the feature space is learned by SVMs from examples of its input/output behavior. Although the learning seems to be computationally infeasible because of high dimensionality of the feature space, e.g. $3^d - 1$ for a d-variable Boolean function, SVMs can perform efficient learning in the high dimensional feature space with the help of a kernel function. A kernel function computes the inner product in a feature space and the use of it allows SVMs to deal with an alternative representation of the target function which does not depend on the dimension of the feature space. This paper presents a particular kernel function called the DNF kernel that enables efficient learning in the feature spaces consisting of all possible conjunctions. For a limited form of DNF consisting of positive Boolean literals, the monotone DNF kernel is also presented.

To explore the capabilities of SVMs employing the DNF kernel, experiments on learning of randomly generated Boolean functions are performed. The experiments show that the resulting algorithm produces higher accuracy than C4.5 does. Furthermore, in comparison with SVMs employing the Gaussian kernel, which is a standard choice of kernels, it is shown that the DNF kernel produces accuracy comparable to best adjusted Gaussian kernels.

2   The Learning Task

In principle, classification in a discrete attribute space can be reduced to the learning of Boolean functions. Firstly, an n-class classification task is reduced to n 2-class classification tasks of discriminating each class from the other classes. Secondly, by assigning a Boolean variable x_{ik} to the proposition $A_i = v_{ik}$ for each value v_{ik} of an attribute A_i ($1 \leq k \leq \ell_i$), each 2-class classification task can be reduced to the learning of Boolean functions $f : \{0,1\}^d \to \{0,1\}$, where $d = \sum_i \ell_i$.

Furthermore, the learning of Boolean functions can be generally stated as binary classification [3]:

given a training set $S \subseteq X \times Y$ and a hypothesis space H, where let X be an input space and $Y = \{\text{P,N}\}$ a set of class labels,
find $g \in H$ such that g minimize *the generalization error* $\text{err}_{\mathcal{D}}(g)$.

The generalization error is the expected misclassification rate for a distribution $\mathcal{D}$ over $X \times Y$ which is defined as

$$\text{err}_{\mathcal{D}}(g) \overset{\text{def}}{=} \int p(\boldsymbol{x}, y) L(g(\boldsymbol{x}), y) d\boldsymbol{x} dy$$

using *zero-one loss*

$$L(g(\boldsymbol{x}), y) \overset{\text{def}}{=} \begin{cases} 1 & g(\boldsymbol{x}) \neq y \\ 0 & \text{otherwise} \end{cases}.$$

From the practical viewpoint, the minimization of the generalization error cannot be performed because it depends on an impractical assumption that a probability distribution over $X \times Y$ is known. Therefore, instead of minimizing it, practical learning machines minimize the following *training-set error* err_S:

$$\text{err}_S(g) \overset{\text{def}}{=} \frac{1}{|S|} \sum_{(\boldsymbol{x},y) \in S} L(g(\boldsymbol{x}), y).$$

However, minimizing the training-set error causes a well known problem *overfitting*: the risk that learning machines select a hypothesis that fits the training data well but captures the underlying model poorly. As a result of the overfitting, learning machines produce high generalization error even though they produce low training-set error.

C4.5 avoids overfitting by pruning of decision trees, that is, given two trees with the same training-set error, it prefers simpler one based on the assumption that overfitting is caused by overly complex trees. This way of overfitting avoidance is known as Occam's razor and is widely used. However, this empirical wisdom is not supported theoretically, and is shown not to be always effective as a practical heuristic [6]. In the literature, the author argues that overfitting arises not because of complexity, but because testing a large number of hypotheses leads to a high probability of finding a hypothesis that fits training data well purely by chance.

The cardinality of the hypothesis space of a learning machine is referred to as *capacity*, and preventing overfitting by allowing just the right amount of capacity is known as *capacity control*. As we will see in the next section, SVMs control their capacity by minimizing a statistical bound of the generalization error based on the statistical learning theory [16]. Within the limited hypothesis space by the minimization, SVMs find a hypothesis with a low training-set error, which is also expected to produce a low generalization error.

Instead of searching for a hypothesis $g \in H$ directly, SVMs search for the following real-valued function f in order to use continuous optimization techniques.

$$g(x) = \begin{cases} P & f(\boldsymbol{x}) \geq 0 \\ N & f(\boldsymbol{x}) < 0 \end{cases}$$

Such a function f is called a *discriminant function*.

As a notational convenience, SVMs use the set $\{+1, -1\}$ of class labels. Accordingly, positive examples of a Boolean function are labeled $+1$ and negative ones -1. That is, in the case of the learning of d-variable Boolean functions, Y is set to $\{+1, -1\}$ and X is set to $\{0, 1\}^d$.

3   Support Vector Machines

This section serves as a brief introduction to the learning principle of SVMs. For a more complete introduction, consult the literatures [15,4].

SVMs learn non-linear discriminant functions in an input space. This is achieved by learning linear discriminant functions in a high-dimensional feature space. A feature mapping ϕ from the input space to the feature space maps the training data $S = \{(\boldsymbol{x}_i, y_i)\}_{i=1}^n$ into $\phi(S) = \{(\phi(\boldsymbol{x}_i), y_i)\}_{i=1}^n = \{(\boldsymbol{z}_i, y_i)\}_{i=1}^n$. In the feature space, SVMs learn a linear discriminant function $f(\boldsymbol{z}) = \langle \boldsymbol{w} \cdot \boldsymbol{x} \rangle + b$ so that the hyperplane $f(\boldsymbol{z}) = 0$ separates the positive examples $\{\boldsymbol{z}_i \mid y_i = 1\}$ from the negative ones $\{\boldsymbol{z}_i \mid y_i = -1\}$. For any hyperplane $f(\boldsymbol{z}) = \langle \boldsymbol{w} \cdot \boldsymbol{z} \rangle + b = 0$, the Euclidean distance of the closest point $\boldsymbol{z}^* \in \{\boldsymbol{z}_1, \ldots, \boldsymbol{z}_n\}$ is called the *margin* of the hyperplane. If we normalize hyperplanes so that $|f(\boldsymbol{z}^*)| = 1$, then the margin of the hyperplane is $\frac{1}{\|\boldsymbol{w}\|}$. Among normalized hyperplanes, SVMs find the *maximal margin hyperplane* that has the maximal margin and separates positive examples from negative ones. Thus, the learning task of SVMs can be stated as the following convex quadratic programming problem:

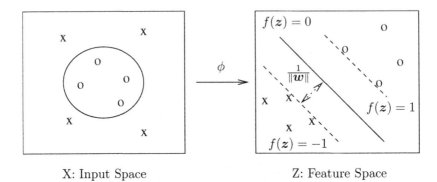

X: Input Space   Z: Feature Space

Fig. 1. The maximal margin hyperplane in a feature space

$$\text{minimize} \quad \|\boldsymbol{w}\|^2, \tag{1}$$

$$\text{subject to} \quad y_i f(\boldsymbol{z}_i) \geq 1 \ (1 \leq i \leq n). \tag{2}$$

The choice of the maximal margin hyperplane is justified by Theorem 4.18 in [4].

Theorem 1. *([4]) For any probability distribution $\mathcal{D}$ on $Z \times Y$ and sufficiently large n, if $y_i f(\boldsymbol{z}_i) \geq \gamma \|\boldsymbol{w}\|$ holds for all $(\boldsymbol{z}_i, y_i)(1 \leq i \leq n)$ and $\gamma > 0$, then the following inequality holds with probability $1 - \delta$*

$$\text{err}_{\mathcal{D}}(f) \leq \frac{2}{n} \left(\frac{64R^2}{\gamma^2} \log \frac{en\gamma}{8R^2} \log \frac{32n}{\gamma^2} + \log \frac{4}{\delta} \right),$$

where R is the radius of a sphere that contains Z.

Because $\gamma \|\boldsymbol{w}\| = 1$ in our context, the minimization of $\|\boldsymbol{w}\|^2$ amounts to the minimization of the statistical bound of the generalization error.

According to the optimization theory, the above convex quadratic programming problem is transformed into the following dual problem:

$$\text{maximize} \quad \sum_{i=1}^{n} \alpha_i - \frac{1}{2} \sum_{i=1}^{n} \sum_{j=1}^{n} \alpha_i \alpha_j y_i y_j \langle \boldsymbol{z}_i \cdot \boldsymbol{z}_j \rangle, \tag{3}$$

$$\text{subject to} \quad \alpha_i \geq 0 \ (1 \leq i \leq n), \ \sum_{i=1}^{n} \alpha_i y_i = 0, \tag{4}$$

where parameters α_i are called *Lagrange multipliers*. It is known that the above convex quadratic programming can be solved efficiently [2,11]. For a solution $\alpha_1^*, \ldots, \alpha_n^*$, the maximal margin hyperplane $f^*(\boldsymbol{z}) = 0$ can be expressed in the dual representation in terms of these parameters:

$$f^*(\boldsymbol{z}) = \sum_{i=1}^{n} \alpha_i^* y_i \langle \boldsymbol{z}_i \cdot \boldsymbol{z} \rangle + b^* \tag{5}$$

$$b^* = y_s - \sum_{i=1}^{n} \alpha_i^* y_i \langle \boldsymbol{z}_i \cdot \boldsymbol{z}_s \rangle \text{ for some } \alpha_s^* \neq 0 \tag{6}$$

An advantage of using the dual representation is that we can side-step evaluation of the feature mapping ϕ, which is infeasible when the dimension of the feature space is quite high. Notice that, in the dual representation, the feature mapping ϕ appears only in the form of inner products

$$\langle \boldsymbol{z}_i \cdot \boldsymbol{z}_j \rangle = \langle \phi(\boldsymbol{x}_i) \cdot \phi(\boldsymbol{x}_j) \rangle .$$

Therefore, if we have a way of computing the inner product in the feature space directly as a function of the input points, i.e.

$$K(\boldsymbol{x}_i, \boldsymbol{x}_j) = \langle \phi(\boldsymbol{x}_i) \cdot \phi(\boldsymbol{x}_j) \rangle ,$$

then we can side-step the computational problem inherent in evaluating the feature mapping. Such functions K are called *kernel functions*. The use of kernel functions makes it possible to map the data implicitly into a high dimensional feature space and to find the maximal margin hyperplane in the feature space.

The next section considers a feature space appropriate for learning Boolean functions and a kernel function for the feature space.

4   The DNF Kernel

For the learning of a Boolean function, it is desirable that a feature space is pertinent to the function enough to linearly separate its positive examples from negative ones. In this section, we considers a feature space whose features are all conjunctions of negated or non-negated Boolean variables. For instance, the following $3^2 - 1$ dimensional feature space is used for 2-variable Boolean functions.

$$x_1, \ x_2, \ 1 - x_1, \ 1 - x_2, \ x_1 x_2, \ x_1(1 - x_2), \ (1 - x_1)x_2, \ (1 - x_1)(1 - x_2)$$

The feature space is formally defined as follows.

Definition 1. *Let* idx *be a bijection from* $\{D, 1, 0\}^d$ *to* $\{0, \ldots, 3^d - 1\}$ *such that* $\text{idx}(D, \ldots, D) = 0$. *For any Boolean variable* x *and any* $p \in \{D, 1, 0\}$, L *is defined as follows.*

$$\text{L}(x, p) = \begin{cases} x & p = 1 \\ 1 - x & p = 0 \\ 1 & p = D \end{cases}$$

Definition 2. $\phi(\boldsymbol{x}) \stackrel{\text{def}}{=} (\phi_1(\boldsymbol{x}), \ldots, \phi_\ell(\boldsymbol{x}))$, *where* $\ell = 3^d - 1$ *and*

$$\phi_i(\boldsymbol{x}) = \prod_{j=1}^{d} \text{L}(x_j, p_j), \ \text{idx}^{-1}(i) = (p_1, \ldots, p_d).$$

In the feature space induced by ϕ defined above, this paper considers hyperplanes with the zero threshold. The following proposition shows that such a class of hyperplanes is sufficient for separating the data of any Boolean function.

Proposition 1. *For any Boolean function $g(\boldsymbol{x})$, there exists a hyperplane $f(\boldsymbol{z}) = \sum_{i=1}^{3^d-1} w_i z_i = 0$ that satisfies the following conditions for any $\boldsymbol{x} \in \{0,1\}^d$.*

$$g(\boldsymbol{x}) = 1 \Leftrightarrow f(\phi(\boldsymbol{x})) = 1 \text{ and } g(\boldsymbol{x}) = 0 \Leftrightarrow f(\phi(\boldsymbol{x})) = -1$$

Proof. Let us consider the hyperplane $\sum_{i=1}^{3^d-1} w_i z_i = 0$ where

$$\boldsymbol{u} = \text{idx}^{-1}(i), \ w_i = \begin{cases} 1 & \boldsymbol{u} \in \{0,1\}^d \text{ and } g(\boldsymbol{u}) = 1 \\ -1 & \boldsymbol{u} \in \{0,1\}^d \text{ and } g(\boldsymbol{u}) = 0 \\ 0 & \text{otherwise.} \end{cases}$$

For this hyperplane, we can show that $w_i \phi_i(\boldsymbol{x}) \neq 0$ iff $i = \text{idx}(\boldsymbol{x})$, and thus $f(\phi(\boldsymbol{x})) = w_i \phi_i(\boldsymbol{x})$.

From this fact, we see that the first condition holds as follows. If $g(\boldsymbol{x}) = 1$ then $w_i = 1$ and $\phi_i(\boldsymbol{x}) = 1$ holds from the definition of w_i and ϕ_i. Therefore, $f(\phi(\boldsymbol{x})) = w_i \phi_i(\boldsymbol{x}) = 1$. Conversely, if $f(\phi(\boldsymbol{x})) = w_i \phi_i(\boldsymbol{x}) = 1$ then w_i must be 1, and thus $g(\boldsymbol{x}) = 1$.

In the same way, we see that the hyperplane satisfies the second condition.

$\square$

According to the way of construction of hyperplanes above, we obtain the following hyperplane separating the data of the Boolean function $x_1 \vee \overline{x_2}$.

$$f(\phi(x_1, x_2)) = x_1 x_2 + x_1(1 - x_2) - (1 - x_1)x_2 + (1 - x_1)(1 - x_2) = 0$$

As the way of construction shows, the conjunctions with a smaller length than d are not necessarily required for the separability. Such features are required for generalization ability of hyperplanes. For example, in a feature space consisting of conjunctions with length d, the following hyperplane has the maximal margin for the training data $\{((1,1),1), ((0,1),-1), ((0,0),1)\}$.

$$f^*(\phi(x_1, x_2)) = x_1 x_2 - (1 - x_1)x_2 + (1 - x_1)(1 - x_2) = 0$$

However, this hyperplane cannot classify $\boldsymbol{x}' = (1, 0)$ because $f^*(\phi(\boldsymbol{x}')) = 0$. That is, SVMs using this feature space are a rote learner. On the other hand, in the feature space consisting of all possible conjunctions, the following hyperplane has the maximal margin for the same data.

$$f^*(\phi(x_1, x_2)) = \alpha_3 x_1 + (\alpha_1 + \alpha_2)(1 - x_1) + (\alpha_2 + \alpha_3)x_2$$
$$+ \alpha_1(1 - x_2) + \alpha_2(1 - x_1)x_2$$
$$+ \alpha_1(1 - x_1)(1 - x_2) + \alpha_3 x_1 x_2 = 0,$$

where $\alpha_1 \approx 0.57, \alpha_2 \approx -0.71, \alpha_3 \approx 0.57$. Note that this hyperplane gains generalization ability, i.e. $f^*(\phi(\boldsymbol{x}')) \approx 1$.

Because the above representation of hyperplanes have $3^d - 1$ terms for d-variable Boolean functions, it is difficult to deal with the representation directly from a computational viewpoint. As we have seen in the previous section, the use of kernel functions in the dual representation resolves the difficulty. In the following, we consider a particular kernel function for the feature space induced by the feature mapping ϕ.

Definition 3 (The DNF Kernel).

$$K(\boldsymbol{u}, \boldsymbol{v}) \stackrel{\text{def}}{=} -1 + \prod_{j=1}^{d} (2u_j v_j - u_j - v_j + 2).$$

The following theorem says that K is a kernel function.

Theorem 2. $\langle \phi(\boldsymbol{u}) \cdot \phi(\boldsymbol{v}) \rangle = K(\boldsymbol{u}, \boldsymbol{v})$.

Proof. $\langle \phi(\boldsymbol{u}) \cdot \phi(\boldsymbol{v}) \rangle + 1 = \sum_{i=1}^{3^d-1} \phi_i(\boldsymbol{u})\phi_i(\boldsymbol{v}) + 1$

$$= \sum_{(p_1,\dots,p_d)\in\{D,1,0\}^d} \prod_{j=1}^{d} \mathrm{L}(u_j, p_j) \prod_{j=1}^{d} \mathrm{L}(v_j, p_j) = \sum_{(p_1,\dots,p_d)} \prod_{j=1}^{d} \mathrm{L}(u_j, p_j)\mathrm{L}(v_j, p_j)$$

$$= \{\mathrm{L}(u_1, 1)\mathrm{L}(v_1, 1) + \mathrm{L}(u_1, 0)\mathrm{L}(v_1, 0) + \mathrm{L}(u_1, D)\mathrm{L}(v_1, D)\}$$

$$\sum_{(p_2,\dots,p_d)} \prod_{j=2}^{d} \mathrm{L}(u_j, p_j)\mathrm{L}(v_j, p_j)$$

$$= (2u_1 v_1 - u_1 - v_1 + 2) \cdot \sum_{(p_2,\dots,p_d)} \prod_{j=2}^{d} \mathrm{L}(u_j, p_j)\mathrm{L}(v_j, p_j)$$

$$\vdots$$

$$= \prod_{j=1}^{d} (2u_j v_j - u_j - v_j + 2) = K(\boldsymbol{u}, \boldsymbol{v}) + 1$$

$\square$

We should notice that the computational complexity of K depends on the dimension d of the input space and not on the dimension $3^d - 1$ of the feature space. Therefore, the use of the kernel function enables efficient learning in the high dimensional feature space.

In some application, negation of Boolean variables is not necessary needed. We can limit the expressive power by using the feature space whose features are all conjunctions of positive Boolean literals. By considering only $\mathrm{L}(x, 1)$ and $\mathrm{L}(x, D)$ in the proof of Theorem 2, we easily see that the following function is a kernel function for the feature space.

Definition 4 (The Monotone DNF Kernel).

$$K_m(\boldsymbol{u}, \boldsymbol{v}) \overset{\text{def}}{=} -1 + \prod_{j=1}^{d} (u_j v_j + 1).$$

The DNF kernel and the monotone DNF kernel are applicable to points on $\mathcal{R}^d$. By restricting their domains to $\{0,1\}^d \times \{0,1\}^d$, their computation is simplified as follows. For any $\boldsymbol{u}, \boldsymbol{v} \in \{0,1\}^d$, we denote by same01 $(\boldsymbol{u}, \boldsymbol{v})$ the number of bits that have the same value in $\boldsymbol{u}$ and $\boldsymbol{v}$. In addition, same1 $(\boldsymbol{u}, \boldsymbol{v})$ denotes the number of active bits common to both $\boldsymbol{u}$ and $\boldsymbol{v}$.

Proposition 2. *For any* $\boldsymbol{u}, \boldsymbol{v} \in \{0,1\}^d$,

$$K(\boldsymbol{u}, \boldsymbol{v}) = -1 + 2^{\text{same01}(\boldsymbol{u},\boldsymbol{v})} \quad and \quad K_m(\boldsymbol{u}, \boldsymbol{v}) = -1 + 2^{\text{same1}(\boldsymbol{u},\boldsymbol{v})} \quad hold.$$

These kernel functions are independently discovered by [8].

5   Experiments

To explore the capabilities of the learning method described above, I conducted experiments on learning of random Boolean functions in the same way as in [5]. The experimental system SVM+DNF implements a SVM using the DNF kernel that finds maximal margin hyperplanes with the zero threshold. To find the maximal margin hyperplane with the fixed threshold, it uses the stochastic gradient ascent algorithm described in [4, Table 7.1] as a convex quadratic programming solver.

The random d-variable Boolean functions were generated in disjunctive normal form as follows. Each variable was included in a disjunct with probability $\frac{a}{d}$ and negated with probability $\frac{1}{2}$. Therefore, the average length of disjuncts is a. The number of disjuncts was set to 2^{a-2} so as to produce approximately equal numbers of positive and negative examples. In the following experiments, d was set to 16 and a was set to 8.

For each Boolean function, n training data and 1000 test data were independently drawn from the uniform distribution. After a learning algorithm was trained using the training data, the misclassification rate of the learning algorithm was measured for the test data. The misclassification rate was averaged across 200 different Boolean functions.

5.1   Comparison with C4.5

Figure 2 illustrates dependency of the misclassification rates on sample size n, where SVM+DNF is compared with C4.5 and Naive Bayes Classifier (NBC).

The result of the experiments shows that SVM+DNF achieves the highest performance. In comparison with C4.5, SVM+DNF is 7.5% more accurate than C4.5 at the sample size $n = 5000$. Also, we see that SVM+DNF is most accurate

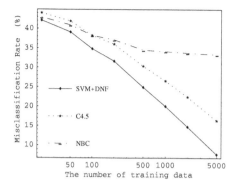

Fig. 2. Comparison with C4.5 and NBC

even at the small sample sizes. This is remarkable in the light of the fact that the capacity of SVM+DNF is larger than that of C4.5 because every decision tree can be represented as a hyperplane with equal separability. In general, the larger the capacity, the higher the risk of overfitting, and the overfitting is especially visible at small sample sizes. The tendency is exhibited by the results that C4.5 is less accurate than NBC at the sample size $n = 20, 50$. As discussed in [5], the phenomenon can be explained as C4.5 overfits the small samples more strongly than NBC does while limited capacity of NBC alleviates overfitting. According to the argument, SVM+DNF has higher risk of overfitting because it has larger capacity than C4.5 has. However, the result shows that SVM+DNF is more accurate than C4.5 even at the small sample sizes. This means that the capacity control of SVM+DNF is effective.

5.2   Comparison with Gaussian Kernels

To test the effectiveness of the DNF kernel, SVM+DNF is compared with SVMs using Gaussian kernels $K_G(\boldsymbol{x}_i, \boldsymbol{x}_j) = \exp(-\|\boldsymbol{x}_i - \boldsymbol{x}_j\|^2/\sigma^2)$.

Figure 3 illustrates dependency of the misclassification rates on sample size, where the DNF kernel is compared with Gaussian kernels with different values of σ^2. From the figure, we see that SVM+DNF has accuracy comparable to SVMs using Gaussian kernels with appropriately adjusted width parameters. This can be explained as follows. Assume that same01 $(\boldsymbol{x}_i, \boldsymbol{x}_j) = c$. Then $K(\boldsymbol{x}_i, \boldsymbol{x}_j) = 2^c - 1$. On the other hand,

$$K_G(\boldsymbol{x}_i, \boldsymbol{x}_j) = e^{\frac{c-d}{\sigma^2}} = e^{\frac{-d}{\sigma^2}} \cdot 2^{\frac{\log_2 e}{\sigma^2} c}.$$

Since the constant $e^{\frac{-d}{\sigma^2}}$ is absorbed in the Lagrange multipliers, K and K_G behave similarly provided σ^2 is appropriately chosen.

As described above, the DNF kernel tells a value of the parameter of the Gaussian kernel appropriate for learning Boolean functions. However the DNF

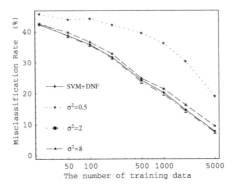

Fig. 3. Comparison with SVMs using Gaussian kernels

kernel has a more crucial advantage: comprehensibility of its features. That is, for the DNF kernel, the corresponding feature mapping is explicitly defined and each feature ϕ_i is considered as a conjunction. This contrasts with the Gaussian kernel; the corresponding feature mapping is defined implicitly and features induced by the kernel are hard to interpret. By virtue of this comprehensibility, we can see that a coefficient w_i of hyperplanes quantify importance of the conjunction ϕ_i for classification. The author believes that the use of the DNF kernel enables to extract crucial features, and these features are helpful to obtain a more accurate or comprehensible classifier.

6   Conclusions and Future Work

This paper considered a feature space appropriate for the learning of Boolean functions. The feature space consists of all possible conjunctions of Boolean literals, and is appropriate in the sense that any Boolean function can be represented as a hyperplane in the space. Furthermore, for the feature space, we can develop the DNF kernel that computes the inner product without depending on high dimensionality of the space. It enables SVMs to efficiently find optimal hyperplanes in the high dimensional feature space. Also, for a limited form of DNF consisting of positive Boolean literals, the monotone DNF kernel was presented. To explore the capabilities of the SVM employing the DNF kernel, experiments on the learning of randomly generated Boolean functions were conducted. The experiments showed that the resulting learning system outperforms C4.5 and has accuracy comparable to SVMs using best adjusted Gaussian kernels. Although the experiments are not extensive, the SVM employing the DNF kernel seems to have relative superiority over other learning algorithms. Further empirical studies to confirm the hypothesis are needed.

Although the SVMs efficiently find the optimal hyperplane for any given data of Boolean functions, it does not mean that they can learn any Boolean function efficiently because they may require exponentially many examples in order to attain high accuracy. The learnability of Boolean formulae has been studied extensively [14,7,10,1]. While efficient learnability of DNF is one of the main open problem in the learning theory, these studies have shown that even a simple class of formulae is not efficiently learnable. Therefore, it seems to be difficult to learn DNF for large d. In that case, we have to limit the class of DNF. It is worth investigating to explore use of the DNF kernel in order to obtain an appropriate limiting parameter.

From a practical point of view, it is important to make the learning method tolerate towards noise. For instance, if a point x appearing more than once in a training set has different class labels due to the classification noise, then the training set is not linearly separable. In this case, the optimization problem can not be solved because the constraint on separability is never satisfied. To cope with the difficulty, one can use soft margin optimization techniques [4] that allow a given amount of violation of the constraint. We should investigate capabilities of these techniques.

Another interesting future research concerns comprehensibility of learned classifiers. In some applications, explanation for the decision made by learned classifiers is important as well as accuracy of the classifiers. To obtain the explanation, features induced by the DNF kernel might be helpful. As mentioned in the previous section, a coefficient w_i of hyperplanes quantifies importance of the conjunction ϕ_i for classification. By extracting crucial features, a more accurate or comprehensible classifier might be obtainable. The author believes that it is a meaningful research direction to study a SVM using a logic-related kernel that can learn accurate models and generate an explanation for a specific decision.

References

1. D. Angluin. Queries and concept learning. *Machine Learning*, 2:319–342, 1988.
2. M. Bellare and P. Rogaway. The complexity of approximating a nonlinear program. In *Complexity of Numerical Optimization*, pages 16–32. World Scientific, 1993.
3. V. Cherkassky and F. Mulier. *Learning from Data*. Wiley, 1998.
4. N. Cristianini and J. Shawe-Taylor. *An Introduction to Support Vector Machines*. Cambridge Press, 2000.
5. P. Domingos. On the optimality of the simple Bayesian classifier under zero-one loss. *Machine Learning*, 29:103–130, 1997.
6. P. Domingos. The role of Occam's razor in knowledge discovery. *Data Mining and Knowledge Discovery*, 3:409–425, 1999.
7. M. Kearns, Ming Li, L. Pitt, and L.G. Valiant. On the learnability of Boolean formulae. *ACM*, pages 285–295, 1987.
8. R. Khardon, D. Roth, and R. Servedio. Efficiency versus convergence of Boolean kernels for on-line learning algorithms. Manuscript, 2001.
9. H. Liu and H. Motoda. Feature transformation and subset selection. *IEEE Intelligent Systems*, 13(2):26–28, 1998.
10. L. Pitt and L.G. Valiant. Computational limitations on learning from examples. *Journal of the Association for Computing Machinery*, 35(4):965–984, 1988.

11. J.C. Platt. Fast training of support vector machines using sequential minimal optimization. In *Advances in Kernel Methods – Support Vector Learning*, pages 185–208. MIT Press, 1998.
12. J.R. Quinlan. An empirical comparison of genetic and decision-tree classifiers. In *Proceedings of International Conference on Machine Learning*, pages 135–141, 1988.
13. J.R. Quinlan. *C4.5: Programs for Machine Learning*. Morgan Kaufmann, 1993.
14. L.G. Valiant. A theory of the learnable. *Communications of the ACM*, 27(11):1134–1142, 1984.
15. V. Vapnik. *The Nature of Statistical Learning Theory*. Springer-Verlag, 1995.
16. V. Vapnik. *Statistical Learning Theory*. Wiley, 1998.

A Random Sampling Technique for Training Support Vector Machines*
For Primal-Form Maximal-Margin Classifiers

Jose Balcázar[1]**, Yang Dai[2]***, and Osamu Watanabe[2]†

[1] Dept. Llenguatges i Sistemes Informatics, Univ. Politecnica de Catalunya
balqui@lsi.upc.es
[2] Dept. of Mathematical and Computing Sciences, Tokyo Institute of Technology
{dai, watanabe}@is.titech.ac.jp

Abstract. Random sampling techniques have been developed for combinatorial optimization problems. In this note, we report an application of one of these techniques for training support vector machines (more precisely, primal-form maximal-margin classifiers) that solve two-group classification problems by using hyperplane classifiers. Through this research, we are aiming (I) to design efficient and theoretically guaranteed support vector machine training algorithms, and (II) to develop systematic and efficient methods for finding "outliers", i.e., examples having an inherent error.

1 Introduction

This paper proposes a new training algorithm of *support vector machines* (more precisely, primal-form maximal-margin classifiers) for two-group classification problems. We use one of the random sampling techniques that have been developed and used for combinatorial optimization problems; see, e.g., [7,1,10]. Through this research, we are aiming (I) to design efficient and theoretically guaranteed support vector machine training algorithms, and (II) to develop systematic and efficient methods for finding "outliers", i.e., examples having an inherent error. Our proposed algorithm, though not perfect, is a good step towards the first goal (I). We show, under some hypothesis, that our algorithm

---

* This work was started when the first and third authors visited Centre de Recerca Mathemática, Spain.
** Supported in part by EU ESPRIT IST-1999-14186 (ALCOM-FT), EU EP27150 (Neurocolt II), Spanish Government PB98-0937-C04 (FRESCO), and CIRIT 1997SGR-00366.
*** Supported in part by a Grant-in-Aid (C-13650444) from the Ministry of Education, Science, Sports and Culture of Japan.
† Supported in part by a Grant-in-Aid for Scientific Research on Priority Areas "Discovery Science" from the Ministry of Education, Science, Sports and Culture of Japan.

N. Abe, R. Khardon, and T. Zeugmann (Eds.): ALT 2001, LNAI 2225, pp. 119–134, 2001.
© Springer-Verlag Berlin Heidelberg 2001

terminates within a reasonable[1] number of training steps. For the second goal (II), we propose, though only briefly, some approach based on this random sampling technique.

Since the present form of support vector machine (SVM in short) was proposed [8], SVMs have been used in various application areas, and their classification power has been investigated in depth from both experimental and theoretical points of view. Also many algorithms and implementation techniques have been developed for training SVMs efficiently; see, e.g., [14,5]. This is because quadratic programming (QP in short) problems need to be solved for training SVMs (as in the original form) and such a QP problem is, though polynomial-time solvable, not so easy. Among speed-up techniques, those called "subset selection" [14] have been used as effective heuristics from the early stage of the SVM research. Roughly speaking, a *subset selection* is a technique to speed-up SVM training by dividing the original QP problem into small pieces, thereby reducing the size of each QP problem. Well known subset selection techniques are chunking, decomposition, and sequential minimal optimization (SMO in short). (See [8,13,9] for the detail.) In particular, SMO has become popular because it outperforms the others in several experiments. Though the performance of these subset selection techniques has been extensively examined, no theoretical guarantee has been given on the efficiency of algorithms based on these techniques. (As far as the authors know, the only positive theoretical results are the convergence (i.e., termination) of some of such algorithms [12,6,11].)

In this paper, we propose a subset selection type algorithm based on a randomized sampling technique developed in the combinatorial optimization community. It solves the SVM training problem by solving iteratively small QP problems for randomly chosen examples. There is a straightforward way to apply the randomized sampling technique to design some SVM training algorithm. But this may not work well for data with many errors. Here we use some geometric interpretation of the SVM training problem [3] and derive a SVM training algorithm for which we can prove much faster convergence. Unfortunately, though, a heavy "book keeping" task is required if we implement this algorithm naturally, and the total running time may become very large despite of its good convergence speed. Here we propose some implementation technique to get around this problem and obtain an algorithm with reasonable running time. Our obtained algorithm is not perfect in two points: (i) some hypothesis is needed (so far) to guarantee its convergence speed, and (ii) the obtained algorithm (so far) works only for training SVMs as a primal-form, and it is not suitable for the kernel technique. But we think that it is a good starting point towards efficient and theoretically guaranteed algorithms.

---

[1] By "reasonable bound", we mean some low polynomial bound w.r.t. n, m, and ℓ, where n, m, and ℓ are respectively the number of attributes, the number of examples, and the number of errorneous examples.

2   SVM and Random Sampling Techniques

Here we explain basic notions on SVM and random sampling techniques. Due to the space limit, we only explain those necessary for our discussion. For SVM, see, e.g., a good textbook [9], and for random sampling techniques, see, e.g., an excellent survey [10].

For support vector machine formulations, we will consider, in this paper, only the binary classification by a hyperplane of the example space; in other words, we regard training SVM for a given set of labeled examples as the problem of computing a hyperplane separating positive and negative examples with the largest margin.

Suppose that we are given a set of m examples x_i, $1 \leq i \leq m$, in some n dimension space, say $\mathbb{R}^n$. Each example x_i is labeled by $y_i \in \{1, -1\}$ denoting the classification of the example. The *SVM training problem* (of the separable case) we will discuss in this paper is essentially to solve the following optimization problem. (Here we follow [3] and use their formulation. But the above problem can be restated by using a single threshold parameter as given in [8].)

$$
\begin{aligned}
&\underline{\text{Max Margin (P1)}} \\
&\text{min. } \frac{1}{2}\|w\|^2 - (\theta_+ - \theta_-) \\
&\text{w.r.t. } w = (w_1, ..., w_n),\ \theta_+,\ \text{and } \theta_-, \\
&\text{s.t. } \quad w \cdot x_i \geq \theta_+ \quad \text{if } y_i = 1, \quad \text{and} \\
&\qquad\quad w \cdot x_i \leq \theta_- \quad \text{if } y_i = -1.
\end{aligned}
$$

Remark 1. Throughout this note, we use X to denote the set of examples, and let n and m denote the dimension of the example space and the number of examples. Also we use i for indexing examples and their labels, and x_i and y_i to denote the ith example and its label. The range of i is always $\{1, ..., m\}$.

By the *solution* of (P1), we mean the hyperplane that achieves the minimum cost. We sometimes consider a partial problem of (P1) that minimizes a target cost under some subset of constrains. A solution to such a partial problem of (P1) is called a *local solution* of (P1) for the subset of constraints.

We can solve this optimization problem by using a standard general QP (i.e., quadratic programming) solver. Unfortunately, however, such general QP solvers are not scale well. Note, on the other hand, that there are cases where the number n of attributes is relatively small, while m is quite large; that is, the large problem size is due to the large number of examples. This is the situation where randomized sampling techniques are effective.

We first explain intuitively our[2] random sampling algorithm for solving the problem (P1). The idea is simple. Pick up a certain number of examples from X and solve (P1) under the set of constraints corresponding to these examples. We choose examples randomly according to their "weights", where initially all

---

[2] This algorithm is not new. It is obtained from a general algorithm given in [10].

examples are given the same weight. Clearly, the obtained local solution is, in general, not the global solution, and it does not satisfy some constraints; in other words, some examples are misclassified by the local solution. Then double the "weight" of such misclassified examples, and then pick up some examples again randomly according to their weights. If we iterate this process several rounds, the weight of "important examples", which are support vectors in our case, would get increased, and hence, they are likely to be chosen. Note that once all support vectors are chosen at some round, then the local solution of this round is the real one, and the algorithm terminates at this point. By using the *Sampling Lemma*, we can prove that the algorithm terminates in $O(n \log m)$ rounds on average. We will give this bound after explaining necessary notions and notations and stating our algorithm.

We first explain the abstract framework for discussing randomized sampling techniques that was given by Gärtner and Welzl [10]. (Note that the idea of this Sampling Lemma can be found in the paper by Clarkson [7], where a randomized algorithm for linear programming has been proposed. Indeed a similar idea has been used [1] to design an efficient randomized algorithm for quadratic programming.)

Randomized sampling techniques, particularly, the Sampling Lemma, is applicable for many "LP-type" problems. Here we use $(\mathcal{D}, \phi)$ to denote an abstract LP-type problem, where $\mathcal{D}$ is a set of elements and ϕ is a function mapping any $\mathcal{R} \subseteq \mathcal{D}$ to some value space. In the case of our problem (P1), for example, we can regard $\mathcal{D}$ as X and define ϕ as a mapping from a given subset R of X to the local solution of (P1) for the subset of constraints corresponding to R. As a LP-type problem, we require $(\mathcal{D}, \phi)$ to satisfy certain conditions. Here we omit the explanation and simply mention that our example case clearly satisfies these conditions.

For any $\mathcal{R} \subseteq \mathcal{D}$, a *basis* of $\mathcal{R}$ is an inclusion-minimal subset $\mathcal{B}$ of $\mathcal{R}$ such that $\phi(\mathcal{B}) = \phi(\mathcal{R})$. The *combinatorial dimension* of $(\mathcal{D}, \phi)$ is the size of the largest basis of $\mathcal{D}$. We will use δ to denote the combinatorial dimension. For the problem (P1), the largest basis is the set of all support vectors; hence, the combinatorial dimension of (P1) is at most $n + 1$. Consider any subset $\mathcal{R}$ of $\mathcal{D}$. A *violator* of $\mathcal{R}$ is an element e of $\mathcal{D}$ such that $\phi(\mathcal{R} \cup \{e\}) \neq \phi(\mathcal{R})$. An element e of $\mathcal{R}$ is *extreme* (or, simply called an *extremer*) if $\phi(\mathcal{R} - \{e\}) \neq \phi(\mathcal{R})$. Consider our case. For any subset R of X, let $(\boldsymbol{w}^*, \theta_+^*, \theta_-^*)$ be a local solution of (P1) obtained for R. Then $\boldsymbol{x}_i \in X$ is a *violator* of R (or, more directly, a *violator* of $(\boldsymbol{w}^*, \theta_+^*, \theta_-^*)$) if the constraint corresponding to $\boldsymbol{x}_i$ is not satisfied with $(\boldsymbol{w}^*, \theta_+^*, \theta_-^*)$.

Now we state our algorithm as Figure 1. In the algorithm, we use u to denote a weight scheme that assigns some integer weight $u(\boldsymbol{x}_i)$ to each $\boldsymbol{x}_i \in X$. For this weight scheme u, consider a multiple set U containing each example $\boldsymbol{x}_i$ exactly $u(\boldsymbol{x}_i)$ times. Note that U has $u(X)$ $(= \sum_i u(\boldsymbol{x}_i))$ elements. Then by "choose r examples randomly from X according to u", we mean to select a set of examples randomly from all $\binom{u(X)}{r}$ subsets of U with equal probability.

For analyzying the efficiency of this algorithm, we use the Sampling Lemma that is stated as follows. (We omit the proof that is given in [10].)

procedure OptMargin
    set weight $u(\boldsymbol{x}_i)$ to be 1 for all examples in X;
    $r \leftarrow 6\delta^2$;   % $\delta = n + 1$.
    repeat
        $R \leftarrow$ choose r examples from X randomly according to u;
        $(\boldsymbol{w}^*, \theta_+^*, \theta_-^*)$ is a solution of (P1) for R;
        $V \leftarrow$ the set of violators in X of the solution;
        if $u(V) \leq u(X)/(3\delta)$ **then** double the weight $u(\boldsymbol{x}_i)$ for all $\boldsymbol{x}_i \in V$;
    until $V = \emptyset$;
    return the last solution;
end-procedure.

Fig. 1. Randomized SVM Training Algorithm

Lemma 1. *Let $(\mathcal{D}, \phi)$ be any LP-type problem. Assume some weight scheme u on $\mathcal{D}$ that gives an integer weight to each element of $\mathcal{D}$. Let $u(\mathcal{D})$ denote the total weight. For a given r, $0 \leq r < u(\mathcal{D})$, we consider the situation where r elements of $\mathcal{D}$ are chosen randomly according to their weights. Let $\mathcal{R}$ denote the set of chosen elements, and let $v_{\mathcal{R}}$ be the weight of violators of $\mathcal{R}$. Then we have the following bound. (Notice that $v_{\mathcal{R}}$ is a random variable. Let $\mathrm{Exp}(v_{\mathcal{R}})$ to denote its expectation.)*

$$\mathrm{Exp}(v_{\mathcal{R}}) \leq \frac{u(\mathcal{D}) - r}{r + 1} \cdot \delta. \tag{1}$$

Using this lemma, we can prove the following bound. (For this theorem, we state the proof below, though it is again immediate from the explanation in [10].)

Theorem 1. *The average number of iterations executed in the OptMargin algorithm is bounded by $6\delta \ln m = O(n \ln m)$. (Recall $|X| = m$ and $\delta \leq n + 1$.)*

Proof. We say a repeat-iteration is *successful* if the if-condition holds in the iteration.

We first bound the number of successful iterations. For this, we analyze how the total weight $u(X)$ increases. Consider the execution of any successful iteration. Since $u(V) \leq u(X)/3\delta$, by doubling the weight of all examples in V, i.e., all violators, $u(X)$ increases by at most $u(X)/(3\delta)$. Thus, after t successful iterations, we have $u(X) \leq m(1 + 1/(3\delta))^t$. (Note that $u(X)$ is initially m.)

Let $X_0 \subseteq X$ be the set of support vectors of (P1). Note that if all elements of X_0 are chosen to R, i.e., $X_0 \subseteq R$, then there should be no violator for R. Thus, at each successful iteration (if it is not the end) some $\boldsymbol{x}_i$ of X_0 must not be in R, which in turn is a violator of R. Hence, $u(\boldsymbol{x}_i)$ gets doubled. Since $|X_0| \leq \delta$, there is some $\boldsymbol{x}_i$ in X_0 that gets doubled at least once every δ successful iterations. Therefore, after t successful iterations, $u(\boldsymbol{x}_i) \geq 2^{t/\delta}$.

Therefore, we have the following upper and lower bounds for $u(X)$.

$$2^{t/\delta} \leq u(X) \leq m(1 + 1/(3\delta))^t.$$

This implies that $t < 3\delta \ln m$ (if the repeat-condition does not hold after t successful iterations). That is, the algorithm terminates within $3\delta \ln m$ successful iterations.

Next estimate how often successful iteration occurs. Here we use the Sampling Lemma. Consider the execution of any repeat-iteration. Let u be the current weight on X, and let R and V be the set chosen at this iteration and the set of violators of R. Then this R corresponds to $\mathcal{R}$ in the Sampling Lemma, and we have $u(V) = v_{\mathcal{R}}$. Hence from (1), we can bound the expectation v_r of $u(V)$ by $(u(X) - r)\delta/(r + 1)$, which is smaller than $u(X)/(6\delta)$ by our choice of r. Thus, the probability that the if-condition is satisfied is at least $1/2$. This implies that the expected number of iterations is at most twice as large as the number of successful iterations. Therefore, the algorithm terminates *on average* within $2 \cdot 3\delta \ln m$ steps.

Thus, while our randomized OptMargin algorithm needs to solve (P1) for about $6n \ln m$ times on average, the number of constraints needed to consider at each time is about $6n^2$. Hence, if n is much smaller than m, then this algorithm is faster than solving (P1) directly. For example, the fastest QP solver up to date needs *roughly* $O(mn^2)$ time. Hence, if n is smaller than $m^{1/3}$, then we can get (at least asymptotic) speed-up. (Of course, one does not have to use such a general purpose solver, but even for an algorithm designed specifically for solving (P1), it is better if the number of constrains is smaller.)

3   A Nonseparable Case and a Geometrical View

For the separable case, the randomized sampling approach seems to help us by reducing the size of the optimization problem we need to solve for training SVM. On the other hand, the important feature of SVM is that it is also applicable for the nonseparable case. More precisely speaking, the nonseparable case includes two subcases: (i) the case where the hyperplane classifier is too weak for classifying given examples, and (ii) the case where there are some erroneous examples, namely outliers. The first subcase is solved by the SVM approach by mapping examples into a much higher dimension space. The second subcase is solved by relaxing constraints by introducing slack variables or "soft margin error". In this paper, we will discuss a way to handle the second subcase; that is, the nonseparable case with outliers.

First we generalize the problem (P1) and state the soft margin hyperplane separation problem.

$$\underline{\text{Max Soft Margin (P2)}}$$
$$\min. \frac{1}{2}\|\boldsymbol{w}\|^2 - (\theta_+ - \theta_-) + D \cdot \sum_i \xi_i$$
$$\text{w.r.t. } \boldsymbol{w} = (w_1, ..., w_n),\ \theta_+,\ \theta_-,\ \text{and } \xi_1, ..., \xi_m$$
$$\text{s.t. } \boldsymbol{w} \cdot \boldsymbol{x}_i \geq \theta_+ - \xi_i \quad \text{if } y_i = 1,$$
$$\boldsymbol{w} \cdot \boldsymbol{x}_i \leq \theta_- + \xi_i \quad \text{if } y_i = -1, \quad \text{and } \xi_i \geq 0.$$

Here $D < 1$ is a parameter that determines the degree of influence from outliers. Note that D should be fixed in advance; that is, D is a constant throughout the training process. (There is a more generalized SVM formulation, where one can change D and furthermore use different D for each example. We left such a generalization for our future work.)

At this point, we can formally define the notion of outliers we are considering in this paper. For a given set X of examples, suppose we solve the problem (P2) and obtain the optimal hyperplane. Then an example in X is called an *outlier* if it is misclassified with this hyperplane. Throughout this paper, we use ℓ to denote the number of outliers. Notice that this definition of outlier is quite relative; that is, relative to the hypothesis class and relative to the soft margin parameter D.

The problem (P2) is again a quadradic programming with linear constraints; thus, it is possible to use our random sampling technique. More specifically, by choosing δ appropriately, we can use the algorithm OptMargin of Figure 1 here. But while $\delta \leq n + m + 1$ is trivial, it does not seem[3] trivial to derive a better bound for δ. On the other hand, the bound $\delta \leq n + m + 1$ is useless in the algorithm OptMargin because the sample size $6\delta^2$ is much larger than m, the number of all examples given. Thus, some new approach seems necessary.

Here we introduce a new algorithm by reformulating the problem (P2) in a different way. We will make use of an intuitive geometric interpretation to (P2) that has been given by Bennett and Bredensteiner [3].

Bennett and Bredensteiner [3] proved that (P2) is equivalent to the following problem (P3); more precisely, (P3) is the Wolfe dual of (P2).

Reduced Convex Hull (P3)

$$\text{min.} \ \frac{1}{2} \left\| \sum_i y_i s_i \boldsymbol{x}_i \right\|^2 \qquad \text{w.r.t.} \ s_1, ..., s_m$$

$$\text{s.t.} \ \sum_{i: y_i = 1} s_i = 1, \qquad \sum_{i: y_i = -1} s_i = 1, \quad \text{and} \ 0 \leq s_i \leq D.$$

Note that $\| \sum_i y_i s_i \boldsymbol{x}_i \|^2 = \| \sum_{i: y_i = 1} s_i \boldsymbol{x}_i - \sum_{i: y_i = -1} s_i \boldsymbol{x}_i \|^2$. That is, the value minimized in (P3) is the distance between two points in the convex hull of positive and negative examples. In the separable case, it is the distance between two closest points in two convex hulls. On the other hand, in the nonseparable case, we give some restriction to the influence of each example; each example cannot contribute to the closest point more than D.

As mentioned in [3], the meaning of D is intuitively explained by considering its inverse $k = 1/D$. (Here we assume that $1/D$ is an integer. Throughout this note, we use k to denote this constant.) Instead of the original convex hulls, we consider the convex hulls of points composed from k examples. Then resulting convex hulls are reduced ones and they may be separable by some hyperplane; in the extreme case where $k = m_+$ (where m_+ is the number of positive examples), the reduced convex hull for positive examples consists of only one point.

---

[3] In the submission version of this paper, we claim that $\delta \leq n + \ell + 1$, thereby deriving an algorithm by using the algorithm OptMargin. We, however, noticed later that it is not that trivial. Fortunately, the bound $n + \ell + 1$ is still valid, which we found quite recently, and we will report this fact in our future paper [2].

More formally, we can reformulate (P3) as follows. Let Z be the set of *composed examples* z_I that is defined by $z_I = (x_{i_1} + x_{i_2} + \cdots + x_{i_k})/k$, with some k distinct elements $x_{i_1}, x_{i_2}, ..., x_{i_k}$ of X with the same label (i.e., $y_{i_1} = y_{i_2} = \cdots = y_{i_k}$). The label y_I of the composed example z_I inherits its members'. Throughout this note, we use I for indexing elements of Z and their labels. The range of I is $\{1, ..., M\}$, where $M \stackrel{\text{def}}{=} |Z|$. Note that $M \leq \binom{m}{k}$. For each z_I, we use z_I to denote the set of original examples from which z_I is composed. Then (P3) is equivalent to the following problem (P4).

Convex Hull of Composed Examples (P4)

$$\text{min.} \quad \frac{1}{2} \left\| \sum_I y_I s_I z_I \right\|^2 \quad \text{w.r.t. } s_1, ..., s_M$$

$$\text{s.t.} \quad \sum_{I:\, y_I = 1} s_I = 1, \quad \sum_{I:\, y_I = -1} s_I = 1, \quad \text{and } 0 \leq s_I \leq 1.$$

Finally we consider the Wolfe primal of this problem. Then we came back to our favorite formulation!

Max Margin for Composed Examples (P5)

$$\text{min.} \quad \frac{1}{2} \|w\|^2 - (\eta_+ - \eta_-)$$
$$\text{w.r.t. } w = (w_1, ..., w_n), \eta_+, \text{ and } \eta_-$$
$$\text{s.t.} \quad w \cdot z_I \geq \eta_+ \quad \text{if } y_I = 1, \quad \text{and}$$
$$\qquad w \cdot z_I \leq \eta_- \quad \text{if } y_I = -1.$$

Note that the combinatorial dimension of (P5) is $n + 1$, the same as that of (P1). The difference is that we have now $M = O(m^k)$ constraints, which is quite large. But this situation is suitable for the sampling technique. Suppose that we use our algorithm based on the randomized sampling technique (OptMargin of Figure 1) for solving (P5). Since the combinatorial dimension is the same, we can use $r = 6(n + 1)^2$ as before. On the other hand, from our analysis, the expected number of iterations is $O(n \ln M) = O(kn \ln m)$. That is, we need to solve QP problems with $n + 2$ variables and $O(n^2)$ constraints for $O(kn \ln m)$ times.

Unfortunately, however, there is a serious problem. The algorithm needs, at least as it is, a large amount of time and space for "book keeping" computation. For example, we have to keep and update weights of all M composed examples in Z, which requires at least $O(M)$ steps and $O(M)$ space. But M is huge.

4   A Modified Random Sampling Algorithm

As we have seen in Section 4, we cannot simply use the algorithm OptMargin for (P5). It takes too much time and space to maintain the weight of all composed examples and to generate them according to their weights. Here we propose a way to get around this problem by giving weight to original examples; this is our second algorithm.

Before stating our algorithm and its analysis, let us first examine solutions to the problems (P2) and (P5). For a given example set X, let Z be the set of composed examples. Let $(\boldsymbol{w}^*, \theta_+^*, \theta_-^*)$ and $(\boldsymbol{w}^*, \eta_+^*, \eta_-^*)$ be the solutions of (P2) for X and (P5) for Z respectively. Note that two solutions share the same $\boldsymbol{w}^*$; this is because (P2) and (P5) are essentially equivalent problems [3]. Let $X_{\text{err},+}$ and $X_{\text{err},-}$ denote the sets of positive/negative outliers. That is, $\boldsymbol{x}_i$ belongs to $X_{\text{err},+}$ (resp., $X_{\text{err},-}$) if and only if $y_i = 1$ and $\boldsymbol{w}^* \cdot \boldsymbol{x}_i < \theta_+^*$ (resp., $y_i = -1$ and $\boldsymbol{w}^* \cdot \boldsymbol{x}_i > \theta_-^*$). We use ℓ_+ and ℓ_- to denote the number of positive/negative outliers. Recall that we are assuming that our constant k is larger than both ℓ_+ and ℓ_-. Let $X_{\text{err}} = X_{\text{err},+} \cup X_{\text{err},-}$.

The problem (P5) is regarded as the LP-type problem $(\mathcal{D}, \phi)$, where the correspondence is the same as (P1) except that Z is used as $\mathcal{D}$ here. Let Z_0 be the basis of Z. (In order to simplify our discussion, we assume nondegeneracy throughout the following discussion.) Note that every element of the basis is extreme in Z. Hence, we call elements of Z_0 *final extremers*. By definition, the solution of (P5) for Z is defined by the constraints corresponding to these final extremers.

By analyzing the Karush-Kuhn-Tucker (in short, KKT) condition for (P2), we can show the following facts. (Though the lemma is stated only for the positive case, i.e., the case $y_I = 1$, the corresponding properties hold for the negative case $y_I = -1$.)

Lemma 2. *Let z_I be any positive final extremer, i.e., an element of Z_0 such that $y_I = 1$. Then the following properties hold: (a) $\boldsymbol{w}^* \cdot z_I = \eta_+^*$. (b) $X_{\text{err},+} \subseteq z_I$. (c) For every $\boldsymbol{x}_i \in z_I$, if $\boldsymbol{x}_i \notin X_{\text{err},+}$, then we have $\boldsymbol{w}^* \cdot \boldsymbol{x}_i = \theta_+^*$.*

Proof. (a) Since Z_0 is the set of final extremers, (P5) can be solved only with the constraints corresponding to elements in Z_0. Suppose that $\boldsymbol{w}^* \cdot z_J > \eta_+^*$ (resp., $\boldsymbol{w}^* \cdot z_J < \eta_-^*$) for some positive (resp., negative) $z_J \in Z_0$ including z_I of the lemma. Let Z' be the set of such z_J's of Z_0. If Z' indeed contained all positive examples in Z_0, then we could set θ_+ with $\theta_+^* - \epsilon$ for some $\epsilon > 0$ and still satisfy all the constraints, which contradicts the optimality of the solution. Hence, we may assume that $Z_0 - Z'$ still has some positive example. Then it is well known (see, e.g., [4]) that a local optimal solution to the problem (P5) with the constraints corresponding to elements in Z_0 is also locally optimal to the problem (P5) with the constraints corresponding to only elements in $Z_0 - Z'$. Furthermore, since (P5) is a convex programming, a local optimal solution is globally optimal. Thus, the original problem (P5) is solved with the constrains corresponding to elements in $Z_0 - Z'$. This contradicts our assumption that Z_0 is the set of final extremers.

(b) Consider the KKT-point $(\boldsymbol{w}^*, \theta_+^*, \theta_-^*, \boldsymbol{\xi}^*, \boldsymbol{s}^*, \boldsymbol{u}^*)$ of (P2). Then the point must satisfy the following so called KKT-condition. (Below we use i to denote indices of examples, and let P and N respectively denote indices i of examples such that $y_i = 1$ and $y_i = 0$. We use $\boldsymbol{e}$ to denote the vector with 1 at every entry.)

$$w^* - \sum_{i \in P} s_i x_i + \sum_{i \in N} s_i^* x_i = 0, \qquad De - s^* - u^* = 0,$$

$$-1 + \sum_{i \in P} s_i^* = 0, \qquad -1 + \sum_{i \in N} s_i^* = 0,$$

$$\forall i \in P \,[\, s_i^*(w^* \cdot x_i - \theta_+^* + \xi_i^*) = 0 \,], \qquad \forall i \in N \,[\, s_i^*(w^* \cdot x_i - \theta_-^* - \xi_i^*) = 0 \,],$$

$u^* \cdot \xi^* = 0$ (which means $(De - s^*) \cdot \xi^* = 0$), and $\xi^*, u^*, s^* \geq 0$.

Note that $(w^*, \theta_+^*, \theta_-^*, \xi^*)$ is an optimal solution of (P2), since (P2) is a convex minimization problem. From these requirements, we have the following relation. (Note that the condition $s^* \leq De$ below is derived from the requirements $De - s^* - u^* = 0$ and $u^* \geq 0$.)

$$w^* = \sum_{i \in P} s_i^* x_i - \sum_{i \in N} s_i^* x_i,$$

$$\sum_{i \in P} s_i^* = 1, \quad \sum_{i \in N} s_i^* = 1, \quad \text{and } 0 \leq s^* \leq De.$$

In fact, s^* is exactly the optimal solution of (P3).

Here by the equivalence of (P4) and (P5), we see that the final extremers are exactly points contributing to the solution of (P4). That is, we have $z_I \in Z_0$ if and only if $s_I^* > 0$, where s_I^* is the Ith element of the solution of (P4). Furthermore, it follows the equivalence between (P3) and (P4), for any i, we have

$$\frac{1}{k} \cdot \sum_{I : x_i \in z_I} s_I^* = s_i^*. \tag{2}$$

Recall that each z_I is defined as the center of k examples of X. Hence, to show that every $x_i \in X_{\mathrm{err},+}$ appears in all positive final extremers, it suffices to show that $s_i^* = 1/k$ for every $x_i \in X_{\mathrm{err},+}$, which follows from the following argument. For any $x_i \in X_{\mathrm{err},+}$, since $\xi_i^* > 0$, it follows from the requirements $(De - s^*) \cdot \xi^* = 0$ and $De - s^* \geq 0$ that $D - s_i^* = 0$; that is, $s_i^* = 1/k$ for any $x_i \in X_{\mathrm{err},+}$.

(c) Consider any index i in P such that x_i appears in some of the final extremer $z_I \in Z_0$. Since $s_I^* > 0$, we can show that $s_i^* > 0$ by using the equation (2). Hence, from the requirement $s_i(w^* \cdot x_i - \theta_+^* + \xi_i^*) = 0$, we have

$$w^* \cdot x_i - \theta_+^* + \xi_i^* = 0.$$

Thus, if $x_i \notin X_{\mathrm{err}}$, i.e., it is not an outlier or $\xi_i^* = 0$, then we have $w^* \cdot x_i = \theta_+^*$.

Let us give some intuitive interpretation to the facts given in this lemma. (Again we only consider, for the simplicity, the positive examples.) First note that the fact (b) of the lemma shows that all final extremers share the set $X_{\mathrm{err},+}$ of outliers. Next it follows from the fact (a) that all final extremers are located on some hyperplane whose distance from the base hyperplane $w^* \cdot z = 0$ is η_+^*. On the other hand, the fact (c) states that all original *normal* examples in a final extremer z_I (i.e., examples not in $X_{\mathrm{err},+}$) are located again on some hyperplane whose distance from the base hyperplane is $\theta_+^* > \eta_+^*$. Here consider the point $v_+ \stackrel{\text{def}}{=} \left(\sum_{x_i \in X_{\text{err},+}} x_i \right) / \ell_+$, i.e., the center of positive outliers, and define $\mu_+^* = w^* \cdot v_+$. Then we have $\theta_+^* > \eta_+^* > \mu_+^*$; that is, the hyperplane defined by the final extremers is located between the one having all normal examples in the final extremers and the one having the center v_+ of outliers. More specifically, since every final extremer is composed from all ℓ_+ positive outliers and $k - \ell_+$ normal examples, we have

$$\theta_+^* - \eta_+^* : \eta_+^* - \mu_+^* = k - \ell_+ : \ell_+.$$

Next we consider local solutions of (P5). We would like to solve (P5) by using the random sampling technique. That is, choose some small subset R of Z randomly according to current weight, and solve (P5) for R. Thus, let us examine local solutions obtained by solving (P5) for such a subset R of Z.

For any set R of composed examples in Z, let $(\widetilde{w}, \widetilde{\eta}_+, \widetilde{\eta}_-)$ be the solution of (P5) for R. Similar to the above, we consider $\widetilde{Z}_0$ to be the set of extremers of R w.r.t. the solution $(\widetilde{w}, \widetilde{\eta}_+, \widetilde{\eta}_-)$. On the other hand, we define here $\widetilde{X}$ to be the set of original examples appearing in some extremers in $\widetilde{Z}_0$.

As before, we will discuss about only positive composed/original examples. Let $\widetilde{Z}_{0,+}$ be the set of positive extremers. Different from the case where all composed examples are examined to solve (P5), here we cannot expect, for example, that all extremers in $\widetilde{Z}_{0,+}$ share the same set of misclassified examples. Thus, instead of sets like $X_{\text{err},+}$, we consider a subset $\widetilde{X}_+'$ of the following set $\widetilde{X}_+$. (It may be the case that $\widetilde{X}_+$ is empty.)

$\widetilde{X}_+$ = the set of positive examples appearing in all extremers in $\widetilde{Z}_{0,+}$.

Intuitively, we want to discuss by using the set $\widetilde{X}_+'$ of "misclassified" examples appearing in all positive extremers. But such a set cannot be defined at this point because no threshold corresponding to θ_+^* has been given. Thus, for a while, let us consider any subset $\widetilde{X}_+'$ of $\widetilde{X}_+$. Let $\widetilde{\ell}_+' = |\widetilde{X}_+'|$, and define $v_+ = \left(\sum_{x_i \in \widetilde{X}_+'} x_i \right) / \widetilde{\ell}_+'$. Also for each $z_I \in \widetilde{Z}_0$, we define a point v_I that is the center of all original examples in $z_I - \widetilde{X}_+'$. That is,

$$v_I \stackrel{\text{def}}{=} \frac{\sum_{x_i \in z_I - \widetilde{X}_+'} x_i}{k - \widetilde{\ell}_+'}.$$

Then we can prove the following fact that corresponds to Lemma 2 and that is proved similarly.

Lemma 3. *For any subset R of Z, we use the symbols defined as above. There exists some $\widetilde{\theta}_+'$ such that for any extremer z_I in $\widetilde{Z}_{0,+}$, we have $\widetilde{w} \cdot v_I = \widetilde{\theta}_+'$.*

Now for our $\widetilde{X}_{\mathrm{err},+}$, we use a subset $\widetilde{X}'_{+}$ of $\widetilde{X}_{+}$ defined by $\widetilde{X}'_{+} = \{\; \boldsymbol{x}_i \in \widetilde{X}_{+} \;:\; \widetilde{\boldsymbol{w}} \cdot \boldsymbol{x}_i < \widetilde{\theta}'_{+} \;\}$, where θ'_{+}, which we denote $\widetilde{\theta}_{\mathrm{err},+}$, is the threshold given in Lemma 3 for $\widetilde{X}'_{+}$. Such a set (while it could be empty) is well-defined. (In the case that $\widetilde{X}_{\mathrm{err},+}$ is empty, we define $\widetilde{\theta}_{\mathrm{err},+} = \widetilde{\eta}_{+}$.)

For any original positive example $\boldsymbol{x}_i \in X$, we call it a *missed example* (w.r.t. the local solution $(\widetilde{\boldsymbol{w}}, \widetilde{\eta}_{+}, \widetilde{\eta}_{-})$) if $\boldsymbol{x}_i \notin \widetilde{X}_{\mathrm{err},+}$ and it holds that

$$\widetilde{\boldsymbol{w}} \cdot \boldsymbol{x}_i \;<\; \widetilde{\theta}_{\mathrm{err},+}. \tag{3}$$

We will use such a missed example as an evidence that there exists a "violator" to $(\widetilde{\boldsymbol{w}}, \widetilde{\eta}_{+}, \widetilde{\eta}_{-})$, which is guaranteed by the following lemma.

Lemma 4. *For any subset R of Z, let $(\widetilde{\boldsymbol{w}}, \widetilde{\eta}_{+}, \widetilde{\eta}_{-})$ be the solution of (P5) for R. Then if there exists a missed example w.r.t. $(\widetilde{\boldsymbol{w}}, \widetilde{\eta}_{+}, \widetilde{\eta}_{-})$, then we have some composed example in Z that is misclassified w.r.t. $(\widetilde{\boldsymbol{w}}, \widetilde{\eta}_{+}, \widetilde{\eta}_{-})$. On the other hand, for any composed example $\boldsymbol{z}_I \in Z$, if it is misclassified w.r.t. $(\widetilde{\boldsymbol{w}}, \widetilde{\eta}_{+}, \widetilde{\eta}_{-})$, then $\boldsymbol{z}_I$ contains some missed example.*

Proof. We consider again only the positive case. Suppose that some missed positive example $\boldsymbol{x}_i$ exists. By definition, we have $\widetilde{\boldsymbol{w}} \cdot \boldsymbol{x}_i < \widetilde{\theta}_{\mathrm{err},+}$, and there exists some extremer $\boldsymbol{z}_I \in \widetilde{Z}_{0,+}$ that does not contain $\boldsymbol{x}_i$. Clearly, $\boldsymbol{z}_I$ contains some example $\boldsymbol{x}_j$ such that $\widetilde{\boldsymbol{w}} \cdot \boldsymbol{x}_j \geq \widetilde{\theta}_{\mathrm{err},+}$. Then we can see that a composed elements $\boldsymbol{z}_J$ consisting of $z_I - \{\boldsymbol{x}_j\} \cup \{\boldsymbol{x}_i\}$ does not satisfy the constraint $\widetilde{\boldsymbol{w}} \cdot \boldsymbol{z}_J \geq \widetilde{\eta}_{+}$.

For proving the second statement, note first that any "misclassified" original example $\boldsymbol{x}_i$, i.e., an example for which the inequality (3) holds, is either a missed example or an element of $\widetilde{X}_{\mathrm{err},+}$. Thus, if a composed element $\boldsymbol{z}_I$ does not contain any missed example, then it cannot contain any misclassified examples other than those in $\widetilde{X}_{\mathrm{err},+}$. Then it is easy to see that $\widetilde{\boldsymbol{w}} \cdot \boldsymbol{z}_I \geq \widetilde{\eta}_{+}$; that is, $\boldsymbol{z}_I$ is not misclassified w.r.t. $(\widetilde{\boldsymbol{w}}, \widetilde{\eta}_{+}, \widetilde{\eta}_{-})$.

We explain the idea of our new random sampling algorithm. As before, we choose (according to some weight) a set R consisiting of r composed examples in Z, and then solve (P5) for R. In the original sampling algorithm, this sampling is repeated until no violator exists. Recall that we are regarding (P5) as an LP-type problem and that by "a violator of R", we mean a composed example that is misclassified with the current solution $(\widetilde{\boldsymbol{w}}, \widetilde{\eta}_{+}, \widetilde{\eta}_{-})$ of (P5) obtained for R. Thanks to the above lemma, we do not have to go through all composed examples in order to search for a violator. A violator exists if and only if there exists some missed example w.r.t. $(\widetilde{\boldsymbol{w}}, \widetilde{\eta}_{+}, \widetilde{\eta}_{-})$. Thus, our first idea is to use the existence of missed example for the stopping condition. That is, the sampling procedure is repeated until no missed example exists.

The second idea is to use the weight of examples $\boldsymbol{x}_i$ in X to define the weight of composed examples. Let u_i denote the weight of the ith example $\boldsymbol{x}_i$. Then for each composed example $\boldsymbol{z}_I \in Z$, its weight U_I is defined as the total of weights of all examples contained in z_I; that is, $U_I = \sum_{\boldsymbol{x}_i \in z_I} u_i$. We use symbols u and U to refer these two weight schemes; we sometimes, use these symbols to denote

procedure OptMarginComposed
    $u_i \leftarrow 1$, for each i, $1 \le i \le m$;
    $r \leftarrow 6\alpha\beta n$;   % For α and β, see the explanation in the text.
    repeat
        $R \leftarrow$ choose r elements from Z randomly according to their weights;
        $(\widetilde{w}, \widetilde{\eta}_+, \widetilde{\eta}_-) \leftarrow$ the solution of (P5) for R;
        $\widetilde{X}_{\mathrm{err}} \leftarrow$ the set of missed examples w.r.t. the above solution;
        if $u(\widetilde{X}_{\mathrm{err}}) \le u(X)/(3\beta)$ **then** $u_i \leftarrow 2u_i$ for each $\boldsymbol{x}_i \in \widetilde{X}_{\mathrm{err}}$;
    until no missed example exists;
    return the last solution;
end-procedure.

Fig. 2. A Modified Random Sampling Algorithm

mapping from a set of (composed) examples to its total weight. For example, $u(X) = \sum_i u_i$, and $U(Z) = \sum_I U_I$. As explained below, it is computationally easy to generate each z_I with probability $U_I/U(Z)$.

Our third idea is to increase weights u_i if it is a missed example w.r.t. the current solution. More specifically, we double the weight u_i if $\boldsymbol{x}_i$ is a missed example w.r.t. the current solution for R. Lemma 4 guarantees that the weight of some element of a final extremer gets doubled so long as there is some missed example. This property is crucial to estimate the number of iterations.

Now we state our new algorithm in Figure 2. In the following, we explain some important points on this algorithm.

Random Generation of R

We explain how to generate each z_I proportional to U_I. Again we only consider the generation of positive composed examples, and we assume that all positive examples are re-indexed as $\boldsymbol{x}_1, ..., \boldsymbol{x}_m$. Also for simplifying our notation, we reuse m amd M to denote m_+ and M_+ respectively.

Recall that each z_I is defined as $(\boldsymbol{x}_{i_1} + \cdots + \boldsymbol{x}_{i_k})/k$, where $\boldsymbol{x}_{i_j}$ is an element of z_I. Here we assume that $i_k < i_{k-1} < \cdots < i_1$. Then each z_I uniquely corresponds to some k-tuple $(i_k, ..., i_1)$, and we identify here the index I of z_I and this k-tuple. Let $\mathcal{I}$ be the set of all such k-tuples $(i_k, ..., i_1)$ that satisfy $1 \le i_j \le m$ (for each j, $1 \le j \le k$) and $i_k < \cdots < i_1$. Here we assume the standard lexcographic order in $\mathcal{I}$.

As stated in the above algorithm, we keep the weights $u_1, ..., u_m$ of examples in X. By using these weights, we can calculate the total weight $U(Z) = \sum_i u_i$. Similarly, for each $z_I \in Z$, we consider the following accumulated weight $\overline{U}(I)$.

$$\overline{U}(I) \stackrel{\mathrm{def}}{=} \sum_{J \le I} U_J.$$

As explained below, it is easy to compute this weight for given $z_I \in Z$. Thus, for generating z_I, (i) choose p randomly from $\{1, ..., U(Z)\}$, and (ii) search for the smallest element I of $\mathcal{I}$ such that $\overline{U}(I) \ge p$. The second step can be done by the standard binary search in $\{1, ..., M\}$, which needs $\log M$ ($\le k \log m$) steps.

We explain a way to compute $\overline{U}(I)$. First we prepare some notations. Define $\overline{V}(I) = \sum_{J \geq I} U_J$. Then it is easy to see that (i) $U_0 = \overline{V}((1, 2, 3, ..., k))$, and (ii) $\overline{U}(I) = U_0 - \overline{V}(I) + (u_{i_k} + u_{i_{k-1}} + \cdots + u_{i_1})$ for each $I = (i_k, i_{k-1}, ..., i_1)$. Thus, it suffices to show how to compute $\overline{V}(I)$.

Consider any given $I = (i_k, i_{k-1}, ..., i_1)$ in $\mathcal{I}$. Also for any j, $1 \leq j \leq k$, we consider the prefix $I'_j = (i_j, i_{j-1}, ..., i_1)$ of I, and define the following values.

$$N_j \stackrel{\text{def}}{=} \text{\# of } I' \text{ such that } I' \geq I'_j, \quad \text{and}$$
$$V_j \stackrel{\text{def}}{=} \sum_{I'=(i'_j,...,i'_1) \geq I'_j} (u_{i'_j} + u_{i'_j - 1} + \cdots + u_{i'_1}).$$

Then clearly we have $\overline{V}(I) = V_k$, and our task is to compute V_k, which can be done inductively as shown in the following lemma. (The proof is omitted.)

Lemma 5. *Consider any given $I = (i_k, i_{k-1}, ..., i_1)$ in $\mathcal{I}$, and use the symbols defined above. Then for each j, $1 \leq j \leq k$, the following relations hold.*

$$N_j = N_{j-1} + \binom{m - i_j}{j}, \quad \text{and} \quad V_j = u_{i_j} \cdot N_{j-1} + \sum_{i_j + 1 \leq i \leq m} u_i \cdot \binom{m - i}{j - 1}.$$

Stopping Condition and Number of Successful Iterations

The correctness of our stopping condition is clear from Lemma 4. We estimate the number of the repeat-iterations. Here again we say that the repeat-iteration is *successful* if the if-condition holds. We give an upper bound for the number of successful iterations.

Lemma 6. *Set $\beta = k(n + 1)$ in the algorithm. Then the number of successful iterations is at most $3k(n + 1) \ln m$.*

Proof. For any $t > 0$, we consider the total weight $u(X)$ after t successful iterations. As before, we can give an upper bound $u(X) \leq m(1 + 1/(3\beta))^t$. On the other hand, some missed example exists at each repeat-iteration, and from Lemma 4, we can indeed find it in any violator, in particular, some final extremer $z_I \in Z_0$. Thus, there must be some element x_i of $\cup_{z_I \in Z_0} z_I$ whose weight u_i gets doubled at least once every $k(n + 1)$ steps. (Recall that $|Z_0| \leq n + 1$.) Hence, we have

$$2^{t/k(n+1)} \leq u(X) \leq m(1 + 1/(3\beta))^t.$$

This implies, under the above choice of β, that $t < 3k(n + 1) \ln m$.

Our Hypothesis and the Sampling Lemma

Finally, the most important point is to estimate how often we would have successful iterations. At each repeat-iteration of our algorithm, we consider the ratio $\rho_{\text{miss}} = u(\widetilde{X}_{\text{err}})/u(X)$. Recall that the repeat-iteration is successful if this ratio is at most $1/(3\beta)$. Our hypothesis is that the ratio ρ_{miss} is, on average, bounded by $1/(3\beta)$. Here we discuss when and for which parameter β, this hypothesis would hold.

For the analysis, we consider "violators" to the local solution of (P5) obtained at each repeat-iteration. Let R be the set of r' composed examples randomly chosen from Z with the probability proportional to their weights determined by U. Recall a violator of R is a composed example $z_I \in Z$ that is misclassified with the obtained solution for R. Let V be the set of violators, and let v_R be its weight under U. Recall also that the total weight of Z is $U(Z)$. Thus, by the Sampling Lemma, the ratio $\rho_{\text{vio}} \overset{\text{def}}{=} v_R/U(Z)$ is bounded as follows.

$$\text{Exp}(\rho_{\text{vio}}) \leq \frac{(n+1)(U(Z) - r')}{r' + 1} \cdot \frac{1}{U(Z)} \leq \frac{n}{r'}.$$

From Lemma 4, we know that every violator should contain at least one missed example. On the other hand, every missed example would contribute to some violator. Hence, it seems reasonable to expect that the ratio ρ_{miss} is bounded by $\alpha \cdot \rho_{\text{vio}}$ for some constant $\alpha \geq 1$, or at least it holds quite often if it is not always true. (It is still o.k. even if α is a low degree polynomial w.r.t. n.) Here we propose the following technical hypothesis.

(Hypothesis) $\qquad\qquad\qquad \rho_{\text{miss}} \leq \alpha \cdot \rho_{\text{vio}}$, for some $\alpha \geq 1$.

Under this hypothesis, we have $\rho_{\text{miss}} \leq n/r'$ on average; thus, by taking $r' = 6\alpha\beta n$, we can show that the expected ratio ρ_{miss} is at most $1/6\beta$, which implies as before that the expected number of iterations is at most twice as the number of successful iterations. Therefore the average number of iterations is bounded by $6k(n+1)\ln m$.

5 Concluding Remarks: Finding Outliers

In computational learning theory, one of the recent important topics is to develop an effective method for handling data with inherent errors. Here by an "inherent error", we mean an error or noise that cannot be corrected by resampling. Typically, an example that is mislabeled and this mislabeled situation does not change even though we resample this example again. Many learning algorithms fail to work under the existence of such inherent errors. SVMs are more robust against errors, but it is still the state of art to determine parameters for erroneous examples. More specifically, the complexity of classifiers and the degree D of the influence of errors are usually selected based on the experts' knowledge and experiences.

Let us fix a hypothesis class as the set of hyperplanes of the sample domain. Also suppose, for the time being, that the parameter D is somehow appropriately chosen. Then we can formally define erroneous examples — outliers — as we did in this paper. Clearly, outliers can be identified by solving (P2); by using the obtained hyperplane, we can check whether a given example is an outlier or not. But it would be nice if we can find outliers on the course of our computation.

As we discussed in Section 5, outliers are not only misclassified examples but also misclassified examples that commonly appear in support vector composed examples. Thus, if there is a good iterative way to solve (P5), we may be able to identify outliers by checking for commonly appearing misclassified examples in support vector composed examples of each local solution. We think that our second algorithm can be used for this purpose.

Also a randomized sampling algorithm for solving (P5) can be used to determine the parameter $D = 1/k$. Note that if we use k that is not large enough, then (P5) does not have a solution; there is no hyperplane separating composed examples. In this case, we would have more violators than we expect. Thus, by running a randomized sampling algorithm for (P5) several rounds, we can detect that the current choice of k is too small if an *unsuccessful iteration* (i.e., an iteration where the if-condition fails) occurs frequently. Thus, we can revise k at an earlier stage.

References

1. I. Adler and R. Shamir, A randomized scheme for speeding up algorithms for linear and convex programming with high constraints-to-variable ratio, *Math. Programming* 61, 39−52, 1993.
2. J. Balcázar, Y. Dai, and O. Watanabe, in preparation.
3. K.P. Bennett and E.J. Bredensteiner, Duality and geometry in SVM classifiers, in *Proc. the 17th Int'l Conf. on Machine Learning* (ICML'2000), 57−64, 2000.
4. D.P. Bertsekas, *Nonlinear Programming*, Athena Scientific, 1995.
5. P.S. Bradley, O.L. Mangasarian, and D.R. Musicant, Optimization methods in massive datasets, in *Handbook of Massive Datasets* (J. Abello , P.M. Pardalos, and M.G.C. Resende, eds.) Kluwer Academic Pub., 2000, to appear.
6. C.J. Lin, On the convergence of the decomposition method for support vector machines, *IEEE Trans. on Neural Networks*, 2001, to appear.
7. K.L. Clarkson, Las Vegas algorithms for linear and integer programming, *J.ACM* 42, 488−499, 1995.
8. C. Cortes and V. Vapnik, Support-vector networks, *Machine Learning* 20, 273−297, 1995.
9. N. Cristianini and J. Shawe-Taylor, *An Introduction to Support Vector Machines*, Cambridge University Press 2000.
10. B. Gärtner and E. Welzl, A simple sampling lemma: Analysis and applications in geometric optimization, *Discr. Comput. Geometry*, 2000, to appear.
11. S.S. Keerthi and E.G. Gilbert, Convergence of a generalized SMO algorithm for SVM classifier design, Technical Report CD-00-01, Dept. of Mechanical and Production Eng., National University of Singapore, 2000.
12. E. Osuna, R. Freund, and F. Girosi, An improved training algorithm for support vector machines, in *Proc. IEEE Workshop on Neural Networks for Signal Processing*, 276−285, 1997.
13. J. Platt, Fast training of support vector machines using sequential minimal optimization, in *Advances in Kernel Methods – Support Vector Learning* (B. Scholkopf, C.J.C. Burges, and A.J. Smola, eds.), MIT Press, 185−208, 1999.
14. A.J. Smola and B. Scholkopf, A tutorial on support vector regression, NeuroCOLT Technical Report NC-TR-98-030, Royal Holloway College, University of London, 1998.

Learning Coherent Concepts

Ashutosh Garg and Dan Roth

Department of Computer Science and the Beckman Institute,
University of Illinois,
Urbana, IL 61801,
ashutosh@uiuc.edu,danr@cs.uiuc.edu

Abstract. This paper develops a theory for learning scenarios where multiple learners co-exist but there are mutual *coherency constraints* on their outcomes. This is natural in cognitive learning situations, where "natural" constraints are imposed on the outcomes of classifiers so that a valid sentence, image or any other domain representation is produced. We formalize these learning situations, after a model suggested in [11] and study generalization abilities of learning algorithms under these conditions in several frameworks. We show that the mere existence of coherency constraints, even without the learner's awareness of them, deems the learning problem easier than predicted by general theories and explains the ability to generalize well from a fairly small number of examples. In particular, it is shown that within this model one can develop an understanding to several realistic learning situations such as highly biased training sets and low dimensional data that is embedded in high dimensional instance spaces.

1 Introduction

A fundamental research effort in learning theory has been the study of generalization abilities of learning algorithms and their dependence on sample complexity. The importance of this research direction goes beyond intellectual curiosity. Understanding the inherent difficulty of learning problems allows one to evaluate whether learning is at all possible in certain situations, estimate the degree of confidence in the predictions made by learned classifiers and is crucial in understanding and analyzing learning algorithms. In particular, these theoretical considerations played a crucial role in the development of practical learning approaches[7,9,6].

One puzzling problem from a theoretical and a practical point of view is the contrast between the hardness of learning problems, as suggested by various bounds on sample complexity and generalization - even for fairly simple concepts - and the apparent ease at which the cognitive systems seem to learn those concepts. Cognitive systems seem to use far less examples and learn more robustly than is predicted by the theoretical models developed so far.

This work develops a learning theory that explains this phenomenon. Following [11] our approach is based on the observation that cognitive learning

N. Abe, R. Khardon, and T. Zeugmann (Eds.): ALT 2001, LNAI 2225, pp. 135–150, 2001.

problems do not usually occur in isolation. Rather, the input is observed by multiple learners that may learn different functions on the same input. We pursue this direction by developing a theory for learning scenarios where multiple learners co-exist but there are mutual compatibility constraints on their outcomes. We believe that this is natural in cognitive learning situations, where "natural" compatibility constraints are imposed on the outcomes of classifiers so that a valid sentence, image or other domain representation is produced. In particular, this model can be viewed as a theoretical framework for learning in multi-modal situations.

Assume, for example, that one is trying to learn a function that determines, given a sentence which contains one of {*weather, whether*} which of the two should actually occur in the sentence. E.g., given the sentence I did not know weather to laugh or cry determine if weather should be replaced by whether. The function learned to perform this task may be fairly complicated; it could depend on a huge number of features such as words neighboring the target words in sentences, their syntactic tags, etc. [9]. Notice, however, that the same sentence could be supplied as input to a different function that predicts the part-of-speech (pos) of the word weather (and others) in this sentence. However, the *predictions* of these functions are not independent. For example, if the pos function determines, in a given context, that the target word is a noun, then the spelling function cannot determine that the correct spelling is whether. Other more intricate constraints exist with other functions that can receive this sentence as input. Consequently, perhaps, even though the data for problems of these sort typically reside in very high dimensional space (e.g., 10^3 to 10^6), one is able to achieve good classification performance (on test data) by looking at relatively few training examples; *very* few relative to what is expected by theory and is needed in simulations of synthetic data of this dimensionality. Similar phenomena exist when learning to detect faces or properties of faces (e.g., gender) in visual learning problems.

This exemplifies our notion of *coherency constraints*: given that these two functions need to produce coherent outputs, the input sentence may not take *any* possible value in the input space (that it could have taken when the function's learnability is studied in isolation) but rather may be restricted to a subset of the inputs on which the functions outcomes are coherent. In this paper we model these learning situations and develop a learning theory that attempts to explain these phenomena.

Notations: We consider the standard scenario of concept learning from examples. A learner is trying to identify a binary classifier $c : X \to \{0, 1\}$ when presented with examples (x, y), where instances $x \in X (= \Re^n)$ are drawn according to a fixed (but unknown) distribution on X and labeled $y = c(x)$. m denotes the number of training examples. $\mathcal{H}$ denotes the hypothesis space (the class of functions from which a hypothesis is selected), $|\mathcal{H}|$ is its cardinality and $h \in \mathcal{H}$ refers to the learned hypothesis.

While our goal is to learn a single target concept, $c : \Re^n \to \{0, 1\}$, we are interested in studying situations in which the learning scenario involves several concepts $c_1, c_2, \ldots, c_k$. We further assume that the concepts are subject to a *constraint* g ($g : X \times \{0,1\}^k \rightarrow \{0,1\}$) which is fixed (but could be probabilistic) and unknown to the learner. The constraint reflects the fact that all these functions represent different aspects of some natural data, as in the example above. We formalize this learning scenario and show that the mere existence of the other functions along with the constraints Nature imposes on the relations between these functions – all unknown to the learner – contribute to the effective simplification of the task of learning c_1.

The effect of constraints on the learning is analyzed by studying three models, with increased generality. We start by a pac analysis of the finite hypothesis class case, under coherency constraints. We then relax some of the assumptions and move to study constraints in the more general equivalence class framework. This allows us to develop a view of coherency as an equivalence relation on the hypothesis class. This view is beneficial in understanding conditions under which learning becomes easier and supports better generalization, even when the same hypothesis class is used. Finally, we develop a general VC-dimension view of coherency constraints. We show that these can be analyzed as a way to restrict the effective number of dichotomies and thus VC-dimensions techniques can be used to derive generalization bounds.

We also provide some examples that serve to motivate the framework and exemplify its power as well as some experimental evidence to its validity. In particular, we show that within this framework one can study and develop an understanding to several realistic learning situations such as highly biased training sets and low dimensional data embedded in high dimensional instance spaces.

2   Coherency Constraints

The usual way to constrain the learning task is to explicitly restrict the concept class. Instead, here we are concerned with the case in which the restriction is imposed implicitly via interaction among concepts. More precisely, we are interested in learning the concept c_1 in a situation that involves several concepts $c_1, c_2, \ldots, c_k$; $c_i : X \rightarrow \{0,1\}$, and a global constraint $g : X \times \{0,1\}^k \rightarrow \{0,1\}$ on the outcomes of these concepts.

The concept of coherency constraints has been formalized in [11] where it was shown that it can be used to explain the "easiness" and robustness of learning in some restricted situations. Several semantics for *coherency* were discussed there. The notion of *Class Coherency* was developed to indicate coherency at the level of the outcome of the classifiers; this turns out to be too restrictive in that it restricted the hypothesis class to include only functions which are coherent with each other over all samples. This notion was then relaxed to define *Distributional Coherency*. In this case the hypothesis space is not restricted; rather, the effect of distributional coherency is in disallowing some of the instances – those on which the constraints are not satisfied – to occur in the input. Results are given for the case of mistake bound learning of half spaces under specific constraints. It was also shown that learning concepts under this model results in hypothesis that are more robust to attribute noise. Similar ideas on robustness have also been discussed in [2,8].

The model studied in this paper builds on the distributional coherency model but extends it in several directions. First, we generalize it to general constraints; we extend it to a probabilistic setting and allow constraints to apply only with some probability; and, under these conditions we develop techniques to analyze general classifiers

Although we are interested in learning a single function c_1, in the following definition we will consider it along with the (possibly) constraining functions $c_2, \ldots c_k$, and denote $\bar{c} = (c_1, c_2, \ldots c_k)$. Thus the constraints in the following definition are imposed on the direct product $\mathcal{C}^k$. The semantics is that for each $\bar{c} \in \mathcal{C}^k$, we restrict the domain of $\bar{c}$ to X' where, with high probability, the constraint is satisfied; that is, $\forall x \in X', g(\bar{c}(x)) = 1$. Moreover, we allow g to depend on x (denoted g_x), so that the constraints can take a very general form.

Definition 1 (Distributional Coherency). *Let $\mathcal{C}$ be a class of functions $c : X \to \{0,1\}$, $g : X \times \{0,1\}^k \to \{0,1\}$ a Boolean constraint, and $\alpha \in [0,1]$ a constant. We define the class of g-coherent functions $\mathcal{C}_g^*$ to be the collection of all functions $\bar{c}^* : X \to \{0,1\}^k \cup \{\star\}$ in $\mathcal{C}^k$ defined by*

$$\bar{c}^*(x) = \begin{cases} \bar{c}(x) \ \textit{if } g_x(\bar{c}(x)) = 1 \\ \star \quad \textit{otherwise} \end{cases}$$

The value "$\star$" is interpreted as a forbidden value for the function $\bar{c}$. Thus we restrict the domain of $\bar{c}$ to the subset X' of X satisfying the constraint g.

The above definition restricts the set of functions we study. Equivalently, we can say that all functions can be studied, but the distribution of the data observed is restricted to respect the coherency constrains. This is made explicit in the following definition for coherency, the one used in the rest of the paper.

Definition 2. *The functions $\bar{c} = (c_1, c_2, \ldots c_k)$ are α-coherent if*

$$P\{x | g_x(c_1, c_2, \ldots c_k)\} = \alpha, \tag{1}$$

where P is the probability according to which instances in X are drawn.

In the pac learning model the above constraint can be interpreted as restricting the class of distributions when learning a function $c_1 \in \mathcal{C}$. Only distributions giving zero (or small, depending on α) weight to the region $X \setminus X'$ are allowed.

We note that this is different from the model of distribution specific learning (e.g., [3]). There, the learner is explicitly aware of the underlying distribution and can utilize it directly. Our model is based on assuming that this is unrealistic; instead, we assume a distribution free model in which the distribution could be constrained in intricate ways. The learner is unaware of this. However, as we show, under this model the learning problem nevertheless becomes easier and we can justify the generalization abilities of the learned hypothesis even in the presence of relatively small number of training examples.

3   PAC Analysis of Coherency Constraints

Consider the pac model [12] analysis for the admissible case when the hypothesis space is finite. That is, it is assumed that during the training phase one is provided with m training examples drawn independently according to P and labeled according to some target concept c_1. The learning algorithm chooses a hypothesis $h \in \mathcal{H}$ that is consistent with target function on the training data. In this setting [5] we know that for the true error of h (that is, $Pr_P(h(x) \neq c_1(x))$) to be bounded by ϵ with probability at least $1 - \delta$, the number of training examples required needs to be greater than

$$m \geq \frac{\ln|\mathcal{H}| + \ln\frac{1}{\delta}}{\epsilon}. \tag{2}$$

This analysis can be extended to the non admissible case (when the target function is not in $\mathcal{H}$) and the assumption on $|\mathcal{H}|$ being finite can be relaxed to a finite VC dimension. Eqn. 2 gives the relation between the true error and the sample complexity. On fixing the confidence (δ) and the hypothesis class ($\mathcal{H}$), the sample complexity is inversely proportional to the true error.

We prove next an analogous result that exhibits the effect of the coherency constraints. W.l.o.g we present it for the case $k = 2$. As above, our goal is to learn a hypothesis h that approximates c_1 ; the hypothesis is chosen such that it is consistent on m training examples with the target concept c_1 and thus, based on the above, (with confidence δ, which we fix for the rest of the discussion) it has a true error of ϵ_1. We now analyze the effect the presence of the coherency constraint has on h's performance. Before we do that, and in order to simplify the discussion that follows, we note that it is always possible to think about the coherency constraint as an *equality* constraint. The reason is that we can always replace c_2 by c_2' deterministically, via the graph of g. Namely, c_2' is defined so that when $g_x(c_1(x), c_2(x)) = 1$, $c_2'(x) = c_2(x)$ if $c_1(x) = c_2(x)$ and $c_2'(x) = \neg c_2(x)$ otherwise. When $g_x(c_1(x), c_2(x)) = 0$ we define c_2' exactly in the opposite way, yielding $\forall x, g_x(c_1, c_2) \equiv [c_1 \equiv c_2]$.

Assume the existence of a concept c_2, such that the learned hypothesis h has a true error of ϵ_2 w.r.t. c_2. Also, we assume that c_2 coheres with the target function c_1 via g, that is:

$$P\{x|g_x(c_1, c_2)\} = \alpha. \tag{3}$$

Consequently, we care about the performance of h only under these constraints. In the following discussion we assume that the outcomes of the concepts c_1, c_2 are independent given the outcome of the hypothesis h[1] In addition, we make the technical assumption that the labels of c_2 are symmetric with respect to h,

---

[1] Note that we assume that c_1, c_2 are independent *given* h; in fact, they may be very dependent. This is a reasonable assumption in many situations, e.g., those presented in Sec. 1. Specifically, this is the situation in cases that involve multiple classifiers (e.g., learning across modalities).

namely, we assume that[2] $Pr(c_2 = 0|h = 1) = Pr(c_2 = 1|h = 0)$. As shown in the next theorem, under these conditions, the hypothesis h learned to approximate c_1, actually achieves true error – relative to instances that are subject to coherency constraints – that is smaller than ϵ_1. Equivalently, in order to achieve true error of ϵ_1 one needs to train on less than the m examples of Eqn. 2.

Theorem 1. *Let c_1 be a target concept and h a learned hypothesis that has true error ϵ_1 relative to it, based on Eqn. 2. Assume that h has true error ϵ_2 with respect to c_2. Then, the true error of h with respect to c_1 on the data satisfying the constraint g (Eqn. 3,), and under the conditions given, is given by*

$$\epsilon = \frac{\epsilon_1\epsilon_2\alpha}{(1 - \epsilon_1)(1 - \epsilon_2) + \epsilon_1\epsilon_2} + \frac{\epsilon_1(1 - \epsilon_2)(1 - \alpha)}{\epsilon_1(1 - \epsilon_2) + (1 - \epsilon_1)\epsilon_2}. \tag{4}$$

The proof is given in Appendix 1. Note that

Lemma 1. $\forall\epsilon_1$, *if* $(\epsilon_2 - 0.5)(\alpha - (1 - \epsilon_1)(1 - \epsilon_2) + \epsilon_1\epsilon_2) < 0$ *then the bound on ϵ in Eqn. 4 satisfies $\epsilon < \epsilon_1$.*

The lemma simply means that for values of α which actually constraints the instances, $\epsilon < \epsilon_1$. The proof is by direct algebraic manipulation. Lemma. 1 and Thm. 1 together show that for coherency constrained data, the true error of h w.r.t. c_1 is lower than the true error in general. Equivalently, one can achieve the same generalization using a smaller number of training examples. This reduction in sample complexity depends on (1) the degree (α) of coherency and (2) the performance (ϵ_2) of (the g-map of) h on c_2. An important point to note is that we do not assume that the learning algorithm knows c_2. It is the mere existence of this concept, which makes the learning of c_1 easier. For the special case of a deterministic constraint, when $\alpha = 1$, the number of examples required for h to have a true error of ϵ_1 with respect to c_1 on the constrained data, is given by

$$m \geq \frac{\ln|\mathcal{H}| + \ln\frac{1}{\delta}}{\frac{\epsilon_1(1-\epsilon_2)}{\epsilon_1(1-\epsilon_2)+(1-\epsilon_1)\epsilon_2}} \tag{5}$$

It is straightforward to see that for $0 \leq \epsilon_2 < 0.5$, this is a better bound than the one given in Eqn. 2.

This case is similar to the one presented in [4]. They have introduced the concept of *co-training* and have shown that the presence of unlabeled data can help under some consistency assumptions. They consider the example of labeling web pages, and it is argued that in this case two independent concepts exist which provide consistent labels. Their example can be mapped to our framework which then provides the guarantees missing in [4]. What is further highlighted by our

---

[2] This can be relaxed; we can assume that these quantities are different and split the region measured by ϵ_2 above to two regions, one given $h = 1$ and the other given $h = 0$; then we can define, for the proof, that $Pr(h \neq c_2) = max\{Pr(c_2 = 0|h = 1), Pr(c_2 = 1|h = 0)\}$.

framework is the realization that the mere existence of the constraint makes the original learning problem easier (even without using it).

The importance of this sample complexity result is the following interpretation of it. The presence of constraints reduces the number of training examples needed in order to achieve a certain generalization performance, relative to a constraint-free scenario. Stated differently, it directly addresses one of our concerns in the introduction: in these situations, one can believe the results of the learned predictor even though it was learned using a small number of examples. This can also be thought of as the PAC analysis of the case discussed in [11].

4   Equivalence Class Analysis

In this section we relax one of the assumptions used in Sec. 3. Rather than assuming a finite hypothesis space we consider the more general case in which the hypothesis class is countably infinite and one assumes a probability distribution Q over it. For the standard learning model this case has been analyzed in [10] and others. Consider the following example.

Example 1 *Assume one is trying to learn a target function c_1 in the presence of c_2 and that c_2 coheres with with c_1 on the observed data. Let $\mathcal{H}$ be the class of monotone Boolean conjunctions over $\{0,1\}^n$ and assume that c_1, c_2 are also in $\mathcal{H}$. We can thus think of c_1, c_2 as elements in $\{0,1\}^n$ with the interpretation that $c_i(j) = 1$ iff the conjunction x_i contains the variable x_j (i=1,2; j=1,...n). Assume now that c_1 differs from c_2 on k bits. Given the coherency constraint then, for all observed instances $x \in \{0,1\}^n$, the corresponding k bits must be zero. As a result, all functions in $\mathcal{H}$ which differ only on these bits are equivalent for this learning problem. The size of the equivalence class will depend on the number of bits k on which c_1, c_2 differ.*

The assumptions made in the above example can be relaxed in several ways. In particular, we can assume coherency with high probability and can still get a similar result in terms of an equivalence class with high probability. Some of the examples in [11] can also be analyzed via the equivalence class view.

Assume that there is some probability distribution Q over the hypothesis space. An equivalence class over this hypothesis space would then mean that one can consider a smaller effective hypothesis space. Figure 1 shows the probability distribution over the hypothesis class. Figure 2 maps the equivalence class view over this hypothesis space. That is, all hypotheses belonging to an equivalence class are indistinguishable due to the presence of a constraint or, equivalently, due to a property of the data. The effective probability distribution assigns to the equivalence classes weights which are proportional to their size. Below we use the pac-Bayes framework to quantify this and show that this view indeed implies tighter generalization bounds.

We assume a countably infinite hypothesis class $\mathcal{H}$ with known probability distribution Q over it and study the effects of coherency constraints. Let $\mathcal{C}$ be the

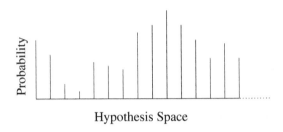

Fig. 1. Probability distribution over the hypothesis space

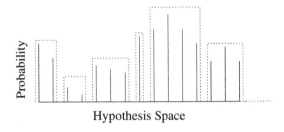

Fig. 2. Probability distribution over the hypothesis space. Dotted lines show the equivalence class, i.e. all the hypotheses that fall in one group of the dotted lines are indistinguishable on the given data and are assigned probability equivalent to the sum of the probabilities of their equivalence class.

class of hypotheses consistent with the data; $c \in C$. Using [10], the generalization error is bounded by

$$\epsilon(c) \leq \frac{\ln \frac{1}{Q(c)} + \ln \frac{1}{\delta}}{m}. \tag{6}$$

Let $\mathcal{H}_c \subseteq \mathcal{H}$, such that $\forall h \in \mathcal{H}_c$, the constraint is satisfied with high probability. We can think of $\mathcal{H}_c$ as the class of hypotheses that are representatives of the equivalence class, although the discussion that follows will apply to any projection (filtering) of the hypothesis class. We are interested in solving for $\epsilon(c|c \in \mathcal{H}_c)$, that is, the probability of a consistent hypothesis making an error given that it satisfies the constraints. To do that we need $Q(c \in C|c \in \mathcal{H}_c)$. (I.e., we restrict our learning algorithm to consider only those hypotheses which satisfy some constraints). This is a more general case than the one discussed in the previous section. As discussed in [11], the constraints have the effect of reducing the size of the hypotheses space and this is what is observed here too. We first compute the term $Q(c|c \in \mathcal{H}_c)$.

$$Q(c|c \in \mathcal{H}_c) = \frac{Q(c, c \in \mathcal{H}_c)}{Q(c \in \mathcal{H}_c)} = \frac{Q(c)Q(c \in \mathcal{H}_c|c)}{Q(\mathcal{H}_c)} = \frac{\gamma Q(c)}{Q(\mathcal{H}_c)}, \tag{7}$$

where γ is the probability that a consistent hypothesis belongs to the subset of the hypotheses class satisfying the constraint. This leads to the following Lemma:

Lemma 2.

$$\epsilon(c|c \in \mathcal{H}_c) \leq \frac{\ln \frac{1}{Q(c)} + \ln Q(\mathcal{H}_c) + \ln \frac{1}{\gamma} + \ln \frac{1}{\delta}}{m} \tag{8}$$

Note that here we are considering a weaker constraint; only with high probability a hypothesis consistent with the data satisfies the constraint. This can also be seen as modifying the probability distribution over the concept class which is governed by the presence of constraints.

5   VC-Dimension Based Bounds

In this section we consider the general case where the hypothesis class may contain infinite number of hypotheses. For the present analysis we will assume that the class has finite VC-dimension. We first introduce the basic principles of the VC theory and then develop related results under coherency constraints. Finally we discuss applications of these to some realistic learning scenario.

The VC-dimension based bounds can be intuitively viewed as extensions of the bounds for the case of finite hypothesis class (Sec. 3) only that the size of the hypothesis class is replaced by *annealed entropy*. The *annealed entropy* is a distribution dependent concept which is then bounded from above by a function of the VC-dimension (using Sauer's lemma) and thus gives distribution free bounds. The annealed entropy is given as

$$H_{ann} = \int \Delta^{\wedge}(x^1, x^2, ..., x^L) dF(\mathbf{x}) \tag{9}$$

where $\Delta^{\wedge}(x^1, x^2, ..., x^L)$ is the maximum number of dichotomies the sample $x^1, x^2, ..., x^L$ can have when using a given set of hypothesis. The integral is taken over all possible samples of size L thus giving the expected number of dichotomies that are possible for a given distribution over the data and a given hypothesis class. Given the annealed entropy, the bound on the generalization error is given by

$$P\{\sup_{\alpha \in \Lambda} |R(\alpha) - R_{emp}(\alpha)| > \epsilon\}$$
$$< 4exp\left\{\left(\frac{H_{ann}(2l)}{l} - \left(\epsilon - \frac{1}{l}\right)^2\right)l\right\}, \tag{10}$$

where $R(R_{emp})$ is the expected (empirical, resp.) risk associated with the target function α. The bound is developed in [14] (Theorem 4.1). It gives the explicit dependence of the true error bound on the annealed entropy. The smaller the annealed entropy, the tighter the bound is. This can also be thought of as the capacity of the hypothesis class as a function of the distribution over the data.

Indeed, this is a much better bound than the most commonly used VC-dimension bound. Consider a hypothesis class $\mathcal{H}$ which consists of all hyperplane in $\Re^n$, and assume that the distribution that governs the data generation supports only data points on the x-axis. For this case, while the VC-dimension of the hypothesis class is directly related to the dimensionality of the space $(n + 1)$ and is not effected by the distribution of the data, the annealed entropy of $\mathcal{H}$ is independent of the space in which the data lies, yielding a much better and more realistic bound. The VC-dimension can thus be thought of as a function of annealed entropy for the worst case probability distribution on the data. However, since, in general, computing the annealed entropy is not feasible, the VC-dimension bound is commonly used.

Next we show that one can use limited information on the data distribution to obtain the *effective annealed entropy*. Our goal is related in spirit to the one studied in [13]. While they give a method of calculating the effective VC-dimension given observed data we, instead, use similar techniques to bound the effective annealed entropy H_{ann}^{eff} within the coherency constraints framework.

5.1   A General Framework for Constraints

This section develops a general framework for modeling the effect of the constraints in terms of the effective annealed entropy; this can then be mapped to the effective VC-dimension of the data. Recall the coherency constraints definition (1). Denote

$$\Gamma_1 \subseteq \Gamma = \{x | g_x(\bar{c}) = 1\} \quad \Gamma_2 = \neg \Gamma_1. \tag{11}$$

This generalizes the discussion in Sec. 2. We assume that the constraint is satisfied only by a particular labeling of the data for Γ_1 instances, however, for the case when $x \in \Gamma_2$, data can take any label.

Eqn. 9 can be written in terms of Γ_1, Γ_2. The expected value is taken over the space of all samples. Since one is looking at the number of dichotomies that can be achieved for the given set of samples, this integral is over the L fold distribution. The annealed entropy can therefore be written as:

$$H_{ann} = \int_{\Gamma_1} \Delta^\wedge(x^1, ..., x^L) dF(\mathbf{x}) + \int_{\Gamma_2} \Delta^\wedge(x^1, ..., x^L) dF(\mathbf{x}) \tag{12}$$

Denote $P(x \in \Gamma_1) = \alpha$, the probability that a sample satisfies the constraint. The probability that not all the samples came from Γ_1 is $1 - \alpha^L$. When all the samples are from Γ_1, then only one labeling of samples is possible; otherwise a large number of dichotomies are possible. We get the following bound on the *effective* annealed entropy:

$$H_{ann} \leq H_{ann}^{eff} = (1 - \alpha^L) H_{ann}^\wedge, \tag{13}$$

where $H_{ann}^\wedge$ gives the maximum number of dichotomies of any set of L samples using the hypothesis from the given class. This bound gives a much smaller value of the effective annealed entropy for small values of L. However, for large values of L, α^L goes to zero as does the effect of constraints (in the formulation given). Thus, as the number of samples grow, the effect of the constraints as played in the simple argument above, on the generalization performance, goes down. To understand this, note that, intuitively, with infinite amount of data, if the constraints affect only a small portion of the instance space (α is small) the number of "observed" dichotomies will be almost as large as the number of possible dichotomies. However, the more interesting case might be that of small values of L, and of large α. Note that in the natural examples alluded to earlier in the paper, α is large. Also, this analysis is still very general and makes no assumptions on the structure of the constraints. Recall, for example, the case discussed at the beginning of this section, where all the instances lie on the x-axis. It would be desirable to exploit general structural constraints to explicitly bound the annealed entropy. These ideas are exemplified in two concrete cases.

5.2   Highly Biased Class Probability

In many realistic learning problems the probability of observing positive examples is very small relative to that of the negative examples. Consider the problem of face detection in Computer Vision. One may see only a few 10's of positive examples and may see millions of negative examples. Similar phenomena occurs in many natural language and information extraction learning situations. The considerations developed earlier can be used to show that the generalization performance in these cases is better than predicted by current theories. To show that, we will compute the effective annealed entropy.

Denote by α the probability of the positive class is α, $1 - \alpha$ is the probability of the negative class. Without loss of generality, we will assume that $\alpha \ll 1$. To model the highly biased class probability as a coherency constraint, one can think of the equality constrain $g(\bar{c})$ with c_1 as the target function and $c_2(x) \equiv 0$. And, we assume that this constraint holds with high probability $(1 - \alpha)$. Using the analysis given for Eqn. 13, we obtain:

Corollary 1. *Assume a highly biased class probability case, with the probability of the positive class being $\alpha \ll 1$. Then the effective annealed entropy for a data set of L samples is*

$$H_{ann}^{eff} \leq (1 - (1 - \alpha)^L) H_{ann}^{\wedge} \tag{14}$$

where H_{ann} is the annealed entropy (no assumptions).

For small values of L, we see that $H_{ann}^{eff} \ll H_{ann}^{\wedge}$. Although as $L \to \infty, H_{ann}^{eff} \to H_{ann}^{\wedge}$, we argue that the interesting case is when L is not too large, since,

$$\lim_{L \to \infty} \frac{H_{ann}^{\wedge}(L)}{L} \to 0 \tag{15}$$

(This is a simple consequence of uniform convergence as the number of samples observed approaches infinity.)

We note that in this case one can observe the effect of the constraints not only as a consequence of the smaller effective annealed entropy but also directly by looking more closely on the form of Chernoff bound. In general, the binary classification problem is modeled as the convergence of the observed frequencies, in a Bernoulli experiment with mean p, to the true frequencies. The standard formulation used for the bound is that of Hoeffding Bound:

$$P(S > (p + \epsilon)m) \leq e^{-2m\epsilon^2},$$

which gives a bound which is independent of p. However, an exact analysis of the Chernoff bound for the Bernoulli case results in the tighter bound:

Lemma 3.

$$P(S > (p+\epsilon)m) \le e^{-n(\epsilon+p)\log\frac{\epsilon+p}{p}-n(1-\epsilon-p)\log\frac{1-\epsilon-p}{1-p}} \qquad (16)$$

This can be easily verified using the standard definition of the Chernoff bound. Fig. 3(a) compares the standard bound given above to the tighter one given by Eqn. 16 as a function of the class probability. It is evident that the bound is significantly better for small values of p.

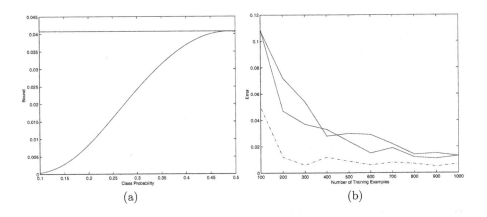

(a)   (b)

Fig. 3. (a) The dotted line gives the bound for the standard Chernoff bound; the solid line is the tighter version of the bound. (b) Learning Curve for the noiseless case. The dotted curve shows the learning case in the presence of the constraint and the solid lines show the learning curves of the individual classifiers in the absence of constraints.

5.3   Linear Mapping to Higher Dimensional Space

As a second example consider learning a linear classifier for a data lying in a high dimensional space (say M). Due to the high dimensionality it is very likely that the training data is linearly separable. In fact, in many natural language and visual learning problems the dimensionality is larger than the number of training instances. The basic question is to understand the generalization properties of the resulting classifier, given that it was learned based on a small number of examples relative to the dimensionality.

For simplicity, we assume that there exists a one-to-one mapping of the M dimensional data to a lower dimensional space, N, through a linear transformation. In this case, we show that the data is linearly separable in the N dimensional space. (E.g., think of a case in which the the data is originally in a lower dimensional space N but is being observed in a higher dimensional space.) and the generalization performance is thus governed by it. Notice that even in this case, the problem of recovering the transformation matrix and using it to map the data back to the lower dimensional space is intractable. However, our claim is that this is not necessary and learning in the high dimensional space does not require to see more data. To see that, let $x = (x_1, x_2, ..., x_M)$ be a training example and $h = (h_1, h_2, ..., h_M)$ the linear classifier in the higher dimensional space. Denote $z = (z_1, z_2, ..., z_N)$ the data point in the N dimensional space such that $x = Az$ where A is the (unknown) $M \times N$ transformation matrix. The outcome of the classifier is $y = h^t x$, which can also be written as

$$y = h^t x = h^t A z = (A^t h)^t z = (h')^t z$$

That is, there exists a linear classifier h' in the lower dimensional space that will achieve the same performance as h in the higher dimensional space. The idea is that one doesn't need to know either A or h'. This scenario is also directly representable in the coherency constraint framework, as in Def. 1. To do that, let $c_1 \equiv h$, the target function in the M dimensional space, $c_2 \equiv h' \circ A^{-1}$, and let the constraint be the equality constraint. Clearly, this simple scenario can be relaxed to the full generality of the definition, but the outcome is essentially the same. That is, there is no need to recover the transformation, but rather the fact that it exists implies that the generalization properties are as good as they could be in the lower dimensional case. The constraints can also be used directly to show that the VC-dimension in this case is actually $N + 1$ and not $M + 1$ as was originally thought.

Recent work on random projection also makes use of the same idea and a number of tighter bounds have been proposed [2,8]. As has been pointed in [11], coherency constraints may also imply increased margin when the classification is done using a linear hyperplane. Applying ideas from the theory of Random Projection, this implies that one can project the data to a lower dimension, without compromising the performance (with high probability). Our recent work [8] makes use of these ideas to develop tighter bounds by analyzing the data in this reduced space.

6   Experiments

We describe some preliminary experiments used to exhibit and evaluate the implications of the insights gained in this work. We considered the problem of learning a half space in the presence of another, constraining, half space. Specifically, data was sampled from an n dimensional space, but the (randomly chosen) classifiers c_1, c_2 actually depend only on $n/2$ dimensions: c_1 depends on $x_1, \ldots x_{n/2}$ and c_2 on $x_{n/2+1}, \ldots x_n$. We show learning curves for learning c_1 given data sampled uniformly from $\Re^n$, and also of learning c_1 when the data observed is filtered to satisfy the equality constraint, that is, for all input instances x, $c_1(x) = c_2(x)$. (For completeness we also show the curves for c_2.)

Figure 3(b) shows the learning rate, for the noise free case, with and without the constraints. We used data in $\Re^{24}$), and tested on 1000 examples. The curves give the errors as a function of the number of training examples; the solid curve – for the individual half-spaces and the dot-dash curve for learning in presence of the equality constraint.

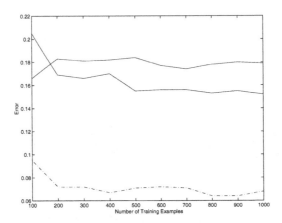

Fig. 4. Learning Curve for the noisy case. The dotted curve shows the learning case in the presence of the constraint and the solid lines show the learning curves of the individual classifiers in the absence of constraints.

Fig. 4 depicts the results of the same experiment for noisy data (this time, data lied in $\Re^{10}$). It is clearly evident from the learning curves shown that the classifier is able to learn much faster in the presence of the constraint. As we have pointed out throughout the paper, the learning algorithm is unaware of the existence of form of the constraints.

7   Conclusions

The power of existing models of learning [12,14] stems from the distribution-free nature of the model. The underlying assumption is that the probability distribution governing the occurrences of instances is too complex to model and a theory should be developed without making explicit assumptions on it. The resulting theories, however, cannot explain well a wide range of phenomena, in which learning can be done robustly from a relatively small number of examples.

In this work we have developed a learning model within which we attempt to explain these phenomena. The key observation underling this model is that, in many situations, learning problems do not occur in isolation. Our model is therefore concerned with learning scenarios where multiple learners co-exist but there are mutual coherency constraints on their outcomes. Within this model, we have developed generalization bounds and have shown that in the presence of coherency constraints the learning problem indeed becomes easier than predicted by the general theories. This could explain the ability to generalize well from a fairly small number of examples and can help in understanding several realistic learning situations.

While several works (e.g., [1]) have criticized the distribution free pac learning model as being too restrictive this work still pursues the distribution free approach (see discussion in Sec. 2). In some sense, our model can be viewed as an intermediate model between the worst case distribution free model that is commonly studied in learning theory and the simpler, but unrealistic, distribution specific model (in which one assumes a complete knowledge of the distribution, and can utilize it when learning). We assume, instead, a distribution free model in which the distribution could be constrained in natural, but intricate ways. The learner is unaware of this. This view opens up a number of questions; in particular, an interesting direction could be to understand generalization under specific families of constraints.

References

1. J. Amsterdam. Some philosophical problems with formal learning theory. In *National Conference on Artificial Intelligence*, pages 580–584, 1988.
2. R. I. Arriaga and S. Vempala. An algorithmic theory of learning: Robust concepts and random projection. In *Proc. of the 40th Foundations of Computer Science*, 1999.
3. G. Benedek and A. Itai. Learnability with respect to fixed distributions. *Theoret. Comput. Sci.*, 86(2):377–389, 1991.
4. A. Blum and T. Mitchell. Combining labeled and unlabeled data with co-training. In *Proc. of the Annual ACM Workshop on Computational Learning Theory*, pages 92–100, 1998.
5. A. Blumer, A. Ehrenfeucht, D. Haussler, and M. K. Warmuth. Occam's razor. *Information Processing Letters*, 24:377–380, April 1987.
6. C. Cortes and V. Vapnik. Support-vector networks. *Machine Learning*, 20:273–297, 1995.
7. H. Druker, R. Schapire, and P. Simard. Improving performance in neural networks using a boosting algorithm. In *Neural Information Processing Systems 5*, pages 42–49. Morgan Kaufmann, 1993.
8. A. Garg, S. Har-Peled, and D. Roth. Generalization bounds for linear learning algorithms. Technical Report UIUCDCS-R-2001-2232, University of Illinois at Urbana Champaign, June 2001.
9. A. R. Golding and D. Roth. A Winnow based approach to context-sensitive spelling correction. *Machine Learning*, 34(1-3):107–130, 1999. Special Issue on Machine Learning and Natural Language.
10. D. A. McAllester. Some PAC-Bayesian theorems. *Machine Learning*, 37(3):355–363, 1999.
11. D. Roth and D. Zelenko. Towards a theory of coherent concepts. In *National Conference on Artificial Intelligence*, pages 639–644, 2000.
12. L. G. Valiant. A theory of the learnable. *Communications of the ACM*, 27(11):1134–1142, November 1984.
13. V. Vapnik, E. Levin, and Y. Le Cun. Measuring the VC-dimension of a learning machine. *Neural Computation*, 6(5):851–876, 1994.
14. V. N. Vapnik. *Statistical Learning Theory*. John-Wiley and Sons Inc., New York, 1998.

8   Appendix

Proof (Proof of Thm. 1). Given the discussion, before the beginning of the theorem, it is sufficient to prove the theorem for the case of g being the equality constraint. We denote by G the constraint set. I.e. $x \in G$ implies that the sample x follows the constraint. Also denote $C = \{x|c_1(x) = c_2(x)\}$ and $\neg C$ its compliment. Similarly $H_c^i = \{x|h(x) = c_i(x)\}$.

The true error of h w.r.t. c_1 on a sample satisfying the constraint is given by

$$
\begin{aligned}
P(h(x) \neq c_1(x)|x \in G) &= P(\neg H_c^1|x \in G) = P(\neg H_c^1, C|x \in G) + P(\neg H_c^1, \neg C|x \in G) \\
&= P(\neg H_c^1|C, x \in G)P(C|x \in G) + P(\neg H_c^1|\neg C, x \in G)P(\neg C|x \in G) \\
&= P(\neg H_c^1|C)P(C|x \in G) + P(\neg H_c^1)|\neg C)P(\neg C|x \in G) \\
&= \frac{P(\neg H_c^1, C)\alpha}{P(C)} + \frac{P(\neg H_c^1, C)(1-\alpha)}{P(\neg C)} \\
&= \frac{P(\neg H_c^1, \neg H_c^2)\alpha}{P(C)} + \frac{P(\neg H_c^1, H_c^2)(1-\alpha)}{P(\neg C)} \\
&= \frac{\epsilon_1\epsilon_2\alpha}{(1-\epsilon_1)(1-\epsilon_2) + \epsilon_1\epsilon_2} + \frac{\epsilon_1(1-\epsilon_2)(1-\alpha)}{(1-\epsilon_1)\epsilon_2 + \epsilon_1(1-\epsilon_2)} \equiv \epsilon
\end{aligned}
$$

The fourth equality follows from the fact that conditioned upon the C or $\neg C$, whether $h(x)$ agrees with $c_1(x)$ or not is independent of whether $x \in G$. The reason is that the effect of the constraint is simply in determining the probability of C. The sixth equality is due to set equality (e.g., $\neg H_c^1 \cap C = \neg H_c^1 \cap \neg H_c^2$). The seventh equality uses the fact that decisions made by concepts c_1, c_2, are independent of each other given h. To see it more specifically, one has to go through a series of probabilistic inequalities. Let H refers to the set of all x, such that $h(x) = 1$ and $\neg H$ refers to the set of x such that $h(x) = 0$.

$$
\begin{aligned}
P(\neg H_c^1, \neg H_c^2) &= \\
&= P(c_1(x) \neq h(x), c_2(x) \neq h(x)|H)P(H) + P(c_1(x) \neq h(x), c_2(x) \neq h(x)|\neg H)P(\neg H) \\
&= P(c_1(x) \neq h(x)|H)P(c_2(x) \neq h(x)|H)P(H) + P(c_1(x) \neq h(x)|\neg H))P(c_2(x) \neq h(x)|\neg H)P(\neg H) \\
&= P(c_2(x) \neq h(x)|H)\{P(c_1(x) \neq h(x)|H)P(H) + P(c_1(x) \neq h(x)|\neg H)P(\neg H)\} \\
&= \epsilon_1\epsilon_2
\end{aligned}
$$

Where we have used the fact that c_2 is a symmetric concept with respect to h (i.e. $P(c_2(x) = 1|h(x) = 0) = P(c_2(x) = 0|h(x) = 1)$,) which means that one can write $P(c_2(x) = 1|h(x) = 0) = \epsilon_2$. Using the same argument, one can derive the other two term $P(C)$ and the term $P(\neg H_c^1, H_c^2)$. The analysis of the latter follows exactly the same step as given above. In case of analysis of $P(c)$, one can write it as a summation of four terms (two conditioned upon $h(x) = 1$ and other two conditioned upon $h(x) = 0$) and can then follow the same argument as above. We have also used the fact that $P(x : c_1(x) = c_2(x)|x \in G) = \alpha$ (Eqn. 3). This proves the theorem.

Learning Intermediate Concepts

(Extended Abstract)

Stephen S. Kwek

Division of Computer Science
University of Texas at San Antonio
San Antonio, TX 78249
kwek@cs.utsa.edu
http://www.eecs.wsu.edu/~kwek

Abstract. In most concept learning problems considered so far by the learning theory community, the instances are labeled by a single unknown target. However, in some situations, although the target concept may be quite complex when expressed as a function of the attribute values of the instance, it may have a simple relationship with some intermediate (yet to be learned) concepts. In such cases, it may be advantageous to learn both these intermediate concepts and the target concept in parallel, and use the intermediate concepts to enhance our approximation of the target concept.

In this paper, we consider the problem of learning multiple interrelated concepts simultaneously. To avoid stability problem, we assume that the dependency relations among the concepts are not cyclical and hence can be expressed using a directed acyclic graph (not known to the learner). We investigate this learning problem in various popular theoretical models: mistake bound model, exact learning model and probably approximately correct (PAC) model.

Keywords: multiple concepts, mistake bound algorithm, exact learning, PAC learning, membership queries

1 Motivation

In a typical concept learning problem, an instance $x = \langle x_1, ..., x_n \rangle$ is classified according to a single unknown target concept f. The learner's task is to find a good hypothesis h that approximates f. In some practical situations, the target concept may be very complex when expressed as a function of only the attribute values of the instance. However, it may be expressible in a simpler form using some intermediate concepts in addition to the attributes of the instance.

As a pedagogical example, suppose you want to predict tomorrow's perceived temperature, which can be different from the air temperature depending on tomorrow's humidity, wind and other factors. However, you can only measure the current weather indicators. It may be difficult to predict the perceived temperature directly from these indicators as they may bear a complex relationship with

N. Abe, R. Khardon, and T. Zeugmann (Eds.): ALT 2001, LNAI 2225, pp. 151–166, 2001.

the future perceived temperature. However, the prediction task may be made easier if we were to learn to predict tomorrow's humidity, wind pattern and other factors (which may have a simpler relationship with the current weather indicators), and then use them to predict tomorrow's perceived temperature. In such scenario, it may be advantages to also learn the intermediate concepts (various weather indicators) and use these intermediate predictions to enhance our approximation of the target concept (perceived temperature). Similarly, it may be easier to predict humidity level if we can also learn to predict wind speed and direction, air pressure and other indicators.

Another example found in [Car98] is the problem of predicting mortality risk from diseases like pneumonia. The goal here is to identify patients accurately and economically so as to decide whether they need to be hospitalized to receive aggressive treatment. Note that the goal is not to diagnose pneumonia as the diagnosis has already been made. Here, we (or rather the Home Managed Care Organization) are interested in determining how much risk the illness poses to the patient and whether the cost of aggressive treatment is necessary. Unfortunately, the task is made complicated by the fact that many of the useful but expansive tests (like white blood cell count, Hematocrit test, Potassium count, etc) for predicting pneumonia risk are performed only after one is hospitalized. It would be more cost effective if we can separate the low-risk patients from the moderate and high-risk patients through the cheaper measurements (like age, sex, diabetic, asthmatic, chest pain, wheezing, blood pressure, temperature, hear murmur, etc) made prior to admission to hospital. One possible way of enhancing pneumonia mortality rate prediction is to approximate the expansive test results using the initial low-cost measurements, and then learns how mortality rate depends on both test results and initial measurements. Further plausible applications in the medical and image processing domains can also be found in [Car96,CPT97, Car98,DHB95,SK90,SH91].

In this paper, we study how to exploit these intermediately related concepts to enhance prediction accuracy. Although the problem of learning multiple related concepts simultaneously has not been well investigated in the learning theory community, the problem has been extensively studied empirically in the neural network community [Car96,CPT97,Car98,DHB95,SK90,SH91]. Instead of having a neural net with a single output node learning a single concept, these empirical studies showed that better results can be achieved by having a neural net with multiple output nodes each trying to learn a different, but closely related, concept. Subsequently, Baxter [Bax95,Bax97] provided theoretical justifications of this phenomenon. The main theme for this type of research is that by learning multiple closely related concepts simultaneously, the learner is better at constructing useful features (the activation functions of the hidden notes). The difference of our work here is that these earlier results did not assume that there is a dependency relationship among the concepts. Further, in our case, we assume the values of the interrelated concepts are specified in the label.

2   The Intermediate Concepts Learning Model

To make the learning problem more general and easier to analyze, we assume that the learner's task is to learn a collection of concepts $\mathcal{F} = \{f_1, ..., f_k\}$, instead of a single target concept. As in standard concept learning, we assume that each concept in $\mathcal{F}$ comes from a given concept class C. Further, we assume that each concept in $\mathcal{F}$ may depend on the other concepts in $\mathcal{F}$, in addition to the attributes. To avoid circular dependency, we also assume that there is a linear ordering $f_{j_1}, ..., f_{j_k}$ of $\mathcal{F}$ such that each concept f_{j_i} is defined by the attributes $X = \{x_1, ..., x_n\}$ of the instance and $\mathcal{F} = \{f_{j_1}(x), ..., f_{j_{i-1}}(x)\}$, but not $\{f_{j_{i+1}}(x), ..., f_{j_k}(x)\}$. However, the learner does not know which are the intermediate concepts in $\mathcal{F}$ that each f_i is dependent on. In other words, the learner does not know the (linear) ordering $f_{j_1}, ..., f_{j_k}$.

Often a concept class that is not very expressive can be used to represent complex concept via this notion of intermediate concepts. For example, a DNF formula can be viewed as a disjunction of some intermediate concepts where each intermediate concept is a conjunction of some attributes of the instance. In our learning setting, we are learning the class of disjunctions union conjunctions. Here, we are assuming that the label of an instance x contains the values of the individual terms in addition to the value of the target DNF. Therefore, although Theorem 2 (see Section 3) implies that disjunctions union conjunctions can be learned efficiently (in the mistake bound model), it does not mean that DNF can be learned efficiently. Theorem 7, 8 and 9 provide further examples of how a complex concept can be represented as a simple concept using a collection of intermediate concepts.

In this model, the intermediate concepts are treated as Boolean values in those concepts that they affect. That is, in measuring the complexity (i.e. length) of a concept represented in terms of both attributes and intermediate concepts, we do not expand the representations of the intermediate concepts. The latter would defeat the motivation of this paper. Further, we assume that the intermediate concepts are somewhat 'related'[1], which in practice entails that the size of $\mathcal{F}$ is polynomially bounded by the number of base attributes X.

The relationship among the concepts can be described by a *dependency DAG* $G(X, \mathcal{F})$ where the nodes are labeled using $X \cup \mathcal{F}$ where X is the set of attributes $\{x_1, ..., x_n\}$. There is an arc $\langle a, b \rangle, a \in X \cup \mathcal{F}, b \in \mathcal{F}$ in $G(X, \mathcal{F})$ if and only if the value of b is directly dependent on a. Clearly, the graph does not contain any cycle due to the ordering of $\mathcal{F}$. The *depth* of G is the length of the longest directed path in $G(X, \mathcal{F})$. The *level* $l(f_i)$ of a function f_i is the length of the longest directed path in $G(X, \mathcal{F})$ that ends in f_i. Although in practice, a learner is typically interested in learning a subset of $\mathcal{F}$, for the sake of simplicity, we assume that the learner is interested in learning all the functions in $\mathcal{F}$. We consider this *intermediate concepts learning* (ICL) problem under various popular concept learning process.

---

[1] The notion of relatedness is somewhat subjective. For further discussion on this issue, we refer the reader to Caruana [Car98].

Littlestone's [Lit88] mistake bound process: In this process, learning proceeds in a sequence of trials. In each trial, the learner is given an instance $x = \langle x_1, ..., x_n \rangle$ in each trial. The learner's task is to predict the classification of x, according to some target function f in a given concept class C. In return, the learner receives a feedback on whether the prediction is a mistake. For the intermediate concepts learning problem, instead of predicting a single concept, the learner has to predict the values of all the functions in $\mathcal{F}$ on x. The objective is to make as few mistakes as possible in any, possibly infinite, sequence of trials. When some of the intermediate predictions are wrong in a trial, we count it as one mistake (not multiple mistakes).

Valiant's [Val84] probably approximately correct (PAC) process: In the single target concept version of the PAC model, the learner's goal is to infer an unknown target concept c from some class of concepts C. To obtain information about c, the learning algorithm is provided access to labeled (positive and negative) examples of c, drawn randomly according to some unknown probability distribution D over the instance space X. The learner is also given two parameters ϵ and δ as input. The learner's goal is to output, with probability at least $1 - \delta$, the description of a concept c' that has probability at most ϵ of disagreeing with c on a randomly drawn example from D (thus, c' has *error* at most ϵ). If such a learning algorithm A exists (that is, an algorithm A meeting the goal for any target concept c, any target distribution D and any $\epsilon, \delta > 0$), we say that C is *PAC-learnable*. We say that a PAC learning algorithm is a *polynomial-time* (or *efficient*) algorithm if the number of examples drawn and computation time are polynomial in n, $1/\epsilon$, $1/\delta$, and perhaps other natural parameters.

We extend the standard PAC model to the ICL environment by requiring the learner to output with probability at least $1 - \delta$, a set of hypothesis $\{h_1, ..., h_k\}$ such that the probability that for all i, the probability that at least one of the hypotheses h_i disagrees with f_i on a randomly drawn example from D is at most ϵ.

Angluin's [Ang88] exact learning process: Here, the learner is given access to some oracles and the learner's task is to exactly identify the target concept f. The two most commonly used oracles are equivalence and membership query oracles. In a single concept learning environment, an *equivalence query oracle* takes a hypothesis h from some hypothesis class H as input. If h is not equivalent to f, then it returns a labeled counterexample which h and f classify differently, otherwise it returns yes. If the hypothesis class H and the concept class C are the same then the equivalence query oracle is said to be *proper*, and *improper* otherwise. A *membership query oracle* takes an arbitrary instance x of the learner's choosing as input and returns its classification $f(x)$. A concept class is said to be efficiently learnable in the exact model with the given oracles if the target concept can be identified in time (and hence the number of queries posed) polynomial in n, the size of the target concept and possibly other natural parameters. For the ICL problem, the learner is supposed to identify all the concepts in $\mathcal{F}$.

Here, a membership query oracle takes an instance x as input and returns $\langle f_1(x), \cdots, f_k(x) \rangle$.

In the above adaptations of the traditional models, we count multiple errors in predicting $f_1(x), ..., f_k(x)$ as one error for the sake of making the analysis simple. Some of the bounds obtained in this paper also apply when we do not count these errors as a single error but multiple errors. Since single concept learning is a restricted case of multiple concepts learning, we have the following trivial observation.

Observation 1 *Efficient learning of intermediate concepts in a concept class C simultaneously implies efficient learning of C in the standard single concept learning setting.*

The main theme of this paper is to show that the converse of Observation 1 holds for the three models when membership queries are not allowed. However, Theorem 7, 8 and 9 in Section 4 show that the converse may not be true when membership queries are allowed. Some ideas from this theoretical research have been implemented and studied empirically using synthetic data. The results seem to be promising. We plan to run our experiments on other standard benchmark data sets and applications found in [Car96,CPT97,Car98,DHB95,SK90,SH91]. Another plan is to adapt our algorithms to deal with missing attribute values and perform experiments on UC Irvine database.

3   Efficient Algorithms for Mistake Bound Learning

For the online mistake bound model, we have the following results.

Theorem 2. *Suppose there is an online algorithm A that learns a single target concept from some concept class C using some monotone hypothesis class C with mistake bound M. Then there is an algorithm that learns multiple intermediate concepts $\mathcal{F} = \{f_1, ..., f_k\} \subset C$ with mistake bound kM.*

Proof: The learner runs one copy of A, denote here as A_i, to learn each function f_i in $\mathcal{F}$. We denote the hypothesis maintained by A_i by h_i. The learner assumes that $f_i(x)$ depends on $X \cup \mathcal{F}(x) \backslash \{f_i(x)\}$.

To make a classification on an instance $x = \langle x_1, ..., x_n \rangle$, we assume initially that each $f_i(x)$ is '0'. To avoid confusion with the actual value of $f_i(x)$, let us denote this assumed value as y_i. With these assumed values, if each $h_i(x_1, ..., x_n, y_1, ..., y_k)$ is the same as its corresponding assumed value y_i, then the learner stops and predicts $h_i(x_1, ..., x_n, y_1, ..., y_k), i = 1, ..., k$. Otherwise, the learner update y_i to $h_i(x_1, ..., x_n, y_1, ..., y_k)$, and continue to attempt to make its classification. Note that since the concept is monotone, y_i can only flip from '0' to '1', but not vice versa. Thus, the learner needs at most k iterations for the output to stabilize and output its prediction.

If the learner makes a mistake, it will receive the correct labeling $\langle f_1(x),$ ..., $f_k(x)\rangle$ of x. The learner updates its hypotheses by checking for each h_i, if $h_i(x_1, ..., x_n, f_1(x), ..., f_k(x)) = f_i(x)$. If not, then we feed $\langle x_1, ..., x_n, f_1(x), ..., f_k(x)\rangle$ as a counterexample to $\mathcal{A}_i$ which will then update the hypothesis h_i. (Note that none of the $\mathcal{A}_i$ will receive a wrong counterexample.)

Suppose there is at least one hypothesis that makes a false positive mistake. Then among all such hypotheses, the one that makes the false positive prediction in the earliest iteration will surely be updated. This is because the target functions are monotone, and the other false-positive mistakes do not affect this particular false positive prediction (since they are made in later iterations). Similarly, if the mistakes are all false negative mistakes then due to monotonicity, all the hypotheses that make mistake will get updated. Note that the mistake bound in Theorem 2 can be lowered further by repeatedly classifying x and performing the above update, until all the predictions $h_1(x), ..., h_k(x)$ are correct.   □

Unfortunately, the proof does not apply when the hypothesis class is not monotone. For non-monotone hypothesis classes, we have the following corresponding theorem where the mistake bound also depends on the depth of the dependency DAG.

Theorem 3. *Suppose there is an online algorithm $\mathcal{A}$ that learns a single target concept from some concept class C with mistake bound M. Further, suppose the depth of the dependency DAG is d. Then there is an algorithm that learns multiple concepts $\mathcal{F} = \{f_1, ..., f_k\} \subset C$ with number of mistakes bounded by $k^2 dM$. Note that we do not require that the hypothesis class and concept class to be the same.*

Proof: The learner runs one copy of $\mathcal{A}$, call it $\mathcal{A}_i$, to learn each function f_i. (See Figure 1.) Initially, $\mathcal{A}_i$ makes an initial guess l_i of the actual level $l(f_i)$ to be 1. That is, the functions only depend on the variables X. When the number of mistakes made by $\mathcal{A}_i$ exceeds M, then we rerun $\mathcal{A}_i$, setting the mistake count to 0 and increment l_i by one at the same time.

Suppose a mistake is made on $f_i(x)$. If we predict all those values $f_j(x)$ with $l_j < l_i$ correctly then we feed x as a counterexample to $\mathcal{A}_i$ so that its hypothesis can be updated. Otherwise, we do not update the hypothesis maintained by $\mathcal{A}_i$. Intuitively, we are changing the cost of the mistake made to some function at lower level. Further, if f_i is at level l and there is another function f_j whose level is incremented from $l - 1$ to l, then f_j may be irrelevant to f_i. The hypothesis h_i constructed by $\mathcal{A}_i$ may contain f_j as a relevant variable and we will have to discard h_i and rerun $\mathcal{A}_i$. This is because we may not able to evaluate $f_i(x)$ without knowing $f_j(x)$ which is currently at the same level.

Our estimate of $l(f_i)$, will not exceed the actual $l(f_i)$. This can be proven easily by induction on the $l(f_i)$. This is clearly true if $l(f^i) = 1$ in which case, we are simply learning a concept with domain X. For $l(f_i) > 1$, we simply note that once l_i reaches $l(f_i)$, all the estimates of the levels of the relevant intermediate concepts of f_i^+ are lower than l_i. Hence, at this stage, the values of

---

initialize:
    for $i \in \{1, \cdots, k\}$
      $l_i := 1$
      run a copy $\mathcal{A}_i$ of $\mathcal{A}$
      initialize the hypothesis h_i in $\mathcal{A}_i$
      set mistake count for h_i, $m_i := 0$

predict $x = \langle x_1, \cdots, x_n \rangle$:
    $relevant_0 := X$
    for $l := 1$ to d
      $relevant_l := relevant_{l-1}$
      for each h_i such that $l_i = l$
        predict $f_i(x) = h_i(relevant_{l-1})$
        $relevant_l := relevant_l \cup \{f_i(x)\}$

update:
    find the smallest l s.t. $\exists h_i$ where $l = l_i$ and $f_i(x) \neq h_i(relevant_{l-1})$
    for all h_i where $l = l_i$ and $f_i(x) \neq h_i(relevant_{l-1})$ **do**
      feed $\langle x_1, \cdots, x_n, f_1(x), \cdots f_k(x) \rangle$ as counterexample to $\mathcal{A}_i$
      $m_i := m_i + 1$
      if $m_i > M$
        restart $\mathcal{A}_i$ with $m_i := 0$
        $l_i := l_i + 1$
    for all h_j s.t. $l_j = l + 1$, restart $\mathcal{A}_j$ with $m_j = 0$.

Fig. 1. Transforming a single concept learning algorithm to one that learns multiple intermediate concepts

these relevant intermediate concepts in a counterexample fed to $\mathcal{A}_i$ are correct. Thus, the counterexamples are all valid and we make at most M mistakes. The number of mistakes made by $\mathcal{A}_i$ when the estimate of $l(f_i)$ remains at some value smaller than $l(f_i)$ is at most kM. Thus, the total number of counterexamples needed to learn a single concept is kdM. Therefore, the total number of mistakes made is bounded by $k^2 dM$.   □

Clearly, the algorithm in Theorem 3 is not very efficient as we need to rerun $\mathcal{A}_i$ each time a function moves to the same level as f_i. We show in the following theorem that for the class of decision lists, this need not be necessary. A decision list is a linearly ordered sequence of nodes $\langle \langle l_1, \alpha_1 \rangle, ..., \langle l_s, \alpha_s \rangle \rangle$ where the l_is are literals and $\alpha_i \in \{+, -\}$. To predict the classification of an unlabeled instance x, we traverse the list from the front until we reached a literal l_i which is evaluated to true, and predict the label of x as α_i. If none of the literals in the list is evaluated to true, then x is labeled using some default label.

Theorem 4. *The class of decision lists can be learned exactly in the ICL setting by making at most*

$$dk2(n + k)^2$$

equivalence queries. Here, $|f_i|$ is the length of the decision list f_i, and d is the depth of the decision DAG.

Proof: We begin by reviewing Rivest's algorithm for learning a single decision list [Riv87] with μ variables. Rivest's algorithm maintains an ordered collection of decision sublists $h = \langle \mathcal{L}_1, ..., \mathcal{L}_\mu, false \rangle$. The actual hypothesis is obtained by concatenating the sublists into a decision list. Initially, $\mathcal{L}_1$ is a list that contains all the 2μ possible nodes while the rest of the sublists are empty (i.e. false). When a prediction mistake is made by a node, say in sublist $\mathcal{L}_i$, then the node is moved to the end of the sublist $\mathcal{L}_{i+1}$. It is trivial to show that if the target decision list is of length l then the number of mistakes made is at most $l2\mu$. Note that since the learner does not know l and thus can only be sure that the learning is complete after making $2\mu^2$ mistakes.

The proof is a very simple modification of the the algorithm described in Theorem 3. We use Rivest's decision lists learning algorithm [Riv87] as the base learning algorithm in the proof of Theorem 3. However, we do not need to restart $\mathcal{A}_i$ when there is a function f_j that moves to the same level as f_i. Instead, we simply remove the four nodes with label f_j or $\overline{f_j}$ from our hypothesis of f_i. This new hypothesis is the same one as if the learner was told beforehand that f_j does not affect f_i and encounter the sequence of trials obtained from the original sequence of trials by ignoring those trials that the learner made a wrong prediction using one of these four nodes. This is because a node is moved from sublist $\mathcal{L}_i$ to sublist $\mathcal{L}_{i+1}$ in the original learning process if and only if it is moved from sublist $\mathcal{L}_i$ to sublist $\mathcal{L}_{i+1}$ in the latter scenario.

As the learner does not need to restart $\mathcal{A}_i$, the bound obtained in Theorem 3 can be trimmed by a factor of k.   □

We show in the following that for the concept class of conjunctions union disjunctions, we do not even need to restart $\mathcal{A}_i$ whenever f_i moves one level up. Clearly, if the class is simply disjunctions (or conjunctions), then we can treat each function in $\mathcal{F}$ as a disjunction (conjunction) and learn $\mathcal{F}$ individually. However, with disjunctions union conjunctions, the functions in $\mathcal{F}$ become Boolean circuits with and-or gates, which are difficult to learn individually.

For each function f_i, either f_i or $\overline{f_i}$ is a disjunction. We maintain a pair of disjunctions h_i^+ and h_i^- as our hypotheses of f_i and $\overline{f_i}$. That is, $h_i^+(x) = +$ signifies that we should classify x as positive, while $h_i^-(x) = +$ means we should classify x as negative. Initially, both h_i^+ and h_i^- are disjunctions of all the literals formed by X (but none of $\mathcal{F}$) and are assigned a level of 1. Each h_i^+ (h_i^-) maintains a list of forbidden functions, initially empty, that are the subset of $\mathcal{F}$ which we are sure do not appear in f_i. We predict $f_i(x)$ using the pair $\langle h_i^+, h_i^- \rangle$ and update $\langle h_i^+, h_i^- \rangle$ according to the following two cases.

Case 1: if $h_i^+(x) = -$ and $h_i^-(x) = -$. We predict according to the hypothesis that has the smallest mistake count. Regardless of whether our guess is correct, we keep incrementing the estimate of $l(f^i)$ (and hence the levels of h_i^+ and h_i^-) until there is some function f_j at one level lower that is not in the forbidden list. We add the these functions and their negations as literals to both h_i^- and h_i^+. We call the literals formed by $\mathcal{F}$ or their negations, *functional literals*.

Case 2: Either $h_i^+(x) = +$ or $h^-(x) = +$. We make our prediction according to which of $h_i^+(x)$ and $h_i^-(x)$ is "+". When both of them predict "+", we pick the one with the smallest mistake count. Suppose we make a mistake. Say we predict "+"(i.e. $h_i^+(x) = +$.) In this case, we remove from h_i^+ all the literals, including functional literals, that agree with $\langle x, f_1(x), ..., f_k(x) \rangle$. We then add to the h_i^+'s forbidden list those functional literals that are set to true.

Theorem 5. *Suppose the target functions $\mathcal{F}$ is a set of k conjunctions or disjunctions with the dependency graph having depth d. Then $\mathcal{F}$ can be learned exactly by making at most $2k(2(n + k) + d)$ mistakes or equivalence queries.*

Proof Sketch: Let us consider an arbitrary function f_i in $\mathcal{F}$. Without lost of generality, assume that f_i is a disjunction and not a conjunction (otherwise, the same argument holds if we assume that we are learning $\overline{f_i}$, which is a disjunction.) We have the following straightforward facts.

Fact 1: Any relevant attribute from X that appears in f_i will not be removed from h_i^+.

Fact 2: An intermediate concept (or its negation) that appears in the forbidden list of h_i^+ definitely does not appear in f_i.

Fact 3: When a Case 2 mistake is made, at least one literal in X is eliminated or one functional literal is added to the forbidden list.

Fact 4: The level of $\langle h_i^+, h_i^- \rangle$, i.e., our estimate of $l(f_i)$, will not exceed the actual $l(f_i)$. This can be proved easily by induction on $l(f_i)$. This is clearly true if $l(f^i) = 1$ in which case, we are simply learning a disjunction over the attributes X. For $l(f_i) > 1$, we simply note that once l_i reaches $l(f_i)$, all the estimates of the levels of the relevant intermediate concepts of f_i^+ are lower than l_i and hence will appear as literals in f_i^+.

Fact 4 implies that in learning f_i^+, Case 1 update is performed at most $l(f_i)$ times. Facts 1, 2 and 3 imply that after at most $2(n + k)$ Case 2 updates, f_i^+ is exactly determined. Thus, the number of mistakes made by predicting according to h_i^+ is at most $2(n + k) + d$. Further, once the number of mistakes made by predicting wrongly according to h_i^- exceeds $2(n + k) + d$, the future predictions of h_i^+ precede those of h_i^-. Thus, the number of mistakes made in predicting $f_i(x)$ is at most $2k(2(n + k) + d)$. □

4 Exact Learning

We show in Section 3 that learning results in the mistake bound can be translated to our ICL model. Since an online algorithm with mistake bound M is essentially equivalent to an exact learning algorithm using $M + 1$ (possibly improper) equivalence queries, we have the following corollary.

Observation 6 *The results presented in Section 3 holds for the intermediate concepts exact learning model with a (possibly improper) equivalence query oracle.*

However, it is not clear whether efficient learning algorithms that make use of membership queries can be translated to efficient algorithms in the ICL settings. The difficulty here is that we have no control over the values of the intermediate target functions on an instance. That is, values of the attributes X of an instance completely determine the values of $\mathcal{F}$. This prevents the learner from posing an arbitrary membership queries on instance where not only all the attribute values are specified, but all the function values, except one, are also specified. This is because the specified function values may not be the same as the actual function values determined by the attributes.

Even for the fundamental algorithm of Angluin for learning monotone DNFs, it is not clear how we can translate it to learn multiple monotone DNFs. One immediate observation is that each function in $\mathcal{F}$ can be expressed as a monotone DNFs over X only. It seems that we can simply learn each function as a monotone DNF over X without regard to the intermediate concepts. However, the representation size may be exponential in the size of the representation using both X and $\mathcal{F}$. For example, consider $|X| = (k-1)m$. Suppose $\forall i \in \{1, ..k-1\}$, $f_i = x_{(i-1)m+1} \vee ... \vee x_{im}$ and $f_k = f_1 \wedge ... \wedge f_{k-1}$ then the DNF representation of f_k using only X has m^{k-1} terms!

In the presence of equivalence and membership query oracles, *unate DNFs* (where each attribute does not appear as both positive literal and negative literal in the target DNF) [AHK93], *horn DNFs* (where each term can have at most one negated literal) [AFP92], *read-once formulas* (where each variable appears exactly once) [AHK93] and ordered binary decision diagrams (decision DAGs, a.k.a. branching program, such that the labels along any directed path respects a linear ordering of the attributes) [GG95] have been shown to be learnable in the single-task learning setting. However, the following theorems 7, 8 and 9 show that efficient learnability of these classes in the intermediate concepts setting would imply efficient learnability of DNFs. The latter is one of the more challenging problem in learning theory.

Theorem 7. *Efficient learnability of unate DNFs and Horn DNFs, using equivalence and/or membership queries in the intermediate concepts setting would imply efficient learnability of DNFs using equivalence and membership queries in the single concept setting.*

Proof: Suppose unate DNFs are learnable in the intermediate concepts learning setting with membership and equivalence queries. Then we can use the unate DNFs learning algorithm to learn a DNF boolean formula f, by introducing intermediate concepts $f_{2i-1}(x) = x_i$ and $f_{2i}(x) = \overline{x_i}$ for each attribute x_i. Any boolean DNF can then be expressed as a monotone DNF using these intermediate concepts. Since we know what these intermediate concepts are, it is clear that we can simulate the equivalence and membership query oracles for the intermediate concepts learning problem by using the standard equivalence and membership query oracles for f. The same argument also holds for Horn DNFs.

$\square$

Theorem 8. *Efficient learnability of read-twice DNFs, read-once formulas and ordered binary branching programs using equivalence and/or membership queries in the ICL setting would imply efficient learnability of DNFs using equivalence and membership queries in the standard single concept setting.*

Proof: Without loss of generality, suppose we know k the maximum number of times the same literal appears in the target read-twice DNF in the single-task learning problem. Then we simply introduce k intermediate concepts that are equivalent to x_i and k intermediate concepts that are equivalent to $\overline{x_i}$. Clearly, any boolean DNF formula can be expressed as a read-once monotone DNF formula with these intermediate concepts, and hence as a read-once formula and read-twice DNF over these intermediate concepts. Similar argument can be used to show ordered binary decision diagrams is as hard as learning unordered binary decision diagrams (a.k.a branching programs). The latter concept class can be used to represent any boolean formula [BTW96,Bar89] of at most the same size. Thus, learning ordered binary decision diagrams is also hard. $\square$

We have the following hardness result for learning monotone DNFs. At first sight, the following proof seems to imply that an efficient algorithm for learning monotone DNFs using EQs and MQs in the standard exact model can be transformed to an algorithm for learning general DNFs. However, this is not the case. The reason being that the MQ oracle cannot be properly simulated, unlike in the transformation presented below.

Theorem 9. *Efficient learnability of monotone DNFs in the intermediate concepts mistake bound learning model with membership queries would imply efficient learnability of DNFs in the standard (single concept) mistake bound model using membership queries*[2].

Proof: As before, we reduce the problem of learning a single general DNF formula to learning multiple monotone formulas. We introduce one new variable y_i for each negated literal $\overline{x_i}$. Clearly, the single target (general) DNF f would appear as a monotone DNF f' with the original set of variables and the new variables. An instance $x = \langle x_1, ..., x_n \rangle$ will be transformed to $\widehat{x} = \langle x_1, ..., x_n, y_1, ..., y_n \rangle$ where $y_i = \overline{x_i}$. For each pair of variables $\{x_i, y_i\}$, we introduce the intermediate concepts $f_i(x) = x_i \vee y_i$. We also introduce another intermediate function $\widehat{f}(\tilde{x}) = x_1 y_1 \vee ... \vee x_n y_n \vee (f_1(\tilde{x}) \wedge ... \wedge f_n(\tilde{x}) \wedge f'(\tilde{x}))$.

We claim that $f(x) = \widehat{f}(\widehat{x})$. Clearly, $f_i(\widehat{x}) = +$ for each $1 \le i \le n$, since in $\widehat{x}$ exactly one of x_i and y_i $(= \overline{x_i})$ is equal to 1. It is also easy to verify that $\widehat{f}(\widehat{x}) = f'(\widehat{x}) = f(x)$. Therefore, to learn the single DNF formula f, we can

---

[2] The following proof is supplied by an anonymous referee.

simply assume that we are learning f in the transformed instance space with the intermediate concepts $f_1, ..., f_n, \tilde{f}$.

Next, since the f_i's are known fixed functions, we can answer membership queries on $f_i(\tilde{x})$. It suffices to show that the membership query oracle MQ_f for f can be used to simulate the membership query oracle $MQ_{\widehat{f}}$ for $\widehat{f}$. On input $\tilde{x}$, $MQ_{\widehat{f}}$ first checks whether there exists an i such that $x_i = y_i = 1$. If so, it returns '+'. Otherwise, $\widehat{f}$ is reduced to $f_1 \wedge ... \wedge f_n \wedge f'$. It proceeds to check whether there is an f_i such that $f_i(\tilde{x}) = x_i \vee y_i = 0$. If so, it returns '-'. Otherwise, $\widehat{f}$ is reduced to f'. Now, if $MQ_{\widehat{f}}$ reaches this stage then for each i, we do not have $x_i = y_i = 1$ but we have either x_i or y_i is 1. In other words, we have $y_i = \overline{x_i}$ and we can map (inversely) $\tilde{x}$ to $x = \langle x_1, ..., x_n \rangle$ so that $\widehat{x} = \tilde{x}$. Now, to determine $\widehat{f}(\tilde{x})$ we simply ask MQ_f for $f(x)$, which is equal to $f'(\widehat{x}) = \widehat{f}(\tilde{x})$ as desired.   □

In applications of intermediate concepts learning, we would typically expect that the number of target concepts to be much less than the number of attributes. The next natural question to ask is what concept class can be learned if there is a bound on the size of $\mathcal{F}$. When the size of $\mathcal{F}$ is some small constant k and $\mathcal{F}$ are monotone DNF formulas, then clearly all the concepts can be represented as a monotone DNFs over X with a polynomial (but exponential in $|\mathcal{F}|$) blowout in representation size. Thus, we have the following result.

Observation 10 *Suppose $|\mathcal{F}|$ is a constant. Then monotone DNFs can be efficiently exactly learned in the intermediate concepts learning setting using equivalence and membership queries.*   □

5   PAC Learning Results

Recall that the *VC-dimension* of a concept class $\mathcal{C}$, denoted by VC-dim$(\mathcal{C})$, is the size of the largest sample that can be labeled in all possible ways by concepts in $\mathcal{C}$. The following theorem due to Blumer *et al.* [BEHW89] gives a sufficient condition for learning a single target concept in the PAC model.

Theorem 11. *[BEHW89] Let $\mathcal{C}$ be an arbitrary concept class with finite VC-dimension. Suppose also that there is an algorithm $\mathcal{A}$ such that for all possible choices of target concept $f \in \mathcal{C}$, given any sample S of examples labeled according to f, with size of S at least*

$$\max \left(\frac{2}{\epsilon} \log \frac{2}{\delta}, \frac{8 \, VC\text{-}dim\,(\mathcal{C})}{\epsilon} \log \frac{13}{\epsilon} \right),$$

$\mathcal{A}$ outputs a hypothesis in $\mathcal{C}$ that classifies S the same way as f. Then $\mathcal{A}$ learns $\mathcal{C}$ in the PAC model.

In the above theorem, the *consistency problem* that $\mathcal{A}$ is solving can be generalized naturally to the intermediate concept learning setting. In our learning environment, each example x in the sample S are labeled according to k concepts $f_1, ..., f_k$. These concepts are from a given concept class $\mathcal{C}$ and satisfy the dependency relation defined by some dependency DAG G. An immediate (but not quite 'correct') objective is to output a set of hypotheses $H = h_1, ..., h_k \in C$ such that for each x in S, $\forall i$, $h_i(x, f_1(x), .., f_{i-1}(x), f_{i+1}(x), ..., f_k(x)) = f_i(x, f_1(x), .., f_{i-1}(x), f_{i+1}(x), ..., f_k(x))$. Note that this is somewhat well-defined for S since the instances in S are labeled. However, for an unlabeled instance x, the learner does not know the values of the $f_i(x)$s. Therefore, in order to use H in making prediction, we require H to satisfy a dependency DAG that has depth smaller than that of G. Note that by our assumption of the PAC learning process, we know that such H exists. Under this dependency DAG constraint, the number of parameters that each f_i is dependent on is smaller than $n + k$. Hence, the VC-dimension of f_i is smaller than that of C defined over $X \cup \mathcal{F}$.

We have the following extension of Theorem 11 in the intermediate concepts learning environment.

Corollary 1. *Suppose a concept class $C_{n,k}$ has VC-dimension polynomial in n and k where n is the number of attributes in X and k is the number of intermediate concepts (in $\mathcal{F}$). Let S be an arbitrary sample of k-labeled examples labeled according to an ordered set $\mathcal{F} = \{f_1, ..., f_k\}$, with size of S at least*

$$\max\left(\frac{2k}{\epsilon}\log\frac{2k}{\delta}, \frac{8k\,VC\text{-}dim\,(C_{n,k})}{\epsilon}\log\frac{13k}{\epsilon}\right).$$

If there is an algorithm $\mathcal{A}$ such that for all possible choices of target concept $f \in C$, given any sample S of $\mathcal{A}$ outputs an ordered set of hypothesis $\{h_1, ..., h_k\}$ in C that classifies S the same way as $\mathcal{F}$, then $\mathcal{A}$ PAC learns C in the intermediate concepts learning setting.

Proof: Let D be the distribution in which we draw the sample S. Let h_i be a hypothesis for f_i that is consistent with S and satisfies the dependency DAG constraint. By Theorem 11, with probability at least $1 - \frac{\delta}{k}$, the probability of $h_i(x) \neq f_i(x)$ for an instance x drawn from D is at most $\frac{\epsilon}{k}$. Therefore, with probability at least $1 - \delta$, the probability that there exists i such that $h_i(x) \neq f_i(x)$ for an instance x drawn from D is at most ϵ. $\square$

Hence, to PAC-learn a concept class C in the intermediate concepts learning setting, it suffices to be able to solve our version of the consistency problem. The following theorem states that efficient algorithm for solving the single task consistency problem can be converted to solve the intermediate concepts consistency problem.

Theorem 12. *If there is an efficient algorithm $\mathcal{A}$ for solving the consistency problem for a concept class C in the single task setting then there is an efficient algorithm $\mathcal{A}'$ for solving the consistency problem for the concept class C in the ICL setting.*

Proof: The algorithm has the same flavor as the algorithms presented in Section 3 and Section 4. As before, we start with an initial guess l_i of the level of each f_i as 1. We then run $\mathcal{A}$ to find a consistent hypothesis h_i for the sample in the same way as f_i. If we cannot find such a hypothesis then we increment l_i by 1. We then repeat the same process of finding a consistent h_i where the attributes being considered are those in X plus those intermediate concepts where the levels are smaller than l_i.

In the first iteration, we can output a consistent hypothesis for each of the concepts with actual level 1. As before, it is easy to verify by induction that the we never overestimate the level of f_i. This ensures that in the subsequent ith iteration, the set of concepts where a consistent hypothesis has been constructed contains all those concepts of level less than l. This guarantees that the relevant functions that we consider in the ith iteration include the latter concepts. Therefore, we can construct a consistent concept that is of level i. □

6   Future Work

In this paper, we show that efficient single-task learning algorithms without membership queries can be extended to efficient multi-task learning in most commonly studied models. However, in the presence of a membership query oracle, this may not be true. In particular, Theorem 7, 8 and 9 suggest that most concept classes are difficult to learn in the intermediate concepts learning setting with equivalence and membership queries.

Problem 1. An interesting question is whether one can give a characterization of these concept classes that are difficult to learn in the intermediate concepts learning setting with membership queries. Is there any concept class that can be learned in the ICL model with equivalence and membership queries?

In most situations, we would expect the number of target concepts to be much smaller than the number of attributes. However, the only positive result obtained when $|\mathcal{F}|$ is bounded, is only for the case where $|\mathcal{F}|$ is constant and the concept class is monotone DNFs (See Observation 10).

Problem 2. Is there any concept class that can be learned when $|\mathcal{F}|$ is $O(\log n)$?

Most results [Lit88,CBLW95,KW94,HKW96] obtained in the mistake bound model is relative to the best hypothesis. That is, the number of mistakes made by the best hypothesis appears as an additive term. For example, Littlestone's winnow algorithm makes at most $O(k \log n + M_{opt})$ mistakes in learning k-disjunctions. Here, n is the number of variables and M_{opt} is the number of mistakes made by the best k-disjunctions. However, in transforming these efficient online algorithm for learning single concept to intermediate concept learning setting (as in Section 3), the number of mistakes made by the best hypothesis appears as a multiplicative factor.

Problem 3. Can any concept class be learned where the total mistakes made by the best ordered collection of hypotheses appears as an additive term in the mistake bound?

In this preliminary research on intermediate concepts learning, we only examine the three most popular learning models. A natural direction for future work is to investigate such learning in other learning models.

Problem 4. Can efficient single task learning algorithms in various variations of PAC and exact model be translated to efficient intermediate concepts learning algorithms in the corresponding models? Exact learning model with various types of 'imperfect' membership query oracles [AS91,AK94,AKST97,BCGS95], agnostic PAC model [KSS94] and statistical PAC model [Kea93] are some examples of interesting models to consider here.

Acknowledgements. The author thanks Dan Roth, Vijay Raghavan for helpful discussions. I also want to thank the anonymous reviewers for their valuable comments which helped me to improve the paper. This research is supported by UTSA Faculty Research Award 14-7518-01.

References

[AFP92]   D. Angluin, M. Frazier, and L. Pitt. Learning conjunctions of Horn clauses. *Machine Learning*, 9:147–164, 1992.

[AHK93]   D. Angluin, L. Hellerstein, and M. Karpinski. Learning read-once formulas with queries. *J. ACM*, 40:185–210, 1993.

[AK94]   D. Angluin and M. Kriķis. Learning with malicious membership queries and exceptions. In *Proc. 7th Annu. ACM Workshop on Comput. Learning Theory*, pages 57–66. ACM Press, New York, NY, 1994.

[AKST97] Dana Angluin, Mārtiņš Krikis, Robert H. Sloan, and György Turán. Malicious omissions and errors in answers to membership queries. *Machine Learning*, 28:211–255, 1997.

[Ang88]   D. Angluin. Queries and concept learning. *Machine Learning*, 2(4):319–342, April 1988.

[AS91]   D. Angluin and D. K. Slonim. Learning monotone DNF with an incomplete membership oracle. In *Proc. 4th Annu. Workshop on Comput. Learning Theory*, pages 139–146, San Mateo, CA, 1991. Morgan Kaufmann.

[Bar89]   David Barrington. Bounded-width polynomial-size branching programs recognize exactly those language in nc. *JCSS*, 38:150–164, 1989.

[Bax95]   Jonathan Baxter. Learning internal representations. In *Proc. 8th Annu. Conf. on Comput. Learning Theory*, pages 311–320. ACM Press, New York, NY, 1995.

[Bax97]   Jonathan Baxter. A Bayesian/information theoretic model of learning to learn via multiple task sampling. *Machine Learning*, 28:7–39, 1997.

[BCGS95] Avrim Blum, Prasad Chalasani, Sally A. Goldman, and Donna K. Slonim. Learning with unreliable boundary queries. In *Proc. 8th Annu. Conf. on Comput. Learning Theory*, pages 98–107. ACM Press, New York, NY, 1995.

[BEHW89] A. Blumer, A. Ehrenfeucht, D. Haussler, and M. K. Warmuth. Learnability and the Vapnik-Chervonenkis dimension. *J. ACM*, 36(4):929–965, 1989.

[BTW96] Nader H. Bshouty, Christino Tamon, and David K. Wilson. On learning width two branching programs. In *Proc. 9th Annu. Conf. on Comput. Learning Theory*, pages 224–227. ACM Press, New York, NY, 1996.

[Car96] Rich Caruana. Algorithms and applications for multitask learning. In *Proc. 13th International Conference on Machine Learning*, pages 87–95. Morgan Kaufmann, 1996.

[Car98] R. Caruana. A dozen tricks with multitask learning. *Lecture Notes in Computer Science*, 1524:165–187, 1998.

[CBLW95] N. Cesa-Bianchi, P. Long, and M. K. Warmuth. Worst-case quadratic loss bounds for on-line prediction of linear functions by gradient descent. *IEEE Transactions on Neural Networks*, 1995. To appear. An extended abstract appeared in COLT '93.

[CPT97] Rich Caruana, Lorien Pratt, and Sebastian Thrun. Multitask learning. *Machine Learning*, 28:41, 1997.

[DHB95] Thomas G. Dietterich, Hermann Hild, and Ghulum Bakiri. A comparison of ID3 and backpropagation for english text-to-speech mapping. *Machine Learning*, 18:51–80, 1995.

[GG95] Ricard Gavaldà and David Guijarro. Learning ordered binary decision diagrams. In *Proc. 6th Int. Workshop on Algorithmic Learning Theory*, pages 228–238. Springer-Verlag, 1995.

[HKW96] D. P. Helmbold, J. Kivinen, and M. K. Warmuth. Worst-case loss bounds for sigmoided linear neurons. In *Proc. 1996 Neural Information Processing Conference*, 1996. To appear.

[Kea93] M. Kearns. Efficient noise-tolerant learning from statistical queries. In *Proc. 25th Annu. ACM Sympos. Theory Comput.*, pages 392–401. ACM Press, New York, NY, 1993.

[KSS94] Michael J. Kearns, Robert E. Schapire, and Linda M. Sellie. Toward efficient agnostic learning. *Machine Learning*, 17(2/3):115–142, 1994.

[KW94] J. Kivinen and M. K. Warmuth. Exponentiated gradient versus gradient descent for linear predictors. Technical Report UCSC-CRL-94-16, University of California, Santa Cruz, Computer Research Laboratory, June 1994. Revised December 7, 1995. An extended abstract to appeared in the STOC 95, pp. 209-218.

[Lit88] N. Littlestone. Learning when irrelevant attributes abound: A new linear-threshold algorithm. *Machine Learning*, 2:285–318, 1988.

[Riv87] Ronald L. Rivest. Learning decision lists. *Machine Learning*, 2:229–246, 1987.

[SH91] Steven C. Suddarth and Alistair D. C. Holden. Symbolic-neural systems and the use of hints for developing complex systems. *International Journal of Man-Machine Studies*, 35(3):291–311, 1991.

[SK90] S. C. Suddarth and Y. L. Kergosien. Rule-injection hints as a means of improving network performance and learning time. In *Proceedings of the EURASIP Workshop on Neural Networks*, pages 120–129, Sesimbra, Portugal, February 1990. EURASIP.

[Val84] L. G. Valiant. A theory of the learnable. *Commun. ACM*, 27(11):1134–1142, November 1984.

Real-Valued Multiple-Instance Learning with Queries

Daniel R. Dooly[1], Sally A. Goldman[1], and Stephen S. Kwek[2]

[1] Washington University, St. Louis MO 63130, USA,
{drd1, sg}@cs.wustl.edu,
http://www.cs.wustl.edu
[2] University of Texas, San Antonio, San Antonia, TX 78249, USA
kwek@cs.utsa.edu,
http://www.cs.utsa.edu

Abstract. The multiple-instance model was motivated by the drug activity prediction problem where each example is a possible configuration for a molecule and each bag contains all likely configurations for the molecule. While there has been a significant amount of theoretical and empirical research directed towards this problem, most research performed under the multiple-instance model is for concept learning. However, binding affinity between molecules and receptors is quantitative and hence a real-valued classification is preferable.

In this paper we initiate a theoretical study of real-valued multiple instance learning. We prove that the problem of finding a target point consistent with a set of labeled multiple-instance examples (or bags) is NP-complete. We also prove that the problem of learning from real-valued multiple-instance examples is as hard as learning DNF. Another contribution of our work is in defining and studying a multiple-instance membership query (MI-MQ). We give a positive result on exactly learning the target point for a multiple-instance problem in which the learner is provided with a MI-MQ oracle and a single adversarially selected bag.

1   Introduction

The *multiple-instance* learning model is becoming increasingly important within machine learning. Unlike standard supervised learning in which each instance is labeled in the training data, in this model each example is a set (or *bag*) of instances which is labeled as to whether any single instance within the bag is positive. The individual instances are not given a label. The goal of the learner is to generate a hypothesis to accurately predict the label of previously unseen bags.

The multiple-instance model was motivated by the *drug activity prediction problem* where each example is a possible configuration (or shape) for a molecule of interest and each bag contains all low-energy (and hence likely) configurations for the molecule [6]. There has been a significant amount of theoretical and empirical research directed towards this problem. Other applications for the

N. Abe, R. Khardon, and T. Zeugmann (Eds.): ALT 2001, LNAI 2225, pp. 167–180, 2001.

multiple-instance model have been studied. For example, Maron and Raton[12] applied the multiple-instance model to the task of learning to recognize a person from a series of images that are labeled positive if they contain the person and negative otherwise. They have also applied this model to learn descriptions of natural images (such as a waterfall) and then used the learned concept to retrieve similar images from a large image database. More recently, Ruffo [14] has used this model for data mining applications.

Most prior research performed under the multiple-instance model is for concept learning (i.e. boolean labels). The first empirical study of Dietterich et al. [6] used real data for the problem of predicting whether or not a synthetic molecule binds to the musk receptor. However, binding affinity between molecules and receptors is quantitative, borne out in quantities such as the energy released by the molecule-receptor pair upon binding and hence a real-valued classification of binding strength in these situations is preferable. Dietterich et al. say "The only aspect of the musk problem that is substantially different from typical pharmaceutical problems is that the musk strength is measured qualitatively by expert human judges, whereas drug activity binding is usually measured quantitatively through biochemical assays."

Furthermore, the previous work has just considered learning from a given set of labeled bags. However, in the real drug-discovery application, obtaining the label for a bag (which corresponds to making the drug and then running a laboratory experiment) is very time consuming. Thus the most appropriate learning model is that of on-line learning with membership queries. More specifically, you begin with a random labeled example. Then a new drug is selected and created followed by an experiment to obtain its affinity value (i.e. the label), and so on. Selecting the next drug to test is very much like a membership query (which outputs a real-valued label) except one cannot select an arbitrary set of points to define a bag.

Our goal here is to initiate a theoretical study on real-valued multiple instance learning which includes the introduction of a multiple-instance membership query (MI-MQ). We prove that the problem of finding a target point consistent with a set of labeled multiple-instance examples (or bags) is NP-complete. We also prove that the problem of learning from real-valued multiple-instance data is as hard as learning DNF. A key contribution of this paper is a positive result on exactly learning the target point for a multiple-instance problem in which the learner is provided with a MI-MQ and a single adversarially selected bag $b = \{p_1, \ldots, p_r\}$.

2   The Real-Valued Multiple-Instance Model

Consider the standard PAC learning problem of learning an axis-aligned box in $\Re^n$. In this model each labeled example is a point in $\Re^n$ (drawn according to some unknown distribution $\mathcal{D}$) and labeled as positive if and only if it is in the target box. A boolean multiple-instance example is a collection of r points in $\Re^n$ (often called a *bag* or *r-example*) which is labeled as positive if and only if at least one of the points in the bag is in the target box. For the drug discovery application, each bag corresponds to a drug and each point in the bag corresponds to the shapes that it is likely to take.

We extend this model to the real-valued setting in the following manner. We assume that there is a target point t in $\Re^n$ which corresponds to the ideal shape. The label for bag $b = \{p_1, \ldots, p_r\}$ is $\max\limits_{i=1,\ldots,r} V(dist(t, p_i))$ where $dist(t, p)$ is the distance between t and p_i in the L_2 norm and V is some function that relates distance with binding strength. For example, V could be defined by the widely used empirical potential for intermolecular interactions, the Lennard-Jones potential $V(d) = 4\epsilon \left(\left(\frac{\sigma}{d} \right)^{12} - \left(\frac{\sigma}{d} \right)^6 \right)$ where ϵ is the depth of the potential well, σ is the distance at which $V(d) = 0$, and d is the internuclear distance for two monoatomic molecules[4]. The Lennard-Jones model is nice because of its mathematical simplicity and ability to qualitatively mimic the real interaction between molecules. For the purposes of this paper, the only property we assume about the computation of the binding strength between p and q is that from it $dist(p, q)$ can be obtained and that the binding strength diminishes as the distance to the target increases. An alternate definition for the label of $b = \{p_1, \ldots, p_r\}$ is to compute

$$d_{min}(b) = \min_{i=1,\ldots,r} dist(t, p_i)$$

and then return $V(d_{min}(b))$ as the label. We will use this view and further, assume that d_{min} itself is given. In general, one can extend this model by using a weighted L_2 norm but in this work we assume that an unweighted L_2 norm is used.

We now define a multiple-instance membership oracle (MI-MQ). There are several reasons why we do not want to allow as input to our membership oracle an arbitrary bag (even of a some fixed size r). First, if allowed to do this then by perturbing the individual points in a given bag b, the learning algorithm could determine which point is closest to the target which would effectively reduce the problem to a single-instance problem. Secondly, as discussed earlier, in reality one can select a drug (which could be a small variation of an earlier drug tested). However, the set of bags that correspond to real drugs are limited and in general there will not exist a drug that would have as its likely conformations the desired r points. The problem of defining a multiple-instance membership query that captures the physical constraints of the underlying chemistry is challenging and we do not claim to have solved that problem here. However, we propose the following model which we feel is a good starting point for developing a theory of learning with queries for real-valued multiple-instance learning. Given a bag $b = \{p_1, \ldots, p_r\}$ where b is provided by an adversary, we define the MI-MQ oracle to be one that takes as input any n-dimensional shift vector v and returns the real-valued label for $b + v = \{p_1 + v, \ldots, p_r + v\}$. One can think of this as a very rough approximation of what happens when the chemical structure of one of the previously tested drugs is slightly altered and thus creates a similar set of points in the bag but with some variations (which we model as a simple shift). Since the molecule smoothly moves between conformations (shapes) an interesting problem is to find an alternate way to capture this dependence in the learning model.

3   Prior Work

We begin with a summary of the prior work on learning the (boolean) multiple-instance concept class of axis-aligned boxes in n-dimensional space. Long and Tan [9] described an efficient PAC algorithm under the restriction that each point in the bag is drawn independently from a product distribution, $\mathcal{D}_{product}$. Hence the resulting distribution over r-examples[1] is $\mathcal{D}_{product}^r$. Auer et al. [2] gave an efficient PAC algorithm that allows each point to be drawn independently from an arbitrary distribution. Hence each r-example is drawn from $\mathcal{D}^r$ for an arbitrary $\mathcal{D}$. In their paper, Auer et al. also proved that if the distributional requirements are further relaxed to be arbitrary distributions over r-examples then learning axis-aligned boxes is as hard as learning DNF formulas in the PAC model. Blum and Kalai [5] described a simple reduction from the problem of PAC learning from multiple-instance examples to that of PAC learning with one-sided random classification noise when the r-examples are drawn from $\mathcal{D}^r$ for $\mathcal{D}$ any distribution. They also described a more efficient (and more involved) reduction to the statistical-query model [8] that yields the most efficient PAC algorithm known for learning axis-aligned boxes in the multiple-instance model. Their algorithm has sample complexity $\tilde{O}(n^2 r/\epsilon^2)$, roughly a factor of r faster than the result of Auer et al.

   To understand some of the difficulties that occur when switching from the boolean to real-valued setting, we briefly overview the basic technique used to obtain these results. They all use the key property that all regions in $\Re^n$ not intersecting with the target box have the same value for the fraction of examples in the region that are positive (since they must be false positives which occurs if none of the other $r - 1$ points are in the target box). Hence one can obtain a PAC algorithm as follows. In each dimension, consider the axis-aligned halfspace defined by each point. Since all points in the target region are positive, the halfspace that cuts off roughly $\epsilon/(2n)$ weight from the target region can be detected by comparing the fraction of the positive and negative examples of a sequence of halfspaces moving towards one of the $2n$ box boundaries (from infinity) at discrete locations as defined by the points in the sample. It is easily seen that the distributional assumptions can be slightly relaxed. Namely, suppose that each r-example is drawn from $\mathcal{D}_1 \times \cdots \times \mathcal{D}_r$. Let $\mathcal{D}_i^+$ be the weight of the positive examples in $\mathcal{D}_i$. As long as $\mathcal{D}_1^+ = \mathcal{D}_2^+ = \cdots \mathcal{D}_r^+$ this key property still holds and hence the class of axis-aligned boxes is PAC learnable in this model. If we relax the distribution assumptions more and no longer require all $\mathcal{D}_i^+$ to be the same then this technique of individually finding each of the $2n$ halfspaces breaks down.

---

[1] We use r-example versus bag when it is required that all bags contain exactly r examples.

We now consider the real-valued setting where the label for bag b is a function of the distance between the closest point in the b and the target. In this setting, the sharp change that occurs in the fraction of positive examples as a halfspace crosses the boundary of the box (in the boolean domain) is no longer present. Hence, a completely different approach is needed. However, in order to ensure that we obtain an algorithm that is polynomial for an arbitrary number of dimensions, we must in some way be able to independently work with each dimension (or at least a constant number of dimensions at a time).

The only theoretical work which we are aware of that studies real-valued multiple-instance learning is work by Goldman and Scott [7]. Similar to our work here, they associate a real-valued label with each point in the multiple-instance example. These values are then combined using a real-valued aggregation operator to obtain the classification for the example. Here we only consider the minimum for the aggregation operator. They provide on-line agnostic algorithms for learning real-valued multiple-instance geometric concepts defined by axis-aligned boxes in *constant* dimensional space by reducing the learning problem to one in which the exponentiated gradient (or gradient descent) algorithm can be used. However, their work (and their basic technique) assumes that d is constant which is not feasible for the drug discovery application since d is typically in the hundreds.

Most empirical work also considers the boolean setting. Recently, Amar, Dooly, Goldman, and Zhang [1] empirically studied diverse-density based and k-citation nearest neighbor based algorithms for learning in the real-valued multiple-instance model. However, even for the original versions of the diverse density [11] and k-citation nearest neighbor algorithms [15] for the boolean domain, no theoretical results have been shown. Also, Ray and Page [13] studied multiple-instance linear regression using artificial data to empirically evaluate their algorithm which uses an inductive logic programming based approach combined with a linear regression algorithm supplemented with EM. Again, no theoretical results are given in their work. The goal of our work here is to begin developing theoretical foundations for the real-valued multiple-instance model for high-dimensional spaces.

4   Results for the Real-Valued Multiple-Instance Model

For the reminder of this paper we study the real-valued multiple instance problem when we assume that each bag is drawn from an arbitrary distribution $\mathcal{D}$ and can have any number of examples within it. We define the *Real-Valued Multiple-Instance L2-Consistency Problem* as the following problem. As input you are given a set S of r-examples each labeled with a real-value. The problem is to determine whether or not there is some target point $t \in \Re^n$ such that the label given to each bag is consistent with target t where we assume bag $b = \{p_1, \ldots, p_r\}$ for target t would receive the label $\min_{i=1,\ldots,r} dist(t, p_i)$ with the L_2 norm for the distance metric.

4.1   Negative Results

In this section we present some negative results demonstrating the the general multiple-instance learning problem is hard.

Theorem 1. *The Real-Valued Multiple-Instance L2-Consistency problem is NP-complete.*

Proof. The proof is by reduction from 3-Sat. The instance space has n dimensions, one for each variable. The 3-Sat formula is transformed into a collection of bags as follows. For each clause in the formula, we introduce a bag of 3 points and assign it a label corresponding to a distance of $\sqrt{n-1}$. Each of these points corresponds to a literal in the clause with all coordinates set to 0 except for the coordinate that corresponds to the literal. If the corresponding literal is a negated literal $\overline{x}_i$ then the ith coordinate is set to -1, otherwise it is set to 1. In addition, we also add to this collection a bag containing only the origin with a label corresponding to a distance of $\sqrt{n}$.

Suppose the point $\boldsymbol{t} = (t_1, ..., t_n)$ labels these bags consistently. Let $\boldsymbol{s} = (s_1, ..., s_n)$ be an arbitrary point in a bag corresponding to a clause such that $dist(\boldsymbol{t}, \boldsymbol{s}) = \sqrt{n-1}$. WLOG, suppose $s_i \neq 0$. Then,

$$dist(\boldsymbol{t}, \boldsymbol{p}) = \sqrt{(s_i - t_i)^2 + \sum_{j \neq i}(t_j)^2} = \sqrt{n-1}.$$

On the other hand,

$$dist(\boldsymbol{t}, \boldsymbol{0}) = \sqrt{\sum_{j=1}^{n}(t_j)^2} = \sqrt{n}.$$

From these two equations, we can deduce that $t_i = s_i$.

Therefore, if there is a point which labels the bags consistently, we transform it into an assignment of variables which satisfies all the clauses as follows: If the coordinate of the point in dimension i is $= -1$, assign false to variable x_i. If the coordinate of the point in dimension i is $= 1$, assign true to variable x_i. Otherwise assign either true or false, at random. For each clause, at least one of the three relevant coordinates of the point will cause an assignment to a variable which makes that clause true. So the assignment satisfies all the clauses.

If there is an assignment of variables which satisfies all the clauses, then the point with coordinate 1 in dimensions corresponding to true variables and coordinate -1 in dimensions corresponding to false variables will meet all the distance criteria, since it is at distance $\sqrt{n}$ from the origin, and there will be at least one of the three points in each bag for which it is at distance $\sqrt{n-1}$.   □

Theorem 1 does not indicate that learning is hard, but only that any learning algorithm that requires the consistency problem to be solved is not feasible. We now give a hardness result showing that the real-valued multiple-instance learning problem is as hard as learning DNF even if the learner is allowed to use a hypothesis class that is not simply a point in $\Re^n$. The statement of this result is very similar to the hardness result for the boolean multiple-instance model of Auer et al. [2]. We note that our result does not follow from their results since each bag in the boolean model is labeled as positive iff it is in the target box. Here, each bag must be labeled with the distance between its closest point and the target point. Hence, neither results subsumes the other.

Theorem 2. *Learning in the real-valued multiple-instance setting is as hard as learning DNF.*

Proof. This proof is by reduction from the problem of learning r-term DNF to the problem of learning in the real-valued multiple-instance setting. Without loss of generality, we assume the target concept does not classify every instance as false. For ease of exposition, we assume that $n > 2$.

First, consider the extremely simple case where there is only a single variable x_1. In this case, the target DNF formula ϕ can only be x_1, $\overline{x}_1$ or $\emptyset$ (i.e., true). These candidate formulas are represented using the vertices P (for positive), N (for negative) and I (for irrelevant) respectively of an equilateral triangle in the two-dimensional Euclidean plane. The origin O is also the center of this triangle is distance 1 away from the vertices (see Figure 1). Let $\epsilon = \frac{1}{2n}$. Let T (for true) be a point that lies outside the triangle and is $\sqrt{1-\epsilon}$ away from both points P and I. Similarly, let F (for false) be a point that lies outside the triangle and is $\sqrt{1-\epsilon}$ away from both points N and I. An instance $\boldsymbol{x}$ is then mapped to T if $x_1 = 1$ and F otherwise. Let $g(\boldsymbol{x})$ and $g(\phi)$ be the points obtained by transforming $\boldsymbol{x}$ and ϕ as described above. Since $n > 2$ (and hence $\epsilon < 1/4$), it is straightforward to verify that $dist(g(\boldsymbol{x}), g(\phi)) = \sqrt{1-\epsilon}$ if $\boldsymbol{x}$ satisfies ϕ since T and F are outside of the triangle defined by I, N, and P. (See Figure 1.)

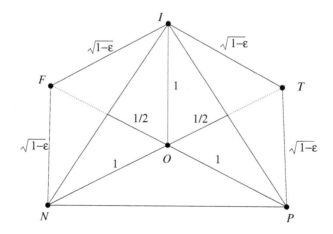

Fig. 1. The geometry of points I, P, N, F, T, O for the proof of Theorem 2.

Next, we extend this reduction to conjunctions. Here, each literal is represented by a point in some 2-dimensional Euclidean plane. That is, the transformed instance space is of dimension $2n$. The coordinates of the target ϕ corresponding to the variable x_i are set to the point $g(\phi_i) = P$, N, or I depending on whether the literal x_i is present as positive literal, present as negative literal or is absent in ϕ, respectively. Similarly, the coordinates corresponding to the value of the variable x_i in an instance $\boldsymbol{x}$ are set to the point $g(x_i) = T$ or F depending on whether $x_i = 1$ or $x_i = 0$. As before, if x_i does not falsify the target ϕ, then $dist(g(x_i), g(\phi_i)) = \sqrt{1 - \epsilon}$ otherwise $dist(g(x_i), g(\phi_i)) \geq 3/2$. In other words, if $\boldsymbol{x}$ satisfies ϕ then $dist(g(\boldsymbol{x}), g(\phi)) = \sqrt{n(1 - \epsilon)}$, otherwise $dist(g(\boldsymbol{x}), g(\phi)) \geq \sqrt{\frac{9}{4} + (n - 1)(1 - \epsilon)} > \sqrt{n}$. To change the latter inequality to an equality so that all the negative instances in the DNF learning problem are mapped into points with unique values, we treat $g(\boldsymbol{x})$ as a bag and add another point $\boldsymbol{o} = \langle 0, ..., 0 \rangle$. Clearly, $dist(g(\phi), \boldsymbol{o}) = \sqrt{n}$ for all possible choices of ϕ and hence $dist(g(\boldsymbol{x}), g(\phi)) = \sqrt{n}$ if $\boldsymbol{x}$ does not satisfy ϕ.

Finally, we extend the reduction to r-term DNF. The transformed instance space is of dimension $2n \times r$. An instance $\boldsymbol{x}$ is mapped into a bag of $B(\boldsymbol{x})$ of $r + 1$ points. This bag contains the origin $\boldsymbol{o} = \langle O, ..., O \rangle$. For each T_i, we introduce a point p_i into the bag. The values of the $(2n(i - 1) + 1)$th to $(2ni)$th coordinates of p_i are set as described in the previous paragraph. The other coordinates are set to O. Viewed another way, in our translation of the problem, we have a 2-dimensional subspace for each combination of boolean variable and term of the DNF formula, giving rn such subspaces in all. We use S_{ij} to denote the subspace associated with the ith variable of term j. We transform the given r-term DNF formula ϕ into a target point in $2rn$-dimensional space as follows. If the jth term in ϕ contains a positive variable x_i, we set the coordinates for subspace S_{ij} to P. If the j term contains $\overline{x}_i$ we set S_{ij} to N. Finally, if variable x_i does not appear in the jth term of ϕ, we set S_{ij} to I. As an example if $\phi = (x_1 \wedge \overline{x}_2 \wedge x_4) \vee (x_1 \wedge x_3)$ (so $n = 4$ and $r = 2$) then the target point $g(\phi) = PNIP \; PIPI$ where the first four pairs correspond to the first term and the second four pairs correspond to the second term.

We translate an assignment of boolean variables as follows. The assignment $x_1, x_2, \ldots, x_n$ is transformed into a bag containing $r + 1$ points. For $1 \leq j \leq r$, in the jth of these points, for each variable $x_i = 0$, we set the coordinates in subspace S_{ij} to F. For each variable $x_i = 1$, we set the coordinates in subspace S_{ij} to T. For all $k \neq j$, we set the coordinates in subspace S_{ik} to O. For the last point, we set the coordinates in all subspaces to O. So continuing our example, assignment $\boldsymbol{x} = 1001$ would be translated to the bag $g(\boldsymbol{x}) = \{TFFT \; OOOO, OOOO \; TFFT, OOOO \; OOOO\}$. Each of the first r points tests to see if this assignment satisfies term j, while the last is a reference point known to be closer to the target than the point corresponding to any unsatisfied term. To complete the transformation, we give the positive bags the value $\sqrt{rn - n\epsilon} = \sqrt{rn - 1/2}$ and the negative bags the value $\sqrt{rn}$. We also include rn bags containing three points each. In each group of three, the coordinates in one of the subspaces S_{ij} are assigned to P, N, or I, and the coordinates in all other subspaces are assigned to O. Each of these rn bags has value $\sqrt{rn-1}$. Finally, we have a bag containing one point o. In all of the subspaces S_{ij} the coordinates are assigned to O. This bag has value $\sqrt{rn}$.

As for the case of conjunctions it can be easily verified that if x satisfies ϕ, then $dist(g(x), g(\phi)) = \sqrt{n(1-\epsilon) + (r-1)n} = \sqrt{rn - \epsilon n} = \sqrt{rn - 1/4}$. Conversely, if x falsifies T_i then

$$dist(g(x), g(\phi)) \geq \sqrt{(n-1)(1-\epsilon) + 9/4 + (r-1)n} > \sqrt{rn}$$

since $\epsilon = 1/(2n)$. Further, since $dist(o, g(\phi)) = \sqrt{rn}$,

$$dist(g(x), g(\phi)) = \begin{cases} \sqrt{rn - \epsilon}, & x \text{ satisfies } \phi \\ \sqrt{rn}, & x \text{ does not satisfy } \phi \end{cases}$$

as desired.

Suppose that we have an algorithm which is able to find a $2rn$-dimensional point p which has a distance to each provided bag where the distance equals the specified label. For any $2rn$-dimensional point p, we use p_{ij} to denote the value of p for subspace S_{ij}. Let q_{ij} be the one of P, N, or I which is closest to p_{ij}. We now argue that the distance between p_{ij} and q_{ij} is zero. That is, p_{ij} must be one of P, N, or I. From the bag with O for all subspaces, we have $\sum_{i,j} dist(p_{ij}, O)^2 = rn$. Multiplying both sides by $rn - 1$ yields

$$(rn - 1) \sum_{i,j} dist(p_{ij}, O)^2 = rn(rn - 1). \tag{1}$$

From the rn bags with three points each we have that $dist(p_{k\ell}, q_{k\ell})^2 + \sum_{i \neq k, j \neq \ell} dist(p_{ij}, O)^2 = rn - 1$. Summing over the rn subspaces we get: $\sum_{k\ell} dist(p_{k\ell}, q_{k\ell})^2 + \sum_{k\ell} \sum_{i \neq k, j \neq \ell} dist(p_{ij}, O)^2 = rn(rn - 1)$. Using the observation that, $\sum_{k\ell} \sum_{i \neq k, j \neq \ell} dist(p_{ij}, O)^2 = (rn - 1) \sum_{ij} dist(p_{ij}, O)^2$ gives

$$\sum_{k\ell} dist(p_{k\ell}, q_{k\ell})^2 + (rn - 1) \sum_{ij} dist(p_{ij}, O)^2 = rn(n - 1). \tag{2}$$

Combining Equations 1 and 2 gives that $\sum_{k\ell} dist(p_{k\ell}, q_{k\ell})^2 = 0$ and hence $p_{k\ell}$ must be one of P, N, or I.

Let us now consider a positive bag (i.e. a bag with label $\sqrt{rn - n\epsilon}$). One of the points in this bag must be at distance $\sqrt{rn - n\epsilon}$ from the target point $t = g(\phi)$. Let it correspond to term j and let us call it z. Since we know that $dist(z_{ik}, O) = 1$, we can subtract the distance in all the subspaces except those corresponding to term j to get $\sum_i dist(t_{ij}, z_{ij})^2 = n(1 - \epsilon)$. So each variable i must satisfy term j. Let us consider a negative bag. All of the points in this bag must be at least distance $\sqrt{rn}$ from t. Let us pick a point w corresponding to term j. There must be at least one subspace for which $dist(t_{ij}, w_{ij})^2 > 1$. The only way this can happen is for variable i to fail to satisfy term j. So we can read the terms of the DNF from the values that t takes in the subspaces. If t_{ij} has location P, then term j contains literal x_i. If t_{ij} has location N, then term j contains the literal $\bar{x}_i$. Finally, if t_{ij} has location I, then term j does not contain include x_i (or its negation). $\qquad \square$

4.2   Our Positive Result

In this section we present a positive result. Let b be an arbitrary bag provided by an adversary. We assume that we have access to a MI-MQ oracle and that from the label provided by this oracle we can then compute the distance between the closest point in $b + v$ and the target t where v is the input given to the MI-MQ. It is important to remember that although we can compute the distance between the target and the closest point from $b + v$ this provides no information as to which point in $b + v$ is closest to the target.

The high-level approach used by our algorithm is to (working one dimension at a time) determine the coordinate in each dimension of the target point. We do this by finding a set of vectors for which we can determine the coordinate of the point which is closest to the target point, and using these to determine the coordinate of the target point. If we could guarantee that we have a unique closest point in a bag, and we pick small enough distances in each dimension, we can use this technique to determine the gradient of the distance function. From that, we can determine an offset from the bag which reaches the target. From that we can determine r such offsets, one from each point in the bag. This uniquely identifies the target. If this process fails (because there was not a unique closest point), one could randomly move the bag. With high probability, one would then have a unique closest point, since failure occurs only when the target lies on a hyperplane equidistant from two closest points. This probabilistic algorithm is more intuitive, but is not guaranteed to halt. Hence, we instead present a somewhat more complex polynomial-time deterministic algorithm.

In order to describe our algorithm in more depth, the following definitions are needed. For any target t, any vector v, and any point p, we define the function $d_{t,p}(v) = \|t - (p + v)\|^2$. For a bag $b = \{p_1, \ldots, p_r\}$ of points, we define $d_{t,b}(v) = \min_{i=1,\ldots,r} d_{t,p}(v)$.

For each dimension $1 \le j \le n$, we consider the function $s_{t,p}^{(j)}(x) = d_{t,p}(x \cdot v_j)$ where v_j is the unit vector in dimension j and x is a scalar. That is, $s_{t,p}^{(j)}(x) = (p_1, \ldots, p_{j-1}, p_j + x, p_{j+1}, \ldots, p_n)$. Observe that

$$s_{t,p}^{(j)}(x) = \sum_{k \ne j}(t_k - p_k)^2 + (t_j - (p_j + x))^2 = \sum_{k \ne j}(t_k - p_k)^2 + (x - (t_j - p_j))^2 = \ell + (x - x')^2$$

for constants (with respect to x) of $\ell = \sum_{k \ne j}(t_k - p_k)^2$ and $x' = (t_j - p_j)$, which is a parabola. Finally, let $s_{t,b}^{(j)}(x) = \min_{p \in b} s_{t,p}^{(j)}(x)$.

Figure 2 shows a visualization of $s_{t,b}^{(j)}(x)$. First, notice that it is obtained by combining the r parabolas given by $s_{t,p}^{(j)}(x)$. For each value of x, the value of $s_{t,b}^{(j)}(x)$ is that of the parabola that has the lowest value at x. We let $f_i^{(j)}$ denote the ith parabola (for dimension j) that defines $s_{t,b}^{(j)}(x)$ going from left to right.

Let $f_r^{(j)}$ be the rightmost parabola. Suppose for a moment that we could determine which point $p_j^{(j)}$ corresponds to $f_r^{(j)}$. If this were the case, then the value at which $f_r^{(j)}$ attains its minimum would give us the translation for which

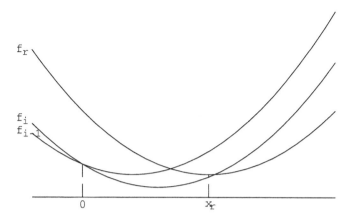

Fig. 2. A visualization of $s_{t,b}^{(j)}(x)$. Notice that the y-intercept ℓ_0 of f_i corresponds to the label of bag b.

p_j is closest to the target. From this we can determine the coordinate of the target in that dimension.

Our goal is now to independently, for each dimension j, find the minimum of the parabola corresponding to $p_j^{(j)}$. For ease of exposition, suppose this parabola was $f_r^{(j)}$ and that its minimum value occurred at a value of x_r. We now demonstrate how we can use the MI-MQ oracle to find $f_r^{(j)}$. Once we have done this, we have found a shift x_j for dimension j for which $p_j^{(j)} + x_j \cdot v_j = t_j$. By then repeating this in each dimension, we have enough information to compute the point $t = \{p_1^{(1)} + x_1, p_2^{(2)} + x_2, \ldots, p_n^{(n)} + x_n\}$.

As discussed above, in $s_{t,b}^{(j)}(x)$ there are r parabolas, one for each point in b. For each parabola it reaches a minimum value for the value of x that represents the dimension j shift for which $t_j - p_j = 0$. It is important to note (as shown above) that all r parabolas are of the form $\ell + (x - x')^2$ where ℓ and x' may be different for each of the points. In particular, for point p, ℓ is the label for bag b that would be obtained if bag b were shifted in dimension j so that $t_j - p_j = 0$ and x' is the value of x where this parabola reaches its minimum value. Our first lemma shows that as we translate far enough in a given dimension, the closest point to the target will eventually be one of those with the smallest coordinate in that dimension. We now formalize this intuition in the following lemma.

Lemma 1. *Let bag b have r points and let v be any vector. Let v_u be the unit vector corresponding to v. Let P_m be the set of points in b for which $p \cdot v$ is minimized for $p \in b$. Let d_1 be the minimal non-zero value of the projection along v of the vectors from points in P_m to points in P. That is, $d_1 = \min_{p \in b}(p - p_m) \cdot v_u$ for p_m any point in P_m. Similarly, let d_2 be the maximal projection of the distance along the hyperplane, normal to v, between any p_m and any other point*

$p \in b$. Let d_0 be the distance between b and the target. Then for any translation x greater than $\frac{(d_0+d_2)^2}{2d_1} + d_0 + d_1$, the closest point in $b + xv$ from the target will be a point in P_m.

Proof Sketch: The distance between any point in $b + xv$ and the target can be expressed in terms of the component along v and the component normal to v. Let us denote the component along v from any point $p_m \in P_m$ to the target as $d_v = (p_m - t) \cdot v$. For such a translation x, $d_v \geq \frac{(d_0+d_2)^2}{2d_1}$. The distance from any other point p to the target is at least that of its component along v, which is at least $d_v + d_1$, while the distance from some point $p_m \in P_m$ to the target is at most $\sqrt{d_v^2 + (d_0 + d_2)^2} \leq \sqrt{d_v^2 + 2d_1 d_v} < \sqrt{d_v^2 + 2d_1 d_v + d_1^2} = d_v + d_1$.   □

Procedure Find_Coordinate (j, b)

> Let d_0 be the label of bag b
> Find all points P_m with minimal j coordinate x_m
> Find a point p_i with second-minimal j coordinate x_i
> Let $d_1 = x_m - x_i$
> Find the point p_j with maximal value of $d_2 = \sqrt{distance^2(p_m, p_j) - d_1^2}$
> For $z = 1, 2, 3$
>> Let $v = 0$ except set $v_j = \frac{(d_0+d_2)^2}{2d_1} + d_0 + d_1 + z$
>> $\ell_z = \mathtt{MI} - \mathtt{MQ}(b, v)$
>> Let y_z be the distance corresponding to label ℓ_z
> Let $f_r^{(j)}$ be the parabola of form $\ell_1 + (x - x_1)^2$ that contains the
> points $(x_0, y_0), (x_1, y_1), (x_2, y_2)$
> Let x_r be the point at which $f_r^{(j)}$ is minimized.
> Return $x_r + x_m$

Fig. 3. The procedure Find_Coordinate searches for the coordinate of the target in dimension j.

We now describe how we use this lemma in the procedure Find_Coordinate (see the detailed pseudo-code in Figure 3). We find the set of leftmost starting points and a translation large enough to make one of them the closest point to the target. We then use the MI-MQ oracle to query the value of $s_{t,b}^{(j)}(x)$ for 3 points, farther out. These points will lie on a parabola. The minimal value of the parabola gives us the j-coordinate of the target.

We now consider the procedure Find_Target which is the overall procedure to learn the target point (see Figure 4). It independently finds the coordinates of the target in each each of the n dimensions.

Theorem 3. *Assuming that each call to the MI-MQ oracle takes constant time, Find_Target has a worst-case time complexity of $O(nr^3)$ and is guaranteed to output the target point t.*

Algorithm Find_Target (b)
    Find distances between all points of b
    For each of the n dimensions $k = 1, \ldots, n$
        Let $v_i = $ Find_Coordinate(k, b)
    Return $\boldsymbol{v} = (v_1, \ldots, v_n)$

Fig. 4. The algorithm Find_Target. Note that all bags created are linear transformations of the original bag b provided by the adversary.

Proof Sketch: Find_Coordinate takes $O(r^2)$ time to find the x_j. So each repetition of the loop in Find_Target takes $O(r^2)$ time. Since there are n repetitions of the loop, the total time taken is $O(nr^2)$.   ☐

5   Concluding Remarks

In this paper, we present some hardness results and a positive result for learning in a real-valued multiple-instance learning model. We hope that this work will be the beginning of a theoretical study of learning in the real-valued multiple instance model and eventually lead to improved algorithms for applications such as drug discovery. There are many interesting open problems. For example, are there non-trivial distributional assumptions, for which there is an efficient PAC learning (or on-line learning) algorithm to approximate the target point from real-valued multiple-instance data? Similarly, can hardness results be shown for more restricted distribution? Finally, are there alternate definitions for a multiple-instance membership query that better capture the physical constraints of the drug-discovery application.

Acknowledgments. We thank the anonymous referees for their many useful comments. Dr. Goldman is supported in part by NSF Grant CCR-9988314 and a Boeing-McDonnell Foundation grant. Dan Dooly is supported in part by NSF Grant CCR-9988314. Dr. Kwek is supported by UTSA Faculty Research Award 14-7518-01.

References

1. R.A. Amar, D.R. Dooly, S.A. Goldman, and Q. Zhang. Multiple-Instance Learning of Real-Valued Data. In *Proc. 18th International Conference on Machine Learning*, pages 3–10. Morgan Kaufmann, 2001.
2. P. Auer, P. M. Long, and A. Srinivasan. Approximating hyper-rectangles: Learning and pseudo-random sets. In *Proceedings of the Twenty-Ninth Annual ACM Symposium on Theory of Computing*, pages 314–323. ACM, 1997.
3. P. Auer. On learning from multi-instance examples: Empirical evaluation of a theoretical approach. In *Proc. 14th International Conference on Machine Learning*, pages 21–29. Morgan Kaufmann, 1997.

4. R.S. Berry, S.A. Rice, and J. Ross. *Physical Chemistry*, Chapter 10 (Intermolecular Forces). John Wiley & Sons, 1980.

5. A. Blum and A. Kalai. A note on learning from multiple-instance examples. *Machine Learning*, 30:23–29, 1998.

6. T. G. Dietterich, R. H. Lathrop, and T. Lozano-Pérez. Solving the multiple-instance problem with axis-parallel rectangles. *Artificial Intelligence*, 89(1-2):31–71, 1997.

7. S.A. Goldman and S.D. Scott. Multiple-Instance Learning of Real-Valued Geometric Patterns. To appear in *Annals of Mathematics and Artificial Intelligence*.

8. M. Kearns. Efficient noise-tolerant learning from statistical queries. In *Proc. 25th Annu. ACM Sympos. Theory Comput.*, pages 392–401. ACM Press, New York, NY, 1993.

9. P. M. Long and L. Tan. PAC learning axis-aligned rectangles with respect to product distributions from multiple-instance examples. *Machine Learning*, 30:7–21, 1998. Earlier version in COLT96.

10. O. Maron. *Learning from Ambiguity*. PhD thesis, MIT, 1998. AI Technical Report 1639.

11. O. Maron and T. Lozano-Pérez. A framework for multiple-instance learning. *Neural Information Processing Systems*, 10, 1998.

12. O. Maron and A. Lakshmi Ratan. Multiple-instance learning for natural scene classification. In *Proc. 15th International Conf. on Machine Learning*, pages 341–349. Morgan Kaufmann, San Francisco, CA, 1998.

13. S. Ray and D. Page. Multiple instance regression. In *Proc. 18th International Conference on Machine Learning*, pages 425–432. Morgan Kaufmann, 2001.

14. G. Ruffo. *Learning single and multiple instance decision trees for computer security applications*. Doctoral dissertation. Department of Computer Science, University of Turin, Torino, Italy, 2000.

15. Wang and Zucker. Multiple-instance learning for natural scene classification. In *Proc. 17th Int. Conf. on Machine Learning*, pages 1119–1125. Morgan Kaufmann, San Francisco, CA, 2000.

Loss Functions, Complexities, and the Legendre Transformation*

Yuri Kalnishkan, Michael V. Vyugin, and Volodya Vovk

Department of Computer Science, Royal Holloway, University of London,
Egham, Surrey, TW20 0EX, United Kingdom. {yura,misha,vovk}@cs.rhul.ac.uk

Abstract. The paper introduces a way of re-constructing a loss function from predictive complexity. We show that a loss function and expectations of the corresponding predictive complexity w.r.t. the Bernoulli distribution are related through the Legendre transformation. It is shown that if two loss functions specify the same complexity then they are equivalent in a strong sense.

1 Introduction

Predictive complexity was introduced in [8] as a natural development of prediction with expert advice. Predictive complexity bounds the cumulative error suffered by any on-line learning algorithm on a sequence. It may be considered an inherent measure of "learnability" of a string in the same way as Kolmogorov complexity reflects the "simplicity" of a string.

Different measures of error (loss functions) specify different variants of predictive complexity; some of them do not have any corresponding predictive complexity at all. This paper shows how a loss function may be recovered from the predictive complexity $\mathcal{K}$ it generates. The loss function λ and the expectations $E\mathcal{K}(\zeta)$, where ζ is a random variable distributed according to the Bernoulli law, are related via the Legendre transformation. Appendix A contains a brief introduction to the theory of the Legendre transformation in the one-dimensional case.

We show that if two loss functions specify the same complexity then they are equivalent in a very strong sense (virtually equal up to a parametrisation). This observation allows us to show that the variants of Kolmogorov complexity, namely, plain, prefix, and monotone, do not correspond to any game and thus are not predictive complexities. Another variant of Kolmogorov complexity, the minus logarithm of Levin's a priori semimeasure, is known to be the predictive complexity specified by the logarithmic game.

---

* Some results from this paper form a part of the technical report "The Existence of Predictive Complexity and the Legendre Transformation", CLRC-TR-00-04, Computer Learning Research Centre, Royal Holloway College, University of London; these results were presented at Fourth French Days on Algorithmic Information Theory, TAI2000.

N. Abe, R. Khardon, and T. Zeugmann (Eds.): ALT 2001, LNAI 2225, pp. 181–189, 2001.

2   Preliminaries

2.1   Games and Superpredictions

A *game* $\mathfrak{G}$ is a triple $(\Omega, \Gamma, \lambda)$, where Ω is called an *outcome space*, Γ stands for a *prediction space*, and $\lambda : \Omega \times \Gamma \to \mathbb{R} \cup \{+\infty\}$ is a *loss function*. We suppose that a definition of computability over Ω and Γ is given and λ is computable according to this definition.

   In this paper we are interested in the binary case $\Omega = \mathbb{B}$. We will denote elements of $\mathbb{B}^*$ (i.e. finite strings of elements of $\mathbb{B}$) by bold letters, e.g. $\boldsymbol{x}, \boldsymbol{y}$. By log we denote logarithm to the base 2.

   We impose the following restrictions in order to exclude degenerated games:

1. The set of possible predictions Γ is a compact topological space.
2. For every $\omega \in \Omega$, the function $\lambda(\omega, \gamma)$ is continuous (w.r.t. the extended topology of $[-\infty, +\infty]$) in the second argument.
3. There exists $\gamma \in \Gamma$ such that, for every $\omega \in \Omega$ the inequality $\lambda(\omega, \gamma) < +\infty$ holds.
4. If there are $\gamma_0 \in \Gamma, \omega_0 \in \Omega$ such that $\lambda(\omega_0, \gamma_0) = +\infty$, then there is a sequence of $\gamma_n \in \Gamma$, $n = 1, 2, \ldots$, such that $\gamma_n \to \gamma_0$ as $n \to \infty$ and $\lambda(\omega_0, \gamma_n) < +\infty$.

Conditions 1–3 have been taken from [7]. Condition 4 essentially means that λ accepts the infinite value only in exceptional cases which can be approximated by final cases.

   We say that a pair $(s_0, s_1) \in [-\infty, +\infty]^2$ is a *superprediction* if there exists a prediction $\gamma \in \Gamma$ such that $s_0 \geq \lambda(0, \gamma)$ and $s_1 \geq \lambda(1, \gamma)$. If we let $P = \{(p_0, p_1) \in [-\infty, +\infty]^2 \mid \exists \gamma \in \Gamma : p_0 = \lambda(0, \gamma) \text{ and } p_1 = \lambda(1, \gamma)\}$ (cf. the canonical form of a game in [6]), the set S of all superpredictions is the set of points that lie "north-east" of P.

   The set S is of fundamental importance and many interesting properties of a game may be described in terms of S. This observation leads to the definition:

Definition 1. *Two games are equivalent if they have the same set of superpredictions.*

The following simple lemma describes the class of sets S which may occur as sets of superpredictions.

Lemma 1. *A set $S \subseteq [-\infty, +\infty]^2$ is the set of superpredictions for some game $\mathfrak{G}$ satisfying conditions 1–4 if and only if the following conditions hold:*

- *for every $(x, y) \in S$ and every $a, b \in [0, +\infty]$, we have $(x + a, y + b) \in S$,*
- *there are $a, b > -\infty$ such that $S \subseteq [a, +\infty] \times [b, +\infty]$,*
- *$S \cap \mathbb{R}^2 \neq \varnothing$, and*
- *the set S is the closure of its final part $S \cap \mathbb{R}^2$ w.r.t. the extended topology of $[-\infty, +\infty]^2$.*

The last item is the direct counterpart of Condition 4.

Let us describe the intuition behind the concept of a game. Consider a prediction algorithm $\mathfrak{A}$ working according to the following protocol:

```
FOR t = 1, 2, ...
    (1) 𝔄 chooses a prediction γₜ ∈ Γ
    (2) 𝔄 observes the actual outcome ωₜ ∈ Ω
    (3) 𝔄 suffers loss λ(ωₜ, γₜ)
END FOR.
```

Over the first T trials, $\mathfrak{A}$ suffers the total loss

$$\text{Loss}_{\mathfrak{A}}(\omega_1, \omega_2, \dots, \omega_T) = \sum_{t=1}^{T} \lambda(\omega_t, \gamma_t) \ . \tag{1}$$

By definition, put $\text{Loss}_{\mathfrak{A}}(\Lambda) = 0$, where Λ denotes the empty string.

The function $\text{Loss}_{\mathfrak{A}}(\boldsymbol{x})$ can be treated as the predictive complexity of $\boldsymbol{x}$ in the game $\mathfrak{G}$ w.r.t. $\mathfrak{A}$. We will call these functions *loss processes*. Sadly, the set of loss processes has no universal elements unless in degenerated cases. Let us now proceed to defining a universal complexity measure.

2.2   Predictive Complexity

Let us fix a game $\mathfrak{G}$. A function $L : \Omega^* \to \mathbb{R} \cup \{+\infty\}$ is called a *superloss process* w.r.t. $\mathfrak{G}$ (see [8]) if the following conditions hold:

- $L(\Lambda) = 0$,
- for every $\boldsymbol{x} \in \Omega^*$, the pair $(L(\boldsymbol{x}0) - L(\boldsymbol{x}), L(\boldsymbol{x}1) - L(\boldsymbol{x}))$ is a superprediction w.r.t. $\mathfrak{G}$, and
- L is semicomputable from above.

We will say that a superloss process K is *universal* if for any superloss process L there exists a constant C such that $\forall \boldsymbol{x} \in \Omega^* : K(\boldsymbol{x}) \leq L(\boldsymbol{x}) + C$. The difference between two universal superloss processes w.r.t. $\mathfrak{G}$ is bounded by a constant. If universal superloss processes w.r.t. $\mathfrak{G}$ exist we may pick one and denote it by $\mathcal{K}^{\mathfrak{G}}$. It follows from the definition that, for every prediction algorithm $\mathfrak{A}$, there is a constant C such that for every $\boldsymbol{x}$ we have $\mathcal{K}^{\mathfrak{G}}(\boldsymbol{x}) \leq \text{Loss}_{\mathfrak{A}}^{\mathfrak{G}}(\boldsymbol{x}) + C$, where $\text{Loss}^{\mathfrak{G}}$ denotes the loss w.r.t. $\mathfrak{G}$. One may call $\mathcal{K}^{\mathfrak{G}}$ *(predictive) complexity* w.r.t. $\mathfrak{G}$.

3   Expectations of Complexity

Theorem 1. *Let $\mathfrak{G}$ be a game satisfying the conditions 1–4. Let $\mathfrak{G}$ specify complexity $\mathcal{K}$ and let S be the set of superpredictions for $\mathfrak{G}$. Then for every $p \in (0,1)$*

(i) there exists a finite limit

$$\tilde{f}(p) = \lim_{n \to \infty} \frac{\boldsymbol{E}}{\mathcal{K}(\xi_1^{(p)} \dots \xi_n^{(p)})} n \;, \tag{2}$$

where $\xi_1^{(p)}, \dots, \xi_n^{(p)}$ are results of n independent Bernoulli trials with the probability of 1 being equal to p, and
(ii) the equality

$$\tilde{f}(p) = -pf^* \left(\frac{p-1}{p} \right) \;, \tag{3}$$

holds, where f^* is the function conjugated to f specified by $f(x) = \inf\{y \mid (x,y) \in S\}^1$ for every $x \in \mathbb{R}$.

Proof. In order to apply the Legendre transformation, we should make sure that f is convex. This fact is implied by the following lemma.

Lemma 2. *If a game $\mathfrak{G}$ satisfying conditions 1–4 specifies predictive complexity, then the intersection of its set of superpredictions S and $\mathbb{R}^2$ is convex.*

The proof is in Appendix B.
    The following proposition allows us to estimate the expectations.

Proposition 1 ([2]). *Let $\mathfrak{G}$ be a game with the set of superpredictions S. Suppose that $p \in (0,1)$, the game $\mathfrak{G}$ specifies complexity $\mathcal{K}$, and the numbers $\rho_1 \leq \rho_2$ are such that*

$$\forall (x,y) \in S \cap \mathbb{R}^2 : (1-p)x + py \geq \rho_1 \;, \tag{4}$$

but

$$\exists (x_0, y_0) \in S \cap \mathbb{R}^2 : (1-p)x_0 + py_0 \leq \rho_2 \;. \tag{5}$$

Then there is $C > 0$ such that, for every $n \in \mathbb{N}$, we have

$$\rho_1 n \leq \boldsymbol{E}\mathcal{K}(\xi_1^{(p)} \dots \xi_n^{(p)}) \leq \rho_2 n + C \;, \tag{6}$$

where $\xi_1^{(p)}, \dots, \xi_n^{(p)}$ are results of n independent Bernoulli trials with the probability of 1 being equal to p.

    It follows from Proposition 1 that there is $C > 0$ such that, for every $p \in (0,1)$ and every positive integer n, we have

$$\alpha(p)n \leq \boldsymbol{E}\mathcal{K}(\xi_1^{(p)} \dots \xi_n^{(p)}) \leq \alpha(p)n + C \;, \tag{7}$$

where

---

[1] We (by definition) assume that $\inf \varnothing = +\infty$.

$$\alpha(p) = \inf_{(x,y)\in S} [(1-p)x + py] \tag{8}$$

$$= \inf_{x\in\mathbb{R}} [(1-p)x + pf(x)] \tag{9}$$

$$= -p \sup_{x\in\mathbb{R}} \left[\frac{p-1}{p}x - f(x)\right] \tag{10}$$

$$= -pf^*\left(\frac{p-1}{p}\right) . \tag{11}$$

□

Corollary 1. *Let two games $\mathfrak{G}_1$ and $\mathfrak{G}_2$ satisfy conditions 1–4. Suppose they have the sets of superpredictions S_1 and S_2 and specify complexities $\mathcal{K}^1$ and $\mathcal{K}^2$. If there is a function $\delta(n) = o(n)$ as $n \to \infty$ such that for every $\boldsymbol{x} \in \mathbb{B}^*$ the inequality*

$$|\mathcal{K}^1(\boldsymbol{x}) - \mathcal{K}^2(\boldsymbol{x})| \leq \delta(|\boldsymbol{x}|) \tag{12}$$

holds, then $S_1 = S_2$ and complexities $\mathcal{K}^1$ and $\mathcal{K}^2$ are equal up to a constant.

Proof. For every $p \in (0,1)$ we have

$$\lim_{n\to\infty} \left| \frac{E}{\left[\mathcal{K}^1(\xi_1^{(p)}\ldots\xi_n^{(p)}) - \mathcal{K}^2(\xi_1^{(p)}\ldots\xi_n^{(p)})\right]} n \right| \leq \frac{\delta(n)}{n} = o(1) \tag{13}$$

as $n \to \infty$, where $\xi_1^{(p)},\ldots,\xi_n^{(p)}$ are as above. This implies that for every $p \in (0,1)$ the equality $\tilde{f}_1(p) = \tilde{f}_2(p)$ holds, where $\tilde{f}_1$ and $\tilde{f}_2$ are defined for the games $\mathfrak{G}_1$ and $\mathfrak{G}_2$ by (2). Thus $f_1^*(t) = f_2^*(t)$ for all $t \in (-\infty,0)$, where f_1 and f_2 are defined in the same way as f in (ii) of Theorem 1. We have $f_1^*(0) = f_2^*(0)$ by continuity; for every $t > 0$ the equality $f_1^*(t) = f_2^*(t) = +\infty$ holds. It follows from a fundamental property of conjugated functions, namely, $f^{**} = f$ (Proposition 2 from Appendix A), that the functions f_1 and f_2 coincide, where f_1 and f_2 are defined in the same way as f in (ii) of Theorem 1. This implies that $S_1 = S_2$. □

Corollary 2. *There is no game specifying plain Kolmogorov complexity K, prefix complexity KP, or monotone complexity Km as its predictive complexity.*

Proof. The difference between any of this functions and the negative logarithm of Levin's a priori semimeasure is bounded by a term of logarithmic order of the length of a string. If one of the functions had been predictive complexity for a game, this game would have been equivalent to the logarithmic game, which has

$$\lambda(\omega,\gamma) = \begin{cases} -\log(1-\gamma) & \text{if } \omega = 0 \\ -\log\gamma & \text{if } \omega = 1 \end{cases}, \tag{14}$$

$\gamma \in [0,1]$, and complexity would have coincided with logarithmic complexity $\mathcal{K}^{\log}$. But $\mathcal{K}^{\log}$ coincides with the negative logarithm of Levin's a priori semimeasure (see [8]). However neither of the differences between these functions and KM can be bounded by a constant (see [9,3]). □

Acknowledgements. Volodya Vovk and Yuri Kalnishkan are supported by EPSRC through the grant GR/M14937. Yuri Kalnishkan and Michael Vyugin also hold Overseas Research Students Awards Scheme grants. The authors are grateful to anonymous ALT reviewers for their insightful and detailed comments.

References

[1] V. M. Alekseev, V. M. Tikhomirov, and S. V. Fomin. *Optimal Control.* Plenum, New York, 1987.

[2] Y. Kalnishkan. General linear relations among different types of predictive complexity. In *Proc. 10th International Conference on Algorithmic Learning Theory — ALT '99*, volume 1720 of *Lecture Notes in Artificial Intelligence*, pages 323–334. Springer-Verlag, 1999.

[3] M. Li and P. Vitányi. *An Introduction to Kolmogorov Complexity and Its Applications.* Springer, New York, 2nd edition, 1997.

[4] A. Wayne Roberts and Dale E. Varberg. *Convex Functions.* Academic Press, 1973.

[5] R. Tyrrell Rockafellar. *Convex Analysis.* Princeton University Press, 1970.

[6] V. Vovk. Aggregating strategies. In M. Fulk and J. Case, editors, *Proceedings of the 3rd Annual Workshop on Computational Learning Theory*, pages 371–383, San Mateo, CA, 1990. Morgan Kaufmann.

[7] V. Vovk. A game of prediction with expert advice. *Journal of Computer and System Sciences*, 56:153–173, 1998.

[8] V. Vovk and C. J. H. C. Watkins. Universal portfolio selection. In *Proceedings of the 11th Annual Conference on Computational Learning Theory*, pages 12–23, 1998.

[9] V. V. V'yugin. Algorithmic entropy (complexity) of finite objects and its applications to defining randomness and amount of information. *Selecta Mathematica formerly Sovietica*, 13:357–389, 1994.

Appendix A: Legendre Transformation

The *Legendre(-Young–Fenchel) transformation* may be defined for functionals on a locally convex space. However everything we need in this paper is just the simplest one-dimensional case. We will follow the treatment of the one-dimensional case in [4]; the general theory of this transformation and conjugated functions may be found in [5,1].

Consider a convex function $f : \mathbb{R} \to [-\infty, +\infty]$. The *conjugated* function $f^* : \mathbb{R} \to [-\infty, +\infty]$ is defined by

$$f^*(t) = \sup_{x \in \mathbb{R}} (xt - f(x)) \ . \tag{15}$$

A function $g : \mathbb{R} \to [-\infty, +\infty]$ is called *proper* if $\forall x \in \mathbb{R} : g(x) > -\infty$ and $\exists x \in \mathbb{R} : g(x) < +\infty$. A proper g is *closed* if for each real α the *level set* $L_\alpha = \{x \in \mathbb{R} \mid g(x) \leq \alpha\}$ is closed w.r.t. the standard topology of $\mathbb{R}$.

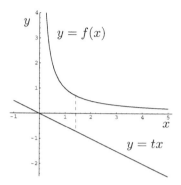

Fig. 1. Evaluation of the Legendre transformation.

Figure (1) provides an example. In the picture we have

$$f(x) = \begin{cases} \frac{1}{x} & \text{if } x > 0, \\ +\infty & \text{otherwise} \end{cases}$$

and we evaluate $f^*(-1/2)$. The supremum from (15) is achieved at $x = \sqrt{2}$.

Proposition 2 (see [4,5]). *If $f : \mathbb{R} \to [-\infty, +\infty]$ is a proper convex function, the following properties hold:*

(i) f^* is convex, proper and closed, and
(ii) if f is closed, $f^{**} = f$.

Appendix B: On a Necessary Condition for the Existence of Predictive Complexity

Proof (of Lemma 2). Assume the converse. Consider a game $\mathfrak{G}$ with the set of superpredictions S such that $S \cap \mathbb{R}^2$ is not convex but there exists complexity $\mathcal{K}$ w.r.t. $\mathfrak{G}$.

There exist points $B_0, B_1 \in S$ such that the segment $[B_0, B_1]$ is not a subset of S. Without loss of generality we may assume that $B_0 = (b_0, 0), B_1 = (0, b_1)$ (see Fig. 2). Indeed, a game $\mathfrak{G}$ with the set of superpredictions S specify complexity if and only if a game $\mathfrak{G}'$ with the set of superpredictions S' which is a shift of S (i.e. there are $a, b \in \mathbb{R}$ such that $S' = \{(x', y') \in (-\infty, +\infty]^2 \mid \exists (x, y) \in S : x' = x + a, y' = y + b\}$) specifies complexity.

There exists a point $A = (a_0, a_1)$ with $a_1, a_2 > 0$ on the boundary of S and above the straight line passing through B_0 and B_1. Let us denote this line by l and let us assume that it has the equation $\alpha_0 x + \alpha_1 y = \rho$, where $\alpha_0, \alpha_1, \rho > 0$.

Let us denote the numbers of 1s an 0s in a string $\boldsymbol{x}$ by $\sharp_1 \boldsymbol{x}$ and $\sharp_0 \boldsymbol{x}$, respectively. Since $b_0 \sharp_0 \boldsymbol{x}$ and $b_1 \sharp_1 \boldsymbol{x}$ are superloss processes, there is $C > 0$ such that,

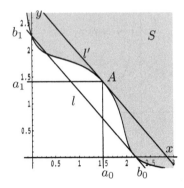

Fig. 2. The set S is coloured grey.

for every $x \in \mathbb{R}^2$, the inequalities

$$\mathcal{K}(x) \le b_0 \natural_0 x + C \qquad (16)$$
$$\mathcal{K}(x) \le b_1 \natural_1 x + C \qquad (17)$$

holds. At the same time, there is a sequence of strings $x_1, x_2, \ldots$ such that for any $n \in \mathbb{N}$ we have $|x_n| = n$ and

$$\mathcal{K}(x_n) \ge a_0 \natural_0 x + a_1 \natural_1 x \ . \qquad (18)$$

The construction of x_n is by induction. Let $x_0 = \Lambda$. Suppose we have constructed x_n. The point $(\mathcal{K}(x_n 0) - \mathcal{K}(x_n), \mathcal{K}(x_n 1) - \mathcal{K}(x_n))$ should lie in at least one of the half-planes $\{(x, y) \mid x \ge a_0\}$ or $\{(x, y) \mid y \ge a_1\}$ i.e. at least one of the inequalities

$$\mathcal{K}(x_n 0) - \mathcal{K}(x_n) \ge a_0 \qquad (19)$$
$$\mathcal{K}(x_n 1) - \mathcal{K}(x_n) \ge a_1 \qquad (20)$$

hold. We define x_{n+1} to be either $x_n 0$ or $x_n 1$ accordingly.

Combining (16), (17) and (18) we get

$$a_0 \natural_0 x_n + a_1 \natural_1 x_n \le b_0 \natural_0 x_n + C \qquad (21)$$
$$a_0 \natural_0 x_n + a_1 \natural_1 x_n \le b_1 \natural_1 x_n + C \qquad (22)$$

for every $n \in \mathbb{N}$. Since $(b_0, 0)$ and $(0, b_1)$ lie below l', where l' is parallel to l and passes through A, we have

$$b_0 = \frac{\alpha_0 a_0 + \alpha_1 a_1}{\alpha_0} - \delta_0 \qquad (23)$$
$$b_1 = \frac{\alpha_0 a_0 + \alpha_1 a_1}{\alpha_1} - \delta_1 \ , \qquad (24)$$

where $\delta_0, \delta_1 > 0$. If we multiply (21) by α_0/a_1, (22) by α_1/a_0 and then add them together, we obtain

$$\frac{\alpha_0 \delta_1}{a_1} \natural_0 \boldsymbol{x}_n + \frac{\alpha_1 \delta_0}{a_0} \natural_1 \boldsymbol{x}_n \leq C_1 \ , \tag{25}$$

where $C_1 > 0$ is a constant. This is a contradiction since $\alpha_0 \delta_1/a_1 > 0$, $\alpha_1 \delta_0/a_0 > 0$, and at least one of the values $\natural_0 \boldsymbol{x}_n$, $\natural_1 \boldsymbol{x}_n$ is unbounded. $\qquad \square$

Non-linear Inequalities between Predictive and Kolmogorov Complexities

Michael V. Vyugin[1] and Vladimir V. V'yugin[2,3]

[1] Department of Computer Science, Royal Holloway, University of London, Egham, Surrey TW20 0EX, England. misha@cs.rhul.ac.uk
[2] Institute for Information Transmission Problems, Russian Academy of Sciences, Bol'shoi Karetnyi per. 19, Moscow GSP-4, 101447, Russia. vld@vyugin.mccme.ru
[3] Computer Learning Research Centre, Royal Holloway, University of London, Egham, Surrey TW20 0EX, England.

Abstract. Predictive complexity is a generalization of Kolmogorov complexity. It corresponds to an "optimal" prediction strategy which gives a lower bound to ability of any algorithm to predict elements of a sequence of outcomes. A variety of types of loss functions makes it interesting to study relations between corresponding predictive complexities. Non-linear inequalities (with variable coefficients) between predictive complexity $KG(x)$ of non-logarithmic type and Kolmogorov complexity $K(x)$ (which is close to predictive complexity for logarithmic loss function) are the main subject of consideration in this paper. We deduce from these inequalities an asymptotic relation $\sup\limits_{x:l(x)=n} \frac{K(x)}{KG(x)} \sim \frac{1}{a}\log n$, when $n \to \infty$, where a is a constant and $l(x)$ is the length of a sequence x. An analogous asymptotic result holds for relative complexities $K(x)/l(x)$ and $KG(x)/l(x)$. To obtain these inequalities we present estimates of the cardinality of all sequences of given predictive complexity.

1 Introduction

A central problem considered in machine learning (and statistics) is the problem of predicting future event x_i based on past observations $x_1 x_2 \ldots x_{i-1}$, where $i = 1, 2 \ldots$. The simplest case is when x_i is either 0 or 1. A prediction algorithm makes its prediction on-line in a form of a real number p_i between 0 and 1. We suppose that the quality of prediction is measured by a specific loss function $\lambda(x_i, p_i)$. The total loss of prediction suffered on a sequence of events $x_1 x_2 \ldots x_n$ is measured by the sum of all values $\lambda(x_i, p_i)$, $i = 1, \ldots, n$.

Various loss functions are considered in literature on machine learning and prediction with expert advice (see, for example, [1,2,8,10,12]). The most important of them are logarithmic loss function and square-loss function. Logarithmic loss function, $\lambda(\sigma, p) = -\log p$ if $\sigma = 1$ and $\lambda(\sigma, p) = -\log(1 - p)$ otherwise, leads to the log-likelihood function. Square-loss function $\lambda(\sigma, \gamma) = (\sigma - \gamma)^2$ is important to applications.

The main goal of prediction is to find a method of prediction which minimizes the total loss suffered on a sequence $x_1 x_2 \ldots x_i$ for $i = 1, 2 \ldots$. This "minimal"

N. Abe, R. Khardon, and T. Zeugmann (Eds.): ALT 2001, LNAI 2225, pp. 190–204, 2001.

possible total loss of prediction was formalized by Vovk [10] in a notion of predictive complexity. The corresponding method of prediction gives a lower bound to ability of any algorithm to predict elements of a sequence of outcomes. Predictive complexity is a generalization of the notion of Kolmogorov complexity and has analogous asymptotic properties. In the case of logarithmic loss function predictive complexity coincides with a variant of Kolmogorov complexity [4]. Predictive complexity corresponding to square-loss function gives a lower limit to the quality of regression under square loss.

A variety of types of loss functions defines the problem of comparative study of corresponding predictive complexities. By comparing predictive complexities corresponding to different loss functions, we compare learnability of strings under different learning environments. We continue the investigation initiated by Kalnishkan in [4]. Paper [4] provided necessary and sufficient conditions on constant coefficients a_1, a_2 and b_1, b_2, b_3 under which the inequalities

$$a_1 K^1(x) + a_2 l(x) + c_1 \geq K^2(x) \quad \text{and} \quad b_1 K^1(x) + b_2 K^2(x) \leq b_3 l(x) + c_2$$

hold for some additive constants c_1, c_2. Here $K^1(x)$ and $K^2(x)$ are predictive complexities of different types, $l(x)$ is the length of a sequence x. Logarithmic KG^{log} and square-loss KG^{sq} complexities can be among K^1 and K^2, in particular inequality $KG^{sq}(x) \leq \frac{1}{4} KG^{log}(x) + c$ holds for some positive constant c. Converse inequalities with constant coefficients between these complexities which can be obtained by Kalnishkan's method have additive term of order $O(l(x))$. To avoid these addends we explore non-linear inequalities. These inequalities hold up to factors $O(\log l(x))$ and present relations between corresponding complexities more exactly.

By its definition below $KG^{log}(x)$ coincides with the minus logarithm of the Levin's [11] "a priori" semimeasure (see also [5]) which is close to Kolmogorov complexity $K(x)$ up to addend $O(\log l(x))$. By this reason and by general fundamental importance of Kolmogorov complexity we compare $KG^{sq}(x)$ with $K(x)$.

To obtain these inequalities we estimate the number of all sequences of length n with given upper bound k on predictive complexity (Proposition 5). We deduce from this combinatorial estimation non-linear inequalities between Kolmogorov complexity and predictive complexity of non-logarithmic type (Propositions 6, 7). More advanced estimates for predictive complexity are given in Theorems 9, 10.

Main results of this paper in an asymptotic form are formulated in Theorems 3 and 4. We compare Kolmogorov complexity $K(x)$ and a predictive complexity $KG(x)$ of non-logaritnmic type. Theorem 3 asserts that

$$\sup_{x: l(x)=n} \frac{K(x)}{KG(x)} \sim \frac{1}{a} \log n,$$

where a is a constant (relation $f(n) \sim g(n)$ means that $\lim_{n \to \infty} f(n)/g(n) = 1$). Theorem 4 gives an analogous relation between relative complexities $K(x)/l(x)$ and $KG(x)/l(x)$.

2 Predictive Complexity

We consider only simplest case, where events $x_1, x_2, \ldots, x_i \ldots$ are simple binary outcomes from $\{0, 1\}$, nevertheless, our results trivially can be extended to the case of arbitrary finite set of all possible outcomes $\{0, 1, \ldots, L-1\}$, where $L > 1$. It is natural to suppose that all predictions are given according to a *prediction strategy* (or *prediction algorithm*) $p_i = S(x_1, x_2, \ldots x_{i-1})$. We will suppose also that our loss functions are computable, and hence, they are continuous in p in the interval $[0, 1]$. The total loss incurred by Predictor who follows the strategy S over the first n trials is defined

$$\mathrm{Loss}_S(x_1 x_2 \ldots x_n) = \sum_{i=1}^{n} \lambda(x_i, S(x_1, x_2, \ldots x_{i-1})).$$

The main problem is to find a method of prediction S which minimizes the total loss $L_S(x)$ suffered on a sequence x of outcomes. In machine learning theory several "aggregating algorithms" achieving this goal in the case of finite number of experts were developed [7,1,12,2,8].

Vovk [8,10] proposed a condition that is sufficient to optimal efficiency of his aggregating algorithm AA. This condition is a concavity of the exponent from the loss function considered. More precise, we fix the *learning rate* $\eta > 0$ and put $\beta = e^{-\eta} \in (0, 1)$. A loss function $\lambda(\sigma, p)$ is called η-mixable if for any sequence of predictions $\gamma_1, \gamma_2, \ldots$ and for any sequence of weights $p_1, p_2, \ldots$ with sum ≤ 1 a prediction $\hat{\gamma}$ exists such that

$$\lambda(\sigma, \hat{\gamma}) \leq \log_\beta \sum_i p_i \beta^{\lambda(\sigma, \gamma_i)} \tag{1}$$

for all σ. By [8] the log-loss function is η-mixable for any $0 < \eta \leq 1$, and square difference is also η-mixable for any $0 < \eta \leq 2$.

In [10] Vovk extended his AA to infinite pool of all "computationally efficient" experts. He introduced a notion of *predictive complexity*, which is a generalization of the notion of Kolmogorov complexity. A function $KG(x)$ is a *measure of predictive complexity* if the following two conditions hold:

1. $KG(\Lambda) = 0$ (where Λ is the empty sequence) and for every x there exists a p such that for each σ $KG(x\sigma) \geq KG(x) + \lambda(\sigma, p)$;
2. $KG(x)$ is *semicomputable from above*, which means that there exists a computable sequence of simple functions $KG^t(x)$ such that, for each x, $KG(x) = \inf_t KG^t(x)$.

By a simple function we mean a nonnegative function which takes rational values or $+\infty$ and equals $+\infty$ for almost all $x \in \Xi$.

Requirement 1) means that the measure of predictive complexity must be valid: there must exists a prediction strategy that achieves it. We consider the *universal* prediction strategy $\Lambda(x) = p$ (which is possible uncomputable), where $p = p(x)$ is the prediction from the item 1) of the definition of a measure of predictive complexity. By definition $\mathrm{Loss}_\Lambda(x) \leq KG(x)$ for each x. Notice that if $\geq$ in 1) is replaced by $=$, the definition of a total loss function will be obtained. Requirement 2) means that $KG(x)$ must be "computable in the limit".

The main advantage of this definition is that a semicomputable from above sequence $KG_i(x)$ of all measures of predictive complexity exists. This means that there exists a computable from i, t, x sequence of simple functions $KG_i^t(x)$ such that

1. $KG_i^{t+1}(x) \leq KG_i^t(x)$ for all i, t, x;
2. $KG_i(x) = \inf_t KG_i^t(x)$ for all i, x;
3. for each measure of predictive complexity $KG(x)$ there exists an i such that $KG(x) = KG_i(x)$ for all x.

We call i an enumeration program of $KG_i(x)$ (for details see Section 6). In particular, for any computable prediction strategy S an enumeration program i exists such that $\mathrm{Loss}_S(x) = KG_i(x)$ for each finite sequence x. We can refine this as follows. We fix some universal programming language. Let $K(S)$ be the length of the shortest program computing for any x a rational approximation of $S(x)$ with given degree of precision. Evidently, there exists a computable function $f(p)$ which transform any program p computing S into an enumerating program $i = f(p)$ such that $\mathrm{Loss}_S(x) = KG_i(x)$. We have also $K(i) = K(f(p)) \leq K(p) + c$, where c is a constant.

Let us mention some analogy with Kolmogorov complexity. In the theory of Kolmogorov complexity computable methods of decoding of finite binary sequences are considered. By this method F we can reconstruct any finite sequence x using its binary program p: $x = F(p)$. Each method of decoding F defines some measure of complexity $K_F(x) = \min\{l(p) : F(p) = x\}$ of finite sequences x. It is easy to verify that this function is semicomputable from above. Kolmogorov's idea was to "mix" all these measures of complexity in one "universal" measure. A computable sequence F_i of all methods of decoding can be constructed by the methods of the theory of algorithms [6]. An universal method of decoding can be defined $U(< i, p >) = F_i(p)$, where i is a program computing F_i, and $< i, p >$ is a suitable code of a pair of programs. Then for any semicomputable from above method of decoding F it holds $K_U(x) \leq K_F(x) + O(1)$ for each x, where a constant $O(1)$ depends on F. We fix some $K_U(x)$, denote it $K(x)$, and call Kolmogorov complexity of a finite sequence x. For technical reason it is convenient to consider prefix-free methods of decoding: if $F(p)$ and $F(q)$ are defined and distinct then codes p and q are incompatible. From this follows $\sum 2^{-K(x)} \leq 1$. In this case the prefix Kolmogorov complexity can also be defined analytically (see [5])

$$K_U(x) = \log_{1/2} \sum_{i=1}^{\infty} r_i 2^{-K_{F_i}(x)},$$

where $r_1, r_2, \ldots$ is a computable sequence of nonnegative weights with sum ≤ 1. For example, we can take $r_i = 2^{-i}$, $i = 1, 2, \ldots$.

Analogously the mixture of all measures of predictive complexity $KG_i(x)$ in the case of η-mixable loss function is defined

$$KG(x) = \log_\beta \sum_{i=1}^{\infty} r_i \beta^{KG_i(x)}, \tag{2}$$

where $r_i = 2^{-K(i)}$. We check that $KG(x)$ is a measure of predictive complexity in Section 6. The following proposition (which is an easy consequence of the formulae (2)) shows that the function $KG(x)$ defined by (2) is a measure of predictive complexity minimal up to an additive constant.

Proposition 1. *[10] Let a loss function $\lambda(\omega, p)$ be computable and η-mixable for some $\eta > 0$. Then there exists a measure of predictive complexity $KG(x)$ such that for any measure of predictive complexity $KG_i(x)$*

$$KG(x) \leq KG_i(x) + (\ln 2/\eta)K(i)$$

for all x, besides, a constant c exists such that

$$KG(x) \leq \mathrm{Loss}_S(x) + (\ln 2/\eta)(K(S) + c)$$

for each computable prediction strategy S and each x.

Let some η-mixable loss function is given. We fix some $KG(x)$ satisfying conditions of Proposition 1 and call its value the *predictive complexity* of x.

The inequality

$$KG(x) \leq (\ln 2/\eta)(K(x) + c)$$

between complexities $KG(x)$ and $K(x)$ can be obtained from Proposition 1, where c is a positive constant depending on γ. To prove it consider prediction strategy S defined by x such that $S(z) = x_i$ for each z of the length $i - 1$, where $1 \leq i \leq l(x) - 1$, and $S(z) = 0$, otherwise (here we also used the requirement 2) from Section 3).

3   Bounded Loss Functions

We prove our results for a wide class of bounded loss functions. A typical representative of this class is the square-loss function. We impose the following restrictions on a loss function $\lambda(\sigma, p)$:

1. $b = \inf_p \sup_\sigma \lambda(\sigma, p) > 0$;
2. $\lambda(0, 0) = \lambda(1, 1) = 0$;
3. the loss function $\lambda(\sigma, p)$ is η-mixable for some $\eta > 0$;
4. $\lambda(\sigma, p)$ is strict monotonic by p, i.e. $\lambda(0, p) > \lambda(0, p')$ and $\lambda(1, p) < \lambda(1, p')$ if $p > p'$ for all $p, p' \in [0, 1]$ (the log-loss function and squared difference satisfy conditions 1)–4) with $b = 1$ and $b = \frac{1}{4}$, accordingly);

5. the loss function $\lambda(\sigma, p)$ is bounded (square-loss function is bounded, but log-loss function fails this condition).

Denote $a = \lambda(1,0)$ and $a' = \lambda(0,1)$. In the following we suppose without loss of generality that $0 < a \leq a'$. We will use the following technical proposition.

Proposition 2. *Let a loss function $\lambda(\sigma, p)$ satisfies conditions 1)–5). Then there exists a computable monotonically increasing function $\delta(\epsilon)$ such that $\delta(\epsilon) > 0$ if $\epsilon > 0$ and such that for each $0 \leq \epsilon \leq 1$ and $0 \leq p \leq 1$ if $\lambda(0, p) \leq a'(1 - \epsilon)$ and $\lambda(1, p) \leq a(1 - \epsilon)$ then $\lambda(0, p) \geq a\delta(\epsilon)$ and $\lambda(1, p) \geq a\delta(\epsilon)$.*

The proof of this proposition is strightforward. In the following it is sufficient to use this proposition instead of 4) and 5).

By definition $a \geq b \geq a\delta(\epsilon)$ for all $0 < \epsilon < 1$.

The normalized by $a > 0$ square-loss function $\lambda(\sigma, p) = a(\sigma - p)^2$ satisfies these conditions with $a' = a$ and $\delta(\epsilon) = \epsilon^2/4$.

4   Summary of Results

In this section we summarize main results in an asymptotic form. These results follow from the results of next section.

Let $\lambda(\sigma, p)$ be a loss function satisfying restrictions 1) – 5) (restrictions 4) and 5) can be replaced on the condition of Proposition 1), and let $KG(x)$ be the corresponding predictive complexity. We call $\lambda(\sigma, p)$ the bounded loss function.

Let us define a *worst-case ratio* function

$$f(n) = \sup_{x:l(x)=n} \frac{K(x)}{KG(x)}. \tag{3}$$

The next theorem follows directly from Theorem 9 (below).

Theorem 3. *The worst-case ratio function $f(n)$ defined by (3) satisfies*

$$\lim_{n \to \infty} \frac{f(n)}{\frac{1}{a} \log n} = 1.$$

This theorem estimates the deviation in the worst case between two complexities on all sequences of length n. The following theorem shows that an analogous deviation takes place for relative complexities $K(x)/l(x)$ and $KG(x)/l(x)$. Let

$$h_n(t) = \sup_{x \in B_{n,t}} \frac{K(x)}{n}. \tag{4}$$

where

$$B_{n,t} = \{x | l(x) = n, \frac{KG(x)}{n} \leq t\}. \tag{5}$$

Define *relative complexities comparing* functions

$$\underline{h}(t) = \liminf_{n \to \infty} h_n(t) \tag{6}$$

$$\overline{h}(t) = \limsup_{n \to \infty} h_n(t) \tag{7}$$

The following theorem is a direct corollary of Theorem 10 (below).

Theorem 4. *The relative complexities comparing functions $\underline{h}(t)$ and $\overline{h}(t)$ defined by (6) and (7) satisfy*

$$\lim_{t \to 0} \left(\frac{\underline{h}(t)}{-\frac{t}{a} \log \frac{t}{a}} \right) = \lim_{t \to 0} \left(\frac{\overline{h}(t)}{-\frac{t}{a} \log \frac{t}{a}} \right) = 1.$$

5   Non-linear Inequalities

In this section we explore some possible connections between Kolmogorov complexity $K(x)$ and predictive complexity $KG(x)$.

A very natural problem arises: to estimate the cardinality of all sequences of predictive complexity less than k? A trivial property of Kolmogorov complexity and predictive complexity for log-loss function is that the cardinality of all binary sequences x of complexity less than k is bigger than 2^{k-c} and less than 2^k for some positive constant c. In the case of predictive complexity of non-logarithmic type the cardinality of the set of all sequences of bounded complexity is infinite. We can estimate the number of sequences of length n having predictive complexity less than k. We denote by $\#A$ the cardinality of a finite set A. Let us consider a set

$$A_{n,k} = \{y \,|\, l(y) = n, KG(y) \le k\}. \tag{8}$$

Let $\lambda(\sigma, p)$ be a bounded loss function and $KG(x)$ be the corresponding predictive complexity.

Proposition 5. *Let $0 < \epsilon < 1$ be a rational number. Then there exists a constant c such that for all n and k such that $k \le \min\{na\delta(\epsilon), na(1 - \epsilon)\}$ the following inequalities hold*

$$\sum_{i \le (k-c)/a} \binom{n}{i} \le \#A_{n,k} \le \sum_{i \le k/b} \binom{k/(a\delta(\epsilon))}{i} \sum_{i \le k/(a(1-\epsilon))} \binom{n}{i}. \tag{9}$$

Proof. Let a sequence x of length n has no more than m ones. Consider prediction strategy $S(z) = 0$ for all z. Then by 4) there are at least $\sum_{i \le m} \binom{n}{i}$ of x such that $KG(x) \le \text{Loss}_S(x) + c \le am + c \le k$, where c is a constant. Then $m \le (k - c)/a$ and we obtain the left-hand side of the inequality (9).

To explain the main idea of the proof of right-hand side of (9) at first we consider a proof of a more simple upper bound

$$\#A_{n,k} \le \sum_{i \le k/b} \binom{n}{i}, \tag{10}$$

which is valid for all $k \le bn$.

We consider a binary tree whose vertices are all finite binary sequences, and edges defined by all pairs $(x, x0)$ and $(x, x1)$, where x is a finite binary sequence.

We consider the universal prediction strategy $\Lambda(x) = p$ defined above. By restriction 1) on a loss function for any x we have $\lambda(0, \Lambda(x)) \geq b$ or $\lambda(1, \Lambda(x)) \geq b$. By this property we assign new labelling to edges of the binary tree using letters A and B. We assign A to $(x, x0)$ and B to $(x, x1)$ if $\lambda(0, \Lambda(x)) \geq b$, and assign B to $(x, x0)$ and A to $(x, x1)$ otherwise. Evidently, two different sequences of length n have different labellings. For each edge $(x, x\sigma)$ labeled by A it holds $\lambda(\sigma, \Lambda(x)) \geq b$ and, hence, for any sequence x of length n having more than m As it holds $KG(x) \geq \text{Loss}_\Lambda(x) \geq bm$. Therefore, the bound (10) holds.

To prove the upper bound (9) assign some labelling to edges $(x, x0)$ and $(x, x1)$ of the binary tree using letters A, B and C, D as follows. For any x consider two cases.

Case 1. There is an edge $(x, x\sigma)$ such that $\lambda(\sigma, \Lambda(x)) \geq a(1 - \epsilon)$. In this case we assign C to $(x, x\sigma)$ and D to $(x, x\hat\sigma)$, where $\hat\sigma = 1$ if $\sigma = 0$, and $\hat\sigma = 0$ otherwise.

Case 2. Case 1 does not hold, i.e. $\lambda(\sigma, \Lambda(x)) \leq a(1 - \epsilon)$ for all σ. In this case we assign the letter A to $(x, x0)$ and letter B to $(x, x1)$ if $\lambda(0, \Lambda(x)) \geq b$ and assign these letters vise versa, otherwise.

Evidently, two different sequences of length n have different labellings.

If some edge $(x, x\sigma)$ labeled by C then $\lambda(\sigma, \Lambda(x)) \geq a(1 - \epsilon)$ and, hence, for any path x of length n having more than $\frac{k}{a(1-\epsilon)}$ letters C it holds $KG(x) \geq \text{Loss}_\Lambda(x) \geq k$.

By definition if some edge $(x, x\sigma)$ labeled by A or by B then $\lambda(\sigma, \Lambda(x)) \leq a(1 - \epsilon)$ for all σ. Then by Proposition 2 we have $\lambda(\sigma, \Lambda(x)) \geq a\delta(\epsilon)$ for all σ. Hence, for any path x of the length n having more than $k/(a\delta(\epsilon))$ letters A or B it holds $KG(x) \geq \text{Loss}_\Lambda(x) \geq k$.

Hence, any sequence x of length n, on which $KG(x) \leq k$, can have no more than $k/(a\delta(\epsilon))$ letters A or B and no more than $\frac{k}{a(1-\epsilon)}$ letters C, the rest part of x are letters D. It also has no more than $\frac{k}{b}$ letters A.

By means of this labelings, every sequence $x \in A_{n,k}$ can be recovered from the following pair (α, β) of sequences. The first element of this pair is the sequence α of all letters A and B assigned to edges on x in the original order. This sequence contains no more than $\frac{k}{b}$ letters A. It is also can not be longer than $k/(a\delta(\epsilon))$. The second element of the pair is the sequence β of all letters C and D assigned to edges on x in the original order. This sequence contains no more than $\frac{k}{a(1-\epsilon)}$ letters C. Given these two sequences (α, β), the whole sequence x can be recovered as follows. Let $x^{i-1} = x_1 \ldots x_{i-1}$, where $1 \leq i \leq n$, be already recovered by some initial fragments α^{s-1} and β^{q-1} of sequences α and β. We can place x^{i-1} in the binary tree supplied by new labellings and so define letters assigned to edges $(x^{i-1}, x^{i-1}0)$ and $(x^{i-1}, x^{i-1}1)$. Comparing these letters with α_s and β_q we can define which sequence must be used in recovering of the next member of x. The corresponding letter α_s or β_q of this sequence determines the member x_i of the sequence x.

Note, that the labelling and, hence, our method of recovering are incomputable. It gives us only a possibility to estimate the number of elements of the set $A_{n,k}$. The method of recovering shows that to do this, it is enough to estimate the number of all such pairs (α, β). It can be estimated as follows:

$$\#A_{n,k} \leq \sum_{i \leq k/b} \binom{k/(a\delta(\epsilon))}{i} \sum_{i \leq k/(a(1-\epsilon))} \binom{n}{i}.$$

□

Note, that upper bound (9) is valid for k much smaller than n for small ϵ.

Proposition 6. Let $0 < \epsilon < \delta^{-1}(\frac{b}{2a})$.

- (i) If in addition $\epsilon \leq \frac{1}{2}$ then a positive constant c exists such that for all x

$$K(x) \leq \frac{KG(x)}{a(1-\epsilon)} \left(\log l(x) - \log \frac{KG(x)}{4a(1-\epsilon)} \right) - \tag{11}$$

$$2 \log \left(\frac{a\delta(\epsilon)}{b} \right) \frac{KG(x)}{b} + c. \tag{12}$$

- (ii) For all sufficiently large n for all x of length n if $KG(x) \leq \frac{n}{2}a(1-\epsilon)$
  then

$$\frac{K(x)}{n} \leq H \left(\frac{KG(x)}{na(1-\epsilon)} \right) - 2 \log \left(\frac{a\delta(\epsilon)}{b} \right) \frac{KG(x)}{bn} + \frac{7 \log n}{n}, \tag{13}$$

where $H(p) = -p \log p - (1-p) \log(1-p)$ is the Shannon entropy.

Proof. Let us consider the recursively enumerable set $A_{n,k}$ defined by (8) above. We can specify any $x \in A_{n,k}$ by n, k and the ordinal number of x in the natural enumeration of $A_{n,k}$, i.e. $K(x) \leq \log \#A_{n,k} + 2 \log n + 2 \log k + c$, for some constant c. After that we make some transformations of the upper bound (9) of Proposition 5 and replace k on $KG(x)$.

We will use the following estimates of the binomial coefficients from [3], Section 6.1.

$$\left(\frac{n}{k} \right)^k \leq \binom{n}{k} \leq \left(\frac{en}{k} \right)^k \tag{14}$$

and estimates

$$\sum_{i \leq m} \binom{n}{i} \leq (m+1) \binom{n}{m}, \tag{15}$$

$$\log \binom{n}{s} \leq nH \left(\frac{s}{n} \right) \tag{16}$$

for any $m \leq \frac{n}{2}$ and $s \leq n$. We use also inequality

$$\frac{H(p)}{p} \leq -2 \log p \tag{17}$$

for all $0 < p < \frac{1}{2}$.

Let $k \leq \frac{n}{2}a(1-\epsilon)$. We have also $\frac{k}{b} \leq \frac{1}{2}\frac{k}{a\delta(\epsilon)}$ for all $\epsilon < \delta^{-1}(\frac{b}{2a})$.

To prove inequality (11) let us consider the recursively enumerable set $A_{n,k}$ defined by (8). We can specify any $x \in A_{n,k}$ by n, k and the ordinal number of x in the natural enumeration of $A_{n,k}$. Using an appropriate encoding of all triples of positive integer numbers by upper bound (9) of Proposition 5 and using (14), (15), (16), (17) we obtain for all $x \in A_{n,k}$

$$K(x) \leq \log \#A_{n,k} + 2\log n + 2\log k + c \leq \tag{18}$$

$$\log \frac{k}{b}\binom{k/(a\delta(\epsilon))}{k/b} + \log \frac{k}{a(1-\epsilon)}\binom{n}{k/(a(1-\epsilon))} + \tag{19}$$

$$2\log n + 2\log k + c \leq \tag{20}$$

$$\log \frac{k}{b} + \frac{k}{a\delta(\epsilon)}H\left(\frac{a\delta(\epsilon)}{b}\right) + \tag{21}$$

$$\log \frac{k}{a(1-\epsilon)} + \log\left(\frac{en}{k/(a(1-\epsilon))}\right)^{k/(a(1-\epsilon))} + \tag{22}$$

$$2\log n + 2\log k + c' = \tag{23}$$

$$\log \frac{k}{b} + \frac{k}{a\delta(\epsilon)}H\left(\frac{a\delta(\epsilon)}{b}\right) + \log \frac{k}{a(1-\epsilon)} + \tag{24}$$

$$\frac{k}{a(1-\epsilon)}\left(\log n + \log e - \log \frac{k}{a(1-\epsilon)}\right) + \tag{25}$$

$$2\log n + 2\log k + c' \leq \tag{26}$$

$$\left(\frac{k}{a(1-\epsilon)} + 2\right)\left(\log n - \log \frac{k}{a(1-\epsilon)} + 2\right) - \tag{27}$$

$$\frac{2k}{b}\log \frac{a\delta(\epsilon)}{b} + c'', \tag{28}$$

where c, c' and c'' are positive constants.

Put $k = KG(x)$. Then by inequalities (18)–(28), we obtain in the case $KG(x) \leq \frac{1}{2}na(1-\epsilon) + 2a(1-\epsilon) = a(1-\epsilon)(\frac{n}{2}+2)$ the following inequality

$$K(x) \leq \left(\frac{KG(x)}{a(1-\epsilon)} + 2\right)\left(\log n - \log \frac{KG(x)}{4a(1-\epsilon)}\right) - \frac{2KG(x)}{b}\log \frac{a\delta(\epsilon)}{b} + c \tag{29}$$

for some positive constant c. We can omit the term $+2$ in (29), since $KG(x)$ is defined up to an additive constant.

Consider two strategies $S_1(z) = 0$ and $S_2(z) = 1$ for all z. Then for each x of length n it holds $Loss_{S_1}(x) \leq \frac{a}{2}n$ or $Loss_{S_2}(x) \leq \frac{a}{2}n$. Therefore the inequality $KG(x) \leq \frac{1}{2}an + c$ holds for some positive constant c. If $KG(x) \geq \frac{n}{2}a(1-\epsilon)$ we have for all n and all x of length n

$$K(x) \leq n + 2\log n + c_1 \leq \frac{n}{2}\log n - \frac{n}{2}\log \frac{n}{8} + c_2 \leq \tag{30}$$

$$\frac{KG(x)}{a(1-\epsilon)}\left(\log n - \log \frac{KG(x)}{4a(1-\epsilon)}\right) + c_3, \tag{31}$$

where c_1, c_2, c_3 are positive constants. Inequality (11), (12) follows from (30), (31) when $\epsilon \leq \frac{1}{2}$. Item (i) is proved.

Let us consider the item (ii). In the case $KG(x) \leq \frac{n}{2}a(1 - \epsilon)$ inequality (13) can be obtained by applying inequality (16) to the second binomial coefficient of (19) as follows.

$$K(x) \leq \frac{k}{a\delta(\epsilon)} H\left(\frac{a\delta(\epsilon)}{b}\right) + nH\left(\frac{k}{na(1 - \epsilon)}\right) + 6 \log n + c, \qquad (32)$$

where c is a positive constant.

Putting $k = KG(x)$ in (32) and dividing on n we obtain for any $\epsilon < \delta^{-1}(\frac{b}{2a})$ for all sufficiently large n

$$\frac{K(x)}{n} \leq H\left(\frac{KG(x)}{na(1 - \epsilon)}\right) + \frac{KG(x)}{na\delta(\epsilon)} H\left(\frac{a\delta(\epsilon)}{b}\right) + \frac{7 \log n}{n} \leq$$
$$H\left(\frac{KG(x)}{na(1 - \epsilon)}\right) - 2 \log\left(\frac{a\delta(\epsilon)}{b}\right) \frac{KG(x)}{bn} + \frac{7 \log n}{n}.$$

□

Proposition 7. *Let $0 < \gamma < 1$, $0 < \epsilon < \delta^{-1}(\frac{b}{2a})$. Then a positive constant c exists such that for each sufficiently large n and each $k \leq \frac{1}{2}na(1 - \epsilon)$ a binary sequence x of length n exists such that*

$$k(1 - \gamma)(1 - \epsilon) \leq KG(x) \leq k + c, \qquad (33)$$
$$K(x) \geq \log\binom{n}{k/a} - 1 \geq nH\left(\frac{KG(x)}{an}\right) - 2 \log n \qquad (34)$$

and also

$$K(x) \geq \frac{KG(x)}{a}\left(\log n - \log \frac{KG(x)}{a}\right) - 2. \qquad (35)$$

Proof. We will find x satisfying the condition of this proposition in the set $A_{n,k}$ defined by (8). We must estimate minimal k' such that $\#A_{n,k} \geq \binom{n}{(k-c)/a} > 2\#A_{n,k'}$. We will show that this inequality holds for all sufficiently large n if $k' = (k - c)(1 - \gamma)(1 - \epsilon)$, where c is a constant from lower bound (9). By incompressibility property of Kolmogorov complexity (see [5]) and lower bound (9) an $x \in A_{n,k} - A_{n,k'}$ exists such that $K(x) \geq \log\binom{n}{(k-c)/a} - 2$. After that, using appropriate estimates of binomial coefficients and replacing k on $k - c$ we obtain inequalities (33), (34) and (35).

We will find x satisfying the condition of this proposition in the set $A_{n,k}$ defined by (8). We must find some k' such that $\#A_{n,k} > 2\#A_{n,k'}$.

By the upper and lower bounds (9) of Proposition 5 it is sufficient that k' be satisfy

$$\binom{n}{(k-c)/a} > 2 \sum_{i \leq k'/(a(1-\epsilon))} \binom{n}{i} \sum_{i \leq k'/b} \binom{k'/(a\delta(\epsilon))}{i}, \qquad (36)$$

where c is a constant from the lower bound (9).

We will find k' satisfying $k' \le \frac{n}{2}a(1-\epsilon)$. By (14) inequality (36) follows from

$$\left(\frac{na}{k-c}\right)^{\frac{k-c}{a}} \ge \frac{4k'}{b}\left(\frac{eb}{a\delta(\epsilon)}\right)^{\frac{k'}{b}}\left(\frac{ena(1-\epsilon)}{k'}\right)^{\frac{k'}{a(1-\epsilon)}}\frac{k'}{a(1-\epsilon)}. \quad (37)$$

Inequality (37) holds for all sufficiently large n if $k' = (k-c)(1-\gamma)(1-\epsilon)$. Then for each sufficiently large n we have $\#A_{n,k} > 2\#A_{n,k'}$ and

$$(k-c)(1-\gamma)(1-\epsilon) \le KG(x) \le k \quad (38)$$

for all $x \in A_{n,k} - A_{n,k'}$. We have also $k' \le \frac{n}{2}a(1-\epsilon)$ if $k \le \frac{1}{2}na(1-\epsilon)+c$.

By incompressibility property of Kolmogorov complexity we have that an $x \in A_{n,k} - A_{n,k'}$ exists such that

$$K(x) \ge \log\binom{n}{(k-c)/a} - 2 \ge nH\left(\frac{k-c}{an}\right) - 2\log n. \quad (39)$$

Here we used the last inequality on the page 66 of [5]. We obtain also by (14)

$$K(x) \ge \log\binom{n}{(k-c)/a} - 2 \ge \frac{k-c}{a}\log n - \frac{k-c}{a}\log\frac{k-c}{a} - 2 = \quad (40)$$

$$\frac{k-c}{a}\left(\log n - \log\frac{k-c}{a}\right) - 2. \quad (41)$$

Now replacing in the proof of the proposition k on $k+c$ and putting $k = KG(x)$ we obtain from (39) and (41) inequalities (34) and (35). Inequality (33) follows from (38). $\square$

The next corollary from propositions 6 and 7 gives precise relations between normalized Kolmogorov and predictive complexities. This result is too technical and it is reformulated in the Section 4 in a more convenient form.

Corollary 8. *Let $0 < \epsilon < \delta^{-1}(\frac{b}{2a})$. Then for all sequences x of sufficiently large length if $KG(x) \le \frac{1}{2}na(1-\epsilon)$ then*

$$\frac{K(x)}{l(x)} \le H\left(\frac{KG(x)}{a(1-\epsilon)l(x)}\right) - 2\log\left(\frac{a\delta(\epsilon)}{b}\right)\frac{KG(x)}{bl(x)} + \frac{7\log l(x)}{l(x)}$$

and for each sufficiently large n there is some x of length n such that

$$\frac{K(x)}{l(x)} \ge H\left(\frac{KG(x)}{al(x)}\right) - \frac{2\log l(x)}{l(x)}$$

Proof. This corollary follows from (13) and (34). $\square$

Theorem 9. *Let $0 < \epsilon < \min\{\frac{1}{2}, \delta^{-1}(\frac{b}{2a})\}$. Then there exists a constant c such that for all n*

$$\frac{1}{a}\log n - c \le f(n) \le \frac{1}{a(1-\epsilon)}\log n - \frac{2}{b}\log\delta(\epsilon) + c$$

where $f(n)$ is the worst-case ratio function defined by (3).

Proof. The right-hand inequality follows directly from (11). The left-hand inequality can be derived from (33) and (35) of Proposition 7. It is enough to let $k = n^\epsilon$. Taking $\epsilon \to 0$ we obtain the needed inequality. $\square$

Theorem 10. *Let* $0 < \epsilon < \delta^{-1}(\frac{b}{2a})$. *Then for each real number* $t \leq \frac{1}{2}a(1 - \epsilon)$

$$H\left(\frac{t}{a}\right) \leq \underline{h}(t) \leq \overline{h}(t) \leq H\left(\frac{t}{a(1-\epsilon)}\right) - \frac{2}{b}\log\frac{a\delta(\epsilon)}{b}t. \qquad (42)$$

where $\underline{h}(t)$ *and* $\overline{h}(t)$ *are relative complexities comparing functions defined by (6) and (7).*

Proof. This theorem follows directly from Corollary 8. $\square$

Acknowledgements. Authors are grateful to Volodya Vovk and Yuri Kalnishkan for useful discussions. Volodya Vovk also made insightful suggestions about formulating of main results of the paper.

References

[1] Haussler, D., Kivinen, J., Warmuth, M.K.: Tight worst-case loss bounds for predicting with expert advice. Technical Report UCSC-CRL-94-36, University of California at Santa Cruz, revised December 1994. Short version in P. Vitányi, editor, Computational Learning Theory, Lecture Notes in Computer Science **904** (1995) 69–83 Springer Berlin

[2] Cesa-Bianchi, N., Freund, Y., Helmbold, D.P., Haussler, D., Schapire, R.E., Warmuth, M.K.: How to use expert advice Journal of the ACM **44** (1997) 427–485

[3] Cormen, H., Leiserson, E., Rivest, R.: Introduction to Algorithms New York: McGraw Hill 1990

[4] Kalnishkan, Y.: General linear relations among different types of predictive complexity In Proc. 10th international Conference on Algorithmic Learning Theory–ALT '99 **1720** (1999) of Lecture Notes in Artificial Intelligence 323–334 Springer–Verlag

[5] Li, M., Vitányi, P.: *An Introduction to Kolmogorov Complexity and Its Applications* Springer New York 2nd edition 1997

[6] Rogers, H.: Theory of recursive functions and effective computability New York: McGraw Hill 1967

[7] Vovk, V.: Aggregating strategies In M. Fulk and J. Case, editors Proceedings of the 3rd Annual Workshop on Computational Learning Theory 371–383 San Mateo CA Morgan Kaufmann 1990

[8] Vovk, V.: A game of prediction with expert advice J. Comput. Syst. Sci. **56** (1998) 153–173

[9] Vovk, V., Gammerman, A.: Complexity estimation principle The Computer Journal **42** (1999) 318–322

[10] Vovk, V., Watkins, C.J.H.C.: Universal portfolio selection Proceedings of the 11th Annual Conference on Computational Learning Theory (1998) 12–23

[11] Zvonkin, A.K., Levin, L.A.: The complexity of finite objects and the algorithmic concepts of information and randomness Russ. Math. Surv. **25** (1970) 83–124

[12] Yamanishi, K.: Randomized approximate aggregating strategies and their applications to prediction and discrimination, in Proceedings 8th Annual ACM Conference on Computational Learning Theory 83–90 Assoc. Comput. Mach. New
York 1995

Appendix: Proof of Proposition 1

A semicomputable from above sequence $KG_i(x)$ of all measures of predictive
complexity satisfying items 1)–3) of Section 2 can be defined as follows. We will
consider the recursively enumerable (r.e.) sets as consisting of pairs (x, r), where
x is a finite binary sequence and r is a nonnegative rational number (all such pairs
can be effectively encoded using all natural numbers). Let W be an universal r.e.
set such that for each r.e. set A (consisting of pairs (x, r) as mentioned above)
there exists a natural number i such that $A = W_i = \{(x, r)|(i, x, r) \in W\}$. The
existence of this set is the central result of the theory of algorithms (see Rogers
[6]).

By computability of $\lambda(\sigma, p)$ a computable sequence of simple functions
$\lambda^t(\sigma, p)$ exists such that $\lambda^{t+1}(\sigma, p) \leq \lambda^t(\sigma, p)$ for all t, σ, p and $\lambda(\sigma, p) =
\inf_t \lambda^t(\sigma, p)$.

Let W^t be a finite subset of W enumerated in t steps. Define

$$W_i^t = \{(x, r)|\exists r'((i, x, r') \in W^t, r \geq r')\} \cup (\Xi \times \{+\infty\}).$$

It is easy to define a computable sequence of simple functions $KG_i^t(x)$ such that
$KG_i^0(x) = \infty$ and $KG_i^{t+1}(x) \leq KG_i^t(x)$ for all x. Besides, $KG_i^t(x)$ is a minimal
(under $\leq$) simple function whose graph is a subset of W_i^t and such that for each
x a rational p exists for which

$$KG_i^t(x\sigma) - KG_i^t(x) \geq \lambda^t(\sigma, p) \tag{43}$$

holds for each $\sigma = 0, 1$. Define $KG_i(x) = \inf_t KG_i^t(x)$ for each i and x. It follows
from (43) and continuity of $\lambda(\sigma, p)$ in p that for any i the function $KG_i(x)$ is a
measure of predictive complexity.

Let a function $KG(x)$ satisfies the conditions (i), (ii) of the definition of a
measure of predictive complexity and $W_i = \{(x, r)|r > KG(x)\}$, where r is a
rational number. It is easy to verify that $KG(x) = KG_i(x)$ for all x.

Let r_i be a semicomputable from below sequence of real numbers such that
$\sum_{i=1}^{\infty} r_i \leq 1$. For instance, we can take $r_i = 2^{-K(i)}$, where $K(i)$ is the Kolmogorov
prefix complexity of i.

We prove that $KG(x)$ defined by (2) is a measure of predictive complexity.
By definition $KG(x)$ is semicomputable from above, i.e (ii) holds. We must verify
(i). Let $\beta = e^{-\eta}$, η is a learning rate. Indeed, by (2) for every x and $j = 0, 1$

$$KG(xj) - KG(x) = \log_\beta \sum_{i=1}^{\infty} q_i \beta^{KG_i(xj)-KG_i(x)} \geq \tag{44}$$

$$\log_\beta \sum_{i=1}^{\infty} q_i \beta^{\lambda(j,\gamma_i)} \geq \lambda(j,\gamma), \qquad (45)$$

where

$$q_i = \frac{r_i \beta^{KG_i(x)}}{\sum\limits_{s=1}^{\infty} r_s \beta^{KG_s(x)}}.$$

Here for any i a prediction γ_i satisfying

$$KG_i(xj) - KG_i(x) \geq \lambda(j,\gamma_i)$$

exists since each element of the sequence $KG_i(x)$ satisfies the condition (i) of the measure of predictive complexity. A prediction γ satisfying (45) exists by η-mixability. For further details see [10], Section 7.6.

Learning by Switching Type of Information

Sanjay Jain[*1] and Frank Stephan[**2]

[1] School of Computing, National University of Singapore, Singapore 119260,
sanjay@comp.nus.edu.sg
[2] Mathematisches Institut, Im Neuenheimer Feld 294, Ruprecht-Karls-Universität
Heidelberg, 69120 Heidelberg, Germany, fstephan@math.uni-heidelberg.de

Abstract. The present work is dedicated to the study of modes of data-presentation between text and informant within the framework of inductive inference. The model is such that the learner requests sequences of positive and negative data and the relations between the various formalizations in dependence on the number of switches between positive and negative data is investigated. In particular it is shown that there is a proper hierarchy of the notions of learning from standard text, in the basic switching model, in the newtext switching model and in the restart switching model. The last one of these turns out to be equivalent to the standard notion of learning from informant.

1 Introduction

One central question studied in inductive inference is the relation between learning from all data, that is learning from informant, and learning from positive data only, that is, learning from text. Learning from text is much more restrictive than learning from informant; already Gold [7] gave an easy example of a class which can be learned from informant but not from text: the collection consisting of one infinite set together with all its finite subsets. Sharma [16] showed that combining learning from informant with a restrictive convergence requirement, namely that the first hypothesis has already to be the correct one, implies also learnability from text, provided that then the usual convergence requirement is applied and the hypothesis may be changed finitely often before converging to the correct one.

The main motivation for this work is to explore the gap between these two extreme forms of data-presentation. Previous authors have already proposed several methods to investigate this gap: Using non-recursive oracles as an additional method cannot completely cover the gap since even the most powerful ones do not permit to learn all sets [8] while the oracle K does this for learning from informant; restrictions on the texts reduce their non-regularity and permit to pass on further information implicitly [13,17]; strengthening the text by permitting

---

[*] Supported in part by NUS grant number RP3992710.
[**] Supported by the Deutsche Forschungsgemeinschaft (DFG) under the Heisenberg grant Ste 967/1–1

N. Abe, R. Khardon, and T. Zeugmann (Eds.): ALT 2001, LNAI 2225, pp. 205–218, 2001.

additional queries [11] to retrieve information not contained in standard texts. Ascending texts permit to reconstruct the complete negative information in the case of infinite sets but might fail to do so in the case of finite sets; thus the class of one infinite set and all its finite subsets still is unlearnable from ascending text.

Motoki [12] and later Baliga, Case and Jain [2] added to the positive information of the text some but not all negative information on the language to be learned. They considered two notions of supplying the negative data: (a) there is a finite set of negative information $S \subseteq \overline{L}$ such that the learner always succeeds learning the set L from input S plus a text for L; (b) there is a finite set $S \subseteq \overline{L}$ such that the learner always succeeds learning the set L from a text for L plus a text for a set H disjoint to L which contains S, that is, which satisfies $S \subseteq H \subseteq \overline{L}$. As one can in case (a) learn all recursively enumerable sets by a single learner, the notion (b) is the more interesting one.

The present work treats positive and negative data symmetrically and several of its notions are much less powerful than those notions from [2] just discussed. The most convenient way to define these notions is to use the idea of a minimum adequate teacher as, for example, described by Angluin [1]. A learner requests positive or negative data-items from a teacher which has – depending on the exact formalization – to fulfill certain requirements in the limit. These formalizations and also the number of switches permitted define then the model. The naturalness of this approach is witnessed by the fact that all classes separating the various formalizations can be defined in easy topological terms. Thus these separating classes are as fundamental as Gold's text-non-learnability example in the sense that they witness the same separations also in the case that the learners may use non-recursive oracles.

2   Notation and Preliminaries

Notation. Any unexplained recursion theoretic notation is from [14]. The symbol Nat denotes the set of natural numbers, $\{0, 1, 2, 3, \ldots\}$. Symbols $\emptyset$, $\subseteq$, $\subset$, $\supseteq$, and $\supset$ denote empty set, subset, proper subset, superset, and proper superset, respectively. Cardinality of a set S is denoted by $\mathrm{card}(S)$.

dom(η) and range(η) denote the domain and range of partial function η, respectively. Sequences are partial functions η where the domain is either Nat or $\{y \in \mathrm{Nat} : y < x\}$ for some x. In the first case, the length of η (denoted $|\eta|$) is ∞, in the second case its length is x. Although sequences may take a special value $\#$ to indicate a pause (when considered as a source of data), this pause-sign is omitted from range(η) for the ease of notation. Furthermore, if $x \leq |\sigma|$, then $\sigma[x]$ denotes the restriction of σ to the domain $\{y \in \mathrm{Nat} : y < x\}$. We let η, σ and τ range over finite sequences. We denote the sequence formed by the concatenation of τ at the end of σ by $\sigma\tau$. Furthermore, we use σx to denote the concatenation of sequence σ and the sequence of length 1 which contains the element x.

By φ we denote a fixed *acceptable* programming system for the partial computable functions mapping Nat to Nat [10,14]. By φ_i we denote the partial computable function computed by the program with number i in the φ-system. Such a program i is a (characteristic) index for a set L if $\varphi_i(x) = 1$ for $x \in L$ and $\varphi_i(x) = 0$ for $x \notin L$; programs for enumeration procedures (so call r.e. indices) are not considered in the present work. From now on, we call the recursive subsets of Nat just languages and do therefore only consider characteristic indices and not enumeration procedures. The symbols L, H range over languages and $\overline{L}$ denotes the complement Nat $- L$ of L. The symbol $\mathcal{L}$ ranges over classes of languages.

Although learning theory also often considers learning non-recursive but still recursively enumerable set, we restrict ourselves to the recursive case since, for notions of learning considered in this paper, this case already permits to construct all counterexamples for interesting separations of learning criteria while all inclusions hold for the case of recursive sets iff they hold for the case of recursively enumerable sets. This is due to the fact that all proofs use mainly the information-theoretic properties but not on recursion-theoretic properties of the concepts. Furthermore, recursive sets have compared to recursively enumerable sets the advantage, that also their complement possesses a recursive enumeration, see Remark 2.8.

Notation from Learning Theory. The main scenario of inductive inference is that a learner reads more and more data on an object and outputs a sequence of hypotheses which eventually converge to the object to be learned. The formalization of the data-presentation uses the concept of a *sequence* introduced above and such data sequences are usually denoted by T (for "text").

Definition 2.1. [7] A *text* T for a language L is an infinite sequence such that its range is L, that is, T contains all elements of L but none of $\overline{L}$. $T[n]$ denotes the finite initial sequence of T with length n.

Definition 2.2. [7] A *learner* (or learning machine) is an algorithmic device which computes a mapping from finite sequences into Nat.

We let $\mathbf{M}$ range over learning machines. $\mathbf{M}(T[n])$ is interpreted as the index for the language conjectured by the learning machine $\mathbf{M}$ on the initial sequence $T[n]$. We say that $\mathbf{M}$ converges on T to i, (written $\mathbf{M}(T) \downarrow = i$) iff $(\forall^\infty n)\,[\mathbf{M}(T[n]) = i]$.

There are several criteria for a learning machine to be successful on a language. Below we define learning in the limit introduced by Gold [7].

Definition 2.3. [7] (a) $\mathbf{M}$ **TxtEx**-learns a text T for a language L iff almost all outputs $\mathbf{M}(T[n])$ are the same index i for L.
(b) $\mathbf{M}$ **TxtEx**-learns a language L (written: $L \in \mathbf{TxtEx}(\mathbf{M})$) just in case $\mathbf{M}$ **TxtEx**-learns each text for L.
(c) $\mathbf{M}$ **TxtEx**-learns a class $\mathcal{L}$ of recursive languages (written: $\mathcal{L} \subseteq \mathbf{TxtEx}(\mathbf{M})$) just in case $\mathbf{M}$ **TxtEx**-learns each language from $\mathcal{L}$.
(d) **TxtEx** is the collection of all classes $\mathcal{L}$ which have a computable **TxtEx**-learner.

The following propositions on learning from text are useful in proving some of our results.

Proposition 2.4. [13, Based on Proposition 2.2A] *Let L be any infinite set and Pos be a finite subset of L. Then $\{H : Pos \subseteq H \subseteq L \wedge card(L - H) \leq 1\}$ $\notin$ **TxtEx**.*

Proposition 2.5. [7] *Let L be any infinite language. If $\mathcal{L}$ contains L and the sets $L \cap \{0, 1, \ldots, n\}$, for infinitely many $n \in Nat$, then $\mathcal{L} \notin$ **TxtEx**.*

We now generalize the concept of learning and permit the learners to request explicitly positive or negative data from a teacher in order to define learning by switching between type of information received.

Definition 2.6. Learning is a game between a learner **M** and a teacher T. Both send alternately informations in the following way: in the k-th round, the learner first sends a request $r_k \in \{+, -\}$. Then the teacher answers with an information x_k. Afterwards the learner outputs a hypothesis e_k. There are three types of interactive protocols between the learner and the teacher; every teacher satisfying the protocol is permitted.

(a) The basic switch-protocol. The teacher has two texts T_+, T_- of L and $\overline{L}$, respectively. After receiving r_k the teacher transmits $T_{r_k}(k)$.

(b) The restarting switch-protocol. The teacher has two texts T_+, T_- of L and $\overline{L}$, respectively. After receiving r_k the teacher computes the current position $l = card(\{h : 0 \leq h < k \wedge r_h = r_k\})$ and transmits $T_{r_k}(l)$.

(c) The newtext switch-protocol. The teacher always either sends an $x_k \in L \cup \{\#\}$ if $r_k = +$ and $x_k \in \overline{L} \cup \{\#\}$ if $r_k = -$. Furthermore, if there is a k such that $r_h = r_k$, for all $h \geq k$, and either $k = 0$ or $r_{k-1} \neq r_k$, then the sequence $x_k, x_{k+1}, \ldots$ is a text for either L (if $r_k = +$) or $\overline{L}$ (if $r_k = -$).

A class $\mathcal{L}$ is learnable according to the given protocol iff there is a computable machine **M** such that for every $L \in \mathcal{L}$ and for every teacher satisfying the protocol for this L, the hypotheses of the learner **M** converge to an index e of L. The corresponding learning-criteria are denoted by **BasicSwEx**, **RestartSwEx** and **NewSwEx**, respectively.

Note that **M** is a **TxtEx**-learner iff M always requests positive data ($r_k = +$ for all k). Therefore, all three notions are generalizations of **TxtEx**-learning.

In the following we define similar restrictions on the number of switches as has been done for the number of mind changes [5,6]. We also consider counting switches by ordinals: the learner has a counter for an ordinal, which is down-counted at every switch and which due to the well-ordering of the ordinals can be downcounted only finitely often. In order to guarantee that the learner is computable, we consider throughout this work only recursive ordinals. In particular, we use a fixed notation system, Ords, and a partial ordering of ordinal notations. A method to define such a notation is, for example, given by Kleene [9,14,15]. Let $\preceq, \prec, \succeq$ and $\succ$ on ordinal notations below refer to the partial ordering of ordinal notations in this system. We do not go into the details of the notation system used, but instead refer the reader to [4,6,9,14,15].

Definition 2.7. **BasicSw$_*$Ex** denotes the variant of **BasicSwEx**, where also the requests of **M** have to converge to some r whenever **M** deals with a teacher following basic switch-protocol, for any given $L \in \mathcal{L}$.

For an ordinal notation α, the variant **BasicSw$_\alpha$Ex** denotes that the learner is equipped with a counter for an ordinal notation and that the number of switches is restricted by requiring that the counter is initialized as α and that it is downcounted exactly whenever a switch occurs: If $r_{k+1} = r_k$ then $\alpha_{k+1} = \alpha_k$ and if $r_{k+1} \neq r_k$ then $\alpha_{k+1} \prec \alpha_k$ where α_k, α_{k+1} are the values of the ordinal counter at rounds $k, k+1$.

Similarly one defines **RestartSw$_*$Ex**, **NewSw$_*$Ex**, **RestartSw$_\alpha$Ex** and **NewSw$_\alpha$Ex**. It is furthermore possible, to use other convergence-criteria than **Ex** for the hypotheses.

Remark 2.8. These notions might change a bit if instead of arbitrary texts some restrictive variants are used.

A *fat text* is a text whose elements occur all infinitely often. Therefore, arbitrary long initial segments of the text may be missing without loosing essential information. Therefore, one can to a certain degree compensate the loss of information when switching in a basic text: **BasicSw$_*$Ex** = **NewSw$_*$Ex** when only fat texts are permitted. The notions **NewSw$_*$Ex** and **RestartSw$_*$Ex** do not change if one feeds fat texts instead of normal texts, but the notion of **BasicSw$_*$Ex** increases its power and becomes equivalent to **NewSw$_*$Ex**. The same applies to the notions obtained by bounding the number of switches by ordinals.

A *recursive text* does not give an advantage for classes of recursive languages, since one can construct counterexample texts always such that they are recursive. As all separations constructed below involve only classes of recursive sets, these separations remain valid if the texts are required to be recursive.

Gold [7] showed that the class of all recursively enumerable sets can be learned from *primitive recursive text* which has to be generated by a primitive recursive function. Then, no switches are necessary at all and all the notions coincide with Gold's notion of learning from text.

Remark 2.9. Let $\mathcal{L}$ contain the four subsets of $\{0,1\}$. This class is **TxtEx**-learnable but it is not learnable by a **BasicSwEx**-learner which is required to make at least one switch on every possible data-sequence.

To see this, assume that the learner starts with requesting positive examples, then 0^∞ is a valid text for $\{0\}$ and the learner has to make eventually on it a switch after some (say n) examples. But then the learner cannot distinguish the sets $\{0\}$ and $\{0,1\}$: In case $\{0\}$, let $T_+ = 0^\infty$ and $T_- = 1\,2\,3\,\ldots$ and in case $\{0,1\}$, let $T_+ = 0^n\,1\,0^\infty$ and $T_- = 2\,2\,3\,\ldots$; so the T_- differ at the first position and the T_+ differ at the $n+1$-st position. Both positions are not seen by the learner and so the learner cannot find out, which case holds. If the learner starts by requesting negative data, it can be trapped similarly.

Although **BasicSwEx** is more powerful than **TxtEx**, it still has a severe restriction since information might be lost and it might happen, that a given learner receives – due to switches – a data sequence which satisfies the protocol for several possible languages. This cannot occur for the criteria of **NewSwEx**-learning and **RestartSwEx**-learning which from this point of view are more natural.

3 Basic Relations between the Concepts

Within this section, we investigate the basic relations between the various criteria of learning by switching type of information.

Proposition 3.1.
(a) *For all ordinals α,* **BasicSw$_\alpha$Ex** $\subseteq$ **NewSw$_\alpha$Ex** $\subseteq$ **RestartSw$_\alpha$Ex**.
(b) **BasicSw$_*$Ex** $\subseteq$ **NewSw$_*$Ex** $\subseteq$ **RestartSw$_*$Ex**.
(c) **BasicSwEx** $\subseteq$ **NewSwEx** $\subseteq$ **RestartSwEx**.

Proof. First note that any teacher using the newtext switch-protocol also satisfies the basic switch-protocol. Also note that any teacher using the restart switch-protocol can be easily modified to give answers using a newtext switch-protocol – by appropriately repeating the already given positive / negative elements before giving any new elements presented in the restart switch-protocol. The proposition follows.   □

In the following it is shown that the hierarchy from Proposition 3.1 (c) is strict, that is,

$$\textbf{TxtEx} \subset \textbf{BasicSwEx} \subset \textbf{NewSwEx} \subset \textbf{RestartSwEx}.$$

Besides this main goal, the influence of restricting the number of switches to be finite or even to respect an ordinal bound, is investigated.

Note that the inclusion **TxtEx** $\subseteq$ **BasicSw$_0$Ex** follows directly from the definition. Furthermore, the class $\{L : \text{card}(\overline{L}) \leq 1\}$, using Proposition 2.4, is not **TxtEx**-learnable but since it contains only cofinite sets it can be learned via some learner requesting always negative data. Thus the inclusion **TxtEx** $\subset$ **BasicSw$_0$Ex** is strict.

Combining finite and cofinite sets is the basic idea to separate newtext switching from basic switching using parts (a) and (c) of Theorem 3.2 below. The class used to show this separation is quite natural and thus also interesting on its own right:

$$\mathcal{L}_{fin,cofin} = \{L : \text{card}(L) < \infty \text{ or } \text{card}(\overline{L}) < \infty\}.$$

Theorem 3.2 below also characterizes the optimal number of switches needed to learn $\mathcal{L}_{fin,cofin}$ (where possible): one can do it for the criteria **NewSw$_*$Ex** and **RestartSw$_*$Ex** with finitely many switches but an ordinal bound on the number of switches is impossible.

Theorem 3.2. (a) $\mathcal{L}_{fin,cofin} \in$ **NewSw$_*$Ex**.
(b) *For all ordinals α,* $\mathcal{L}_{fin,cofin} \notin$ **RestartSw$_\alpha$Ex**.
(c) $\mathcal{L}_{fin,cofin} \notin$ **BasicSwEx**.

Proof. (a) The machine **M** works in stages. At any point of time it keeps track of elements in L and $\overline{L}$ that it has received.

Construction.

Initially let Pos $= \emptyset$, Neg $= \emptyset$ and go to stage 0.

Stage s: If $|\text{Pos}| \leq |\text{Neg}|$
Then request a positive example x;
    update Pos $=$ Pos $\cup \{x\} - \{\#\}$;
    conjecture the finite set Pos;
Else request for negative data x;
    update Neg $=$ Neg $\cup \{x\} - \{\#\}$;
    conjecture the cofinite set Nat $-$ Neg.
Go to stage $s + 1$

It is straight forward to enforce that the learner always represents each conjectured set with the same index. Having this property, it is easy to verify that **M NewSw$_*$Ex**-learns $\mathcal{L}_{fin,cofin}$.

(b) Suppose by way of contradiction that **M RestartSw$_\alpha$Ex**-learns the class $\mathcal{L}_{fin,cofin}$. Since every finite sequence of data can be extended to the one of a set in $\mathcal{L}_{fin,cofin}$, **M** has to behave correctly on all data sequences and does not switch without downcounting the ordinal. There is a minimal ordinal β which **M** can reach in some downcounting process. For this β, there is a corresponding round k, a sequence of requests by **M** and a sequence of answers given by a teacher such that **M**'s ordinal counter is β after the k-th round; let Pos be the positive data and Neg be the negative data provided by the teacher until reaching β. As β is minimal, **M** does not make any further downcounting but stabilizes to one type request, say to requesting positive data; the case of requesting only negative data is similar. Let $L = \overline{\text{Neg}}$. If H satisfies Pos $\subseteq H \subseteq L$ and $\text{card}(L - H) \leq 1$ then H is cofinite and **M** is required to learn H without a further switch. So **M** would be a **TxtEx**-learner for $\{H : \text{Pos} \subseteq H \subseteq L \wedge \text{card}(L - H) \leq 1\}$, a contradiction to Proposition 2.4.

(c) Suppose by way of contradiction that **M BasicSwEx**-learns $\mathcal{L}_{fin,cofin}$. Due to symmetry-reasons one can assume that the first request of **M** is $+$ and assume that the teacher gives $\#$. Now consider the special case that T_- is either $\#^\infty$ or $y\#^\infty$ for some number y. The set to be learned is either Nat or Nat $- \{y\}$ and the only remaining relevant information is the text T_+. Thus if one could learn $\mathcal{L}_{fin,cofin}$ under the criterion **BasicSwEx**, then one could also **TxtEx**-learn the class $\{L : \text{card}(\overline{L}) \leq 1\}$, a contradiction to Proposition 2.4.   □

The result in (c) can be improved to show that even classes which are very easy for **NewSwEx** cannot be **BasicSwEx**-learned.

Corollary 3.3.   NewSw$_1$Ex $\not\subseteq$ BasicSwEx.

Proof. The proof of Theorem 3.2 (c) shows even that the class

$$\{L : \text{card}(L) \leq 1 \text{ or } \text{card}(\overline{L}) \leq 1\}$$

is not **BasicSwEx**-learnable; the sets with card$(L) \leq 1$ are added for the case that the request r_0 in the proof of (c) is $-$. It remains an easy verification that the considered class is **NewSw$_1$Ex**-learnable: A machine first asks for positive examples and outputs an index for the set consisting of the examples seen so far, unless it discovers that there are at least two elements in the language. At which point it switches to requesting negative examples to find the at most one negative example. □

The following theorem shows the strength of restarting switch protocol by showing that it has the same learning power as the criterion **InfEx** where the learner gets the full information on the set L to be learned by reading its characteristic function instead of a text for it [7].

Theorem 3.4. RestartSwEx = InfEx.

Proof. Clearly, **RestartSwEx** $\subseteq$ **InfEx**. In order to show that **InfEx** $\subseteq$ **RestartSwEx**, we show how to construct an informant for the input language using a teacher which follows the restart switch-protocol. Clearly, this suffices to prove the theorem. The learner requests alternatingly, positive and negative information. This gives the learner a text for L as well as for $\overline{L}$, which allows one to construct an informant for the input language L. □

The following theorem shows that newtext switching protocol can simulate restart switching protocol, if the number of switches is required to be finite.

Theorem 3.5. *For all ordinals α,* **RestartSw$_\alpha$Ex = NewSw$_\alpha$Ex.**
RestartSw$_*$Ex = NewSw$_*$Ex.

Proof. By Proposition 3.1, it suffices to show the direction that **RestartSw$_\alpha$Ex** $\subseteq$ **NewSw$_\alpha$Ex**, and **RestartSw$_*$Ex** $\subseteq$ **NewSw$_*$Ex**. Note that for languages in the class being learned, if the machine makes only finitely many switches, then any teacher following the newtext switch-protocol also follows the restart switch-protocol. Theorem follows. □

In contrast to Theorem 3.5 the following theorem shows the advantage of restarting switching protocol, compared to newtext switching protocol if the number of switches is not required to be finite.

Theorem 3.6. RestartSwEx $\not\subseteq$ NewSwEx.

Proof. Let $\mathcal{L}$ contain all finite variants of the set Odd of odd numbers. Clearly, $\mathcal{L} \in$ **RestartSwEx = InfEx**. Suppose by way of contradiction that $\mathcal{L} \in$ **NewSwEx** as witnessed by **M**. Let Even denote the set Nat $-$ Odd of even numbers. We then consider the following cases.

Case 1: There exists a way of answering the requests of **M** such that positive requests are answered by elements from Odd, negative requests are answered by elements from Even $- \{0\}$ and **M** makes infinitely many switches.

In this case, clearly **M** cannot distinguish between the cases of input language being Odd and input language being Odd $\cup \{0\}$.

Case 2: Not case 1. Let $x_0, x_1, \ldots, x_k$ be an initial sequence of answers such that

- for $i \leq k$, if $r_i = +$, then $x_i \in \text{Odd}$,
- for $i \leq k$, if $r_i = -$, then $x_i \in \text{Even} - \{0\}$,
- if the teacher is consistent with Odd and $\text{Odd} \cup \{0\}$, then **M** does not make a further switch, that is, the following two conditions hold:
  - if $r_{k+1} = +$ and the teacher takes its future examples $x_{k+1}, x_{k+2}, \ldots$ from the set Odd then $r_j = r_{k+1}$ for all $j > k$;
  - if $r_{k+1} = -$ and the teacher takes its future examples $x_{k+1}, x_{k+2}, \ldots$ from the set $\text{Even} - \{0\}$ then $r_j = r_{k+1}$ for all $j > k$.

Note that there exists such k, $x_0, x_1, \ldots, x_k$ since one could otherwise construct an infinite sequence as in case 1 by infinitely often extending a given sequence such that infinitely many switches occur.

Case 2a: $r_{k+1} = +$.

In this case, **M** has to learn the set Odd and every set $\text{Odd} - \{2x + 1\}$ where $2x + 1 \notin \{x_0, x_1, \ldots, x_k\}$ from positive data. This is impossible by Proposition 2.4.

Case 2b: $r_{k+1} = -$.

This is similar to Case 2a. **M** needs to learn the set Odd and every set $\text{Odd} \cup \{2x\}$ with $2x \notin \{0, x_0, x_1, \ldots, x_k\}$ from negative data. Again this is impossible by symmetric version of Proposition 2.4. $\qquad\square$

The previous result completes the proof that all inclusions of the hierarchy **TxtEx** $\subset$ **BasicSwEx** $\subset$ **NewSwEx** $\subset$ **RestartSwEx** are proper.

4   Counting the Number of Switches

Theorem 4.1 and Corollary 4.2 show a hierarchy with respect to number of switches.

Theorem 4.1. *For $\alpha \succ \beta$, $\text{NewSw}_\alpha\text{Ex} \not\subseteq \text{RestartSw}_\beta\text{Ex}$.*

Proof. Extend $\prec$ to $\text{Ords} \cup \{-1\}$ by letting $-1 \prec \beta$, for every $\beta \in \text{Ords}$. There is a computable function od from Nat to $\text{Ords} \cup \{-1\}$ such that

- for every $\beta \preceq \alpha$ there are infinitely many $x \in \text{Nat}$ such that $\text{od}(x) = \beta$;
- there are infinitely many $x \in \text{Nat}$ such that $\text{od}(x) = -1$;
- the set $\{(x, y) : \text{od}(x) \prec \text{od}(y)\}$ is recursive.

A set $F = \{x_1, x_2, \ldots, x_k\} \subseteq \text{Nat}$ is α-admissible iff

- $0 < x_1 < x_2 < \ldots < x_k$;
- $\alpha \succ \text{od}(x_1) \succ \text{od}(x_2) \succ \ldots \succ \text{od}(x_k) \succeq -1$.

The empty set is also α-admissible, but no infinite set is since the second condition postulates a descending chain of ordinals which is always finite. Now the class $\mathcal{L}$ is defined by the equations

$$L_F = \{x : \mathrm{card}(\{0, 1, \ldots, x\} \cap F) \text{ is odd}\};$$
$$\mathcal{L}_\alpha = \{L_F : F \text{ is } \alpha\text{-admissible}\}.$$

Note that the set $L_\emptyset$ is just $\emptyset$. Now it is shown that the class $\mathcal{L}_\alpha$ witnesses the separation.

Claim. $\mathcal{L}_\alpha \in \mathbf{NewSw}_\alpha\mathbf{Ex}$.

Proof of Claim. The machine $\mathbf{M}$ has variables n for the number of switches done so far, E for the finite set of examples seen after the last switch, m_n for the maximal element seen so far and γ_n the value of the ordinal-counter after n switches. The initialization before stage 0 is $E = \emptyset$, $n = 0$, $m_0 = 0$ and $\gamma_0 = \alpha$; $\max_{ordinals} Y$ just denotes the maximum element of a non-empty finite set Y of ordinals with respect to their ordering.

Construction. Stage s (what is done when the s-th example x is read).

(1) If n is even, request x to be a positive example x;
    If n is odd, request x to be a negative example x.
(2) If $x \notin \{\#, 0, 1, \ldots, m_n\}$ and $X = \{y \leq x : 0 \preceq \mathrm{od}(y) \prec \gamma_n\}$ is not empty
    Then switch the data type by doing the following:
        Reset $E = \emptyset$;
        Let $\beta = \max_{ordinals}\{\mathrm{od}(y) : y \in X\}$;
        Update $n = n + 1$;
        Let $m_n = x$ and $\gamma_n = \beta$;
    Else let $E = E \cup \{x\} - \{\#\}$.
(3) If $E \not\subseteq \{0, 1, \ldots, m_n\}$ then let a be the first example outside $\{0, 1, \ldots, m_n\}$ which had shown up after the n-th switch else let $a = m_n$.
(4) If n is even and $a = m_n$ then conjecture E;
    If n is even and $a > m_n$ then conjecture $E \cup \{a, a + 1, \ldots\}$;
    If n is odd and $a = m_n$ then conjecture $\overline{E}$;
    If n is odd and $a > m_n$ then conjecture $\{0, 1, \ldots, a\} - E$.

It is clear that the ordinal is downcounted at every switch of the data presentation. Thus the ordinal bound on the number of mind changes is satisfied.

Assume that F is α-admissible, $k = \mathrm{card}(F)$ and $F = \{x_1, x_2, \ldots, x_k\}$. Below let n denote the limiting value of n in the above algorithm. At every switch, $\mathbf{M}$ downcounts the ordinal from α through $\gamma_1, \gamma_2, \ldots$ to γ_n and thus keeps the ordinal bound. The values $m_0, m_1, \ldots, m_n$ satisfy the condition that $L_F(m_h) \neq L_F(m_{h+1})$ since the values m_h with odd h are positive and the values m_h with even h are negative examples; $m_0 = 0$ and thus $m_0 \notin L_F$ by definition. Due to the definition of F it follows that $m_1 \geq x_1, m_2 \geq x_2, \ldots, m_n \geq x_n$. By induction, one can verify that $\gamma_h \succeq \mathrm{od}(x_h)$ for $h = 1, 2, \ldots, n$.

When making the n-th switch, the learner knows that m_n has the opposite type of information as from now on observed.

Thus if no information $x \geq m_n$ arrives after that switch, it follows that $x_0, x_1, \ldots, x_k < m_n$ and thus E will eventually contain all y such that the type of information of y is opposite to the one of m_n. If n is even then $L_F = E$ and the algorithm is correct. If n is odd then $L_F = \overline{E}$ and the algorithm is correct again.

If some $x > m_n$ arrives after the last switch, then one knows that $\mathbf{M}$ abstains from switching due to the fact that whenever an example $x > m_n$ arrives then $X = \emptyset$. As infinitely many of these examples satisfy $\mathrm{od}(x) = \gamma$, for all ordinals $\gamma \in \mathrm{Ords}$, it follows that already $\mathrm{od}(m_n) = 0$ and therefore these examples cannot qualify to go into X. As $\gamma_h \succeq \mathrm{od}(x_h)$ for $h = 1, 2, \ldots, n$ one has that $\gamma_n = 0 \succeq \mathrm{od}(x_n)$. It follows that $\mathrm{od}(x_n) = 0$ and $n = k - 1$. The first example $a > m_n$ to show up satisfies $a \geq x_k$. Thus every $x \geq a$ satisfies that $L_F(x) = L_F(a)$ and it is sufficient to know which of the $x \leq a$ are in L_F and not. This is found out in the limit and thus the sets conjectured by $\mathbf{M}$ are correct.

It is straight forward to ensure that $\mathbf{M}$ always outputs the same index for the same set and thus does not only semantically but also syntactically converge to an index of L_F.

Claim. If a $\mathbf{RestartSw_\alpha Ex}$-learner $\mathbf{M}$ starts with requesting a negative example first, then $\mathbf{M}$ cannot $\mathbf{RestartSw_\alpha Ex}$-learn the whole class $\mathcal{L}_\alpha$.

Proof of Claim. Let data of type n be negative data if n is even and positive data if n is odd. So, for this claim, data of type n is what $\mathbf{M}$ requests after n switches. In the following, a set F is constructed such that $\mathbf{M}$ does not $\mathbf{RestartSw_\beta Ex}$-learn L_F.

Construction of F. The inductive construction starts with $F = \emptyset$, $n = \mathrm{card}(F)$ and $\mathbf{M}$ requesting examples of type n. There is a finite sequence $\sigma_0 \sigma_1 \ldots \sigma_n$ defined inductively such that one of the following cases applies:

Switch: $\mathbf{M}$ makes a switch and requests an example of type $n + 1$;
LS: $\sigma_0 \sigma_1 \ldots \sigma_n$ is a locking-sequence for L_F in the sense that for every sequence τ of examples of type n for F, $\mathbf{M}$ behaves after having seen the input $\sigma_0 \sigma_1 \ldots \sigma_n \tau$ as follows:
  – $\mathbf{M}$ does not make a switch and continues to request examples of type n;
  – $\mathbf{M}$ conjectures L_F.
Fail: There is a text T of data of type n for L_F such that $\mathbf{M}$, on the sequence $\sigma_0 \sigma_1 \ldots \sigma_n T$, does not converge to a hypothesis for L_F.

Now the construction of F is continued as follows:

Switch: After having seen $\sigma_0 \sigma_1 \ldots \sigma_n$, $\mathbf{M}$ downcounts the ordinal to a new value $\gamma' \prec \gamma$. Now one takes an x_{n+1} such that
  – $\mathrm{od}(x_{n+1}) = \gamma'$;
  – $x_{n+1} > y$ for all $y \in F \cup \mathrm{range}(\sigma_0 \sigma_1 \ldots \sigma_n) \cup \{0\}$
  and adds x_{n+1} to F.

LS: Similarly as in the previous case one can choose a number x_{n+1} such that
- $\text{od}(x_{n+1}) = -1$;
- $x_{n+1} > y$ for all $y \in F \cup \text{range}(\sigma_0 \sigma_1 \ldots \sigma_n) \cup \{0\}$
and completes the construction by adding x_{n+1} to F.

Fail: One leaves F untouched and finishes the construction.

Verification. Note that in the inductive process, adding a number x_n to F never makes any previously examples invalid, therefore it is legal to do these modifications during the construction. Furthermore, in the case that it is not possible to satisfy the case "Switch" in the construction at some stage n, one has that after having seen the example-sequence $\sigma_0 \sigma_1 \ldots \sigma_{n-1}$ (which is the empty sequence in the case $n = 0$) $\mathbf{M}$ requests only data of type n as long as it sees examples from L_F. Therefore there is a finite sequence σ_n of examples of type n for L_F such that $\sigma_0 \sigma_1 \ldots \sigma_n$ is a locking sequence for L_F by the construction of Blum and Blum [3], that is, either case "LS" or case "Fail" holds. So it is possible to continue the inductive definition in every step.

As the sequence $\text{od}(x_1), \text{od}(x_2), \ldots$ is a falling sequence of ordinals, it must be finite and therefore the construction eventually ends in the cases "LS" or "Fail". In the case "Fail" it is clear that the F constructed gives an L_F not learned by $\mathbf{M}$.

Let F' contain those elements of F which are already in F when the construction enters the case "LS". Note that all $y \geq x_{n+1}$ are examples of type n for $L_{F'}$ and that L_F and $L_{F'}$ do not differ on any $z \in \{0, 1, \ldots, x_{n+1} - 1\}$ and that thus the information seen so far is consistent with L_F and $L_{F'}$. It follows that, given any text T of type n for L_F, $\mathbf{M}$ converges on $\sigma_0 \sigma_1 \ldots \sigma_n T$ to an index of $L_{F'}$ and thus does not learn L_F. □

The first claim shows that $\mathcal{L}_\alpha$ is $\mathbf{RestartSw}_\alpha\mathbf{Ex}$-learnable while the second claim shows that such a learner cannot start by requesting a negative example first. Therefore, if $\mathbf{M}$ would be a $\mathbf{RestartSw}_\beta\mathbf{Ex}$-learner for $\mathcal{L}_F$ and $\beta \prec \alpha$, then $\mathbf{M}$ has to start with requesting a positive example. Now one could consider a new $\mathbf{RestartSw}_\alpha\mathbf{Ex}$-learner which first requests a negative example, then switches to positive data and downcounts the ordinal from α to β and from that on copycats the behaviour of $\mathbf{M}$ with an empty prehistory. It would follow that $\mathbf{M}$ can $\mathbf{RestartSw}_\beta\mathbf{Ex}$-learn $\mathcal{L}_F$ iff the new learner $\mathbf{RestartSw}_\alpha\mathbf{Ex}$-learns $\mathcal{L}_F$ and starts with requesting a negative example. As this contradicts the second Claim above, the assertion that $\mathcal{L}_F$ witnesses $\mathbf{RestartSw}_\alpha\mathbf{Ex} \not\subseteq \mathbf{RestartSw}_\beta\mathbf{Ex}$ for all $\beta \prec \alpha$ is completed. □

Corollary 4.2. *Suppose $\alpha \succ \beta$. Then $\mathbf{BasicSw}_\alpha\mathbf{Ex} \not\subseteq \mathbf{RestartSw}_\beta\mathbf{Ex}$, in particular:*
(a) $\mathbf{BasicSw}_\alpha\mathbf{Ex} \not\subseteq \mathbf{BasicSw}_\beta\mathbf{Ex}$.
(b) $\mathbf{NewSw}_\alpha\mathbf{Ex} \not\subseteq \mathbf{NewSw}_\beta\mathbf{Ex}$.
(c) $\mathbf{RestartSw}_\alpha\mathbf{Ex} \not\subseteq \mathbf{RestartSw}_\beta\mathbf{Ex}$.

Proof. The main idea is to use the cylinderification $\mathcal{L}_\alpha^{cyl}$ of the class $\mathcal{L}_\alpha$ from Theorem 4.1 in order to show that

$$\mathcal{L}_\alpha^{cyl} \in \mathbf{BasicSw}_\alpha\mathbf{Ex} - \mathbf{RestartSw}_\beta\mathbf{Ex}.$$

Then (a), (b) and (c) follow immediately.

Let $\langle \cdot, \cdot \rangle$ code pairs of natural numbers bijectively into natural numbers: $\langle x, y \rangle = \frac{(x+y) \cdot (x+y+1)}{2} + x$. The cylinderification of a set L is then defined by $L^{cyl} = \{ \langle x, y \rangle : x \in L, y \in \text{Nat} \}$ and $\mathcal{L}_\alpha^{cyl} = \{ L^{cyl} : L \in \mathcal{L}_\alpha \}$, where $\mathcal{L}_\alpha$ is as defined in Theorem 4.1.

Note that any text for L^{cyl} is essentially a fat text for L. Therefore the fact $\mathcal{L} \in \mathbf{NewSw}_\alpha\mathbf{Ex}$ implies that $\mathcal{L}^{cyl} \in \mathbf{BasicSw}_\alpha\mathbf{Ex}$ by using Remark 2.8. On the other hand, $\mathcal{L}^{cyl} \notin \mathbf{RestartSw}_\beta\mathbf{Ex}$ since $\mathcal{L} \notin \mathbf{RestartSw}_\beta\mathbf{Ex}$ and by using Remark 2.8 again. $\qquad\square$

5   Conclusion

The starting point of the present work was the fact, that there is a large gap between the data-presentation by a text and by an informant: a text gives only positive data while an informant gives complete information on the set to be learned. So notions of data presentation between these two extreme cases were proposed and the relations between them were investigated. The underlying idea of these notions is that the learner may switch between receiving positive and negative data, but these switches are either restricted in the number or may cause the loss of information.

For example, the **BasicSwEx**-learner can at every stage only follow one of the text T_+ and T_- of positive and negative information on the set L to be learned and might therefore miss important information on the other side.

The results of the present work resolve all the relationships between different switching criteria proposed in this paper. In particular it was established that the inclusion

$$\mathbf{TxtEx} \subset \mathbf{BasicSwEx} \subset \mathbf{NewSwEx} \subset \mathbf{RestartSwEx}$$

is everywhere proper. Furthermore, the notion **RestartSwEx** coincides with learning from informant. In case of restricting the number of switches to be finite or to meet an ordinal bound, $\mathbf{RestartSw}_*\mathbf{Ex}$ and $\mathbf{RestartSw}_\alpha\mathbf{Ex}$ coincide with $\mathbf{NewSw}_*\mathbf{Ex}$ and $\mathbf{NewSw}_\alpha$, respectively. The hierarchy induced by measuring the number of switches with recursive ordinals is proper.

In summary, the notion **NewSwEx** and its variant by bounding the number of switches turned out to be the most natural definition in the gap between **TxtEx**-learning and learning from informant. The notion of **BasicSwEx**-learning is between **TxtEx**-learning and learning from informant, but has some strange side-effects as pointed out in Remark 2.9.

Note that these criteria differ from learning from negative open text from [2] which was called notion (b) in the introduction: Learning from open negative text is weaker than learning from informant and thus different from **RestartSwEx**. On the other hand, the class $\mathcal{L}_{fin,cofin}$ and the class $\mathcal{L}$ from Theorem 3.6 are both learnable from negative open text and so separate this notion from the other switching criteria mentioned in this paper.

Acknowledgment. We would like to thank the anonymous referees of the conference ALT for useful comments.

References

1. Dana Angluin. Learning regular sets from queries and counter-examples. *Information and Computation*, 75:87–106, 1987.
2. Ganesh Baliga, John Case and Sanjay Jain. Language learning with some negative information. *Journal of Computer and System Sciences*, 51(5):273–285, 1995.
3. Lenore Blum and Manuel Blum. Toward a mathematical theory of inductive inference. *Information and Control*, 28:125–155, 1975.
4. John Case, Sanjay Jain and Mandayam Suraj. Not-so-nearly-minimal-size program inference. In Klaus P. Jantke and Steffen Lange, editors, *Algorithmic Learning for Knowledge-Based Systems*, volume 961 of *Lecture Notes in Artificial Intelligence*, pages 77–96. Springer-Verlag, 1995.
5. John Case and Carl Smith. Comparison of identification criteria for machine inductive inference. *Theoretical Computer Science*, 25:193–220, 1983.
6. Rūsiņš Freivalds and Carl Smith. On the role of procrastination in machine learning. *Information and Computation*, pages 237–271, 1993.
7. E. Mark Gold. Language identification in the limit. *Information and Control*, 10:447–474, 1967.
8. Sanjay Jain and Arun Sharma. On the non-existence of maximal inference degrees for language identification. *Information Processing Letters*, 47:81–88, 1993.
9. Stephen Kleene. Notations for ordinal numbers. *Journal of Symbolic Logic*, 3:150–155, 1938.
10. M. Machtey and Paul Young. *An Introduction to the General Theory of Algorithms*. North Holland, New York, 1978.
11. Wolfgang Merkle and Frank Stephan. Refuting learning revisited. Technical Report Forschungsberichte Mathematische Logik 52/2001, Mathematisches Institut, Universität Heidelberg, 2001. Extended abstract to appear in *Proceedings of the Twelfth International Conference on Algorithmic Learning Theory*, 2001.
12. Tatsuya Motoki. Inductive inference from all positive and some negative data. *Information Processing Letters*, 39(4):177–182, 1991.
13. Daniel Osherson, Michael Stob and Scott Weinstein. *Systems that Learn: An Introduction to Learning Theory for Cognitive and Computer Scientists*. MIT Press, 1986.
14. Hartley Rogers. *Theory of Recursive Functions and Effective Computability*. McGraw-Hill, 1967. Reprinted by MIT Press in 1987.
15. Gerald E. Sacks. *Higher Recursion Theory*. Springer-Verlag, 1990.
16. Arun Sharma. A note on batch and incremental learnability. *Journal of Computer and System Sciences*, 56(3):272–276, 1998.
17. Rolf Wiehagen. Identification of formal languages. In *Mathematical Foundations of Computer Science*, volume 53 of *Lecture Notes in Computer Science*, pages 571–579. Springer-Verlag, 1977.

Learning How to Separate

Sanjay Jain[*,1] and Frank Stephan[**,2]

[1] School of Computing, National University of Singapore, Singapore 119260,
`sanjay@comp.nus.edu.sg`
[2] Mathematisches Institut, Im Neuenheimer Feld 294, Ruprecht-Karls-Universität
Heidelberg, 69120 Heidelberg, Germany, `fstephan@math.uni-heidelberg.de`

Abstract. The main question addressed in the present work is how to
find effectively a recursive function separating two sets drawn arbitrarily
from a given collection of disjoint sets. In particular, it is investigated in
which cases it is possible to satisfy the following additional constraints:
confidence where the learner converges on all data-sequences; conservativeness where the learner abandons only definitely wrong hypotheses;
consistency where also every intermediate hypothesis is consistent with
the data seen so far; set-driven learners whose hypotheses are independent of the order and the number of repetitions of the data-items supplied; learners where either the last or even all hypotheses are programs
of total recursive functions.

The present work gives an overview of the relations between these
notions and succeeds to answer many questions by finding ways to carry
over the corresponding results from other scenarios within inductive inference. Nevertheless, the relations between conservativeness and set-
driven inference needed a novel approach which enabled to show the
following two major results:

(1) There is a class for which recursive separators can be found in
a confident and set-driven way, but no conservative learner finds a (not
necessarily total) separator for this class.

(2) There is a class for which recursive separators can be found in
a confident and conservative way, but no set-driven learner finds a (not
necessarily total) separator for this class.

1 Introduction

Consider the scenario in which a subject is attempting to learn its environment.
At any given time, the subject receives a finite piece of data about its environment, and based on this finite information, conjectures an explanation about
the environment. The subject is said to *learn* its environment just in case the
explanations conjectured by the subject become fixed over time, and this fixed
explanation is a correct representation of the subject's environment. Inductive
Inference, a subfield of computational learning theory, provides a framework for

---

[*] Supported in part by NUS grant number RP3992710.
[**] Supported by the Deutsche Forschungsgemeinschaft (DFG) under the Heisenberg
grant Ste 967/1–1

N. Abe, R. Khardon, and T. Zeugmann (Eds.): ALT 2001, LNAI 2225, pp. 219–234, 2001.

the study of the above scenario when the subject is an algorithmic device. The above model of learning is based on the work initiated by Gold [11] and has been used in inductive inference of both functions and languages. This model is often referred to as *explanatory learning*, in short: **Ex**-learning. We refer the reader to [2,5,9,13,17] for background material in this field.

In recursion theory, recursive separability of disjoint languages has been extensively explored [22]. A prominent fact is that there are disjoint recursively enumerable sets which cannot be separated by a total recursive function which takes 0 on the first and 1 on the second set. Indeed, the question: relative to which oracles any two disjoint and recursively enumerable sets are separable has been investigated; these oracles turned out to be those which allow to compute a complete extension of Peano-Arithmetic [20].

In the present work, we consider a combination of learning and separation. Thus a machine receives, as input data about two disjoint languages. The machine is then expected to come up with, in the limit, a procedure to separate the two input languages. A machine is able to *separate* languages from a class of disjoint languages, if it is able to separate any pair of languages from the class. The above can be used to model situations such as follows. Consider an employee in an embassy which receives letters in various languages. The job of the employee is to pass it to appropriate interpreter for translating but may ignore junk letters not written in any relevant language. We may expect the employee to become an expert in the above process after having seen enough examples from each of the languages used in the embassy. This is essentially the model of separation we are considering.

In addition to just separability we also consider various constraints on the machine such as reliability, consistency, conservativeness, etc, and study how it affects the power of machine to separate pairs of disjoint languages.

2   Notation and Preliminaries

Any unexplained recursion theoretic notation is from [22]. The symbol N denotes the set of natural numbers, $\{0, 1, 2, 3, \ldots\}$. Cardinality of a set S is denoted by $\text{card}(S)$. The maximum and minimum of a set are denoted by $\max(\cdot), \min(\cdot)$, respectively, where $\max(\emptyset) = 0$ and $\min(\emptyset) = \infty$. $\text{domain}(\eta)$ and $\text{range}(\eta)$ denote the domain and range of partial function η respectively. Sequences are partial functions η where the domain is either N or $\{y \in N : y < x\}$ for some x. In the first case, the length of η (denoted $|\eta|$) is ∞, in the second case its length is x. Although sequences may take a special value $\#$ to indicate a pause (when considered as a source of data), this pause-sign is omitted from $\text{range}(\eta)$ for the ease of notation. Furthermore, if $x \leq |\sigma|$, then $\sigma[x]$ denotes the restriction of σ to the domain $\{y \in N : y < x\}$. We let SEQ denote the set of all finite sequences and let σ and τ range over SEQ. We denote the sequence formed by the concatenation of τ at the end of σ by $\sigma\tau$. Furthermore, we use σx to denote the concatenation of sequence σ and the sequence of length 1 which contains the element x.

We let $\langle \cdot, \cdot \rangle$ stand for an arbitrary, computable, bijective mapping from $N \times N$ onto N [22]. We assume without loss of generality that $\langle \cdot, \cdot \rangle$ is monotonically increasing in both of its arguments. We extend $\langle \cdot, \cdot \rangle$ to n-tuples in a natural way (including $n = 1$, where $\langle x \rangle$ may be taken to be x). Due to the above isomorphism between N^k and N, we often identify the tuple $(x_1, \cdots, x_n)$ with $\langle x_1, \cdots, x_n \rangle$.

By φ we denote a fixed *acceptable* programming system for the partial computable functions mapping N to N [22,18]. An example for an acceptable programming system is any enumeration of all Turing machines. Further examples are standard programming languages such as Basic, Pascal, Fortran ... provided that the data-type of normal variables is N (without upper bound on the values). By φ_i we denote the partial computable function computed by the program with number i in the φ-system. Symbol $\mathcal{R}$ denotes the set of all recursive functions, that is total computable functions. Symbol $\mathcal{R}_{0,1}$ denotes the set of all recursive functions with range subset of $\{0, 1\}$. By Φ we denote an arbitrary fixed Blum complexity measure [6,12] for the φ-system. By W_i we denote domain(φ_i). W_i is, then, the recursively enumerable (r.e.) set/language $(\subseteq N)$ accepted (or equivalently, generated) by the φ-program i. We also say that i is a grammar for W_i. Symbol $\mathcal{E}$ will denote the set of all r.e. languages. Symbol L, with or without decorations, ranges over $\mathcal{E}$. By $\overline{L}$, we denote the complement of L, that is $N - L$.

Symbol $\mathcal{L}$, with or without decorations, ranges over subsets of $\mathcal{E}$. By $W_{i,s}$ we denote the set $\{x < s \mid \Phi_i(x) < s\}$.

A class $\mathcal{L} \subseteq \mathcal{E}$ is said to be recursively enumerable (r.e.) [22], iff $\mathcal{L} = \emptyset$ or there exists a recursive function f such that $\mathcal{L} = \{W_{f(i)} \mid i \in N\}$. In this latter case we say that $W_{f(0)}, W_{f(1)}, \ldots$ is a recursive enumeration of $\mathcal{L}$. $\mathcal{L}$ is said to be 1–1 enumerable iff (I) $\mathcal{L}$ is finite or (II) there exists a recursive function f such that $\mathcal{L} = \{W_{f(i)} \mid i \in N\}$ and $W_{f(i)} \neq W_{f(j)}$, if $i \neq j$. In this latter case we say that $W_{f(0)}, W_{f(1)}, \ldots$ is a 1–1 recursive enumeration of $\mathcal{L}$.

K denotes the diagonal halting set, that is $\{x \mid \varphi_x(x)\downarrow\}$. A pair of disjoint languages, L and L', are said to be recursively separable iff there exists a recursive function f such that for all $x \in L$, $f(x) = 0$ and for all $x \in L'$, $f(x) = 1$. If a pair of disjoint languages is not recursively separable, then the pair is said to be recursively inseparable. It is well known that there are pairs of disjoint recursively enumerable languages which are recursively inseparable.

Let **Disjoint** $= \{\mathcal{L} \mid (\forall L, L' \in \mathcal{L})[L \cap L' = \emptyset \text{ or } L = L']\}$. That is, classes in **Disjoint** consist only of disjoint languages.

A function $f(\cdot)$ is said to be limiting recursive, if there exists a recursive function g such that, for all x, $f(x) = \lim_{t \to \infty} g(x, t)$. A function F is said to dominate a function f, iff for all but finitely many x, $F(x) \geq f(x)$. Computations using oracles can be defined in the usual way [12,22], by allowing machine access to an oracle. Note that there exists a K-recursive function f which dominates every recursive function and which is approximable from below. That is, there exists a recursive sequence of recursive functions f_s, such that for all s, x, $f_s(x) \leq f_{s+1}(x)$, and $f(x) = \max(\{f_s(x) : s \in N\})$. We now present concepts from language learning theory.

Definition 1. [11] (a) A *text* T for a language L is a mapping from N into $(N \cup \{\#\})$ such that L is the set of natural numbers in the range of T.

(b) The *range* of a text T, denoted by range(T), is the set of natural numbers occuring in T; that is, the language which T is a text for.

(c) $T[n]$ denotes the finite initial sequence of T with length n.

We let T, with or without decorations, range over texts.

Definition 2. A *language learning machine* [11] is an algorithmic device which computes a mapping from SEQ into $N \cup \{?\}$.

Intuitively, "?" above denotes the case when the machine may not wish to make a conjecture. Although it is not necessary to consider learners that issue "?" for identification/separation in the limit, it becomes useful when the number of mind changes a learner can make is bounded. We let $\mathbf{M}$, with or without decorations, range over learning machines. $\mathbf{M}(T[n])$ is interpreted as the grammar (index for an accepting program) conjectured by the learning machine $\mathbf{M}$ on the initial sequence $T[n]$. We say that $\mathbf{M}$ converges on T to i, (written $\mathbf{M}(T){\downarrow} = i$) iff $(\forall^\infty n)\,[\mathbf{M}(T[n]) = i]$.

There are several criteria for a learning machine to be successful on a language. Below we define identification in the limit introduced by Gold [11].

Definition 3. [11] (a) $\mathbf{M}$ **TxtEx**-identifies a text T just in case $(\exists i \mid W_i = \text{range}(T))\,(\forall^\infty n)\,[\mathbf{M}(T[n]) = i]$.

(b) $\mathbf{M}$ **TxtEx**-identifies a recursively enumerable language L (written: $L \in$ **TxtEx(M)**) just in case $\mathbf{M}$ **TxtEx**-identifies each text for L.

(c) $\mathbf{M}$ **TxtEx**-identifies a class $\mathcal{L}$ of recursively enumerable languages (written: $\mathcal{L} \subseteq$ **TxtEx(M)**) just in case $\mathbf{M}$ **TxtEx**-identifies each language from $\mathcal{L}$.

(d) **TxtEx** $= \{\mathcal{L} \subseteq \mathcal{E} \mid (\exists \mathbf{M})[\mathcal{L} \subseteq \textbf{TxtEx(M)}]\}$.

By the definition of convergence, only finitely many data points from a function f have been observed by $\mathbf{M}$ at the (unknown) point of convergence. Hence, some form of learning must take place in order for $\mathbf{M}$ to learn f. For this reason, hereafter the terms *identify*, *learn* and *infer* are used interchangeably.

3   Separability

We now consider the notion of separating the languages. In this case, $\mathbf{M}$ receives as input texts for two disjoint languages L and L'. $\mathbf{M}$ is required to converge on the input to a program i such that, $\varphi_i(x) = 0$, for $x \in L$ and $\varphi_i(x) = 1$, for $x \in L'$. For $x \in \overline{L \cup L'}$, it doesn't matter what φ_i outputs. Thus, for this kind of learning, we require the learning machines to be a mapping from SEQ $\times$ SEQ to $N \cup \{?\}$. For ease of presentation, we assume that the two inputs to the machine are of the same length. That is when we consider $\mathbf{M}(\sigma, \sigma')$, we assume that $|\sigma| = |\sigma'|$. This is without loss of generality since one can always use padding by #'s to make the length same. We further assume, without explicitly stating at all places, that the two inputs are disjoint: that is range(σ) $\cap$ range(σ') $= \emptyset$.

We say that $\mathbf{M}$ on (T, T') converges to i (written: $\mathbf{M}(T, T')\!\downarrow = i$) iff for all but finitely many n, $\mathbf{M}(T[n], T'[n]) = i$.

Definition 4. (a) $\mathbf{M}$ **Resep**-*identifies* (T, T') iff $\mathbf{M}(T, T')$ converges to an index i such that $\mathrm{range}(T) \subseteq \varphi_i^{-1}(0)$ and $\mathrm{range}(T') \subseteq \varphi_i^{-1}(1)$.

(b) $\mathbf{M}$ **Resep**-*identifies* (L, L') iff for any text T for L and any text T' for L', $\mathbf{M}$ **Resep**-identifies (T, T').

(c) $\mathbf{M}$ **Resep**-*identifies* $\mathcal{L}$ iff $\mathbf{M}$ **Resep**-identifies all pairs (L, L') where L and L' are disjoint sets in $\mathcal{L}$.

(d) **Resep** $= \{\mathcal{L} \mid \mathcal{L} \in \mathbf{Disjoint} \wedge (\exists \mathbf{M})\,[\mathbf{M}\ \mathbf{Resep}\text{-identifies } \mathcal{L}]\}$.

Definition 5. [5,7,13,19,21,27]

(a) $\mathbf{M}$ is *Popperian* iff for all σ, σ' such that $\mathrm{range}(\sigma) \cap \mathrm{range}(\sigma') = \emptyset$ and $|\sigma| = |\sigma'|$, the function computed by $\mathbf{M}(\sigma, \sigma')$ is total.

(b) $\mathbf{M}$ is *consistent* iff for all σ, σ' such that $\mathrm{range}(\sigma) \cap \mathrm{range}(\sigma') = \emptyset$ and $|\sigma| = |\sigma'|$, $\mathrm{range}(\sigma) \subseteq \varphi_{\mathbf{M}(\sigma, \sigma')}^{-1}(0)$, and $\mathrm{range}(\sigma') \subseteq \varphi_{\mathbf{M}(\sigma, \sigma')}^{-1}(1)$.

(c) $\mathbf{M}$ is *reliable* iff for all T, T' such that $\mathrm{range}(T) \cap \mathrm{range}(T') = \emptyset$, and $\mathbf{M}(T, T')$ converges, $\mathbf{M}$ **Resep**-identifies (T, T').

(d) $\mathbf{M}$ is *conservative* iff for all σ, σ' and all τ, τ' such that $|\sigma| = |\sigma'|$, $|\tau| = |\tau'|$, and $\mathrm{range}(\sigma\tau) \cap \mathrm{range}(\sigma'\tau') = \emptyset$, if $\mathrm{range}(\sigma\tau) \subseteq \varphi_{\mathbf{M}(\sigma, \sigma')}^{-1}(0)$ and $\mathrm{range}(\sigma'\tau') \subseteq \varphi_{\mathbf{M}(\sigma, \sigma')}^{-1}(1)$, then $\mathbf{M}(\sigma, \sigma') = \mathbf{M}(\sigma\tau, \sigma'\tau')$.

(e) $\mathbf{M}$ is *set driven* iff $\mathbf{M}$ is total and for all $\sigma, \sigma', \tau, \tau'$, such that $|\sigma| = |\sigma'|$ and $|\tau| = |\tau'|$, if $\mathrm{range}(\sigma) = \mathrm{range}(\tau)$ and $\mathrm{range}(\sigma') = \mathrm{range}(\tau')$, then $\mathbf{M}(\sigma, \sigma') = \mathbf{M}(\tau, \tau')$.

(f) $\mathbf{M}$ is *finite* iff $\mathbf{M}$ is total and for all $\sigma, \sigma', \tau, \tau'$ such that $|\sigma| = |\sigma'|$ and $|\tau| = |\tau'|$, if $\mathbf{M}(\sigma, \sigma') \neq ?$ then $\mathbf{M}(\sigma\tau, \sigma'\tau') = \mathbf{M}(\sigma, \sigma')$. That is, a once established hypothesis is never changed.

(g) $\mathbf{M}$ is *confident* iff for all T, T' such that $\mathrm{range}(T) \cap \mathrm{range}(T') = \emptyset$, $\mathbf{M}(T, T')$ converges.

We say that $\mathbf{M}$ is consistent on (σ, σ') to mean that $\mathrm{range}(\sigma) \subseteq \varphi_{\mathbf{M}(\sigma, \sigma')}^{-1}(0)$, and $\mathrm{range}(\sigma') \subseteq \varphi_{\mathbf{M}(\sigma, \sigma')}^{-1}(1)$. We say that $\mathbf{M}$ is consistent on (T, T') to mean that $\mathbf{M}$ is consistent on $(T[n], T'[n])$, for all n. We say that $\mathbf{M}$ is consistent on (L, L') to mean that $\mathbf{M}$ is consistent on all (T, T'), where T is a text for L and T' is a text for L'.

Similarly, we say that $\mathbf{M}$ is conservative on (γ, γ'), if for all $\sigma, \tau, \sigma', \tau'$ such that $|\sigma| = |\sigma'|$, $|\tau| = |\tau'|$, $\sigma\tau \subseteq \gamma$, $\sigma'\tau' \subseteq \gamma'$, and $\mathrm{range}(\sigma\tau) \cap \mathrm{range}(\sigma'\tau') = \emptyset$, if $\mathrm{range}(\sigma\tau) \subseteq \varphi_{\mathbf{M}(\sigma, \sigma')}^{-1}(0)$ and $\mathrm{range}(\sigma'\tau') \subseteq \varphi_{\mathbf{M}(\sigma, \sigma')}^{-1}(1)$, then $\mathbf{M}(\sigma, \sigma') = \mathbf{M}(\sigma\tau, \sigma'\tau')$.

Definition 6. $\mathbf{M}$ conservatively **Resep**-identifies (L, L') iff $\mathbf{M}$ is conservative and $\mathbf{M}$ **Resep**-identifies (L, L').

Conservativesep $= \{\mathcal{L} \in \mathbf{Disjoint} \mid (\exists \mathbf{M})\,[\mathbf{M}$ is conservative, and $\mathbf{M}$ **Resep**-identifies $\mathcal{L}]\}$.

One can similarly define **Popperiansep**, **Reliablesep**, **Setdrivensep**, **Consistentsep** and **Finitesep**.

Definition 7. **M Recsep**-identifies (T, T') iff **M Resep**-identifies (T, T') and $\varphi_{M(T,T')}$ is a total function.

One can similarly define **Recsep** identification of pairs of languages and disjoint classes and the class **Recsep**.

It is not more difficult to separate k disjoint sets instead of 2. For example, given 3 sets L, L', L'' by their texts T, T', T'', one can simulate the **Resep**-identifier for each pair of 2 sets coming up with programs e, e', e'' to separate the pairs (L, L'), (L, L'') and (L', L''), respectively. Then one has that the program d given as

$$\varphi_d(x) = \begin{cases} 0, & \text{if } \varphi_e(x)\!\downarrow = 0 \wedge \varphi_{e'}(x)\!\downarrow = 0; \\ 1, & \text{if } \varphi_e(x)\!\downarrow = 1 \wedge \varphi_{e''}(x)\!\downarrow = 0; \\ 2, & \text{if } \varphi_{e'}(x)\!\downarrow = 1 \wedge \varphi_{e''}(x)\!\downarrow = 1; \\ u, & \text{if } \varphi_e(x), \varphi_{e'}(x), \varphi_{e''}(x) \text{ are defined} \\ & \text{and no previous case applies;} \\ \uparrow, & \text{otherwise;} \end{cases}$$

where u is an arbitrary number in $\{0, 1, 2\}$, it does not matter which one. It is easy to verify then that $L \subseteq \varphi_d^{-1}(0)$, $L' \subseteq \varphi_d^{-1}(1)$, $L'' \subseteq \varphi_d^{-1}(2)$ and φ_d is total if the functions $\varphi_e, \varphi_{e'}, \varphi_{e''}$ are total. Similar arguments deal with the case of $4, 5, \ldots$ sets.

Furthermore, one can also show that for the considered variants **Finite-sep**-identification, **Consistentsep**-identification, **Recsep**-identification, **Confidentsep**-identification, **Reliablesep**-identification and **Conservativesep**-identification, the notion does not depend on the number of sets used in the definition. So one can without loss of generality restrict oneself to defining everything with separating pairs.

The only special case is if there is a function ψ separating all sets. But then the learning task for pairs becomes trivial since one only has to identify the numbers i and j such that L is mapped by ψ to i and L' to j. So the existence of such a ψ allows to separate pairs easily. The converse does not hold: if one takes the class containing all sets $\{2x\}, \{2x + 1\}$ with $x \notin K$ and all sets $\{2x, 2x + 1\}$ with $x \in K$, then it is **Resep**-identifiable by an easy algorithm but no ψ separates all the sets of this class.

The notion of stabilizing and locking sequence is useful.

Definition 8. (Based on [5,10]) (σ, σ') is a stabilizing sequence for **M** on (L, L'), iff (I) $|\sigma| = |\sigma'|$, (II) range$(\sigma) \subseteq L$, (III) range$(\sigma') \subseteq L'$, and (IV) for all τ, τ' such that $|\tau| = |\tau'|$, range$(\tau) \subseteq L$ and range$(\tau') \subseteq L'$, $[\mathbf{M}(\sigma\tau, \sigma'\tau') = \mathbf{M}(\sigma, \sigma')]$.

Definition 9. (Based on [5,10]) (σ, σ') is a **Resep**-locking sequence for **M** on (L, L') iff (σ, σ') is a stabilizing sequence for **M** on (L, L') and $L \subseteq \varphi_{M(\sigma,\sigma')}^{-1}(0)$ and $L' \subseteq \varphi_{M(\sigma,\sigma')}^{-1}(1)$.

Lemma 10. (Based on [5,10]) *If* **M** **Resep**-*identifies* (L, L'), *then*
(a) *There exists a* **Resep**-*locking sequence for* **M** *on* L.
(b) *Every stabilizing sequence for* **M** *on* (L, L') *is a* **Resep**-*locking sequence for* **M** *on* L.

Note that a similar lemma applies for other criteria of separation discussed in this paper. For ease of notation sometimes we drop "**Resep**" from **Resep**-locking sequence.

4   First Results

A central question within the theory of inductive inference is the relation between the various criteria of identification. With respect to the theory of separation, the inclusions turn out to be easily provable. The below inclusions either follow immediately from the definition or are straightforward. Note that **TxtFin** denotes identification by a finite machine which never revises its first hypothesis; **TxtFin** is the notion corresponding to **Finitesep**. Below **TxtDecEx** is a notion similar to **TxtEx**, except that the machine **M** is supposed to converge to a decision procedure for input language, instead of grammar for input language [8].

Proposition 11. TxtEx ∩ Disjoint ⊆ Resep.
TxtDecEx ∩ Disjoint ⊆ Recsep.
TxtFin ∩ Disjoint ⊆ Finitesep.
Finitesep ⊆ Conservativesep ∩ Confidentsep ⊆ Resep.
Popperiansep ⊆ Conservativesep.
Popperiansep ⊆ Recsep ⊆ Resep.

If one can learn a class $\mathcal{L}$ as a class of sets from positive data, one can also separate the disjoint sets within $\mathcal{L}$ since, for any given $L, L' \in \mathcal{L}$, the learner takes the hypotheses for L as separators for L, L'. But the next result shows that this connection does not hold for the converse direction.

Theorem 12. *There is a class $\mathcal{L}$ such that*
(a) *$\mathcal{L} \notin$ **TxtEx**.*
(b) *$\mathcal{L}$ is finitely (and thus confidently and conservatively) **Resep**-identifiable;*
(c) *$\mathcal{L}$ is reliably **Resep**-identifiable.*

Proof. Let $\mathbf{M}_0, \mathbf{M}_1, \ldots$ denote a listing of all the learning machines. Let $L_i \subseteq \{\langle i, x \rangle \mid x \in N\}$ be a recursive set such that $\mathbf{M}_i$ does not **TxtEx**-identify L_i. Let $\mathcal{L} = \{L_i \mid i \in N\}$. Then, $\mathcal{L}$ witnesses the theorem.   □
Bārzdiņš [3,9] introduced the notion of behaviourally correct learning where the learner outputs infinitely many guesses of which almost all describe the function or set to be learned correctly. Behaviourally correct identification is a proper generalization of **TxtEx**-learning. Note that in the previous theorem, the non-learnability could even be strengthened by constructing $\mathcal{L}$ such that L_i is not behaviourally correct identified by the i-th machine; then the resulting class is not behaviourally correct identifiable.

The next theorem establishes that the notions of reliable, consistent and Popperian separation coincide. The notions of (globally) consistent and Popperian learning also coincide for learning sets from positive data while this is no longer true for reliable learning: only finite sets are reliably learnable from positive data [13, Proposition 5.42]. Nevertheless, the three notions also coincide in the world of learning $\{0, 1\}$-valued functions from complete data [28].

Theorem 13. *Whenever some* **Resep**-*identifier* **M** *of a class* $\mathcal{L}$ *of disjoint sets satisfies one of the properties below, one can replace* **M** *by a better* **Resep**-*identifier* **M'** *satisfying all of them.*
(a) **M** *is consistent.*
(b) **M** *is reliable.*
(c) **M** *is Popperian.*
In particular, **Reliablesep** = **Consistentsep** = **Popperiansep** $\subseteq$ **Recsep**.

Proof. If **M** is consistent or reliable, then for every σ, σ', such that $|\sigma| = |\sigma'|$, let each of the functions $t_{\sigma,\sigma'}$ and $d_{\sigma,\sigma'}$ take the first case in the below case-distinctions which applies:

$$
t_{\sigma,\sigma'}(x) = \begin{cases} 0, & \text{if } x \in \text{range}(\sigma) \cup \text{range}(\sigma'); \\ s, & \text{the first } s \text{ such that either} \\ & \mathbf{M}(\sigma\#^s, \sigma'x^s) \neq \mathbf{M}(\sigma, \sigma') \text{ or } \mathbf{M}(\sigma x^s, \sigma'\#^s) \neq \mathbf{M}(\sigma, \sigma'); \\ \uparrow, & \text{otherwise}; \end{cases}
$$

$$
d_{\sigma,\sigma'}(x) = \begin{cases} 0, & \text{if } t_{\sigma,\sigma'}\!\downarrow = 0 \wedge x \in \text{range}(\sigma) \\ & \text{or } t_{\sigma,\sigma'}(x)\!\downarrow > 0 \wedge \mathbf{M}(\sigma x^{t_{\sigma,\sigma'}(x)}, \sigma'\#^{t_{\sigma,\sigma'}(x)}) \neq \mathbf{M}(\sigma, \sigma'); \\ 1, & \text{if } t_{\sigma,\sigma'}\!\downarrow = 0 \wedge x \in \text{range}(\sigma') \\ & \text{or } t_{\sigma,\sigma'}(x)\!\downarrow > 0 \wedge \mathbf{M}(\sigma x^{t_{\sigma,\sigma'}(x)}, \sigma'\#^{t_{\sigma,\sigma'}(x)}) = \mathbf{M}(\sigma, \sigma'); \\ \uparrow, & \text{otherwise, that is, } t_{\sigma,\sigma'}(x)\!\uparrow. \end{cases}
$$

If **M** is either consistent or reliable, then for all σ, σ', the functions $t_{\sigma,\sigma'}$ and $d_{\sigma,\sigma'}$ are total. Furthermore, if (σ, σ') is a separating locking sequence for **M** on (L, L'), then $L \subseteq d_{\sigma,\sigma'}^{-1}(0)$ and $L' \subseteq d_{\sigma,\sigma'}^{-1}(1)$.

If **M** is Popperian, then let $d_{\sigma,\sigma'}$ denote $\varphi_{\mathbf{M}(\sigma,\sigma')}$.

Thus, if **M** is Popperian, reliable or consistent, then for $d_{\sigma,\sigma'}$ defined as above, (I) for all σ, σ': $d_{\sigma,\sigma'}$ is total and (II) if **M** **Resep**-identifies (L, L'), then there exists a σ, σ' such that $L \subseteq d_{\sigma,\sigma'}^{-1}(0)$ and $L' \subseteq d_{\sigma,\sigma'}^{-1}(1)$.

Let $p_0, p_1, \ldots$ be a recursive sequence of programs such that $\{\varphi_{p_i} \mid i \in N\} = \{d_{\sigma,\sigma'} \mid \sigma, \sigma' \in \text{SEQ} \wedge |\sigma| = |\sigma'|\} \cup \{\chi \mid \chi \text{ is the characteristic function of some finite set}\}$. Note that such an enumeration of programs exists.

Now define **M'** as follows. $\mathbf{M}'(\tau, \tau') = p_i$, where i is minimal such that $\text{range}(\tau) \subseteq \varphi_i^{-1}(0)$ and $\text{range}(\tau') \subseteq \varphi_i^{-1}(1)$. Since the sequence p_i's contains programs for characteristic function of every finite set, above **M'** is total.

It is easy to verify that **M'** **Resep**-identifies $\mathcal{L}$ and **M'** is Popperian, consistent and reliable. (Thus **M'** also **Recsep**-identifies $\mathcal{L}$.)   □

Note that **M'** defined in above proof is set-driven. Thus, we also have

Corollary 14. Consistentsep $\subseteq$ **Setdrivensep**.
Popperiansep $\subseteq$ **Setdrivensep**.
Reliablesep $\subseteq$ **Setdrivensep**.

For the following proposition we need concepts from function learning, which are similar to language learning, but where the inputs are graphs of functions, and outputs are programs for computing the function. Alternatively, these criteria can be considered as restriction of language learning to the cases, where the input is from the class of single valued total languages only; where a language L is single valued total, iff it satisfies the following properties

(I) single valuedness: $(\forall x)(\forall y, z) [[\langle x, y \rangle \in L \text{ and } \langle x, z \rangle \in L] \Rightarrow y = z]$;
(II) totality: $(\forall x)(\exists y) [\langle x, y \rangle \in L]$.

We refer the reader to [9,11,13] for the details on function learning.

Proposition 15. *Suppose $\mathcal{C} \subseteq \mathcal{R}_{0,1}$ be given. Then one can define an enumeration $f_0, f_1, \ldots$ of functions in $\mathcal{C}$, such that the class $\mathcal{L}_{\mathcal{C}}$ given by*

$$L_i = \{\langle i, x, f_i(x) \rangle \mid x \in N\},$$
$$L'_i = \{\langle i, x, 1 - f_i(x) \rangle \mid x \in N\},$$
$$\mathcal{L}_{\mathcal{C}} = \{L_i \mid i \in N\} \cup \{L'_i \mid i \in N\}$$

satisfies the following:
(a) $\mathcal{C} \in \mathbf{ReliableEx} \Leftrightarrow \mathcal{L}_{\mathcal{C}} \in \mathbf{Reliablesep}$.
(b) $\mathcal{C} \in \mathbf{Ex} \Leftrightarrow \mathcal{L}_{\mathcal{C}} \in \mathbf{Recsep}$.
(c) $\mathcal{C} \in \mathbf{ConfidentEx} \Leftrightarrow \mathcal{L}_{\mathcal{C}} \in \mathbf{Confidentsep}$.
(d) $\mathcal{C} \in \mathbf{Fin} \Leftrightarrow \mathcal{L}_{\mathcal{C}} \in \mathbf{Finitesep}$.
(e) $\mathcal{C} \in \mathbf{PopperianEx} \Leftrightarrow \mathcal{L}_{\mathcal{C}} \in \mathbf{Popperiansep}$.

Proof. Let $\mathbf{M}_0, \mathbf{M}_1, \ldots$ denote a listing of all learning machines. It is easy to see that for arbitrary enumeration $f_0, f_1, \ldots$ of functions in $\mathcal{C}$, $\Rightarrow$ of (a) to (d) above holds.

For $\Leftarrow$ we show part (a) only. Other parts can be similarly shown. Suppose that $\mathcal{C} \notin \mathbf{ReliableEx}$. Let $L_{i,f} = \{\langle i, x, f(x) \rangle \mid x \in N\}$ and $L'_{i,f} = \{\langle i, x, 1 - f(x) \rangle \mid x \in N\}$. Note that for all i, such that $\mathbf{M}_i$ is reliable separator, there exists an $f \in \mathcal{C}$, such that $\mathbf{M}_i$ does not **Resep**-identify $(L_{i,f}, L'_{i,f})$ (otherwise, one can easily modify $\mathbf{M}_i$ to show that $\mathcal{C} \in \mathbf{ReliableEx}$). If $\mathbf{M}_i$ is not reliable, then let f_i be arbitrary function in $\mathcal{C}$. Otherwise let f_i be a function in $\mathcal{C}$ such that $\mathbf{M}_i$ does not **Resep**-identify (L_{i,f_i}, L'_{i,f_i}). Let $\mathcal{L}_{\mathcal{C}} = \{L_{i,f_i} \mid i \in N\} \cup \{L'_{i,f_i} \mid i \in N\}$. It follows that $\mathcal{L}_{\mathcal{C}} \notin \mathbf{Reliablesep}$. $\Leftarrow$ of Part (a) follows. $\square$

The proof of Proposition 15 permits now to transfer the following noninclusions from the theory of learning functions [1,4,9,19,21,23,24,26] to the theory of learning separations.

Corollary 16. Recsep $\not\subseteq$ Reliablesep.
Reliablesep $\not\subseteq$ Confidentsep.
Confidentsep $\not\subseteq$ Reliablesep.
Popperiansep $\not\subseteq$ Confidentsep.
Confidentsep $\not\subseteq$ Finitesep.

Osherson, Stob and Weinstein [21, Exercise 4.4.2C] noted that a class which consists only of infinite sets has already a set-driven learner. This result directly transfers to the above separation-problems derived from function-classes. Thus one has, that the classes witnessing the non-inclusions in Corollary 16 are also set-driven separable.

Corollary 17. Setdrivensep $\not\subseteq$ Confidentsep.
Setdrivensep $\not\subseteq$ Reliablesep.
Setdrivensep $\not\subseteq$ Finitesep.

Proposition 18. *If L and L' are a recursively inseparable pair, then the class $\mathcal{L} = \{L, L'\}$ is finitely (and thus confidently) **Resep**-identifiable but not **Recsep**-identifiable (and thus also neither consistently nor reliably **Resep**-identifiable).*

However, above proposition uses the fact that there doesn't exist any recursive separator for (L, L'). The following theorem shows that one can do the separation of **TxtFin** and **Recsep** (and thus of **Finitesep** and **Recsep**) even if all languages in $\mathcal{L}$ are recursive. The proof uses a modification of the technique from Proposition 15, combined with the fact that there is even no limiting-recursive procedure to remove undefined places from programs, even if it does not matter which values are filled in at these places.

Theorem 19. Finitesep $\cap$ Setdrivensep $\cap$ TxtFin $\not\subseteq$ Recsep.
Furthermore, some class $\mathcal{L} \subseteq \mathcal{R}$ witnesses this separation.

Proof. Let $L_x = \{\langle x, y\rangle \mid \varphi_x(y)\downarrow = 0\}$, $L'_x = \{\langle x, y\rangle \mid \varphi_x(y)\downarrow = 1\}$ and $\mathcal{L} = \{L_x, L'_x \mid L_x \neq \emptyset$ and $L'_x \neq \emptyset$ and $\mathrm{card}(\{y \mid \langle x, y\rangle \notin L_x \cup L'_x\}) \leq 1\}$. Note that all sets in $\mathcal{L}$ are recursive.

Given two disjoint sets H, H' from $\mathcal{L}$ one can give a program for the below function ψ being 0 on H and 1 on H' after just knowing one element $\langle x, y\rangle$ and $\langle x', y'\rangle$ of H and H' as follows:

$$\psi(\langle v, w\rangle) = \begin{cases} 0, & \text{if } v = x \text{ and } \varphi_v(w)\downarrow = \varphi_x(y)\downarrow; \\ 1, & \text{if } v = x' \text{ and } \varphi_v(w)\downarrow = \varphi_{x'}(y')\downarrow; \\ \uparrow, & \text{otherwise.} \end{cases}$$

It is straightforward to extend the definition of the learner such that it becomes a **Finitesep**-identifier (by omitting any further mind change) or a **Setdrivensep**-identifier (by taking always the least pairs $\langle x, y\rangle$ and $\langle x', y'\rangle$ available from the input). Similarly one can show that $\mathcal{L}$ is **TxtFin**-learnable.

If there were a **Recsep**-identifier **M** for $\mathcal{L}$, then one could construct a procedure which, using oracle K, transforms a given program p, such that φ_p is defined and 0 or 1 at all but at most one place, into a program for a total extension of φ_p— but such a K-recursive algorithm does not exist. Thus $\mathcal{L} \notin$ **Recsep**. $\square$

5   Conservative Separability

The most involved separations are linked to conservativeness, the corresponding results are the main results of this work. Before investigating them in detail, recall that the following two inclusions were already mentioned in Proposition 11:

- **Finitesep $\subseteq$ Conservativesep.**
- **Popperiansep $\subseteq$ Conservativesep.**

They can be used to obtain the following noninclusions which have previously been obtained for **Finitesep** and **Popperiansep**, respectively.

Corollary 20. Conservativesep $\not\subseteq$ Recsep.
Conservativesep $\not\subseteq$ Confidentsep.

Although one can show that every procedure to learn separations can be transformed into one to learn these separations conservatively, this transformation is not effective and gives a noncomputable **Conservativesep**-identifier. Later below (Theorem 22) it will also be shown that this loss of recursiveness is unavoidable since there is a class which is **Recsep**-identifiable but not **Conservativesep**-identifiable. In the following, let **NonCompConservativesep** denote the class of languages that can be **Conservativesep**-identified, by dropping the constraint that learner has to be computable.

Theorem 21. Resep $\subseteq$ NonCompConservativesep.

Proof. This proof is almost identical to the proof for the corresponding result which Osherson, Stob and Weinstein [21, Proposition 4.5.1A] stated in the context of learning sets from positive data. Suppose **M** **Resep**-identifies $\mathcal{L}$. Define **F** as follows.

$$\mathbf{F}(\sigma x, \sigma' y) = \begin{cases} \mathbf{F}(\sigma, \sigma'), & \text{if } \mathrm{range}(\sigma x) \subseteq \varphi^{-1}_{\mathbf{F}(\sigma,\sigma')}(0) \\ & \text{and } \mathrm{range}(\sigma' y) \subseteq \varphi^{-1}_{\mathbf{F}(\sigma,\sigma')}(1); \\ \mathbf{M}(\sigma x, \sigma' y), & \text{otherwise.} \end{cases}$$

It is easy to verify that **F** is conservative, and **Resep**-identifies any (L, L') which is **Resep**-identified by **M**. $\square$

The next two results are the main results of the paper, which establish that the notions of conservative and set-driven separation are incomparable; moveover the two classes witnessing the two non-inclusions have a **Setdrivensep**-identifier and **Conservativesep**-identifier, respectively, which in addition is also a confident **Recsep**-identifier. Note that this result stands in contrast to the situation of learning sets from text where every set-driven learnable class is also conservatively learnable [16, Theorem 7.1].

Theorem 22. Confidentsep$\cap$Recsep$\cap$Setdrivensep $\not\subseteq$ Conservativesep.

Proof. Let $\mathbf{M}_0, \mathbf{M}_1, \ldots$ denote an enumeration of total machines such that for all **M**, there exists an i such that, if **M** conservatively **Resep**-identifies $\mathcal{L}$, then $\mathbf{M}_i$ conservatively **Resep**-identifies $\mathcal{L}$. Note that there exists such an enumeration of machines (see for example, [13], for similar result for **TxtEx**-identification).

Let $O_{x,y} = \{\langle x, y, 2z + 1 \rangle \mid z \in N\}$, $E_{x,y} = \{\langle x, y, 2z \rangle \mid z \in N\}$ and $U_{x,y} = O_{x,y} \cup E_{x,y}$.

Following an argument of Jockusch [15], there exist recursive functions g, h such that, for all x, y,

(A) $W_{g(x,y)}$ and $W_{h(x,y)}$ are infinite disjoint subsets of $O_{x,y}$.

(B) If W_y is infinite, then $W_{g(x,y)}$ and $W_{h(x,y)}$ partition the set $O_{x,y}$.

(C) If W_y is finite, then $W_{g(x,y)}$ and $W_{h(x,y)}$ form a recursively inseparable pair.

Let $ConsM = \{x \mid (\forall y) (\forall \text{ finite } L_x, L'_x \subseteq U_{x,y} \mid L_x \cap L'_x = \emptyset) [\mathbf{M}_x \text{ is conservative on } (L_x, L'_x)]\}$. Note that $\overline{ConsM}$ is recursively enumerable. We will later construct a recursive f such that for all x and y, $W_{f(x,y)}$ is a recursive subset of $E_{x,y}$. In addition, for all x, we will define L_x and L'_x. We will ensure that, for all x, there exists a y such that:

(D) $L_x, L'_x \subseteq U_{x,y}$.

(E) $\mathbf{M}_x$ does not **Conservativesep**-identify (L_x, L'_x).

(F) If $x \in ConsM$ and $(L_x \cup L'_x) \cap W_{f(x,y)} \neq \emptyset$, then L_x and L'_x are both finite subsets of $U_{x,y}$, and $\text{card}(L_x \cup L'_x) \leq 2 + \min((L_x \cup L'_x) \cap W_{f(x,y)})$ and $(L_x \cup L'_x) \cap W_{f(x,y),\max(L_x \cup L'_x)} \neq \emptyset$.

(G) If $x \in ConsM$ and $(L_x \cup L'_x) \cap W_{f(x,y)} = \emptyset$, then W_y is infinite, $L_x = W_{g(x,y)} \cup E_{x,y} - W_{f(x,y)}$, and $L'_x = W_{h(x,y)}$.

(H) If $x \notin ConsM$, then $L_x = \text{range}(\sigma) \cup \{d\}$ and $L'_x = \text{range}(\sigma')$, where (σ, σ') is the least pair such that $\text{range}(\sigma)$ and $\text{range}(\sigma')$ are disjoint subsets of $U_{x,y}$ and $\mathbf{M}_x$ is not conservative on (σ, σ'), and $d \in O_{x,y}$ is the least number such that x is enumerated in $\overline{ConsM}$ within d steps and $d > \max(\text{range}(\sigma) \cup \text{range}(\sigma'))$.

Now let $\mathcal{L} = \{L_x \mid x \in N\} \cup \{L'_x \mid x \in N\}$.

By (E), $\mathcal{L} \notin$ **Conservativesep**. Using (A), (B), (D), (F), (G) and (H) above, we easily have that $\mathcal{L} \in$ **Confidentsep** $\cap$ **Setdrivensep** $\cap$ **Recsep**.

Construction of f. We now construct $W_{f(x,y)}$. After the construction, we will define suitable L_x and L'_x, and show that (D) to (H) are satisfied.

Initially let $\sigma_0 = \sigma'_0 = \Lambda$. Let $W^s_{f(x,y)}$ denote the set of those elements which are enumerated into $W_{f(x,y)}$ before stage s. Go to stage 0.

Stage s

1. Dovetail steps 2 and 3, until search in one of them succeeds. If search in step 2 succeeds (before the search in step 3), then go to step 4. If search in step 3 succeeds (before the search in step 2), then go to step 5.

2. Search for $z \in E_{x,y}$ such that $z > \max(\text{range}(\sigma_s) \cup \text{range}(\sigma'_s) \cup \{s\})$ and $\varphi_{\mathbf{M}(\sigma_s,\sigma'_s)}(z)\!\downarrow = 0$.

3. Search for τ_s and τ'_s such that the following conditions are satisfied.
   $|\tau_s| = |\tau'_s|$.
   $\sigma_s \subseteq \tau_s$ and $\text{range}(\tau_s) \subseteq W_{g(x,y)} \cup E_{x,y} - W^s_{f(x,y)}$.
   $\sigma'_s \subseteq \tau'_s$ and $\text{range}(\tau'_s) \subseteq W_{h(x,y)}$.
   $\mathbf{M}(\sigma_s, \sigma'_s) \neq \mathbf{M}(\tau_s, \tau'_s)$.

4. Enumerate z into $W_{f(x,y)}$.
   Search for τ_s and τ'_s such that the following conditions are satisfied.
   $|\tau_s| = |\tau'_s|$.
   $\sigma_s \subseteq \tau_s$ and $\text{range}(\tau_s) \subseteq W_{g(x,y)} \cup E_{x,y} - (W^s_{f(x,y)} \cup \{z\})$.
   $\sigma'_s \subseteq \tau'_s$ and $\text{range}(\tau'_s) \subseteq W_{h(x,y)}$.
   $\mathbf{M}(\sigma_s, \sigma'_s) \neq \mathbf{M}(\tau_s, \tau'_s)$.

If and when such τ_s and τ_s' are found, go to step 5.

5. Let $\sigma_{s+1} = \tau_s$ and $\sigma_{s+1}' = \tau_s'$.

Go to stage $s + 1$.

End stage s

Verification of the properties (D) through (H). Note that either $W_{f(x,y)}$ is finite, or there exist infinitely many stages, and $s \in W_{f(x,y)}$, iff $s \in W_{f(x,y)}^s$. Thus $W_{f(x,y)}$ is recursive.

For each $x \in N$, we now consider the following cases.

Case 1: $x \notin ConsM$.

In this case, let σ, σ' be the least pair such that, for some y, range(σ) and range(σ') are disjoint subsets of $U_{x,y}$ and $\mathbf{M}_x$ is not conservative on (σ, σ'). Let $L_x = \text{range}(\sigma) \cup \{d\}$ and $L_x' = \text{range}(\sigma')$, where $d \in O_{x,y}$ is the least number such that x is enumerated into $\overline{ConsM}$ in less than d steps and d is larger than any element of range$(\sigma) \cup$ range(σ'). Note that there is a partial-recursive function which computes explicit lists of the elements of L_x and L_x' for every $x \notin ConsM$.

Thus, (D), (E) and (H) are satisfied, and (F) and (G) do not apply.

*Case 2: $x \in ConsM$ and there exists a y such that W_y is infinite and $\mathbf{M}_x$ does not **Resep**-identify $(W_{g(x,y)} \cup E_{x,y} - W_{f(x,y)}, W_{h(x,y)})$.*

In this case, let $L_x = W_{g(x,y)} \cup E_{x,y} - W_{f(x,y)}$, and $L_x' = W_{h(x,y)}$. Now, $\mathbf{M}_x$ does not **Resep**-identify (L_x, L_x').

Thus, (D), (E) and (G) are satisfied, and (F) and (H) do not apply.

*Case 3: $x \in ConsM$ and for all y such that W_y is infinite, $\mathbf{M}_x$ **Resep**-identifies $(W_{g(x,y)} \cup E_{x,y} - W_{f(x,y)}, W_{h(x,y)})$.*

In the following we will select finite L_x, L_x' with $L_x \cap W_{f(x,y)} \neq \emptyset$, for some y, satisfying conditions (D), (E) and (F).

Now we deal with Case 3 in detail: Let $I_1 = \{y \mid (\exists s)[$ in the construction of $W_{f(x,y)}$, step 4 of stage s is started but does not end $]\}$. Note that, $\{y \mid W_y$ is infinite$\} \subseteq I_1$. Furthermore, I_1 is recursively enumerable relative to the oracle K. Thus, for every $y \in I_1$ one can find s, z and σ_s, σ_s' (depending on y) using the oracle K, where in the definition of $W_{f(x,y)}$, s is the stage in which step 4 is started but does not end, and z is as defined in step 4 of stage s.

Using the oracle K, one can also test whether the following two conditions hold:

(P1) $\mathbf{M}_x(\sigma_s z d^n, \sigma_s' \#^{n+1}) = \mathbf{M}_x(\sigma_s, \sigma_s')$, for all $d \in W_{g(x,y)}$ and all n;

(P2) $\mathbf{M}_x(\sigma_s z \#^n, \sigma_s' d^{n+1}) = \mathbf{M}_x(\sigma_s, \sigma_s')$, for all $d \in W_{h(x,y)}$ and all n.

Let $I_2 = \{y \in I_1 \mid$ (P1) and (P2) are satisfied$\}$. Note that I_2 is recursively enumerable relative to the oracle K. Note that, if W_y is infinite, and $\mathbf{M}_x$ conservatively **Resep**-identifies $(W_{g(x,y)} \cup E_{x,y} - W_{f(x,y)}, W_{h(x,y)})$, then

$\varphi^{-1}_{\mathbf{M}_x(\sigma_s,\sigma'_s)}(0) \supseteq W_{g(x,y)} \cup \{z\}$ and $\varphi^{-1}_{\mathbf{M}_x(\sigma_s,\sigma'_s)}(1) \supseteq W_{h(x,y)}$. Thus, y must satisfy (P1) and (P2). Thus, $I_2 \supseteq \{y \mid W_y \text{ is infinite}\}$. Since I_2 is recursively enumerable relative to oracle K, and $\{y \mid W_y \text{ is infinite}\}$ is Π_2-complete, there must exist a y such that W_y is finite, and $y \in I_2$. For the following, fix such a y, and corresponding s, z, σ_s and σ'_s, where s is the stage in which step 4 of $W_{f(x,y)}$ starts but does not finish, and z is as defined in stage s. Let $A = \varphi^{-1}_{\mathbf{M}_x(\sigma_s,\sigma'_s)}(0)$, and $B = \varphi^{-1}_{\mathbf{M}_x(\sigma_s,\sigma'_s)}(1)$.

Case 3.1: At least one of the sets $W_{g(x,y)} - A$ and $W_{h(x,y)} - B$ is infinite.

If $\mathrm{card}(W_{g(x,y)} - A) = \infty$, then let $d \in W_{g(x,y)} - A$ be such that $z \in W_{f(x,y),d}$. Now, $\mathbf{M}_x$ does not **Resep**-identify $(\mathrm{range}(\sigma_s) \cup \{z,d\}, \mathrm{range}(\sigma'_s))$, since y satisfies (P1). Thus, we define that $L_x = \mathrm{range}(\sigma_s) \cup \{z,d\}$ and $L'_x = \mathrm{range}(\sigma'_s)$. Note that $\mathrm{card}(L_x \cup L'_x) \leq 2 + \mathrm{card}(\mathrm{range}(\sigma_s) \cup \mathrm{range}(\sigma'_s)) \leq 2 + z$, and $z \in L_x \cap W_{f(x,y),\max(L_x \cup L'_x)}$.

Similarly, if $\mathrm{card}(W_{h(x,y)} - B) = \infty$, then let $d \in W_{h(x,y)} - B$ be such that $z \in W_{f(x,y),d}$. Now, $\mathbf{M}_x$ does not **Resep**-identify $(\mathrm{range}(\sigma_s) \cup \{z\}, \mathrm{range}(\sigma'_s) \cup \{d\})$, since y satisfies (P2). Thus, let $L_x = \mathrm{range}(\sigma_s) \cup \{z\}$ and $L'_x = \mathrm{range}(\sigma'_s) \cup \{d\}$. Note that $\mathrm{card}(L_x \cup L'_x) \leq 2 + \mathrm{card}(\mathrm{range}(\sigma_s) \cup \mathrm{range}(\sigma'_s)) \leq 2 + z$, and $z \in L_x \cap W_{f(x,y),\max(L_x \cup L'_x)}$.
Thus, (D), (E) and (F) are satisfied, and (G) and (H) do not apply.

Case 3.2: $\mathrm{range}(\sigma_s) \not\subseteq A$ or $\mathrm{range}(\sigma'_s) \not\subseteq B$.

Let $d \in W_{g(x,y)} - \mathrm{range}(\sigma_s)$ be such that $z \in W_{f(x,y),d}$. Let $L_x = \mathrm{range}(\sigma_s) \cup \{z,d\}$, $L'_x = \mathrm{range}(\sigma'_s)$.
It is easy to verify that (D), (E) and (F) are satisfied and (G) and (H) do not apply.

Case 3.3: $\mathrm{range}(\sigma_s) \subseteq A$, $\mathrm{range}(\sigma'_s) \subseteq B$, and the two sets $W_{g(x,y)} - A$ and $W_{h(x,y)} - B$ are both finite.

Since $W_{g(x,y)}$ and $W_{h(x,y)}$ form a recursively inseparable pair, we must have that $A \cap O_{x,y}$ and $B \cap O_{x,y}$ are not recursive. Since $x \in ConsM$, the set

$$C = \{d \in O_{x,y} \mid (\exists n,m)\ [\mathbf{M}_x(\sigma_s z d^n, \sigma'_s \#^{n+1}) \neq \mathbf{M}_x(\sigma_s, \sigma'_s)]$$
$$\wedge\ [\mathbf{M}_x(\sigma_s z \#^m, \sigma'_s d^{m+1}) \neq \mathbf{M}_x(\sigma_s, \sigma'_s)]\}$$

is disjoint to A and B. However, $\mathrm{card}(O_{x,y} - (A \cup B \cup C)) = \infty$, due to non-recursiveness of $A \cap O_{x,y}$ and $B \cap O_{x,y}$. Thus, there exists a $d \in O_{x,y} - (A \cup B \cup C)$, such that $z \in W_{f(x,y),d}$. If for all n, $\mathbf{M}_x(\sigma_s z d^n, \sigma'_s \#^{n+1}) = \mathbf{M}_x(\sigma_s, \sigma'_s)$, then let $L_x = \mathrm{range}(\sigma_s) \cup \{z,d\}$, $L'_x = \mathrm{range}(\sigma'_s)$.
Otherwise, for all n, $\mathbf{M}_x(\sigma_s z \#^n, \sigma'_s d^{n+1}) = \mathbf{M}_x(\sigma_s, \sigma'_s)$. In this case let $L_x = \mathrm{range}(\sigma_s) \cup \{z\}$, $L'_x = \mathrm{range}(\sigma'_s) \cup \{d\}$.
Thus, (D), (E) and (F) are satisfied, and (G) and (H) do not apply.

From the above cases 1, 2, 3.1, 3.2 and 3.3, we have that (D) to (H) are satisfied. Thus proving the theorem. $\qquad \square$

Theorem 23. Confidentsep∩Conservativesep∩Recsep ⊈ Setdrivensep.

A proof of Theorem 23 is given in the technical report of this paper [14, Theorem 24].

6   Conclusion

Blum and Blum [5] considered the model of learning extensions of partial recursive functions. The separations considered in the present work can be viewed as a special case of this type of learning, since one could map the class $\mathcal{L}$ to the class $\mathcal{F}$ of all functions $\Psi_{L,L'}$ with Ψ being 0 on L and being 1 on L' and being undefined everywhere else. Now $\mathcal{L}$ is (conservatively) **Resep**-identifiable iff $\mathcal{F}$ is (conservatively) learnable in the model of Blum and Blum [5]. An application of the construction of a class $\mathcal{L}$ which is **Resep**-identifiable but not **Conservativesep**-identifiable is, that the corresponding $\mathcal{F}$ witnesses, that in the model of Blum and Blum some class of partial-recursive functions is learnable in the limit but is not conservatively learnable. This gives a contrast to the case of learning total recursive functions where Stephan and Zeugmann [25] showed that conservativeness is not restrictive.

Although every separation problem is the special case of a learning problem in the model of Blum and Blum [5], there is no general correspondence between these worlds. For example, there are reliably but not consistently learnable classes of functions while these notions coincide in the case of separating languages.

Acknowledgments. We would like to thank John Case for helpful discussions and proposing research on learning how to separate sets.

References

1. A. Ambainis, S. Jain, and A. Sharma. Ordinal mind change complexity of language identification. *Theoretical Computer Science*, 220(2):323–343, 1999.
2. D. Angluin and C. Smith. Inductive inference: Theory and methods. *Computing Surveys*, 15:237–289, 1983.
3. J. Bārzdiņš. Two theorems on the limiting synthesis of functions. In *Theory of Algorithms and Programs, vol. 1*, pages 82–88. Latvian State University, 1974. In Russian.
4. J. Bārzdiņš and R. Freivalds. On the prediction of general recursive functions. *Soviet Mathematics Doklady*, 13:1224–1228, 1972.
5. L. Blum and M. Blum. Toward a mathematical theory of inductive inference. *Information and Control*, 28:125–155, 1975.
6. M. Blum. A machine-independent theory of the complexity of recursive functions. *Journal of the ACM*, 14:322–336, 1967.
7. J. Case, S. Jain, and S. Ngo Manguelle. Refinements of inductive inference by Popperian and reliable machines. *Kybernetika*, 30:23–52, 1994.

8. J. Case and C. Lynes. Machine inductive inference and language identification. In M. Nielsen and E. M. Schmidt, editors, *Proceedings of the 9th International Colloquium on Automata, Languages and Programming*, volume 140 of *Lecture Notes in Computer Science*, pages 107–115. Springer-Verlag, 1982.

9. J. Case and C. Smith. Comparison of identification criteria for machine inductive inference. *Theoretical Computer Science*, 25:193–220, 1983.

10. M. Fulk. Prudence and other conditions on formal language learning. *Information and Computation*, 85:1–11, 1990.

11. E. M. Gold. Language identification in the limit. *Information and Control*, 10:447–474, 1967.

12. J. Hopcroft and J. Ullman. *Introduction to Automata Theory, Languages, and Computation*. Addison-Wesley, 1979.

13. S. Jain, D. Osherson, J. Royer, and A. Sharma. *Systems that Learn: An Introduction to Learning Theory*. MIT Press, Cambridge, Mass., second edition, 1999.

14. S. Jain and F. Stephan. Learning how to separate. Technical Report Forschungsberichte Mathematische Logik 51/2001, Mathematical Institute, University of Heidelberg, 2001.

15. C. Jockusch. Degrees in which recursive sets are uniformly recursive. *Candadian Journal of Mathematics*, 24:1092–1099, 1972.

16. E. Kinber and F. Stephan. Language learning from texts: Mind changes, limited memory and monotonicity. *Information and Computation*, 123:224–241, 1995.

17. R. Klette and R. Wiehagen. Research in the theory of inductive inference by GDR mathematicians – A survey. *Information Sciences*, 22:149–169, 1980.

18. M. Machtey and P. Young. *An Introduction to the General Theory of Algorithms*. North Holland, New York, 1978.

19. E. Minicozzi. Some natural properties of strong identification in inductive inference. *Theoretical Computer Science*, 2:345–360, 1976.

20. P. Odifreddi. *Classical Recursion Theory*. North-Holland, Amsterdam, 1989.

21. D. Osherson, M. Stob, and S. Weinstein. *Systems that Learn: An Introduction to Learning Theory for Cognitive and Computer Scientists*. MIT Press, 1986.

22. H. Rogers. *Theory of Recursive Functions and Effective Computability*. McGraw-Hill, 1967. Reprinted by MIT Press in 1987.

23. G. Schäfer-Richter. *Über Eingabeabhängigkeit und Komplexität von Inferenzstrategien*. PhD thesis, RWTH Aachen, 1984.

24. A. Sharma, F. Stephan, and Y. Ventsov. Generalized notions of mind change complexity. In *Proceedings of the Tenth Annual Conference on Computational Learning Theory*, pages 96–108. ACM Press, 1997.

25. F. Stephan and T. Zeugmann. On the uniform learnability of approximations to non-recursive functions. In O. Watanabe and T. Yokomori, editors, *Algorithmic Learning Theory: Tenth International Conference (ALT' 99)*, volume 1720 of *Lecture Notes in Artificial Intelligence*, pages 276–290. Springer-Verlag, 1999.

26. K. Wexler and P. Culicover. *Formal Principles of Language Acquisition*. MIT Press, 1980.

27. R. Wiehagen and W. Liepe. Charakteristische Eigenschaften von erkennbaren Klassen rekursiver Funktionen. *Journal of Information Processing and Cybernetics (EIK)*, 12:421–438, 1976.

28. T. Zeugmann. On Bārzdiņš' conjecture. In K. P. Jantke, editor, *Analogical and Inductive Inference, Proceedings of the International Workshop*, volume 265 of *Lecture Notes in Computer Science*, pages 220–227. Springer-Verlag, 1986.

Learning Languages in a Union

Sanjay Jain[1], Yen Kaow Ng[2], and Tiong Seng Tay[3]

[1] School of Computing
National University of Singapore
Singapore 119260
sanjay@comp.nus.edu.sg
[2] School of Computing
National University of Singapore
Singapore 119260
ngyenkao@comp.nus.edu.sg
[3] Department of Mathematics
National University of Singapore
Singapore 119260
mattayts@nus.edu.sg

Abstract. In inductive inference, a machine is given words in a language and the machine is said to identify the language if it correctly names the language. In this paper we study classes of languages where the unions of up to a fixed number (n say) of languages from the class are identifiable. We distinguish between two different scenarios: in one scenario, the learner need only to name the language which results from the union; in the other, the learner must individually name the languages which make up the union (we say that the unioned language is *discerningly* identified). We define three kinds of identification criteria based on this and by the use of some naturally occurring classes of languages, demonstrate that the inferring power of each of these identification criterion decreases as we increase the number of languages allowed in the union, thus resulting in an infinite hierarchy for each identification criterion. A comparison between the different identification criteria also yielded similar hierarchies. We show that for each n, there exists a class of disjoint languages where all unions of up to n languages from this class can be discerningly identified, but there is no learner which identifies every union of $n+1$ languages from this class. We give sufficient conditions for classes of languages where the unions can be discerningly identified. We also present language classes which are complete with respect to weak reduction (in terms of intrinsic complexity) for our identification criteria.

1 Introduction

We continue a line of enquiry explored in [Wri89,SA00,GK99], where the learner is required to learn unions of languages drawn from a class of languages.

What is different from previous studies is that we distinguish between two different scenarios. In one scenario, the learner is only required to name the

N. Abe, R. Khardon, and T. Zeugmann (Eds.): ALT 2001, LNAI 2225, pp. 235–250, 2001.
© Springer-Verlag Berlin Heidelberg 2001

language which results from the union; in the other, we want the learner to individually name the languages which make up the union — in a sense, the learner is discerning between the languages in the union. Our study is motivated by the abundance of situations where learners are presented with information that is some sort of mixture. For example, children in a multi-lingual environment are frequently exposed to more than one (natural) languages at the same time, but are nonetheless able to tell what are the languages they hear; or, in a physical experiment, radiations collected by the same detector may originate from many different source processes, for which scientists are often put to the task of discerning. We are also interested in devising mechanisms which will allow us to distinguish between languages that has to be presented as a mixture.

In the course of identifying the languages which make up a union, what happens when there are two (or more) possible sets of languages from the class which unions to the same language? Should the learner be required to name both possibilities, or should the learner be allowed to choose any one? Or perhaps such a situation should be simply declared unlearnable? We formalize different identification criteria based on these considerations.

It can be said in general that the inferring power of learners lessen when more languages are allowed in the union, and moreover, there are naturally occurring classes of languages which hold up these hierarchies. We also noticed hierarchies between each of the different identification criteria. More notably, for each n, there exists a class of *disjoint* languages where all the unions of up to n languages from this class can be *discerningly identified*, but there is no learner that can identify every union of $n + 1$ languages from this class.

In our attempt to characterize these identification criteria, we discovered two sufficient conditions for classes of languages where the unions can be discerningly identified. We demonstrate that one of these conditions is difficult to be further relaxed, by showing how some weaker conditions are insufficient to hold up the same results. Finally, we give natural classes of languages which are complete with respect to weak reduction in terms of so-called intrinsic complexity [FKS95] for the identification criteria we defined.

Due to space constraints, we omit proofs for some of the results. Some of our results can also be generalized for other identification criteria.

2   Notation and Preliminaries

Any unexplained recursion-theoretic notation is from [Rog67]. N denotes the set of natural numbers. N^+ denotes the set of positive integers. Let *rat* denote the set of non-negative rational numbers. $\emptyset$, $\in$, $\subset$, $\subseteq$, $\supset$, $\supseteq$ respectively denote empty set, element of, proper subset, subset, proper superset, superset. max(.), min(.) denote maximum and minimum of a set, where by convention $\max(\emptyset) = 0$ and $\min(\emptyset) = \infty$. Cardinality of a set S is denoted by $card(S)$. $D_0, D_1, \ldots$ stand for a computable sequence of all finite sets [Rog67]. $A - B$ denotes the set $\{x \mid x \in A \text{ and } x \notin B\}$.

$\langle \cdot, \cdot \rangle$ stands for an arbitrary, computable bijective mapping from $N \times N$ onto N. For all x and y, $\pi_1(\langle x, y \rangle) = x$ and $\pi_2(\langle x, y \rangle) = y$. We assume without loss of generality that $\langle \cdot, \cdot \rangle$ is monotonically increasing in both of its arguments. $\langle \cdot, \cdot \rangle$ can be extended to n-tuples in a natural way (including $n = 1$, where $\langle x \rangle$ may be taken to be x). Projection functions $\pi_1, \ldots, \pi_n$ corresponding to n-tuples can be defined similarly (where the tuple size would be clear from context). Due to the above isomorphism between N^k and N, we often identify the tuple $(x_1, \ldots, x_n)$ with $\langle x_1, \ldots, x_n \rangle$. The quantifiers $\overset{\infty}{\forall}$, $\overset{\infty}{\exists}$ and $\exists!$ denote, for all but finitely many, there exists infinitely many and there exists a unique, respectively.

A computable numbering is a partial computable function from N^2 to N. The symbol ψ ranges over computable numberings. We denote by ψ_i, the partial function, $\lambda x. \psi(i, x)$. Thus ψ_i denotes the partial function computed by the program with index i in the numbering ψ. Ψ denotes an arbitrary Blum complexity measure for ψ. W_i^ψ denotes $domain(\psi_i)$. W_i^ψ is, then, the r.e. set/language ($\subseteq N$) accepted (or equivalently, generated) by the ψ-program i. We also say that i is a ψ-grammar for W_i^ψ. $W_{i,s}^\psi$ denotes the set $\{x \leq s \mid \Psi_i(x) \leq s\}$. We say that numbering ψ is reducible to numbering ψ' (written $\psi \prec \psi'$) if and only if there exists a recursive function h such that $(\forall i)[\psi_i = \psi'_{h(i)}]$. In this case we say that h witnesses that $\psi \prec \psi'$. An acceptable numbering is a computable numbering to which every computable numbering can be reduced. The symbol φ denotes a standard acceptable numbering [Rog67] and the symbol Φ denotes an arbitrary fixed Blum complexity measure for the φ-system [Blu67]. In this paper we abbreviate W_i^φ to W_i, and $W_{i,s}^\varphi$ to $W_{i,s}$.

$\mathcal{E}$ denotes the class of all r.e. languages. $\mathcal{R}$ denotes the set of all recursive functions, that is total computable functions. Symbol L, with or without decorations, ranges over $\mathcal{E}$. The symbol $\mathcal{L}$, with or without decorations, ranges over subsets of $\mathcal{E}$. K denotes the diagonal halting problem set, that is, $K = \{x \mid x \in W_x\}$. (K is a recursively enumerable, non-recursive set.) $SINGLE$ denotes the set $\{\{x\} \mid x \in N\}$. FIN denotes the set $\{D \subset N \mid D \text{ is finite}\}$. $INIT$ denotes the set $\{\{x \in N \mid x \leq n\} \mid n \in N\}$.

A class $\mathcal{L}$ of r.e. languages is said to be *recursively enumerable* [Rog67] if there is $S \in \mathcal{E}$ such that $\mathcal{L} = \{W_i \mid i \in S\}$. For each infinite, recursively enumerable class of languages $\mathcal{L}$, there exists a total recursive function f such that $\mathcal{L} = \{W_{f(i)} \mid i \in N\}$. $\mathcal{L}$ is said to be 1–1 recursively enumerable if and only if (i) $\mathcal{L}$ is finite or (ii) there exists a recursive function f such that $\mathcal{L} = \{W_{f(i)} \mid i \in N\}$ and $W_{f(i)} \neq W_{f(j)}$, for $i \neq j$. In this latter case we say that $W_{f(0)}, W_{f(1)}, \ldots$ is a 1–1 recursive enumeration of $\mathcal{L}$.

A partial function d from N to N is said to be partial limiting recursive, if and only if there exists a recursive function F from $N \times N$ to N such that for all x, $d(x) = \lim_{y \to \infty} F(x, y)$. Here if $d(x)$ is not defined then $\lim_{y \to \infty} F(x, y)$, must also be undefined. A partial limiting recursive function d is called (total) limiting recursive, if d is total. $\downarrow$ denotes defined or converges. $\uparrow$ denotes undefined or diverges.

We now present concepts from language learning theory. The next definition introduces the concept of a *sequence* of data.

Definition 1. [Gol67] (a) A *sequence* σ is a mapping from an initial segment of N into $(N \cup \{\#\})$. The empty sequence is denoted by Λ.
(b) The *content* of a sequence σ, denoted $content(\sigma)$, is the set of natural numbers in the range of σ.
(c) The *length* of σ, denoted by $|\sigma|$, is the number of elements in σ. So, $|\Lambda| = 0$.
(d) For $n \leq |\sigma|$, the initial sequence of σ of length n is denoted by $\sigma[n]$. So, $\sigma[0] = \Lambda$.

Intuitively, $\#$'s represent pauses in the presentation of data. We let σ, τ, and γ, with or without decorations, range over finite sequences. SEQ denotes the set of all finite sequences.

Definition 2. [Gol67] (a) A *text* T for a language L is a mapping from N into $(N \cup \{\#\})$ such that L is the set of natural numbers in the range of T.
(b) The *content* of a text T, denoted by $content(T)$, is the set of natural numbers in the range of T; that is, the language which T is a text for.
(c) $T[n]$ denotes the finite initial sequence of T with length n.

We let T, with or without decorations, range over texts. We let $\mathcal{T}$ range over sets of texts.

Definition 3. [Gol67] An *inductive inference machine* (**IIM**) is an algorithmic device which computes a mapping from SEQ into N.

$M(T[n])$ is interpreted as the grammar (index for an accepting program) conjectured by the machine M on the initial sequence $T[n]$. We say that M converges on T to i (written $M(T)\downarrow = i$) if $(\overset{\infty}{\forall} n)[M(T[n]) = i]$.

Let $M_0, M_1, \ldots$ denote a sequence of the **IIM**s, such that every class in **TxtEx** is identifies by at least one of the machines in the sequence [OSW86].

Gold [Gol67] introduced the following language learning criterion known as **TxtEx**-identification.

Definition 4. [Gol67] (a) M **TxtEx**-identifies a text T just in case $(\exists i \mid W_i = content(T))$ $(\overset{\infty}{\forall} n)[M(T[n]) = i]$.
(b) M **TxtEx**-identifies an r.e. language L (written $L \in$ **TxtEx**(M)) just in case M **TxtEx**-identifies each text for L.
(c) M **TxtEx**-identifies a class $\mathcal{L}$ of r.e. languages (written $\mathcal{L} \subseteq$ **TxtEx**(M)) just in case M **TxtEx**-identifies each language from $\mathcal{L}$.
(d) **TxtEx** $= \{\mathcal{L} \subseteq \mathcal{E} \mid (\exists M)[\mathcal{L} \subseteq$ **TxtEx**$(M)]\}$.

3   Identification of Unions of Languages

Definition 5. [SA00] Let $\mathcal{L} \subseteq \mathcal{E}$.
(a) *The union language of $\mathcal{L}$, $L_{\mathcal{L}} = \bigcup_{L \in \mathcal{L}} L$.*
(b) *The class of at most k unions of $\mathcal{L}$, $\mathcal{L}^k = \{ L_{\mathcal{L}'} \mid \mathcal{L}' \subseteq \mathcal{L} \wedge card(\mathcal{L}') \leq k \}$.*

We now define an identification criterion for the learning of unions of languages.

Definition 6. Let $k \in N^+$ and $\mathcal{L} \subseteq \mathcal{E}$.
(a) M **U^kTxtEx**-identifies $\mathcal{L}$ just in case $\mathcal{L}^k \subseteq$ **TxtEx**(M).
(b) **U^kTxtEx** $= \{\mathcal{L} \subseteq \mathcal{E} \mid (\exists M)[M$ **U^kTxtEx**-identifies $\mathcal{L}]\}$.

UTxtEx coincides with the definition of "identification of unions of languages" in [Wri89,SA00].

Wright [Wri89,MSW91] showed a sufficient condition (finite elasticity) for indexed families [Ang80] of recursive languages to be in **U^nTxtEx** for all n. Shinohara and Arimura noted that this result does not apply to the unions of unbounded number of languages and provided a sufficient condition for **U^*TxtEx** membership in [SA00].

We now define an identification criterion, where the learner must furthermore, individually identify each of the languages in the union.

Definition 7. Given $\mathcal{L} \subseteq \mathcal{E}$ where $card(\mathcal{L}) < \infty$.
(a) We say a set of indices $\{x_1, x_2, \ldots, x_{card(\mathcal{L})}\} \subseteq N$ is a *representation index set* of $\mathcal{L}$ just in case $\{W_{x_1}, W_{x_2}, ..., W_{x_{card(\mathcal{L})}}\} = \mathcal{L}$.
(b) Let $\mathcal{I}_{\mathcal{L}} = \{I \mid I$ is a representation index set of $\mathcal{L}\}$.
(c) Let $\mathcal{I} = \{I \mid (\exists \mathcal{L} \subseteq \mathcal{E}, card(\mathcal{L}) < \infty)[I \in \mathcal{I}_{\mathcal{L}}]\}$.

Any representation index set $\{x_1, x_2, \ldots, x_{card(\mathcal{L})}\}$ can be represented by a natural number k where $D_k = \{x_1, x_2, \ldots, x_{card(\mathcal{L})}\}$. This representation is implicit whenever the context requires such an interpretation.

Definition 8. Let $k \in N^+$ and $\mathcal{L} \subseteq \mathcal{E}$.
(a) M **DU^kTxtEx**-identifies $\mathcal{L}$ just in case $(\forall \mathcal{L}' \subseteq \mathcal{L} \mid card(\mathcal{L}') \leq k)$ $(\forall\, T$ for $L_{\mathcal{L}'})$ $[M(T)\downarrow \wedge M(T) \in \mathcal{I}_{\mathcal{L}'}]$.
(b) **DU^kTxtEx** $= \{\mathcal{L} \subseteq \mathcal{E} \mid (\exists M)[M$ **DU^kTxtEx**-identifies $\mathcal{L}]\}$.

The **D** in **DUTxtEx** stands for *discernible*. It is clear from the definitions that **DU^1TxtEx** $\equiv$ **U^1TxtEx** $\equiv$ **TxtEx**.

Proposition 1. *Given $\mathcal{L} \subseteq \mathcal{E}$. If there exists $\mathcal{L}', \mathcal{L}'' \subseteq \mathcal{L}$, $\mathcal{L}' \neq \mathcal{L}''$, but $L_{\mathcal{L}'} = L_{\mathcal{L}''}$, then $\mathcal{L} \notin DU^k TxtEx$ for $k = \max(card(\mathcal{L}'), \ card(\mathcal{L}''))$.*

Definition 9. Let $\mathcal{L} \subseteq \mathcal{E}$ and $k \in N^+$. The class of languages $\mathcal{L}^k$ is said to be *uniquely definable from* $\mathcal{L}$ just in case $(\forall L \in \mathcal{L}^k)(\exists! \mathcal{L}' \subseteq \mathcal{L} \mid card(\mathcal{L}') \leq k)[L_{\mathcal{L}'} = L]$.

We now introduce an identification criteria where the complications of Proposition 1 is avoided. The learner is considered correct by simply naming any set of (up to) n languages in the class which make up the language of the input text.

Definition 10. Let $k \in N^+$ and $\mathcal{L} \subseteq \mathcal{E}$.
(a) M **WDU**^{k}**TxtEx**-identifies $\mathcal{L}$ just in case $(\forall L \in \mathcal{L}^k)$ $(\forall T$ for $L)$ $[M(T)\downarrow \wedge (\exists \mathcal{L}' \subseteq \mathcal{L} \mid card(\mathcal{L}') \leq k)$ $[M(T) \in \mathcal{I}_{\mathcal{L}'} \wedge T$ happens to be a text for $L_{\mathcal{L}'}]]$.
(b) **WDU**^{k}**TxtEx** $= \{\mathcal{L} \subseteq \mathcal{E} \mid (\exists M)[M$ **WDU**^{k}**TxtEx**-identifies $\mathcal{L}]\}$.

The **W** in **WDUTxtEx** stands for *weak*.

To avoid Proposition 1, we may also require the learner to name all possible unions of languages in the class which result in the language of the input text. We do not consider this alternative in this abstract.

4   Hierarchy Results

We now describe a natural class of languages which give rise to our hierarchy results.

Fix $n \in N^+$, $n \geq 2$. Let $v_1, v_2, \ldots, v_{n-1}$ be unit vectors along each axis of an $(n-1)$-dimensional space. Let G_n be a simplex with n vertices, respectively at $-v_1, v_1, v_2, \ldots, v_{n-1}$. (For $n = 2$, the vertices are at v_1 and $-v_1$.)

Let RAT_n be the set of all the points in an $(n-1)$-dimensional space with only rational valued coordinates, and let $coderat_n(.)$ be an effective bijective mapping from RAT_n to N. Let $T_n = \{\sum_{i=1}^{n-1} \epsilon_i v_i \mid \epsilon_i \in rat\}$ and let $\Lambda_n = \{G_n + T \mid T \in T_n\}$.

For each $G \in \Lambda_n$, the polytope of G, denoted $P(G)$, can be defined as the set of all points X which satisfy n linear equations $\overrightarrow{\nu_k} \cdot X \leq b_k$, $k = 1, 2, \ldots, n$ where for each k, the coefficient b_k and the vector $\overrightarrow{\nu_k}$ can be obtained by solving $n-1$ linear equations (each formed by substituting in the equation a vertex of G). [1] [Cox63]

Let $Lang(G) = \{coderat_n(X) \mid X \in P(G) \wedge X \in RAT_n\}$. Let $TRANSIM_n = \{Lang(G) \mid G \in \Lambda_n\}$.

We now give some properties of Λ_n (and hence $TRANSIM_n$) which we shall use to demonstrate our hierarchy results.

Claim (1). Given $G \in \Lambda_n$ with vertices at $A_1, A_2, \ldots, A_n$. Let $V = \{A_1, A_2, \ldots, A_n\}$. Let each outward normal for the hyperplane formed by $V - \{A_i\}$ be denoted $\overrightarrow{\nu_i}$. Let $G' = G + T$ where $T \in T_n$, then $T \cdot \overrightarrow{\nu_i} < 0 \Rightarrow (V - \{A_i\}) \cap P(G') = \emptyset$.

---

[1] Intuitively, the inequality for each k represents a bounding hyperplane for the polytope, where each vector $\overrightarrow{\nu_k}$ is the outward normal for the bounding hyperplane.

Claim (2). Let $n \geq 2$. Given $G \in \Lambda_n$ with vertices at $A_1, A_2, \ldots, A_n$. Let C be a point in $P(G)$. For each $i \in N$, $1 \leq i \leq n$, let $\overrightarrow{\mu_i} = (1/|\overrightarrow{CA_i}|)\overrightarrow{CA_i}$ and $G_i(\delta) = G + \delta \overrightarrow{\mu_i}$. There exists a collection of n simplexes $G_1(\epsilon_1'), G_2(\epsilon_2'), \ldots, G_n(\epsilon_n')$ where each $\epsilon_i' > 0$ and n numbers $\xi_1, \xi_2, \ldots, \xi_n$ where $0 < \xi_i \leq \epsilon_i'$ such that $(\forall \delta_i, 0 \leq \delta_i \leq \xi_i)[P(G_i(\delta_i)) \subseteq \bigcup_{j=1}^{n} P(G_j(\epsilon_j'))]$.

Proposition 2. $(\forall n \in N^+)[DU^n \, TxtEx - U^{n+1} \, TxtEx \neq \emptyset]$.

Proof. The case of $n = 1$ is shown by the class of languages $\{K\} \cup SINGLE$. We now show the case for $n \geq 2$.

Let $PRIMES$ be the set of all the prime numbers and $p_1, p_2, \ldots$ be an enumeration of $PRIMES$ in ascending order. Let ψ be a computable numbering for which $(\forall i \in N)[W_{p_i}^{\psi} = W_i]$.

For each $G \in \Lambda_n$, let $X_1(G) = T \cdot v_1$, where $T \in T_n$ is such that $G = G_n + T$, and let $L_G = \{\langle 0, x \rangle \mid x \in Lang(G)\} \cup \{\langle 1, y \rangle \mid y \in W_{h(X_1(G))}^{\psi}\}$, where $h(a)$ is the denominator of a in reduced form. Clearly, h is a recursive function. Let $ExtTRANSIM_n = \{L_G \mid G \in \Lambda_n\}$. Using Claim (1), it can be verified that $ExtTRANSIM_n \in DU^n TxtEx$.

Let $\Lambda \subset \Lambda_n$ be a collection of n simplexes as in Claim (2). Without loss of generality, we require that the numbering ψ has it that $(\forall G \in \Lambda)$ $[W_{h(X_1(G))}^{\psi} = \emptyset]$. Let $G_a \in \Lambda_n$ and $\xi \in rat$ be such that $(\forall \delta, 0 \leq \delta \leq \xi)$ $[P(G_a + \delta v_1) \subseteq \bigcup_{G \in \Lambda} P(G)]$. By Claim (2), such G_a and ξ exists. Let $G_b = G_a + \xi v_1$. Let $\Lambda' = \{G_a + \alpha v_1 \mid 0 \leq \alpha \leq \xi \wedge \alpha \in rat\}$. Let $\mathcal{L}' = \{L_{G'} \cup \bigcup_{G \in \Lambda} L_G \mid G' \in \Lambda'\}$.

For each $z \in rat$, $X_1(G_a) < z < X_1(G_b)$ there exists a language in $\mathcal{L}'$ which differ from $\bigcup_{G \in \Lambda} L_G$ by the set $\{\langle 1, y \rangle \mid y \in W_{h(z)}^{\psi}\}$. Since there exists an $m \in N$ such that $(\forall p \in PRIMES \ where \ p > m)(\exists l \in N \mid l$ is co-prime with $p)[X_1(G_a) < \frac{l}{p} < X_1(G_b)]$, the set $\{W_{h(z)}^{\psi} \mid z \in rat, X_1(G_a) < z < X_1(G_b)\}$ includes all the r.e. languages. Thus if $\mathcal{L}'$ is in **TxtEx**, then the set of all the r.e. languages would be in **TxtEx**. It follows that $\mathcal{L}'$ cannot be in **TxtEx**. Since $\mathcal{L}' \subseteq ExtTRANSIM_n^{n+1}$, $ExtTRANSIM_n \notin U^{n+1}TxtEx$.   ∎

Corollary 1. *For all $n \in N^+$.*
(a) $U^{n+1} TxtEx \subset U^n TxtEx$.
(b) $DU^{n+1} TxtEx \subset DU^n TxtEx$.
(c) $WDU^{n+1} TxtEx \subset WDU^n TxtEx$.

Proposition 3. *For all $n \in N^+$.*
(a) $(WDU^* TxtEx \cap DU^n TxtEx) - DU^{n+1} TxtEx \neq \emptyset$.
(b) $(U^* TxtEx \cap WDU^n TxtEx) - WDU^{n+1} TxtEx \neq \emptyset$.

Proof. For part (a), the case of $n = 1$ is shown by FIN. Let $n \in N$ and $n \geq 2$. Let $\{G_1, G_2, \ldots, G_n\} \subset \Lambda_n$ be a collection of n simplexes and let

G_0 be such that $P(G_0) \subseteq \bigcup_{i=1}^{n} P(G_i)$. Such $G_0, G_1, \ldots, G_n$ exists by Claim (2). Let $\mathcal{L} = \{Lang(G_i) \mid 0 \le i \le n\}$. It is easy to verify that $\mathcal{L} \in$ **DU^{n}TxtEx** $\cap$ **WDU*TxtEx**. However, since a text for $\bigcup_{i=0}^{n} Lang(G_i)$ is also a text for $\bigcup_{i=1}^{n} Lang(G_i)$, by Proposition 1, $\mathcal{L} \notin$ **DU^{n+1}TxtEx**.

For part (b), let $n \in N^+$. For $i, k \in N$, let $A_{i,k} = \{\langle \lfloor i/(n+1) \rfloor \cdot (n+1) + j, \langle i, k \rangle \rangle \mid j \in N \wedge 0 \le j \le n\} \cup \{\langle i, x \rangle \mid x \in N\}$.

Given total $g : N \to N$ and $i \in N$, let $L_{i,g} = A_{i,g(i)}$. Let $\mathcal{L}_g = \{L_{i,g} \mid i \in N\}$. It is easy to verify that $\{\mathcal{L}_g \mid g : N \to N\} \subseteq$ **U*TxtEx** $\cap$ **WDU^{n}TxtEx**. Note that for all g, g', $\bigcup_{j \le n} L_{(n+1)*e+j,g} = \bigcup_{j \le n} L_{(n+1)*e+j,g'} = \{\langle i, x \rangle \mid (n+1)*e \le i < (n+1)*(e+1)$ and $x \in N\}$.

Now define g such that for all e, $\{L_{(n+1)*e+j,g} \mid j \le n\}$ is not the set of languages to which M_e converges on $\{\langle i, x \rangle \mid (n+1)*e \le i < (n+1)*(e+1)$ and $x \in N\}$. Note that such g can be easily defined.

Thus, $\mathcal{L}_g \notin$ **WDU^{n+1}TxtEx**.   ∎

Corollary 2. $(\forall n \in N, n \ge 2)[\boldsymbol{DU^n \, TxtEx} \subset \boldsymbol{WDU^n \, TxtEx} \subset \boldsymbol{U^n \, TxtEx}]$.

4.1 Disjointness

It may be argued that languages in a union only fail to be discerningly identifiable as a result of crucial information regarding one language being lost within the other languages; that is, when all the "important" members (such as $Lang(G)$ in the proof of Proposition 2) of one language are also members of some other languages in the union. It is natural to ask if disjointness would be a sufficient condition for unions of languages to be discerningly identifiable. The following result answers this in the negative.

Theorem 1. For all $n \in N^+$, there exists $\mathcal{L} \in \boldsymbol{DU^n \, TxtEx}$ where

(a) $\emptyset \notin \mathcal{L}$,

(b) $(\forall L, L' \in \mathcal{L})[L \cap L' = \emptyset]$,

such that $\mathcal{L} \notin \boldsymbol{U^{n+1} \, TxtEx}$.

Proof. Unless stated otherwise, let e, i, j, with or without decorations, range over N, and S, with or without decorations, range over finite sets. For each **IIM** M_e, we construct $S_e, L_e^0, L_e^1, \ldots, L_e^n$ where

$$L_e^0 = \{\langle e, 0, 0 \rangle\} \cup \{\langle e, i, j \rangle \mid 1 \le i \le n, \ j \in S_e\}$$

and for $1 \le i \le n$, L_e^i satisfies the following two properties:

(1) $L_e^i = \{\langle e, i, j \rangle \mid j \in W_{\min(\{\pi_3(x) \mid x \in L_e^i\})}\}$
(2) $\min(\{\pi_3(x) \mid x \in L_e^i\}) > \max(S_e)$.

Let $\mathcal{L} = \{L_e^0, L_e^1, ..., L_e^n \mid e \in N\}$. It is clear that for all $L, L' \in \mathcal{L}$, $L \cap L' = \emptyset$. We now show that $\mathcal{L} \in \mathbf{DU}^n\mathbf{TxtEx}$. Let $g : N^3 \mapsto N$ be a recursive function such that for each $e \in N$,

$$W_{g(e,0,S)} = \{\langle e, 0, 0 \rangle\} \cup \{\langle e, i, j \rangle \mid i \in N, 1 \le i \le n \wedge j \in S]\}$$

and for each $i \in N^+$,

$$W_{g(e,i,j)} = \{\langle e, i, k \rangle \mid k \in W_j\}.$$

Now $\mathcal{L} \in \mathbf{DU}^n\mathbf{TxtEx}$ is witnessed by following M.

$M(T[m]):$
    $S \leftarrow \emptyset$.
    $A \leftarrow \{j \in N \mid (\exists w \in content(T[m]))[\pi_1(w) = j]\}$.
    For each $e \in A$ do
        $B \leftarrow content(T[m])$.
        If $\langle e, 0, 0 \rangle \in content(T[m])$ then
            $C \leftarrow \{j \mid (\forall i, 1 \le i \le n)[\langle e, i, j \rangle \in content(T[m])]\}$.
            $S \leftarrow S \cup \{g(e, 0, C)\}$.
            $B \leftarrow B - W_{g(e,0,C)}$.
        For $i \leftarrow 1$ to n do
            If exists j_0 such that $\langle e, i, j_0 \rangle \in B$, then
                For minimum such j_0, let $S \leftarrow S \cup \{g(e, i, j_0)\}$.
    Output S.

It is easy to verify that M $\mathbf{DU}^n\mathbf{TxtEx}$-identifies $\mathcal{L}$.

We now show that $\mathcal{L} \notin \mathbf{U}^{n+1}\mathbf{TxtEx}$. For each M_e here is the construction to show that M_e does not $\mathbf{U}^{n+1}\mathbf{TxtEx}$-identify $\mathcal{L}$. By Kleene's Recursion Theorem there exists an index e' such that $W_{e'}$ may be defined in stages $s = 0, 1, 2 \ldots$, as below. For each s, $W_{e'}^s$ denotes the finite portion of $W_{e'}$ enumerated just before stage s.

    Stage 0: Let $\sigma^1 = \langle e, 0, 0 \rangle \diamond \langle e, 1, e' \rangle \diamond \langle e, 2, e' \rangle \diamond \ldots \diamond \langle e, n, e' \rangle$. Let $W_{e'}^1 = \{e'\}$.
        Go to stage 1.
    Stage s: Search for τ where $content(\tau) \subseteq \{\langle e, i, j \rangle \mid 1 \le i \le n \wedge j > \max(W_{e'}^s)\}$ such that $M_e(\sigma^s) \ne M_e(\sigma^s \diamond \tau)$. If and when τ is found, enumerate $\{j \mid (\exists i', 1 \le i' \le n)[\langle e, i', j \rangle \in content(\tau)]\}$ into $W_{e'}$, and let σ^{s+1} be an extension of σ^s such that $content(\sigma^{s+1}) = \{\langle e, 0, 0 \rangle\} \cup \{\langle e, i, j \rangle \mid 1 \le i \le n \wedge j \in W_{e'}$ enumerated up to now$\}$. Go to stage $s + 1$.

If the search for τ failed at any stage s, then let $L_e^0 = content(\sigma^s)$, let $e'' > \max(W_{e'}^s)$ be such that $\min(W_{e''}) = e''$. For each $i \in N$, $1 \le i \le n$, let $L_e^i = \{\langle e, i, j \rangle \mid j \in W_{e''}\}$. Since stage s does not succeed, M_e does not identify at least one of L_e^0 and $L_e^0 \cup \bigcup_{i=1}^n L_e^i$. If the search is successful at all stages, let

$L_e^0 = \{\langle e, 0, 0\rangle\}$ and for each i let $L_e^i = \{\langle e, i, x\rangle \mid x \in W_{e'}\}$, then M_e fails to converge on the input $\bigcup_s \sigma^s$, a text for $L_e^0 \cup \bigcup_{i=1}^n L_e^i$.   ∎

In obtaining the above result we have used a class of languages that is not recursively enumerable. It remains to be seen if for recursively enumerable classes of languages, disjointness can be sufficient as a condition for $\mathbf{U}^n\mathbf{TxtEx}$ identification for any $n > 1$. The following, however, shows the contrary.

Example 1. Let
$$L_{x,0} = \{\langle x, 0\rangle\} \cup \{\langle x, y\rangle \mid (\forall z \leq y)[\varphi_x(z)\downarrow]\}$$
$$L_{x,y+1} = \begin{cases} \{\langle x, y+1\rangle\} & \text{if } \langle x, y+1\rangle \notin L_{x,0} \\ L_{x,0} & \text{otherwise} \end{cases}$$

Let $\mathcal{L} = \{L_{x,i} \mid x, i \in N\}$. Clearly, $\mathcal{L} \in \mathbf{TxtEx}$. Now suppose there exists M such that $\mathcal{L}^2 \in \mathbf{TxtEx}(M)$, then $(\exists \sigma \mid content(\sigma) \subseteq L_{x,0}) [(\forall \tau \mid content(\tau) \subseteq \{\langle x, i\rangle \mid i \in N\})[M(\sigma) = M(\tau)]] \Leftrightarrow \varphi_x \in \mathcal{R}$. The condition on the left hand side is Σ_2 to check. However, the set $\{x \mid \varphi_x \text{ is recursive}\}$ is not Σ_2, a contradiction.

We note that the class of languages in Example 1 is not 1–1 recursively enumerable. As will be shown by our next result, for a 1–1 recursively enumerable class of languages, disjointness is a sufficient condition for the class to be in $\mathbf{DU}^*\mathbf{TxtEx}$.

5   Sufficient Conditions for DUTxtEx Identification

5.1   Functions That Enumerate Distinguishing Elements

Let recursively enumerable $\mathcal{L} \subseteq \mathcal{E}$ be given. Suppose for all $L \in \mathcal{L}$, there is an effective procedure to enumerate an element which is uniquely in L, that is, no other language in $\mathcal{L}$ contains this element. Can we then identify every collection of languages drawn from $\mathcal{L}$? An answer is attempted in the following proposition.

Proposition 4. *Let $\mathcal{L}$ be a 1–1 recursively enumerable class of languages as witnessed by the computable numbering ψ. If there exists a limiting recursive function d and total recursive F for which $d(i) = \lim_{t\to\infty} F(i,t)$ such that*
(a) $(\forall i \in N)[d(i) \in W_i^\psi]$,
(b) $(\forall i, j \in N)[d(i) \in W_j^\psi \Rightarrow i = j]$, and
(c) $(\forall j \in N)[card(\{F(i,t) \mid i, t \in N\} \cap W_j^\psi) < \infty]$.
Then $\mathcal{L} \in \mathbf{DU}^*\mathbf{TxtEx}$.

Proof. Let recursive function h witnesses that $\psi \prec \varphi$. Define M as follows.

$M(T[m]):$
$\qquad S \leftarrow \emptyset.$
$\qquad \text{For } i = 0 \text{ to } m \text{ do}$

If $[F(i, m) \in content(T[m]) \cap W_{i,m}^{\psi}]$ and
$$\neg[(\exists i', j')[i' < m \;\wedge\; j' < m \;\wedge\; i' \neq j' \;\wedge\; F(i, m) \in W_{i',m}^{\psi} \cap W_{j',m}^{\psi}]]$$
    Then $S \leftarrow S \cup \{h(i)\}$.

Output S.

Let T be a text for $L = \bigcup_{i \in D} W_i^{\psi}$, a union of $card(D)$ languages from $\mathcal{L}$ and let $A = range(F) \cap L$. Since each language in L intersects with only finitely many outputs of F, $card(A) < \infty$. Intuitively, A contains all the potential "distinguishing element"s M will encounter during the identification process. Since D and A are finite, there exists $n \in N$ so large that

(1) $(\forall t > n)\ (\forall i \in D)\ [F(i, t) = d(i) \wedge d(i) \in content(T[t]) \cap W_{i,t}^{\psi}]$.

(2) $(\forall n' > n)(\forall x \in A - \{d(k) \mid k \in D\})[(\exists j \in N - D)[x \in W_{j,n'}^{\psi}] \Rightarrow (\exists i', j' < n)[i' \neq j' \wedge x \in W_{i',n'}^{\psi} \cap W_{j',n'}^{\psi}]]$

Clause (1) ensures that all $i \in D$ will eventually be output by M. Clause (2) ensures that all programs $j \notin D$, which enumerate some element in A are excluded from consideration (note that every element in A is enumerated by some program in D).

Hence for all $n' > n$, $i \in D$ if and only if $i \in M(T[n'])$. It follows that M **DU*TxtEx**-identifies $\mathcal{L}$. ∎

Corollary 3. *Let $\mathcal{L}$ be a class of languages for which there exists a 1–1 numbering and*
>   *(a) $\emptyset \notin \mathcal{L}$,*
>   *(b) $(\forall L, L' \in \mathcal{L})[L \neq L' \Rightarrow L \cap L' = \emptyset]$.*
> *Then $\mathcal{L} \in \boldsymbol{DU^* TxtEx}$.*

Proof. Let $\mathcal{L} = \{W_i^{\psi} \mid i \in N\}$ where ψ is a 1–1 numbering for $\mathcal{L}$. Let $F(i, t) = \min(W_{i,t}^{\psi})$ and let $d(i) = \lim_{t \to \infty} F(i, t)$. Clearly, (a) $(\forall i \in N)[d(i) \in W_i^{\psi}]$, (b) $(\forall i, j \in N)[d(i) \in W_j^{\psi} \Rightarrow i = j]$, and (c) $(\forall j \in N)[card(\{F(i, t) \mid i, t \in N\} \cap W_j^{\psi}) < \infty]$. Thus d fulfills all the conditions for Proposition 4. Hence $\mathcal{L} \in \mathbf{DU^*TxtEx}$. ∎

Corollary 4. *Let $\mathcal{L}$ be an indexed family of recursive languages where*
>   *(a) $\emptyset \notin \mathcal{L}$,*
>   *(b) $(\forall L, L' \in \mathcal{L})[L \neq L' \Rightarrow L \cap L' = \emptyset]$.*
> *Then $\mathcal{L} \in \boldsymbol{DU^* TxtEx}$.*

In Proposition 4, some weaker conditions for (a) and (b) may not be sufficient, even if we strengthen (c) to require that d is a recursive function. For instance, if we have only the following conditions (where the requirement for (b) is relaxed):
>   (a) $(\forall i \in N)[d(i) \in W_i^{\psi}]$
>   (b) $(\forall i \in N)[card(\{W_j^{\psi} \mid d(i) \in W_j^{\psi}\}) < \infty]$,
>   (c) d is recursive.

then identifiability for $\mathcal{L}^2$ cannot be guaranteed, as the following example shows.

Example 2. Let
$$L_0 = \{\langle 0, x\rangle \mid x \in N\} \cup \{\langle 1, x\rangle \mid x \in K\}$$
$$L_{i+1} = \begin{cases} \{\langle 0, i+1\rangle\} \cup \{\langle 1, i\rangle\} \cup \{\langle 2, i\rangle\} & \text{if } i \in K \\ \{\langle 0, i+1\rangle\} \cup \{\langle 1, i\rangle\} & \text{otherwise} \end{cases}$$

Let $\mathcal{L} = \{L_i \mid i \in N\}$ and define d such that $(\forall x \in N)[d(x) = \langle 0, x\rangle]$. It is easy to verify that (a) $\mathcal{L}$ is 1–1 recursively enumerable, (b) $\mathcal{L} \in \mathbf{TxtEx}$, (c) $\mathcal{L}^2$ is uniquely definable from $\mathcal{L}$, and (d) d satisfies the weaker condition given above for $\mathcal{L}$. However, for all $k \in N$, the language $\{\langle 0, i\rangle \mid i \in N\} \cup \{\langle 1, x\rangle \mid x \in K \cup \{k\}\}$ is in $\mathcal{L}^2$, hence $\mathcal{L}^2$ is unidentifiable.

A similar weakening of these conditions, where instead of a single unique element d is required to name only a set of elements which is unique to each language in the class, as in the following:

(a) $(\forall i \in N)[D_{d(i)} \subseteq W_i^\psi]$

(b) $(\forall i, j \in N)[D_{d(i)} \subseteq W_j^\psi \Rightarrow i = j]$.

(c) d is recursive.

then such a function will also fail to guarantee that $\mathcal{L}^2 \in \mathbf{TxtEx}$, as demonstrated by the following example.

Example 3. Let
$$L_0 = \{\langle 0, 0\rangle\} \cup \{\langle 1, x\rangle \mid x \in N\}$$
$$L_1 = \{\langle 1, 1\rangle\} \cup \{\langle 0, x\rangle \mid x \in N\} \cup \{\langle 2, x\rangle \mid x \in K\}$$
$$L_{i+2} = \begin{cases} \{\langle 0, i+2\rangle\} \cup \{\langle 1, x\rangle \mid x \in N\} \cup \{\langle 2, i\rangle\} \cup \{\langle 3, i\rangle\} & \text{if } i \in K \\ \{\langle 0, i+2\rangle\} \cup \{\langle 1, x\rangle \mid x \in N\} \cup \{\langle 2, i\rangle\} & \text{otherwise} \end{cases}$$

Let $\mathcal{L} = \{L_i \mid i \in N\}$ and define d such that $(\forall x \in N)[d(x) = \{\langle 0, x\rangle, \langle 1, x\rangle\}]$. It is easy to verify that $\mathcal{L}$ is a 1–1 recursively enumerable class of languages in $\mathbf{TxtEx}$ where all the languages in $\mathcal{L}^2$ are uniquely definable from $\mathcal{L}$, and that d satisfies all the prescribed conditions for $\mathcal{L}$. However, for all $k \in N$, $\{\langle 0, i\rangle, \langle 1, i\rangle \mid i \in N\} \cup \{\langle 2, x\rangle \mid x \in K \cup \{k\}\}$ is in $\mathcal{L}^2$, thus $\mathcal{L}^2$ is not in $\mathbf{TxtEx}$.

5.2   Restrictions on Structures of Languages

Proposition 5. *Given* $n \in N^+$. *Let* $\mathcal{L}$ *be a class of languages such that*

(a) *every language in* $\mathcal{L}^n$ *is uniquely definable from* $\mathcal{L}$,

(b) $(\forall L \in \mathcal{L})[card(\{L' \in \mathcal{L} \mid L' \cap L \neq \emptyset\}) < \infty]$,

(c) *there exists a computable numbering* ψ *for* $\mathcal{L}$ *such that:*

   (1) $(\forall L \in \mathcal{L})[card(L) = \infty \Rightarrow card(\{i \mid W_i^\psi = L\}) = 1]$.

   (2) $(\forall L \in \mathcal{L})[card(L) < \infty \Rightarrow card(\{i \mid W_i^\psi = L\}) < \infty]$.

then $\mathcal{L} \in \mathbf{DU}^n\,\mathbf{TxtEx}$.

Proof. We let A and B, with or without decorations, range over FIN. Let h witnesses that $\psi \prec \varphi$.

$M(T[m])$:

Let $\mathcal{C}^m = \{i \mid i \le m \;\wedge\; W^\psi_{i,m} \cap content(T[m]) \neq \emptyset\}$.

Let $Candidates^m = \{S \subseteq \mathcal{C}^m \mid card(S) \le n\}$.

Let $s_0 = \max(\{s \mid (\exists S \in Candidates^m)[\;\bigcup_{i \in S} W^\psi_{i,s} \subseteq content(T[m])$
$$\wedge\; \bigcup_{i \in S} W^\psi_{i,m} \supseteq content(T[s])]\}).$$

Output $\{h(i) \mid i \in D_{k_0}\}$, where $k_0 = \min(\{k \mid D_k \in Candidates^m$
$$\wedge\; \bigcup_{i \in D_k} W^\psi_{i,s_0} \subseteq content(T[m])$$
$$\wedge\; \bigcup_{i \in D_k} W^\psi_{i,m} \supseteq content(T[s_0])\}).$$

Intuitively, M outputs the seemingly best grammar set in $Candidates^m$ which describes the input text. Let T be a text for $L = \bigcup_{i \in B} W^\psi_i$, a union of $card(B) \le n$ languages from $\mathcal{L}$. We divide B into two groups, $B_1 = \{i \in B \mid W^\psi_i$ is finite$\}$ and $B_2 = \{i \in B \mid W^\psi_i$ is infinite$\}$. By the requirement of ψ, for each $i \in B_1$, there exist only finitely many j such that $W^\psi_i = W^\psi_j$, and for each $i \in B_2$, for all $j \neq i$, $W^\psi_i \neq W^\psi_j$. Let $\mathcal{A} = \{A \mid \bigcup_{i \in A} W^\psi_i = \bigcup_{i \in B_1} W^\psi_i\}$. Since $\mathcal{L}^n$ is uniquely definable from $\mathcal{L}$, the only sets of languages which are capable of generating L are $\{B_2 \cup A \mid A \in \mathcal{A}\}$. Let $CorrectInd = \{B_2 \cup A \mid A \in \mathcal{A}\}$.

Let $\mathcal{C}' = \{i \mid W^\psi_i \cap content(T) \neq \emptyset\}$. Since each language in $\{W^\psi_i \mid i \in B\}$ intersects with only finitely many other languages in $\mathcal{L}$, $\mathcal{C}'$ is finite. It is easy to verify that there exists $n_0 \in N$ such that for all $n' > n_0$, $\mathcal{C}^{n'} = \mathcal{C}^{n'+1} = \mathcal{C}'$. Let $n_1 \in N$, $n_1 > n_0$ be so large that

$$(\forall i \in \mathcal{C}')[W^\psi_i \text{ is finite} \Rightarrow W^\psi_i = W^\psi_{i,n_1} \wedge W^\psi_i \subseteq content(T[n_1])]$$

Let $Candidates' = Candidates^{n_0}$. Clearly, for all $n' > n_0$, $Candidates^{n'} = Candidates^{n'+1} = Candidates'$. Let $n_2 > n_1$ be so large that

$$\neg[(\exists A \in Candidates' - CorrectInd)[\;(\bigcup_{i \in A} W^\psi_{i,n_2} \subseteq L)$$
$$\wedge(\bigcup_{i \in A} W^\psi_i \supseteq content(T[n_2]))]]$$

Let $n_3 > n_2$ be so large that

$$[\;\bigcup_{i \in B} W^\psi_{i,n_2+1} \subseteq content(T[n_3]) \wedge \bigcup_{i \in B} W^\psi_{i,n_3} \supseteq content(T[n_2 + 1])]$$

Clearly, for all $n' > n_3$, $\{D \in Candidates' \mid \bigcup_{i \in D} W^\psi_{i,n_2+1} \subseteq content(T[n'])$ $\wedge \bigcup_{i \in D} W^\psi_{i,n'} \supseteq content(T[n_2 + 1])\} = CorrectInd$. Hence for all $n' > n_3$, M outputs $\min(\{k \mid D_k \in CorrectInd\})$. It follows that M $\mathbf{DU^n TxtEx}$-identifies $\mathcal{L}$.   ∎

Corollary 5. *Fix* $n \in N^+$. *Let* $\mathcal{L} = \{L_i \mid i \in N\}$ *be a 1–1 recursively enumerable class of languages where*

(a) every language in $\mathcal{L}^n$ *is uniquely definable from* $\mathcal{L}$.

(b) $(\forall i \in N)[card(\{j \mid L_i \cap L_j \neq \emptyset\}) < \infty]$.

Then $\mathcal{L} \in \mathbf{DU^n TxtEx}$.

The conditions in Proposition 5 are clearly not necessary — as is evident by $TRANSIM_n$, which is 1–1 recursively enumerable but every language in the class intersects with infinitely many other languages within the class.

6   Intrinsic Complexity

The concept of *intrinsic complexity* [FKS95,JS96,KPSW99,JKW00,JK01] is an attempt to describe the relative hardness of identifying a class of languages under the requirement given by an identification criterion. The idea is to reduce the task of $\mathcal{I}$-identifying a class of languages to the task of $\mathcal{J}$-identifying another class. To be able to reduce the identification of $\mathcal{L}$ to that of identifying $\mathcal{L}'$, we should be able to transform $\mathcal{I}$-admissible texts T for languages in $\mathcal{L}$ to $\mathcal{J}$-admissible texts T' for languages in $\mathcal{L}'$ and further transform $\mathcal{J}$-admissible sequences for T' into $\mathcal{I}$-admissible sequences for T.

An *enumeration operator* (or just operator), Θ, is an algorithmic mapping from SEQ into SEQ such that for all $\sigma, \tau \in$ SEQ, if $\sigma \subseteq \tau$, then $\Theta(\sigma) \subseteq \Theta(\tau)$. We further assume that for all texts T, $\lim_{n\to\infty} |\Theta(T[n])| = \infty$. By extension, we think of Θ as also defining a mapping from T to T such that $\Theta(T) = \bigcup_n \Theta(T[n])$. If for a language L, there exists an L' such that, for each text T for L, $\Theta(T)$ is a text for L', then we write $\Theta(L) = L'$.

[JS96] distinguished between two kinds of reductions, called *weak* and *strong reductions*. We consider only the former here.

We extend the definition for weak reduction as follow, so that instead of just reducing the task of identifying every language in a class, $\mathcal{L}_1$ say, to tasks of identifying languages in another class $\mathcal{L}_2$, we want to reduce the task for identifying every language in $\mathcal{L}_1^n$ to tasks of identifying languages in $\mathcal{L}_2^m$, for some $m, n \in N$.

Definition 11.   Let $\mathcal{L}_1, \mathcal{L}_2 \subseteq \mathcal{E}$ be given. Let $\mathcal{K}_1, \mathcal{K}_2 \in \{\mathbf{U}, \mathbf{DU}, \mathbf{WDU}\}$ and $n, m \in N^+$ be given. Let $\mathcal{T}_1 = \{T \mid T$ is a text for $L \in \mathcal{L}_1^n\}$. Let $\mathcal{T}_2 = \{T \mid T$ is a text for $L \in \mathcal{L}_2^m\}$. We say that $\mathcal{L}_1 \leq_{weak}^{\mathcal{K}_1^n \boldsymbol{TxtEx}, \mathcal{K}_2^m \boldsymbol{TxtEx}} \mathcal{L}_2$ just in case there exist operators Θ and Ξ such that for all $T \in \mathcal{T}_1$ and for all infinite sequences of conjectures $\mathcal{G}$ the following hold:
(a) $\Theta(T) \in \mathcal{T}_2$, and
(b) if $\mathcal{G}$ is a $\mathcal{K}_2^m \boldsymbol{TxtEx}$-admissible sequence for $\Theta(T)$, then $\Xi(\mathcal{G})$ is a $\mathcal{K}_1^n \boldsymbol{TxtEx}$-admissible sequence for T.
We say that $\mathcal{L}_1 \leq_{weak}^{\mathcal{K}^n \boldsymbol{TxtEx}} \mathcal{L}_2$ if and only if $\mathcal{L}_1 \leq_{weak}^{\mathcal{K}^n \boldsymbol{TxtEx}, \mathcal{K}^n \boldsymbol{TxtEx}} \mathcal{L}_2$.

Definition 12. [JKW00] Let $\mathcal{I}$ be an identification criterion. Let $\mathcal{L} \subseteq \mathcal{E}$ be given.
(a) If for all $\mathcal{L}' \in \mathcal{I}$, $\mathcal{L}' \leq_{weak}^{\mathcal{I}} \mathcal{L}$, then $\mathcal{L}$ is $\leq_{weak}^{\mathcal{I}}$-hard.
(b) If $\mathcal{L}$ is $\leq_{weak}^{\mathcal{I}}$-hard and $\mathcal{L} \in \mathcal{I}$, then $\mathcal{L}$ is $\leq_{weak}^{\mathcal{I}}$-complete.

Proposition 6. *For all $n \in N^+$,*

(a) INIT is $\leq_{\text{weak}}^{\mathbf{U}^n\mathbf{TxtEx}}$-complete.

(b) INIT is $\leq_{\text{weak}}^{\mathbf{WDU}^n\mathbf{TxtEx}}$-complete.

(c) INIT is $\leq_{\text{weak}}^{\mathbf{DU}^n\mathbf{TxtEx}}$-hard.

Proposition 7. $(\forall n \in N, n \geq 2)[TRANSIM_n$ *is* $\leq_{\text{weak}}^{\mathbf{DU}^n\mathbf{TxtEx}}$*-complete*]*.*

Acknowledgements. Sanjay Jain was supported in part by NUS grant number RP3992710.

References

[Ang80]   D. Angluin. Inductive inference of formal languages from positive data. *Information and Control*, 45:117–135, 1980.

[Blu67]   M. Blum. A machine-independent theory of the complexity of recursive functions. *Journal of the ACM*, 14:322–336, 1967.

[Cox63]   H.S.M. Coxeter. *Regular Polytopes (2nd ed.)*. Methuen & Co. Ltd., London, 1963.

[FKS95]   R. Freivalds, E. Kinber, and C. Smith. On the intrinsic complexity of learning. *Information and Computation*, 123(1):64–71, 1995.

[GK99]   S. Goldman and S. Kwek. On learning unions of pattern languages and tree patterns. *Algorithmic Learning Theory: Tenth International Conference (ALT' 99)*, 1720:347–363, 1999.

[Gol67]   E. M. Gold. Language identification in the limit. *Information and Control*, 10:447–474, 1967.

[JK01]   S. Jain and E. Kinber. On intrinsic complexity of learning geometrical concepts from texts. In *Proceedings of the Fourteenth Annual Conference on Computational Learning Theory*, 2001. To appear.

[JKW00]   S. Jain, E. Kinber, and R. Wiehagen. Language learning from texts: Degrees of intrinsic complexity and their characterizations. In Nicolo Cesa-Bianchi and Sally Goldman, editors, *Proceedings of the Thirteenth Annual Conference on Computational Learning Theory*, pages 47–58. Morgan Kaufmann, 2000.

[JS96]   S. Jain and A. Sharma. The intrinsic complexity of language identification. *Journal of Computer and System Sciences*, 52:393–402, 1996.

[KPSW99] E. Kinber, C. Papazian, C. Smith, and R. Wiehagen. On the intrinsic complexity of learning recursive functions. In *Proceedings of the Twelfth Annual Conference on Computational Learning Theory*, pages 257–266. ACM Press, 1999.

[MSW91]   T. Motoki, T. Shinohara, and K. Wright. The correct definition of finite elasticity: Corrigendum to identification of unions. In L. Valiant and M. Warmuth, editors, *Proceedings of the Fourth Annual Workshop on Computational Learning Theory*, page 375. Morgan Kaufmann, 1991.

[OSW86]   D. Osherson, M. Stob, and S. Weinstein. *Systems that Learn: An Introduction to Learning Theory for Cognitive and Computer Scientists*. MIT Press, 1986.

[Rog67]   H. Rogers. *Theory of Recursive Functions and Effective Computability.* McGraw-Hill, 1967. Reprinted by MIT Press in 1987.

[SA00]   T. Shinohara and H. Arimura. Inductive inference of unbounded unions of pattern languages from positive data. *Theoretical Computer Science A*, 241:191–209, 2000. Special Issue for ALT'96.

[Wri89]   K. Wright. Identification of unions of languages drawn from an identifiable class. In R. Rivest, D. Haussler, and M. Warmuth, editors, *Proceedings of the Second Annual Workshop on Computational Learning Theory*, pages 328–333. Morgan Kaufmann, 1989.

On the Comparison of Inductive Inference Criteria for Uniform Learning of Finite Classes

Sandra Zilles

Fachbereich Informatik
Universität Kaiserslautern
Postfach 3049
D - 67653 Kaiserslautern
zilles@informatik.uni-kl.de

Abstract. We consider a learning model in which each element of a class of recursive functions is to be identified in the limit by a computable strategy. Given gradually growing initial segments of the graph of a function, the learner is supposed to generate a sequence of hypotheses converging to a correct hypothesis. The term correct means that the hypothesis is an index of the function to be learned in a given numbering. Restriction of the basic definition of learning in the limit yields several inference criteria, which have already been compared with respect to their learning power.

The scope of uniform learning is to synthesize appropriate identification strategies for infinitely many classes of recursive functions by a uniform method, i.e. a kind of meta-learning is considered. In this concept we can also compare the learning power of several inference criteria. If we fix a single numbering to be used as a hypothesis space for all classes of recursive functions, we obtain results similar to the non-uniform case. This hierarchy of inference criteria changes, if we admit different hypothesis spaces for different classes of functions. Interestingly, in uniform identification most of the inference criteria can be separated by collections of finite classes of recursive functions.

1 Introduction

Inductive Inference is concerned with theoretical models simulating learning processes. A model of quite simple mathematical description is for example identification of classes of recursive functions. This concept in general includes three main components:

- a partial-recursive function S – also called strategy – simulating the learner,
- a class U of total recursive functions which have to be identified by S,
- a partial-recursive numbering ψ – called hypothesis space – which enumerates at least all functions in U.

In each step of the identification process S is presented a finite subgraph of some unknown arbitrary function f contained in U; the strategy S then returns

N. Abe, R. Khardon, and T. Zeugmann (Eds.): ALT 2001, LNAI 2225, pp. 251–266, 2001.

a hypothesis which is interpreted as an index of a function in the given numbering ψ. It is the learner's job to eventually return a single correct hypothesis, i.e. the sequence of outputs ought to converge to a ψ-number of f. This model – called identification in the limit – has first been analyzed by Gold in [5] and gave rise to the investigation and comparison of several new learning models ("inference criteria") basing on that principle. The common idea was to restrict the definition of identifiability by means of additional – and in some way natural – demands concerning the properties of the hypotheses. The corresponding models have been compared with respect to the resulting identification power; for some more background the reader is referred to [3], [4] and [7].

This paper studies Inductive Inference on a meta-level. Considering collections of infinitely many classes U of recursive functions we are looking for meta-learners synthesizing an appropriate strategy for each class U to be learned. For that purpose we agree on a method to describe a class U, because for the synthesis of a learner our meta-strategy should be given some description of U. That means we do not only try to solve a learning problem by an expert learner but to design a higher-level learner which constructs a method for solving a learning problem from a given description. Thus the meta-learner is able to simulate all the expert learners.

Uniform learning of classes of recursive functions has already been studied by Jantke in [6]. Unfortunately, his results are rather negative; he proves that there is no strategy which – given any description of an arbitrary class U consisting of just a single recursive function – synthesizes a learner which identifies U with respect to a fixed hypothesis space. Even if we allow different hypothesis spaces for the different classes of recursive functions, no meta-learner is successful for all descriptions of finite classes (cf. [12]). Since in the non-uniform case finite classes can be identified easily with respect to any common inference criterion, these results might suggest that the model of uniform learning yields a concept the investigation of which is not worthwile. As we will see, the results in this paper allow a more optimistic point of view. Of course it is quite natural to consider the same inference criteria known from the non-uniform model also in our meta-level. The aim of this paper is to investigate whether the comparison of these criteria concerning the resulting identification power yields hierarchies analogous to those approved in the classical context. In most cases we will see, that the classical separation results can be transferred to uniform learning. And we can prove even more. If we consider uniform learning with respect to fixed hypothesis spaces, all separations of inference criteria can be achieved by collections of *finite* classes of recursive functions. The resulting hierarchies correspond to the non-uniform case. If we drop the restrictions concerning the hypothesis spaces, we obtain slightly different results, although many of the criteria can still be separated by finite classes. So whereas finite classes are very simple regarding their identifiability in Gold's model, they are in most cases sufficient for the separation of inference criteria in uniform learning. Furthermore we conclude that the hierarchies obtained are very much influenced by the choice of the hypothesis spaces. Now, since the hierarchies of inference criteria do not collapse in our meta-level – even if we restrict ourselves to the choice of simple learning problems – we conclude that the concept of uniform learning is neither trivial nor fruitless. Furthermore this paper corroborates the interpretation that our different inference criteria possess some really substantial specific properties, which yield separations of such a strong nature that they still hold for uniform learning of finite classes.

In [12] the reader may also find positive results encouraging further research. It is shown that the choice of descriptions for the classes U has more influence on the uniform identifiability than the classes themselves, i.e. many meta-strategies fail rather because of a bad description of the learning problem than because of the complexity of the problem. So it might be interesting to find out what kinds of descriptions are suitable for uniform learnability and whether they can be characterized by any specific properties.

Further research on uniform identification has also been made in the context of language learning, see for example [8], [9] and [2]. Because of its numerous positive results, in particular the work of Baliga, Case and Jain [2] motivates the investigation of meta-strategies.

2   Preliminaries

Recursion theoretic terms used without explicit definition can be found in [10].

By $\mathbb{N}$ we denote the set of all nonnegative integers, $\mathbb{N}^*$ is the set of all finite tuples over $\mathbb{N}$; the variable n always ranges over $\mathbb{N}$. For fixed n, the notion $\mathbb{N}^n$ is used for the set of all n-tuples of integers. By implicit use of a bijective computable function cod : $\mathbb{N}^* \mapsto \mathbb{N}$ we will identify any $\alpha \in \mathbb{N}^*$ with its coding $\text{cod}(\alpha) \in \mathbb{N}$. A statement is quantified with $\forall^\infty n$ in order to indicate that the statement is fulfilled for all but finitely many n; quantifiers $\forall$ and $\exists$ are used in the common way.

For any set X the expression card X denotes the cardinality of X; $\wp X$ denotes the set of all subsets of X. As a symbol for set inclusion we use $\subseteq$, proper inclusion is indicated by $\subset$. Incomparability of sets is expressed by $\#$.

The set of all partial-recursive functions is denoted by $\mathcal{P}$, the set of total recursive functions by $\mathcal{R}$. In order to refer to functions of a fixed number n of input variables, we sometimes add the superscript n to these symbols. For any $f \in \mathcal{P}$, $x \in \mathbb{N}$ we write $f(x)\downarrow$, if f is defined on input x; $f(x)\uparrow$ otherwise. If $f \in \mathcal{P}$ and n fulfill $f(0)\downarrow, \ldots, f(n)\downarrow$ we set $f[n] := \text{cod}(f(0), \ldots, f(n))$, i.e. $f[n]$ corresponds to the initial segment of length $n + 1$ of f. Comparing $f, g \in \mathcal{P}$ we write $f =_n g$, if $\{(x, f(x)) \mid x \leq n, \ f(x)\downarrow\} = \{(x, g(x)) \mid x \leq n, \ g(x)\downarrow\}$; otherwise $f \neq_n g$. By the notion $f \subseteq g$ we indicate that $\{(x, f(x)) \mid x \in \mathbb{N}, \ f(x)\downarrow\} \subseteq \{(x, g(x)) \mid x \in \mathbb{N}, \ g(x)\downarrow\}$ and use proper inclusion by analogy. But $f \in \mathcal{P}$ may also be identified with the sequence $(f(n))_{n \in \mathbb{N}}$, so we sometimes write $f = 0^n 1\uparrow^\infty$ and the like. We often identify a tuple $\alpha \in \mathbb{N}^*$ with the function $\alpha\uparrow^\infty$ implicitly. By $\text{rng}(f)$ we refer to the range $\{f(x) \mid x \in \mathbb{N}, \ f(x)\downarrow\}$ of a function $f \in \mathcal{P}$.

A function $\psi \in \mathcal{P}^{n+1}$ is used as a numbering for the set $\mathcal{P}_\psi := \{\psi_i \mid i \in \mathbb{N}\}$, where $\psi_i(x) := \psi(i, x)$ for all $i \in \mathbb{N}$, $x \in \mathbb{N}^n$ as usual. i is called ψ-number of the function ψ_i. In order to refer to the set of all total functions in $\mathcal{P}_\psi$, we use the notion $\mathcal{R}_\psi$, i.e. $\mathcal{R}_\psi := \mathcal{P}_\psi \cap \mathcal{R}$. $\mathcal{R}_\psi$ is called the recursive core or "$\mathcal{R}$-core" of $\mathcal{P}_\psi$. If $\psi \in \mathcal{P}^{n+2}$, every $b \in \mathbb{N}$ corresponds to a numbering $\psi^b \in \mathcal{P}^{n+1}$, if we define $\psi^b(i, x) := \psi(b, i, x)$ for all $i \in \mathbb{N}$, $x \in \mathbb{N}^n$. Again i is a ψ^b-number for the function ψ_i^b defined in the common way.

Now we introduce our basic Inductive Inference criterion called identification in the limit, which was first defined in [5]. It may be regarded as a fundamental learning model from which we define further restrictive inference criteria (see Definitions 2 and 3). The notation EX in Definition 1 abbreviates the term "explanatory identification" which is also used to refer to learning in the limit.

Definition 1. *Let $U \subseteq \mathcal{R}$, $\psi \in \mathcal{P}^2$. The class U belongs to EX_ψ and is called identifiable in the limit wrt the hypothesis space ψ iff there is a function $S \in \mathcal{P}$ (called strategy) such that for any $f \in U$:*

1. $S(f[n])\!\downarrow$ for all $n \in \mathbb{N}$ ($S(f[n])$ is called hypothesis on $f[n]$),
2. there is some $j \in \mathbb{N}$ such that $\psi_j = f$ and $\forall^\infty n \ [S(f[n]) = j]$.

If S is given, we also write $U \in EX_\psi(S)$. We set $EX := \bigcup_{\psi \in \mathcal{P}^2} EX_\psi$.

On any function $f \in U$ the strategy S must generate a sequence of hypotheses converging to a ψ-number of f. But a user reading the hypotheses generated by S up to a certain time will never know whether the actual hypothesis is correct or not, because he cannot decide whether the time of convergence is already reached. If there was a bound on the number of mind changes, he could at least rely on the actual hypothesis whenever the bound is reached. Learning with such bounds has first been studied in [3].

Definition 2. *Assume $U \subseteq \mathcal{R}$, $\psi \in \mathcal{P}^2$, $m \in \mathbb{N}$. U belongs to $(EX_m)_\psi$ and is called identifiable (in the limit) with no more than m mind changes wrt ψ iff there exists an $S \in \mathcal{P}$ satisfying*

1. $U \in EX_\psi(S)$ (where S is additionally permitted to return the sign "?"),
2. for all $f \in U$ there is an $n_f \in \mathbb{N}$ satisfying
 * $-\ \forall x < n_f \ [S(f[x]) = ?]$,*
 * $-\ \forall x \geq n_f \ [S(f[x]) \in \mathbb{N}]$,*
3. $\mathrm{card}\{n \in \mathbb{N} \mid ? \neq S(f[n]) \neq S(f[n+1])\} \leq m$ for all $f \in U$.

We use the notations $(EX_m)_\psi(S)$ and EX_m by analogy with Definition 1. A class $U \subseteq \mathcal{R}$ is identifiable with a bounded number of mind changes iff there is an $m \in \mathbb{N}$ such that $U \in EX_m$.

The output "?" allows our strategy to indicate that its hypothesis is left open for the actual time being, in order not to waste a mind change in the beginning of the learning process.

It is also a natural thought to strengthen the demands concerning the intermediate hypotheses themselves. A successful learning behaviour might be to generate intermediate hypotheses agreeing with the information received up to the actual time of the learning process ("consistent" hypotheses, cf. [1]). In order to be less demanding, one could also ask for hypotheses which do not disagree convergently (i.e. in their *defined* values) with the actual information ("conform" hypotheses, see [11]). Since any hypothesis representing a function not contained in $\mathcal{R}$ must be wrong, another natural demand would be to allow only ψ-numbers of total recursive functions ("total" hypotheses, cf. [7]) as outputs of S. Since in general the halting problem in ψ is not decidable, it might be hard for our strategy to detect the incorrectness of a hypothesis, if the corresponding function differs from the function to be learned only by being undefined for some arguments. For learning with "convergently incorrect" hypotheses (cf. [4]) such outputs are forbidden.

Definition 3. *Choose a pair $(I, \mathcal{C}_I)$ from those listed below. Let $U \subseteq \mathcal{R}$, $\psi \in \mathcal{P}^2$. U is called identifiable under the criterion I wrt ψ iff there exists a strategy $S \in \mathcal{P}$ such that $U \in EX_\psi(S)$ and for all $f \in U$, $n \in \mathbb{N}$ condition $\mathcal{C}_I$ is satisfied.*

I	$\mathcal{C}_I$
$CONS$	$\psi_{S(f[n])} =_n f$
$CONF$	$\forall x \leq n \ [\psi_{S(f[n])}(x)\!\downarrow \ \Rightarrow \ \psi_{S(f[n])}(x) = f(x)]$
$TOTAL$	$\psi_{S(f[n])} \in \mathcal{R}$
CEX	$\psi_{S(f[n])} \not\subseteq f$

We use the phrases "identification with consistent (conform, total, convergently incorrect) intermediate hypotheses" respectively. The notations I, I_ψ, $I_\psi(S)$ are used in the common way.

For the inference criteria introduced here the following comparison results have been proved:

Theorem 1. *1. $\forall m \in \mathbb{N} \ [EX_m \subset EX_{m+1} \subset EX]$ (see [3]).*
2. $TOTAL \subset CONS \subset CONF \subset EX \subset \wp\mathcal{R}$ (see [7], [11] and [5]).
3. $TOTAL \subset CEX \subset EX$ (see definitions and [4]).
4. $CEX \# CONS$ (see [4]).

For convenience $\mathcal{I} := \{EX, CONS, CONF, TOTAL, CEX\} \cup \{EX_m \mid m \in \mathbb{N}\}$ denotes the set of all inference criteria declared in this section. Furthermore let

– $J^* := \{U \subseteq \mathcal{R} \mid U \text{ is finite}\}$,
– $J^1 := \{U \subseteq \mathcal{R} \mid \text{card } U = 1\} \ (= \{\{f\} \mid f \in \mathcal{R}\})$.

3   Uniform Learning – Definition and Basic Results

From now on let $\varphi \in \mathcal{P}^3$ be a fixed acceptable numbering of $\mathcal{P}^2$ and $\tau \in \mathcal{P}^2$ an acceptable numbering of $\mathcal{P}^1$. As φ is acceptable, it might be regarded as a numbering of all numberings $\psi \in \mathcal{P}^2$: every $b \in \mathbb{N}$ corresponds to the function φ^b which is defined by $\varphi^b(i, x) := \varphi(b, i, x)$ for any $i, x \in \mathbb{N}$. Thus b also describes a class $\mathcal{R}_b$ of recursive functions, where $\mathcal{R}_b := \mathcal{R}_{\varphi^b} = \mathcal{P}_{\varphi^b} \cap \mathcal{R}$; i.e. $\mathcal{R}_b$ is the recursive core of $\mathcal{P}_{\varphi^b}$. Therefore any set $B \subseteq \mathbb{N}$ will be called *description set* for the collection $\{\mathcal{R}_b \mid b \in B\}$ of recursive cores corresponding to the indices in B. Considering each recursive core as a set of functions to be identified, any description set $B \subseteq \mathbb{N}$ may be associated to a collection of learning problems. Now we are looking for a meta-learner which – given any description $b \in B$ – develops a special learner coping with the learning problem described by b, i.e. the special learner must identify each function in $\mathcal{R}_b$.

Definition 4. *Let $J \subseteq \wp\mathcal{R}$, $I \in \mathcal{I}$, $J \subseteq I$, $B \subseteq \mathbb{N}$. The set B is called suitable for uniform learning wrt J and I iff the following conditions are fulfilled:*

1. $\forall b \in B \; [\mathcal{R}_b \in J]$,
2. $\exists S \in \mathcal{P}^2 \; \forall b \in B \; \exists \psi \in \mathcal{P}^2 \; [\mathcal{R}_b \in I_\psi(\lambda x.S(b,x))]$.

We abbreviate this by $B \in suit(J,I)$ and write $B \in suit(J,I)(S)$, if S is given.

So $B \in suit(J,I)$ iff every recursive core described by some index $b \in B$ belongs to the class J and additionally there is a strategy $S \in \mathcal{P}^2$ which, given $b \in B$, synthesizes an I-learner successful for $\mathcal{R}_b$ with respect to some appropriate hypothesis space ψ. Note that the synthesis of these appropriate hypothesis spaces is *not* required. This means in particular, that in general the output of a meta-learner cannot be interpreted practically, because we might not know which numbering is actually used as a hypothesis space. Of course we might restrict our definition of suitable description sets by demanding uniform learnability with respect to the acceptable numbering τ for all classes $\mathcal{R}_b$. Another possibility is to use the numberings φ^b, $b \in B$, already given by the description set B as hypothesis spaces for I-identification of the classes $\mathcal{R}_b$.

Definition 5. *Let $I \in \mathcal{I}$, $J \subseteq I$, $B \subseteq \mathbb{N}$, $S \in \mathcal{P}^2$. Assume $B \in suit(J,I)(S)$. We write $B \in suit_\tau(J,I)(S)$ if $\mathcal{R}_b \in I_\tau(\lambda x.S(b,x))$ for all $b \in B$. The notation $B \in suit_\varphi(J,I)(S)$ shall indicate that $\mathcal{R}_b \in I_{\varphi^b}(\lambda x.S(b,x))$ for all $b \in B$. We also use the notations $suit_\tau(J,I)$ and $suit_\varphi(J,I)$ in the usual way.*

Of course it would be nice to find characterizations of the sets suitable for uniform learning with respect to J, I, where $I \in \mathcal{I}$ and $J \subseteq I$ are given. This paper compares the uniform identification power of several criteria $I \in \mathcal{I}$ and concentrates on the case $J = J^*$, i.e. all recursive cores to be identified are finite. Our first result follows obviously from our definitions.

Proposition 1. *Let $I \in \mathcal{I}$, $J \subseteq I$. Then $suit_\varphi(J,I) \subseteq suit_\tau(J,I) \subseteq suit(J,I)$.*

Whether these inclusions are proper inclusions or not depends on the choice of J and I. If they turned out to be equalities for all J and I, then Definition 5 would be superfluous. But in fact, as Theorem 5 will show, we have proper inclusions in the general case. That means that a restriction in the choice of the hypothesis spaces results in a restriction of the learning power of meta-strategies.

Any strategy identifying a class $U \subseteq \mathcal{R}$ with respect to some criterion $I \in \mathcal{I}\backslash\{\text{CONS}, \text{CONF}\}$ can be replaced by a *total* recursive strategy without loss of learning power. This new strategy is defined by computing the values of the old strategy for a bounded number of steps and a bounded number of input examples with increasing bounds. As long as no hypothesis is found, some temporary hypothesis agreeing with the restrictions in the definition of I is produced. Afterwards the hypotheses of the former strategy are put out "with delay".[1] Now we transfer these observations to the level of uniform learning and get the following result, which we will use in several proofs:

Proposition 2. *Let $I \in \mathcal{I}\backslash\{CONS, CONF\}$, $J \subseteq I$, $B \subseteq \mathbb{N}$. Assume $B \in suit(J, I)$ ($suit_\tau(J, I)$). Then there is a total recursive function S such that $B \in suit(J, I)(S)$ ($suit_\tau(J, I)(S)$ respectively).*

Let us now collect some simple examples of description sets suitable or not suitable for uniform learning. First we consider the identification of classes consisting of just one recursive function. Any set describing such classes turns out to be suitable for identification under any of our criteria:

Theorem 2. *Let $I \in \mathcal{I}$. Then $suit(J^1, I) = \{B \subseteq \mathbb{N} \mid \mathcal{R}_b \in J^1 \text{ for all } b \in B\}$.*

Proof. Let $B \subseteq \mathbb{N}$ fulfill $\mathcal{R}_b \in J^1$ for all $b \in B$. Since for all $f \in \mathcal{R}$ there exists a numbering $\psi \in \mathcal{P}^2$ with $\psi_0 = f$, the strategy constantly zero yields $B \in \text{suit}(J^1, I)$. Thus $\{B \subseteq \mathbb{N} \mid \mathcal{R}_b \in J^1 \text{ for all } b \in B\} \subseteq \text{suit}(J^1, I)$. The other inclusion is obvious. $\square$

Unfortunately, we would rather not regard the strategy defined in this proof as an "intelligent" learner, because its output does not depend on the input at all. Its success lies just in the choice of appropriate hypothesis spaces. If such a choice of hypothesis spaces is forbidden, we obtain an absolutely negative result:

Theorem 3. *$\{b \in \mathbb{N} \mid \mathcal{R}_b \in J^1\} \notin suit_\tau(J^1, EX)$.*
In particular even $\{b \in \mathbb{N} \mid card \{i \in \mathbb{N} \mid \varphi_i^b \in \mathcal{R}\} = 1\} \notin suit_\tau(J^1, EX)$.

For a proof see [6] or [12]. So, if we fix our hypothesis spaces in advance, not even the classes consisting of just one element can be identified in the limit uniformly. Regarding the identification of arbitrary finite classes (the learnability of which is trivial in the non-uniform case), the situation gets worse still. Even by free choice of the hypothesis spaces we cannot achieve uniform EX-identifiability.

Theorem 4. *$\{b \in \mathbb{N} \mid \mathcal{R}_b \in J^*\} \notin suit(J^*, EX)$.*

A proof can be found in [12]. How can we interpret these results? Is the concept of uniform learning fruitless and further research on this area not worthwile? Fortunately, many results in [2] and [12] allow a more optimistic point of view.

---

[1] This does not work for CONS and CONF, since in general after the delay the hypotheses are no longer consistent or conform with the information in the actual time of the learning process.

For example, [12] shows that some constraints on the descriptions $b \in B$ – especially concerning the topological structure of the numberings φ^b – yield uniform learnability of huge classes of functions, even with consistent *and* total intermediate hypotheses and also with respect to our acceptable numbering τ. The sticking point seems to be that uniform identifiability is not so much influenced by the classes to be learned, but by the numberings φ^b chosen as representations for these classes. So the numerous negative results should be interpreted carefully. For example the reason that there is no uniform EX-learner for $\{b \in \mathbb{N} \mid \mathcal{R}_b \in J^*\}$ is not so much the complexity of finite classes but rather the need to cope with *any* numbering possessing a finite $\mathcal{R}$-core. Based on these aspects we should not tend to a pessimistic view concerning the fruitfulness of the concept of uniform learning. Our results in the following sections will substantiate this opinion.

Theorems 2 and 3 now enable the proof of the following example of a strict version of Proposition 1.

Theorem 5. $\mathrm{suit}_\varphi(J^1, I) \subset \mathrm{suit}_\tau(J^1, I) \subset \mathrm{suit}(J^1, I)$ *for all* $I \in \mathcal{I}$.

Proof. $\mathrm{suit}_\tau(J^1, I) \subset \mathrm{suit}(J^1, I)$ is obtained as follows: by Theorem 3 we know that $B_1 := \{b \in \mathbb{N} \mid \mathcal{R}_b \in J^1\} \notin \mathrm{suit}_\tau(J^1, I)$ (otherwise B_1 was also an element of $\mathrm{suit}_\tau(J^1, \mathrm{EX})$). Thus by Theorem 2 we obtain $B_1 \in \mathrm{suit}(J^1, I) \backslash \mathrm{suit}_\tau(J^1, I)$.

It remains to prove $\mathrm{suit}_\varphi(J^1, I) \subset \mathrm{suit}_\tau(J^1, I)$. Again by Theorem 3 we know that there exists a set $B \subseteq \mathbb{N}$ such that card $\{i \in \mathbb{N} \mid \varphi_i^b \in \mathcal{R}\} = 1$ for all $b \in B$ and $B \notin \mathrm{suit}_\varphi(J^1, \mathrm{EX})$. Now let $g \in \mathcal{R}$ be a computable function satisfying

$$\varphi_i^{g(b)}(x) = \begin{cases} 0 & \text{if } \varphi_i^b(y)\!\downarrow \text{ for all } y \leq x \\ \uparrow & \text{otherwise} \end{cases} \quad \text{for any } b, i, x \in \mathbb{N} \ .$$

Let $B' := \{g(b) \mid b \in B\}$. Since $\mathcal{R}_{g(b)} = \{0^\infty\}$ for $b \in B$, we get $B' \in \mathrm{suit}_\tau(J^1, I)$ (via a strategy which constantly returns a τ-index of the function 0^∞).

Obviously $\{i \in \mathbb{N} \mid \varphi_i^{g(b)} \in \mathcal{R}\} = \{i \in \mathbb{N} \mid \varphi_i^b \in \mathcal{R}\}$ for all $b \in \mathbb{N}$. If there was a strategy $S \in \mathcal{P}^2$ satisfying $B' \in \mathrm{suit}_\varphi(J^1, I)(S)$, we would achieve $B \in \mathrm{suit}_\varphi(J^1, \mathrm{EX})(T)$ by defining $T(b, f[n]) := S(g(b), 0^n)$ for $f \in \mathcal{R}$, $b, n \in \mathbb{N}$. This contradicts the choice of B, so $B' \in \mathrm{suit}_\tau(J^1, I) \backslash \mathrm{suit}_\varphi(J^1, I)(S)$. Hence $\mathrm{suit}_\varphi(J^1, I) \subset \mathrm{suit}_\tau(J^1, I)$. $\qquad \square$

4 Separation of Inference Criteria – Special Hypothesis Spaces

From now on we will compare the learning power of our inference criteria for uniform learning of finite classes of recursive functions, i.e. we try to find results in the style of Theorem 1, where the criteria $I \in \mathcal{I}$ are replaced by the sets $\mathrm{suit}(J^*, I)$, $\mathrm{suit}_\tau(J^*, I)$ or $\mathrm{suit}_\varphi(J^*, I)$. Please note that a separation like for example $\mathrm{suit}_\tau(\mathrm{CONS}, \mathrm{CONS}) \subset \mathrm{suit}_\tau(\mathrm{CONS}, \mathrm{EX})$ is not a very astonishing result. The remarkable point is that even collections of *finite* classes of recursive functions suffice for a separation (note that in the non-uniform case finite classes can be identified under *any* criterion $I \in \mathcal{I}$ easily).

Since all proofs for the theorems stated in Section 4 proceed in a similar manner and include rather long constructions, we will omit most of them and just give sketches of the proofs for Theorem 7 and Theorem 9.

In this section we concentrate on uniform learning with respect to fixed hypothesis spaces, i.e. according to Definition 5. Our aim is to show that all the comparison results in Theorem 1 hold analogously for these concepts, even if all classes to be learned are finite. Lemma 1 summarizes some simple observations.

Lemma 1. *1. $suit_\varphi(J^*, EX_m) \subseteq suit_\varphi(J^*, EX_{m+1}) \subseteq suit_\varphi(J^*, EX)$ for arbitrary $m \in \mathbb{N}$,*
2. $suit_\varphi(J^*, TOTAL) \subseteq suit_\varphi(J^*, CONS) \subseteq suit_\varphi(J^*, CONF) \subseteq suit_\varphi(J^*, EX)$,
3. $suit_\varphi(J^*, TOTAL) \subseteq suit_\varphi(J^*, CEX) \subseteq suit_\varphi(J^*, EX)$.
These results hold analogously if we substitute $suit_\varphi$ by $suit_\tau$.

Proof. All these inclusions except for $suit_\varphi(J^*, TOTAL) \subseteq suit_\varphi(J^*, CONS)$ (or analogously with τ instead of φ) follow immediately from the definitions. If a set $B \subseteq \mathbb{N}$ fulfills $B \in suit_\varphi(J^*, TOTAL)(S)$ for some strategy $S \in \mathcal{P}^2$, we can easily define $T \in \mathcal{P}^2$ such that $B \in suit_\varphi(J^*, CONS)(T)$. On input $(b, f[n])$ the strategy T just has to check the hypothesis $S(b, f[n])$ for consistency wrt φ^b. For $b \in B$, $f \in \mathcal{R}_b$ this is possible, because the function $\varphi^b_{S(b,f[n])}$ is total. If consistency is verified, T returns the same index as S, otherwise it returns some consistent hypothesis (which can be found, if $f \in \mathcal{R}_b$). Convergence to a correct hypothesis follows from the choice of S. The τ-case is proved by analogy.   □

Now we want to prove that all these inclusions are in fact proper inclusions. For that purpose consider Theorem 6 first.

Theorem 6. $suit_\varphi(J^*, EX_{m+1}) \setminus suit(J^*, EX_m) \neq \emptyset$ *for any $m \in \mathbb{N}$.[2]*

Note that this result is even stronger than required. We just needed to prove $suit_\varphi(J^*, EX_{m+1}) \setminus suit_\varphi(J^*, EX_m) \neq \emptyset$ and the corresponding statement for the τ-case. Besides we have not only verified $suit(J^*, EX_{m+1}) \setminus suit(J^*, EX_m) \neq \emptyset$, but we observe a further fact: though we know uniform learning with respect to the hypothesis spaces given by φ to be much more restrictive than uniform learning without special demands concerning the hypothesis spaces, we still can find collections of class-descriptions which are

- restrictive enough to describe finite classes of recursive functions only,
- suitable for uniform EX_{m+1}-identification with respect to the hypothesis spaces corresponding to their descriptions,
- but *not* suitable for uniform EX_m-identification even if the hypothesis spaces can be chosen without restrictions.

Similar strict separations are obtained by the following theorems.

Theorem 7. $suit_\varphi(J^*, EX) \setminus suit(J^*, CONF) \neq \emptyset$.

---

[2] The proof is omitted but proceeds similar to the proof of Theorem 7.

Proof. We will just give a sketch of the relevant parts of the proof; details and formal constructions are not needed to explain the general idea common to most of the proofs of our results. We use a strategy $T \in \mathcal{R}$ to define a description set $B \subseteq \mathbb{N}$ suitable for uniform identification in the limit by T. The set B shall describe only finite recursive cores and will not be suitable for uniform conform identification. The choice of the strategy T may seem rather arbitrary, but it will enable an indirect proof.

Define $T \in \mathcal{R}$ by

$$T(f[n]) := \begin{cases} 0 & \text{if } f[n] \in \{0,1\}^* \\ \max\{f(0), \ldots, f(n)\} - 1 & \text{otherwise} \end{cases}$$

for arbitrary $f \in \mathcal{R}$ and $n \in \mathbb{N}$.
Then set $B := \{b \in \mathbb{N} \mid \mathcal{R}_b \text{ is finite and } \mathcal{R}_b \in \mathrm{EX}_{\varphi^b}(T)\}$.

We will prove $B \in \mathrm{suit}_\varphi(J^*, \mathrm{EX}) \setminus \mathrm{suit}(J^*, \mathrm{CONF})$. By definition of B we obviously have $B \in \mathrm{suit}_\varphi(J^*, \mathrm{EX})$. Now $B \notin \mathrm{suit}(J^*, \mathrm{CONF})$ is verified by way of contradiction.

Assumption. $B \in \mathrm{suit}(J^*, \mathrm{CONF})$.
Then there is some $S \in \mathcal{P}^2$ such that $\mathcal{R}_b \in \mathrm{CONF}(\lambda x.S(b,x))$ for all $b \in B$.

Aim. Construct an integer b_0, such that $b_0 \in B$, but $\mathcal{R}_{b_0} \notin \mathrm{CONF}(\lambda x.S(b_0,x))$, in contradiction to our assumption. The strategy $\lambda x.S(b_0,x)$ will fail for at least one function $f \in \mathcal{R}_{b_0}$ by either

- changing its hypothesis for f infinitely often or
- not terminating its computation on input of some initial segment of f or
- violating the conformity demand on input of some initial segment of f.

Construction of b_0. We define $\eta^b \in \mathcal{P}^2$ uniformly in $b \in \mathbb{N}$. First we define $\eta_0^b(0) := 0$. If we set $y_0 := 0$, the segment $\eta_0^b[y_0]$ is already defined. We start in stage 0.

In general, in stage k we proceed as follows:
For the definition of further values of η_0^b one computes $S(b, \eta_0^b[y_k])$, $S(b, \eta_0^b[y_k]0)$ and $S(b, \eta_0^b[y_k]1)$. If one of these values is undefined, then $\eta_0^b = 0{\uparrow}^\infty$. Else, if these values are all equal, we append zeros until we observe that the strategy $\lambda x.S(b,x)$ changes its mind on the initial segment constructed so far. Otherwise we just append one value $t \in \{0,1\}$, such that $S(b, \eta_0^b[y_k]) \neq S(b, \eta_0^b[y_k]t)$.
The functions η_{2k+1}^b and η_{2k+2}^b are defined as follows:
$\eta_{2k+1}^b[y_k + 2] := \eta_0^b[y_k]0(2k+2)$, $\eta_{2k+2}^b[y_k + 2] := \eta_0^b[y_k]1(2k+3)$. Both functions will be extended by zeros until the values $S(b, \eta_0^b[y_k]0)$ and $S(b, \eta_0^b[y_k]1)$ are computed and the definition of η_0^b is stopped temporarily because of a mind change of $\lambda x.S(b,x)$ on the initial segment of η_0^b constructed so far (if

these conditions are never satisfied, we obtain $\eta^b_{2k+1} = \eta^b_0[y_k]0(2k+2)0^\infty$ and $\eta^b_{2k+2} = \eta^b_0[y_k]1(2k+3)0^\infty)$. If the definition of η^b_0 is stopped temporarily, let y_{k+1} be the maximal argument for which η^b_0 is defined. If y_{k+1} exists, go to stage $k+1$.

The Recursion Theorem then yields an integer $b_0 \in \mathbb{N}$ satisfying $\varphi^{b_0} = \eta^{b_0}$.

Claim. 1. We have $\mathrm{rng}(\varphi^{b_0}_0) \subseteq \{0,1\}$; if $x \in \mathbb{N}$, then $\max(\mathrm{rng}(\varphi^{b_0}_{x+1})) = x + 2$ or $\mathrm{rng}(\varphi^{b_0}_{x+1}) = \emptyset$.
2. If in the construction of φ^{b_0} all stages are reached, then $\mathcal{R}_{b_0} = \{\varphi^{b_0}_0\}$. If stage k ($k \in \mathbb{N}$) is the last stage to be reached, then $\mathcal{R}_{b_0} = \{\varphi^{b_0}_0, \varphi^{b_0}_{2k+1}, \varphi^{b_0}_{2k+2}\}$ or $\mathcal{R}_{b_0} = \{\varphi^{b_0}_{2k+1}, \varphi^{b_0}_{2k+2}\}$.

This claim implies $b_0 \in B$. For the proof of $\mathcal{R}_{b_0} \notin \mathrm{CONF}(\lambda x.S(b_0, x))$ we assume by way of contradiction that $\mathcal{R}_{b_0} \in \mathrm{CONF}_\psi(\lambda x.S(b_0, x))$ for some numbering $\psi \in \mathcal{P}^2$. By Claim 2 it suffices to consider the following three cases:

Case 1. $\mathcal{R}_{b_0} = \{\varphi^{b_0}_0\}$.
Then all stages are reached in our construction. We observe that in the identification process for $\varphi^{b_0}_0$ the strategy $\lambda x.S(b_0, x)$ changes its hypothesis infinitely often.

Case 2. $\mathcal{R}_{b_0} = \{\varphi^{b_0}_{2k+1}, \varphi^{b_0}_{2k+2}\}$ for some $k \in \mathbb{N}$.
In this case we have $S(b_0, \varphi^{b_0}_{2k+1}[y_k + 1])\uparrow$ or $S(b_0, \varphi^{b_0}_{2k+2}[y_k + 1])\uparrow$ (with y_k as in our construction), so $\lambda x.S(b_0, x)$ cannot be successful for both $\varphi^{b_0}_{2k+1}$ and $\varphi^{b_0}_{2k+2}$.

Case 3. $\mathcal{R}_{b_0} = \{\varphi^{b_0}_0, \varphi^{b_0}_{2k+1}, \varphi^{b_0}_{2k+2}\}$ for $k \in \mathbb{N}$.
Then stage k is reached; stage $k + 1$ is not reached. Furthermore

$$S(b_0, \varphi^{b_0}_{2k+1}[y_k + 1]) = S(b_0, \eta^{b_0}_0[y_k]0) = S(b_0, \eta^{b_0}_0[y_k]1) = S(b_0, \varphi^{b_0}_{2k+2}[y_k + 1]) \,,$$

although $\varphi^{b_0}_{2k+1}[y_k + 1] \neq \varphi^{b_0}_{2k+2}[y_k + 1]$. Thus $i := S(b_0, \varphi^{b_0}_{2k+1}[y_k + 1])$ cannot be a ψ-number for both $\varphi^{b_0}_{2k+1}$ and $\varphi^{b_0}_{2k+2}$. There are two possibilities:

Case 3.1. $\psi_i(y_k + 1)\uparrow$.
Then the sequence of hypotheses produced by $\lambda x.S(b_0, x)$ on the function $\varphi^{b_0}_0$ converges to an index incorrect for $\varphi^{b_0}_0$ with respect to ψ.

Case 3.2. $\psi_i(y_k + 1)\downarrow$.
Then i is not conform for both $\varphi^{b_0}_{2k+1}[y_k + 1]$ and $\varphi^{b_0}_{2k+2}[y_k + 1]$ wrt ψ.

We conclude $\mathcal{R}_{b_0} \notin \mathrm{CONF}_\psi(\lambda x.S(b_0, x))$; thus $\mathcal{R}_{b_0} \notin \mathrm{CONF}(\lambda x.S(b_0, x))$. The properties of b_0 now contradict our assumption, so $B \notin \mathrm{suit}(J^*, \mathrm{CONF})$. This completes the proof. □

A separation of the criteria CONF and CONS in the uniform learning model can be verified with similar methods; the proof is omitted.

Theorem 8. $suit_\varphi(J^*, CONF) \setminus suit(J^*, CONS) \neq \emptyset.$

So, the results CONS $\subset$ CONF $\subset$ EX can also be transferred to uniform learning with respect to τ and the numberings given a priori by φ. Again, finite classes are sufficient for the separations.

In order to prove $suit_\varphi(J^*, \text{TOTAL}) \subset suit_\varphi(J^*, \text{CONS})$ (and the same result for $suit_\tau$) we use Theorem 9. Since $suit_\tau(J^*, \text{TOTAL}) \subseteq suit_\tau(J^*, \text{CEX})$, we even obtain $suit_\varphi(J^*, \text{CONS}) \setminus suit_\tau(J^*, \text{TOTAL}) \neq \emptyset$.

Theorem 9. $suit_\varphi(J^*, CONS) \setminus suit_\tau(J^*, CEX) \neq \emptyset.$

Proof. We will omit some formal details and concentrate on the main ideas. Again we use a strategy $T \in \mathcal{P}^2$ to define a description set $B \subseteq \mathbb{N}$ suitable for uniform consistent identification by T. Though B describes only finite recursive cores, it will not be suitable for uniform CEX-identification with respect to τ.

Define $T \in \mathcal{P}^2$ by

$$
T(b, f[n]) := \begin{cases} 0 & \text{if } 0 \notin \{f(0), \ldots, f(n)\} \\ \min\{i \geq 1 \mid \exists \alpha \in (\mathbb{N} \setminus \{0\})^* & \text{if } 0 \in \{f(0), \ldots, f(n)\} \text{ and} \\ \quad [\alpha 0 \subseteq \varphi_i^b \text{ and } \alpha 0 \subseteq f]\} & \text{such a minimum is found} \\ \uparrow & \text{otherwise} \end{cases}
$$

for $f \in \mathcal{R}$ and $b, n \in \mathbb{N}$.
Then set $B := \{b \in \mathbb{N} \mid \mathcal{R}_b \text{ is finite and } \mathcal{R}_b \in \text{CONS}_{\varphi^b}(\lambda x.T(b, x))\}$.

We will prove $B \in suit_\varphi(J^*, \text{CONS}) \setminus suit_\tau(J^*, \text{CEX})$. The definitions imply $B \in suit_\varphi(J^*, \text{CONS})$. The claim $B \notin suit_\tau(J^*, \text{CEX})$ is verified by way of contradiction.

Assumption. $B \in suit_\tau(J^*, \text{CEX})$,
i.e. there is some $S \in \mathcal{R}^2$ such that $\mathcal{R}_b \in \text{CEX}_\tau(\lambda x.S(b, x))$ for any $b \in B$.

Aim. Construction of an integer $b_0 \in B$ with $\mathcal{R}_{b_0} \notin \text{CEX}_\tau(\lambda x.S(b_0, x))$, in contradiction to our assumption. The strategy $\lambda x.S(b_0, x)$ will fail for at least one $f \in \mathcal{R}_{b_0}$ by either

- changing its hypothesis for f infinitely often or
- generating a hypothesis incorrect for f with respect to τ for infinitely many initial segments of f or
- guessing a τ-number of a proper subfunction of f on input of some initial segment of f.

Construction of b_0.
Define a function $\psi \in \mathcal{P}^3$ with the help of initial segments α_k^b ($b, k \in \mathbb{N}$) as follows: for arbitrary $b \in \mathbb{N}$ set $\alpha_0^b := 1$ and begin in stage 0.

In general, in stage k we proceed as follows:
$e := S(b, \alpha_k^b)$. Start a parallel check until *(i)* or *(ii)* turns out to be true.

(i). There is some $y < |\alpha_k^b|$ such that $\tau_e(y)$ is defined and $\tau_e(y) \neq \alpha_k^b(y)$.
(ii). There is some $y \geq |\alpha_k^b|$ such that $\tau_e(y)$ is defined.

The function ψ_{k+1}^b shall have the initial segment $\alpha_k^b 0$ which will be extended by a sequence of 0's, until *(i)* or *(ii)* turns out to be true. If condition *(i)* turns out to be true first, then ψ_0^b shall have the initial segment α_k^b which will be extended by a sequence of 1's, until $\lambda x.S(b, x)$ is forced to change its mind on ψ_0^b; then α_{k+1}^b shall be the initial segment of ψ_0^b constructed so far. If condition *(ii)* turns out to be true first – with $\tau_e(y_k)\!\downarrow$, $y_k > n$ – then $\alpha_{k+1}^b := \alpha_k^b 1 \ldots 1(\tau_e(y_k) + 1)$, where the last argument in the domain of α_{k+1}^b is y_k. In case α_{k+1}^b is defined go to stage $k + 1$. If neither *(i)* nor *(ii)* is fulfilled, ψ_0^b remains initial.

The Recursion Theorem then yields an integer $b_0 \in \mathbb{N}$ satisfying $\varphi^{b_0} = \psi^{b_0}$.

Claim. The construction in stage k implies

1. $\varphi_{k+1}^{b_0} \in \mathcal{R}$ iff $[\alpha_k^{b_0}$ is defined and $\tau_{S(b_0, \alpha_k^{b_0})} \subseteq \alpha_k^{b_0}\uparrow^\infty \; (\subset \varphi_{k+1}^{b_0})]$,
2. if $\varphi_{k+1}^{b_0} \notin \mathcal{R}$ and $\alpha_{k+1}^{b_0}\uparrow$, then $\varphi_0^{b_0} = \alpha_k^{b_0} 1^\infty \in \mathcal{R}$ and the sequence of hypotheses produced by $\lambda x.S(b_0, x)$ on $\varphi_0^{b_0}$ converges to an index incorrect for $\varphi_0^{b_0}$ with respect to τ,
3. if $\varphi_{k+1}^{b_0} \notin \mathcal{R}$ and $\alpha_{k+1}^{b_0}\!\downarrow$, then $\alpha_k^{b_0} \subseteq \alpha_{k+1}^{b_0} \subseteq \varphi_0^{b_0}$; furthermore
    a) $S(b_0, \alpha_{k+1}^{b_0}) \neq S(b_0, \alpha_k^{b_0})$ or
    b) $S(b_0, f[|\alpha_k^{b_0}| - 1])$ is incorrect wrt τ for any $f \in \mathcal{R}$ satisfying $\alpha_{k+1}^{b_0} \subset f$,
4. if $\varphi_0^{b_0} \in \mathcal{R}$, then $\varphi_{k+1}^{b_0} \notin \mathcal{R}$ for all $k \in \mathbb{N}$. Furthermore $0 \notin \text{rng}(\varphi_0^{b_0})$.
5. There is exactly one index i such that $\varphi_i^{b_0} \in \mathcal{R}$.

With this claim and our construction we can verify $b_0 \in B$. Now we assume by way of contradiction that $\mathcal{R}_{b_0} \in \text{CEX}_\tau(\lambda x.S(b_0, x))$. It suffices to regard two cases.

Case 1. $\mathcal{R}_{b_0} = \{\varphi_0^{b_0}\}$.
Then on $\varphi_0^{b_0}$ the strategy $\lambda x.S(b_0, x)$ changes its hypothesis infinitely often or returns a hypothesis incorrect with respect to τ infinitely often. We obtain $\mathcal{R}_{b_0} \notin \text{CEX}_\tau(\lambda x.S(b_0, x))$.

Case 2. $\mathcal{R}_{b_0} = \{\varphi_i^{b_0}\}$ with $i \geq 1$.
With Claim 1 we have $\tau_{S(b_0, \varphi_i^{b_0}[n])} \subseteq \alpha_{i-1}^{b_0}\uparrow^\infty \subset \alpha_{i-1}^{b_0} 0^\infty = \varphi_i^{b_0}$ for some $n \in \mathbb{N}$.
Hence $S(b_0, \varphi_i^{b_0}[n])$ is a τ-number of a proper subfunction of $\varphi_i^{b_0}$. We conclude $\mathcal{R}_{b_0} \notin \text{CEX}_\tau(\lambda x.S(b_0, x))$.

In each case we have $\mathcal{R}_{b_0} \notin \text{CEX}_\tau(\lambda x.S(b_0, x))$. As $b_0 \in B$, this contradicts our initial assumption; so $B \notin \text{suit}_\tau(J^*, \text{CEX})$. This completes the proof. □

Thus it only remains to show that the separations in Lemma 1.3 are proper inclusions. From Theorem 9 and $\text{suit}_\varphi(J^*, \text{CONS}) \subseteq \text{suit}_\varphi(J^*, \text{EX})$ (analogously for suit_τ) we obtain that the second inclusion $\text{suit}_\varphi(J^*, \text{CEX}) \subseteq \text{suit}_\varphi(J^*, \text{EX})$ and its τ-version are indeed proper. For the first inclusion regard Theorem 10.

Theorem 10. $suit_\varphi(J^*, CEX) \setminus suit(J^*, CONS) \neq \emptyset.$[3]

Together with $\text{suit}_\tau(J^*, \text{TOTAL}) \subseteq \text{suit}_\tau(J^*, \text{CONS})$ this theorem yields $\text{suit}_\varphi(J^*, \text{CEX}) \setminus \text{suit}_\tau(J^*, \text{TOTAL}) \neq \emptyset$ and in particular $\text{suit}_\varphi(J^*, \text{TOTAL}) \subset \text{suit}_\varphi(J^*, \text{CEX})$, where again suit_φ may be replaced by suit_τ.

With Theorems 9 and 10 we have also verified the following corollary.

Corollary 1.   1. $suit_\varphi(J^*, CEX) \# suit_\varphi(J^*, CONS),$
2. $suit_\tau(J^*, CEX) \# suit_\tau(J^*, CONS).$

Now we can summarize our separation results for uniform learning of finite classes with respect to fixed hypothesis spaces.

Theorem 11.   1. $suit_\varphi(J^*, EX_m) \subset suit_\varphi(J^*, EX_{m+1}) \subset suit_\varphi(J^*, EX)$ *for arbitrary* $m \in \mathbb{N}$,
2. $suit_\varphi(J^*, TOTAL) \subset suit_\varphi(J^*, CONS) \subset suit_\varphi(J^*, CONF) \subset suit_\varphi(J^*, EX),$
3. $suit_\varphi(J^*, TOTAL) \subset suit_\varphi(J^*, CEX) \subset suit_\varphi(J^*, EX).$
   These results hold analogously if we substitute $suit_\varphi$ *by* $suit_\tau$.

Thus we have transferred the comparison results of Theorem 1 to the concept of meta-learning in fixed hypothesis spaces. Each separation is achieved already by restricting ourselves to the synthesis of strategies for finite classes of recursive functions.

5   Separation of Inference Criteria – General Hypothesis Spaces

In this section we investigate the hierarchies of inference criteria for uniform learning without restrictions in the choice of the hypothesis spaces. Again we will concentrate on description sets corresponding to collections of finite classes of recursive functions. Some of the comparison results in Section 4 hold analogously for this concept, but there are differences, too. Our first simple observations in Lemma 2 follow immediately from the definitions.

Lemma 2.   1. $suit(J^*, EX_m) \subseteq suit(J^*, EX_{m+1}) \subseteq suit(J^*, EX)$ *for all* $m \in \mathbb{N}$,
2. $suit(J^*, CONS) \subseteq suit(J^*, CONF) \subseteq suit(J^*, EX),$
3. $suit(J^*, TOTAL) \subseteq suit(J^*, CEX) \subseteq suit(J^*, EX).$

---

[3] The proof is omitted but proceeds similar to the proof of Theorem 7.

Note that we dropped the inclusion for TOTAL-identification in the second line. Since in general a uniform strategy S satisfying $B \in \text{suit}(J^*, \text{TOTAL})(S)$ for some $B \subseteq \mathbb{N}$ can *not* synthesize an appropriate hypothesis space for $\mathcal{R}_b$ from $b \in B$, the hypotheses returned by S cannot be checked for consistency. Therefore the proof of Lemma 1 cannot be transferred. By Theorems 6, 7, 8 all inclusions in Lemma 2.1 and 2.2 are proper inclusions. But for the other separations we observe a different connection, as Theorem 12 states.

Theorem 12. $\text{suit}(J^*, TOTAL) = \text{suit}(J^*, CEX) = \text{suit}(J^*, EX)$.

Proof. $\text{suit}(J^*, \text{TOTAL}) \subseteq \text{suit}(J^*, \text{CEX}) \subseteq \text{suit}(J^*, \text{EX})$ follows by definition. It remains to prove $\text{suit}(J^*, \text{EX}) \subseteq \text{suit}(J^*, \text{TOTAL})$. For that purpose fix a description set $B \in \text{suit}(J^*, \text{EX})$. Then we know

1. $\mathcal{R}_b$ is finite for all $b \in B$,
2. there is a strategy $S \in \mathcal{P}^2$ such that for any $b \in B$ there is a hypothesis space $\psi^{[b]} \in \mathcal{P}^2$ satisfying $\mathcal{R}_b \in \text{EX}_{\psi^{[b]}}(\lambda x.S(b, x))$.

Note that the hypothesis spaces $\psi^{[b]}$ do not have to be computable uniformly in b. Now we want to prove that $B \in \text{suit}(J^*, \text{TOTAL})$. We even will see that our given strategy S is already an appropriate strategy for uniform TOTAL-identification from B. This requires a change of the hypothesis spaces $\psi^{[b]}$ for $b \in B$.

Idea. Assume $b \in B$ was fixed. Since $\lambda x.S(b, x)$ identifies the finite class $\mathcal{R}_b$ in the limit, there are only finitely many initial segments of functions in $\mathcal{R}_b$ which force the strategy $\lambda x.S(b, x)$ into a "non-total" guess. If we replace the functions in $\psi^{[b]}$ associated with these non-total guesses by an element of $\mathcal{R}$ (for example 0^∞), we obtain a hypothesis space appropriate for TOTAL-identification of $\mathcal{R}_b$ by $\lambda x.S(b, x)$.

More formally: Fix $b \in B$. From 2 we obtain card $\{n \in \mathbb{N} \mid \psi^{[b]}_{S(b, f[n])} \notin \mathcal{R}\} < \infty$ for all $f \in \mathcal{R}_b$. Defining the set of "forbidden" hypotheses on "relevant" initial segments by

$$H^{[b]} := \{i \in \mathbb{N} \mid \psi^{[b]}_i \notin \mathcal{R} \wedge \exists f \in \mathcal{R}_b \, \exists n \in \mathbb{N} \, [S(b, f[n]) = i]\} \, ,$$

we conclude with statement 1, that $H^{[b]}$ is finite. Now we define a new hypothesis space $\eta^{[b]}$ by

$$\eta^{[b]}_i := \begin{cases} \psi^{[b]}_i & \text{if } i \notin H^{[b]} \\ 0^\infty & \text{if } i \in H^{[b]} \end{cases} \quad \text{for all } i \in \mathbb{N} \, .$$

Since $\psi^{[b]} \in \mathcal{P}^2$ and $H^{[b]}$ is finite, $\eta^{[b]}$ is computable. The definition of $\eta^{[b]}$ then implies $\mathcal{R}_b \in \text{TOTAL}_{\eta^{[b]}}(\lambda x.S(b, x))$. As $b \in B$ was chosen arbitrarily, we conclude $B \in \text{suit}(J^*, \text{TOTAL})$. $\qquad\square$

With this result we also observe a difference to our separation of TOTAL and CONS in the classical learning model.

Corollary 2. $suit(J^*, CONS) \subset suit(J^*, CONF) \subset suit(J^*, TOTAL)$.

Proof. This fact follows immediately from Theorem 7 and Theorem 8 and by the result $suit(J^*, EX) = suit(J^*, TOTAL)$ in Theorem 12. □

Obviously, a further change in the hierarchies of inference criteria is witnessed by the fact $suit(J^*, CONS) \subset suit(J^*, CEX)$, which follows by the same argumentation as in the proof of Corollary 2. We summarize:

Theorem 13. *1. $suit(J^*, EX_m) \subset suit(J^*, EX_{m+1}) \subset suit(J^*, EX)$ for arbitrary $m \in \mathbb{N}$,*
2. $suit(J^*, CONS) \subset suit(J^*, CONF) \subset suit(J^*, TOTAL) = suit(J^*, CEX) = suit(J^*, EX)$.

So in contrast to uniform identification of finite classes with respect to fixed hypothesis spaces the separations in Theorem 1 cannot be transferred to the unrestricted concept of uniform learning. Still it is remarkable, how many inference criteria for uniform identification can be separated by collections of finite classes of functions – even with very strong results (cf. the remarks below Theorem 6).

References

1. Barzdins, J. (1974); *Inductive Inference of Automata, Functions and Programs*, In: Proceedings International Congress of Mathematicians, 455-460.
2. Baliga, G.; Case, J.; Jain, S. (1996); *Synthesizing Enumeration Techniques for Language Learning*, In: Proceedings of the Ninth Annual Conference on Computational Learning Theory, ACM Press, 169-180
3. Case, J.; Smith, C. (1983); *Comparison of Identification Criteria for Machine Inductive Inference*, Theoretical Computer Science 25, 193-220.
4. Freivalds, R.; Kinber, E.B.; Wiehagen, R. (1995); *How Inductive Inference Strategies Discover Their Errors*, Information and Computation 118, 208-226.
5. Gold, E.M. (1967); *Language Identification in the Limit*, Information and Control 10, 447-474.
6. Jantke, K.P. (1979); *Natural Properties of Strategies Identifying Recursive Functions*, Elektronische Informationsverarbeitung und Kybernetik 15, 487-496.
7. Jantke, K.P.; Beick, H. (1981); *Combining Postulates of Naturalness in Inductive Inference*, Elektronische Informationsverarbeitung und Kybernetik 17, 465-484.
8. Kapur, S.; Bilardi, G. (1992); *On Uniform Learnability of Language Families*, Information Processing Letters 44, 35-38.
9. Osherson, D.N.; Stob, M.; Weinstein, S. (1988); *Synthesizing Inductive Expertise*, Information and Computation 77, 138-161.
10. Rogers, H. (1987); *Theory of Recursive Functions and Effective Computability*, MIT Press, Cambridge, Massachusetts.
11. Wiehagen, R. (1978); *Zur Theorie der algorithmischen Erkennung*, Dissertation B, Humboldt-University, Berlin (in German).
12. Zilles, S. (2000); *On Uniform Learning of Classes of Recursive Functions*, Technical Report LSA-2000-05E, Centre for Learning Systems and Applications, University of Kaiserslautern.

Refutable Language Learning with a Neighbor System

Yasuhito Mukouchi and Masako Sato

Department of Mathematics and Information Sciences
College of Integrated Arts and Sciences
Osaka Prefecture University, Sakai, Osaka 599-8531, Japan
{mukouchi, sato}@mi.cias.osakafu-u.ac.jp

Abstract. We consider inductive language learning and machine discovery from examples with some errors. In the present paper, the error or incorrectness we consider is the one described uniformly in terms of a distance over strings. Firstly, we introduce a notion of a recursively generable distance over strings, and for a language L, we define a k-neighbor language L' as a language obtained from L by (i) adding some strings *not* in L each of which is at most k distant from some string in L and by (ii) deleting some strings in L each of which is at most k distant from some string *not* in L. Then we define a k-neighbor system of a base language class as the collection of k-neighbor languages of languages in the class, and adopt it as a hypothesis space. We give formal definitions of k-neighbor (refutable) inferability, and discuss necessary and sufficient conditions on such kinds of inference.

1 Introduction

In the present paper, we consider inductive language learning and machine discovery from examples with some errors. Inductive inference is a process of hypothesizing a general rule from examples. As a correct inference criterion for inductive inference of formal languages and models of logic programming, we have mainly used Gold's identification in the limit [8]. An inference machine M is said to identify a language L in the limit, if the sequence of guesses from M, which is successively fed a sequence of examples of L, converges to a correct expression of L. In this criterion, a target language, whose examples are fed to an inference machine, is assumed to belong to a hypothesis space which is given in advance. However, this assumption is not appropriate, if we want an inference machine to infer or to discover an unknown rule which explains examples or data obtained from scientific experiments. That is, the behavior of an inference machine is not specified, in case we feed examples of a target language not in the hypothesis space in question.

In their previous paper, as a computational logic of machine discovery, Mukouchi and Arikawa [15,17] focused refutability of the hypothesis space concerned, and discussed both refutability and inferability from examples. That is, for every target language, if it is a member of the hypothesis space concerned, then

N. Abe, R. Khardon, and T. Zeugmann (Eds.): ALT 2001, LNAI 2225, pp. 267–282, 2001.
© Springer-Verlag Berlin Heidelberg 2001

an inference machine should identify the target language in the limit, otherwise it should refute the hypothesis space itself in a finite time. They showed that there are some rich hypothesis spaces that are refutable and inferable from complete examples (i.e., positive and negative examples, or an informant), but refutable and inferable classes from only positive examples (i.e., text) are very small. In relation to refutable inference, Sato [21] discussed general conditions for a class to be refutably inferable from complete examples. Lange and Watson [13] and Mukouchi [18] also proposed inference criteria relaxing the requirements of inference machines, and Jain [10] also deals with the problem for recursively enumerable languages. On the other hand, Mukouchi [16] and Kobayashi and Yokomori [11] also proposed inference criterion requiring an inference machine to infer an admissible approximate language within the hypothesis space concerned, even when the target language is not in the hypothesis space.

In many real-world applications of machine discovery or machine learning from examples, we have to deal with incorrect examples. In the present paper, we consider language learning from observed incorrect examples together with correct examples, i.e., from imperfect examples. When we are considering language learning from complete examples, i.e., from positive and negative examples, some positive examples may be presented to the learner as negative examples, and vice versa. It is natural to consider that each observed incorrect example has some connection with a certain correct example on a target language to be learned. The incorrect examples we consider here are the ones described uniformly in terms of a distance over strings. Assume that the correct example is a string v and the observed example is a string w. In case we are considering the so-called Hamming distance and two strings v and w have the same length but differ just one symbol, then we estimate the incorrectness as their distance of one. In case we are considering the edit distance and w can be obtained from v by deleting just one symbol and inserting one symbol in another place, then we estimate the incorrectness as their distance of two. Mukouchi and Sato [19] introduced a notion of a recursively generable distance over strings, and defined k-neighbor closure of a language L as the collection of strings each of which is at most k distant from some string in L. Then they discussed inferability of a k-neighbor closure of a language in the hypothesis space from positive examples.

There are various approaches to language learning from incorrect examples (cf. e.g. Jain [9], Stephan [24], and Case and Jain [7]). Stephan [24] has formulated a model of noisy data, in which a correct example crops up infinitely often, and an incorrect example only finitely often. There is no connection between incorrect examples considered there and correct examples.

In the present paper, for a language L, we define a k-neighbor language L' as a language obtained from L by (i) adding some strings *not* in L each of which is at most k distant from some string in L and by (ii) deleting some strings in L each of which is at most k distant from some string *not* in L. Formally, a language L' is a k-neighbor language of L, if L' is a subset of the k-neighbor closure of L and L'^c is a subset of the k-neighbor closure of L^c, where L^c is the complement of L. Then we define a k-neighbor system of a base language class as the collection of all k-neighbor languages of languages in the class, and adopt it as a hypothesis space. We consider refutability and inferability of a k-neighbor system from complete examples and present some conditions on language classes to be refutable and inferable from complete examples.

2   Preliminaries

2.1   A Language and a Distance

Let Σ be a fixed finite alphabet. Each element of Σ is called a *constant symbol*. Let Σ^+ be the set of all nonnull constant strings over Σ and let $\Sigma^* = \Sigma^+ \cup \{\varepsilon\}$, where ε is the null string. A subset L of Σ^* is called a *language*. The length of a string $w \in \Sigma^*$ is denoted by $|w|$. For $n \in N$, Σ^n denotes the set of all strings whose length is n, and $\Sigma^{\leq n}$ denotes the set of all strings whose length is at most n, that is, $\Sigma^n = \{w \in \Sigma^* \mid |w| = n\}$ and $\Sigma^{\leq n} = \{w \in \Sigma^* \mid |w| \leq n\}$.

A language $L \subseteq \Sigma^*$ is said to be *recursive*, if there is a computable function $f : \Sigma^* \to \{0, 1\}$ such that $f(w) = 1$ iff $w \in L$ for $w \in \Sigma^*$.

We consider a distance between two strings defined as follows:

Definition 1. *Let $N = \{0, 1, 2, \cdots\}$ be the set of all natural numbers.*

A function $d : \Sigma^* \times \Sigma^* \to N \cup \{\infty\}$ is called a distance *over strings, if it satisfies the following three conditions:*

   (i) For every $v, w \in \Sigma^*$, $d(v, w) = 0$ iff $v = w$.
   (ii) For every $v, w \in \Sigma^*$, $d(v, w) = d(w, v)$.
   (iii) For every $u, v, w \in \Sigma^*$, $d(u, v) + d(v, w) \geq d(u, w)$.

A distance d is said to be recursive, *if there is an effective procedure that computes $d(v, w)$ for every $v, w \in \Sigma^*$ with $d(v, w) \neq \infty$.*

Then we define the k-neighbor closure of a language as follows:

Definition 2 (Mukouchi and Sato [19]). *Let $d : \Sigma^* \times \Sigma^* \to N \cup \{\infty\}$ be a distance over strings and let $k \in N$.*

The k-neighbor closure $\overline{w}^{(d,k)}$ of a string $w \in \Sigma^*$ w.r.t. d is the set of all strings each of which is at most k distant from w, that is, $\overline{w}^{(d,k)} = \{v \in \Sigma^* \mid d(v, w) \leq k\}$.

The k-neighbor closure $\overline{L}^{(d,k)}$ of a language $L \subseteq \Sigma^*$ w.r.t. d is the set of all strings each of which is at most k distant from some string in L, that is, $\overline{L}^{(d,k)} = \bigcup_{w \in L} \overline{w}^{(d,k)} = \{v \in \Sigma^* \mid \exists w \in L \text{ s.t. } d(v, w) \leq k\}$.

By the definition, we see that $\{w\} = \overline{w}^{(d,0)} \subseteq \overline{w}^{(d,1)} \subseteq \overline{w}^{(d,2)} \subseteq \cdots$ and $L = \overline{L}^{(d,0)} \subseteq \overline{L}^{(d,1)} \subseteq \overline{L}^{(d,2)} \subseteq \cdots$.

The following lemma is obvious:

Lemma 1. *Let d be a distance, and let $k \in N$.*

For a language $L \subseteq \Sigma^*$ and for a string $w \in \Sigma^*$, $w \in \overline{L}^{(d,k)}$ if and only if $\overline{w}^{(d,k)} \cap L \neq \phi$.

For a set S, we denote by $\sharp S$ the cardinality of S. A procedure is said to *generate* a finite set S, if the procedure enumerates all elements in S and then stops.

Definition 3 (Mukouchi and Sato [19]). *A distance d is said to* have finite thickness, *if for every* $w \in \Sigma^*$, $\sharp \overline{w}^{(d,k)}$ *is finite.*

A distance d is said to be recursively generable, *if d has finite thickness and there exists an effective procedure that on inputs* $k \in N$ *and* $w \in \Sigma^*$ *generates* $\overline{w}^{(d,k)}$.

We note that the notion of a recursively generable finite-set-valued function was introduced by Lange and Zeugmann [12].

Example 1. (1) We consider a distance known as the Hamming distance. For a string w and for a number i with $1 \leq i \leq |w|$, by $w[i]$, let us denote the i-th symbol appearing in w. For two strings $v, w \in \Sigma^*$, let

$$d(v,w) = \begin{cases} \sharp\{i \mid 1 \leq i \leq |v|, \; v[i] \neq w[i]\}, & \text{if } |v| = |w|, \\ \infty, & \text{if } |v| \neq |w|. \end{cases}$$

Clearly, this distance d is recursively generable.

(2) Next, we consider a distance known as the edit distance. Roughly speaking, the edit distance d over two strings $v, w \in \Sigma^*$ is the least number of editing steps needed to convert v to w. Each editing step consists of a rewriting step of the form $a \to \varepsilon$ (a deletion), $\varepsilon \to b$ (an insertion), or $a \to b$ (a change), where $a, b \in \Sigma$.

Clearly, this distance d is recursively generable.

Let d be a recursively generable distance, and let $k \in N$. Then, for every $v, w \in \Sigma^*$, by checking $v \in \overline{w}^{(d,k)}$, whether $d(v,w) \leq k$ or not is recursively decidable. Therefore d turns to be a recursive distance. Let $L \subseteq \Sigma^*$ be a recursive language. Then, for every $w \in \Sigma^*$, by checking $\overline{w}^{(d,k)} \cap L \neq \phi$, whether $w \in \overline{L}^{(d,k)}$ or not is recursively decidable. Therefore $\overline{L}^{(d,k)}$ is also a recursive language.

In the present paper, we exclusively deal with a *recursively generable distance*, and simply refer it as a *distance* without any notice.

2.2   Inferability from Examples

We briefly introduce the basic notions necessary for defining our framework of neighbor inference.

Definition 4 (Angluin [2]). *A class* $\mathcal{L} = \{L_i\}_{i \in N}$ *of languages is said to be an* indexed family of recursive languages, *if there is a computable function* $f : N \times \Sigma^* \to \{0,1\}$ *such that* $f(i,w) = 1$ *iff* $w \in L_i$.

In the present paper, we adopt an indexed family of recursive languages as a base hypothesis space.

Definition 5 (Gold [8]). *A* complete presentation, *or an* informant, *of a language* $L \subseteq \Sigma^*$ *is an infinite sequence* $(w_0, v_0), (w_1, v_1), \cdots \in \Sigma^* \times \{0,1\}$ *such that* $\{w_i \mid i \in N, v_i = 1\} = L$ *and* $\{w_i \mid i \in N, v_i = 0\} = L^c \, (= \Sigma^* \setminus L)$.

In what follows, σ *or* δ *denotes a complete presentation, and* $\sigma[n]$ *denotes the* σ's *initial segment of length* $n \in N$. *For a complete presentation* σ *and for* $n \in N$, *we put* $\sigma[n]^+ = \{w_i \mid (w_i, 1) \in \sigma[n]\}$ *and* $\sigma[n]^- = \{w_i \mid (w_i, 0) \in \sigma[n]\}$.

An *inductive inference machine* (*IIM*, for short) is an effective procedure, or a certain type of Turing machine, which requests inputs from time to time and produces natural numbers from time to time. An *inductive inference machine that can refute hypothesis spaces* (*RIIM*, for short) is an effective procedure which requests inputs from time to time and either (i) produces natural numbers from time to time forever or (ii) refutes the class and stops in a finite time after producing some natural numbers. The outputs produced by the machine are called *guesses*.

For an IIM M or an RIIM M, for a complete presentation σ and for $n \in N$, by $M(\sigma[n])$ we denote the last guess or the refutation sign produced by M which is successively presented examples in $\sigma[n]$ on its input requests.

An IIM M or an RIIM M is said to *converge to a number i for a complete presentation* σ, if there is an $n \in N$ such that for every $m \geq n$, $M(\sigma[m]) = i$. An RIIM M is said to *refute a class* $\mathcal{L}$ *from a complete presentation* σ, if there is an $n \in N$ such that $M(\sigma[n])$ is the refutation sign. In this case we also say that M refutes the class $\mathcal{L}$ from $\sigma[n]$.

Then we define the ordinary inferability of a class of languages as follows:

Definition 6 (Gold [8]). *Let* $\mathcal{L} = \{L_i\}_{i \in N}$ *be a class of languages.*

An IIM M *is said to* infer *a language* $L_i \in \mathcal{L}$ *in the limit from complete examples, if for every complete presentation* σ *of* L_i, M *converges to an index* j *for* σ *such that* $L_j = L_i$.

An IIM M *is said to* infer *a class* $\mathcal{L}$ *in the limit from complete examples, if for every* $L_i \in \mathcal{L}$, M *infers* L_i *in the limit from complete examples.*

A class $\mathcal{L}$ *is said to be* inferable *in the limit from complete examples, if there is an IIM which infers* $\mathcal{L}$ *in the limit from complete examples.*

In the definition above, the behavior of an inference machine is not specified, when we feed a complete presentation of a language which is *not* in the class concerned.

Definition 7 (Mukouchi and Arikawa [15,17]). *An RIIM* M *is said to* refutably infer *a class* $\mathcal{L}$ *from complete examples, if it satisfies the following condition: For every* $L \subseteq \Sigma^*$, *(i) if* $L \in \mathcal{L}$, *then* M *infers* L *in the limit from complete examples, (ii) otherwise* M *refutes* $\mathcal{L}$ *from every complete presentation of* L.

A class $\mathcal{L}$ *is said to be* refutably inferable *from complete examples, if there is an RIIM which refutably infers* $\mathcal{L}$ *from complete examples.*

Now, we introduce our successful learning criterion we consider in the present paper.

Definition 8. *Let* d *be a distance, and let* $k \in N$.

A language $L' \subseteq \Sigma^*$ *is said to be a* k-neighbor language *of a language* $L \subseteq \Sigma^*$ w.r.t. d, *if* $L' \subseteq \overline{L}^{(d,k)}$ *and* $L'^c \subseteq \overline{L^c}^{(d,k)}$.

The set of all k-neighbor languages of L w.r.t. d *is denoted by* $[L]^{(d,k)}$. *The* k-neighbor system $[\mathcal{L}]^{(d,k)}$ *of a class* $\mathcal{L} = \{L_i\}_{i \in N}$ w.r.t. d *is the collection of all* k-neighbor languages of languages in $\mathcal{L}$ w.r.t. d, *that is,* $[\mathcal{L}]^{(d,k)} = \bigcup_{i \in N} [L_i]^{(d,k)}$.

In the definition above, we note that $L' \subseteq \overline{L}^{(d,k)}$ and $L'^c \subseteq \overline{L^c}^{(d,k)}$, if and only if $(\overline{L^c}^{(d,k)})^c \subseteq L' \subseteq \overline{L}^{(d,k)}$.

Example 2. (1) Let $\Sigma = \{a, b\}$, let d be the Hamming distance, and let $k = 2$. For a string $w \in \Sigma^*$, let us denote by $o(w, b)$ the number of b's appearing in w. We consider the language $L = \{w \in \Sigma^* \mid 3 \leq o(w, b) \leq 7\}$. Then $\overline{L}^{(d,k)} = \{w \in \Sigma^* \mid 1 \leq o(w, b) \leq 9\}$. On the other hand, $L^c = \{w \in \Sigma^* \mid o(w, b) < 3 \text{ or } o(w, b) > 7\}$, and thus $\overline{L^c}^{(d,k)} = \{w \in \Sigma^* \mid o(w, b) \neq 5\}$ and $(\overline{L^c}^{(d,k)})^c = \{w \in \Sigma^* \mid o(w, b) = 5\}$. Therefore $L' \in [L]^{(d,k)}$ if and only if $\{w \in \Sigma^* \mid o(w, b) = 5\} \subseteq L' \subseteq \{w \in \Sigma^* \mid 1 \leq o(w, b) \leq 9\}$.

(2) Let $\Sigma = \{a\}$, let d be the edit distance, and let $k = 1$. We consider the language $L = \{a, aaa, \cdots, a^{2n+1}, \cdots\}$. As easily seen, $\overline{L}^{(d,k)} = \{\varepsilon, a, aa, aaa, \cdots, a^n, \cdots\} = \Sigma^*$. On the other hand, $L^c = \{\varepsilon, aa, aaaa, \cdots, a^{2n}, \cdots\}$, and thus $\overline{L^c}^{(d,k)} = \Sigma^*$ and $(\overline{L^c}^{(d,k)})^c = \phi$. Therefore $[L]^{(d,k)}$ consists of all languages over Σ.

(3) Let d be an arbitrary distance, and let $k \in N$. We consider the language $L = \Sigma^*$. As easily seen, $\overline{L}^{(d,k)} = \Sigma^*$. On the other hand, $L^c = \phi$, and thus $\overline{L^c}^{(d,k)} = \phi$ and $(\overline{L^c}^{(d,k)})^c = \Sigma^*$. Therefore $[L]^{(d,k)} = \{L\}$.

In a similar way, we see that $[L']^{(d,k)} = \{L'\}$, where $L' = \phi$.

We note that in case L is a recursive language, $\overline{L}^{(d,k)}$ and $\overline{L^c}^{(d,k)}$ are also recursive languages, while $L' \in [L]^{(d,k)}$ is not a recursive language in general. Furthermore neither the class $[L]^{(d,k)}$ nor $[\mathcal{L}]^{(d,k)}$ is indexable in general.

Definition 9. *Let $\mathcal{L} = \{L_i\}_{i \in N}$ be a class of languages, let d be a distance, and let $k \in N$.*

For a language $L \subseteq \Sigma^*$, a pair $(i, j) \in N \times N$ is said to be a weak k-neighbor *answer for L, if $j \leq k$ and $L \in [L_i]^{(d,j)}$.*

For a language $L \subseteq \Sigma^*$, a pair $(i, j) \in N \times N$ is said to be a k-neighbor answer for L, if (i) (i, j) is a weak k-neighbor answer for L and (ii) for every pair (i', j') with $j' < j$, $L \notin [L_{i'}]^{(d,j')}$.

An IIM M is said to k-neighborly (resp., weak k-neighborly) infer a class $\mathcal{L}$ w.r.t. d from complete examples, if for every $L \in [\mathcal{L}]^{(d,k)}$ and every complete presentation σ of L, M converges to a number $\langle i, j \rangle$ for σ such that (i, j) is a k-neighbor (resp., weak k-neighbor) answer for L, where $\langle \cdot, \cdot \rangle$ represents the Cantor's pairing function.

A class $\mathcal{L}$ is said to be k-neighborly (resp., weak k-neighborly) inferable w.r.t. d from complete examples, if there is an IIM which k-neighborly (resp., weak k-neighborly) infers $\mathcal{L}$ w.r.t. d from complete examples.

A class $\mathcal{L}$ is said to be neighborly (resp., weak neighborly) inferable w.r.t. d from complete examples, if for every $k \in N$, $\mathcal{L}$ is k-neighborly (resp., weak k-neighborly) inferable w.r.t. d from complete examples.

We also omit the phrase 'w.r.t. d', if it holds for every distance d.

Furthermore, we take the refutability of the class into consideration as follows:

Definition 10. *Let d be a distance, and let $k \in N$.*

An RIIM M is said to k-neighbor-refutably (resp., weak k-neighbor-refutably) infer a class $\mathcal{L}$ w.r.t. d from complete examples, if it satisfies the following condition: For every $L \subseteq \Sigma^*$, (i) if $L \in [\mathcal{L}]^{(d,k)}$, then M k-neighborly (resp., weak k-neighborly) infers L from complete examples, (ii) otherwise M refutes $\mathcal{L}$ from every complete presentation of L.

A class $\mathcal{L}$ is said to be k-neighbor-refutably (resp., weak k-neighbor-refutably) inferable w.r.t. d from complete examples, if there is an RIIM which k-neighbor-refutably (resp., weak k-neighbor-refutably) infers $\mathcal{L}$ w.r.t. d from complete examples.

A class $\mathcal{L}$ is said to be neighbor-refutably (resp., weak neighbor-refutably) inferable w.r.t. d from complete examples, if for every $k \in N$, $\mathcal{L}$ is k-neighbor-refutably (resp., weak k-neighbor-refutably) inferable w.r.t. d from complete examples.

We also omit the phrase 'w.r.t. d', if it holds for every distance d.

The rest of this section is devoted to summarize some known results related to this study.

Since we are considering an indexed family of recursive languages, the following theorem is valid:

Theorem 1 (Gold [8]). *Every class $\mathcal{L}$ is inferable in the limit from complete examples.*

Definition 11 (Mukouchi and Arikawa [15,17]). *A pair (T, F) of subsets of Σ^* is said to be consistent with a language L, if $T \subseteq L$ and $F \subseteq L^c$.*

The econs function e for a class $\mathcal{L}$ is the function such that for two finite sets $T, F \subseteq \Sigma^*$,

$$
e(T, F) = \begin{cases} 1, & \text{if there exists an } L \in \mathcal{L} \\ & \quad \text{such that } (T, F) \text{ is consistent with } L, \\ 0, & \text{otherwise.} \end{cases}
$$

Definition 12 (Mukouchi [14]). *A pair (T, F) of finite subsets of Σ^* is said to be a pair of definite finite tell-tale sets of a language L within a class $\mathcal{L}$, if (i) (T, F) is consistent with L and (ii) (T, F) is inconsistent with every $L' \in \mathcal{L}$ with $L' \neq L$.*

Theorem 2 (Mukouchi and Arikawa [15,17]). *A class $\mathcal{L}$ is refutably inferable from complete examples, if and only if it satisfies the following two conditions (C1) and (C2):*

(C1) The econs function for $\mathcal{L}$ is computable.

(C2) For every $L \notin \mathcal{L}$, there is a pair of definite finite tell-tale sets of L within $\mathcal{L}$.

The condition (C2) above means that for every $L \notin \mathcal{L}$, there is a pair (T, F) of finite subsets of Σ^* such that (i) (T, F) is consistent with L and that (ii) (T, F) is inconsistent with every language in $\mathcal{L}$.

3   Inferability

3.1   Characterizations

The following theorem can be shown by a simple enumerative method:

Theorem 3. *For every $k \in N$ and every distance d, every class is weak k-neighborly inferable w.r.t. d from complete examples, and thus every class is weak neighborly inferable from complete examples.*

Proof. Let d be a distance, and let $k \in N$. We consider the algorithm in Figure 1.

Procedure IIM M
begin
       let $T_0 := \phi$ and $F_0 := \phi$;
       let $n := 0$ and $i := 0$;
       repeat
           let $n := n + 1$;
           read the next example (w, v);
           if $v = 1$ **then** let $T_n := T_{n-1} \cup \{w\}$ and $F_n := F_{n-1}$
           else let $T_n := T_{n-1}$ and $F_n := F_{n-1} \cup \{w\}$;
           while $T_n \not\subseteq \overline{L_i}^{(d,k)}$ or $F_n \not\subseteq \overline{L_i^c}^{(d,k)}$ **do** $i := i + 1$;
           output $\langle i, k \rangle$;
       forever;
end.

Fig. 1. An IIM which weak k-neighborly infers a class w.r.t. d from complete examples

It is easy to see that the algorithm weak k-neighborly infers every class w.r.t. d from complete examples. □

On k-neighbor inferability, the following theorem is valid:

Theorem 4. *Let d be a distance, and let $k \in N$.*
    A class $\mathcal{L}$ is k-neighborly inferable w.r.t. d from complete examples, if and only if $\mathcal{L}$ satisfies the following condition (C3):
    (C3) There is a computable function f which satisfies the following condition: For every $L \in [\mathcal{L}]^{(d,k)}$ and every complete presentation σ of L, there is an $n \in N$ such that for every $m \geq n$, $f(\sigma[m]) = k'$, where $k' \in N$ is the least number such that $L \in [\mathcal{L}]^{(d,k')}$.

Proof. The 'only if' part is obvious.
    The 'if' part. We assume that there is a computable function f which satisfies the condition above. Then we consider the algorithm in Figure 2.

Procedure IIM M
begin

    let $T_0 := \phi$ and $F_0 := \phi$;
    let δ be the empty sequence;
    let $n := 0$;
    repeat

        let $n := n + 1$;
        read the next example (w, v);
        let $\delta := \delta \cdot (w, v)$;
        if $v = 1$ **then** let $T_n := T_{n-1} \cup \{w\}$ and $F_n := F_{n-1}$
        else let $T_n := T_{n-1}$ and $F_n := F_{n-1} \cup \{w\}$;
        let $k' := f(\delta)$;
        search for the least index $i \leq n$ such that $T_n \subseteq \overline{L_i}^{(d,k')}$ and $F_n \subseteq \overline{L_i^c}^{(d,k')}$;
        if such an index i is found **then** output $\langle i, k' \rangle$
        else output $\langle n, k \rangle$;

    forever;

end.

Fig. 2. An IIM which k-neighborly infers a class w.r.t. d from complete examples

Let $L \in [\mathcal{L}]^{(d,k)}$, and we assume that a complete presentation σ of L is fed to the procedure. Let k_0 be the least number k such that $L \in [\mathcal{L}]^{(d,k)}$, and then let (i_0, k_0) be the k-neighbor answer for L such that for every $i < i_0$, (i, k_0) is not a k-neighbor answer for L. Then it is easy to see that the algorithm converges to $\langle i_0, k_0 \rangle$.

Therefore the algorithm k-neighborly infers $\mathcal{L}$ w.r.t. d from complete examples. $\qquad\square$

Corollary 1. *Let d be a distance, and let $k \in N$.*

If a class $\mathcal{L}$ is $(k + 1)$-neighborly inferable w.r.t. d from complete examples, then $\mathcal{L}$ is also k-neighborly inferable w.r.t. d from complete examples.

In a similar way to Mukouchi and Arikawa [15,17], we can show the following theorem:

Theorem 5. *Let d be a distance, and let $k \in N$.*

A class $\mathcal{L}$ is weak k-neighbor-refutably inferable w.r.t. d from complete examples, if and only if $\mathcal{L}$ satisfies the following two conditions (C4) and (C5):

(C4) The econs function for the class $[\mathcal{L}]^{(d,k)}$ is computable.

(C5) For every $L \notin [\mathcal{L}]^{(d,k)}$, there is a pair of definite finite tell-tale sets of L within the class $[\mathcal{L}]^{(d,k)}$.

Theorem 6. *Let d be a distance, and let $k \in N$.*

A class $\mathcal{L}$ is k-neighbor-refutably inferable w.r.t. d from complete examples, if and only if $\mathcal{L}$ satisfies the conditions (C3), (C4) and (C5).

Theorem 7. *Let d be a distance, and let $k \in N$.*

If a class $\mathcal{L}$ satisfies the following two conditions (C4') and (C5'), then $\mathcal{L}$ also satisfies the condition (C3), and thus $\mathcal{L}$ is k-neighborly inferable w.r.t. d from complete examples:

(C4') For every $k' < k$, the econs function for the class $[\mathcal{L}]^{(d,k')}$ is computable.

(C5') For every $k' < k$ and every $L \notin [\mathcal{L}]^{(d,k')}$, there is a pair of definite finite tell-tale sets of L within the class $[\mathcal{L}]^{(d,k')}$.

Proof. Assume that a class $\mathcal{L}$ satisfies the conditions (C4') and (C5').

For $k' < k$, let $e_{k'}$ be the econs function for the class $[\mathcal{L}]^{(d,k')}$. Then we construct an algorithm for computing $f(\sigma[n])$ as follows:

    (i) Search for the least $k' < k$ such that $e_{k'}(\sigma[n]^+, \sigma[n]^-) = 1$.

    (ii) If such an index k' is found then output k', otherwise output k.

Then it is easy to see that the algorithm witnesses the condition (C3).   □

By Theorems 6 and 7, the following corollary is valid:

Corollary 2. *Let d be a distance, and let $k \in N$.*

If a class $\mathcal{L}$ satisfies the conditions (C4), (C5), (C4') and (C5'), then $\mathcal{L}$ is k-neighbor-refutably inferable w.r.t. d from complete examples.

Furthermore, by Theorem 5 and Corollary 2, the following corollary is valid:

Corollary 3. *Let d be a distance.*

A class $\mathcal{L}$ is neighbor-refutably inferable w.r.t. d from complete examples, if and only if $\mathcal{L}$ is weak neighbor-refutably inferable w.r.t. d from complete examples.

On the other hand, by Theorems 2 and 7, the following corollary is valid:

Corollary 4. *If a class $\mathcal{L}$ is refutably inferable from complete examples, then $\mathcal{L}$ is also 1-neighborly inferable from complete examples.*

3.2 Some Other Conditions

In the previous section, we showed that every class is weak neighborly inferable from complete examples. On neighbor inferability, there is a class that is not neighborly inferable from complete examples.

Theorem 8. *Let $k \geq 1$.*

There is a class $\mathcal{L}$ and a distance d such that $\mathcal{L}$ is not k-neighborly inferable w.r.t. d from complete examples.

Example 3. We consider the class $\mathcal{FL}$ of all finite languages over Σ. Then, as easily seen, for every distance d and every $k \in N$, the class $[\mathcal{FL}]^{(d,k)}$ also consists of all finite languages.

(1) For every distance d and every $k \in N$, the class $\mathcal{FL}$ is k-neighborly inferable w.r.t. d from complete examples, that is, the class $\mathcal{FL}$ is neighborly inferable from complete examples.

(2) For every distance d and every $k \in N$, the class $\mathcal{FL}$ is not (weak) k-neighbor-refutably inferable w.r.t. d from complete examples.

This is because there is no pair of definite finite tell-tale sets of an infinite language within $\mathcal{L}$.

For a set $T \subseteq \Sigma^*$, let us put $\mathcal{X}^{(d,k)}(T) = \{T' \subseteq \overline{T}^{(d,k)} \mid T \subseteq \overline{T'}^{(d,k)}\}$.

Lemma 2. *Let d be a distance, and let $k \in N$, let $\mathcal{L}$ be a class of languages, and let $T, F \subseteq \Sigma^*$ be two sets such that $T \cap F = \phi$.*

There exists an $L \in [\mathcal{L}]^{(d,k)}$ such that (T, F) is consistent with L, if and only if there exists an $L' \in \mathcal{L}$, a $T' \in \mathcal{X}^{(d,k)}(T)$ and an $F' \in \mathcal{X}^{(d,k)}(F)$ such that (T', F') is consistent with L'.

Proposition 1. *Let d be a distance.*

If the econs function for a class $\mathcal{L}$ is computable, then for every $k \in N$, the econs function for the class $[\mathcal{L}]^{(d,k)}$ is also computable.

Proof. Assume that e is the computable econs function for a class $\mathcal{L}$.

Let $k \in N$, and let T, F be two finite subsets of Σ^*. Then we see that $\mathcal{X}^{(d,k)}(T)$ is a finite class of finite subsets of Σ^*, and so is $\mathcal{X}^{(d,k)}(F)$. Thus we see by Lemma 2 that we can recursively decide whether or not there is an $L \in [\mathcal{L}]^{(d,k)}$ such that (T, F) is consistent with L by checking $T \cap F = \phi$ and $e(T', F') = 1$ for some $(T', F') \in \mathcal{X}^{(d,k)}(T) \times \mathcal{X}^{(d,k)}(F)$.

Therefore the econs function for the class $[\mathcal{L}]^{(d,k)}$ is computable.   □

On the other hand, the converse is not valid in general.

Proposition 2. *There is a distance d and a class $\mathcal{L}$ such that for every $k \geq 1$, the econs function for the class $[\mathcal{L}]^{(d,k)}$ is computable and that the econs function for $\mathcal{L}$ is not computable.*

Proof. Let $\varphi_0, \varphi_1, \varphi_2, \cdots$ be all partial recursive functions of one variable with acceptable numbering (cf. Rogers [20]), and then let $\Phi_0, \Phi_1, \Phi_2, \cdots$ be computational complexity measures (cf. Blum [6]), that is, the following conditions hold:

(i) For every $i, x \in N$, $\varphi_i(x)$ is defined, if and only if $\Phi_i(x)$ is defined.

(ii) For every $i, x, y \in N$, whether $\Phi_i(x) \leq y$ or not is recursively decidable.

Let $\Sigma = \{a, b\}$ and let us put

$$L_{\langle i,j \rangle} = \begin{cases} \{a^{i+1}, b^{i+1}\}, & \text{if } \Phi_i(i) \leq j, \\ \{a^{i+1}\}, & \text{otherwise}, \end{cases}$$

where $\langle \cdot, \cdot \rangle$ represents the Cantor's pairing function. Then we consider the class $\mathcal{L} = \{L_i\}_{i \in N}$.

Suppose that the econs function for $\mathcal{L}$ is computable. Then, for every $i \in N$, by testing there is an $L \in \mathcal{L}$ such that $(\{b^{i+1}\}, \phi)$ is consistent with L, we can recursively decide whether or not $\varphi_i(i)$ is defined. This contradicts the halting problem.

Hence the econs function for $\mathcal{L}$ is not computable.

Let $k \geq 1$ and let d be the distance such that

$$d(v, w) = \begin{cases} 0, & \text{if } v = w, \\ 1, & \text{if } v \neq w \text{ and } |v| = |w|, \\ \infty, & \text{otherwise.} \end{cases}$$

Then, for every $i, j \in N$, $\overline{L_{\langle i,j \rangle}}^{(d,k)} = \Sigma^{i+1}$ and $\overline{L_{\langle i,j \rangle}^c}^{(d,k)} = \Sigma^*$, and thus $[L_{\langle i,j \rangle}]^{(d,k)} = \{L \mid L \subseteq \Sigma^{i+1}\}$. Hence the econs function e for the class $[\mathcal{L}]^{(d,k)}$ is such that for two finite sets $T, F \subseteq \Sigma^*$,

$$e(T, F) = \begin{cases} 1, & \text{if } \exists i \in N \text{ s.t. } T \subseteq \Sigma^{i+1} \text{ and } F \subseteq (\Sigma^{i+1})^c, \\ 0, & \text{otherwise,} \end{cases}$$

and thus it is computable. $\square$

By Theorem 2 and Proposition 1, the following corollary is valid:

Corollary 5. *If a class $\mathcal{L}$ is refutably inferable from complete examples, then the econs function for $\mathcal{L}$ is computable, and thus for every distance d and every $k \in N$, the econs function for the class $[\mathcal{L}]^{(d,k)}$ is computable.*

The following lemma is basic:

Lemma 3. *Let d be a distance, let $k, n \in N$, let $L_1, \cdots, L_n \subseteq \Sigma^*$, and let $L \subseteq \Sigma^*$ be a language such that $L \notin [L_1]^{(d,k)} \cup \cdots \cup [L_n]^{(d,k)}$.*
There is a pair (T, F) of finite subsets of Σ^* such that (i) (T, F) is consistent with L and that (ii) (T, F) is inconsistent with every $L' \in [L_1]^{(d,k)} \cup \cdots \cup [L_n]^{(d,k)}$.

Definition 13 (Mukouchi and Arikawa [15,17]). *Let $\mathcal{L} = \{L_i\}_{i \in N}$ be a class of languages, and let $\mathcal{S}$ be a subclass of $\mathcal{L}$.*
A set $I \subseteq N$ of indices is said to be a cover-index set *of $\mathcal{S}$, if the collection of all languages each of which has an index in I is equal to $\mathcal{S}$, that is, $\mathcal{S} = \{L_i \in \mathcal{L} \mid i \in I\}$.*

Proposition 3 (Mukouchi and Arikawa [15,17]). *If a class $\mathcal{L}$ satisfies the following two conditions (C6) and (C7), then $\mathcal{L}$ is refutably inferable from complete examples:*
(C6) There is an effective procedure which on input $w \in \Sigma^*$ generates a finite cover-index set of the subclass $\{L_i \in \mathcal{L} \mid w \in L_i\}$ of $\mathcal{L}$.
(C7) The class $\mathcal{L}$ contains the empty language as its member.

Theorem 9. *If a class $\mathcal{L}$ satisfies the conditions (C6) and (C7), then $\mathcal{L}$ satisfies the following two conditions (C4") and (C5"):*

(C4") For every distance d and every $k \in N$, the econs function for the class $[\mathcal{L}]^{(d,k)}$ is computable.

(C5") For every distance d, every $k \in N$ and every $L \notin [\mathcal{L}]^{(d,k)}$, there is a pair of definite finite tell-tale sets of L within the class $[\mathcal{L}]^{(d,k)}$.

Proof. Assume that a class $\mathcal{L}$ satisfies the conditions (C6) and (C7). Then, by Proposition 3 and Corollary 5, we see $\mathcal{L}$ satisfies the condition (C4") above.

Let d be a distance, let $k \in N$, and let $L \notin [\mathcal{L}]^{(d,k)}$. By the condition (C7), $\mathcal{L}$ contains the empty language as its member, and so does $[\mathcal{L}]^{(d,k)}$. Thus L is nonempty, and let $w \in L$.

Let us put $\mathcal{T} = \{L' \in \mathcal{L} \mid \overline{w}^{(d,k)} \cap L' \neq \phi\}$. Then, for every $L'' \in [\mathcal{L}]^{(d,k)}$, if $w \in L''$, then $L'' \in [\mathcal{T}]^{(d,k)}$. In fact, let $L'' \in [\mathcal{L}]^{(d,k)}$ be a language such that $w \in L''$, and let $L' \in \mathcal{L}$ be a language such that $L'' \in [L']^{(d,k)}$. Since $w \in L'' \subseteq \overline{L'}^{(d,k)}$, we see by Lemma 1 that $\overline{w}^{(d,k)} \cap L' \neq \phi$, and thus $L' \in \mathcal{T}$. Hence $L'' \in [\mathcal{T}]^{(d,k)}$ holds.

Since the distance d has finite thickness and $\mathcal{L}$ satisfies the condition (C6), we see that $\mathcal{T}$ is a finite subclass of $\mathcal{L}$. Appealing to Lemma 3, we see that there is a pair (T, F) of finite subsets of Σ^* such that (i) (T, F) is consistent with L and that (ii) (T, F) is inconsistent with every $L'' \in [\mathcal{T}]^{(d,k)}$.

Finally, we put $T' = T \cup \{w\}$ and $F' = F$. Then, as easily seen, (T', F') is a pair of definite finite tell-tale sets of L within the class $[\mathcal{L}]^{(d,k)}$.   □

By Theorems 5, 7 and 9 and Corollary 2, we have the following corollary:

Corollary 6. *Assume that a class $\mathcal{L}$ satisfies the conditions (C6) and (C7).*

(1) The class $\mathcal{L}$ is weak neighbor-refutably inferable from complete examples.

(2) The class $\mathcal{L}$ is neighbor-refutably inferable from complete examples.

(3) The class $\mathcal{L}$ is neighborly inferable from complete examples.

Example 4. Here, we consider the class $\mathcal{PAT}$ of pattern languages.

We briefly recall a pattern and a pattern language. For more details, please refer to Angluin [1,2].

Fix a finite alphabet Σ. A pattern π is a nonnull finite string of constant and variable symbols. The pattern language $L(\pi)$ generated by a pattern π is the set of all strings obtained by substituting nonnull strings of constant symbols for the variables in π. Since two patterns that are identical except for renaming of variables generate the same pattern language, we do not distinguish one from the other. We can enumerate all patterns recursively and whether $w \in L(\pi)$ or not is recursively decidable. Therefore we can consider the class of pattern languages as an indexed family of recursive languages, where the pattern itself is considered to be an index.

As easily seen, the empty language $L = \phi$ does not belong to $\mathcal{PAT}$ and there is no pair of definite tell-tale sets of L within $\mathcal{PAT}$. Thus the class $\mathcal{PAT}$ is not refutably inferable from complete examples (cf. Mukouchi and Arikawa [15,17]).

However the class $\mathcal{PAT}$ satisfies the condition (C6). In fact, fix an arbitrary constant string w. As easily seen, if $w \in L(\pi)$, then π is not longer than w. There is an effective procedure that on input a fixed length generates the set of all patterns shorter than the length, and whether $w \in L(\pi)$ or not is recursively decidable. Therefore there is an effective procedure that on input $w \in \Sigma^+$ generates the set $\{\pi \mid w \in L(\pi)\}$.

Let $\mathcal{PAT}'$ be the class of all pattern languages and the empty language. Then the class $\mathcal{PAT}'$ satisfies the conditions (C6) and (C7), and thus by Corollary 6, we see that the following propositions are valid:

(1) The class $\mathcal{PAT}'$ is weak neighbor-refutably inferable from complete examples.

(2) The class $\mathcal{PAT}'$ is neighbor-refutably inferable from complete examples.

(3) The class $\mathcal{PAT}'$ is neighborly inferable from complete examples.

4   EFS Definable Classes

In this section, we consider neighbor inference and neighbor-refutable inference of languages classes defined by *elementary formal systems* (*EFSs*, for short).

The EFSs were originally introduced by Smullyan [23] to develop his recursion theory. In a word, EFSs are a kind of logic programming language which uses patterns instead of terms in first order logic [25], and they are shown to be natural devices to define languages [3].

In this paper, we briefly review the related known results and the obtained results on neighbor inferability and neighbor-refutable inferability of language classes definable by the so-called length-bounded EFSs. For detailed definitions and properties of EFSs, please refer to Smullyan [23], Arikawa [3], Arikawa et al. [4,5] and Yamamoto [25].

For $n \in N$, let us put $\mathcal{LBL}^{[\leq n]}$ be the class of languages defined by length-bounded EFSs with at most n axioms.

We note that the class $\mathcal{LBL}^{[\leq n]}$ was introduced by Shinohara [22] as a rich hypothesis space inferable in the limit from positive examples. On refutable inferability, Mukouchi and Arikawa [15,17] have obtained the following theorem:

Theorem 10 (Mukouchi and Arikawa [15,17]). *Let $n \in N$.*

The class $\mathcal{LBL}^{[\leq n]}$ is refutably inferable from complete examples.

We can show the following lemma in a similar way to Mukouchi and Arikawa [15,17].

Lemma 4. *Let $n \in N$.*

The class $\mathcal{LBL}^{[\leq n]}$ satisfies the condition (C5"), that is, for every distance d, every $k \in N$ and every $L \notin [\mathcal{LBL}^{[\leq n]}]^{(d,k)}$, there is a pair of definite finite tell-tale sets of L within the class $[\mathcal{LBL}^{[\leq n]}]^{(d,k)}$.

By Theorems 5, 7 and 10, Corollaries 2 and 5 and Lemma 4, we have the following theorem:

Theorem 11. *Let $n \in N$.*

(1) The class $\mathcal{LBL}^{[\leq n]}$ is weak neighbor-refutably inferable from complete examples.

(2) The class $\mathcal{LBL}^{[\leq n]}$ is neighbor-refutably inferable from complete examples.

(3) The class $\mathcal{LBL}^{[\leq n]}$ is neighborly inferable from complete examples.

5   Concluding Remarks

We have introduced a notion of a k-neighbor language and formalized k-neighbor refutability and inferability of a language class from complete examples. Then we presented some sufficient and necessary conditions for a language class. We also showed that the language class definable by the length-bounded EFSs with at most n axioms is k-neighbor-refutably inferable from complete examples.

As a future work, we should clarify the relations between weak k-neighbor-refutable inferability, k'-neighbor-refutable inferability and k''-neighbor inferability for distinct $k, k', k'' \in N$. As another future investigation, we can consider neighbor inferability from *positive examples* and neighbor *finite* inferability from positive examples as well as from complete examples. We will discuss the issue somewhere.

References

1. D. Angluin: *Finding patterns common to a set of strings*, Journal of Computer and System Sciences **21** (1980) 46–62.
2. D. Angluin: *Inductive inference of formal languages from positive data*, Information and Control **45** (1980) 117–135.
3. S. Arikawa: *Elementary formal systems and formal languages – simple formal systems*, Memoirs of Faculty of Science, Kyushu University, Series A, Math. **24** (1970) 47–75.
4. S. Arikawa, T. Shinohara and A. Yamamoto: *Elementary formal systems as a unifying framework for language learning*, in Proceedings of the Second Annual ACM Workshop on Computational Learning Theory (1989) 312–327.
5. S. Arikawa, T. Shinohara and A. Yamamoto: *Learning elementary formal systems*, Theoretical Computer Science **95** (1992) 97–113.
6. M. Blum: *A machine independent theory of the complexity of the recursive functions*, Journal of the Association for Computing Machinery **14**(2) (1967) 322–336.
7. J. Case and S. Jain: *Synthesizing learners tolerant computable noisy data*, in Proceedings of the Ninth International Conference on Algorithmic Learning Theory, Lecture Notes in Artificial Intelligence **1501** (1998) 205–219.
8. E.M. Gold: *Language identification in the limit*, Information and Control **10** (1967) 447–474.
9. S. Jain: *Program synthesis in the presence of infinite number of inaccuracies*, Journal of Computer and System Sciences **53**(3) (1996) 583–591.
10. S. Jain: *Learning with refutation*, Journal of Computer and System Sciences **57**(3) (1998) 356–365.
11. S. Kobayashi and T. Yokomori: *On approximately identifying concept classes in the limit*, in Proceedings of the Sixth International Workshop on Algorithmic Learning Theory, Lecture Notes in Artificial Intelligence **997** (1995) 298–312.

12. S. Lange and T. Zeugmann: *Types of monotonic language learning and their characterization*, in Proceedings of the Fifth Annual ACM Workshop on Computational Learning Theory (1992) 377–390.
13. S. Lange and P. Watson: *Machine discovery in the presence of incomplete or ambiguous data*, in Proceedings of the Fifth International Workshop on Algorithmic Learning Theory, Lecture Notes in Artificial Intelligence **872** (1994) 438–452.
14. Y. Mukouchi: *Characterization of finite identification*, in Proceedings of the Third International Workshop on Analogical and Inductive Inference, Lecture Notes in Artificial Intelligence **642** (1992) 260–267.
15. Y. Mukouchi and S. Arikawa: *Inductive inference machines that can refute hypothesis spaces*, in Proceedings of the Fourth International Workshop on Algorithmic Learning Theory, Lecture Notes in Artificial Intelligence **744** (1993) 123–136.
16. Y. Mukouchi: *Inductive inference of an approximate concept from positive data*, in Proceedings of the Fifth International Workshop on Algorithmic Learning Theory, Lecture Notes in Artificial Intelligence **872** (1994) 484–499.
17. Y. Mukouchi and S. Arikawa: *Towards a mathematical theory of machine discovery from facts*, Theoretical Computer Science **137** (1995) 53–84.
18. Y. Mukouchi: *Refutable inference with a restricted target class*, Mathematica Japonica **49**(3) (1999) 363–372.
19. Y. Mukouchi and M. Sato: *Language learning with a neighbor system*, in Proceedings of the Third International Conference on Discovery Science, Lecture Notes in Artificial Intelligence **1967** (2000) 183–196.
20. H. Rogers Jr.: "Theory of recursive functions and effective computability," McGraw-Hill, 1967.
21. M. Sato: *Inductive inference of formal languages*, Bulletin of Informatics and Cybernetics **27**(1) (1995) 85–106.
22. T. Shinohara: *Rich classes inferable from positive data: length-bounded elementary formal systems*, Information and Computation **108** (1994) 175–186.
23. R.M. Smullyan: "Theory of formal systems," Princeton University Press, 1961.
24. F. Stephan: *Noisy inference and oracles*, Theoretical Computer Science **185** (1997) 129–157.
25. A. Yamamoto: *Procedural semantics and negative information of elementary formal system*, Journal of Logic Programming **13**(4) (1992) 89–98.

Learning Recursive Functions Refutably[*]

Sanjay Jain[1][**], Efim Kinber[2], Rolf Wiehagen[3], and Thomas Zeugmann[4]

[1] School of Computing, National University of Singapore, Singapore 119260
sanjay@comp.nus.edu.sg
[2] Department of Computer Science, Sacred Heart University, Fairfield, CT
06432-1000, U.S.A.
kinbere@sacredheart.edu
[3] Department of Computer Science, University of Kaiserslautern, PO Box 3049,
67653 Kaiserslautern, Germany
wiehagen@informatik.uni-kl.de
[4] Institut für Theoretische Informatik, Med. Universität zu Lübeck, Wallstraße 40,
23560 Lübeck, Germany
thomas@tcs.mu-luebeck.de

Abstract. Learning of recursive functions refutably means that for *every* recursive function, the learning machine has either to learn this function or to refute it, i.e., to signal that it is not able to learn it. Three modi of making precise the notion of refuting are considered. We show that the corresponding types of learning refutably are of strictly increasing power, where already the most stringent of them turns out to be of remarkable topological and algorithmical richness. All these types are closed under union, though in different strengths. Also, these types are shown to be different with respect to their intrinsic complexity; two of them do not contain function classes that are "most difficult" to learn, while the third one does. Moreover, we present characterizations for these types of learning refutably. Some of these characterizations make clear where the refuting ability of the corresponding learning machines comes from and how it can be realized, in general.

For learning with anomalies refutably, we show that several results from standard learning without refutation stand refutably. Then we derive hierarchies for refutable learning. Finally, we show that stricter refutability constraints cannot be traded for more liberal learning criteria.

1 Introduction

The basic scenario in learning theory informally consists in that a learning machine has to learn some unknown object based on certain information, that is the machine creates one or more hypotheses which eventually converge to a more or less correct and complete description of the object. In learning *refutably* the main goal is more involved. Here, for *every* object from a given universe, the

---

[*] A full version of this paper is available as technical report (cf. [17]).
[**] Supported in part by NUS grant number RP3992710.

N. Abe, R. Khardon, and T. Zeugmann (Eds.): ALT 2001, LNAI 2225, pp. 283–298, 2001.
© Springer-Verlag Berlin Heidelberg 2001

learning machine has either to learn the object or to refute it, that is to "signal" if it is incapable to learn this object. This approach is philosophically motivated by Popper's logic of scientific discovery, (testability, falsifyability, refutability of scientific hypotheses), see [31,24]. Moreover, this approach has also some rather practical implications. If the learning machine signals its inability to learn a certain object, then one can react upon this inability, by modifying the machine, by changing the hypothesis space, or by weakening the learning requirements.

A crucial point of learning refutably is to formally define how the machine is allowed or required to refute a non-learnable object. Mukouchi and Arikawa [29], required refuting to be done in a "one shot" manner, i.e., if after some finite amount of time, the machine concludes that it cannot learn the target object, then it outputs a special "refuting symbol" and stops the learning process forever. Two weaker possibilities of refuting are based on the following observation. Suppose that at some time, the machine feels unable to learn the target object and outputs the refuting symbol. Nevertheless, this time the machine keeps trying to learn the target. It may happen that the information it further receives contains new evidence causing it to change its mind about its inability to learn the object. This process of "alternations" can repeat. It may end in learning the object. Or it may end in refuting it by never revising the machine's belief that it cannot learn the object, i.e., by forever outputting the refuting symbol from some point on. Finally, there may be infinitely many such alternations between trying to learn and believing that this is impossible. In our paper, we will allow and study all three of these modes of learning refutably.

Our universe is the class $\mathcal{R}$ of all recursive functions. The basic learning criterion used is **Ex**, learning in the limit (cf. Definition 1). We study the following types of learning refutably:

RefEx, where refuting a non-learnable function takes place in the *one shot* manner described above (cf. Definition 5).

WRefEx, where both learning and refuting are *limiting* processes, that is on every function from the universe, the learning machine converges either to a correct hypothesis for this function or to the refuting symbol, see Definition 6, (**W** stands for "weak").

RelEx, where a function is considered to be refuted if the learner outputs the refuting symbol *infinitely often* on this function (cf. Definition 7). **Rel** stands for "reliable", since **RelEx** coincides with reliable learning (cf. Proposition 1).

Note that for all types of learning refutably, every function from $\mathcal{R}$ is either learned or refuted by every machine learning refutably. So, it can *not* happen that such a machine converges to an *incorrect* hypothesis (cf. Correctness Lemma).

We show that the types of learning refutably are of strictly increasing power (cf. Theorem 3). Already the most stringent of them, **RefEx**, is of remarkable topological and algorithmical richness (cf. Proposition 3 and Corollary 9). All of these learning types are closed under union, Proposition 5, where **RefEx** and **WRefEx**, on the one hand, and **RelEx**, on the other hand, do not behave completely analogous. Such a difference can also be exhibited with respect to the intrinsic complexity; actually, both **RefEx** and **WRefEx** do not contain function classes that are "most difficult" to learn, while **RelEx** does contain such classes (cf. Theorems 6 and 7). We also present characterizations for our types of learning refutably. Some of these characterizations make it clear where the refuting ability of the corresponding learning machines comes from and how it can be realized, in general (cf. Theorems 12 and 13).

Besides pure **Ex**-learning refutably we also consider **Ex**-learning and **Bc**-learning with *anomalies* refutably (cf. Definitions 18 and 19). We show that many results from learning without refutation stand refutably, see Theorems 15 and 21. Then we derive several hierarchies for refutable learning, thereby solving an open problem from [22], see Corollaries 16 and 22. Finally, we show that, in general, one cannot trade a stricter refutability constraint for a more liberal learning criterion (cf. Corollary 25 and Theorem 26).

Since the pioneering paper [29] learning with refutation has attracted much attention (cf. [30,24,16,28,19,15]).

2   Notation and Preliminaries

Unspecified notations follow [33]. $\mathbb{N}$ denotes the set of natural numbers. We write $\emptyset$ for the empty set and card(S) for the cardinality of the set S. The minimum and maximum of a set S are denoted by $\min(S)$ and $\max(S)$, respectively.

η, with or without decorations ranges over partial functions. If η_1 and η_2 are both undefined on input x, then, we take $\eta_1(x) = \eta_2(x)$. We say that $\eta_1 \subseteq \eta_2$ iff for all x in the domain of η_1, $\eta_1(x) = \eta_2(x)$. We let dom(η) and rng(η), respectively, denote the domain and range of the partial function η. $\eta(x)\downarrow$ and $\eta(x) =\downarrow$ both denote that $\eta(x)$ is defined and $\eta(x)\uparrow$ as well as $\eta(x) =\uparrow$ stand for $\eta(x)$ is undefined. For any partial functions η, η' and $a \in \mathbb{N}$, we write $\eta =^a \eta'$ and $\eta =^* \eta'$ iff card($\{x \mid \eta(x) \neq \eta'(x)\}$) $\leq a$ and card($\{x \mid \eta(x) \neq \eta'(x)\}$) $< \infty$, respectively. We identify a partial function η with its graph $\{(x, \eta(x)) \mid x \in \mathrm{dom}(\eta)\}$.

For $r \in \mathbb{N}$, the r-extension of η denotes the function f defined as $f(x) = \eta(x)$, if $x \in \mathrm{dom}(\eta)$ and $f(x) = r$, otherwise.

$\mathcal{R}$ denotes the class of all *recursive* functions over $\mathbb{N}$. Furthermore, we set $\mathcal{R}_{0,1} = \{f \mid f \in \mathcal{R} \,\&\, \mathrm{rng}(f) \subseteq \{0, 1\}\}$. $\mathcal{C}$ and $\mathcal{S}$, with or without decorations range over subsets of $\mathcal{R}$. For $\mathcal{C} \subseteq \mathcal{R}$, we let $\overline{\mathcal{C}}$ denote $\mathcal{R} \setminus \mathcal{C}$. By $\mathcal{P}$ we denote the class of all *partial recursive* functions over $\mathbb{N}$. f, g, h and F, with or without decorations range over recursive functions unless otherwise specified.

A computable numbering (or just numbering) is a partial recursive function of two arguments. For a numbering $\psi(\cdot, \cdot)$, we use ψ_i to denote the function $\lambda x.\psi(i, x)$, i.e., ψ_i is the function computed by the program i in the numbering ψ. ψ and ϱ range over numberings. $\mathcal{P}_\psi$ denotes the set of partial recursive functions in the numbering ψ, i.e., $\mathcal{P}_\psi = \{\psi_i \mid i \in \mathbb{N}\}$ and $\mathcal{R}_\psi = \{\psi_i \mid i \in \mathbb{N} \,\&\, \psi_i \in \mathcal{R}\}$. That is, $\mathcal{R}_\psi$ stands for the set of all recursive functions in the numbering ψ. A numbering ψ is called one-to-one iff $\psi_i \neq \psi_j$ for any distinct i, j. By φ we denote a *fixed* acceptable programming system (cf. [33]). We write φ_i for the partial recursive function computed by program i in the φ-system. By Φ we denote any Blum [6] complexity measure associated with φ. We assume without loss of generality that $\Phi_i(x) \geq x$, for all i, x.

$\mathcal{C} \subseteq \mathcal{R}$ is said to be *recursively enumerable* (abbr. r.e.) iff there is an r.e. set X such that $\mathcal{C} = \{\varphi_i \mid i \in X\}$. For any r.e. class $\mathcal{C} \neq \emptyset$, there is an $f \in \mathcal{R}$ such that $\mathcal{C} = \{\varphi_{f(i)} \mid i \in \mathbb{N}\}$.

A function g is called *accumulation point* of a class $\mathcal{C} \subseteq \mathcal{R}$ iff $g \in \mathcal{R}$ and $(\forall n \in \mathbb{N})(\exists f \in \mathcal{C})[(\forall x \leq n)[g(x) = f(x)] \;\&\; f \neq g]$. Note that g may or may not belong to $\mathcal{C}$. For $\mathcal{C} \subseteq \mathcal{R}$, we let $\mathrm{Acc}(\mathcal{C}) = \{g \mid g \text{ is an accumulation point of } \mathcal{C}\}$.

The quantifier $\forall^\infty$ stands for all but finitely many. The following function and class are considered below. Zero is the everywhere 0 function, and $FINSUP = \{f \mid f \in \mathcal{R} \;\&\; (\forall^\infty x)[f(x) = 0]\}$ is the class of all functions of finite support.

2.1 Function Learning

We assume that the graph of a function is fed to a machine in canonical order. For a partial function η with $\eta(x)\!\downarrow$ for all $x < n$, we write $\eta[n]$ for the set $\{(x, \eta(x)) \mid x < n\}$, the finite initial segment of η of length n. We set $\mathrm{SEG} = \{f[n] \mid f \in \mathcal{R} \;\&\; n \in \mathbb{N}\}$ and $\mathrm{SEG}_{0,1} = \{f[n] \mid f \in \mathcal{R}_{0,1} \;\&\; n \in \mathbb{N}\}$. We let σ, τ and γ, with or without decorations range over SEG. Λ is the empty segment. We assume a computable ordering of the elements of SEG.

Let $|\sigma|$ denote the length of σ. Thus, $|f[n]| = n$, for every total function f and all $n \in \mathbb{N}$. If $|\sigma| \geq n$, then we let $\sigma[n]$ denote $\{(x, \sigma(x)) \mid x < n\}$. An *inductive inference machine* (IIM) $\mathbf{M}$ is an algorithmic device that computes a total mapping from SEG into $\mathbb{N}$ (cf. [13]). We say that $\mathbf{M}(f)$ converges to i (written: $\mathbf{M}(f)\!\downarrow = i$) iff $(\forall^\infty n)[\mathbf{M}(f[n]) = i]$; $\mathbf{M}(f)$ is undefined if no such i exists. Now, we define several criteria of function learning.

Definition 1 ([13,5,10]). Let $a \in \mathbb{N} \cup \{*\}$, let $f \in \mathcal{R}$ and let $\mathbf{M}$ be an IIM.

(a) $\mathbf{M}$ **$\mathbf{Ex}^a$**-*learns* f (abbr. $f \in \mathbf{Ex}^a(\mathbf{M})$) iff there is an i with $\mathbf{M}(f)\!\downarrow = i$ and $\varphi_i =^a f$.

(b) $\mathbf{M}$ **$\mathbf{Ex}^a$**-*learns* $\mathcal{C}$ iff $\mathbf{M}$ **$\mathbf{Ex}^a$**-learns each $f \in \mathcal{C}$.

(c) $\mathbf{Ex}^a = \{\mathcal{C} \subseteq \mathcal{R} \mid (\exists \mathbf{M})[\mathcal{C} \subseteq \mathbf{Ex}^a(\mathbf{M})]\}$.

Note that for $a = 0$ we omit the upper index, i.e., we set $\mathbf{Ex} = \mathbf{Ex}^0$.

By the definition of convergence, only finitely many data of f were seen by an IIM up to the (unknown) point of convergence. Hence, some learning must have taken place. Thus, we use *identify*, *learn* and *infer* interchangeably.

Definition 2 ([2,10]). Let $a \in \mathbb{N} \cup \{*\}$, let $f \in \mathcal{R}$ and let $\mathbf{M}$ be an IIM.

(a) $\mathbf{M}$ **$\mathbf{Bc}^a$**-*learns* f (written: $f \in \mathbf{Bc}^a(\mathbf{M})$) iff $(\forall^\infty n)[\varphi_{\mathbf{M}(f[n])} =^a f]$.

(b) $\mathbf{M}$ **$\mathbf{Bc}^a$**-*learns* $\mathcal{C}$ iff $\mathbf{M}$ **$\mathbf{Bc}^a$**-learns each $f \in \mathcal{C}$.

(c) $\mathbf{Bc}^a = \{\mathcal{C} \subseteq \mathcal{R} \mid (\exists \mathbf{M})[\mathcal{C} \subseteq \mathbf{Bc}^a(\mathbf{M})]\}$.

We set $\mathbf{Bc} = \mathbf{Bc}^0$. Harrington [10] showed that $\mathcal{R} \in \mathbf{Bc}^*$. Thus, we shall consider mainly $\mathbf{Bc}^a$ for $a \in \mathbb{N}$ in the following.

Definition 3 (Minicozzi [27], Blum and Blum [5]). Let $\mathbf{M}$ be an IIM.

(a) $\mathbf{M}$ is *reliable* iff for all $f \in \mathcal{R}$, $\mathbf{M}(f)\downarrow \Rightarrow \mathbf{M}$ **Ex**-identifies f.
(b) $\mathbf{M}$ **RelEx**-*infers* $\mathcal{C}$ (written: $\mathcal{C} \subseteq \mathbf{RelEx(M)}$) iff $\mathbf{M}$ is reliable and $\mathbf{M}$ **Ex**-infers $\mathcal{C}$.
(c) $\mathbf{RelEx} = \{\mathcal{C} \subseteq \mathcal{R} \mid (\exists \mathbf{M})[\mathbf{M} \ \mathbf{RelEx}\text{-infers } \mathcal{C}]\}$.

Thus, a machine is reliable if it does not converge on functions it fails to identify. For references on reliable learning besides [27,5], see [21,14,22,8].

Definition 4. NUM $= \{\mathcal{C} \mid (\exists \mathcal{C}' \mid \mathcal{C} \subseteq \mathcal{C}' \subseteq \mathcal{R})[\mathcal{C}' \text{ is recursively enumerable}]\}$.

Inductive inference within **NUM** has been studied, e.g. in [13,3]. For the general theory of learning recursive functions, see [1,5,10,11,23,18].

2.2   Learning Refutably

Next, we introduce learning with refutation. We consider three versions of refutation based on how the machine is required to refute a function. First we extend the definition of IIM by allowing it to output a special symbol $\perp$. Thus, now an IIM maps SEG to $\mathbb{N} \cup \{\perp\}$. Convergence of an IIM on a function is defined as before (but now a machine may converge to a number $i \in \mathbb{N}$ or to $\perp$).

Definition 5. Let $\mathbf{M}$ be an IIM. $\mathbf{M}$ **RefEx**-*identifies* a class $\mathcal{C}$ (written: $\mathcal{C} \subseteq$ **RefEx(M)**) iff the following conditions are satisfied.

(a) $\mathcal{C} \subseteq \mathbf{Ex(M)}$.
(b) For all $f \in \mathbf{Ex(M)}$, for all n, $\mathbf{M}(f[n]) \neq \perp$.
(c) For all $f \in \mathcal{R}$ such that $f \notin \mathbf{Ex(M)}$, there exists an $n \in \mathbb{N}$ such that $(\forall m < n)[\mathbf{M}(f[m]) \neq \perp]$ and $(\forall m \geq n)[\mathbf{M}(f[m]) = \perp]$.

The following generalization of **RefEx** places less restrictive constraint on how the machine refutes a function. **WRef** below stands for weak refutation.

Definition 6. Let $\mathbf{M}$ be an IIM. $\mathbf{M}$ **WRefEx**-*learns* a class $\mathcal{C}$ (written: $\mathcal{C} \subseteq$ **WRefEx(M)**) iff the following conditions are satisfied.

(a) $\mathcal{C} \subseteq \mathbf{Ex(M)}$.
(b) For all $f \in \mathcal{R}$ such that $f \notin \mathbf{Ex(M)}$, $\mathbf{M}(f)\downarrow = \perp$.

For weakly refuting a function f, an IIM just needs to converge to $\perp$. Before convergence, it may change its mind finitely often whether or not to refute f. Another way an IIM may refute a function f is to output $\perp$ on f infinitely often.

Definition 7. Let $\mathbf{M}$ be an IIM. $\mathbf{M}$ **RelEx**$'$-*identifies* a class $\mathcal{C}$ (written: $\mathcal{C} \subseteq$ **RelEx**$'$**(M)**) iff the following conditions are satisfied.

(a) $\mathcal{C} \subseteq \mathbf{Ex(M)}$.

(b) For all $f \in \mathcal{R}$ such that $f \notin \mathbf{Ex}(\mathbf{M})$, there exists infinitely many $n \in \mathbb{N}$ such that $\mathbf{M}(f[n]) = \bot$.

Proposition 1. RelEx = RelEx$'$.

As it follows from their definitions, for any of the learning types **RefEx**, **WRefEx** and **RelEx**, we get that any $f \in \mathcal{R}$ has either to be learned or to be refuted. This is made formally precise by the following Correctness Lemma.

Lemma 1 (*Correctness Lemma*). *Let $\mathbf{I} \in \{\mathbf{RefEx}, \mathbf{WRefEx}, \mathbf{RelEx}\}$. For any $\mathcal{C} \subseteq \mathcal{R}$, any IIM $\mathbf{M}$ with $\mathcal{C} \subseteq \mathbf{I}(\mathbf{M})$, and any $f \in \mathcal{R}$, if $\mathbf{M}(f)\!\downarrow \in \mathbb{N}$, then $\varphi_{\mathbf{M}(f)} = f$.*

3   Ex-Learning Refutably

We first derive several properties of the defined types of learning refutably. We then relate these types by their so-called intrinsic complexity. Finally, we present several characterizations for refutable learnability.

3.1   Properties and Relations

First, we exhibit some properties of refutably learnable classes. These properties imply that the corresponding learning types are of strictly increasing power. Already the most stringent of these types, **RefEx**, is of surprising richness. In particular, every class from **RefEx** can be enriched by including all of its accumulation points. This is not possible for the classes from **WRefEx** and **RelEx**, as it follows from the proof of Theorem 3.

Proposition 2. *For all $\mathcal{C} \in \mathbf{RefEx}$, $\mathcal{C} \cup \mathrm{Acc}(\mathcal{C}) \in \mathbf{RefEx}$.*

Proof. Suppose $\mathcal{C} \in \mathbf{RefEx}$ as witnessed by some total IIM $\mathbf{M}$. Let $g \in \mathcal{R}$ be an accumulation point of $\mathcal{C}$. We claim that $\mathbf{M}$ must **Ex**-identify g. Assume to the contrary that for some n, $\mathbf{M}(g[n]) = \bot$. Then, by the definition of accumulation point, there is a function $f \in \mathcal{C}$ such that $g[n] \subseteq f$. Hence $\mathbf{M}(f[n]) = \bot$, too, a contradiction to $\mathbf{M}$ **RefEx**-identifying $\mathcal{C}$. ∎

The next proposition shows that **RefEx** contains "topologically rich", namely *non-discrete* classes, i.e. classes which contain accumulation points. Thus, **RefEx** is "richer" than **Ex**-learning without any mind change, since any class being learnable in that latter sense may not contain any of its accumulation points (cf. [25]). More precisely, **RefEx** and **Ex**-learning without mind changes are set-theoretically *incomparable*; the missing direction follows from Theorem 14 below.

Proposition 3. RefEx *contains non-discrete classes.*

The following proposition establishes some bound on the topological richness of the classes from **WRefEx**.

Definition 8. A class $\mathcal{C} \subseteq \mathcal{R}$ is called *initially complete* iff for every $\sigma \in$ SEG, there is a function $f \in \mathcal{C}$ such that $\sigma \subseteq f$.

Proposition 4. WRefEx *does not contain any initially complete class.*

The following result is needed for proving Theorem 3 below.

Lemma 2. $\mathcal{C} = \{f \in \mathcal{R} \mid (\forall x \in \mathbb{N})[f(x) \neq 0]\} \notin \mathbf{Ex}$.

We are now ready to prove that **RefEx**, **WRefEx** and **RelEx**, respectively, are of strictly increasing power.

Theorem 3. RefEx $\subset$ **WRefEx** $\subset$ **RelEx**.

Proof. **RefEx** $\subseteq$ **WRefEx** $\subseteq$ **RelEx** by their definitions and Proposition 1.

We first show that **WRefEx** $\setminus$ **RefEx** $\neq \emptyset$. For that purpose, we define $\mathrm{SEG}^+ = \{f[n] \mid f \in \mathcal{R} \,\&\, n \in \mathbb{N} \,\&\, (\forall x \in \mathbb{N})[f(x) \neq 0]\}$. Let $\mathcal{C} = \{0\text{-ext}(\sigma) \mid \sigma \in \mathrm{SEG}^+\}$. Then $\mathrm{Acc}(\mathcal{C}) = \{f \in \mathcal{R} \mid (\forall x \in \mathbb{N})[f(x) \neq 0]\}$, which is not in **Ex**, by Lemma 2. Thus, $\mathcal{C} \cup \mathrm{Acc}(\mathcal{C}) \notin \mathbf{Ex}$, and hence, $\mathcal{C} \notin \mathbf{RefEx}$, by Proposition 2.

In order to show that $\mathcal{C} \in \mathbf{WRefEx}$, let prog $\in \mathcal{R}$ be a recursive function such that for any $\sigma \in \mathrm{SEG}^+$, $\mathrm{prog}(\sigma)$ is a φ-program for $0\text{-ext}(\sigma)$. Let **M** be defined as follows.

$$\mathbf{M}(f[n]) = \begin{cases} \perp, & \text{if } f[n] \in \mathrm{SEG}^+; \\ \mathrm{prog}(\sigma), & \text{if } 0\text{-ext}(f[n]) = 0\text{-ext}(\sigma), \text{ for some } \sigma \in \mathrm{SEG}^+; \\ \perp, & \text{otherwise.} \end{cases}$$

It is easy to verify that **M** **WRefEx**-identifies $\mathcal{C}$.

We now show that **RelEx** $\setminus$ **WRefEx** $\neq \emptyset$. *FINSUP* is initially complete and *FINSUP* $\in$ **NUM**. Since **NUM** $\subseteq$ **RelEx**, see [27], we have that *FINSUP* $\in$ **RelEx**. On the other hand, *FINSUP* $\notin$ **WRefEx** by Proposition 4.   ∎

As a consequence from the proof of Theorem 3, we can derive that the types **RefEx**, **WRefEx** and **RelEx** already differ on *recursively enumerable* classes.

Corollary 4. RefEx $\cap$ **NUM** $\subset$ **WRefEx** $\cap$ **NUM** $\subset$ **RelEx** $\cap$ **NUM**.

We next point out that all the types of learning refutably share a pretty rare, but desirable property, namely to be closed under union.

Proposition 5. RefEx, WRefEx *and* **RelEx** *are closed under finite union.*

RelEx is even closed under the union of any effectively given *infinite* sequence of classes (cf. [27]). The latter is not true for both **RefEx** and **WRefEx**, as it can be seen by shattering the class *FINSUP* into its subclasses of *one* element each.

3.2   Intrinsic Complexity

There is another field where **RefEx** and **WRefEx**, on the one hand, and **RelEx**, on the other hand, behave differently, namely that of intrinsic complexity. The intrinsic complexity compares the difficulty of learning by using some reducibility notion, see [12]. With every reducibility notion comes a notion of completeness. A function class is complete for some learning type I, if this class is "most difficult" to learn among all the classes from I. As we show, **RefEx** and **WRefEx** do not contain such complete classes, while **RelEx** does.

Definition 9. A sequence $P = p_0, p_1, \ldots$ of natural numbers is called **Ex**-*admissible* for $f \in \mathcal{R}$ iff P converges to a program p for f.

Definition 10 (Rogers [33]). A *recursive operator* is an effective total mapping, Θ, from (possibly partial) functions to (possibly partial) functions such that:
(a) For all functions η, η', if $\eta \subseteq \eta'$ then $\Theta(\eta) \subseteq \Theta(\eta')$.
(b) For all η, if $(x, y) \in \Theta(\eta)$, then there is a finite function $\alpha \subseteq \eta$ such that $(x, y) \in \Theta(\alpha)$.
(c) For all finite functions α, one can effectively enumerate (in α) all $(x, y) \in \Theta(\alpha)$.

For each recursive operator Θ, we can effectively find a recursive operator Θ' such that

(d) for each finite function α, $\Theta'(\alpha)$ is finite, and its canonical index can be effectively determined from α, and
(e) for all total functions f, $\Theta'(f) = \Theta(f)$.

This allows us to get a nice effective sequence of recursive operators.

Proposition 6. *There exists an effective enumeration, $\Theta_0, \Theta_1, \cdots$ of recursive operators satisfying condition* (d) *above such that, for all recursive operators Θ, there exists an $i \in \mathbb{N}$ satisfying $\Theta(f) = \Theta_i(f)$ for all total functions f.*

Definition 11 (Freivalds et al. [12]). Let $\mathcal{S}, \mathcal{C} \in$ **Ex**. Then $\mathcal{S}$ is called **Ex**-*reducible* to $\mathcal{C}$ (written: $\mathcal{S} \leq_{\textbf{Ex}} \mathcal{C}$) iff there exist two recursive operators Θ and Ξ such that for all $f \in \mathcal{S}$,
(a) $\Theta(f) \in \mathcal{C}$,
(b) for any **Ex**-admissible sequence P for $\Theta(f)$, $\Xi(P)$ is **Ex**-admissible for f.

If $\mathcal{S}$ is **Ex**-reducible to $\mathcal{C}$, then $\mathcal{C}$ is at least as difficult to **Ex**-learn as $\mathcal{S}$ is. Indeed, if **M Ex**-learns $\mathcal{C}$, then $\mathcal{S}$ is **Ex**-learnable by an IIM that, on any function $f \in \mathcal{S}$, outputs $\Xi(\mathbf{M}(\Theta(f)))$.

Definition 12. Let **I** be a learning type and $\mathcal{C} \subseteq \mathcal{R}$. $\mathcal{C}$ is called **Ex**-*complete* in **I** iff $\mathcal{C} \in$ **I**, and for all $\mathcal{S} \in$ **I**, $\mathcal{S} \leq_{\textbf{Ex}} \mathcal{C}$.

Theorem 5. *Let $\mathcal{C} \in$ **WRefEx**. Then there exists a class $\mathcal{S} \in$ **RefEx** such that $\mathcal{S} \not\leq_{\textbf{Ex}} \mathcal{C}$.*

Theorem 5 immediately yields the following result.

Theorem 6. (1) *There is no **Ex**-complete class in **RefEx**.*
    (2) *There is no **Ex**-complete class in **WRefEx**.*

In contrast to Theorem 6, **RelEx** contains an **Ex**-complete class.

Theorem 7. *There is an **Ex**-complete class in **RelEx**.*

3.3   Characterizations

We present several characterizations for **RefEx**, **WRefEx** and **RelEx**. The first group of characterizations relates refutable learning to the established concept of *classification*. The main goal in recursion theoretic classification can be described as follows. Let be given some finite (or even infinite) family of function classes. Then, for an arbitrary function from the union of all these classes, one has to find out which of these classes the corresponding function belongs to, see [4,37,35,34,9]. What we need in our characterization theorems below will be classification where only *two* classes are involved in the classification process, more exactly, a class together with its complement; and semi-classification which is some weakening of classification. Note that the corresponding characterizations using these kinds of classification are in a sense close to the definitions of learning refutably. Nevertheless, these characterizations are useful in that their characteristic conditions are easily testable, i.e. they allow to check, whether or not a given class is learnable with refutation.

Let $\mathcal{R}_{0,?}$ be the class of all total computable functions mapping $\mathbb{N}$ into $\{0,?\}$.

Definition 13. $\mathcal{S} \subseteq \mathcal{R}$ is *finitely semi-classifiable* iff there is $c \in \mathcal{R}_{0,?}$ such that
(a) for every $f \in \mathcal{S}$, there is an $n \in \mathbb{N}$ such that $c(f[n]) = 0$,
(b) for every $f \in \overline{\mathcal{S}}$ and for all $n \in \mathbb{N}$, $c(f[n]) = ?$.

Intuitively, a class $\mathcal{S} \subseteq \mathcal{R}$ is finitely semi-classifiable if for every $f \in \mathcal{S}$ after some finite amount of time one finds out that $f \in \mathcal{S}$, whereas for every $f \in \overline{\mathcal{S}}$, one finds out "nothing".

Theorem 8. *For any* $\mathcal{C} \subseteq \mathcal{R}$, $\mathcal{C} \in$ **RefEx** *iff* $\mathcal{C}$ *is contained in some class* $\mathcal{S} \in$ **Ex** *such that* $\overline{\mathcal{S}}$ *is finitely semi-classifiable.*

Proof. Necessity. Suppose $\mathcal{C} \in$ **RefEx** as witnessed by some total IIM **M**. Let $\mathcal{S} = $ **Ex**(**M**). Clearly, $\mathcal{C} \subseteq \mathcal{S}$. Furthermore, (i) for any $f \in \mathcal{S}$ and any $n \in \mathbb{N}$, $\mathbf{M}(f[n]) \neq \bot$, and (ii) for any $f \in \overline{\mathcal{S}}$, there is $n \in \mathbb{N}$ such that $\mathbf{M}(f[n]) = \bot$.

Now define c as follows.

$$c(f[n]) = \begin{cases} 0, & \text{if } \mathbf{M}(f[n]) = \bot; \\ ?, & \text{if } \mathbf{M}(f[n]) \neq \bot. \end{cases}$$

Clearly, $c \in \mathcal{R}_{0,?}$ and $\overline{\mathcal{S}}$ is finitely semi-classifiable by c.

Sufficiency. Suppose $\mathcal{C} \subseteq \mathcal{S} \subseteq$ **Ex**(**M**), and $\overline{\mathcal{S}}$ is finitely semi-classifiable by some $c \in \mathcal{R}_{0,?}$. Now define **M**$'$ as follows.

$$\mathbf{M}'(f[n]) = \begin{cases} \mathbf{M}(f[n]), & \text{if } c(f[n]) = ?; \\ \bot, & \text{if } c(f[x]) = 0, \text{ for some } x \leq n. \end{cases}$$

It is easy to verify that **M**$'$ **RefEx**-identifies $\mathcal{C}$.   ∎

We can apply the characterization of **RefEx** above in order to show that **RefEx** contains "non-trivial" classes. Therefore, let

$$\mathcal{C} = \{f \mid f \in \mathcal{R} \ \& \ \varphi_{f(0)} = f \ \& \ (\forall x \in \mathbb{N})[\Phi_{f(0)}(x) \leq f(x+1)]\}.$$

Clearly, $\mathcal{C} \in \mathbf{Ex}$ and $\overline{\mathcal{C}}$ is finitely semi-classifiable. Hence, by Theorem 8, $\mathcal{C}$ is **RefEx**-learnable. $\mathcal{C} \notin \mathbf{NUM}$ was shown in [38], Theorem 4.2. Hence, we get the following corollary illustrating that **RefEx** contains "algorithmically rich" classes, that is classes being not contained in any recursively enumerable class.

Corollary 9. RefEx \ NUM $\neq \emptyset$.

We now characterize **WRefEx**. Therefore, we need the special case of classification where the classes under consideration form a partition of $\mathcal{R}$.

Definition 14 ([37]). (1) Let $\mathcal{C}, \mathcal{S} \subseteq \mathcal{R}$, where $\mathcal{C} \cap \mathcal{S} = \emptyset$. $(\mathcal{C}, \mathcal{S})$ is called *classifiable* iff there is $c \in \mathcal{R}_{0,1}$ such that for any $f \in \mathcal{C}$ and for almost all $n \in \mathbb{N}$, $c(f[n]) = 0$; and for any $f \in \mathcal{S}$ and for almost all $n \in \mathbb{N}$, $c(f[n]) = 1$.

(2) A class $\mathcal{C} \subseteq \mathcal{R}$ is called *classifiable* iff $(\mathcal{C}, \overline{\mathcal{C}})$ is classifiable.

Theorem 10. *For any $\mathcal{C} \subseteq \mathcal{R}$, $\mathcal{C} \in \mathbf{WRefEx}$ iff $\mathcal{C} \subseteq \mathcal{S}$ for a classifiable class $\mathcal{S} \in \mathbf{Ex}$.*

Proof. Necessity. Suppose $\mathcal{C} \in \mathbf{WRefEx}$ as witnessed by some total IIM **M**. Let $\mathcal{S} = \mathbf{Ex(M)}$. Clearly, $\mathcal{C} \subseteq \mathcal{S}$ and $\mathcal{S} \in \mathbf{Ex}$. Now define c as follows.

$$c(f[n]) = \begin{cases} 0, & \text{if } \mathbf{M}(f[n]) \neq \bot; \\ 1, & \text{if } \mathbf{M}(f[n]) = \bot. \end{cases}$$

Then, clearly, $\mathcal{S}$ is classifiable by c.

Sufficiency. Suppose $\mathcal{C} \subseteq \mathcal{S} \subseteq \mathbf{Ex(M)}$, and let $\mathcal{S}$ be classifiable by some $c \in \mathcal{R}_{0,1}$. Then, define $\mathbf{M'}$ as follows.

$$\mathbf{M'}(f[n]) = \begin{cases} \mathbf{M}(f[n]), & \text{if } c(f[n]) = 0 \\ \bot, & \text{if } c(f[n]) = 1. \end{cases}$$

Clearly, $\mathbf{M'}$ witnesses that $\mathcal{C} \in \mathbf{WRefEx}$. ∎

Finally, we give a characterization of **RelEx** in terms of semi-classifiability.

Definition 15 ([35]). $\mathcal{S} \subseteq \mathcal{R}$ is *semi-classifiable* iff there is $c \in \mathcal{R}_{0,?}$ such that

(a) for any $f \in \mathcal{S}$ and almost all $n \in \mathbb{N}$, $c(f[n]) = 0$,
(b) for any $f \in \overline{\mathcal{S}}$ and infinitely many $n \in \mathbb{N}$, $c(f[n]) = ?$.

Thus, a class $\mathcal{S}$ of recursive functions is semi-classifiable if for every function $f \in \mathcal{S}$, one can find out in the limit that f belongs to $\mathcal{S}$, while for any $g \in \mathcal{R} \setminus \mathcal{S}$ one is not required to know in the limit where this function g comes from.

Theorem 11. *For all $\mathcal{C} \subseteq \mathcal{R}$, $\mathcal{C} \in \mathbf{RelEx}$ iff $\mathcal{C} \subseteq \mathcal{S}$ for a semi-classifiable class $\mathcal{S} \in \mathbf{Ex}$.*

Proof. Necessity. Suppose $\mathcal{C} \in \mathbf{RelEx}$ by some total IIM **M**. Let $\mathcal{S} = \mathbf{Ex(M)}$. Clearly, $\mathcal{C} \subseteq \mathcal{S}$. In order to show that $\mathcal{S}$ is semi-classifiable, define c as follows.

$$c(f[n]) = \begin{cases} 0, & \text{if } n = 0 \text{ or } \mathbf{M}(f[n-1]) = \mathbf{M}(f[n]); \\ ?, & \text{if } n > 0 \text{ and } \mathbf{M}(f[n-1]) \neq \mathbf{M}(f[n]). \end{cases}$$

Now, for any $f \in \mathcal{S}$, $\mathbf{M}(f)\downarrow$, and thus $c(f[n]) = 0$ for almost all $n \in \mathbb{N}$. On the other hand, if $f \in \overline{\mathcal{S}}$ then $f \notin \mathbf{Ex}(\mathbf{M})$. Consequently, since $\mathbf{M}$ is reliable and total, we have $\mathbf{M}(f[n-1]) \neq \mathbf{M}(f[n])$ for infinitely many $n \in \mathbb{N}$. Hence $c(f[n]) = ?$ for infinitely many n. Thus, $\mathcal{S}$ is semi-classifiable by c.

Sufficiency. Suppose $\mathcal{C} \subseteq \mathcal{S} \subseteq \mathbf{Ex}(\mathbf{M})$. Suppose $\mathcal{S}$ be semi-classifiable by some $c \in \mathcal{R}_{0,?}$. Define $\mathbf{M}'$ as follows.

$$\mathbf{M}'(f[n]) = \begin{cases} \mathbf{M}(f[n]), & \text{if } c(f[n]) = 0; \\ n, & \text{if } c(f[n]) = ?. \end{cases}$$

Now, for any $f \in \mathcal{S}$, for almost all n, $c(f[n]) = 0$. Hence $\mathbf{M}'$ will $\mathbf{Ex}$-learn f, since $\mathbf{M}$ does so. If $f \in \overline{\mathcal{S}}$, then $c(f[n]) = ?$ for infinitely many n. Consequently, $\mathbf{M}'$ diverges on f caused by arbitrarily large outputs. Thus, $\mathbf{M}'$ $\mathbf{RelEx}$-learns $\mathcal{C}$. ∎

There is a kind of "dualism" in the characterizations of $\mathbf{RefEx}$ and $\mathbf{RelEx}$. A class is $\mathbf{RefEx}$-learnable if it is contained in some $\mathbf{Ex}$-learnable class having a *complement* that is finitely semi-classifiable. In contrast, a class is $\mathbf{RelEx}$-learnable if it is subset of an $\mathbf{Ex}$-learnable class that *itself* is semi-classifiable.

The characterizations of the second group, this time for $\mathbf{RefEx}$ and $\mathbf{RelEx}$, significantly differ from the characterizations presented above in two points. First, the characteristic conditions are stated here in terms that formally have nothing to do with learning. Second, the sufficiency proofs are again constructive and they make clear where the "refuting ability" of the corresponding learning machines in general comes from. For stating the corresponding characterization of $\mathbf{RefEx}$, we need the following notions.

Definition 16. A numbering ψ is *strongly one-to-one* iff there is a recursive function $d: \mathbb{N} \times \mathbb{N} \to \mathbb{N}$ such that for all $i, j \in \mathbb{N}$, $i \neq j$, there is an $x < d(i,j)$ with $\psi_i(x) \neq \psi_j(x)$.

Any strongly one-to-one numbering is one-to-one. Moreover, given any distinct ψ-indices i and j, the functions ψ_i and ψ_j do not only differ, but one can compute a bound on the least argument on which these functions differ.

Definition 17 ([32]). A class $\Pi \subseteq \mathcal{P}$ is called *completely r.e.* iff $\{i \mid \varphi_i \in \Pi\}$ is recursively enumerable.

Now, we can present our next characterization.

Theorem 12. *For any $\mathcal{C} \subseteq \mathcal{R}$, $\mathcal{C} \in \mathbf{RefEx}$ iff there are numberings ψ and ϱ such that*

(1) ψ *is strongly one-to-one and* $\mathcal{C} \subseteq \mathcal{P}_\psi$,
(2) $\mathcal{P}_\varrho$ *is completely r.e. and* $\mathcal{R}_\varrho = \overline{\mathcal{R}_\psi}$.

By the proof of Theorem 12, in $\mathbf{RefEx}$-learning the processes of learning and refuting, respectively, can be nicely separated. An IIM can be provided with two spaces, one for learning, ψ, and one for refuting, ϱ. If and when the "search for refutation" in the refutation space has been successful, the learning process can be stopped forever. This search for refutation is based on the fact that the refutation space forms a completely r.e. class $\mathcal{P}_\varrho$ of partial recursive functions. The spaces for learning and refuting are interconnected by the essential property that their recursive kernels, $\mathcal{R}_\psi$ and $\mathcal{R}_\varrho$, disjointly exhaust $\mathcal{R}$. This property guarantees that each recursive function either will be learned or refuted. The above characterization of **RefEx** is "more granular" than the one of **RefEx** by Theorem 8. The characterization of Theorem 8 requires that one should find out *anyhow* if the given function does not belong to the target class. The characterization of Theorem 12 makes precise *how* this task can be done. Moreover, the **RefEx**-characterization of Theorem 12 is incremental to a characterization of **Ex**, since the existence of a numbering with condition (1) above is necessary and sufficient for **Ex**-learning the class $\mathcal{C}$ (cf. [36]). Finally, the refutation space could be "economized" in the same manner as the learning space by making it one-to-one.

The following characterization of **RelEx** is a slight modification of a result from [20].

Theorem 13. *For any $\mathcal{C} \subseteq \mathcal{R}$, $\mathcal{C} \in$ **RelEx** iff there are a numbering ψ and a function $d \in \mathcal{R}$ such that*

(1) *for any $f \in \mathcal{R}$, if $H_f = \{i \mid f[d(i)] \subseteq \psi_i\}$ is finite, then H_f contains a ψ-index of f,*

(2) *for any $f \in \mathcal{C}$, H_f is finite.*

Theorem 13 instructively clarifies where the ability to learn reliably may come from. Mainly, it comes from the properties of a well-chosen space of hypotheses. In any such space ψ exhibited by Theorem 13, for any function f from the class to be learned, there are only finitely many "candidates" for ψ-indices of f, the set H_f. This *finiteness* of H_f together with the fact that H_f then contains a ψ-index of f, make sure that the amalgamation technique [10] succeeds in learning any such f. Conversely, the *infinity* of this set H_f of candidates automatically ensures that the learning machine as defined in the sufficiency proof of Theorem 13 *diverges* on f. This is achieved by causing the corresponding machine to output arbitrarily large hypotheses on every function $f \in \mathcal{R}$ with H_f being infinite.

4 $\mathbf{Ex}^a$-Learning and $\mathbf{Bc}^a$-Learning Refutably

In this section, we consider **Ex**-learning and **Bc**-learning *with anomalies* refutably. Again, we will derive both strengths and weaknesses of refutable learning. As it turns out, many results of standard learning, i.e. without refutation, stand refutably. This yields several hierarchies for refutable learning. Furthermore, we show that in general one cannot trade the strictness of the refutability constraints for the liberality of the learning criteria.

We can now define $\mathbf{IEx}^a$ and $\mathbf{IBc}^a$ for $\mathbf{I} \in \{\mathbf{Ref}, \mathbf{WRef}, \mathbf{Rel}\}$ analogously to Definitions 5, 6, and 7. We only give the definitions of $\mathbf{RefEx}^a$ and $\mathbf{RelBc}^a$ as examples.

Definition 18. Let $a \in \mathbb{N} \cup \{*\}$ and let **M** be an IIM. **M RefEx^a**-*learns* $\mathcal{C}$ iff

(a) $\mathcal{C} \subseteq \mathbf{Ex}^a(\mathbf{M})$.
(b) For all $f \in \mathbf{Ex}^a(\mathbf{M})$, for all n, $\mathbf{M}(f[n]) \neq \perp$.
(c) For all $f \in \mathcal{R}$ such that $f \notin \mathbf{Ex}^a(\mathbf{M})$, there exists an $n \in \mathbb{N}$ such that $(\forall m < n)[\mathbf{M}(f[m]) \neq \perp]$ and $(\forall m \geq n)[\mathbf{M}(f[m]) = \perp]$.

Definition 19 ([22]). Let $a \in \mathbb{N} \cup \{*\}$ and let **M** be an IIM. **M RelBc^a**-*learns* $\mathcal{C}$ iff

(a) $\mathcal{C} \subseteq \mathbf{Bc}^a(\mathbf{M})$.
(b) For all $f \in \mathcal{R}$ such that $f \notin \mathbf{Bc}^a(\mathbf{M})$, there exist infinitely many $n \in \mathbb{N}$ such that $\mathbf{M}(f[n]) = \perp$.

RelEx^a and **RelBc^a** were studied firstly in [21] and [22], respectively.

Our first result points out some weakness of learning refutably. It shows that there are classes which, on the one hand, are easy to learn in the standard sense of **Ex**-learning without any mind change, but, on the other hand, which are not learnable refutably, even if we allow both the most liberal type of learning refutably, namely reliable learning, and the very rich type of **Bc**-learning with an arbitrarily large number of anomalies. For proving this result, we need the following proposition.

Proposition 7. (a) *For any $a \in \mathbb{N}$ and any $\sigma \in \mathrm{SEG}$, $\{f \in \mathcal{R} \mid \sigma \subseteq f\} \notin \mathbf{Bc}^a$.*

(b) *For any $a \in \mathbb{N}$ and any $\sigma \in \mathrm{SEG}_{0,1}$, $\{f \in \mathcal{R}_{0,1} \mid \sigma \subseteq f\} \notin \mathbf{Bc}^a$.*

Next, recall that **Ex**-learning without mind changes is called *finite learning*. Informally, here the learning machine has "one shot" only to do its learning task. We denote the resulting learning type by **Fin**.

Theorem 14. *For all $a \in \mathbb{N}$, $\mathbf{Fin} \setminus \mathbf{RelBc}^a \neq \emptyset$.*

Next we show that allowing anomalies can help in learning refutably. Indeed, while $\mathbf{Ex}^{a+1} \setminus \mathbf{Ex}^a \neq \emptyset$ was shown in [10], we now strengthen this result to **RefEx**-learning with anomalies.

Theorem 15. *For any $a \in \mathbb{N}$, $\mathbf{RefEx}^{a+1} \setminus \mathbf{Ex}^a \neq \emptyset$.*

Theorem 15 implies the following hierarchy results ((3) was already shown in [21]).

Corollary 16. *For every $a \in \mathbb{N}$,*

(1) $\mathbf{RefEx}^a \subset \mathbf{RefEx}^{a+1}$,
(2) $\mathbf{WRefEx}^a \subset \mathbf{WRefEx}^{a+1}$,
(3) $\mathbf{RelEx}^a \subset \mathbf{RelEx}^{a+1}$.

Now a proof similar to the proof of Theorem 15 can be used to show the following result. Notice that $\mathbf{Ex}^* \setminus \bigcup_{a \in \mathbb{N}} \mathbf{Ex}^a \neq \emptyset$ was proved in [10].

Theorem 17. $\mathbf{RefEx}^* \setminus \bigcup_{a \in \mathbb{N}} \mathbf{Ex}^a \neq \emptyset$.

Theorem 15 implies further corollaries. In [10], $\mathbf{Ex}^* \subseteq \mathbf{Bc}$ was shown. This result extends to all our types of refutable learning.

Proposition 8. *For* $\mathbf{I} \in \{\mathbf{Ref}, \mathbf{WRef}, \mathbf{Rel}\}$, $\mathbf{IEx}^* \subseteq \mathbf{IBc}$.

In [10] it was proved that $\mathbf{Bc} \setminus \mathbf{Ex}^* \neq \emptyset$. This result holds refutably.

Corollary 18. $\mathbf{RefBc} \setminus \mathbf{Ex}^* \neq \emptyset$.

The next corollary points out that already $\mathbf{RefEx}^1$ contains "algorithmically rich" classes of *predicates*.

Corollary 19. $\mathbf{RefEx}^1 \cap 2^{\mathcal{R}_{0,1}} \not\subseteq \mathbf{NUM} \cap 2^{\mathcal{R}_{0,1}}$.

Corollary 19 can be even strengthened by replacing $\mathbf{RefEx}^1$ with $\mathbf{RefEx}$. This another time exhibits the richness of already the most stringent of our types of learning refutably.

Theorem 20. $\mathbf{RefEx} \cap 2^{\mathcal{R}_{0,1}} \not\subseteq \mathbf{NUM} \cap 2^{\mathcal{R}_{0,1}}$.

Note that Theorem 20 contrasts a known result on reliable $\mathbf{Ex}$-learning. If we require the $\mathbf{Ex}$-learning machine's reliability not only on $\mathcal{R}$, but even on the set of all *total* functions, then all classes of recursive *predicates* belonging to this latter type are in $\mathbf{NUM}$, see [14].

We now give the analogue to Theorem 15 for $\mathbf{Bc}^a$-learning rather than $\mathbf{Ex}^a$-learning. Note that $\mathbf{Bc}^{a+1} \setminus \mathbf{Bc}^a \neq \emptyset$ was shown in [10].

Theorem 21. *For any* $a \in \mathbb{N}$, $\mathbf{RefBc}^{a+1} \setminus \mathbf{Bc}^a \neq \emptyset$.

Theorem 21 yields the following hierarchies, where (3) solves an open problem from [22].

Corollary 22. *For every* $a \in \mathbb{N}$,

(1) $\mathbf{RefBc}^a \subset \mathbf{RefBc}^{a+1}$,
(2) $\mathbf{WRefBc}^a \subset \mathbf{WRefBc}^{a+1}$,
(3) $\mathbf{RelBc}^a \subset \mathbf{RelBc}^{a+1}$.

Theorem 23. $\mathbf{RefBc}^* \setminus \bigcup_{a \in \mathbb{N}} \mathbf{Bc}^a \neq \emptyset$.

In the proof of Theorem 3 we have derived that *FINSUP* $\notin \mathbf{WRefEx}$. This result is now strengthened for $\mathbf{WRefBc}^a$-learning and then used in the next corollary below.

Theorem 24. *For every* $a \in \mathbb{N}$, *FINSUP* $\notin \mathbf{WRefBc}^a$.

The next corollary points out the relative strength of $\mathbf{RelEx}$-learning over $\mathbf{WRefBc}^a$-learning. In other words, in general, one cannot compensate a stricter refutability constraint by a more liberal learning criterion.

Corollary 25. *For all* $a \in \mathbb{N}$, $\mathbf{RelEx} \setminus \mathbf{WRefBc}^a \neq \emptyset$.

Our final result exhibits the strength of $\mathbf{WRefEx}$-learning over $\mathbf{RefBc}^a$-learning. Thus, it is in the same spirit as Corollary 25 above.

Theorem 26. *For all* $a \in \mathbb{N}$, $\mathbf{WRefEx} \setminus \mathbf{RefBc}^a \neq \emptyset$.

Note that Theorems 14, 24 and 26, and Corollary 25 hold even if we replace $\mathbf{Bc}^a$ by any criterion of learning for which Proposition 7 holds.

References

1. D. Angluin and C. Smith. Inductive inference: Theory and methods. *Computing Surveys*, 15:237–289, 1983.
2. J. Bārzdiņš. Two theorems on the limiting synthesis of functions. In *Theory of Algorithms and Programs, Vol. 1*, pp. 82–88. Latvian State University, 1974. In Russian.
3. J. Bārzdiņš and R. Freivalds. Prediction and limiting synthesis of recursively enumerable classes of functions. *Latvijas Valsts Univ. Zimatm. Raksti*, 210:101–111, 1974.
4. S. Ben-David. Can finite samples detect singularities of real-valued functions? In *24th Annual ACM Symposium on the Theory of Computing*, pp. 390–399, 1992.
5. L. Blum and M. Blum. Toward a mathematical theory of inductive inference. *Inform. and Control*, 28:125–155, 1975.
6. M. Blum. A machine-independent theory of the complexity of recursive functions. *Journal of the ACM*, 14:322–336, 1967.
7. J. Case. Periodicity in generations of automata. *Mathematical Systems Theory*, 8:15–32, 1974.
8. J. Case, S. Jain, and S. Ngo Manguelle. Refinements of inductive inference by Popperian and reliable machines. *Kybernetika*, 30:23–52, 1994.
9. J. Case, E. Kinber, A. Sharma, and F. Stephan. On the classification of computable languages. In *Proc. 14th Symposium on Theoretical Aspects of Computer Science*, Vol. 1200 of *Lecture Notes in Computer Science*, pp. 225–236. Springer, 1997.
10. J. Case and C. Smith. Comparison of identification criteria for machine inductive inference. *Theoretical Computer Science*, 25:193–220, 1983.
11. R. Freivalds. Inductive inference of recursive functions: Qualitative theory. In *Baltic Computer Science*, Vol. 502 of *Lecture Notes in Computer Science*, pp. 77–110. Springer, 1991.
12. R. Freivalds, E. Kinber, and C.H. Smith. On the intrinsic complexity of learning. *Information and Computation*, 123(1):64–71, 1995.
13. E.M. Gold. Language identification in the limit. *Inform. and Control*, 10:447–474, 1967.
14. J. Grabowski. Starke Erkennung. In *Strukturerkennung diskreter kybernetischer Systeme, Teil 1*, pp. 168–184. Seminarbericht Nr. 82, Department of Mathematics, Humboldt University of Berlin, 1986.
15. G. Grieser. Reflecting inductive inference machines and its improvement by therapy. In *Algorithmic Learning Theory: 7th International Workshop (ALT '96)*, Vol. 1160 of *Lecture Notes in Artificial Intelligence*, pp. 325–336. Springer, 1996.
16. S. Jain. Learning with refutation. *Journal of Computer and System Sciences*, 57(3):356–365, 1998.
17. S. Jain, E. Kinber, R. Wiehagen and T. Zeugmann. Refutable inductive inference of recursive functions. Schriftenreihe der Institute für Informatik/Mathematik, Serie A, SIIM-TR-A-01-06, Medical University at Lübeck, 2001.
18. S. Jain, D. Osherson, J.S. Royer, and A. Sharma. *Systems that Learn: An Introduction to Learning Theory*. MIT Press, Cambridge, Mass., second edition, 1999.
19. K. P. Jantke. Reflecting and self-confident inductive inference machines. In *Algorithmic Learning Theory: 6th International Workshop (ALT '95)*, Vol. 997 of *Lecture Notes in Artificial Intelligence*, pp. 282–297. Springer, 1995.
20. W. Jekeli. *Universelle Strategien zur Lösung induktiver Lernprobleme*. MSc Thesis, Dept. of Computer Science, University of Kaiserslautern, 1997.

21. E.B. Kinber and T. Zeugmann. Inductive inference of almost everywhere correct programs by reliably working strategies. *Journal of Information Processing and Cybernetics (EIK)*, 21:91–100, 1985.

22. E. Kinber and T. Zeugmann. One-sided error probabilistic inductive inference and reliable frequency identification. *Information and Computation*, 92(2):253–284, 1991.

23. R. Klette and R. Wiehagen. Research in the theory of inductive inference by GDR mathematicians – A survey. *Information Sciences*, 22:149–169, 1980.

24. S. Lange and P. Watson. Machine discovery in the presence of incomplete or ambiguous data. In *Algorithmic Learning Theory: 4th International Workshop on Analogical and Inductive Inference (AII '94) and 5th International Workshop on Algorithmic Learning Theory (ALT '94)*, Vol. 872 of *Lecture Notes in Artificial Intelligence*, pp. 438–452. Springer, 1994.

25. R. Lindner. *Algorithmische Erkennung*. Dissertation B, University of Jena, 1972.

26. M. Machtey and P. Young. *An Introduction to the General Theory of Algorithms*. North Holland, New York, 1978.

27. E. Minicozzi. Some natural properties of strong identification in inductive inference. *Theoretical Computer Science*, 2:345–360, 1976.

28. T. Miyahara. Refutable inference of functions computed by loop programs. Technical Report RIFIS-TR-CS-112, Kyushu University, Fukuoka, 1995.

29. Y. Mukouchi and S. Arikawa. Inductive inference machines that can refute hypothesis spaces. In *Algorithmic Learning Theory: 4th International Workshop (ALT '93)*, Vol. 744 of *Lecture Notes in Artificial Intelligence*, pp. 123–136. Springer, 1993.

30. Y. Mukouchi and S. Arikawa. Towards a mathematical theory of machine discovery from facts. *Theoretical Computer Science*, 137:53–84, 1995.

31. K. R. Popper. *The Logic of Scientific Discovery*. Harper and Row, 1965.

32. H. Rice. On completely recursively enumerable classes and their key arrays. *The Journal of Symbolic Logic*, 21:304–308, 1956.

33. H. Rogers. *Theory of Recursive Functions and Effective Computability*. McGraw-Hill, 1967. Reprinted by MIT Press in 1987.

34. C.H. Smith, R. Wiehagen, and T. Zeugmann. Classifying predicates and languages. *International Journal of Foundations of Computer Science*, 8(1):15–41, 1997.

35. F. Stephan. On one-sided versus two-sided classification. Technical Report Forschungsberichte Mathematische Logik 25/1996, Mathematical Institute, University of Heidelberg, 1996.

36. R. Wiehagen. Characterization problems in the theory of inductive inference. In *Proc. of the 5th International Colloquium on Automata, Languages and Programming*, Vol. 62 of *Lecture Notes in Computer Science*, pp. 494–508. Springer, 1978.

37. R. Wiehagen and C.H. Smith. Generalization versus classification. *Journal of Experimental and Theoretical Artificial Intelligence*, 7:163–174, 1995.

38. T. Zeugmann. A-posteriori characterizations in inductive inference of recursive functions. *J. of Inform. Processing and Cybernetics (EIK)*, 19:559–594, 1983.

Refuting Learning Revisited

Wolfgang Merkle and Frank Stephan*

Mathematisches Institut, Im Neuenheimer Feld 294, Ruprecht-Karls-Universität
Heidelberg, 69120 Heidelberg, Germany,
{fstephan|merkle}@math.uni-heidelberg.de

Abstract. We consider, within the framework of inductive inference,
the concept of refuting learning as introduced by Mukouchi and Arikawa,
where the learner is not only required to learn all concepts in a given
class but also has to explicitly refute concepts outside the class.

In the first part of the paper, we consider learning from text and
introduce a concept of limit-refuting learning that is intermediate between refuting learning and reliable learning. We give characterizations
for these concepts and show some results about their relative strength
and their relation to confident learning.

In the second part of the paper we consider learning from texts that
for some k contain all positive Π_k-formulae that are valid in the standard
structure determined by the set to be learned. In this model, the following results can be shown. For the language with successor, any countable
axiomatizable class can be limit-refuting learned from Π_1-texts. For the
language with successor and order, any countable axiomatizable class
can be reliably learned from Π_1-texts and can be limit-refuting learned
from Π_2-texts, whereas the axiomatizable class of all finite sets cannot
be limit-refuting learned from Π_1-texts. For the full language of arithmetic, which contains in addition plus and times, for any k there is an
axiomatizable class that can be limit-refuting learned from Π_{k+1}-texts
but not from Π_k-texts. A similar result with $k+3$ in place of $k+1$ holds
with respect to the language of Presburger's arithmetic.

1   Introduction

Inductive Inference [12,25] studies, on an abstract level, the phenomenon of
learning. Gold [7] introduced the following basic formalization of a learning situation. The objects to be learned are the sets within a given class of recursively
enumerable sets. The learner has to identify each set in this class by converging
to a hypothesis that describes the set uniquely while observing longer and longer
prefixes of any text for this set. A learner converges if it changes its hypothesis at
most finitely often, a text for a set is any sequence that contains all elements but
no non-elements of the set, and usually hypotheses are indices with respect to
some fixed acceptable numbering of the partial recursive functions (equivalently

---

* Supported by the Deutsche Forschungsgemeinschaft (DFG) under the Heisenberg
grant Ste 967/1–1

N. Abe, R. Khardon, and T. Zeugmann (Eds.): ALT 2001, LNAI 2225, pp. 299–314, 2001.
© Springer-Verlag Berlin Heidelberg 2001

one could use grammars or programs enumerating the members of the set to be learned). Gold [7] demonstrated that it is impossible to learn the class of all recursively enumerable sets. This restriction holds for topological as well as for recursion theoretical reasons.

(a) For any learner that learns all finite sets and for any infinite set A, there is a text for A on which the learner diverges.
(b) The class of all graphs of computable functions cannot be learned by a computable learner — indeed, Adleman and Blum [1] quantified the problem of learning this class by showing that learning the class requires access to an oracle of high Turing degree.

The topological and computational aspects of learning interact. Gold [7] considered models of learning where in place of arbitrary texts, the learner just receives texts that can be computed in some fixed computation model. Gold showed that a computable learner can learn all recursively enumerable sets from primitive recursive texts (by simply identifying the primitive recursive function that generates the text) while, on the other hand, the collection of all recursive texts is already so complex that a computable learner cannot learn the class of all recursively enumerable sets from recursive texts.

In the present work, the power of learners is not enlarged by restricting texts to computationally simple ones but by increasing their information content. While standard texts essentially just list the elements of the set to be learned, we consider texts that contain positive formulae that are true for the set to be learned. The consideration of such more informative texts relates to the fact that we consider a model of learning where the learner has to recognize and to explicitly refute data-sequences belonging to sets that are not learned. This model is rather restrictive in a setting of standard texts and allows just the learning of classes of finite sets. The model becomes more powerful in the setting where the texts contain formulae and in this setting, we will investigate into the question which kind of classes can be learned from what types of formulae.

Mukouchi and Arikawa [22,23] introduced the learning model where the learner has to refute data-sequences that belong to sets that are not in the class to be learned. Their model is a sharpened version of Minicozzi's reliable learning, where the learner either converges to a correct index or diverges. In the model of Mukouchi and Arikawa, instead of diverging, the learner has to give an explicit refutation signal after a finite number of steps.

Lange and Watson [17], Jantke [14], and Jain [10] considered variants of refuting learning where a learner M for a class $\mathcal{C}$ of sets is not required to refute unless the input text T satisfies both of the following conditions.

– M does not infer the concept to which T belongs.
– There is a prefix $\sigma \preceq T$ such that no data-sequence of any concept in $\mathcal{C}$ extends σ.

These restrictions were meant to overcome the observation that the original definition of "refutable learning" of Mukouchi and Arikawa [22,23] was rather restrictive. In particular, the original conditions permitted only to learn finite sets since, on the one hand, a learner cannot learn an infinite set A and all its subsets and, on the other hand, a refuting learner cannot refute any subset of a set it learns.

The present work takes an alternative approach to improve the power of a refuting learner. First, we consider a model where the learner is only required to "refute in the limit". In a context of language learning from informant, a similar concept has been introduced recently and independently by Jain, Kinber, Wiehagen and Zeugmann [11]. In a context of function-learning, already Grieser [8,9] investigated learners that refute in the limit. In his model of reflecting learning, however, a function f has only to be refuted in case it is incompatible with the class to be learned, i.e., if there is a prefix $\sigma \preceq f$ that is not extended by any function in the class to be learned. Grieser [8,9] notes that with his model in many (but not all) cases the necessity to refute can be avoided by transition to a dense superclass $\mathcal{C}'$ of the class $\mathcal{C}$ to be learned because by definition, $\mathcal{C}$ is learnable with reflection in the limit iff $\mathcal{C}'$ is learnable in the limit with respect to the standard definition of learning.

Second, more powerful variants of texts will be considered in order to overcome the restriction to classes of finite sets. This is achieved by considering a slightly altered form of the logical-based setting originally considered by Mukouchi and Arikawa [22,23]. Informally, our approach can be summarized as follows.

- The learner either has to converge to an index of the set to be learned or to the distinguished refutation symbol "?". It will be shown in Remark 3.5 that this type of learning is more restrictive than reliable learning but is less restrictive than the model used by Mukouchi and Arikawa, where the data is already refuted by outputting a single refutation symbol.
- The data-sequences are sequences of first-order sentences describing the set to be learned. In the special case where the data just contains the atomic facts that hold for the set to be learned, this is equivalent to presenting a standard text for the set. We will, however, also consider models where the data does not just contain atomic sentences but Π_k-sentences of some given level k in the quantifier-alternation-hierarchy.

More detailed accounts of inductive inference, inference in logic and of recursion theory in general can be found in the monographs [3,12,19,24,30].

Notation. For an arbitrary set A, let A^* be the set of finite strings over A. We write $\mathbb{N}$ for the set of natural numbers. Unless explicitly stated otherwise, by the terms *set* and *class* we refer to a set of natural numbers and to a set of such sets, respectively. We fix a canonical indexing of the finite sets and we let F_i denote the finite set with canonical index i. A class $\mathcal{C}$ of finite sets is *computable* (is *recursively enumerable*) iff the set $\{i : F_i \in \mathcal{C}\}$ is computable (is recursively enumerable). Observe that a non-empty class of finite sets is recursively enumerable iff it can be represented as $\{F_{g(i)} : i \in \mathbb{N}\}$ for some recursive function g.

2 Learning from Standard Texts

Before we discuss refuting learning in Section 3, we shortly review some basic concepts and techniques from learning theory. Related to the task of refuting input texts, the learners considered in the following do not just output indices (i.e, natural numbers) but might also output a special refutation symbol.

We fix two distinguished symbols not in $\mathbb{N}$, the pause symbol $\#$ and the refutation symbol $?$. *Texts* and *strings* are infinite and finite, respectively, sequences over $\mathbb{N} \cup \{\#\}$. The *range* of a text or string is the set of all elements appearing in it that are different from the pause symbol. We write $\text{range}(\sigma)$ for the range of a string σ. A text is a *text for* a set A iff A coincides with the range of this text and hence, for example, $\#\# \ldots$ is the only text for the empty set.

Definition 2.1.   An *unrestricted learner* is a mapping from strings to $\mathbb{N} \cup \{?\}$ and a *learner* is such a mapping that is computable. A learner EX-learns or, for short, *learns* a set A iff on every text for A, the learner converges to an index for A. A learner learns a class iff it learns every set in the class.

Remark 2.2.   The numbers output by a learner are meant as hypothesis on the set to be learned with respect to some fixed indexing. In this connection, the usage of *computable* and of *recursively enumerable* indices is most common, i.e., the number i denotes the ith partial recursive function or the ith computational enumerable set W_i. We frequently consider the learning of classes of finite sets, and in this situation we might also use canonical indices as hypotheses.

Most of the results shown below will go through if we simply require that the sets to be learned can be identified by an index at all and that there is an effective mapping from natural description of sets emerging during the learning algorithm to indices of these sets with respect to the indexing used. In fact, we will not presuppose more on the indexing used unless explicitly stated otherwise.

In a context of learners that always output a natural number, Osherson, Stob and Weinstein [25] considered learners that converge on all texts.

Definition 2.3.   [25, Section 4.6.2] A learner is *confident* iff on any text, the learner converges to a natural number. A class is *confidently learnable* iff it is learned by a confident learner.

Standard techniques and results for confident learners extend easily to the type of learners considered here, which besides natural numbers might also output refutation symbol, if we require again that the learner has to converge – to an index or to the refutation symbol – on all texts.

Remark 2.4.   Any class that is learned by a learner that converges on all texts does not contain infinite ascending chains. In particular, the class of all finite sets cannot be learned by such a learner.

For a proof by contradiction, fix a learner M that converges on all texts and consider an ascending chain $A_0, A_1, \ldots$ of sets that are all learned by M. Then one can inductively find strings σ_k such that each σ_k contains only elements from A_k and M outputs an index for A_k on input $\sigma_0 \sigma_1 \ldots \sigma_k$. So M outputs on the text $\sigma_0 \sigma_1 \ldots$ an index for each of the sets A_k and hence does not converge, neither to an index for a set nor to the refutation symbol. (It it not required that $\sigma_0\sigma_1 \ldots$ is a text for the set $A_0 \cup A_1 \cup \ldots$, it may also be a text for a subset.)

Remark 2.5.   Let M_0 be a learner that converges on all texts. Then for any set A there is a string τ that is a stabilizing sequence for M_0 and A in the sense that for all strings γ over $A \cup \{\#\}$ we have $M_0(\tau) = M_0(\tau\gamma)$. For a proof observe that, otherwise, we could construct a text for A on which M_0 diverges.

By searching for such stabilizing sequences we can construct a learner M that learns all sets that are learned by M_0 and has in addition the following properties (for details of this construction see Jain et al. [12, Proposition 5.29 on Page 102]). First, for any set A — including sets that are not learned or are not even indexed by the given indexing — the learner M converges on every text of A to the same value $M_0(\tau)$, where τ is the least stabilizing sequence for M_0 and A (with respect to some appropriate ordering on strings). Second, any text for any set A has a finite prefix that is a stabilizing sequence for M and A.

3   Refuting Learning from Standard Texts

Next we review the definitions of the concepts of refuting and reliable learning that are due to Mukouchi and Arikawa [22] and to Minicozzi [21], respectively, and we introduce the related concept of limit-refuting learning. While a refuting learner continues forever to output refutation symbols after having output a refutation symbol once, a limit-refuting learner might alternate between indices and refutation symbols in an arbitrary way before converging.

Definition 3.1.   A learner *refutes* a set iff on every text for this set, the learner first outputs at most finitely many numbers (without outputting any refutation symbol) and then outputs nothing but refutation symbols. A learner is *refuting* iff for any set A, either the learner refutes A or on every text for A the learner converges to an index for A without ever outputting ?. A learner *limit-refutes* a set iff on every text for this set, the learner converges to ?, and a learner is *limit-refuting* if it either learns or limit-refutes any set.

A class $\mathcal{C}$ is *refuting learnable* iff there is a refuting learner that learns $\mathcal{C}$. A class $\mathcal{C}$ is *sharply refuting learnable* iff there is a refuting learner that learns $\mathcal{C}$ and refutes every set not in $\mathcal{C}$. The concept *limit-refuting learnable* and its sharp variant are defined likewise with refuting replaced by limit-refuting.

A learner is *reliable* iff for any set A, the learner either learns A or has infinitely many mind changes on any text for A, and a class is *reliably learnable* if it is learned by a reliable learner.

The sharply refuting learnable classes are those originally introduced by Mukouchi and Arikawa [22,23]. Observe that a class is refuting learnable iff it is a subclass of some sharply refuting learnable class. This follows because by definition any refuting class is a subclass of a sharply refuting class while, on the other hand, any sharply refuting learnable class is refuting learnable and any subclass of a refuting learnable class is again refuting learnable. In Remarks 3.2 through 3.4, we describe some features of the types of learning described in Definition 3.1 and then, in Remark 3.5, we compare their respective strength.

Remark 3.2. For the scope of this remark, call a class *infinitely-often-refuting* learnable iff the class is learned by a learner that for any set A, either learns A or outputs infinitely many refutation symbols on any text for A. Then by definition, any limit-refuting learnable class is also infinitely-often-refuting learnable. Moreover, it is not so hard to show that the concepts of infinitely-often-refuting learning and of reliable learning coincide.

Remark 3.3. A class of sets is reliably learnable if and only if it consists only of finite sets. In particular, by Remark 3.5 below, any refuting or limit-refuting learnable class consists only of finite sets.

The restriction of reliable learning to classes of finite sets has already been observed by Osherson, Stob and Weinstein [25, Proposition 4.6.1A] and can be shown as follows. A learner that always outputs an index for the finite set seen so far learns all finite sets and is indeed reliable. Next assume that M is a reliable learner and let $a_1 a_2 \ldots$ be any text for an infinite set A. Then each set of the form $\{a_1, \ldots, a_m\}$ is either learned by M or M diverges on any text for this set and consequently there must be infinitely many sets of the former or infinitely many sets of the latter type. But in both cases, by simply repeating elements in the given text, we can construct a text for A on which M does not converge to an index for A, that is, M does not learn A.

Remark 3.4. Limit-refuting learnable classes do not contain infinite ascending chains. The assertion is immediate from Remark 2.4, because by definition a limit-refuting learner converges on all texts.

The following remark extends the observation of Mukouchi and Arikawa [22] that any refuting learnable class is also reliably learnable.

Remark 3.5. For any class $\mathcal{C}$,

$$\mathcal{C} \text{ refuting learnable} \quad \Rightarrow \quad \mathcal{C} \text{ limit-refuting learnable}$$
$$\Rightarrow \quad \mathcal{C} \text{ reliably learnable}, \tag{1}$$

and both implications are strict. In particular, the concepts of refuting learnable, limit-refuting learnable and reliably learnable class are mutually distinct.

The first implication in (1) is immediate by definition, while the second one follows by Remark 3.2. Moreover, the first two concepts are separated by the class considered in Remark 3.9 below, while the class of all finite sets is reliably learnable but is not limit-refuting learnable, as follows by Remarks 3.3 and 3.4.

Remark 3.6. Reliable learners have been introduced by Minicozzi [21] by a slightly different formulation where on any text for a set the learner either learns the set or diverges. Minicozzi's definition is apparently less restrictive than Definition 3.1, because the former allows that a learner fails to learn a set A while it still converges to an index for A on some texts for A. Nevertheless, both definitions yield the same concept of reliably learnable class. A similar statement holds with respect to corresponding less restrictive definitions of refuting and limit-refuting learning where for example in the case of limit-refuting learning one just requires that on any text for a set the learner either converges to an index for this set or converges to the refutation symbol. Proofs can be obtained

by considering stabilizing sequences as in Remark 2.5 or constructions similar
to the ones used for obtaining such sequences.

Remark 3.7.   Minicozzi [21] showed that finite unions of reliably learnable
classes are also reliably learnable. Similar assertions hold for all variants of
refuting learning by the following simple principle. Given k refuting learners
$M_1, M_2, \ldots, M_k$ for the classes $\mathcal{C}_1, \mathcal{C}_2, \ldots, \mathcal{C}_k$, the learner M given by

$$M(\sigma) = \begin{cases} M_l(\sigma) & \text{if } l \text{ is the least index with } M_l(\sigma) \neq ?; \\ ? & \text{otherwise;} \end{cases}$$

learns the union $\mathcal{C}$ of the classes $\mathcal{C}_1, \mathcal{C}_2, \ldots, \mathcal{C}_k$ with respect to the same variant
of refuting learning.

By Remarks 3.3 and 3.4, any refuting learnable class $\mathcal{C}$ contains only finite sets
and any infinite set A contains some finite set $D \notin \mathcal{C}$. Mukouchi and Arikawa [23]
demonstrated that in the case of unrestricted learners, the two latter properties
can be extended to a characterization of the sharply refuting learnable classes,
i.e., in our terms a class $\mathcal{C}$ is sharply refuting learnable by an unrestricted learner
iff there are finite sets $D_0, D_1, \ldots$ such that any infinite set contains some set D_i
while none of the sets D_i is contained in any set in $\mathcal{C}$. The following theorem is
essentially a reformulation of the characterization of Mukouchi and Arikawa. Recall in connection with the theorem that by definition a class is refuting learnable
if and only if it is contained in a sharply refuting learnable class.

Theorem 3.8.   [23] *A class $\mathcal{C}$ is sharply refuting learnable iff $\mathcal{C}$ contains only
finite sets and there is a recursively enumerable class $\{D_0, D_1, \ldots\}$ of finite sets
such that $\mathcal{C}$ coincides with the class $\{X : D_i \nsubseteq X \text{ for all } i\}$.*

Theorem 3.8 implies in particular that sharply refuting learnable classes are
closed under taking subsets.

Proof.   First assume that $\mathcal{C}$ is sharply refuting learnable, that is, $\mathcal{C}$ contains
exactly the sets that are learned by some refuting learner M. Then $\mathcal{C}$ contains
only finite sets by Remark 3.2. Moreover, the class $\mathcal{D}$ of all finite sets D such
that there is a string σ over D where $M(\sigma) = ?$ is obviously recursively enumerable and exactly the sets that are not learned by M contain some set in D.
Conversely, given a recursively enumerable class as in the theorem and a representing function g, a refuting learner for $\mathcal{C}$ is obtained as follows. On input σ, the
learner checks whether $F_{g(i)} \subseteq \text{range}(\sigma)$ for any $i \leq |\sigma|$. If so, the learner outputs
a refutation symbol while, otherwise, it outputs an index for $\text{range}(\sigma)$. ■

Remark 3.9.   Theorem 3.8 does not extend to limit-refuting learning. A
counter-example is given by the class $\mathcal{C}$ of all sets of the form $\{0, 2, 4, \ldots, 2n,$
$2n + 1\}$. The class $\mathcal{C}$ is learned by the limit-refuting learner that outputs an index for the finite set seen so far in case this set is in $\mathcal{C}$ and, otherwise, outputs a
refutation symbol. However, the set of all even numbers is infinite and any of its
finite subsets with maximum m can be extended to the set $\{0, 2, 4, \ldots, m, m+1\}$
in $\mathcal{C}$, i.e., there is no sequence $D_0, D_1, \ldots$ as in Theorem 3.8.

The following theorem shows that also the property of limit-refuting learnable
classes shown in Remark 3.4 can be extended to a characterization.

Theorem 3.10. *A class is limit-refuting learnable iff it is contained in a recursively enumerable class of finite sets that does not contain any infinite ascending chain.*

Proof. Let $\mathcal{C}$ be a class of finite sets that is recursively enumerable with representing function g and does not contain any infinite ascending chain. Consider the learner M that on input σ outputs an index for range(σ) in case the latter set is among $\mathrm{F}_{g(0)}, \ldots, \mathrm{F}_{g(|\sigma|)}$ and, otherwise, outputs ?. Then, obviously, M is computable and learns every set in $\mathcal{C}$. Moreover, M limit-refutes any set $A \notin \mathcal{C}$. In case A is finite, this is immediate by the construction of M. So assume that A is infinite and let $a_1, a_2, \ldots$ be any text for A. As $\mathcal{C}$ contains no infinite chains, $\mathcal{C}$ contains only finitely many sets of the form $\{a_1, a_2, \ldots, a_n\}$ and hence M outputs a refutation symbol on almost all prefixes of the given text.

In order to prove the reverse direction, assume that we are given a class $\mathcal{C}_0$ that is learned by a limit-refuting learner M. Let the class $\mathcal{C}$ contain all finite sets C such that

$$\text{for all } \tau \in (C \cup \{\#\})^* \text{ with } |\tau| \le |C|,$$
$$\text{there is } \gamma \in (C \cup \{\#\})^* \text{ with } M(\tau\gamma) \ne ?. \tag{2}$$

The set of all indices i such that (2) is satisfied with C replaced by F_i is recursively enumerable, that is, $\mathcal{C}$ is a recursively enumerable class of finite sets. Moreover, by construction, $\mathcal{C}$ contains all finite sets that are learned by M, hence $\mathcal{C}_0$ is contained in $\mathcal{C}$. Assume now for a proof by contradiction that $A_0, A_1, A_2, \ldots$ is an infinite ascending chain that is contained in $\mathcal{C}$ and let A be the union of the sets A_i. Then by Remark 3.3, the learner M limit-refutes the infinite set A and hence, by Remark 2.5, there is a stabilizing sequence τ for A and M with range$(\tau) \subseteq A$ and $M(\tau\gamma) = ?$ for any string γ with range$(\tau) \subseteq A$. Thus (2) is false for all finite subsets C of A where range$(\tau) \subseteq C$ and $|\tau| \le |C|$. Consequently, contrary to our assumption, almost all sets A_i are not in $\mathcal{C}$. ∎

Recall that a confident learner is a learner that always converges to a natural number, see Definition 2.3. Given any limit-refuting learner, according to Remark 3.2 this learner can be transformed into an equivalent reliable learner. Similarly, by replacing all refutation symbols by any fixed index, we can transform any limit-refuting learner into a confident learner that learns the same class, that is, any limit-refuting learnable class is also confidently learnable. Theorem 3.11 shows that the reverse implication is true for classes that are closed under taking subsets.

Theorem 3.11. *Let the class $\mathcal{C}$ be closed under taking subsets. Then the following conditions are equivalent.*
(a) *$\mathcal{C}$ is limit-refuting learnable.*
(b) *$\mathcal{C}$ is confidently learnable.*
(c) *$\mathcal{C}$ is learned by a refuting learner that may use the halting problem K as an oracle.*

Theorem 3.12. *In a setting of learners that use canonical indices as hypotheses, any class is limit-refuting learnable if and only if it is confidently learnable.*

4   Refuting Learning in a Logical Setting

In the sequel, we consider learning in a logical setting, that is, the classes to be learned, the data, and occasionally also the hypotheses are given in terms of logical formulae. We will always work with a logical language $\mathcal{L}$ that consists of a unary predicate symbol P plus a subset of the symbols $\{s, <, +, *, \overline{0}, \overline{1}, \ldots\}$. The structures considered all have domain $\mathbb{N}$ and the interpretation of the symbols other than P is always the usual one, that is, $\overline{n}$ is interpreted as number n, s is the successor function, $<$ is the usual strict order on natural numbers, and $+$ and $*$ are interpreted as addition and multiplication over $\mathbb{N}$. We will refer to such structures as *standard structures*. The aim of the learning process is then to identify the interpretation of P. The logical language $\mathcal{L}$ will be chosen among

$\mathcal{B} = \{\mathrm{P}, \overline{0}, \overline{1}, \overline{2}, \ldots\}$, the *basic language*,
$\mathcal{S} = \mathcal{B} \cup \{\mathrm{s}\}$, the *language of successor*,
$\mathcal{O} = \mathcal{B} \cup \{\mathrm{s}, <\}$, the *language of order*,
$\mathcal{P} = \mathcal{B} \cup \{\mathrm{s}, <, +\}$, the *language of Presburger's arithmetic*,
$\mathcal{A} = \mathcal{B} \cup \{\mathrm{s}, <, +, *\}$, the *language of arithmetic*.

With a language $\mathcal{L}$ understood, the standard structure determined by a set A is denoted by $\mathbf{M}(A)$. In the setting considered here, a set A and the structure $\mathbf{M}(A)$ are essentially equivalent. Accordingly, we extend the notation introduced in connection with the learning of sets to the learning of $\mathcal{L}$-structures. For example, given any $\mathcal{L}$-structure $\mathbf{M}(A)$, an $\mathcal{L}$-text for $\mathbf{M}(A)$ or, for short, a *text for* $\mathbf{M}(A)$ is simply a text for the set A and a learner learns $\mathbf{M}(A)$ if on every text for $\mathbf{M}(A)$, the learner converges to an index for A. Moreover, given a sentence Ψ and a set A, we write $\Psi[A]$ for the truth value of Ψ in $\mathbf{M}(A)$.

A class $\mathcal{C}$ of standard structures is called $\mathcal{L}$-*axiomatizable* if and only if there is an $\mathcal{L}$-sentence Ψ such that $\mathcal{C}$ contains exactly those standard structures in which the formula is true, i.e., $\mathcal{C} = \{X : \Psi[X]\}$. Next we review some well-known facts about axiomatizable classes.

Remark 4.1.   Any $\mathcal{P}$-axiomatizable class of finite sets is computable. For a proof, recall that Presburger's arithmetic, i.e., the theory of the natural numbers with addition, is decidable [26,29]. As a consequence, given an index i and a $\mathcal{P}$-formula Φ, we can effectively test whether Φ is true in the standard structure determined by the finite set $F_i = \{n_1, \ldots, n_m\}$ by first replacing in Φ every subformula of the form $\mathrm{P}t$, t a term, by $t = \overline{n_1} \vee \ldots \vee t = \overline{n_m}$, then checking whether the resulting formula is true in Presburger's arithmetic.

Remark 4.2.   For any $\mathcal{O}$-axiomatizable class $\mathcal{C}$, the set

$$I_{\mathcal{C}} = \{i : (\exists C \in \mathcal{C})\, [F_i \subseteq C]\}$$

of canonical indices of all subsets of the sets in $\mathcal{C}$ is computable. A proof can be derived by an argument similar to the one used in Remark 4.1, using Büchi's result [2,31] that the monadic second order theory of the natural numbers with successor and order is decidable.

Remark 4.3. The Theorem of Matiyasevich (see for example Smoryński [29]) states that every recursively enumerable set is Diophantine and thus can be defined by a positive existential $\mathcal{A}$-sentence. More precisely, from an index for a recursively enumerable set W we can compute effectively a constant l and polynomials f and g in $l + 1$ variables and with coefficients in $\mathbb{N}$ such that for all $x \in \mathbb{N}$,

$$x \in W \quad \text{iff} \quad (\exists z_1, \ldots, z_l \in \mathbb{N})\,[f(x, z_1, \ldots, z_l) = g(x, z_1, \ldots, z_l)]. \quad (3)$$

Hence the matrix of the right-hand side of (3) is an $\mathcal{A}$-formula. Furthermore, if W is computable, then its complement is recursively enumerable and so for suitable polynomials f', g' as above we have for all $x \in \mathbb{N}$,

$$x \in W \quad \text{iff} \quad (\forall z_1, \ldots, z_l \in \mathbb{N})\,[f'(x, z_1, \ldots, z_l) \neq g'(x, z_1, \ldots, z_l)]. \quad (4)$$

So we obtain a positive universal $\mathcal{A}$-sentence that defines W because the subformula $f'(\ldots) \neq g'(\ldots)$ is equivalent to $f'(\ldots) < g'(\ldots) \lor g'(\ldots) < f'(\ldots)$.

Now consider any Π_k-set A. Then A and its complement can be represented by formulae in prenex normal form with $k - 1$ alternations of quantifiers and a matrix that corresponds to a computable set W. By replacing these computable sets according to (3) and (4), we infer that for k even and odd, the set A can be represented by

$$x \in A \;\Leftrightarrow\; (\forall y_1 \forall y_2 \ldots \exists y_h\, \exists z_1 \ldots \exists z_l)$$
$$[f(x, y_1, \ldots, y_h, z_1, \ldots, z_l) = g(x, y_1, \ldots, y_h, z_1, \ldots, z_l)],$$
$$x \in A \;\Leftrightarrow\; (\forall y_1 \forall y_2 \ldots \forall y_h\, \forall z_1 \ldots \forall z_l)$$
$$[f'(x, y_1, \ldots, y_h, z_1, \ldots, z_l) \neq g'(x, y_1, \ldots, y_h, z_1, \ldots, z_l)],$$

respectively, i.e., by positive $\mathcal{A}$-sentences with the same number $k - 1$ of alternations of quantifiers. Furthermore, these formulae can be effectively computed from a recursive index of the set W and an appropriate representation of the quantifier prefix for the variables $y_1, \ldots, y_h$.

Remark 4.4. Besides learners that state their hypotheses in the form of canonical, computable or recursively enumerable indices of sets, in the logical setting one can also consider learners that state their hypotheses in the form of logical formulae. We consider two ways of indexing sets by logical formulae, which might be called *coinciding indices* and *subset indices*. A formula used as a coinciding index is true for (and thus identifies) exactly one structure in the class to be learned, while for a formula used as a *subset index*, among all structures in the class to be learned that satisfy the formula there is a unique least structure (with respect to set theoretical inclusion), which is hence identified by the formula. Learning via subset indices has been considered by Martin, Sharma and Stephan [20]. Unless explicitly stated otherwise, the results shown in the sequel hold no matter whether we use canonical, computable, recursively enumerable, coinciding or subset indices, as long as all sets to be learned can be indexed at all by such indices. Accordingly, when stating these results we do not make explicit the indexing used.

The interplay between logic and learning has been considered before in several papers [4,5,6,13,15,16,18,19,20,28]. In connection with the learning of standard structures, the type of texts used above are essentially equivalent to a sequence that contains exactly the atomic $\mathcal{L}$-sentences that are true in the structure to be learned, a type of data presentation considered by Shinohara [28].

Next we state for various models of learning that classes that are axiomatizable in an appropriate language and are learned by an unrestricted learner are in fact learnable. The corresponding proofs use Theorem 4.5, which extends the characterizations of refuting and limit-refuting learnability stated in Theorems 3.8 and 3.10 to unrestricted learners.

Theorem 4.5. [23] *A class $\mathcal{C}$ has an unrestricted sharply refuting learner iff $\mathcal{C}$ contains only finite sets and there is a sequence $D_0, D_1, \ldots$ of finite sets such that $\mathcal{C}$ coincides with the class $\{X : D_i \nsubseteq X \text{ for all } i\}$.*

A class $\mathcal{C}$ has an unrestricted limit-refuting learner iff $\mathcal{C}$ contains only finite sets and $\mathcal{C}$ does not contain any infinite ascending chain of finite sets.

Theorem 4.6. *Any $\mathcal{P}$-axiomatizable class that has an unrestricted limit-refuting learner is limit-refuting learnable.*

Theorem 4.7.
(a) *Any $\mathcal{O}$-axiomatizable class that has an unrestricted refuting learner is refuting learnable.*
(b) *Any $\mathcal{P}$-axiomatizable class that has an unrestricted refuting learner is refuting learnable by a learner that may use the halting problem K as an oracle.*
(c) *There is a $\mathcal{P}$-axiomatizable class that has an unrestricted refuting learner but has no refuting learner.*

5 Learning Axiomatizable Classes from Π_k-Texts

In this section we consider learning models where the information given in the data is not just a listing of all elements of the set A to be learned but in addition contains all formulae of a certain type that are true in $\mathbf{M}(A)$. Similar settings have been considered before, e.g., by Gasarch and Smith [5], Martin and Osherson [18], Martin, Sharma and Stephan [20], and Shinohara [28].

Recall that a Π_0-$\mathcal{L}$-formula is an $\mathcal{L}$-formula without quantifiers while for all $k \geq 1$, a Π_k-$\mathcal{L}$-formula is an $\mathcal{L}$-formula that consists of a quantifier prefix followed by a quantifier-free formula where the prefix starts with a universal quantifier and has at most $k - 1$ alternations between universal and existential quantifiers (e.g., for a quantifier-free $\mathcal{L}$-formula Φ, the formula $(\forall x_1 \forall x_2 \exists x_3)\, [\Phi(x_1, x_2, x_3)]$ is a Π_2-$\mathcal{L}$-formula). The concept of a Σ_k-$\mathcal{L}$-formula is defined almost literally the same except that the quantifier prefix of such a formula starts with an existential quantifier. Recall further that a Π_k-$\mathcal{L}$-sentence is a Π_k-$\mathcal{L}$-formula that does not contain free variables and that an $\mathcal{L}$-formula is *positive* iff it does not contain logical connectives other than $\vee$ and $\wedge$.

Definition 5.1. A Π_k-$\mathcal{L}$-*text* for a set A is a sequence that, besides pause symbols, contains exactly all the positive Π_k-sentences that are valid in $\mathbf{M}(A)$.

For any set A, a text and a Π_0-$\mathcal{L}$-text for A provide essentially the same information, whereas we will see below that for $k > 0$, in general more classes can be learned from Π_k-$\mathcal{L}$-texts than just from texts.

Remark 5.2. As already observed by Martin, Sharma and Stephan [20], there is no need to define Σ_k-texts because the amount of information provided by a Π_k-$\mathcal{L}$-text and by a Σ_{k+1}-$\mathcal{L}$-text is exactly the same. For a proof, observe that for any Π_k-formula $\Psi(x_1, \ldots, x_m)$, in any standard structure the Σ_{k+1}-formula $(\exists x_1 \ldots x_m)[\Psi(x_1 \ldots x_m)]$ is true if and only if for some $n_1, \ldots, n_m$, the Π_k-formula $\Psi(\overline{n_1}, \ldots, \overline{n_m})$ is true.

Remarks 3.3 and 3.5 imply that for any language $\mathcal{L}$, just classes of finite sets can be refuting, limit-refuting, or reliably learned from Π_0-$\mathcal{L}$-text. In contrast to this, Theorem 5.3 shows that Π_2-$\mathcal{O}$-texts permit limit-refuting and reliably learning, respectively, of all countable $\mathcal{O}$-axiomatizable classes or, equivalently, of all classes that for some constant n, contain only sets that are ultimately periodic with period n.

Theorem 5.3.
(a) *Every countable $\mathcal{O}$-axiomatizable class is limit-refuting learnable from Π_2-$\mathcal{O}$-texts.*
(b) *Every countable $\mathcal{O}$-axiomatizable class is reliably learnable from Π_1-$\mathcal{O}$-texts.*
(c) *Some countable $\mathcal{O}$-axiomatizable class, namely the class of all finite sets, is not limit-refuting learnable from Π_1-$\mathcal{O}$-texts.*

Sketch of Proof. Due to a result of Büchi [2], all members L of a given $\mathcal{O}$-axiomatizable and countable class $\mathcal{C}$ are ultimately periodic with a fixed length n, that is they have a prefix δ_L of length n or more such that $L(z) = L(z - n)$ for all z not in the domain of δ_L. Now let $\Gamma_n(\delta_L)$ denote the formula which states that all places x with $\delta_L(x) \downarrow = 1$ satisfy Px and that furthermore, for every $y \geq |\delta_L| - n$, at least j of the n places $z \in \{y, y+1, \ldots, y+n-1\}$ satisfy Pz. The formula $\Gamma_n(\delta_L)$ is satisfied when P is the characteristic predicate of L but not when P is the characteristic predicate of a proper subset of L. Now the following algorithm learns the class reliably from Π_1-$\mathcal{O}$-texts.

Algorithm. On input $\phi_0, \ldots, \phi_h$ find the first formula ϕ_k such that $\phi_k = \Gamma_n(\delta_L)$ with δ_L and L as above such that all formulas ϕ_l are consistent with L. If such a formula ϕ_k is found, then output ϕ_k, else output the refutation-symbol.

In case of divergence, reliable learning means here that no hypothesis is output infinitely often. It can be shown that the algorithm converges to a refutation-symbol even in case the input-text is a Π_2-$\mathcal{O}$-text for a set L that is not of the form $\delta\sigma^\infty$ for any string $\sigma \in \{0,1\}^n$. On the other hand, one can show that every limit-refuting learner for the class of finite sets requires Π_2-$\mathcal{O}$-texts, while Π_1-$\mathcal{O}$-texts are not sufficient. Intuitively speaking, such a learner requires formulae like $(\forall x)(\exists y)[y > x \wedge Py]$ in order to be able to refute texts for infinite sets. $\square$

The proof of Theorem 5.4 uses a result of Thomas [32,33], according to which membership of a set L in an $\mathcal{S}$-axiomatizable class $\mathcal{L}$ can be checked by counting, up to some threshold value m, for all strings of length less than or equal to some number n how often they appear as substring in the characteristic sequence of L.

For example, consider the $\mathcal{S}$-axiomatizable class $0^+1^+0^\infty$ of all sets that have a characteristic function of the form $0^i1^j0^\infty$ for some $i,j > 0$. For $n = 2$ and $m = 2$ we then have

$$L \in 0^+1^+0^\infty \Leftrightarrow L(0) = 0 \wedge (\mathrm{occ}_m(L, 01) = 1 \wedge \mathrm{occ}_m(L, 10) = 1).$$

where $\mathrm{occ}_m(L, \eta)$ denotes the minimum of m and the number of substrings of L that are equal to η.

Theorem 5.4. *Every countable $\mathcal{S}$-axiomatizable class can be limit-refuting learned from Π_1-$\mathcal{S}$-text.*

Remark 5.5. Similarly it holds that any countable $\mathcal{B}$-axiomatizable class is limit-refuting learnable from Π_1-$\mathcal{B}$-texts. The class $\{A : |\overline{A}| \leq 1\}$ is countable and $\mathcal{B}$-axiomatizable via the formula $(\exists x)(\forall y)[x = y \vee Py]$. But this class is not learnable from standard text at all. Since, for all languages $\mathcal{L}$ considered here, Π_0-$\mathcal{L}$-texts are equivalent to standard texts, it follows that results like Theorem 5.4 cannot be improved to learnability from Π_0-$\mathcal{L}$-texts.

In the case of reliable and limit-refuting learning of $\mathcal{A}$-axiomatizable classes, — in contrast to $\mathcal{O}$-axiomatizable classes considered in the last section — for increasing k we can learn more and more classes from Π_k-$\mathcal{A}$-text.

Theorem 5.6. *For every k, the class of all $\emptyset^k$-recursive sets is not reliably learnable from Π_k-$\mathcal{A}$-text but is reliably learnable from Π_{k+1}-$\mathcal{A}$-text. In particular, for every k there is a countable $\mathcal{A}$-axiomatizable class that is not reliably learnable from Π_k-$\mathcal{A}$-texts.*

Sketch of Proof. Fix k and let $\mathcal{C}$ be the class of all $\emptyset^k$-recursive sets. Recall that a set A is in $\mathcal{C}$ iff A and its complement are both Σ_{k+1}-sets or, equivalently, iff A and its complement are both Π_{k+1}-sets. Furthermore, given an index e of an oracle Turing machine that computes A relative to oracle $\emptyset^k$, we can compute representations of A and its complement as Σ_{k+1}- and Π_{k+1}-sets and, by Remark 4.3, from these representations we can compute positive Π_{k+1}-$\mathcal{A}$-formulae Θ_0^e and Θ_1^e such that for all n,

$$(n \notin A \text{ iff } \Theta_0^e(\overline{n})[A]) \quad \text{and} \quad (n \in A \text{ iff } \Theta_1^e(\overline{n})[A]) \tag{5}$$

in case A is computed by the e-th oracle Turing machine relative to oracle $\emptyset^k$. It can be shown that there is a reliable learner N that learns the class $\mathcal{C}$ from Π_{k+1}-$\mathcal{A}$-text by syntactically analyzing the data, i.e., N checks whether certain formulae containing Θ_0^e and Θ_1^e have already appeared in the input text.

Non-Learnability from Π_k-$\mathcal{A}$-text. It remains to show that $\mathcal{C}$ is not reliably learnable from Π_k-$\mathcal{A}$-text. In order to do so, we fix any learner M that is reliable (in the sense that for any set Y, either M converges on any Π_k-$\mathcal{A}$-text for Y to a subset index for Y or M diverges on any Π_k-$\mathcal{A}$-text for Y) and show that there is a $\emptyset^k$-recursive set R, i.e., $R \in \mathcal{C}$, such that M does not learn R.

Let $\Psi_0, \Psi_1, \ldots$ be an enumeration of all positive Π_k-$\mathcal{A}$-sentences where, in order to simplify notation, we assume that Ψ_0 is true for all sets. Recall that these sentences are monotone in the sense that whenever $A \subseteq B$ and $\Psi_n[A]$ is true, then so is $\Psi_n[B]$. We define inductively for all $\alpha \in \{0,1\}^*$ computable sets A_α, B_α, C_α and corresponding intervals $I_\alpha = \{X : A_\alpha \subseteq X \subseteq B_\alpha\}$. These intervals are chosen such that whenever β extends α, then I_β is contained in I_α. Moreover, we will ensure for all α,

$$\Psi_i[A_\alpha] = \Psi_i[B_\alpha] \qquad \text{for all } i \leq |\alpha|, \qquad (6)$$

and hence, by monotonicity of the Ψ_i, all sets in I_α agree with respect to the predicates Ψ_0 through $\Psi_{|\alpha|}$.

The inductive definition starts with the interval I_λ bounded by $A_\lambda = \emptyset$ and $B_\lambda = \mathbb{N}$. Then given A_α and B_α, in order to define $A_{\alpha 0}$, $A_{\alpha 1}$, $B_{\alpha 0}$ and $B_{\alpha 1}$, we proceed as follows.

- Let $n = |\alpha|$. Let C_α be the union of A_α and the set containing every second element in $B_\alpha \setminus A_\alpha$, i.e., if $c_1, c_2, \ldots$ is a strictly ascending enumeration of the elements of $B_\alpha - A_\alpha$, then $C_\alpha = A_\alpha \cup \{c_2, c_4, \ldots\}$.
  So we have $A_\alpha \subset C_\alpha \subset B_\alpha$ and in this chain of inclusions, any set contains infinitely many more numbers than its predecessors.
- Let

$$(D_\alpha, E_\alpha) = \begin{cases} (C_\alpha, B_\alpha) & \text{in case } \Psi_n[C_\alpha] \text{ holds,} \\ (A_\alpha, C_\alpha) & \text{otherwise.} \end{cases}$$

  (By monotonicity of Ψ_n, if the first case applies then Ψ_n is true for all sets between C_α and B_α, if the second case applies then Ψ_n is false for all sets between A_α and C_α. Hence by construction, $\{X : D_\alpha \subseteq X \subseteq E_\alpha\}$ is an infinite subinterval of I_α and all sets in this interval agree with respect to Ψ_n.)
- Let x_α be the first element in $E_\alpha \setminus D_\alpha$. Define two infinite and disjoint subintervals $I_{\alpha 0}$ and $I_{\alpha 1}$ of I_α by letting $A_{\alpha 0} = D_\alpha$, $B_{\alpha 0} = E_\alpha \setminus \{x_\alpha\}$, and $A_{\alpha 1} = D_\alpha \cup \{x_\alpha\}$, $B_{\alpha 1} = E_\alpha$.

By construction, for all α the sets A_α, B_α and C_α are computable. Furthermore, for any given α, the inductive definition of these sets is computable relative to the oracle $\emptyset^k$, hence with access to this oracle we can compute programs that do not use an oracle and decide the sets A_α, B_α, and C_α. Furthermore, for any set F there is a unique set X_F that is contained in the intersection of all classes I_α such that α is a prefix of the characteristic function of F. If we let

$$\Psi_n^F = \begin{cases} \Psi_n & \text{if } \Psi_n[X] \text{ for all } X \in I_{F(0)F(1)\ldots F(n)}, \\ \# & \text{otherwise (that is, } \neg \Psi_n[X] \text{ for all } X \in I_{F(0)F(1)\ldots F(n)}) , \end{cases}$$

then $\Psi_0^F, \Psi_1^F, \ldots$ is a Π_k-$\mathcal{A}$-text for X_F. Note that Ψ_n^F corresponds to the value of the formula $\Psi_n[C_\alpha]$ where α is equal to $F(0)F(1)\ldots F(n-1)$. For any string α, let $t_\alpha = \Psi_0^F \Psi_1^F \ldots \Psi_n^F$ where F is any extension α and the actual choice of F does not affect the value of t_α. Then t_α can be computed from α relative to $\emptyset^k$.

Given any reliable learner M, there is a set F such that F and X_F are both computable relative to oracle $\emptyset^k$, but M does not learn the set X_F. Given any string α, the learner M cannot learn all of the uncountably many sets X_F with $F \succeq \alpha$ and so, as M is reliable, we can pick an extension $\beta \succeq \alpha$ with

$M(t_\alpha) \neq M(t_\beta)$. If we start from the empty string, we obtain a set F and a text $\Psi_0^F, \Psi_1^F, \ldots$ for X_F on which M changes its mind infinitely often.

By similar methods, Theorem 5.6 can be extended to the following result.

Theorem 5.7.   *For every k, there is a countable $\mathcal{A}$-axiomatizable class that is limit-refuting learnable from Π_{k+1}-$\mathcal{A}$-text but not from Π_k-$\mathcal{A}$-text.*

It is possible to define multiplication in the language $\mathcal{P}$ of Presburger's arithmetic if the language is augmented by a predicate for the square numbers. This technique is due to Putnam [27] and can be used to obtain results for $\mathcal{P}$-axiomatizable classes that correspond to, but are slightly weaker than Theorems 5.6 and 5.7.

Corollary 5.8.   *For any k, there is a countable $\mathcal{P}$-axiomatizable class that is limit-refuting learnable from Π_{k+3}-$\mathcal{P}$-text but is not reliably learnable from Π_k-$\mathcal{P}$-text.*

Acknowledgements   We like to thank Thomas Wilke for very helpful discussion about his work on $\mathcal{S}$-axiomatizable classes. Furthermore, we are grateful to the anonymous referees of *Algorithmic Learning Theory 2001* and *Theoretical Computer Science* for their comments and corrections.

References

1. Leonard M. Adleman and Manuel Blum: Inductive inference and unsolvability. *The Journal of Symbolic Logic*, 56:891–900, 1991.
2. J. Richard Büchi: On a decision method in restricted second order arithmetic. *Proceedings of the International Congress on Logic, Methodology and Philosophy of Science*, Standford University Press, Standford, California, 1960.
3. Heinz-Dieter Ebbinghaus, Jörg Flum and Wolfgang Thomas: *Mathematical Logic*, Springer, 1994.
4. William I. Gasarch, Mark G. Pleszkoch and Robert Solovay: Learning via queries in $[+, <]$. *The Journal of Symbolic Logic*, 57:53–81, 1992.
5. William I. Gasarch and Carl H. Smith: Learning via queries, *Journal of the Association of Computing Machinery*, 39:649–674, 1992.
6. Clark Glymour: Inductive Inference in the limit. *Erkenntnis* 22:23–31, 1985.
7. E. Mark Gold: Language identification in the limit. *Information and Control*, 10: 447–474, 1967.
8. Gunter Grieser: *Reflexion in der Induktiven Inferenz*. Diploma Thesis, Technische Hochschule Leipzig, 1996.
9. Gunter Grieser: Reflecting Inductive Inference Machines and its Improvement by Therapy. *Seventh Annual International Workshop on Algorithmic Learning Theory* (ALT), *Lecture Notes in Artificial Intelligence* 1160:325–336, Springer, 1996.
10. Sanjay Jain: Learning with refutation. *Journal of Computer and Systems Sciences*, 57:356–365, 1998.
11. Sanjay Jain, Efim Kinber, Rolf Wiehagen, Thomas Zeugmann: *On learning of functions refutably*, Theoretical Computer Science, to appear.
12. Sanjay Jain, Daniel Osherson, James Royer and Arun Sharma: *Systems that Learn*, revised edition of [25]. The MIT Press, Cambridge, Massachusetts, 1999.
13. Sanjay Jain and Arun Sharma: Elementary formal systems, intrinsic complexity and procrastination. *Information and Computation*, 132:65–84, 1997.

14. Klaus-Peter Jantke: Reflecting and self-confident inductive inference machines. *Sixth Annual International Workshop on Algorithmic Learning Theory* (ALT), *Lecture Notes in Artificial Intelligence* 997:282–297, Springer, 1995.
15. Kevin T. Kelly: *The Logic of Reliable Inquiry*. Oxford University Press, New York, 1996.
16. Kevin T. Kelly and Clark Glymour: Inductive inference from theory-laden data. *Journal of Philosophical Logic*, 21:391–444, 1992.
17. Steffen Lange and Phil Watson: Machine discovery in the presence of incomplete or ambiguous data. *Joint Proceedings of the Fourth International Workshop on Analogical and Inductive Inference* (AII) *and of the Fifth Workshop on Algorithmic Learning Theory* (ALT), *Lecture Notes in Artificial Intelligence* 872:438–452, Springer, 1994.
18. Eric Martin and Daniel N. Osherson: Scientific discovery based on belief revision. *The Journal of Symbolic Logic*, 62:1352-1370, 1997.
19. Eric Martin and Daniel N. Osherson: *Elements of Scientific Inquiry*. The MIT Press, Cambridge, Massachusetts, 1998.
20. Eric Martin, Arun Sharma and Frank Stephan: *Learning Power and Language Expressiveness*. Forschungsbericht Mathematische Logik 49, Mathematisches Institut, Universität Heidelberg, Heidelberg, 2000.
21. Eliana Minicozzi. Some natural properties of strong-identification in inductive inference. *Theoretical Computer Science*, 2:345–360, 1976.
22. Yasuhito Mukouchi and Setsuo Arikawa: Inductive inference machines that can refute hypothesis spaces. *Fourth Annual International Workshop on Algorithmic Learning Theory* (ALT), *Lecture Notes in Artificial Intelligence* 744:123–136, Springer, 1993.
23. Yasuhito Mukouchi and Setsuo Arikawa: Towards a mathematical theory of machine discovery from facts. *Theoretical Computer Science*, 137:53–84, 1995.
24. Piergiorgio Odifreddi: *Classical Recursion Theory, Volumes* I *and* II. North Holland and Elsevier, Amsterdam, 1989 and 1999.
25. Daniel Osherson, Michael Stob and Scott Weinstein: *Systems That Learn. An Introduction to Learning Theory for Cognitive and Computer Scientists*. Bradford — The MIT Press, Cambridge, Massachusetts, 1986.
26. Mojzesz Presburger: Über die Vollständigkeit eines gewissen Systems der Arithmetik der ganzen Zahlen in welchem die Addition als einzige Operation hervortritt. *C. R. 1er Congrès des Mathématiciens des Pays Slaves* (Warsaw) 92–101, 395, 1930.
27. Hilary Putnam: Decidability and essential undecidability. *The Journal of Symbolic Logic*, 22:39–54, 1957.
28. Takeshi Shinohara: Inductive inference of monotonic formal systems from positive data. *New Generation Computing*, 8:371–384, 1991.
29. Craig Smoryński: *Logical Number Theory I. An Introduction*. Springer, 1991.
30. Robert I. Soare: *Recursively Enumerable Sets and Degrees. A Study of Computable Functions and Computably Generated Sets*. Springer, 1987.
31. Wolfgang Thomas: Automata on Infinite Objects. *Handbook of Theoretical Computer Science*, Vol. B, edited by Jan van Leeuwen, p. 133–191, Elsevier, Amsterdam, 1990.
32. Wolfgang Thomas: Classifying regular events in symbolic logic, *Journal of Computer and System Sciences*, 25:360–376, 1982.
33. Thomas Wilke: Locally threshold testable languages of infinite words. *Tenth Annual Symposium on Theoretical Aspects of Computer Science* (STACS), *Lecture Notes in Computer Science* 665:607–616, Springer, 1993.

Efficient Learning of Semi-structured Data from Queries

Hiroki Arimura[1,2], Hiroshi Sakamoto[1], and Setsuo Arikawa[1]

[1] Dept. of Informatics, Kyushu University,
Fukuoka 812-8581, Japan
[2] PRESTO, Japan Science and Technology Co., Japan
{arim, hiroshi, arikawa}@i.kyushu-u.ac.jp

Abstract. This paper studies the polynomial-time learnability of the classes of *ordered gapped tree patterns* (OGT) and *ordered gapped forests* (OGF) under the into-matching semantics in the query learning model of Angluin. The class OGT is a model of semi-structured database query languages, and a generalization of both the class of ordered/unordered tree pattern languages and the class of non-erasing regular pattern languages. First, we present a polynomial time learning algorithm for μ-OGT, the subclass of OGT without repeated tree variables, using equivalence queries and membership queries. By extending this algorithm, we present polynomial time learning algorithms for the classes μ-OGF of forests without repeated variables and *OGT* of trees with repeated variables using equivalence queries and subset queries. We also give representation-independent hardness results which indicate that both of equivalence and membership queries are necessary to learn μ-OGT.

1 Introduction

Huge amount of electronic data have been available on the Web as the form of HTML and XML data for this decade [19]. These heterogeneous collections of electronic data are called *semi-structured data* and modeled as ordered node-labeled trees [1,9]. In database and network communities, there are remarkable attention in data mining and information extraction methods to extract useful information as simple patterns from these semi-structured data [14,18]. However, there are small number of formal studies on the complexity of learning patterns from semi-structured data.

In this paper, we introduce the class *OGT* of *ordered gapped tree patterns* (OGT) *with the into-match semantics* as a formal model of recently emerging query languages for semi-structured data [1,9,20]. Then, we study its learnability in the exact learning model of Angluin [5]. An OGT is a labeled ordered tree with tree and gap variables, where arbitrary trees and paths are substituted for the tree and the gap variables, resp., to match the pattern tree to a data tree In Fig. 1, we show examples of a constant tree and an OGT. We refer to an OGT without repeated tree variables as μ-OGT. The class of OGT is a generalization

N. Abe, R. Khardon, and T. Zeugmann (Eds.): ALT 2001, LNAI 2225, pp. 315–331, 2001.
© Springer-Verlag Berlin Heidelberg 2001

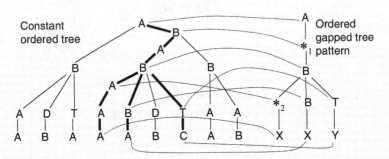

Fig. 1. An ordered tree and an ordered gapped tree pattern, where dotted lines indicates an into-matching from the pattern to the tree.

of the class of ordered tree patterns with the into-match semantics of Amoth, Cull, and Tadepalli [2] and the class of regular pattern languages [4,8,15]. We also introduce ordered gapped forests OGF with the into-match semantics as sets of OGTs, whose semantics is defined as the unions of tree pattern languages.

We start with analyzing the complexity of the membership problem. We show that the membership problems for μ-OGT and thus μ-OGF are polynomial time solvable. On the other hand, we show that the membership problem for OGT with repeated variables is NP-complete.

As a main result, we show that the class μ-OGT, the subclass of OGT without repeated variables, is polynomial time learnable using equivalence and membership queries under a finite alphabet. Our algorithm LEARN-INTO-LIN-OGT runs in polynomial time in n using exactly one equivalence queries and $O(n^2)$ membership queries, where n is the size of the initial counterexample. This algorithm does not require the assumption of infinite alphabets. We also give representation-independent hardness results which indicate that both of equivalence and membership queries are necessary to learn μ-OGT.

By extending the previous algorithm for μ-OGT, we present a polynomial time learning algorithm LEARN-INTO-OGF for the class μ-OGF of ordered gapped forests without repeated variables using $O(m)$ equivalence and $O(mn^2)$ subset queries over an infinite alphabet, where m is the cardinality of a target forest. For this result, we develop an efficient, complete, and proper generalization operator for μ-OGT. Finally, we show that the full class OGT of ordered gapped tree patterns with repeated variables is polynomial time learnable from equivalence queries and subset queries by using the partition technique proposed by Amoth, Cull, and Tadepalli [2].

As summary, our results generalize the polynomial time learnability of Amoth *et al.* [2] and Matsumoto and Shinohara [15]. The into-match semantics is originally introduced by [2] for the learning of unordered trees and forests, and well captures the essence of pattern matching for semi-structured data query languages. Although there are a number of researches on the learning of tree-like patterns [17,7,3,12], most of them are based on the onto-match semantics [3] and far from learning of patterns like OGT and OGF. This work seems to be one of the first attempts to analyze the complexity of learning ordered tree patterns with the into-matching semantics, and hence, may provide a theoretical base of information extraction from Web and XML [18], and will indicate possibility and limitations of such tasks.

This paper is organized as follows. In Section 2, we review basic definitions on OGT and OGF. In Section 3, we present a polynomial time learning algorithm for μ-OGT with EQ and MQ. In Section 4, we show that neither EQ and MQ can be eliminated to efficiently learn any super class of μ-OGT. In Section 5, we present a polynomial time learning algorithm for μ-OGF with EQ and SQ. In Section 6, we extend our algorithms in Section 3 and Section 5 for the full class of OGT with repeated variables. In Section 7, we conclude.

2   Preliminaries

2.1   Ordered Tree Patterns

In this section, we first define the class OT of ordered tree patterns, and then the class OGT of ordered gapped tree patterns by generalizing OT.

For a set A, $\#A$ denotes the cardinality of A. Let A be a set of labels. An *ordered tree over* A is a rooted, node labeled acyclic graph $t = (V, E, r, \ell, c)$ with the following properties. V is the set of nodes and $E \subseteq V \times V$ is the set of edges. For each edge $(u, v) \in E$, we say that u is the *parent* of v and v is a *children* of u. The node $r \in V$ is the special node without parent and called the *root* of t. All nodes but the root of t have exactly one parent. Each node is labeled by the labeling function $\ell : V \to A$. For each node u, its children $u_1, \ldots, u_n$ $(n \geq 0)$ are ordered from left to right and numbered consecutively by the numbering function $c : V \to \mathbf{N}$. A node $u \in V$ is a *leaf* if it has no children, and an *internal node* otherwise. A node u is a *chain node* if it has exactly one child.

For an ordered tree $t = (V, E, r, \ell, c)$, we will use the notation V_t, E_t, r_t, ℓ_t, and c_t to denote the associated components V, E, r, ℓ, and c. For an ordered tree s, t and a node $u \in V$, t/u denotes the unique subtree of t whose root is u. We define the *size* of t, denoted by $|t|$, to be the number of nodes in t. We write $s = t$ if they are syntactically identical with its structures and labels.

Next, we define the class of ordered patterns. Let $\Sigma = \{a, b, f, g, \ldots\}$ be a finite alphabet of *constant symbols* and $\mathbf{X} = \{x, y, z, \ldots\}$ be a countable alphabet of *tree variables*. An *ordered tree pattern* (OT) is an ordered tree over $\Sigma \cup \mathbf{X}$, where each internal node is labeled by a constant symbol and each leaf is labeled by either a constant symbol or a tree variable. For an ordered tree pattern t, we denote by $var(t)$ the set of tree variables appearing in t. A node v in t is said to be a *constant node* if $\ell_t(v) \in \Sigma$ and a *variable node* if $\ell_t(v) \in \mathbf{X}$. An ordered tree pattern is *constant* if it contains no tree variables. $\mathcal{T}$ denotes the set of all constant trees over Σ.

We introduce two matching semantics for OT according to Amoth *et al.* [2].

Definition 1. *For OTs s and t, an* into-matching *from s to t is a mapping $\phi : V_s \to V_t$ satisfying the following conditions.*

(1) The mapping ϕ is one-to-one.
(2) The root of s maps to the root of t, i.e., $\phi(r_s) = r_t$.
(3) The mapping ϕ preserves the constant labels. That is, if a constant node $u \in V_s$ maps to $v \in V_t$, then they have the same labels, i.e., $\ell_s(u) = \ell_t(v) \in \Sigma$.
(4) The mapping ϕ maps the variable nodes $u_1, \ldots, u_n \in V_s$ ($n \geq 2$) with the same label $x \in \mathbf{X}$ to nodes $v_1, \ldots, v_n \in V_t$ with the same subtrees. That is, $t/v_1 = \cdots = t/v_n$.
(5) The mapping ϕ preserves the ordering among children. That is, if a constant node $u \in V_s$ with k children maps to a node $v \in V_t$ with n children, then $k \leq n$ and there exists some $1 \leq j_1 < \cdots < j_k \leq n$ such that for every $1 \leq i \leq k$, the i-th child of u maps to the j_i-th child of v.

A variant of the above definition without condition (2) is common in tree pattern matching [13]. Another matching semantics is the *onto-matching* [3], which is the matching semantics for first-order terms when OTs are restricted to be ranked trees [7]. The onto-semantics is defined as the into-matching such that the numbers k and n of children must be the same in the condition (5).

Definition 2 (Amoth *et al.* [2]). *For OT s and t, s into-matches (onto-matches, resp.) t, denoted by $s \sqsupseteq_{in} t$ ($s \sqsupseteq_{on} t$, resp.), if there exists an into-matching ϕ (an onto-matching ϕ, resp.) from s to t.*

Now, we define the class of ordered gapped tree patterns. Let $\Gamma = \{*, \ldots\}$ be a countable alphabet of *gap variables* mutually disjoint from Σ and $\mathbf{X}$.

Definition 3. *An* ordered gapped tree pattern *(OGT) is an ordered tree over $\Sigma \cup \mathbf{X}$ defined as follows. Each internal node is labeled by either a constant symbol or a gap variable. Each leaf is labeled by either a constant symbol or a tree variable. An internal node is labeled by a gap variable only when it is a chain node, i.e., a node with exactly one child. This constraint intuitively means that a gap variable is essentially an edge label that matches any path in a tree. There are no repeated occurrences of the same gap variable in the OGT.*

A node v in t is said to be a *gap node* if $\ell_t(v) \in \Gamma$. Constant and variable nodes are defined similarly as in OT. For an OGT t, we denote by $var(t)$ and $gap(t)$ the sets of the tree and the gap variables appearing in t, resp. We often use the term notation for OGT. For example, the OGT in Fig. 1 can be written as $A(*_1(B(*_2(X), B(X), T(Y))))$. Below, we give the definition of the gapped-matching for OGT. Note that the following definition applies to only gap nodes, while the condition (5) in Definition 1 applies only to constant nodes.

Definition 4. *For OGT s and t, a* gapped into-matching *from s to t is a mapping $\phi : V_s \to V_t$ satisfying the following condition in addition to the conditions (1)–(5) in Definition 1 for the into-matching for OT.*

(6) The mapping ϕ preserves the parent-child relation on gap nodes. That is, if a gap node $u \in V_s$ maps to $v \in V_t$, then the unique child of u maps to a proper descendant of v in t.

Definition 5. *For OGT s and t, s gapped into-matches t, denoted by $s \sqsupseteq_{in} t$, if there exists a gapped into-matching ϕ from s to t.*

See Fig. 1 for an example of the gapped into-matching from an OGT to a constant tree, where dotted lines indicate the matching. Since the gapped into-matching for OGT is conservative extension of the into-matching for OT, we will not distinguish the gapped into-match and the into-match in what follows.

Let $s, t \in OGT$ and $\alpha \in \{in, on\}$ be the underlying matching semantics. If $s \sqsupseteq_\alpha t$ then s is said to be a *generalization* of t or t is said to be an *instance* of s. If $s \sqsupseteq_\alpha t$ and $t \sqsupseteq_\alpha s$ hold then we define $s \equiv t$ and say s is equivalent to t. If $s \sqsupseteq_\alpha t$ but $t \not\sqsupseteq_\alpha s$ then we define $s \sqsupset_\alpha t$, and s is said to be a proper generalization of t or t is said to be a proper instance of s.

Definition 6 ([2,7]). *For an OGT t, the language of t under the underlying semantics $\alpha \in \{in, on\}$ is defined by the set of constant ordered trees*

$$L_\alpha(t) = \{\, w \in T \mid t \sqsupseteq_\alpha w \,\},$$

which consists of all instances of t with the semantics α.

Note that for a constant tree t, $L_{in}(t)$ may be an infinite set while $L_{on}(t)$ is always a singleton set.

Lemma 1. *For any OGT s, t and constant trees $u, w \in T$, the following properties hold.*

1. *The into-match relation $\sqsupseteq_{in}$ is reflexive and transitive.*
2. *$s \equiv_{in} t$ if and only if s and t are identical modulo renaming of variables.*
3. *If $s \sqsupseteq_{in} t$, then $|s| \leq |t|$*
4. *If $w \in L_{in}(s)$, then $|s| \leq |w|$*
5. *If $s \sqsupseteq_{in} t$, then $L_{in}(s) \supseteq L_{in}(t)$.*
6. *If Σ is infinite, then $s \sqsupseteq_{in} t$ if and only if $L_{in}(s) \supseteq L_{in}(t)$.*

An OGT is said to be *linear* if it does not have repeated occurrences of the same variable. We also call a linear OGT a *μ-OGT*. Note that OGT is always *linear* on gap variables by definition.

We denote by OT, OGT, μ-OT, and μ-OGT the classes of OTs, OGTs, linear OTs, and linear OGTs, resp. T is the class of constant ordered trees. Since we will mainly consider the into-matching semantics for OGT, we may write $\sqsupseteq$ instead of $\sqsupseteq_{in}$ if it is clear from context. We assume that all the classes OT, OGT, μ-OT, and μ-OGT contains the bottom tree $\perp$ defined by $L_{in}(\perp) = \emptyset$ and $t \sqsupseteq_{in} \perp$ for every OGT t. The into-matching problems for a class C of OGTs is, given OGT $s, t \in C$, to determine if $s \sqsupseteq_{in} t$ holds.

Lemma 2. *The into-matching problems for μ-OGT is polynomial time solvable.*

Proof. We give a sketch of the algorithm. Removing all gap nodes in pattern s, we can decompose s into a set of small constant trees in $\mathcal{T}$. For these trees, we can mark all points that some tree into-matches in $O(mn)$ total time by technique similar to [13], where $m = |s|$ and $n = |t|$. Then by dynamic programming over t, we can detect the matching points of all subtrees of s in $O(mn)$ time. This gives the proof. $\qquad\square$

Theorem 1. *The into-matching problems for OT and thus for OGT are NP-complete.*

Proof. It is easy to see that the problem belongs to NP. We give a log-space reduction from the one-in-three SAT problem into the into-matching problem for OT as follows. Let $F = C_1 \wedge \cdots \wedge C_m$ be an instance 3-CNF over a set of Boolean variables $\{v_1, \ldots, v_n\}$. Suppose that the alphabet Σ contains $f, g, h, c_1, \ldots, c_m$, $b, 0, 1$ and $\mathbf{X} = \{x_1, \ldots, x_n\}$. We will define the instance (T, P) of the into-matching problem, where $T = g(T_0, T_1, \ldots, T_m)$ and $P = g(P_0, P_1, \ldots, P_m)$, as follows. First, we define a pair (T_0, P_0) by $T_0 = f(b^{(1)}(0, 1), \ldots, b^{(n)}(0, 1))$ and $P_0 = f(b^{(1)}(x_1), \ldots, b^{(n)}(x_n))$. Then, we know that if P_0 into-matches T_0 then the value of $(x_1, \ldots, x_n)$ corresponds with an assignment in $\{0, 1\}^n$. Then, we define (T_j, P_j) for every $1 \le j \le m$. Let $1 \le j \le m$ be any index and let $C_j = L_{i_1} \vee L_{i_2} \vee L_{i_3}$ be the j-th clause in the 3-CNF F, where L_i is either x_i or $\bar{x}_i$. For every $k = 1, 2, 3$, we denote by $\mathbf{1}_{i_k} \in \{0, 1\}$ and $\mathbf{0}_{i_k}$ be the bits that make the i_k-th literal L_{i_k} true and false, resp. Then, we define $T_j = c_j(h(\mathbf{1}_{i_1}, \mathbf{0}_{i_2}, \mathbf{0}_{i_3}), h(\mathbf{0}_{i_1}, \mathbf{1}_{i_2}, \mathbf{0}_{i_3}), h(\mathbf{0}_{i_1}, \mathbf{0}_{i_2}, \mathbf{1}_{i_3}))$ and $P_j = c_j(h(x_{i_1}, x_{i_2}, x_{i_3}))$. For the instance (T, P) above, it is not hard to see that $(b_1, \ldots, b_n) \in \{0, 1\}^n$ is an yes-instance of F in one-in-three SAT if and only if P into-matches T by a matching ϕ that matches each node labeled with x_i to the node labeled with b_i for $i = 1, \ldots, n$. This completes the proof. $\qquad\square$

2.2   Learning Model

As a learning model, we use the exact learning model of Angluin [5], where a learning algorithm accesses the information on the target concept t_* by using the following queries. Let t_* be a target hypothesis. An *equivalence query* for t_* (EQ) is to propose any tree pattern $t \in OGT$ and denoted by $EQ(t)$. The answer is *yes* if $L(t) = L(t_*)$. Otherwise, a *counterexample* $w \in (L(t_*) - L(t)) \cup (L(t) - L(t_*))$ is returned. A counterexample w is *positive* if $w \in L(t_*)$ and *negative* otherwise. A *subset query* (SQ), denoted by $SQ(t)$, is to propose any tree pattern $t \in OGT$, and receives as the answer *yes* if $L(t) \subseteq L(t_*)$ and *no* otherwise. A *membership query* (MQ), denoted by $MQ(w)$, is to propose any constant tree $w \in \mathcal{T}$, and receives as the answer *yes* if $w \in L(t_*)$ and *no* otherwise.

The goal of an *exact learning algorithm* $\mathcal{A}$ is exact identification of the target hypothesis t_* using making equivalence and membership queries for t_*. $\mathcal{A}$ must halt and output a hypothesis $t \in \mathcal{H}$ that is equivalent to t_*, i.e., $L(t) = L(t_*)$, and, at any stage in learning, the running time of $\mathcal{A}$ must be bounded by a polynomial in the size of t_* and of the longest counterexample returned by equivalence queries so far.

MQ and EQ for μ-OGT are polynomial time decidable under the into-match semantics from Lemma 2. Hence, the exact learnability with EQ (and MQ, resp.) implies the learnability in the PAC-learning model (with MQ, resp.) and the prediction learning model (with MQ, resp.) for μ-OGT [5]. Unfortunately, MQ is NP-complete for the full class OGT under the into-match semantics as seen in Theorem 1, while EQ is linear time decidable by 2 of Lemma 1. In all learning algorithms in this paper, the hypotheses belong to the target class.

3   Learning Linear Ordered Gapped Tree Patterns

In this section, we present an efficient algorithm for learning μ-OGT using equivalence and membership queries.

Definition 7. *Let s, t be OGT and ϕ be any into-matching from s to t. Then, a node v in t is said to be an* excess node *w.r.t. ϕ if no nodes in s maps to v. Otherwise, the node v is said to be a* mapped node *w.r.t. ϕ.*

Lemma 3. *Let s, t be OGT such that $s \sqsupseteq t$, and ϕ be any into-matching from s to t. If $|s| \neq |t|$ then there exists at least one excess node in t w.r.t. ϕ.*

Proof. Since $\phi : V_s \to V_t$ is a one-to-one mapping, if there is no excess nodes in t w.r.t. ϕ then $|s| = |t|$ must hold. This is the contradiction. $\square$

We introduce two operations reducing the size of an OGT. Let t be an OGT and $v \in V_t$ be a node. Let v be a leaf in t. Then, the *removal* of v is the operation that removes the leaf v and its incident edge $(parent, v) \in E_t$ from t. Let v be a chain node in t. Then, the *contraction* at v is the operation that removes v from t and replaces a pair of incident edges $(parent, v), (v, child) \in E_t$ with the new edge $(parent, child)$ in E_t. In both cases, we denote by $t \backslash \{v\}$ the tree obtained from t by applying the operation with v to t. Let $v \in V_t$ be any node and $\alpha \in \Sigma \cup \mathbf{X} \cup \Gamma$ be any symbol, the *replacement* at v with α is the operation to replace the label $\ell_t(v)$ with α. We denote the resulting tree by $t[\alpha/v]$.

Lemma 4. *Let s, t be μ-OGT ($t \in \mathcal{T}$) such that $s \sqsupseteq_{in} t$. If there exists either a leaf or a chain node e that is an excess node in t w.r.t. some into-matching ϕ from s to t, then the constant tree t' defined as follows satisfies $s \sqsupseteq_{in} t'$.*

1. *For a leaf e, $t' = t \backslash \{e\}$ is obtained from t by the removal of e.*
2. *For a chain node e, $t' = t \backslash \{e\}$ is obtained from t by the contraction at e.*

Proof. Suppose that $\phi : V_s \to V_t$ is any into-matching from s to t. Let $t' = t \backslash \{e\}$ is the tree obtained by either removal or contraction at e. Then, we show that ϕ is still an into-match from s to t' as follows. We can see that the mapping ϕ satisfies the conditions (1) to (5) in Definition 1 and the condition (6) in Definition 4. Since e is an excess node, i.e., $e \notin \phi(V_s)$, the conditions (1), (2),

---

Algorithm LEARN-INTO-LIN-OGT

Given: Oracles for EQ and MQ for target μ-OGT t_*.

Output: A μ-OGT t equivalent to t_*.

Method:

1 If $(EQ(\perp) = yes)$ then return $\perp$.

2 Let w be a counterexample returned by EQ. /* A positive example of t_* */

3 While t changes, do:

> /* The following steps properly reduce the size of $t = w$ */
>
> (a) If $MQ(w\backslash\{v\}) = yes$ for some leaf or chain node v of w then $w := w\backslash\{v\}$, where $w\backslash\{v\}$ is the constant tree obtained by either the removal or the contraction, resp.
>
> (b) $t := w$.

4 While t changes, do:

> /* The following steps properly reduce the number of constants in t */
>
> (a) If $MQ(w[b/v]) = yes$ for some leaf v of w and a constant label $b \neq \ell_w(v)$, then let $x \in \Sigma\backslash var(t)$ be a new tree variable.
>
> (b) Else if $MQ(w[b/v]) = yes$ for some chain node v of w and a constant label $b \neq \ell_w(v)$, then let $x \in \Gamma\backslash gap(t)$ be a new gap variable.
>
> (c) $t := t[x/v]$.

5 return t;

Fig. 2. A learning algorithm for μ-*OGT* with the into-match semantics using equivalence queries and membership queries

(3) are obviously satisfied. If s is μ-OGT, then the condition (4) is also satisfied. In the case that e is a leaf, the removal of e does not change the order of the sibling of e at all. Thus, the condition (5) follows. In the case that e is a chain node, e is on the path between $\phi(g)$ and $\phi(c)$, where g is a gap node and c is its child in s. Thus, even after the contraction at e, $\phi(c)$ is still a proper descendant of $\phi(g)$, and this satisfies the condition (6) in Definition 4. □

For a pair s, t of isomorphic OGT, a pair of nodes $(u, v) \in V_s \times V_t$ *has the same position* if they have the same numbering with the preorder numbering in the depth-first search.

Lemma 5. *Let s be an OGT and t be an instance of s of the same size. Let $\psi : V_t \to V_s$ be an isomorphism between V_t and V_s. For every node $v \in V_t$, if $s \sqsupseteq_{in} t[a_i/v]$ $(i = 1, 2)$ for a pair of distinct constants $a_1 \neq a_2$, then $\psi(v)$ is a tree variable if v is a leaf and a gap variable if v is a gap node.*

Proof. For ever $i \in \{1, 2\}$, let $t_i = t[a_i/v]$ and let ϕ_i be an into-matching from s to $t[a_i/v]$. Since t_1 and t_2 differ only in their labels, we have $V_{t_1} = V_{t_2} = V_t$. If $|s| = |t|$ then we know that ϕ_1 and ϕ_2 are the same isomorphism from V_s to V_{t_i}. From the condition (3) of Definition 1, the node u cannot be a constant node. Thus, u is either a variable node or a gap node depending on whether it is a leaf or a chain node. □

Theorem 2. *The algorithm LEARN-INTO-LIN-OGT of Fig. 2 exactly learns any linear ordered gapped tree pattern t_* in μ-OGT with the into-match semantics in polynomial time using exactly one EQ and $O(n^2)$ MQ, where n is the size of the initial counterexample given by EQ. This also holds for either finite or infinite alphabet Σ.*

Proof. If $t_* = \bot$ then, the algorithm outputs $t = \bot$, and we are done. Thus, suppose that $t_* \neq \bot$. Then, the algorithm receives a positive counterexample $w \in \mathcal{T}$ of t_* of size $n \geq 1$ such that $t_* \sqsupseteq_{in} w$. First, we see the termination of the algorithm. We can easily see that whenever the first while-loop is executed, the size $|w|$ decreases by at least one, and whenever the second while-loop is executed, the number $var(t) + gap(t)$ increases by at least one while $|t|$ is constant. Thus, the first and the second while-loops can be executed at most $O(n)$ time.

Suppose that we enter the while-loop of step 3. The while-loop is executed while $|w| = |t| > |t_*|$. If $|w| > |t_*|$ then it follows from Lemma 3 that there exists at least one excess node, say v, w.r.t. ϕ that is either a leaf or a chain node. Otherwise, there is an internal node with more than one children. We can follow down this edge and then repeat this process until we eventually reach a leaf or a chain excess node. Thus Lemma 4 shows that step 3.(a) is executed and this repeats until $|w| = |t_*|$ holds.

Now, the algorithm enters the second while-loop. Suppose that $t_* \sqsupseteq_{in} w$ but $t_* \not\sqsupseteq_{in} w$. Since $|w| = |t_*|$, there is a node v such that $\ell_w(v)$ is constant but $\ell_{t_*}(v)$ is either a tree variable or a gap variable. Thus by Lemma 5, the algorithm executes one of steps 4.(a) or 4.(b) and correctly computes the updated pattern $t' = t[x/v]$ such that $t_* \sqsupseteq_{in} t'$ still holds. Therefore, this step is executed until the algorithm reaches $t \equiv_{in} t_*$. Hence, the theorem is proved. □

Corollary 1. *The class μ-OGT under the into-matching semantics is polynomial time learnable in exact learning model using one positive example and MQ.*

4   Necessity of Equivalence and Membership Queries

In the following, we show that membership queries alone is insufficient for learning of μ-OGT. We then show that μ-OGT is prediction preserving hard for DNF formulas. Since the latter hardness result is representation independent and the membership queries for μ-OGT are polynomial time solvable, it also indicates the insufficiency of exact learning with equivalent queries alone or PAC-learning random examples alone assuming the hardness of DNF formulas.

Theorem 3. *Any algorithm that exactly learns all linear ordered gapped tree patterns in μ-OGT using membership queries alone must run in $2^{\Omega(n)}$ times in the worst case, where n is the size of the target hypothesis.*

Proof. Suppose that Σ contains three symbols $0, 1, a$ and f. For any binary sequence $b_1 \cdots b_n \in \{0,1\}^n$ of length n, we have an associated constant ordered tree patterns

$$\overbrace{f(b_1, f(\cdots f(b_n, a) \cdots))}^{n}$$

over Σ. There are 2^n such OT. Then, an adversary maintains a set S of candidate hypotheses as follows. Initially, S is the set of all of 2^n chain trees defined above. Given a membership query $MQ(w)$ with $w \in \mathcal{T}$, let $Path(w)$ be the set of all chain trees contained in w as a path in w. Whenever $S \backslash Path(w)$ is not empty, the adversary returns "no" and set $S := S \backslash Path(w)$, Since $\#Path(w)$ is bounded by the size of w, the adversary can continue this process while the total size $n = \sum_{1 \le i \le k} |w_i|$ of queries does not exceeds 2^n. Since the cost of a query of length $m \ge 0$ is $O(m)$, the time complexity of the algorithm is bounded below by $2^{\Omega(n)}$. □

Theorem 4. *The polynomial time prediction of the class μ-OGT is at least as hard as the polynomial time prediction of DNF formulas.*

Proof. It is sufficient to show that there is a prediction preserving reduction [21] from DNF_n to μ-OGT for every $n \ge 0$. Let $d = T_1 \vee \cdots \vee T_m$ be a DNF formula over the set $\{v_1, \ldots, v_n\}$ of Boolean variables. Suppose that Σ contains constant symbols $0, 1, f$ and g. For each assignment $a = a_1 \cdots a_n \in \{0, 1\}^n$, let $\tilde{a} = g(g(a_1), \ldots, g(a_n))$ and $\tilde{b} = g(g(0), g(1), \ldots, g(0), g(1)) = g((g(0), g(1))^n)$. Then, construct an instance mapping ψ and a hypothesis mapping ξ as follows:

$$\psi(a) = f(\overbrace{\tilde{a}, \tilde{b}, \ldots, \tilde{b}, \tilde{a}}^{2m-1})$$
$$\xi(d) = f(\xi(T_1), \ldots, \xi(T_m)),$$

where $\psi(a)$ contains $(m-1)$ copies of $\tilde{a}$ and m copies of $\tilde{b}$. For each $1 \le j \le m$, the subtree $\xi(T_j)$ of $\xi(d)$ is defined by $\xi(T_j) = g(\alpha_1^j, \ldots, \alpha_n^j)$, where $\alpha_i^j = g(1)$ if the j-th term T_j contains v_j, $\alpha_i^j = g(0)$ if the j-th term T_j contains $\overline{v_j}$, and $\alpha_i^j = g$ otherwise. Then, the following statements hold. (a) $\xi(T_i)$ into-matches $\tilde{a}$ iff a satisfies term T_j. (b) $\xi(T_i)$ always matches $\tilde{b}$. (c) $\tilde{a}$ and $\tilde{b}$ are only the subtrees that $\xi(T_j)$ into-matches. It easily follows from (a) and (b) that if a satisfies at least one term, say T_j, in d then $\xi(d)$ into-matches $\psi(a)$. On the other hand, assume that $\xi(d)$ into-matches $\psi(a)$. Then using (a)–(c) and the pigeon-hole principle, it is not difficult to show that at least one $\xi(T_j)$ into-matches a copy of $\tilde{a}$. Therefore, a satisfies T_j and thus the whole formula d. Combining above arguments, we have that a satisfies d iff $\xi(d)$ into-matches $\psi(a)$ and the theorem follows from [21]. □

5   Extension for Linear Ordered Gapped Forests

In this section, we show a polynomial time learning algorithm for μ-OGF using equivalence and subset queries. An *ordered gapped forest* (OGF, for short) is a finite set $H = \{t_1, \ldots, t_k\}$ ($k \ge 0$) of ordered gapped tree patterns in OGT. An ordered gapped forest H is *linear* (linear OGF or μ-OGF, for short) if every member $t \in H$ is a linear OGT in μ-OGT. We denote by OGF and μ-OGF the classes of OGFs and μ-OGFs, respectively. Forests of OTs with the onto-semantics under a ranked alphabet are called unions of tree patterns in [7].

Definition 8. *For an ordered gapped forest H, we define the* language *of H with the into-semantics as the union $L_{in}(H) = \cup_{t \in H} L_{in}(t)$ of the languages defined by its members.*

The following property is called the compactness [3,2,6,8] and plays an important role in the learning of unions of languages [8].

Lemma 6. *Let Σ be an infinite alphabet. For any ordered gapped forests $P, Q \in OGF$, $L_{in}(P) \supseteq L_{in}(Q)$ if and only if for every $q \in Q$ there exists some $p \in P$ such that $p \sqsupseteq q$.*

Proof. For every OGT $q \in Q$, let w_q be a constant tree obtained from q by *substituting* mutually distinct constants not appearing in any of P for all tree and gap variables in q. Since $w_q \in L(Q)$, if $L_{in}(P) \supseteq L_{in}(Q)$ then there exists some $p \in P$ such that $w_q \in L(P)$. Since any substituted symbols do not appear in P, if $p \sqsupseteq_{in} w_q$ then we have $p \sqsupseteq_{in} q$ by inverting the substitution. $\square$

An intuitive idea behind our learning algorithm for OGF is to identify each member of the target forest H_* one by one using as a subroutine a learning algorithm with MQ or SQ for learning μ-OGT. For this purpose, a property which will be shown in Lemma 8 is essential. Below, we develop a new algorithm LEARN-INTO-LIN-OGT-SQ as such a subprocedure.

A *generalization operator* for OGT is a binary relation $\gamma \subseteq OGT \times OGT$ such that for every $s, t \in OGT$, $(s,t) \in \gamma$ implies $s \sqsubseteq_{in} t$. For γ and any OGT s, we define $\gamma(s) = \{ t \in OGT \mid (s,t) \in \gamma \}$ and denote by γ^+ the transitive closure of γ. Then, γ is called *efficient* if for every $s \in OGT$, $\#\gamma(s)$ is polynomially bounded by $|s|$ and all elements in $\gamma(s)$ can be printed in polynomial time in $|s|$; γ is called *proper* if for every $s, t \in OGT$, $(s,t) \in \gamma$ implies $s \sqsubset_{in} t$, and *complete* if for every $s, t \in OGT$, $s \sqsubset_{in} t$ implies $(s,t) \in \gamma^+$.

Below, we give a generalization operator for μ-OGT.

Definition 9. *Let s, t be μ-OGT. Then, $(s,t) \in \gamma_1$ holds if t is obtained from s by applying one of the following operations O1–O4:*

(O1) If s has a leaf $v \in V_s$, then $t = t \backslash \{v\}$ is the tree obtained by removing v.

(O2) If s has a gap node $v \in V_s$, then $t = s \backslash \{p\}$ is the tree obtained by contracting s at either the non-root parent or the non-leaf child p of v.

(O3) If s has a leaf node $v \in V_s$ with constant label c, then $t = s[x/v]$, where $x \in \mathbf{X} \backslash var(s)$ is a new tree variable.

(O4) If s has a chain node $v \in V_s$ with constant label c, then $t = s[x/v]$, where $x \in \Gamma \backslash gap(s)$ is a new gap variable.

Definition 10. *The operator γ_1 is an efficient and proper generalization operator for μ-OGT.*

Proof. First, we see that γ_1 is proper. Let s, t be any OGT. If $(s,t) \in \gamma_1$ then we have $s \sqsubseteq_{in} t$ by the construction of γ_1. Assume that the converse $s \sqsupseteq_{in} t$ holds. Then, we have $s \equiv_{in} t$ and it follows from 2 of Lemma 1 that s and t are

---

Algorithm LEARN-INTO-LIN-OGT-BY-SQ
Given: Oracles for *EQ* and *SQ* for target μ-OGT t_*.
Output: A μ-OGT t equivalent to t_*.
Method:
  1 If $(EQ(\bot) = yes)$ then return $\bot$.
  2 Let w be a counterexample returned by EQ. Set $t = w$.
    /* w is a positive example of t_* */
  3 While $MQ(t') = yes$ for some $t' \in \gamma_1(t)$, set $t = t'$.
    /* γ_1 is the refinement operator for μ-OGT defined in Definition 9. */
  4 return t;

Fig. 3. A learning algorithm for μ-OGT with the into-match semantics using equivalence queries and subset queries

identical modulo renaming. However, this is not possible by the construction of γ_1. Hence, γ_1 is proper. We can see that for every s, $\#\gamma_1(s) = O(n)$ and $\gamma_1(s)$ is polynomial time computable in $n = |s|$. $\qquad\square$

Lemma 7. *The generalization operator γ_1 is complete for μ-OGT.*

Proof. It is sufficient to show that for any μ-OGT s, t, if $s \sqsubseteq_{in} t$ then there is a sequence $s_0 = s, s_1, \ldots, s_n = t$ $(n \geq 0)$ of μ-OGT where for every $1 \leq i \leq n$, $(s_{i-1}, s_i) \in \gamma_1$ holds. If $s \equiv_{in} t$ then the claim trivially holds. Thus, we assume that $s \sqsubset_{in} t$ with an into-matching ϕ. Then, we see that one of the operators (O1)–(O4) is applicable to obtain an $s' \in \gamma(s)$ such that $s' \sqsubseteq t$ as follows. In the case that $|s| < |t|$, it follows from Lemma 3 that there are excess nodes e w.r.t. ϕ that are a leaf node or a chain node next to a gap node, and we can apply operations (O1) or (O2) to e. In the case that $|s| = |t|$, there exists some constant node e whose label can be changed to either a tree or a gap node by (O3) or (O4). In either case, we obtain $s' \in \gamma_1(s)$ such that $s' \sqsubseteq t$. $\qquad\square$

In Fig. 3, we present a modified algorithm LEARN-INTO-OGT-SQ for learning μ-OGT with EQ and SQ. To see the correctness of the algorithm, we prepare some notations and lemmas. Let $t_* \in \mu$-OGT be the target OGT, $t_0 \in T$ be the initial positive instance returned by EQ, and for every $n \geq 0$, let t_n be the hypotheses generated in the n-th execution of the while loop. Since γ_1 is proper and complete, we have the next lemma crucial for the main result.

Lemma 8. *For any $w \in \mathcal{T}$, the sequence of hypotheses generated by the algorithm LEARN-INTO-OGT-SQ form an properly increasing sequence $t_0 = w \sqsubset_{in} t_1 \sqsubset_{in} \cdots \sqsubset_{in} t_i \sqsubset_{in} \cdots \sqsubseteq_{in} t_*$ $(i \geq 0)$.*

To see the termination, we define the size complexity of an OGT t by $size(t) = 2 \times |t| - (\#var(t) + \#gap(t))$. Obviously, $0 \leq size(t) \leq 2|t|$ holds. The next lemma holds for full class of OGT.

Lemma 9. *For any OGT s, t, if $s \sqsubset_{in} t$ then $size(s) > size(t)$ holds.*

Algorithm LEARN-INTO-LIN-OGF
Given: Oracles for EQ and SQ for the target forest T_*.
Output: An ordered gapped forest H equivalent to T_*.
Method:
  1 $H := \emptyset$;
  2 While $(EQ(H) = no)$, do:
    (a) Let w be a counterexample returned by EQ.
    (b) Run the algorithm LEARN-INTO-OGT-SQ of Fig. 3 with w as the initial
        positive counterexample and using SQ for T_*.
    (c) Let t be the tree pattern returned by LEARN-INTO-OGT-SQ.
    (d) $H := H \cup \{t\}$.
  4 Return H.

Fig. 4. A learning algorithm for μ-OGF with the into-match semantics using equivalence queries and subset queries

Lemma 10. *The algorithm LEARN-INTO-LIN-OGT-SQ of Fig. 3 exactly learns any linear ordered gapped tree pattern t_* in μ-OGT with the into-match semantics in polynomial time in n using exactly one EQ and $O(n^2)$ SQ, where n is the size of the initial counterexample given by EQ. This also holds for either finite or infinite alphabet Σ.*

Proof. By similar arguments as in Theorem 2. □

In Fig. 4, we present the main algorithm LEARN-INTO-LIN-OGF for learning OGF with EQ and SQ, which uses LEARN-INTO-OGT-SQ as a subroutine.

Theorem 5. *Let Σ be an infinite alphabet. The algorithm LEARN-INTO-LIN-OGF of Fig. 4 exactly learns any μ-OGF T_* with the into-match semantics in polynomial time in m and n using $O(m)$ EQ and $O(mn^2)$ SQ, where $m = \#T_*$ and n is the maximum size of the counterexamples given by EQ.*

Proof. In the initial stage, the algorithm received a positive instance of t_* since $L_{in}(\emptyset) = \emptyset$. By induction on the number of stages, we can show that the example given to the subroutine LEARN-INTO-OGT-SQ is always positive. We denote by H the current forest in the main algorithm. Let t_0 and t be the initial example to and hypothesis maintained by the subroutine. We will show that $h_* \sqsupseteq_{in} t$ for some $h_* \in H_*$ but $h \not\sqsupseteq t$ for any $h \in H$ hold, which ensure that the subroutine can correctly simulate SQ for $L_{in}(T_*)\backslash L_{in}(H)$ using SQ for $L_{in}(T_*)$. Suppose contrary that $h \sqsupseteq t$ for some $h \in H$. Since $t \sqsupseteq t_0$ by Lemma 8, this means $h \sqsupseteq t_0$ and thus $t_0 \in L_{in}(H)$. This contradicts the assumption, and we showed the claim. For any counterexample t_0 to $SQ(H)$, $t_0 \in L_{in}(T_*)\backslash L_{in}(H)$, and thus there is some $t_* \in T_*$ such that $t_* \sqsupseteq t_0$ with some matching ϕ. Based on the existence of ϕ, the subroutine eventually identifies one of the t_* such that $t_* \sqsupseteq t_0$. Since the main algorithm identify at least one member of the target forest T_* in each execution of its while loop, the while loop of the main algorithm can be executed at most m times. This completes the proof. □

6   Learning Unrestricted Ordered Gapped Tree Patterns

In this section, we present a modified algorithm for learning OGT with repeated variables in polynomial time using equivalence and subset queries based
on the technique of [2]. Since the membership query for OGT is NP-complete
by Lemma 1, this result may not have practical value. We include this section
for indicating how to learn complex tree patterns in general.

From the next lemma, we know that it is required to simultaneously replace
several subtrees to learn OGT with repeated variables. Let γ_1 be the generalization operator for μ-OGT introduced in Section 5.

Lemma 11. *Let s, t be OGT. Suppose that $s \sqsupseteq_{in} t$ but $s \not\equiv t$. Then, one of the
following condition holds:*

1. *There exists some OGT $t' \in \gamma_1(t)$ such that $s \sqsupseteq_{in} t'$.*
2. *There exists some OGT t' such that $s \sqsupseteq_{in} t'$ and $t' \sqsupseteq_{in} t$ defined as follows:
   For some set of at least two nodes $V = \{v_1, \ldots, v_n\}$ $(n \geq 2)$ with any
   labels which have the identical subtrees $t/v_1 = \cdots = t/v_n$, the OGT $t' =
   t[z/v_1, \ldots, z/v_n]$ is obtained by replacing each t/v_i $(1 \leq i \leq n)$ with the
   nodes labeled with the copies of a new variable $z \in \mathbf{X} \backslash var(t)$.*

Proof. From the definition of the into-matching in Definition 1 and the completeness of the generalization operator γ_1 for μ-OGT in Lemma 7.   □

To overcome this problem, Amoth, Cull, and Tadepalli [2] developed an el-
egant partitioning technique to generalize repeated variables in unordered trees
and forests. For OGT s, t, we denote by $O_t(s)$ the set of all *occurrences* of s in
t, i.e., all nodes $v \in V_t$ that s is the subtree of t with the root v, and by $t \backslash (t/v)$
the tree obtained by removing the subtree of t rooted at node $v \in V_t$. In Fig. 5,
we show a version of their algorithm, *Partition*, modified for OGT.

Example 1. Let us explain the algorithm *Partition* with an example in Fig. 6.
Let $t_* = f(a(x, y), b(x, y, y))$ be an OGT and $t = f(a(a, a), b(a, a, a))$ be an
instance of t_*. Assume that γ_1 is already applied to t and not applicable any
more. In general, a may be either a constant or a tree. (1) First, the algorithm
inserts the copies of new variable z at the right to each occurrences of constant
a. (2) The algorithm first delete an old leaf a and (3) then a new leaf z using SQ.
If these steps succeeds, then the matching from t_* to t have to split the variables
into two groups as shown in (3) since we have more subtrees a and x than any
variable x or y. Finally, the resulting nodes z and x indicate this splitting.

Lemma 12. *Let t_* be a target OGT and t be any OGT such that $t_* \sqsupseteq_{in} t$.
Suppose that $s \sqsupseteq_{in} t$ but $s \not\equiv t$, and there is no OGT $t' \in \gamma_1(t)$ such that
$s \sqsupseteq_{in} t'$. Then, the algorithm Partition in Fig. 5 computes an OGT t' such that
$s \sqsupseteq_{in} t' \sqsupseteq_{in} t$. Furthermore, Partition runs in polynomial time using $O(n^2)$ SQ
in $n = |t|$.*

Procedure Partition(t)

/* Simultaneously changing identical subtrees with the same new variables. */

For each distinct subtree s of t do begin

    $S_s := O_t(s)$ and $k := |S_s|$; let $z \in \mathbf{X} \backslash var(t)$ be a new tree variable;

    For each $v \in S_s$ do:

        Create a new node u labeled with a copy of z;

        Attach u to the parent of v as the adjacent right sibling of v;

    $S_z := O_t(z)$ and $S := S_s \cup S_z$;

    While t changes do: /* executed whenever $|S| > k$ */

        If there is some $v \in S \cap S_s$ such that $SQ(t \backslash (t/v)) = yes$ then

            $t := t \backslash (t/v)$; $S := S \backslash \{v\}$;   /* removing the subtree rooted at v */

        Else if there is some $v \in S \cap S_z$ such that $SQ(t \backslash \{v\}) = yes$ then

            $t := t \backslash \{v\}$; $S := S \backslash \{v\}$;   /* removing the variable node v */

    If ($s \in \mathbf{X}$ and $S \neq S_z$) or ($s \notin \mathbf{X}$ and $S \neq S_s$) then

        Return t;   /* t is properly generalized */

end for;

Return t;   /* t does not change */

Fig. 5. The partitioning algorithm using subset queries

Theorem 6. *There exists some algorithm that exactly learns any unrestricted ordered gapped tree pattern t_* in OGT with the into-match semantics in polynomial time in n using exactly one EQ and $O(n^3)$ SQ, where n is the size of the initial counterexample given by EQ. This also holds for either finite or infinite alphabet Σ.*

Proof. We modify the LEARN-INTO-LIN-OGT-SQ of Fig. 3 used for learning μ-OGT with EQ and SQ. The following is the outline of the modified algorithm, where γ_1 is the refinement operator for μ-OGT defined in Definition 9.

    1 If $(EQ(\bot) = yes)$ then return $\bot$.

    2 Let w be a counterexample returned by EQ. Set $t = w$.

    3 While t changes during the loop, do:

      (a) If $MQ(t') = yes$ for some $t' \in \gamma_1(t)$, then set $t = t'$.

      (b) Else *Partition*(t) returns an answer t', then set $t = t'$.

    4 return t;

From Lemma 7, γ_1 is a proper and complete generalization operator. From Lemma 10, Lemma 7, and Lemma 12, we can show a similar property as Lemma 8 On the other hand, the size complexity is also valid for OGT with repeated variables. This and Lemma 9 show the termination after at most $O(n)$ execution of the while loop, and each execution requires $O(n^2)$ SQ. From Lemma 11, the algorithm terminates only when $t_n \equiv_{into} t_*$. This completes the proof.   □

7 Conclusion

In this paper, we presented efficient algorithms for learning the class of μ-OGT using equivalence and membership queries, and the class of μ-OGF and the class

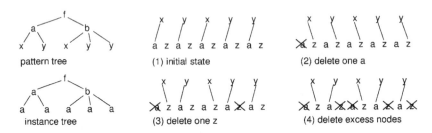

Fig. 6. An example computation of the partition algorithm

of unrestricted OGT with equivalence and subset queries under the into-match semantics. We also showed two hardness results which indicates that above two types of queries are necessary to efficiently learn μ-OGT and μ-OGF. Connection among the learnabilities of OGT, OGF, pattern languages [4,16] and first-order logic [11] is a future problem.

References

1. S. Abiteboul, Quass, McHugh, J. Widom, J. L. Wiener, The Lorel query language for semistructured data, *Int'l. J. on Digital Libraries*, 1(1), 68-88, 1997.
2. T. R. Amoth, P. Cull, and P. Tadepalli, Exact learning of unordered tree patterns from queries, In *Proc. COLT'99*, ACM Press, 323–332, 1999.
3. T. R. Amoth, P. Cull, and P. Tadepalli, Exact learning of tree patterns from queries and counterexamples, In *Proc. COLT'98*, ACM Press, 175-186, 1988.
4. D. Angluin, Finding patterns common to a set of strings, *JCSS*, 21, 46–62, 1980.
5. D. Angluin, Queries and concept learning, *Machine Learning*, 2(4), 319–342, 1988.
6. H. Arimura, H. Ishizaka, T. Shinohara, S. Otsuki, A generalization of the least general generalization, *Machine Intelligence*, 13, 59–85, 1994.
7. H. Arimura, H. Ishizaka, T. Shinohara, Learning unions of tree patterns using queries, *Theoretical Computer Science*, 185(1), 47–62, 1997.
8. H. Arimura, T. Shinohara, S. Otsuki, Finding minimal generalizations for unions of pattern languages and its application to inductive inference from positive data, In *Proc. STACS'94*, LNCS 775, Springer-Verlag, 649–660, 1994.
9. P. Buneman, M. F. Fernandez, D. Suciu, UnQL: A query language and algebra for semistructured data based on structural recursion, *VLDB J.*, 9(1), 76–110, 2000.
10. M. Frazier, L. Pitt, CLASSIC learning, *Machine Learning*, 25 (2-3), 151–193, 1996.
11. R. Khardon, Learning function-free Horn expressions, *Mach. Learn.*, 35(1), 241–275, 1999.
12. K-I. Ko, A. Marron, Tzeng, Learning string patterns and tree patterns from examples, In *Proc. 7th Internat. Conference on Machine Learning*, 384–391, 1990.
13. Kosaraju, S. R., Efficient tree pattern matching, In *Proc. 30th FOCS*, 178–183, 1989.
14. N. Kushmerick, Wrapper induction: efficiency and expressiveness, Artificial Intelligence, Vol.118, pp.15–68, 2000.
15. S. Matsumoto and A. Shinohara, Learning Pattern Languages Using Queries, *Proc. Euro COLT'97*, LNAI, Springer-Verlag, 185–197, 1997.

16. J. Nessel and S. Lange, Learning erasing pattern languages with queries, Proc. ALT2000, LNAI 1968, Springer-Verlag, 86–100, 2000.
17. G. D. Plotkin, A note on inductive generalization, In *Machine Intell.*, 5, Edinburgh Univ. Press, 153–163, 1970.
18. H. Sakamoto, Y. Murakami, H. Arimura, S. Arikawa, Extracting Partial Structures from HTML Documents, In *Proc. FLAIRS 2001*, AAAI Press, 2001.
19. Extensible Markup Language (XML) Version 1.0. *W3C Recommendation 1998.*
20. XML-QL: A Query Language for XML W3C Note, Aug. 1998.
21. L. Pitt, M. K. Warmuth, Prediction-preserving reducibility, J. Comput. System Sci. 41(3) (1990) 430–467.

Extending Elementary Formal Systems[*]

Steffen Lange[1], Gunter Grieser[2], and Klaus P. Jantke[1]

[1] Deutsches Forschungszentrum für Künstliche Intelligenz,
Stuhlsatzenhausweg 3, Saarbrücken, Germany,
{lange,jantke}@dfki.de
[2] Technische Universität Darmstadt, Fachbereich Informatik,
Alexanderstr. 10, 64283 Darmstadt, Germany,
grieser@informatik.tu-darmstadt.de

Abstract. An elementary formal system (EFS) is a logic program such as a Prolog program, for instance, that directly manipulates strings. Arikawa and his co-workers proposed elementary formal systems as a unifying framework for formal language learning.

In the present paper, we introduce advanced elementary formal systems (AEFSs), i.e., elementary formal systems which allow for the use of a certain kind of negation, which is nonmonotonic, in essence, and which is conceptually close to negation as failure.

We study the expressiveness of this approach by comparing certain AEFS definable language classes to the levels in the Chomsky hierarchy and to the language classes that are definable by EFSs that meet the same syntactical constraints.

Moreover, we investigate the learnability of the corresponding AEFS definable language classes in two major learning paradigms, namely in Gold's model of learning in the limit and Valiant's model of probably approximately correct learning. In particular, we show which learnability results achieved for EFSs extend to AEFSs and which do not.

1 Introduction and Motivation

Elementary formal systems (EFSs) have been introduced by Smullyan [20] to develop his theory of recursive functions over strings. In [3] and in a series of subsequent publications like [5,24,4,6,19,25,14], for example, Arikawa and his co-workers proposed elementary formal systems as a unifying framework for formal language learning.

EFSs are a kind of logic programs such as a Prolog programs, for instance. EFSs directly manipulate non-empty strings over some underlying alphabet and can be used to describe formal languages. For instance, the EFS depicted in Figure 1 describes the language that contains all non-empty strings of form $a^n b^n$. More formally speaking, if a ground atom $p(w)$ can be derived from the given rules, then the string w has to be of form $a^n b^n$.

[*] This work has been partially supported by the German Ministry of Economics and Technology (BMWi) within the joint project LExIKON under grant 01 MD 949.

N. Abe, R. Khardon, and T. Zeugmann (Eds.): ALT 2001, LNAI 2225, pp. 332–347, 2001.
© Springer-Verlag Berlin Heidelberg 2001

(1) $p(xy) \leftarrow q(x,y)$.
(2) $q(\mathsf{a},\mathsf{b})$.
(3) $q(\mathsf{a}x,\mathsf{b}y) \leftarrow q(x,y)$.

Fig. 1. An example EFS

Arikawa and his co-workers (cf. [5,4], e.g.) used EFSs as a uniform framework to define acceptors for formal languages. In this context, they discussed the relation of certain EFS definable language classes to the standard levels in the classical Chomsky hierarchy. In addition, they have studied the learnability/non-learnability of EFS definable language classes in different learning paradigms, including Gold's [9] model of learning in the limit as well as Valiant's [23] model of probably approximately correct learning (cf. [5,4,19,25,14], e.g.). For instance, the results in [18,19] impressively show that EFSs provide an appropriate framework to prove that rich language classes are Gold-style learnable from only positive examples.

In the present paper, we follow this line of research. But in generalizing ordinary EFSs, we introduce so-called advanced elementary formal systems (AEFSs, for short). In contrast to EFSs, an AEFS may additionally contain rules of the form $A \leftarrow \underline{not}\ B_1$, where A and B_1 are atoms and $\underline{not}$ stands for a certain kind of negation, which is nonmonotonic, in essence, and which is conceptually close to negation as failure. Even this rather limited approach to use negation has its benefits in that it may seriously simplify the definition of formal languages. For instance, the following rules define the language of all square-free strings[1]. Formally speaking, a ground atom $p(w)$ can be derived only in case that the string w is square-free.

(1) $p(x) \leftarrow \underline{not}\ q(x)$.
(2) $q(xx)$.
(3) $q(xy) \leftarrow q(x)$.
(4) $q(xy) \leftarrow q(y)$.

Fig. 2. An example AEFS

The work reported in the present paper mainly draws its motivation from ongoing research related to knowledge discovery and information extraction (IE) in the World Wide Web. Documents prepared for the Internet in HTML, in XML or in any other syntax have to be interpreted by browsers sitting anywhere in the World Wide Web. For this purpose, the documents do need to contain syntactic expressions which are controlling its interpretation including its visual appearance and its interactive behaviour. While the document's content is embedded into those syntactic expressions which are usually hidden from the user and which are obviously apart from the user's interest, the user is typically in-

---

[1] As usual, a string w is *square-free* if it does not contain a non-empty substring of form vv.

terested in the information itself. Accordingly, the user deals exclusively with the desired contents, whereas a system for IE should deal with the syntax.

In a characteristic scenario of system-supported IE, the user is taking a source document and is highlighting representative pieces of information that are of interest. Now, it is left to the system to understand how the target information is wrapped into syntactic expressions and to learn a procedure (henceforth called wrapper) that allows for an extraction of this information (cf. [12,21,8], e.g.).

AEFSs seem to provide an appropriate framework to describe extraction procedures that naturally comprises the approaches proposed in the IE community (cf. [12,22], e.g.).

For illustration, consider the following table and its LATEX source which contains details about the first half-dozen of workshops on Algorithmic Learning Theory (ALT). The aim of the IE task is to extract all pairs (y,c) that refer to the year y and the corresponding conference site c of a workshop in the ALT series that has proceedings co-edited by Arikawa. So, the pairs (1990,Tokyo) and (1994,Reinhardsbrunn) may serve as illustrating examples.

Year	Editors	Publisher	Conference Site
1990	Arikawa, Goto, Oshuga, Yokomori	Ohmsha Ltd.	Tokyo
1991	Arikawa, Maruoka, Sato	Ohmsha Ltd.	Tokyo
1992	Doshita, Furukawa, Jantke, Nishida	Springer	Tokyo
1993	Jantke, Kobayashi, Tomita, Yokomori	Springer	Tokyo
1994	Jantke, Arikawa	Springer	Reinhardsbrunn
1995	Jantke, Shinohara, Zeugmann	Springer	Fukuoka

Fig. 3. Visual appearance of the sample document

```
\begin{tabular}{|c|c|c|c|}
\hline
Year & Editors & Publisher & Conference Site \\\hline
1990 & Arikawa, Goto, Oshuga, Yokomori & Ohmsha Ltd. & Tokyo \\\hline
1991 & Arikawa, Maruoka, Sato & Ohmsha Ltd. & Tokyo \\\hline
1992 & Doshita, Furukawa, Jantke, Nishida & Springer & Tokyo \\\hline
1993 & Jantke, Kobayashi, Tomita, Yokomori & Springer & Tokyo \\\hline
1994 & Jantke, Arikawa & Springer & Reinhardsbrunn \\\hline
1995 & Jantke, Shinohara, Zeugmann & Springer & Fukuoka \\\hline
\end{tabular}
```

Fig. 4. LATEX source of the sample document

Note that the line breaks in Figure 4 have additionally been inserted to improve readability.

An AEFS that describes how the required information is wrapped into the LATEX source in Figure 4 looks as follows:

(1) extract(y, c, x_0\hliney&x_1&x_2&c\\x_3) ← p(y), p(x_1), p(x_2), p(c), h(x_1).

(2) p(x) ← $\underline{not}$ q(x).   (3) h(Arikawa).

(4) q(&).   (5) h(xy) ← h(x).

(6) q(xy) ← q(x).   (7) h(xy) ← h(y).

(8) q(xy) ← q(y).

Fig. 5. Sample wrapper represented as hereditary AEFS

The first rule can be interpreted as follows: A year y and the conference site c can be extracted from a LATEX source document d in case that (i) d matches the pattern x_0\hliney&x_1&x_2&c\\$x_3$ and (ii) the instantiations of the variables y, x_1, x_2, and c meet certain constraints. For example, the constraint h(x_1) states that the variable x_1 can only be replaced by some string that contains the substring Arikawa. Further constraints like p(y) explicitly state which text segments are suited to be substituted for the variable y, for instance. In this particular case, text segments that do not contain the substring & are allowed. If a document d matches the pattern x_0\hliney&x_1&x_2&c\\$x_3$ and if all specified constraints are fulfilled, then the instantiations of the variables y and c yield the information required.

As the above example shows, the explicit use of logical negation seems to be quite useful, since it may help to describe wrappers in a natural way. In this particular case, the predicate p guarantees that the specified wrapper does not allow for the extraction of pairs (y,c) such that y and c belong to different rows in the table depicted in Figure 3.

The focus of the present paper is twofold. On the one hand, we study the expressiveness of the proposed extention of EFSs by comparing certain AEFS definable language classes to the levels in the Chomsky hierarchy as well as to the language classes that are definable by EFSs that meet the same syntactical constraints. This may help to better understand the strength of the proposed framework.

In the longterm, we are interested in IE systems that automatically infer wrappers from examples. With respect to the illustrating example above, we are targeting at learning systems that are able to infer, for instance, the wrapper of Figure 5 from the source document of Figure 4 together with the two samples (1990,Tokyo) and (1994,Reinhardsbrunn). Therefore, on the other hand, we investigate the learnability of the corresponding AEFS definable language classes in Gold's [9] model of learning in the limit and Valiant's [23] model of probably approximately correct learning. In this context, we systematically discuss the question which learnability results achieved for EFSs lift to AEFSs and which do not.

2   Advanced Elementary Formal Systems

AEFSs generalize Smullyan's [20] elementary formal systems which he introduced to develop his theory of recursive functions over strings.

2.1 Preliminaries

By Σ we denote any fixed finite alphabet. Let Σ^+ be the set of all non-empty words over Σ. Moreover, we let Σ^n denote the set of all words in Σ^+ having length less than or equal to n, i.e., $\Sigma^n = \{w \mid w \in \Sigma^+, |w| \le n\}$. Let $a \in \Sigma$. Then, for all $n \ge 1$, $a^{n+1} = aa^n$, where, by convention, $a^1 = a$.

Any subset $L \subseteq \Sigma^+$ is called a *language*. By $\overline{L}$ we denote the *complement* of L, i.e., $\overline{L} = \Sigma^+ \setminus L$. Furthermore, let $\mathcal{L}$ be a language class. Then, we let $\mathcal{L}^n = \{L \cap \Sigma^n \mid L \in \mathcal{L}\}$.

By $\mathcal{L}_{reg}$, $\mathcal{L}_{cf}$, $\mathcal{L}_{cs}$, and $\mathcal{L}_{re}$ we denote the class of all regular, context free, context sensitive, and recursively enumerable languages, respectively. These are the standard levels in the well-known Chomsky hierarchy (cf. [10], e.g.).

The following lemmata provide standard knowledge about context free languages (cf. [10], e.g.) that is helpful in proving Theorem 8 below.

Lemma 1 *Let $L \subseteq \{a\}^+$. Then, $L \in \mathcal{L}_{cf}$ iff $L \in \mathcal{L}_{reg}$.*

Lemma 2 *Let $L \subseteq \Sigma^+$ be a context free language and let $\Sigma_0 \subseteq \Sigma$. Then, $L' = L \cap \Sigma_0^+$ constitutes a context free language.*

2.2 Elementary Formal Systems

Next, we provide notions and notations that allow for a formal definition of ordinary EFSs.

Assume three mutually disjoint sets – a finite set Σ of characters, a finite set Π of predicate symbols, and an enumerable set X of variables. We call every element in $(\Sigma \cup X)^+$ a pattern and every string in Σ^+ a ground pattern. For a pattern π, we let $v(\pi)$ be the set of variables in π.

Let $p \in \Pi$ be a predicate symbol of arity n and let $\pi_1, \ldots, \pi_n$ be patterns. Let $A = p(\pi_1, \ldots, \pi_n)$. Then, A is said to be an atomic formula (an atom, for short). A is ground, if all the patterns π_i are ground. Moreover, $v(A)$ denotes the set of variables in A.

Let A and $B_1, \ldots, B_n$ be atoms. Then, $r = A \leftarrow B_1, \ldots, B_n$ is a rule, A is the head of r, and all the B_i form the body of r. If all atoms in r are ground, then r is a ground rule. Moreover, if $n = 0$, then r is called a fact. Sometimes, we write A instead of $A \leftarrow$.

Let σ be a non-erasing substitution, i.e., a mapping from X to $(\Sigma \cup X)^+$ such that, for all but finitely many $x \in X$, $\sigma(x) = x$. For any pattern π, $\pi\sigma$ is the pattern which one obtains when applying σ to π. Let $C = p(\pi_1, \ldots, \pi_n)$ be an atom and let $r = A \leftarrow B_1, \ldots, B_n$ be a rule. Then, we set $C\sigma = p(\pi_1\sigma, \ldots, \pi_n\sigma)$ and $r\sigma = A\sigma \leftarrow B_1\sigma, \ldots, B_n\sigma$. If $r\sigma$ is ground, then it is said to be a ground instance of r.

Definition 1 ([6]) *Let Σ, Π, and X be fixed, and let Γ be a finite set of rules over Σ, Π, and X. Then, $S = (\Sigma, \Pi, \Gamma)$ is said to be an EFS.*

EFSs can be considered as particular logic programs without negation. There are two major differences: (i) patterns play the role of terms and (ii) unification has to be realized modulo the equational theory

$$E = \{\circ(x, \circ(y, z)) = \circ(\circ(x, y), z)\},$$

where $\circ$ is interpreted as concatenation of patterns.

As for logic programs (cf. [13], e.g.), the semantics of an ordinary EFS S, denoted by $Sem_o(S)$, can be defined via the operator T_S (see below). In the corresponding definition, we use the following notations. For any EFS $S = (\Sigma, \Pi, \Gamma)$, we let $B(S)$ denote the set of all well-formed ground atoms over Σ and Π. Moreover, we let $G(S)$ denote the set of all ground instances of rules in Γ.

Definition 2 *Let S be an EFS and let $I \subseteq B(S)$. Then, we let $T_S(I) = I \cup \{A \mid A \leftarrow B_1, \ldots, B_n \in G(S)$ for some $B_1 \in I, \ldots, B_n \in I\}$.*

Note that, by definition, the operator T_S is embedding (i.e., $I \subseteq T_S(I)$ for all $I \subseteq B(S)$) and monotonic (i.e., $I \subseteq I'$ implies $T_S(I) \subseteq T_S(I')$ for all $I, I' \subseteq B(S)$).

As usual, we let $T_S^{n+1}(I) = T_S(T_S^n(I))$, where $T_S^0(I) = I$, by convention.

Definition 3 *Let S be an EFS. Then, we let $Sem_o(S) = \bigcup_{n \in \mathbb{N}} T_S^n(\emptyset)$.*

In general, $Sem_o(S)$ is semi-decidable, but not decidable. However, as we will see below, $Sem_o(S)$ turns out to be decidable in case that S meets several natural syntactical constraints.

Finally, by $\mathcal{EFS}$ we denote the collection of all EFSs.

2.3 Beyond Elementary Formal Systems

Informally speaking, an AEFS is an EFS that may additionally contain rules of the form $A \leftarrow \underline{not}\ B_1$, where A and B_1 are atoms and $\underline{not}$ stands for a certain kind of negation, which is nonmonotonic, in essence, and which is conceptually close to negation as failure. The underlying meaning is as follows. If, for instance, $A = p(x_1, \ldots, x_n)$ and $B_1 = q(x_1, \ldots, x_n)$, then the predicate p succeeds iff the predicate q fails.

However, taking the conceptual difficulties into consideration that occur when defining the semantics of logic programs with negation as failure (cf. [13], e.g.), AEFSs are constrained to meet several additional syntactic requirements (cf. Definition 4). The requirements posed guarantee that, similarly to stratified logic programs (cf. [13], e.g.), the semantics of AEFSs can easily be described. Moreover, as a side-effect, it is guaranteed that AEFSs inherit some of the convenient properties of EFSs.

Before formally defining how AEFSs look like, we need some more notations. Let Γ be a set of rules (including rules of the form $A \leftarrow \underline{not}\ B_1$). Then, $hp(\Gamma)$ denotes the set of predicate symbols that appear in the head of any rule in Γ.

Definition 4 *AEFSs and their semantics are inductively defined as follows.*

(1) An EFS S' is also an AEFS and its semantics $Sem(S') = Sem_o(S')$.

(2) If $S_1 = (\Sigma, \Pi_1, \Gamma_1)$ and $S_2 = (\Sigma, \Pi_2, \Gamma_2)$ are AEFSs such that $\Pi_1 \cap \Pi_2 = \emptyset$, then $S = (\Sigma, \Pi_1 \cup \Pi_2, \Gamma_1 \cup \Gamma_2)$ is an AEFS and its semantics is $Sem(S) = Sem(S_1) \cup Sem(S_2)$.

(3) If $S_1 = (\Sigma, \Pi_1, \Gamma_1)$ is an AEFS and $p \notin \Pi_1$ and $q \in \Pi_1$ are n-ary predicate symbols, then $S = (\Sigma, \Pi_1 \cup \{p\}, \Gamma_1 \cup \{p(x_1, \ldots, x_n) \leftarrow \underline{not}\ q(x_1, \ldots, x_n)\})$ is an AEFS and its semantics is $Sem(S) = Sem(S_1) \cup \{p(s_1, \ldots, s_n) \mid p(s_1, \ldots, s_n) \in B(S), q(s_1, \ldots, s_n) \notin Sem(S_1)\}$.

(4) If $S_1 = (\Sigma, \Pi_1, \Gamma_1)$ is an AEFS and $S' = (\Sigma, \Pi', \Gamma')$ is an EFS such that $hp(\Gamma') \cap \Pi_1 = \emptyset$, then $S = (\Sigma, \Pi' \cup \Pi_1, \Gamma' \cup \Gamma_1)$ is an AEFS and its semantics is $Sem(S) = \bigcup_{n \in \mathbb{N}} T_{S'}^n(Sem(S_1))$.

Finally, by $\mathcal{AEFS}$ we denote the collection of all AEFSs.

According to Definition 4, the same AEFS may be constructed either via (2) or (4). Since T_S is both embedding and monotonic, the semantics is the same in both cases.

2.4   Using AEFS for Defining Formal Languages

In the following, we show how AEFSs can be used to describe formal languages and relate the resulting language classes to the language classes of the classical Chomsky hierarchy.

Definition 5 Let $S = (\Sigma, \Pi, \Gamma)$ be an AEFS and let $p \in \Pi$ be a unary predicate symbol. Then, we let $L(S, p) = \{s \mid p(s) \in Sem(S)\}$.

Furthermore, a language $L \subseteq \Sigma^+$ is said to be AEFS definable iff there are a superset Σ_0 of Σ, an AEFS $S = (\Sigma_0, \Pi, \Gamma)$, and a unary predicate symbol $p \in \Pi$ with $L = L(S, p)$.

Intuitively speaking, $L(S, p)$ is the language which the AEFS S defines via the unary predicate symbol p.

Definition 6 Let $\mathcal{M} \subseteq \mathcal{AEFS}$ and let $k \in \mathbb{N}$. Then, $\mathcal{L}(\mathcal{M})$ is the set of all languages that are definable by AEFSs in $\mathcal{M}$. Moreover, $\mathcal{L}(\mathcal{M}(k))$ is the set of all languages that are definable by AEFSs in $\mathcal{M}$ that have at most k rules.

For example, $\mathcal{L}(\mathcal{AEFS}(2))$ is the class of all languages that are definable by unconstrained AEFSs that consist of at most 2 rules.

Our first result puts the expressive power of AEFSs into the right perspective.

Theorem 1 $\mathcal{L}_{re} \subset \mathcal{L}(\mathcal{AEFS})$.

Proof: Since, by definition, $\mathcal{L}(\mathcal{EFS}) \subseteq \mathcal{L}(\mathcal{AEFS})$, and $\mathcal{L}_{re} \subseteq \mathcal{L}(\mathcal{EFS})$ (cf. [6]), we get $\mathcal{L}_{re} \subseteq \mathcal{L}(\mathcal{AEFS})$. Since there are languages $L \in \mathcal{L}_{re}$ that have a complement which is not recursively enumerable (cf. [17]), $\mathcal{L}(\mathcal{AEFS}) \setminus \mathcal{L}_{re} \neq \emptyset$ is an immediate consequence of Theorem 2 below.   □

Moreover, the following closedness properties can be shown.

Theorem 2 $\mathcal{L}(\mathcal{AEFS})$ is closed under the operations union, intersection, and complement.

To elaborate a more accurate picture, similarly to [6], we next introduce several constraints on the structure of the rules an AEFS may contain.

Let r be a rule of form $A \leftarrow B_1, \ldots, B_n$. Then, r is said to be variable-bounded iff, for all $i \leq n$, $v(B_i) \subseteq v(A)$. Moreover, r is said to be length-bounded iff, for all substitutions σ, $|A\sigma| \geq |B_1\sigma| + \cdots + |B_n\sigma|$. Clearly, if r is length–bounded, then r is also variable–bounded. Note that, in general, the opposite does not hold.

Moreover, let r be a rule of form $p(\pi) \leftarrow q_1(x_1), \ldots, q_n(x_n)$, where $x_1, \ldots, x_n$ are mutually distinct variables and π is a regular[2] pattern which contains exactly the variables $x_1, \ldots, x_n$, then r is said to be regular.

In addition, every rule of form $p(x_1, \ldots, x_n) \leftarrow \underline{not}\ q(x_1, \ldots, x_n)$ is both variable–bounded and length–bounded. Moreover, every rule of form $p(x) \leftarrow \underline{not}\ q(x)$ is regular.

Definition 7 *Let $S = (\Sigma, \Pi, \Gamma)$ be an AEFS. Then, S is said to be*
(1) variable–bounded iff all $r \in \Gamma$ are variable–bounded,
(2) length–bounded iff all $r \in \Gamma$ are length–bounded, and
(3) regular iff all $r \in \Gamma$ are regular.

By vb-$\mathcal{AEFS}$ (vb-$\mathcal{EFS}$), lb-$\mathcal{AEFS}$ (lb-$\mathcal{EFS}$), and reg-$\mathcal{AEFS}$ (reg-$\mathcal{EFS}$) we denote the collection of all AEFSs (EFSs) that are variable–bounded, length–bounded, and regular, respectively.

The following three theorems illuminate the expressive power of ordinary EFSs.

Theorem 3 ([6])
(1) $\mathcal{L}(vb\text{-}\mathcal{EFS}) \subseteq \mathcal{L}_{re}$.
(2) For any $L \in \mathcal{L}_{re}$, there is a $L' \in \mathcal{L}(vb\text{-}\mathcal{EFS})$ such that $L = L' \cap \Sigma^+$.

If Σ contains at least two symbols, assertion (2) rewrites to $\mathcal{L}_{re} \subseteq \mathcal{L}(vb\text{-}\mathcal{EFS})$ (cf. [6]).

Theorem 4 ([6])
(1) $\mathcal{L}(lb\text{-}\mathcal{EFS}) \subseteq \mathcal{L}_{cs}$.
(2) For any $L \in \mathcal{L}_{cs}$, there is a $L' \in \mathcal{L}(lb\text{-}\mathcal{EFS})$ such that $L = L' \cap \Sigma^+$.

Theorem 5 ([6]) $\mathcal{L}(reg\text{-}\mathcal{EFS}) = \mathcal{L}_{cf}$.

Concerning AEFSs the situation changes slightly. This is mainly caused by the fact that variable–bounded, length–bounded, and regular AEFSs are closed under intersection.

Theorem 6 $\mathcal{L}(vb\text{-}\mathcal{AEFS})$, $\mathcal{L}(lb\text{-}\mathcal{AEFS})$, *and* $\mathcal{L}(reg\text{-}\mathcal{AEFS})$ *are closed under the operations union, intersection, and complement.*

For AEFSs, Theorems 3 and 4 rewrites as follows.

Theorem 7
(1) $\mathcal{L}_{re} \subset \mathcal{L}(vb\text{-}\mathcal{AEFS})$.
(2) $\mathcal{L}(lb\text{-}\mathcal{AEFS}) = \mathcal{L}_{cs}$.

Proof: First, we show (1). Applying Theorem 6, one sees that assertion (2) of Theorem 3 rewrites to $\mathcal{L}_{re} \subseteq \mathcal{L}(vb\text{-}\mathcal{AEFS})$. Next, $\mathcal{L}(vb\text{-}\mathcal{AEFS}) \setminus \mathcal{L}_{re} \neq \emptyset$ can be shown by applying the same arguments as in the demonstration of Theorem 1.

---

[2] A pattern π is said to be *regular* iff every variable occurs at most once in π.

Second, we verify (2). Again, applying Theorem 6, one directly sees that assertion (2) of Theorem 4 rewrites to $\mathcal{L}_{cs} \subseteq \mathcal{L}(lb\text{-}\mathcal{AEFS})$. Moreover, by definition, for any $L \in \mathcal{L}(lb\text{-}\mathcal{AEFS})$, there are languages $L_0, \ldots, L_n \in \mathcal{L}(lb\text{-}\mathcal{EFS})$ such that L can be defined by applying the operations union and intersection to these languages. Since $\mathcal{L}(lb\text{-}\mathcal{EFS}) \subseteq \mathcal{L}_{cs}$ and since $\mathcal{L}_{cs}$ is closed with respect to the operations union and intersection (cf. [10], e.g.), we may conclude that $\mathcal{L}(lb\text{-}\mathcal{AEFS}) \subseteq \mathcal{L}_{cs}$. $\qquad\square$

In our opinion, assertion (2) of Theorem 7 witnesses the naturalness of our approach to extend EFSs to AEFSs. In contrast to assertion (2) of Theorem 4, there is no need to use auxilary characters in the terminal alphabet.

Theorem 8 $\mathcal{L}_{cf} \subset \mathcal{L}(reg\text{-}\mathcal{AEFS}) \subset \mathcal{L}_{cs}$.

Proof: First, $\mathcal{L}_{cf} \subseteq \mathcal{L}(reg\text{-}\mathcal{AEFS}) \subseteq \mathcal{L}_{cs}$ follows immediately from Theorems 5 and 7.

Second, $\mathcal{L}_{cf} \subset \mathcal{L}(reg\text{-}\mathcal{AEFS})$ follows from the fact that $\mathcal{L}(reg\text{-}\mathcal{AEFS})$ is closed under intersection (cf. Theorem 6), while $\mathcal{L}_{cf}$ is not (cf. [10], e.g.).

Third, we show that $\mathcal{L}_{cs} \setminus \mathcal{L}(reg\text{-}\mathcal{AEFS}) \neq \emptyset$. Let $L \subseteq \{a\}^+$ with $L \in \mathcal{L}_{cs} \setminus \mathcal{L}_{cf}$ (cf. [10], for some illustrating examples). We claim that $L \notin \mathcal{L}(reg\text{-}\mathcal{AEFS})$. Suppose the contrary, i.e., $L \in \mathcal{L}(reg\text{-}\mathcal{AEFS})$. By definition, there are languages $L_0, \ldots, L_n \in \mathcal{L}(reg\text{-}\mathcal{EFS})$ such that L can be defined by applying the operations union and intersection to these languages. Let $i \leq n$. By Theorem 5, $L_i \in \mathcal{L}_{cf}$. Moreover, let $L_i' = L_i \cap \{a\}^+$. By Lemma 2, $L_i' \in \mathcal{L}_{cf}$, and thus, by Lemma 1, $L_i' \in \mathcal{L}_{reg}$. Finally, one easily sees that L can also be defined by applying the operations union and intersection to the languages $L_0', \ldots, L_n'$. Finally, since $\mathcal{L}_{reg}$ is closed with respect to the operations union and intersection, we may therefore conclude that $L \in \mathcal{L}_{reg}$ which in turn yields $L \in \mathcal{L}_{cf}$, a contradiction. $\qquad\square$

3   Learning of AEFSs

3.1   Notions and Notations

First, we briefly review the necessary basic concepts concerning Gold's [9] model of learning in the limit. We refer the reader to the survey papers [2] and [26] as well as to the textbook [11] which contain all missing details.

There are several ways to present information about formal languages to be learned. The basic approaches are defined via the key concept text and informant, respectively. Let L be the target language. A *text for* L is just any sequence of words labelled '+' that exhausts L. An *informant for* L is any sequence of words labelled alternatively either by '+' or '−' such that all the words labelled by '+' form a text for L, while the remaining words labelled by '−' constitute a text for $\overline{L}$. Sometimes, labelled words are called *examples*.

As in [9], we define an *inductive inference machine* (abbr. IIM) to be an algorithmic device working as follows: The IIM takes as its input larger and larger initial segments of a text (an informant). After processing an initial segment σ, the IIM outputs a hypothesis $M(\sigma)$, i.e., a number encoding a certain computer program. More formally, an IIM maps finite sequences of elements from $\Sigma^+ \times \{+, -\}$ into numbers in $\mathbb{N}$.

The numbers output by an IIM are interpreted with respect to a suitably chosen hypothesis space $\mathcal{H} = (h_j)_{j \in \mathbb{N}}$. When an IIM outputs some number j, we interpret it to mean that the machine is hypothesizing h_j.

Now, let $\mathcal{L}$ be a language class, let L be a language, and let $\mathcal{H} = (h_j)_{j \in \mathbb{N}}$ be a hypothesis space. An IIM M $LimTxt_{\mathcal{H}}$ ($LimInf_{\mathcal{H}}$)–learns L iff, for every text t for L (for every informant i for L), there exists a $j \in \mathbb{N}$ such that $h_j = L$, and moreover M almost always outputs the hypothesis j when fed the text t (the informant i). Furthermore, an IIM M $LimTxt_{\mathcal{H}}$ ($LimInf_{\mathcal{H}}$)–learns $\mathcal{L}$ iff, for every $L \in \mathcal{L}$, M $LimTxt_{\mathcal{H}}$($LimInf_{\mathcal{H}}$)–learns L. In addition, we write $\mathcal{L} \in LimTxt$ ($\mathcal{L} \in LimInf$) provided there are a hypothesis space $\mathcal{H}$ and an IIM M that $LimTxt_{\mathcal{H}}$ ($LimInf_{\mathcal{H}}$)–learns $\mathcal{L}$.

Next, we focus our attention on Valiant's [23] model of probably approximately correct learning (PAC model, for short; see also the textbook [16] for further details). In contrast to Gold's [9] model, the focus is now on learning algorithms that, based on randomly chosen positive and negative examples, find, fast and with high probability, a sufficiently good approximation of the target language.

To give a precise definition of the PAC model, we need the following notions and notations. We use a finite alphabet Λ for representing languages. A *representation* for a language class $\mathcal{L}$ is a function $R : \mathcal{L} \to \wp(\Lambda^+)$ such that, for all distinct languages $L, L' \in \mathcal{L}$, $R(L) \neq \emptyset$ and $R(L) \cap R(L') = \emptyset$. Let $L \in \mathcal{L}$. Then, $R(L)$ is the set of representations for L and $\ell_{\min}(L, R)$ is the length of the shortest string in $R(L)$. Moreover, let T be a set of examples. Then, $\ell_{\min}(T, R)$ is the length of a shortest representation in $R(L)$ that is consistent[3] with T.

Definition 8 ([23]) *A language class $\mathcal{L}$ is polynomial-time PAC learnable in a representation R iff there exists a learning algorithm $\mathcal{A}$ such that*

(1) $\mathcal{A}$ takes a sequence of examples as input and runs in polynomial time with respect to the length of the input;

(2) there exists a polynomial $q(\cdot, \cdot, \cdot, \cdot)$ such that, for any $L \in \mathcal{L}$, any $n \in \mathbb{N}$, any $s \geq 1$, any reals e, d with $0 < e, d < 1$, and any probability distribution Pr on Σ^n, if $\mathcal{A}$ takes $q(1/e, 1/d, n, s)$ examples, which are generated randomly according to Pr, then $\mathcal{A}$ outputs, with probability at least $1 - d$, a hypothesis $h \in R$ with $Pr(w \in ((L \setminus h) \cup (h \setminus L))) < e$, when $\ell_{\min}(L, R) \leq s$ is satisfied.

We complete this section by providing some more notions and notations that are of relevance when proving some of the learnability/non-learnability results presented below.

Definition 9 *A pair (S, p) of an AEFS $S = (\Sigma, \Pi, \Gamma)$ and a unary predicate symbol $p \in \Pi$ is said to be reduced with respect to a set T of examples iff $L(S, p)$ is consistent with T and, for any $S' = (\Sigma, \Pi, \Gamma')$ with $\Gamma' \subset \Gamma$, $L(S', p)$ is not consistent with T.*

---

[3] As usual, a language L is said to be *consistent* with T iff, for all $(x, +) \in T$, $x \in L$ and, for all $(x, -) \in T$, $x \notin L$.

The following notion adopts one of the key concepts in [18], where it has been shown that, for classes of elementary formal systems, bounded finite thickness implies that the corresponding language class is learnable in the limit from only positive examples.

Definition 10 ([18]) *Let* $M \subseteq \mathcal{EFS}$. *$M$ is said to have bounded finite thickness iff, for all* $w \in \Sigma^+$, *there are at most finitely many EFS* $S \in M$ *such that (i) S is reduced with respect to* $T = \{(w, +)\}$ *and (ii) the language defined by S is consistent with T.*

Finally, we define the notion *polynomial dimension* which is one of the key notions when studying the learnability of formal languages in the PAC model.

Definition 11 ([15]) *Let* $\mathcal{L}$ *be a language class.* $\mathcal{L}$ *has polynomial dimension iff there is a polynomial* $d(\cdot)$ *such that, for all* $n \in \mathbb{N}$, $\log_2 |\mathcal{L}^n| \leq d(n)$.

3.2 Gold-Style Learning

The following theorem summarizes the known learnability results for EFSs. Recall that, by definition, $\mathcal{L}(lb\text{-}\mathcal{EFS}(k))$ is the collection of all languages that are definable by length-bounded EFSs that consist of at most k rules.

Theorem 9 ([9,19])
(1) $\mathcal{L}(lb\text{-}\mathcal{EFS}) \in LimInf$.
(2) $\mathcal{L}(lb\text{-}\mathcal{EFS}) \notin LimTxt$.
(3) For all $k \in \mathbb{N}$, $\mathcal{L}(lb\text{-}\mathcal{EFS}(k)) \in LimTxt$.

Having in mind that $\mathcal{L}(lb\text{-}\mathcal{EFS}) = \mathcal{L}(lb\text{-}\mathcal{AEFS})$, we may directly conclude:

Corollary 1.
(1) $\mathcal{L}(lb\text{-}\mathcal{AEFS}) \in LimInf$.
(2) $\mathcal{L}(lb\text{-}\mathcal{AEFS}) \notin LimTxt$.

The next theorem points to a major difference concerning the learnability of EFSs and AEFSs, respectively.

Theorem 10
(1) $\mathcal{L}(lb\text{-}\mathcal{AEFS}(1)) \in LimTxt$.
(2) For all $k \geq 2$, $\mathcal{L}(lb\text{-}\mathcal{AEFS}(k)) \notin LimTxt$.

Proof: By definition, $\mathcal{L}(lb\text{-}\mathcal{AEFS}(1)) = \mathcal{L}(lb\text{-}\mathcal{EFS}(1))$, and thus (1) follows from Theorem 9.

Next, let $k = 2$. Let $\Sigma = \{a\}$ and consider the family $\mathcal{L} = (L_i)_{i \in \mathbb{N}}$ such that $L_0 = \{a^n \mid n \in \mathbb{N}\}$ and $L_{i+1} = \{a^n \mid n \leq i+1\}$. $\mathcal{L}$ can be defined via the family of regular AEFSs $(S_i = (\Sigma, \Pi, \Gamma_i))_{i \in \mathbb{N}}$ with $\Pi = \{p, q\}$, $\Gamma_0 = \{p(a), p(ax) \leftarrow p(x)\}$, and $\Gamma_i = \{q(a^i x), p(x) \leftarrow \underline{not}\ q(x)\}$ for all $i \geq 1$. Obviously, for every $i \in \mathbb{N}$, $L(S_i, p) = L_i$. On the other hand, it is well-known that $\mathcal{L} \notin LimTxt$ (cf. [26], e.g.), and therefore we are done. $\qquad\square$

3.3   Probably Approximately Correct Learning

In [4,14], the polynomial-time PAC learnability of several language classes that are definable by EFSs has been studied. It has been shown that even quite simple classes are not polynomial-time PAC learnable – for instance, the class of all regular pattern languages[4]. However, if one bounds the number of variables that may occur in the defining patterns, regular pattern languages become polynomial-time PAC learnable. Moreover, by putting further constraints on the rules that can be used to define EFSs, positive results for even larger EFS definable language classes have been achieved (cf. [4,14]). The relevant technicalities are as follows.

A rule of form $p(\pi_1, \ldots, \pi_n) \leftarrow p_1(\tau_1, \ldots, \tau_{t_1}), \ldots, p_m(\tau_{t_{m-1}+1}, \ldots, \tau_{t_m})$ is said to be *hereditary* iff, for every $j = 1, \ldots, t_m$, the pattern τ_j is a subword of some pattern π_i. Moreover, any rule of form $p(x_1, \ldots, x_n) \leftarrow \underline{not}\ q(x_1, \ldots, x_n)$ is a hereditary one, since it obviously meets the syntactical constraints stated above. Note that, by definition, every hereditary rule is variable–bounded.

Definition 12 *Let $S = (\Sigma, \Pi, \Gamma)$ be an AEFS. Then, S is said to be hereditary iff all $r \in \Gamma$ are hereditary. By h-$\mathcal{AEFS}$ (h-$\mathcal{EFS}$) we denote the collection of all hereditary AEFSs (EFSs).*

In contrast to the general case (cf. Definition 5), hereditary AEFS have the following nice feature. Let $L \subseteq \Sigma^+$ with $L \in \mathcal{L}(h\text{-}\mathcal{AEFS})$. Then, there is a hereditary AEFS for L consisting only of rules that uses exclusively characters from Σ.

Definition 13 *Let $m, k, t, r \in \mathbb{N}$. By h-$\mathcal{AEFS}(m, k, t, r)$ (h-$\mathcal{EFS}(m, k, t, r)$) we denote the collection of all hereditary AEFSs (EFSs) S that satisfy (1) to (4), where*

(1) S contains at most m rules.
(2) the number of variable occurrences in the head of every rule in S is at most k.
(3) the number of atoms in the body of every rule in S is at most t.
(4) the arity of each predicate symbol in S is at most r.

Taking into consideration that $\mathcal{L}(reg\text{-}\mathcal{EFS}) = \mathcal{L}_{cf}$ (cf. Theorem 5), one can easily show that $\mathcal{L}(reg\text{-}\mathcal{EFS}) \subseteq \bigcup_{m \in \mathbb{N}} \mathcal{L}(h\text{-}\mathcal{EFS}(m, 2, 1, 2))$ (cf. [4]). Similarly, it can easily be verified that $\mathcal{L}(reg\text{-}\mathcal{AEFS}) \subseteq \bigcup_{m \in \mathbb{N}} \mathcal{L}(h\text{-}\mathcal{AEFS}(m, 2, 1, 2))$. Hence, hereditary EFSs resp. AEFSs are much more expressive than it might seem.

For hereditary EFSs, the following learnability result is known.

Theorem 11 ([14]) *Let $m, k, t, r \in \mathbb{N}$. Then, the class $\mathcal{L}(h\text{-}\mathcal{EFS}(m, k, t, r))$ is polynomial-time PAC learnable.*

As the results in [14] impressively show, it is inevitable to *a priori* bound all the defining parameters. In other words, none of the resulting language classes is polynomial-time PAC learnable, if at least one of the parameters involved may arbitrarily grow.

---

[4] That is, the class of all languages that are definable by an EFS that consists of exactly one rule of form $p(\pi)$, where π is a regular pattern.

Next, we turn our attention to study the learnability of language classes that are definable by hereditary AEFSs.

Our first result demonstrates that hereditary AEFSs are more expressive than hereditary EFSs.

Theorem 12 $\mathcal{L}(h\text{-}\mathcal{AEFS}(2,1,1,1)) \setminus \bigcup_{m,k,t,r \in \mathbb{N}} \mathcal{L}(h\text{-}\mathcal{EFS}(m,k,t,r)) \neq \emptyset.$

Proof: Consider the language family $\mathcal{L} = (L_i)_{i \in \mathbb{N}}$ such that $L_0 = \{a^n \mid n \in \mathbb{N}\}$ and $L_{i+1} = \{a^n \mid n \leq i+1\}$. Having a closer look at the demonstration of Theorem 10, one directly sees that $\mathcal{L} \in \mathcal{L}(h\text{-}\mathcal{AEFS}(2,1,1,1))$.

We claim that $\mathcal{L}$ witnesses the stated separation. Suppose to the contrary that there are $m,k,t,r \in \mathbb{N}$ such that $\mathcal{L} \in \mathcal{L}(h\text{-}\mathcal{EFS}(m,k,t,r))$. Since $\mathcal{L} \notin Lim\,Txt$ (cf. [26], e.g.), this directly implies $\mathcal{L}(h\text{-}\mathcal{EFS}(m,k,t,r)) \notin Lim\,Txt$. However, by combining results from [18] and [14], it can easily be shown that $\mathcal{L}(h\text{-}\mathcal{EFS}(m,k,t,r)) \in Lim\,Txt$, a contradiction. The relevant details are as follows: It has been shown that, for every $m,k,t,r \in \mathbb{N}$, $\mathcal{L}(h\text{-}\mathcal{EFS}(m,k,t,r))$ has polynomial dimension (cf. [14]; see also Lemma 4 in the demonstration of Theorem 13 below). Moreover, every EFS definable language class with polynomial dimension has bounded finite thickness which in turn implies that this language class is $Lim\,Txt$–identifiable (cf. [18]).[5]   □

Surprisingly, Theorem 11 remains valid in case that one considers hereditary AEFSs instead of EFSs. This nicely contrasts the fact that, in Gold's [9] model, AEFS definable language classes may become harder to learn than EFS definable ones, although they are supposed to meet the same syntactical constraints (cf. Theorems 9 and 10). Moreover, having Theorem 12 in mind, the next theorem establishes the polynomial-time PAC learnability of a language class that properly comprises the class in [14].

Theorem 13 *Let $m,k,t,r \in \mathbb{N}$. Then, the class $\mathcal{L}(h\text{-}\mathcal{AEFS}(m,k,t,r))$ is polynomial-time PAC learnable.*

Proof: Let $m,k,t,r \in \mathbb{N}$. Furthermore, let $\mathcal{L} = \mathcal{L}(h\text{-}\mathcal{AEFS}(m,k,t,r))$ and let R be a mapping that assigns AEFSs in $h\text{-}\mathcal{AEFS}(m,k,t,r)$ to languages in $\mathcal{L}$. Applying results from [7] and [15], it suffices to show:

(1) $\mathcal{L}$ is of polynomial dimension.
(2) There is a polynomial-time finder for R, i.e., there exists a polynomial-time algorithm that, given a finite set T of examples for any $L \in \mathcal{L}$, computes an AEFS $S \in h\text{-}\mathcal{AEFS}(m,k,t,r)$ that is consistent with T.

Due to the space constraints, a formal verification of (1) is provided, only. Note that (2) can be show be adapting ideas used in [14] to demonstrate Theorem 11. The differences rest on the fact that the entailment relation for AEFSs does not meet the monotonicity principle of classical logics.

Lemma 3 *Let T be a set of examples over Σ. Furthermore, let (S,p) be a pair consisting of a hereditary AEFS $S = (\Sigma, \Pi, \Gamma)$ and a unary predicate symbol*

---

[5] Note that, for AEFS definable language classes, an analogue implication does not hold. This is caused by the fact that the entailment relation for AEFSs does not meet the monotonicity principle of classical logics.

$p \in \Pi$. If (S, p) is reduced with respect to T, then for each rule $q_0(\pi_1^0, \ldots, \pi_{r_0}^0) \leftarrow q_1(\pi_1^1, \ldots, \pi_{r_1}^1), \ldots, q_{t'}(\pi_1^{t'}, \ldots, \pi_{r_{t'}}^{t'})$ in Γ there exists a substitution σ such that all the $\pi_i^j \sigma$ are subwords of some labelled word from T.

Proof: Assume the contrary. Let T be a set of examples over Σ, let (S, p) be a pair consisting of a hereditary AEFS $S = (\Sigma, \Pi, \Gamma)$ and a unary predicate symbol p in Π such that (S, p) is reduced with respect to T. Moreover, let $r = q_0(\pi_1^0, \ldots, \pi_{r_0}^0) \leftarrow q_1(\pi_1^1, \ldots, \pi_{r_1}^1), \ldots, q_{t'}(\pi_1^{t'}, \ldots, \pi_{r_{t'}}^{t'})$ be a rule in Γ that violates the assertions stated in Lemma 3.

We claim that $L(S', p)$ with $S' = (\Sigma, \Pi, \Gamma')$ is also consistent with T, where $\Gamma' = \Gamma \setminus \{r\}$. To see this, assume the contrary.

Case 1: There is a word w such that $(w, +) \in T$ and $w \notin L(S', p)$.

Hence, during the derivation[6] of $p(w)$, a ground instance $r\sigma$ of rule r has to be used. Since S is hereditary, each $\pi_1^0 \sigma, \ldots, \pi_{r_0}^0 \sigma$ is a subword of w. Consequently, this implies that all $\pi_i^j \sigma$ are subwords of w, contradicting our assumption.

Case 2: There is a word w such that $(w, -) \in T$ and $w \in L(S', p)$.

Hence, there must be an atom $p'(w_1, \ldots, w_{r'})$ that is used when deriving $p(w)$ such that (i) $p'(w_1, \ldots, w_{r'}) \in Sem(S')$, (ii) $p'(w_1 \ldots, w_{r'}) \notin Sem(S)$, and (iii) there is a rule $p'(x_1, \ldots, x_{r'}) \leftarrow \underline{not}\ q'(x_1, \ldots, x_{r'})$ in Γ' such that $q'(w_1, \ldots, w_{r'}) \in Sem(S)$ and $q'(w_1, \ldots, w_{r'}) \notin Sem(S')$. Since S is hereditary, all $w_1, \ldots, w_{r'}$ are subwords of w. Now, analogously to Case 1, during the derivation of $q'(w_1, \ldots, w_{r'})$ according to the rules in S, a ground instance $r\sigma$ of rule r has to be used. As argued above, all the $\pi_i^j \sigma$ are subwords of the words $w_1, \ldots, w_n$, and therefore they are subwords of w, too. Since $(w, -) \in T$, this contradicts our assumption.

Summing up, $L(S', p)$ must be consistent with T. Hence, S is not reduced with respect to T, a contradiction, and thus Lemma 3 follows.   ◇

Lemma 4 *For any $m, k, t, r \in \mathbb{N}$, the class $\mathcal{L}(h\text{-}\mathcal{AEFS}(m, k, t, r))$ has polynomial dimension.*

Proof: Let $m, k, t, r \in \mathbb{N}$ be fixed. We estimate the cardinality of the class $\mathcal{L}(h\text{-}\mathcal{AEFS}(m, k, t, r))^n$ in dependence on n.

Let (S, p) be a pair of an hereditary AEFS $S = (\Sigma, \Pi, \Gamma) \in h\text{-}\mathcal{AEFS}(m, k, t, r)$ and a predicate symbol $p \in \Pi$ of arity one. Since Γ contains at most m rules, we may assume that $|\Pi| \leq m$. Furthermore, we may assume that (S, p) is reduced with respect to some finite set of examples $T \subseteq \Sigma^n \times \{+, -\}$.

By definition, each rule in Γ is either of form (i) $A \leftarrow B_1, \ldots, B_s$ or of form (ii) $A' \leftarrow \underline{not}\ B_1'$, where $A' = p'(x_1, \ldots, x_j)$ and $B_1' = q'(x_1, \ldots, x_j)$ for some $p', q' \in \Pi$ and variables $x_1, \ldots, x_j$. Because of Lemma 3, the same counting arguments as in [14] can be invoked to show that there at most $O(2^{n^{2r}})$ rules of form (i). Moreover, as a simple calculation shows, there are $O((2mr^r)^2)$ rules of form (ii) (which does not depend on n). Consequently, there are at most $O(2^{n^{2r}})$ rules that can be used when defining an AEFS in $h\text{-}\mathcal{AEFS}(m, k, t, r)$, and thus

---

[6] We abstain from formally defining the term derivation, since an intuitive understanding shall suffice. For the missing details, the interested reader is refered to [6], for instance.

there are at most $O(2^{n^{2r}})$ hereditary AEFS with at most m rules that have to be considered when estimating the cardinality of the class $\mathcal{L}(h\text{-}\mathcal{AEFS}(m,k,t,r))^n$. Hence, the class $\mathcal{L}(h\text{-}\mathcal{AEFS}(m,k,t,r))$ has polynomial dimension, and thus Lemma 4 follows. $\diamond$
Hence, (1) is indeed fulfilled. $\square$

4   Conclusions

Motivated by research related to knowledge discovery and information extraction in the World Wide Web, we introduced advanced elementary formal systems (AEFSs) – a kind of logic programs to manipulate strings.

The authors are currently applying the approach presented here within a joint research and development project named LExIKON on information extraction from the Internet. This project is supported by the German Federal Ministry for Economics and Technology.

Advanced elementary formal systems generalize elementary formal systems (EFSs) in that they allow for the use of a certain kind of negation, which is non-monotonic, in essence, and which is conceptually close to negation as failure. In our approach, we syntactically constrained the use of negation. This guarantees that AEFSs inherit some of the convenient properties of EFSs – for instance, their clear and easy to capture semantics.

Negation as failure allows one to describe formal languages in a more natural and compact manner. Moreover, as Theorems 7 and 8 show, AEFSs are more expressive than EFSs. Naturally, this leads to the question of whether or not the known learnability results for EFS definable language classes remain valid if one considers the more general framework of AEFSs. Interestingly, the answer to this question heavily depends on the underlying learning paradigm.

As we have shown, certain AEFS definable language classes are not Gold-style learnable from only positive data, although the corresponding language classes that are definable by EFSs are known to be learnable (cf. Theorem 10). Surprisingly, in the PAC model, differences of this type cannot be observed (cf. Theorems 11 and 13). Although the considered classes of AEFS definable languages properly comprise the corresponding classes of EFS definable languages – which are the largest classes of EFS definable languages formerly known to be polynomial-time PAC learnable – both language classes are polynomial-time PAC learnable.

References

1. D. Angluin, Inductive inference of formal languages from positive data, Information and Control 45 (1980) 117–135.
2. D. Angluin, C.H. Smith, A survey of inductive inference: Theory and methods, Computing Surveys 15 (1983) 237–269.
3. S. Arikawa, Elementary formal systems and formal languages - Simple formal systems, Memoirs of Faculty of Science, Kyushu University, Series A, Mathematics 24 (1970) 47–75.

4. S. Arikawa, S. Miyano, A. Shinohara, T. Shinohara, A. Yamamoto, Algorithmic learning theory with elementary formal systems, IEICE Trans. Inf. & Syst. E75-D 4 (1992) 405–414.
5. S. Arikawa, T. Shinohara, A. Yamamoto, Elementary formal systems as a unifying framework for language learning, in: Proc. Second Annual Workshop on Computational Learning Theory, Morgan Kaufmann, 1989, pp. 312–327.
6. S. Arikawa, T. Shinohara, A. Yamamoto, Learning elementary formal systems, Theoretical Computer Science 95 (1992) 97–113.
7. A. Blumer, A. Ehrenfeucht, D. Hausler, M. Warmuth, Learnability and the Vapnik-Chervonenkis dimension, Journal of the ACM 36 (1989) 929–965.
8. G. Grieser, K.P. Jantke, S. Lange, B. Thomas, A unifying approach to HTML wrapper representation and learning, in: Proc. Third Int. Conference on Discovery Science, LNAI 1967, Springer-Verlag, 2000, pp. 50–64.
9. E.M. Gold, Language identification in the limit, Information and Control 14 (1967) 447–474.
10. J.E. Hopcroft, J.D. Ullman, Formal Languages and their Relation to Automata, Addison-Wesley Publishing Company, 1979.
11. S. Jain, D. Osherson, J. Royer, A. Sharma, Systems that Learn - 2nd Edition, An Introduction to Learning Theory, MIT Press, 1999.
12. N. Kushmerick, Wrapper induction: efficiency and expressiveness, Artificial Intelligence 118 (2000) 15–68.
13. V. Lifschitz, Foundations of logic programming, in: Principles of knowledge representation, G. Brewka (ed.), CSLI Publications, 1996, pp. 69–127.
14. S. Miyano, A. Shinohara, T. Shinohara, Polynomial-time learning of elementary formal systems, New Generation Computing 18 (2000) 217–242.
15. B.K. Natarajan, On learning sets and functions, Machine Learning 4 (1989) 67–97.
16. B.K. Natarajan, Machine Learning - A Theoretical Approach, Morgan Kaufmann Publ., 1991.
17. H. Rogers Jr., Theory of Recursive Functions and Effective Computability, MIT Press, 1987.
18. T. Shinohara, Inductive inference of monotonic formal systems from positive data, New Generation Computing 8 (1991) 371–384.
19. T. Shinohara, Rich classes inferable from positive data: Length-bounded elementary formal systems, Information and Computation 108 (1994) 175–186.
20. R.M. Smullyan, Theory of Formal Systems, Annals of Mathematical Studies, No. 47, Princeton University, 1961.
21. S. Soderland, Learning information extraction rules from semi-structured and free text, Machine Learning 34 (1997) 233–272.
22. B. Thomas, Token-Templates and Logic Programs for Intelligent Web Search, Journal of Intelligent Information Systems 14 (2000) 241–261.
23. L. Valiant, A theory of the learnable, Communications of the ACM 27 (1984) 1134–1142.
24. A. Yamamoto, Procedural semantics and negative information of elementary formal systems, Journal of Logic Programming 13 (1992) 89–97.
25. C. Zeng, S. Arikawa, Applying inverse resolution to EFS language learning, in: Proc. Int. Conference for Young Computer Scientists, Int. Academic Publishers, 1999, pp. 480–487.
26. T. Zeugmann, S. Lange, A guided tour across the boundaries of learning recursive languages, in: Algorithmic Learning for Knowledge-Based Systems, K.P. Jantke and S. Lange (eds), LNAI 961, Springer-Verlag, 1995, pp. 190–258.

Learning Regular Languages Using RFSA*

François Denis, Aurélien Lemay, and Alain Terlutte

GRAPPA - LIFL
Bât M3, Université de Lille I,
59655 Villeneuve d'Ascq Cedex, FRANCE
{denis, lemay, terlutte}@lifl.fr

Abstract. Residual languages are important and natural components of regular languages. Most approaches in grammatical inference rely on this notion. Classical algorithms such as RPNI try to identify prefixes of positive learning examples which give rise to identical residual languages. Here, we study inclusion relations between residual languages. We lead experiments which show that when regular languages are randomly drawn using non deterministic representations, the number of inclusion relations is very important. We introduced in previous articles a new class of automata which is defined using the notion of residual languages: residual finite state automata (RFSA). RFSA representations of regular languages may have far less states than DFA representations. We prove that RFSA are not polynomially characterizable. However, we design a new learning algorithm, DeLeTe2, based on the search of inclusion relations between residual languages, which produces a RFSA and have both good theoretical properties and good experimental performances.

1 Introduction

The subject of this paper is grammatical inference of regular languages. Most classical approaches in this field represent regular languages by Deterministic Finite State Automata (DFA): operations on DFA are fast, and every regular language admits a unique minimal DFA. However, it is well known that DFA is not the most optimal way of representing regular languages: the size of minimal DFA of languages as simple as $\Sigma^*0\Sigma^n$ is exponential with respect to n: thus these languages cannot be learned by classical algorithms in reasonable time. It seems natural to learn regular languages using non deterministic representations [CF00], [DLT00]. We presented in [DLT01] a new class of non deterministic finite automata, the class of Residual Finite State Automata (RFSA). The residual language of a language L with regard to a word u is the set of words v such that uv is in L. The number of distinct residual languages of a regular language is finite (Myhill-Nerode theorem). The definition of RFSA is based on this notion. RFSA have some interesting properties: for example, every regular language can be represented by a unique minimal canonical RFSA which can be exponentially

---

* This work was partially supported by the "projet TIC du CPER TACT - région Nord - Pas de Calais"

N. Abe, R. Khardon, and T. Zeugmann (Eds.): ALT 2001, LNAI 2225, pp. 348–363, 2001.
© Springer-Verlag Berlin Heidelberg 2001

smaller than its equivalent minimal DFA. A first learning algorithm using this representation has been described in [DLT00].

We first study the notion of residual language. A residual language of a regular language is said to be prime if it is not union of other residual languages. Each state of the canonical RFSA of a language L is associated with one prime residual language of L. We first study the ratio between the number of prime residual languages of L and the total number of residual languages of L. The second aspect we study is the number of inclusion relations between distinct residual languages of L, as this notion is used to build RFSA and can be exploited in learning algorithms. In Section 3, we study theses parameters from an experimental point of view, and show they highly depend on the way regular languages are generated. If languages are generated using random DFA, most residual languages are prime, and there are few inclusion relations between them. But if regular languages are generated using NFA or regular expressions, the number of prime residual languages is often small with regard to the total number of residual languages, and there are a lot of inclusions between them.

These results suggest two families of learning algorithms that we study in Section 4: the first approach would be to seek after prime residual languages: we show in Section 4.1 that this identification is impossible using a sample polynomial with respect to the size of the canonical RFSA. The second approach would be to look after inclusion relations between residual languages: this approach is developed in Section 4.2 where we introduce a new learning algorithm (DeLeTe2). When classical algorithms, like RPNI [OG92], look after equivalent residual languages and merge states to obtain a DFA, DeLeTe2 looks after inclusion of residual languages and uses them to add transitions to the current automaton, and obtain a RFSA. Section 5 presents experimental results of DeLeTe2, and shows that, when regular languages are generated using non deterministic representations, DeLeTe2 has good performances.

2 Preliminaries

The reader may refer to [Yu97], [HU79] for classical definitions and proofs on formal language theory. The notions of prime and composed residual languages and RFSA have been introduced and studied in [DLT01].

2.1 Regular Languages, Regular Expressions, and Automata

Let Σ be a finite alphabet and let Σ^* be the set of words on Σ. We note ε the empty word and $|u|$ the length of a word u. A *language* is a subset of Σ^*. For any word u and any language L, we note $Pref(u) = \{v | \exists w \ vw = u\}$ and $Pref(L) = \cup\{Pref(u) | u \in L\}$. We note $<$ the usual lexicographic order[1]. A *non deterministic finite automaton* (NFA) is a quintuple $A = \langle \Sigma, Q, Q_0, F, \delta \rangle$ where Q is a finite set of states, $Q_0 \subseteq Q$ is the set of initial states, $F \subseteq Q$

---
[1] For example, first words defined on $\Sigma = \{a, b\}$ are ε, a, b, aa, ab, ba, bb, ...

is the set of final states, δ is the transition function defined from a subset of $Q \times \Sigma$ to 2^Q. As usual, we also denote by δ the extended transition function defined from a subset of $2^Q \times \Sigma^*$ to 2^Q. We take the number of states of a NFA as a measure of its size. A NFA is *deterministic* (DFA) if Q_0 contains exactly one element q_0 and if $\forall q \in Q$, $\forall x \in \Sigma$, $Card(\delta(q, x)) \leq 1$. A DFA is *complete* if $\forall q \in Q$, $\forall x \in \Sigma$, $Card(\delta(q, x)) = 1$. A NFA is *trimmed* if $\forall q \in Q$, $\exists w_1$, $w_2 \in \Sigma^*$, $q \in \delta(Q_0, w_1)$ and $\delta(q, w_2) \cap F \neq \emptyset$. A word $u \in \Sigma^*$ is recognized by a NFA if $\delta(Q_0, u) \cap F \neq \emptyset$ and the language L_A recognized by A is the set of the words recognized by A. We denote by $Rec(\Sigma^*)$ the class of recognizable languages over Σ^*. There exists a unique minimal DFA that recognizes a given recognizable language (minimal with regard to the number of states and unique up to an isomorphism). A *regular expression* e denotes a *regular language* L if $e = \emptyset$ and $L(e) = \emptyset$; $e = \varepsilon$ and $L(e) = \{\varepsilon\}$; $e = x$ and $L(e) = \{x\}$ where $x \in \Sigma$; $e = e_1 + e_2$ and $L(e) = L(e_1) \cup L(e_2)$; $e = e_1 \cdot e_2$ and $L(e) = L(e_1)L(e_2)$; $e = e_1^*$ and $L(e) = (L(e_1))^*$. The Kleene theorem proves that the class of regular languages $Reg(\Sigma^*)$ is identical to $Rec(\Sigma^*)$.

2.2   Residual Languages and RFSA

For any language L and any word u over Σ, we note $u^{-1}L = \{v \in \Sigma^* \mid uv \in L\}$ the *residual* language of L associated with u (also called Brzozowski derivative [Brz64]). The set of distinct residual languages of any regular language is finite (Myhill-Nerode theorem). A residual language is *composed* if it is equal to the union of the residual languages it strictly contains i.e. $u^{-1}L$ is composed if and only if $u^{-1}L = \bigcup \{v^{-1}L \mid v^{-1}L \subsetneq u^{-1}L\}$. A residual language is *prime* if it is not composed. Let $A = \langle \Sigma, Q, Q_0, F, \delta \rangle$ be a NFA and let $q \in Q$. We note L_q the language defined by $L_q = \{v \mid \delta(q, v) \cap F \neq \emptyset\}$. If A is a trimmed DFA, L_q is always a residual language of L_A; moreover, if A is minimal, for every non empty residual language $u^{-1}L$, there exists a unique $q \in Q$ such that $L_q = u^{-1}L$. A *Residual Finite State Automaton* (RFSA) is a NFA $A = \langle \Sigma, Q, Q_0, F, \delta \rangle$ such that, for each state $q \in Q$, L_q is a residual language of L_A. Trimmed DFA are RFSA. It can be proved that for each prime residual $u^{-1}L_A$ of a RFSA A, there exists a state q such that $L_q = u^{-1}L_A$. A state q of a RFSA is said to be *prime* (resp. composed) if the residual language it defines is prime (resp. composed). The *saturated* of a RFSA A is $A^s = \langle \Sigma, Q, Q_0^s, F, \delta^s \rangle$ with $Q_0^s = \{q \in Q \mid L_q \subseteq L\}$ and $\forall q \in Q$, $\forall x \in \Sigma$, $\delta^s(q, x) = \{q' \in Q \mid L_{q'} \subseteq x^{-1}L_q\}$. It can be shown that the saturated of a RFSA is a RFSA. A saturated RFSA can be reduced by deleting its composed states. We then obtain a unique minimal (with regard to the number of states) trimmed saturated RFSA which recognizes the same language and which is called the *canonical RFSA* of L. The number of states of a canonical RFSA is exactly the number of non empty prime residual languages of the language it recognizes. Therefore, a canonical RFSA can be much smaller than its equivalent DFA: for example, the canonical RFSA recognizing $\Sigma^* 0 \Sigma^n$ has $n + 2$ states while its equivalent minimal DFA possesses 2^n states. Let $A = \langle \Sigma, Q, Q_0, F, \delta \rangle$ be a canonical RFSA. The *simplified* canonical RFSA of L_A is defined by $A' = \langle \Sigma, Q, Q_0', F, \delta' \rangle$ with $Q_0' = \{q \in Q_0 \mid \nexists q' \in Q_0, L_q \subsetneq L_{q'}\}$

and $\forall q' \in Q$, $\forall x \in \Sigma$, $\delta'(q',x) = \{q \in \delta(q',x) \mid \nexists q'' \in \delta(q',x), L_q \subsetneq L_{q''}\}$. this automaton recognizes L_A. All References about prime residual languages and RFSA can be found in [DLT01].

Example 1. Let A be the minimal DFA described in Fig. 1. The residual languages are $L_{q_0} = \varepsilon + 00^+ + 0^*1\Sigma^+$, $L_{q_1} = 0^+ + 0^*1\Sigma^+$, $L_{q_2} = \Sigma^+$, $L_{q_3} = 0^* + 0^*1\Sigma^+$, $L_{q_4} = \Sigma^*$. We have the following inclusions and compositions $L_{q_1} \subset L_{q_2}$, $L_{q_3} = L_{q_0} \cup L_{q_1}$, $L_{q_4} = L_{q_0} \cup L_{q_1} \cup L_{q_2} \cup L_{q_3}$. The prime states are q_0, q_1, q_2. The saturated of A is described in Fig. 1 and the equivalent canonical RFSA and simplified canonical RFSA are described in Fig. 2.

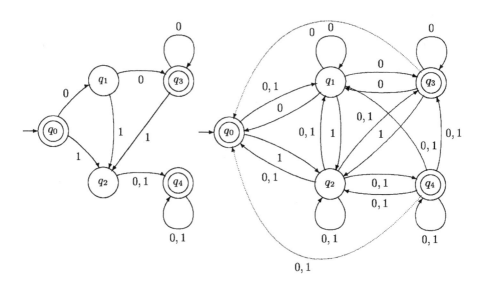

Fig. 1. The minimal DFA recognizing $\varepsilon + 00^+ + 0^*1\Sigma^+$ and its saturated RFSA.

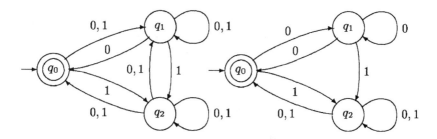

Fig. 2. The equivalent canonical RFSA and simplified canonical RFSA.

2.3   The Model of Learning from Given Data

The learning model from given data has been introduced in [Gol78] where Gold proved that regular languages represented by DFA are polynomially learnable from given data (see also [Hig97]). An *example* of a language L over Σ^* is a pair (u, e) where $e = 1$ if $u \in L$ and $e = 0$ otherwise. A *sample* of L is a finite set of examples of L. The size of a sample is the sum of the length of the words it contains. For any sample S of L, we note $S^+ = \{u|(u, 1) \in S\}$ and $S^- = \{u|(u, 0) \in S\}$.

Here, we only consider the class of regular languages REG. We consider three *representation schemes*: DFA, RFSA and NFA.

Definition 1. *[Hig97] We say that REG is* semi-polynomially learnable *from given data using representation scheme R if there exist two algorithms $\mathcal{T}$ and $\mathcal{L}$ such that for any target language $L \in REG$ and any representation $r \in R(L)$:*

- $\mathcal{T}$ *with input r computes a teaching sample S_L whose size is polynomial in the size of r,*
- *for any sample S of L containing S_L, $\mathcal{L}$ with input S computes a representation of L in time polynomial in the size of S.*

We say that REG is polynomially learnable *from given data if it is semi-polynomially learnable and if $\mathcal{T}$ computes S_L in time polynomial in $|r|$.*

REG is polynomially learnable from given data using the representation scheme by DFA and RPNI is a learning algorithm in this framework [OG92]. De la Higuera gives a necessary condition to be semi-polynomially learnable based on the following notion:

Definition 2. *We say that REG is* polynomially characterizable *using the representation scheme R if there exists a function $\mathcal{T}$ such that*

- *for any language $L \in REG$ and any representation $r \in R(L)$, $\mathcal{T}(r)$ is a sample of L whose size is polynomial in the size of r,*
- *for any pair of distinct languages (L, L') represented by (r, r'), L is not consistent with $\mathcal{T}(r')$ or L' is not consistent with $\mathcal{T}(r)$.*

Proposition 1. *[Hig97] If REG is semi-polynomially learnable from given data using a representation R then it is polynomially characterizable using R. For any non empty alphabet, REG is not polynomially characterizable using representations by NFA.*

3   Experimental Study of Residual Languages

As RFSA are defined using the notion of residual language, a natural first step before building learning algorithm based on this representation is to study properties of residual languages. We focus our study on two aspects of residual languages that are important for RFSA. The first aspect we study is the number of prime residual languages of a regular language, which is also the number of states of the canonical RFSA, and the second aspect is the number of inclusion relations between residual languages, as this notion is used in the definition of the transition function of RFSA. We study these questions from an experimental point of view. We consider here three classical representation schemes of regular languages: DFA, NFA and regular expressions, and we define natural way to draw randomly regular languages using these representations. We observed that results are very different regarding to the generation method which is used: when languages are generated using DFA, there are few inclusion relations between residual languages, and few composed residual languages either. But when languages are generated using NFA or regular expressions, there are a lot of inclusion relations between residual languages, and the number of prime residual languages can be very small with regard to the total number of residual languages. Let us define below the protocol of our experiments:

The procedure DrawDFA(nStates, p_F) takes as input an integer nStates and a probability p_F and outputs a complete DFA whose number of states is chosen randomly between 1 and nStates. The successor of any state reading any letter is chosen randomly among the set of states and each state is chosen to be final with a probability equal to p_F.

The procedure DrawNFA(nStates, nTrans, p_I, p_F) takes as input two integers nStates and nTrans, two probabilities p_I and p_F and outputs a NFA with nStates states. For any state and any letter, the number of possible transitions is chosen randomly between 0 and nTrans. Each state is chosen to be initial (resp. final) with a probability equal to p_I (resp. p_F).

The procedure DrawRegExp(NbOp,$p_\emptyset$, p_0, p_1, p_*, $p_.$, p_+) takes as input an integer NbOp and 6 non negative numbers summing to 1 and outputs a regular expression which has at most NbOp operators; the root operator is chosen among $\{\emptyset, 0, 1, +, \cdot, ^*\}$ using the input probabilities. When the root operator is unary, the procedure is called with parameter NbOp-1 to build its argument and when it is binary, it is called with approximately (NbOp-1)/2 on each branch.

The main procedure Result uses one of the above procedure to draw regular languages and completes two arrays $T1[100 \times 100]$ and $T2[100 \times 100]$: $T1[n, i]$ is the number of prime residual languages of the ith regular language drawn whose minimal DFA has a size equal to n (as a consequence, n is also the total number of residual languages of the language). $T2[n, i]$ is the number of inclusions relations between two distinct residual languages of this language. The procedure stops when arrays are completed.

Fig. 3 and 4 show curves corresponding to the procedure Result when regular languages are drawn using DrawDfa(120,0.1), DrawRegExp(100, 0.025, 0.05, 0.05, 0.125, 0.5, 0.25) and DrawNfa(30,2,0.1,0.1). Other experiments have been performed with other values and similar results have always been obtained. These results indicate that the ratio between the number of prime residual languages and the total number of residual languages of a language - and therefore between the size of a canonical RFSA and a minimal DFA - is highly dependent on the method used to draw regular languages: drawing DFA

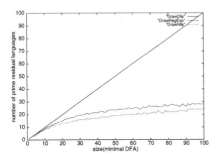

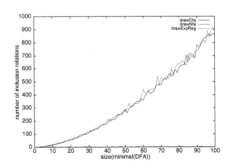

Fig. 3. Number of prime residual languages.

Fig. 4. Inclusions between distinct residual languages.

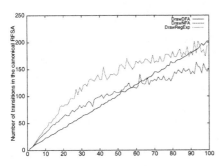

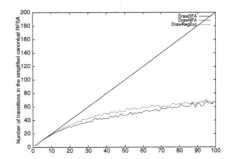

Fig. 5. Number of transitions in the canonical RFSA

Fig. 6. Transitions in the simplified canonical RFSA

provides regular languages such that almost all residual languages are prime while drawing NFA or regular expressions provides regular languages such that most residual languages are composed, which also imply that there is a lot of inclusions relations between residual languages. This can be checked on figure 4 which also indicate that there is nearly no such inclusion relation in languages generated by DFA (the curve is nearly merged with the X-axes).

Note that we use here the number of states of an automaton as a measure of its size. Its number of transitions can also be considered. Fig. 5 and 6 show curves corresponding to the number of transitions for canonical RFSA and simplified canonical RFSA for the same languages as above. Languages obtained using DFA have a number of transitions roughly equal to the number of transitions of the minimal DFA (languages studied here have 2 letters therefore their complete minimal DFA have $2 \times n$ transitions), for other languages, simplified canonical RFSA usually have a number of transitions significantly smaller than minimal DFA. Therefore it is reasonable to say that simplified canonical RFSA is a more economic way than DFA to represent regular languages generated by non-deterministic representations.

These results have to be explained but for now, we can only speculate on their explanations. Our hypothesis is that to generate a DFA with n state is roughly equivalent to generate n distinct languages (one per state) and these languages have low probability to have any inclusion relation or to be composed. When a NFA of n states is generated, the n languages obtained also have a low probability to have inclusion relations, but languages associated to states of the corresponding minimal DFA are composition of these languages, which may be the reason why so many states are composed or have inclusion relations between them. A similar argument can probably be used for regular expressions.

These experiments suggest two approaches in grammatical inference. The first one consists in identifying prime residual languages of target languages (we show in section 4.1 that this identification is not possible with a sample of size polynomial in the size of the canonical RFSA). The second idea would be to seek after inclusion relations between residual languages: this is the approach that we develop in section 4.2.

These results also raises the problem of a natural representation of regular languages: none of the previously described procedures is more natural or more artificial than the others. As a consequence, learning artificial benchmarks should not only be based on procedures that choose DFA. We also raise the naive question: do the regular languages occurring in practical cases belong to the first class (size(canonical RFSA) $\simeq$ size(minimal DFA)) or to the second class (size(canonical RFSA) $<<$ size(minimal DFA))?

4   Learning Using Residual Languages

In this section, we present two ways to use properties of residual languages in grammatical inference. The first approach that seems natural with regard to previous results would be to use the fact that prime residual languages of a regular language can be few among the set of all its residual languages. From this point of view, the canonical RFSA seems to be an interesting target for grammatical inference. However, we prove that the class of regular languages is not polynomially characterizable using RFSA (if the underlying alphabet has at least two letters).

The other interesting property of residual languages that previous experiments point out is the fact that there can be a lot of inclusion relations between them. We present a new learning algorithm based on inclusion detection between residual languages and study its theoretical properties. These results precise the study made in [DLT00].

4.1   RFSA Are Not Polynomially Characterizable

It has been shown in [Hig97] that the class REG is not polynomially characterizable using NFA even if the underlying alphabet contains only one letter. The proof cannot be directly used to show an analogous result for RFSA as it can be proved that the class of RFSA over a one letter alphabet is polynomially learnable from given data. Indeed, it can be shown that the size of the canonical RFSA of a regular language over a one-letter alphabet is not smaller than the square root of the size of the equivalent minimal DFA and algorithms such as RPNI can be used to learn them. The number of states of an automaton is used as a measure of its size, but results presented below are still true if we use the number of transitions (as the number of transitions is less or equal to $|Q| \times |Q| \times |\Sigma|$).

Proposition 2. *The class of regular languages over a two-letters alphabet is not polynomially characterizable using RFSA.*

Proof. Let $p_1,..., p_k$ be distinct prime numbers and let $L_{p_i} = a^* \setminus (a^{p_i})^* = \{a^{np_i+m} \mid n \in \mathbb{N}, 0 < m < p_i\}$, for each i, $1 \leq i \leq k$. Let us consider the two canonical RFSA A_1 and A_2 recognizing the languages

$$L_{A_1} = aa^+ + \cup_{i=1}^k b^i L_{p_i} \text{ and } L_{A_2} = \cup_{i=1}^k (a + b^i) L_{p_i}.$$

Automaton A_1 has $\Sigma_{i=1}^k p_i + k + 1$ states and automaton A_2 has $\Sigma_{i=1}^k p_i + k$ states. For any polynomial P, we can choose prime numbers such that $\Pi_{i=1}^k p_i$ is bigger than $P(\Sigma_{i=1}^k p_i + k + 1)$. We verify that:

$$L_{A_1} \cap a^* = aa^+$$

$$L_{A_2} \cap a^* = a(\bigcup_{i=1}^k L_{p_i}) = a(\bigcup_{i=1}^k (a^* \setminus (a^{p_i})^*)) = a(a^* \setminus \bigcap_{i=1}^k (a^{p_i})^*) = a(a^* \setminus (a^{\Pi_{i=1}^k p_i})^*)$$

$$L_{A_1} \cap b(a+b)^* = L_{A_2} \cap b(a+b)^*$$

$$L_{A_1} \cap (a+b)^{<\Pi_{i=1}^k p_i} = L_{A_2} \cap (a+b)^{<\Pi_{i=1}^k p_i}$$

Therefore any set S with a size smaller than $\Pi_{i=1}^k p_i$ verifies $S \cap L_{A_1} = S \cap L_{A_2}$ and $S \cap \overline{L_{A_1}} = S \cap \overline{L_{A_2}}$.

Suppose now that REG is polynomially characterizable using RFSA. Let $\mathcal{T}$ be the function that computes characteristic samples and let P be a polynomial such that $size(\mathcal{T}(A)) \leq P(size(A))$. Let k be such that $\Pi_{i=1}^k p_i > P(\Sigma_{i=1}^k p_i + k + 1)$ and let $S_1 = \mathcal{T}(A_1)$ and $S_2 = \mathcal{T}(A_2)$. L_{A_1} is consistent with S_2 and L_{A_2} is consistent with S_1 which is contradictory.   □

With proposition 1, we obtain the following corollary:

Corollary 1. *The class of regular languages over a two-letters alphabet is not semi-polynomially learnable using RFSA.*

Although regular languages are polynomially learnable when represented by DFA, they are not polynomially learnable when represented by RFSA. In other words, if $n_r(L)$ is the number of residual languages of a language L and if $n_p(L)$ is the number of its prime residual languages, a number of examples polynomial in $n_r(L)$ is sufficient to learn L whereas a number of example polynomial in $n_p(L)$ is not sufficient. As our experiments showed that when regular languages are generated using non deterministic ways $n_p(L) << n_r(L)$, it would be interesting to know if it is possible to find an intermediary value of the learning parameter.

If we note $p(L)$ the greatest depth of a prime residual language of L (i.e. $p(L) = Max\{Min\{|u| \mid u^{-1}L = R\} \mid R$ prime residual language of $L\}$), we can hope that there exists a learning algorithm polynomial in $p(L) \times n_p(L)$ (which can still be small with regard to $n_r(L)$). But this problem, or the more general problem to know whether there exists another intermediary solution is still open.

4.2   Inclusion Relation Based Learning Algorithm

Classical learning algorithms such as RPNI build a prefix tree acceptor from the positive examples, and evaluate whether languages associated with different states are equivalent; if so, they merge these states. Previous results showed that it could be interesting to go one step further and to look after inclusions of languages instead of equivalences. We present here a learning algorithm (DeLeTe2) based on this approach. We first introduce its target automaton. This automaton has fewer states than the minimal DFA.

Saturated subautomata of the minimal DFA. Let $A = \langle \Sigma, Q, q_0, F, \delta \rangle$ be a minimal trimmed DFA. For every state q of A, we define u_q as being the smallest word of Σ^* such that $\delta(q_0, u_q) = q$ (so, $u_{q_0} = \varepsilon$). We assume that $Q = \{q_0, \ldots, q_n\}$ is ordered using u_q. In other words, $q_i < q_j$ iff $u_{q_i} < u_{q_j}$. Let $A^s = \langle \Sigma, Q, Q_0^s, F, \delta^s \rangle$ be the saturated of A.

For any word u, the automaton A_u is obtained from the saturated A^s of A by deleting the states q such that $u_q > u$. It is defined by $A_u = \langle \Sigma, Q^u, Q_0^u, F^u, \delta^u \rangle$ with $Q^u = \{q \in Q \mid u_q \leq u\}, Q_0^u = Q_0^s \cap Q^u, F^u = F \cap Q^u, \delta^u(q, x) = \delta^s(q, x) \cap Q^u$.

There is a finite number of subautomata A_u. When u is bigger than u_{q_n}, the subautomaton A_u is A^s itself. On the other way, what is the smallest u such that $L_A = L_{A_u}$?

Proposition 3. *Let p be the greatest prime state in A. The word u_p is the smallest word such that the automaton A_{u_p} is equivalent to A.*

Proof. All states greater than p in A are composed. The automaton A_{u_p} is obtained by saturation of A and reduction of the states greater than p. These two operations preserve the language recognized by the automaton A [DLT01].

On the other hand, if u is smaller than u_p, the subautomaton A_u does not contain p. Since p is a prime state, there exists a word w which does not belong to any residual language included in L_{Ap}. The word $u_p w$ is not recognized by the automaton A_u. $\square$

Note that the automaton A_{u_p} only depends on the language L_A. It is possible to build examples where the automaton A_{u_p} is exponentially smaller than A.

Example 2. Let us come back to the automaton described in Fig. 1. The greatest prime state is q_2 and A_{u_2} is the canonical RFSA described in Fig. 2.

A characteristic sample. As in the previous section, we denote by p the greatest prime residual language of the minimal trimmed DFA A. A sample is said *characteristic* if it provides complete informations about inclusion relations between the residual languages associated with the states smaller than p.

We define $SP(L) = \{u_q | q \leq p\}$ and $K(L) = \{u_q x | q \leq p, x \in \Sigma, \delta(q, x) \neq \emptyset\}$.

Definition 3. *A sample S is characteristic for the automaton A_{u_p} if*

- $\forall u \in SP(L) \cup K(L), u \in Pref(S^+)$
- $SP(L) \cap L \subseteq S^+$,
- $\forall u \in SP(L), \forall v \in SP(L) \cup K(L), u^{-1}L \not\subseteq v^{-1}L \Rightarrow \exists w$ *such that* $uw \in S^+$ *and* $vw \in S^-$.

Let S be a sample, let $u, v \in Pref(S^+)$. We note:

- $u \prec v$ if no word w exists such that $uw \in S^+$ and $vw \in S^-$,
- $u \simeq v$ if $u \prec v$ and $v \prec u$.

It is clear that for any sample S and any words $u, v \in Pref(S^+)$, we have $u^{-1}L = v^{-1}L \Rightarrow u \simeq v$ and $u^{-1}L \subseteq v^{-1}L \Rightarrow u \prec v$.

Lemma 1. *Suppose that the sample S is characteristic for the automaton A_{u_p}, and let $u \in SP(L)$, $v \in SP(L) \cup K(L)$. We have $u \prec v \Rightarrow u^{-1}L \subseteq v^{-1}L$.*

Proof. Straightforward since $\forall u \in SP(L), \forall v \in SP(L) \cup K(L), u^{-1}L \not\subseteq v^{-1}L \Rightarrow \exists w$ such that $uw \in S^+$ and $vw \in S^-$. This implies that $u \not\prec v$. $\square$

Example 3. (continued) We have $SP(L) = \{\varepsilon, 0, 1\}$, $K(L) = \{0, 1, 00, 01, 10, 11\}$. The smallest characteristic set is $S = S^+ \cup S^-$ where $S^+ = \{\varepsilon, 00, 11, 010, 10\}$ and $S^- = \{0, 1, 01, 001\}$.

We have the following relations between elements of $SP(L)$ and elements of $SP(L) \cup K(L)$ (if u is the label of a row and v the label of a column, a word w in the array means that $uw \in S^+$ and $vw \in S^-$).

	ε	0	1	00	01	10	11
ε	$\prec$	ε	ε	$\prec$	ε	$\prec$	$\prec$
0	0	$\prec$	$\prec$	$\prec$	$\prec$	$\prec$	$\prec$
1	1	1	$\prec$	1	$\prec$	$\prec$	$\prec$

The conclusion of the previous lemma can be checked on this array.

The *DeLeTe2* Algorithm. We now present an algorithm that builds a NFA from a sample of a target language L. If the sample is characteristic, the algorithm builds the automaton A_{u_p}. Starting with an empty automaton, the algorithm considers prefixes of the sample as characterization of states. A new state is added to the current set of state when it is supposed to be non equivalent with previous ones. The transitions associated with the new state are added.

Input: a sample S of a language L.
Let $Pref = \{u_0, \ldots, u_n\}$ be the set of prefixes of S^+
ordered using the usual order.
Let $Q = Q_0 = F = \delta = \emptyset$.
Let $u = \varepsilon$.
Repeat
   If $\exists u' \in Q$ such that $u \simeq u'$
   Then
      delete $u\Sigma^*$ from $Pref$
   Else
      $Q = Q \cup \{u\}$
      $Q_0 = Q_0 \cup \{u\}$ if $u \prec \varepsilon$
      $F = F \cup \{u\}$ if $u \in S^+$
      $\delta = \delta \cup \{(u', x, u) \mid u' \in Q,\ u'x \in Pref,\ u'x \succ u\}$
      $\cup\{(u, x, u') \mid u' \in Q,\ ux \in Pref,\ ux \succ u'\}$
   End If
   Let $u = $ next word in $Pref$
until $A = \langle \Sigma, Q, Q_0, F, \delta \rangle$ is consistent with S

Output: The automaton $A = \langle \Sigma, Q, Q_0, F, \delta \rangle$.

Example 4. (continued) On the previous example, the algorithm needs three steps to recover the target automaton.

1. In the first step, the state ε is added. As $\varepsilon \prec \varepsilon$, the state ε is initial. The word ε belongs to S^+, the state ε is final. There is no relation $x \succ \varepsilon$ or $\varepsilon \succ x$ for $x \in \{0, 1\}$ and $x \in Pref$; thus no transition has to be added.
2. In the second step, the state 0 is added because $0 \not\simeq \varepsilon$. As $0 \not\prec \varepsilon$, the state 0 is not initial. The word 0 does not belong to S^+, then the state 0 is not final. We have the relations $\varepsilon 0 \succ 0$, $\varepsilon 1 \succ 0$, $00 \succ 0$, $01 \succ 0$ and the relations $00 \succ \varepsilon$, $00 \succ 0$, $01 \succ 0$. The corresponding transitions are added.
3. In the third step, the state 1 is added because $1 \not\simeq \varepsilon$ and $1 \not\simeq 0$. As $1 \not\prec \varepsilon$, the state 1 is not initial. The word 1 does not belong to S^+, then the state 1 is not final. We have the relations $\varepsilon 1 \succ 1$, $01 \succ 1$, $10 \succ 1$, $11 \succ 1$ and the relations $10 \succ \varepsilon$, $10 \succ 0$, $10 \succ 1$, $11 \succ \varepsilon$, $11 \succ 0$, $11 \succ 1$. The corresponding transitions are added.

This automaton is consistent with S.

Theorem 1. *If the input of the DeLeTe2 algorithm is a characteristic sample for the subautomaton A_{u_p}, it outputs the subautomaton A_{u_p}.*

Proof. We can prove that, at each beginning of the loop, we have $u \leq u_p$. At the beginning of the else part, it belongs to $SP(L)$. Then the set Q is included in $SP(L)$. Due to the definition of the characteristic sample and to lemma 1, u is an initial state if $u \prec \varepsilon$, i.e. $u^{-1}L \subseteq L$; u is a final state if $u \in S^+$, i.e. $\varepsilon \in u^{-1}L$. The added transitions are all transitions such that $u'x \succ u$, i.e. $(u'x)^{-1}L \supseteq u^{-1}L$ or

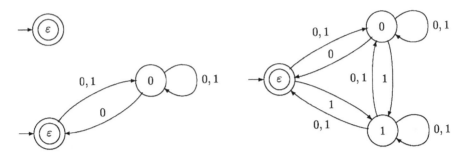

Fig. 7. The three steps.

$ux \succ u'$, i.e. $(ux)^{-1}L \supseteq u'^{-1}L$. Thus, at the end of the loop, the automaton A is the subautomaton A_u of the minimal DFA recognizing L. When the automaton A is consistent with the sample, we have the subautomaton A_{u_p}.   □

Given a minimal DFA, deciding whether a given state is prime is a PSPACE-complete problem [DLT01]. Therefore, computing the smallest characteristic set of a given DFA is not feasible. However, it is always possible to compute within polynomial time from a given DFA *some* characteristic sample: use $SP(L) = \{u_q | q \in Q\}$ and the corresponding $K(L)$. So, the class of regular languages represented by DFA can be polynomially learned from given data by our algorithm.

5   Some Experimental Results

In this section, we compare our algorithm with other grammatical inference algorithms: RPNI [OG92], and Red-Blue (RB) (by H. Juillé and J. B. Pollack, implemented by K. Lang) which is a variant of RPNI that uses evidence driven state merging (EDSM, see [LPP98]).

5.1   Implementation of DeLeTe2

Here, we do not suppose that the input sample is characteristic, and so, to perform our experiments, we use a variant of the algorithm presented above. This variant always computes an automaton which is consistent with the input sample, and is more efficient than the previous algorithm. Modifications used here do not alter theoretical results: the algorithm used here is still a learning algorithm in the conditions mentioned above.

Whenever the algorithm intends to use a $\prec$ to modify the current automaton, it first checks that this modification do not entail inconsistency. In order to do this verification, it first considers all the $\prec$ relations that are derived from the current one: as the inclusion relation is transitive, the set of valid $\prec$ relation should be transitive too. For example, if $q_1 \prec q_2$ is a valid relation, and if we check whether $q_2 \prec q_3$ is valid or not, then we also consider the relation $q_1 \prec q_3$

and modify the automaton accordingly. The same way, if $q_1 \prec q_2$, $L_{q'_1} = x^{-1}L_{q_1}$ and $L_{q'_2} = x^{-1}L_{q_2}$ (because q'_1 and q'_2 are successors of q_1 and q_2 on the prefix tree), we also consider the relation $q'_1 \prec q'_2$. If all these new $\prec$ relations do not entail inconsistency with the input sample, they are all marked as valid and the modification of the current automaton is accepted. Also, whenever two states are considered equivalent, the algorithm merge them.

5.2   Experimental Protocol

We build several benchmarks using generating methods described in Section 3: `DrawNFA(20,2,0.1,0.1)` have been used to generate NFA and `DrawRegExp(50,0.025,0.05,0.05,0.125,0.5,0.25)` to generate regular expressions. Studies have also been made using the procedure `DrawDFA`: in this case DeLeTe2 has worse results than RPNI and Red-Blue, which can be understood easily considering that, for this generation method, there are nearly no inclusion relations between distinct residual languages, so the approach we propose here is less effective than algorithm using equivalence relations. A target language being drawn, examples are drawn the following way: we choose l randomly in $[0, 15]$, and we create a word w of length l, each letter of w being chosen by flipping a coin.

One experiment consists in generating a language, generating a training set, generating a test set containing 1000 words and training each algorithm on the training set. In order to have results significantly higher than majority vote, only experiments the generated language of which has more than 20 % of negative examples and more than 20 % of positive examples in the learning sample have been kept. Each benchmark correspond to 30 experiments. Benchmarks are denoted by the representation chosen to draw its languages and the number of examples in the learning sample.

On each benchmark, we compare the following algorithms: Majority Vote (MAJ), DeLeTe2 (DLT2), RPNI , and Red-Blue (RB). We compare them using two methods: first we observe average recognition rate of the output automaton of each algorithm on the test set, then we do matches (noted *algo1* - *algo2* on the table) where we count the number of experiments where one algorithm is better than another (in term of recognition rate), and we count a tie when the difference is not significative (using the Mc Nemar test, see [Die98]). Results of those matches are noted: won_by_algo1 + won_by_algo2 + nb_tie. We also perform basic statistical tests on each benchmark: $n_r(L)$ is the number of distinct residual languages of the generated language L, $n_p(L)$ its number of prime residual languages, $n_i(L)$ the number of inclusion relations between distinct residual languages of L and $|A_{u_p}(L)|$ is the number of states of the target automaton of DeLeTe2. Average values for generated languages are indicated here for each benchmark.

5.3   Results

Against RPNI, DeLeTe2 has won 130 matches, it has lost 24 matches and there are 86 draws; against RedBlue, it has won 127 matches, it has lost 33 matches

Benchmark	nfa_50	nfa_100	nfa_150	nfa_200	expreg_50	expreg_100	expreg_150	expreg_200
MAJ	68.6 %	68.7 %	65.0 %	67.9 %	65.0 %	66.7 %	62.4 %	62.4 %
RB	66.5 %	68.5 %	70.7 %	70.8 %	77.5 %	82.0 %	88.1 %	90.9 %
RPNI	66.5 %	68.7 %	72.2 %	71.0 %	81.2 %	82.5 %	85.2 %	90.6 %
DLT2	69.3 %	74.4 %	76.7 %	78.9 %	81.3 %	91.4 %	92.0 %	95.7 %
DLT - RPNI	14 + 6 + 10	19 + 3 + 8	18 + 3 + 9	23 + 1 + 6	17 + 2 + 11	19 + 1 + 10	11 + 4 + 15	9 + 4 +17
DLT - RB	16 + 8 + 6	17 + 4 + 9	19 + 4 + 7	21 + 2 + 7	9 + 8 + 13	19 + 3 + 8	15 + 3 + 12	11 + 1 + 18
$[n_r(L)]$	126,4	123,3	131,6	120,3	6,8	7,0	9,7	9,2
$[n_p(L)]$	22,1	22,6	21,4	24,7	5,8	5,8	6,7	6,1
$[n_i(L)]$	2172,7	2124,4	2093,3	1834,5	16,4	16,2	38,3	39,0
$[\|A_{u_p}(L)\|]$	99.5	94.8	91.7	110.0	6.6	6.7	8.6	8.3

and there are 80 draws. So, we can say that DeLeTe2, while very basic, is better than the two other algorithms on benchmarks generated using NFA and regular expressions. Details on the experiments described in this paper can be found at http://www.grappa.univ-lille3.fr/~lemay/alt01/.

6   Conclusion

The most classical strategy used in grammatical inference of regular languages consists in identifying words which define identical residual languages and then merging the corresponding states in the current automaton. This strategy naturally leads to build a DFA in order to identify the target language. We have proposed here an alternative strategy: look for inclusion relations between residual languages and then saturate the current automaton. This new strategy naturally leads to the RFSA representation of regular languages. Both theoretical and experimental results given in this paper show that this new approach is interesting and promising.

This paper also raises the problem of representation of languages: properties of randomly generated regular languages highly depend on the representation used to generate them. Two families of languages are highlighted here : in the first family, most residual languages are prime and there are few inclusion relations between them, in the second one, most residual languages are composed and there are many inclusion relations between them. Both those families should be studied in benchmarks. An interesting question not studied here is the problem of practical cases. We can assume that some cases are mostly constituted by languages of the first family, whereas other cases are mostly composed of languages of the second family. This could determine the kind of learning algorithm to use.

References

[Brz64]   Janusz A. Brzozowski. Derivatives of regular expressions. *Journal of the ACM*, 11:481–494, 1964.

[CF00]   F. Coste and D. Fredouille. Efficient ambiguity detection in c-nfa. In *Grammatical Inference: Algorithms and Applications*, volume 1891 of *Lecture Notes in Artificial Intelligence*. Springer Verlag, 2000.

[Die98]   Thomas G. Dietterich. Approximate statistical tests for comparing supervised classification learning algorithms. *Neural Computation*, 10(7):1895–1923, 1998.

[DLT00]   F. Denis, A. Lemay, and A. Terlutte. Learning regular languages using non deterministic finite automata. In *ICGI'2000*, volume 1891 of *Lecture Notes in Artificial Intelligence*, pages 39–50. Springer Verlag, 2000.

[DLT01]   F. Denis, A. Lemay, and A. Terlutte. Residual finite state automata. In *18th Annual Symposium on Theoretical Aspects of Computer Science*, volume 2010 of *Lecture Notes in Computer Science*, pages 144–157, 2001.

[Gol78]   E.M. Gold. Complexity of automaton identification from given data. *Inform. Control*, 37:302–320, 1978.

[Hig97]   Colin De La Higuera. Characteristic sets for polynomial grammatical inference. *Machine Learning*, 27:125–137, 1997.

[HU79]   J.E. Hopcroft and J.D. Ullman. *Introduction to Automata Theory, Languages, and Computation*. Addison-Wesley, 1979.

[LPP98]   K. J. Lang, B. A. Pearlmutter, and R. A. Price. Results of the Abbadingo one DFA learning competition and a new evidence-driven state merging algorithm. In *Proc. ICGI'98*, volume 1433 of *Lecture Notes in Artificial Intelligence*, pages 1–12. Springer-Verlag, 1998.

[OG92]   J. Oncina and P. Garcia. Inferring regular languages in polynomial update time. In *Pattern Recognition and Image Analysis*, pages 49–61, 1992.

[Yu97]   Sheng Yu. *Handbook of Formal Languages, Regular Languages*, volume 1, chapter 2, pages 41–110. Springer Verlag, 1997.

Inference of ω-Languages from Prefixes

Colin de la Higuera and Jean-Christophe Janodet

EURISE, Université de Saint-Etienne
France
cdlh@univ-st-etienne.fr, janodet@univ-st-etienne.fr

Abstract. Büchi automata are used to recognize languages of infinite words. Such languages have been introduced to describe the behavior of real time systems or infinite games. The question of inferring them from infinite examples has already been studied, but it may seem more reasonable to believe that the data from which we want to learn is a set of finite words, namely the prefixes of accepted or rejected infinite words. We describe the problems of identification in the limit and polynomial identification in the limit from given data associated to different interpretations of these prefixes: a positive prefix is universal (respectively existential) when all the infinite words of which it is a prefix are in the language (respectively when at least one is) ; the same applies to the negative prefixes. We prove that the classes of regular ω-languages (those recognized by Büchi automata) and of deterministic ω-languages (those recognized by deterministic Büchi automata) are not identifiable in the limit, whichever interpretation for the prefixes is taken. We give a polynomial algorithm that identifies the class of safe languages from positive existential prefixes and negative universal prefixes. We show that this class is maximal for polynomial identification in the limit from given data, in the sense that no superclass can even be identified in the limit.

1 Introduction

Grammatical inference [5, 7, 11] deals with the general problem of automatic learning machines (grammars or automata) from structured data, and more usually words. Between the different syntactic objects from formal language theory, most attention has been paid to the case of deterministic finite automata (*dfa*), even if some results on different types of grammars are known. On the other hand the question of learning automata on infinite words has hardly been studied.

The study of these automata was motivated by decision problems in mathematical logic. They provide a normal form for certain monadic second-order theories [4]. Later work concerned the relationship between these automata and the semantics of modal and temporal logics [14]. Today, these automata are used to model critical reactive systems. By reactive is implied a software whose purpose is to interact with its environment, and by critical one where mistakes or anomalies can have serious consequences, that can cost much more than the actual benefit made by the software. This is the case for instance of automatic pilots, operating systems or nuclear station automatic supervisors.

N. Abe, R. Khardon, and T. Zeugmann (Eds.): ALT 2001, LNAI 2225, pp. 364–377, 2001.
© Springer-Verlag Berlin Heidelberg 2001

The development of such software requires automatic program proving capacities. It is wished in particular that properties known as safety, which expresses that something bad will never occur during the execution of the system, are verified. Current examples of safety properties are mutual exclusion or deadlock avoidance [1]. These properties are described formally in temporal logics like *PTL* (*Propositional Temporal Logic*), whose models, Kripke structures, can be modeled by Büchi automata [14]. Consequently, Büchi automata make it possible to model with the same formalism the critical systems and the logical properties that they must satisfy and to develop effective proof algorithms (model checking).

Nevertheless, the formal specifications of the critical software, and more still, their properties, are difficult to write for a non-specialist of automata and temporal logics. Let us take the example of a lock chamber with two gates giving access to a safe deposit. One enters the lock chamber by gate 1 and one leaves it by gate 2 (or vice versa), but gate 2 should be allowed to open only if gate 1 is closed (and vice versa). This system is represented by the automaton below:

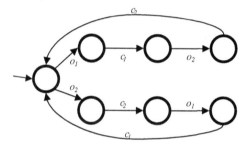

Fig. 1. A two-gate lock chamber (*o*=open, *c*=closed)

The safety property "gates 1 and 2 are never open at the same time" is written, in *PTL*: $\square$(not $p_1 \vee$ not p_2), where property p_i is that "gate i is open". If a non-specialist is not able to describe a system and its properties, he may be able on the other hand to give examples of "good" and "bad" behaviors of the system. These examples are sequences of events, $o_1\ c_1\ o_2\ c_2\ o_2\ c_2\ o_1\ c_1...$ and $o_2\ c_2\ o_1\ c_1...$, which are "good" behaviors, or $o_1\ o_2...$ and $o_1\ c_1\ o_1...$, which are "bad" behaviors. The same applies to the logical properties the system must satisfy. Our objective is thus to learn automatically the Büchi automaton by collecting only positive and negative examples.

The problem of learning automata on infinite words poses a first delicate problem: whatever the way of recovering the data (batch of examples, on line learning, use of an oracle or a teacher), is it reasonable to consider data which would be infinite words? Let us recall that with an alphabet of size 2 the set of infinite words is already uncountable. In previous research, the choice was to use data coming from the countable subset of the ultimately periodic words (of type uv^ω, u and v being finite words). Saoudi and Yokomori [12] define a (restricted) class of local languages, and prove the learnability of these languages from positive examples; Maler and Pnueli [9] adapt Angluin's L^* algorithm [2] and make it possible to learn a particular class of automata with the assistance of a polynomial number of equivalence and membership queries.

Nevertheless, we wish the learning of an automaton to be done from experimental data received from the potential users of a system. The data will therefore necessarily be finite words. And the interpretation of these words can vary. A finite word u can be a positive prefix, in the sense that one will be able to say that all its (infinite) continuations are good, or that one of its continuations at least is. The same kind of interpretations exists for the negative prefixes.

In this article we are thus interested in the inference of various types of machines on infinite words, from prefixes. In section 2 we will give the definitions concerning the ω-languages, and in section 3 those necessary to the comprehension of the learning problems. In section 4 we establish several learnability results, by showing that for the majority of the alternatives, identification in the limit of the classes of ω-regular languages and ω-deterministic languages is not possible. A positive result concerning the polynomial identification of safe languages is given.

2   Definitions

2.1   Finite Words, Languages, and Automata

An alphabet Σ is a finite nonempty set of symbols called letters. Σ^* denotes the set of all finite words over Σ. A language L over Σ is a subset of Σ^*. In the following, letters are indicated by a, b, c..., words by u, v,.., z, and the empty word by λ. Let **N** be the set of all non negative integers.

A deterministic finite automaton (dfa) is a quintuple $A=<Q, \Sigma, \delta, F, q_0>$ where Σ is an alphabet, Q is a finite set of states, $q_0 \in Q$ is an initial state, $\delta: Q \times \Sigma \rightarrow Q$ is a transition function, and $F \subseteq Q$ is a set of marked states, called the final states.

We define recursively:

- $\delta(q_i, \lambda) = q_i$
- $\delta(q_i, a.w) = \delta(\delta(q_i, a), w)$

$L(A)$, the language recognized by automaton A is $\{w \in \Sigma^*: \delta(q_0, w) \in F\}$.

It is well known that the languages recognized by dfas form the family of regular languages. This class is considered as a borderline case for grammatical inference [7].

2.2   Infinite Words and ω-Languages

We mainly use the notations from [13].

An infinite word u (or ω-word) over Σ is a mapping $\mathbf{N} \rightarrow \Sigma$. Such a word is written $u(0)u(1)...u(n)...$, with $u(i) \in \Sigma$. Σ^ω denotes the set of all ω-words over Σ. An ω-language over Σ is a set of infinite words, thus a subset of Σ^ω.

Let L and K be two languages over Σ. We define:

$$L^\omega = \{u \in \Sigma^\omega \ / \ u = u_0 u_1 ...: \forall i \in \mathbf{N} \ u_i \in L\} \qquad \text{and}$$
$$KL^\omega = \{u \in \Sigma^\omega \ / \ u = u_1 u_2: u_1 \in K \text{ and } u_2 \in L^\omega\}$$

An ω-language L is ω-regular *iff* there exists two finite sequences of regular languages $<A_i>_{i \in [n]}$ and $<B_i>_{i \in [n]}$ such that $L = \bigcup_{i=1}^{i=n} A_i B_i^{\omega}$.

Let *Pref(u)* denote the set of all finite prefixes of an infinite word u.

Given an ω-language L, $Pref(L) = \bigcup_{u \in L} Pref(u)$.

2.3   Automata on Infinite Words

Büchi automata [4] are used to recognize languages of infinite words. These languages are actually used to model reactive systems [14] and infinite games [13].

A Büchi automaton is a quintuple $A = <Q, \Sigma, \delta, F, q_0>$ where Σ is an alphabet, Q is a finite set of states, $q_0 \in Q$ is an initial state, $\delta: Q \times \Sigma \to 2^Q$ is a transition function, and $F \subseteq Q$ is a set of marked states.

A run of A on an ω-word u is a mapping $C_u: \mathbf{N} \to Q$ such that:

    (*i*) $C_u(0) = q_0$

    (*ii*) $\forall i \in \mathbf{N}, C_u(i+1) \in \delta(C_u(i), u(i))$

Note that C_u is undefined if at some point $C_u(i)$ is undefined.

An ω-word u is accepted by A *iff* there exists a state of F which appears infinitely often in a run of A on u. Let $L(A)$ be the set of all accepted ω-words by A. We can show [13] that an ω-language L is ω-regular *iff* $L = L(A)$ for some Büchi automaton A.

An automaton is deterministic *iff* $| \delta(q, a) | \leq 1$ for all states q and letters a.

Let $\mathbf{Reg}_\omega(\Sigma)$ be the class of all ω-regular languages and $\mathbf{Det}_\omega(\Sigma)$ the class of all ω-languages which are recognized by a deterministic Büchi automaton. Unlike what happens in the case of finite automata, $\mathbf{Det}_\omega(\Sigma) \subset \mathbf{Reg}_\omega(\Sigma)$ but $\mathbf{Det}_\omega(\Sigma) \neq \mathbf{Reg}_\omega(\Sigma)$. Indeed, consider the language $(b^*a)^\omega$ of words with an infinite number of a. This language is accepted by the deterministic automaton 2a below but its complementary $(a+b)^*b^\omega$ is not deterministic, although it is recognized by the non deterministic automaton 2b.

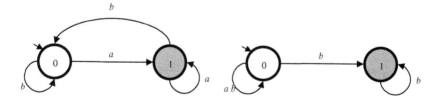

Fig. 2. Büchi automata 2a and 2b recognize $(b^*a)^\omega$ and $(a+b)^*b^\omega$. Their marked states are in gray.

2.4   ω-Safe Languages and *DB*-Machines

An ω-language L is safe [1] *iff*

$$\forall w \in \Sigma^{\omega}, (\forall u \in Pref(w), \exists v \in \Sigma^{\omega}: uv \in L) \Rightarrow w \in L$$

ie

$$\forall w \in \Sigma^{\omega}, Pref(w) \subseteq Pref(L) \Rightarrow w \in L$$

that is to say,

$$\forall w \in \Sigma^{\omega}, w \notin L \Rightarrow (\exists u \in Pref(w): \forall v \in \Sigma^{\omega} uv \notin L)$$

Let **Safe**$_\omega(\Sigma)$ denote the class of all safe ω-regular languages.

b^*a^{ω} is not a safe language. Indeed, every prefix b^n of b^{ω} (which is not in the language) is a prefix of $b^n a^{\omega}$ (which is in the language). On the other hand, $b^*a^{\omega} + b^{\omega}$ is safe. It follows that **Safe**$_\omega(\Sigma) \neq$ **Det**$_\omega(\Sigma)$ and we are going to show (Theorem 1) that **Safe**$_\omega(\Sigma) \subset$ **Det**$_\omega(\Sigma)$.

A *DB*-machine is a deterministic Büchi automaton where $F=Q$.

Theorem 1. *L is a safe ω-regular language iff L is recognized by a DB-machine.*

We introduce the following definitions in order to prove the previous theorem:

Definition 1. *$P \subseteq \Sigma^*$ is a regular prefix language if and only if:*
1. *P is regular;*
2. *every prefix of a word of P is a word of P: $\forall u \in \Sigma^* \ \forall a \in \Sigma: ua \in P \Rightarrow u \in P$;*
3. *every word of P is a proper prefix of another word of P: $\forall u \in P \ \exists a \in \Sigma: ua \in P$.*

Definition 2. *A dfa A is a prefix automaton (or prefix dfa) if and only if*
1. *every state is final;*
2. *every state is alive: $\forall q \in Q, \ \exists a \in \Sigma: \delta(q, a) \in Q$.*

Proposition 1.
1. *If L is an ω-regular language, then Pref(L) is a regular prefix language;*
2. *if P is a regular prefix language, then there exists a prefix automaton which recognizes P;*
3. *if $A = \langle Q, \Sigma, \delta, Q, q_0 \rangle$ is a prefix automaton, then the language $L(M)$ recognized by the DB-machine $M = \langle Q, \Sigma, \delta, Q, q_0 \rangle$ is ω-regular and satisfies $L(A) = Pref(L(M))$.*

Proof. Notice that several different ω-languages can have the same prefix language.

1) Let $P = Pref(L)$. L is ω-regular, so there are sequences of regular languages $\langle A_i \rangle_{i \in [n]}$ and $\langle B_i \rangle_{i \in [n]}$ such that $L = \bigcup_{i=1}^{i=n} A_i B_i^{\omega}$. $Pref(\bigcup_{i=1}^{i=n} A_i B_i^{\omega}) = \bigcup_{i=1}^{i=n} Pref(A_i) \cup A_i B_i^* Pref(B_i)$ is a regular language which is closed by prefixes. Let $u \in P$. As $P = Pref(L)$, there exists $v \in \Sigma^{\omega}$ such that $uv \in L$. Let a be the first letter of v. Then ua is a prefix of uv, so $ua \in P$.

2) Let P be a regular prefix language. P is recognized by a *dfa* A which is minimal but not necessarily complete (*ie*, we remove its dead-state if necessary). As P is prefix, every state of this automaton is final. Finally, let q be a state of A and u a word such that $\delta(q_0, u) = q$. By the definition of a prefix language, there exists $a \in \Sigma$ such that $ua \in P$. So $\delta(q, a) \in Q$, thus q is alive.

3) Let $A=<Q, \Sigma, \delta, Q, q_0>$ be a prefix automaton. Consider the corresponding DB-machine $M=<Q, \Sigma, \delta, Q, q_0>$. Let us prove that $Pref(L(M))=L(A)$. Let $u \in Pref(L(M))$. Then there exists $w \in \Sigma^\omega$ such that $uw \in L(M)$. It is clear that $\delta(q_0, u) \in Q$, so $u \in L(A)$. Conversely, let $u \in L(A)$ and $q=\delta(q_0, u)$. As q is alive, we can build two words v and w such that $\delta(q, v)=q'$ and $\delta(q', w)=q'$. Clearly, the run C_{uvw^ω} goes infinitely often through state q'. So $uvw^\omega \in L(M)$ and $u \in Pref(L(M))$.

Proof of Theorem 1. Let L be a language recognized by a DB-machine $M=<Q, \Sigma, \delta, Q, q_0>$ and $w \in \Sigma^\omega$. Assume that every prefix u_n of w can be continued into a word of L recognized by M. The mapping $C_w: N \to Q$ such that $C_w(0)=q_0$ and $\forall i \in N, C_w(i+1)= \delta(C_w(i), u_i(i))= \delta(C_w(i), w(i))$ is a run of M on w. Since all the states of M are marked, this run is successful, so $w \in L$. Hence, L is a safe ω-regular language. Conversely, let L be a safe ω-regular language. By Proposition 1, $Pref(L)$ is a regular prefix language which is recognized by some prefix automaton $A=<Q, \Sigma, \delta, Q, q_0>$. We claim that L is recognized by the DB-machine $M=<Q, \Sigma, \delta, Q, q_0>$. Indeed, by Proposition 1, the language $L(M)$ satisfies $Pref(L(M))= L(A)$. Moreover, by the first part of this proof, $L(M)$ is a safe language (since M is a DB-machine). So L and $L(M)$ are both safe languages such that $Pref(L)=Pref(L(M))=L(A)$. Assume that there exists a word w in L and not in $L(M)$ (or vice-versa). As $Pref(L)=Pref(L(M))$, every prefix of w is in $Pref(L(M))$. Since $L(M)$ is a safe language, w itself is in $L(M)$, which is impossible. So $L=L(M)$.

Corollary 1. *Let L and L' be two safe ω-regular languages. $Pref(L)=Pref(L')\Leftrightarrow L=L'$.*

Proof. $\Leftarrow$ is straightforward. $\Rightarrow$ is an immediate consequence of the previous proof.

3   Learning ω-Regular Languages from Their Prefixes

One of the main difficulties consists in explaining the meaning of "p is a positive prefix of the ω-language L" and "n is a negative prefix of the ω-language L". The meaning of prefixes and the interesting cases to be studied depend on the context of our problem.

Definition 3.
1. p is an $\exists$-positive prefix of L iff $\exists u \in \Sigma^\omega$, $pu \in L$
2. p is a $\forall$-positive prefix of L iff $\forall u \in \Sigma^\omega$, $pu \in L$
3. n is an $\exists$-negative prefix of L iff $\exists u \in \Sigma^\omega$, $nu \notin L$
4. n is a $\forall$-negative prefix of L iff $\forall u \in \Sigma^\omega$, $nu \notin L$

Given an ω-language L, let $P_\forall(L)$ denote the set of all $\forall$-positive prefixes of L, $P_\exists(L)$ the set of all $\exists$-positive prefixes of L, $N_\forall(L)$ the set of all $\forall$-negative prefixes of L, and $N_\exists(L)$ the set of all $\exists$-negative prefixes of L.

Two finite sets $S+$ and $S-$ of finite words form together a set of (p, n)-examples for an ω-language L if and only if $S+ \subseteq P_p(L)$ and $S- \subseteq N_n(L)$.

For instance, on the automaton 2a, $L=((a+b)*a)^\omega$, $P_\forall(L)=N_\forall(L)=\varnothing$ and $P_\exists(L)=N_\exists(L)=\Sigma^*$.

We can also remark that for all ω-languages L, $P_\exists(L)=Pref(L)$ and
$$P_\exists(L) \cap N_\forall(L) = P_\forall(L) \cap N_\exists(L) = \varnothing \qquad P_\exists(L) \cup N_\forall(L) = P_\forall(L) \cup N_\exists(L) = \Sigma^*$$
$$P_\forall(L) = N_\forall(\Sigma^\omega \backslash L) \qquad\qquad\qquad P_\exists(L) = N_\exists(\Sigma^\omega \backslash L)$$

3.1   On Convergence Criteria

In this section, we adapt the definitions of Gold [5] and de la Higuera [7]. Other paradigms than identification in the limit are known, but they are often either similar to these or harder to establish. A comparison between different models can be found in [11].

It will be useful to systematically consider a class L of languages and an associated class R of representations. The latter one will have to be strong enough to represent the whole class of languages, *i.e.* $\forall L \in L,\ \exists r \in R:\ L(r)=L$.

The size of a representation (denoted $|r|$) is polynomially related to the size of its encoding. In the case of a deterministic automaton, the number of states is a relevant measure, since the alphabet has a constant size.

All the classes we consider are recursively enumerable. Moreover, for Büchi automata and finite words, given $x \in \{\exists, \forall\}$, the problems "$w \in P_x(L(A))$?" and "$w \in N_x(L(A))$?" are decidable, so the definition of identification in the limit from prefixes can be presented as follows:

Definition 4. *A class L of ω-languages is (p, n)-identifiable in the limit for a class R of representations if and only if there exists an algorithm A such that:*
1. *given a finite set <S+, S-> of prefixes, with $S+ \subseteq P_p(L)$ and $S- \subseteq N_n(L)$, A returns h in R consistent with <S+, S->;*
2. *for all representations r of a language L in L, there exists a finite characteristic set <CS+, CS->, such that, on <S+, S-> with $CS+ \subseteq S+ \subseteq P_p(L)$ and $CS- \subseteq S- \subseteq N_n(L)$, A returns a hypothesis h equivalent to r.*

We now adapt the definition of polynomial identification in the limit from fixed data [5, 7] to the case of learning from prefixes. This definition takes better care of practical considerations: for instance with this definition, deterministic finite automata are learnable whereas context-free grammars or non-deterministic automata are not.

Definition 5. *A class L of ω-languages is (p, n)-polynomially identifiable in the limit from fixed finite prefixes for a class R of representations if and only if there exists an algorithm A and two polynomials $\alpha()$ and $\beta()$ such that:*
1. *given a set <S+, S-> of prefixes of size m^1, with $S+ \subseteq P_p(L)$ and $S- \subseteq N_n(L)$, A returns h in R in $O(\alpha(m))$ time and h is consistent with <S+, S->;*
2. *for all representations r of size n of a language L in L, there exists a characteristic set <CS+, CS-> of size at most $\beta(n)$, such that, on <S+, S-> with $CS+ \subseteq S+ \subseteq P_p(L)$ and $CS- \subseteq S- \subseteq N_n(L)$, A returns a hypothesis h equivalent to r.*

---

[1] The size of a set S of finite words is the sum of the length of all the words in S.

3.2   The Problem of Learning ω-Languages from Their Prefixes

We have now defined the different parameters of the problem. The main question is: can the class L of ω-regular languages represented by R be learned following the criterion C from a set of (p, n)-examples?

The classes L we are interested in are those defined in section 2. The representation classes are B-Aut (Büchi automata) for $\mathbf{Reg}_\omega(\Sigma)$, DB-Aut (deterministic Büchi automata) for $\mathbf{Det}_\omega(\Sigma)$ and DB-Mach (DB-machines) for $\mathbf{Safe}_\omega(\Sigma)$. The criteria will be identification in the limit and polynomial identification in the limit from fixed prefixes. The examples of positive and negative prefixes will be defined according to the different combinations of the quantifiers $\exists$ and $\forall$.

Hence a learning problem will be completely specified when given:
1. the class of languages and its representation class;
2. the convergence criterion;
3. the interpretation one gives to positive and negative prefixes.

A problem will thus be a triple <L_R, *criterion*, *interpretation*> where *criterion* will be *idlim* (identification in limit) or *polyid* (polynomial identification in the limit from fixed prefixes) and *interpretation* will be a pair (p, n) such that p and $n \in \{\exists, \forall\}$.

Example. The problem <$\mathbf{Safe}_\omega(\Sigma)_{DB\text{-Mach}}$, *idlim*, $(\exists, \forall)$> is the one of identification in the limit of the class $\mathbf{Safe}_\omega(\Sigma)$ where the languages are represented by DB-machines and a presentation made of existential positive prefixes and universal negative prefixes (see definition 3) is given. Such a problem will have a "positive status" if this class is actually learnable with the chosen criterion, a "negative status" if it is not and an "unknown status" if the problem is unsolved.

4   Results

We give two types of results. The first concerns classes $\mathbf{Reg}_\omega(\Sigma)$ and $\mathbf{Det}_\omega(\Sigma)$, for which identification in the limit from prefixes is impossible. The second concerns the class of safe languages, for which polynomial identification in the limit by fixed prefixes is proved.

4.1   General Properties

We first give a straightforward reduction property; we establish that polynomial identification only holds when identification in the limit also holds: if <L_R, *idlim*, *sign*> has a negative status, so does <L_R, *polyid*, *sign*>.

A necessary condition for the identification of a class of languages is that any pair of languages from the class can be effectively separated by some prefix:

Lemma 1. *Let L be a class of ω-languages and R a class of representations for L. If there exist L_1 and L_2 in L such that $L_1 \neq L_2$, $P_p(L_1) = P_p(L_2)$ and $N_n(L_1) = N_n(L_2)$, then the problem <L_R, idlim, (p, n)> has a negative status.*

Proof. Suppose that an algorithm A identifies class L; then L_1 and L_2 have respective characteristic sets CS_1 and CS_2. But L_1 and L_2 are consistent with $CS_1 \cup CS_2$. Hence either L_1 or L_2 is not identified.

Theorem 2. *For any class of representations R, $\forall p$, $n \in \{\exists, \forall\}$, $<Reg_\omega(\Sigma)_R$, idlim, $(p, n)>$ and $<Det_\omega(\Sigma)_R$, idlim, $(p, n)>$ have negative status.*

Proof. We will use the same counter-example, shown in Figure 3, to prove that neither the class of all ω-regular languages, nor that of all ω-deterministic ones are identifiable in the limit (and furthermore polynomially identifiable from given prefixes). The languages accepted by automata 3a and 3b are respectively $L_1 = a^\omega + a^*ba^*b(a+b)^\omega$ and $L_2 = a^*ba^*b(a+b)^\omega$. Whatever the choice of quantifiers p and n, languages P_p and N_n are identical in both cases.

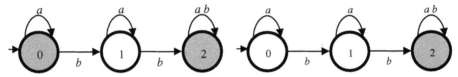

Fig. 3. Automata 3a and 3b accept respectively languages $a^\omega + a^*ba^*b(a+b)^\omega$ and $a^*ba^*b(a+b)^\omega$.

Formally:

$P_\exists(L_1) = P_\exists(L_2) = \Sigma^*$ $N_\exists(L_1) = N_\exists(L_2) = a^* + a^*ba^*$

$P_\forall(L_1) = P_\forall(L_2) = a^*ba^*b(a+b)^*$ $N_\forall(L_1) = N_\forall(L_2) = \emptyset$

4.2   On the Identification of Safe Languages

The previous result is very negative, but hardly surprising. It implies that learning requires either to consider a subclass of languages, and/or to change the convergence criterion. It is surely not reasonable to choose a less demanding criterion than identification in the limit; we will thus concentrate on a subclass of ω-deterministic languages in the sequel: the safe ω-languages. We first prove that the associated class of prefix languages is polynomially identifiable in the limit from given data:

Proposition 2. *The class of regular prefix languages, represented by prefix dfas, is polynomially identifiable in the limit from given prefixes.*

Proof. To prove the above proposition we use algorithm *RPNI*-prefixes1. An alternative and more efficient algorithm, that can return a compatible non trivial prefix automaton, even when the characteristic set is not included in the data is proposed in the appendix. As for *RPNI*-prefixes1, it makes use, as a sub-routine, of *RPNI* [10] which can identify a *dfa* from positive and negative data (typically two finite sets of finite words $S+$ and $S-$).

The first object *RPNI* builds is the prefix tree acceptor (*pta*): this is the largest *dfa* with no useless[2] states recognizing exactly $S+$.

---

[2] A state is useless if it does not lead to an accepting state, or is not accessible from the initial state.

Algorithm *RPNI-prefixes1*

```
Input: S=<S+,S-> (a set of positive words S+, and
of negative words S-)
Output: a prefix automaton (<Q, Σ, δ, F, q₀>)
Begin
 A←RPNI(S+, S-);
 If A is a prefix dfa
    then return A
    else max_neg←max{length(u): u∈S-};
         For all w in S+ s.t. w∈Pref(S-) and
                   w∉(Pref(S+)\{w}) do
                Compute v of length max_neg s.t.
                   Pref(v)∩S-=∅ and w∈Pref(v);
                S+←S+∪{v};
         A←PTA(S+);
         Q←Q∪{q_f}; F←Q;
         For all a in Σ do δ(q_f, a)← q_f;
         For all q in Q such that q is a leaf do
                For all a in Σ do δ(q, a)← q_f;
         Return A
end.
```

If $<S+, S->$ contains a characteristic set of the target language L, *RPNI* returns a prefix automaton A that accepts language L [10]. If $<S+, S->$ does not contain a characteristic set, *RPNI* returns an automaton which is consistent with $<S+, S->$, but may be neither prefix nor even transformable into a prefix automaton. In that case *RPNI*-prefixes1 transforms the *pta* into a consistent prefix automaton.

Indeed function PTA(S+) constructs the *pta* corresponding to $S+$ in which are added extra words whose positive labeling does not introduce inconsistency; testing (w∈Pref(S-) and w∉Pref(S+)\{w}) allows to know which states of the *pta* have no successors; these states must then lead to a new universal[3] state q_f whenever the new transition is not used by some negative word: such a transition always exists since the data is supposed to be consistent. Building a polynomial implementation is straightforward.

Theorem 3. $<Safe_ω(Σ)_{DB-Mach}, polyid, (∃, ∀)>$ *a has positive status.*

Proof. We show that the conditions of definition 5 are met:

i. Let L be a safe language. On any pair of sets $<S+, S->$ of $(∃, ∀)$-prefixes for L, by proposition 2 a prefix *dfa* accepting $S+$ and rejecting $S-$ can be returned in polynomial time. In constant time this automaton is transformed into a *DB-machine* M by changing the acceptance criterion. Furthermore $S+⊆Pref(L(M))$ and $S-∩Pref(L(M))=∅$.

---

[3] A state is universal if by any letter there is a transition to the same state.

ii. Let L be a safe language, and M a DB-machine accepting L. Let A be the prefix automaton associated with M. Let $<CS+, CS->$ be a characteristic set for A and $RPNI$. Let now $<S+, S->$ be such that $CS+\subseteq S+$, $CS-\subseteq S-$, $S+\subseteq L(A)$ and $S-\cap L(A)=\emptyset$. Notice that the size of $<CS+, CS->$ is polynomial in that of A which in turn is the same as the size of M. On input $<S+, S->$ $RPNI$ returns an automaton A' equivalent to A. By construction, the DB-machine M' associated to A' is such that $Pref(L(M'))=L(A')=L(A)=Pref(L(M))$. By corollary 1 $L(M)=L(M')$ holds.

Theorem 4. *If L strictly contains $\mathbf{Safe}_\omega(\Sigma)$ and R is a class of machines for L, $<L_R,$ idlim, $(\exists, \forall)>$ has a negative status.*

Proof. Let L be a class containing strictly $\mathbf{Safe}_\omega(\Sigma)$ and L a language in L but not in $\mathbf{Safe}_\omega(\Sigma)$. $P_\exists(L)$ is a prefix language. But in that case there exists a language L' in $\mathbf{Safe}_\omega(\Sigma)$ such that $P_\exists(L)=P_\exists(L')$ and $N_\forall(L)=N_\forall(L')$. By lemma 1, it follows that L is not identifiable.

Theorems 3 and 4 allow us to deduct a final result concerning learning from $(\forall, \exists)$-prefixes. An ω-language L is co-safe *iff* its complementary $\Sigma^\omega \setminus L$ is a safe language. We denote $\mathbf{Co\text{-}Safe}_\omega(\Sigma)$ the family of co-safe ω-regular languages. Co-safe languages are accepted by co-DB-machines, *i.e.* complete Büchi automata with a unique marked state which is a universal state.

Theorem 5. *$<Co\text{-}Safe_\omega(\Sigma)_{co\text{-}DB\text{-}Mach},$ polyid, $(\forall, \exists)>$ has a positive status. Furthermore for any class L strictly containing $\mathbf{Co\text{-}Safe}_\omega(\Sigma)$, and R a class of machines for L, $<L_R,$ idlim, $(\forall, \exists)>$ has negative status.*

Proof. Any complete prefix presentation by $(\forall, \exists)$ of a co-safe language L is a complete prefix presentation by $(\exists, \forall)$ of the safe language $\Sigma^\omega\setminus L$, since $P_\exists(\Sigma^\omega\setminus L)=N_\exists(L)$ and $N_\forall(\Sigma^\omega\setminus L)=P_\forall(L)$. Moreover the construction of a co-DB-machine from a DB-machine can be done in linear time by completing it with a universal state which becomes the marked state. From theorem 3, the problem $<\mathbf{Safe}_\omega(\Sigma)_{DB\text{-}Mach},$ polyid, $(\exists, \forall)>$ has a positive status, and so has $<\mathbf{Co\text{-}Safe}_\omega(\Sigma)_{co\text{-}DB\text{-}Mach},$ polyid, $(\forall, \exists)>$.

5   Conclusion

This work is a first approach to the problem of learning or identifying automata on infinite words from finite prefixes. A certain number of open questions and new research directions can be proposed. Among those we mention:

The problem $<?_?,$ *criterion*, $(\exists, \exists)>$. It is rather easy to show that for all the classes of languages studied in this paper, the status will be negative. It seems relevant to find a class of languages (undoubtedly rather restricted) for which the status would be positive.

Learning from prefix queries (membership queries on the prefixes) and equivalence queries.

Improvement of the inference algorithm (*RPNI*-prefixes) for the learning of the prefix languages. The algorithm proposed is polynomial. It is however neither easy to implement, nor (probably) does it perform well in practice.

Lastly, the validation of this algorithm on real data (produced by a system), remains to be done. The type of automata corresponding to real world tasks has the characteristic to have an important alphabet, but few outgoing transitions per state. In this context simplification by typing of the alphabet [3] is undoubtedly a track to be retained.

Acknowledgement. The authors would like to thank Maurice Nivat who suggested the problem.

References

1. B. Alpern, A.J. Demers and F.B. Schneider. Defining Liveness. *Information Processing Letters* 21, 181-185, 1985.
2. D. Angluin. On the Complexity of Minimum Inference of Regular Sets. *Information and Control* 39, 337–350, 1978.
3. M. Bernard and C. de la Higuera. Apprentissage de Programmes Logiques par Inférence Grammaticale, *Revue d'Intelligence Artificielle*, 14/3-4, 375-396, 2001.
4. J.R. Büchi. On a decision method in restricted second order arithmetic. *Proc. Cong. Logic Method and Philos. Of Sci.*, Stanford Univ. Press, California, 1960.
5. M.E. Gold. Complexity of Automaton Identification from Given Data, *Information and Control*, 37, 302-320, 1978.
6. C. de la Higuera, J. Oncina and E. Vidal. Identification of dfa's:data dependant vs data-independant algorithms,.*in Proceedings of ICGI '96*, LNAI 1147, Springer-Verlag, 1996.
7. C. de la Higuera. Characteristic Sets for Polynomial Grammatical Inference, *Machine Learning* 27, 125-138, 1997.
8. K. Lang, B.A. Pearlmutter and R.A. Price. Results of the Abbadingo One DFA Learning Competition and a New Evidence-Driven State Merging Algorithm, in Grammatical Inference, *Proceedings of ICGI '98*, LNAI 1433, Springer Verlag, 1-12, 1998.
9. O. Maler and A. Pnueli. On the Learnability of Infinitary Regular Sets, *Proc. 4th COLT*, 128-136, Morgan Kauffman, San Mateo, 1991.
10. J. Oncina and P. Garcia. Identifying Regular Languages in Polynomial Time, in *Advances in Structural and Syntactic Pattern Recognition*, H. Bunke ed., Series in Machine Perception and Artificial Intelligence 5, 99-108, 1992.
11. R.J. Parekh and V. Honavar. On the relationship between Models for Learning in Helpful Environments, in *Proceedings of ICGI 2000*, LNAI 1891, Springer Verlag, 207-220, 2000.
12. A. Saoudi and T. Yokomori. Learning Local and Recognizable ω-languages and Monadic Logic Programs, in *Proceedings of EUROCOLT*, LNCS, Springer Verlag, 1993.
13. W. Thomas. Automata on infinite objects, *Handbook of Theoretical Computer Science* (Van Leewen ed.), 133-191, North-Holland, Amsterdam, 1990.
14. M.Y. Vardi and P. Wolper. Automata-Theoretic Techniques in Modal Logics of Programs, Journal of Computer and Systems Science 32, 183-221, 1986.

Appendix: A Constructive Prefix dfa Inference Algorithm

The algorithm proposed in section 4 identifies polynomially and in the limit from given data any prefix automaton. It is nevertheless practically a useless algorithm: one is never sure to have a characteristic set inside his learning data, and returning the *pta* with some added edges is not convincing. We give here a specific prefix automaton learning algorithm. It is based on *RPNI* [10], and uses notations from [6].

Algorithm *RPNI*-prefixes2 adds to S+ all prefixes of S+, and goes through a typical state merging routine. The only problem is to make sure that every merge leads to an automaton that will be completable into a prefix automaton. To do this each positive state has to stay alive: there must be at least one infinite word leading from this state that avoids every negative state.

Algorithm *RPNI*-prefixes2

```
Input: S=<S+, S->
Output: a prefix automaton (defined by δ, F+, F-)
Begin
  (*Initializations*)
  S+←S+∪Pref(S+); n←0;
  ∀a∈Σ, Tested(q₀, a)←∅; F+←{q₀}; F-←∅;
  While there are some unmarked words in S+∪S- do
     <q, a, q'>←chose_transition();
     If Possible(δ(q, a)=q')
          then δ(q, a)←q';
               For all unmarked w in S+ do
                    If δ(q₀, w)=q" then mark (w);
                                          F+←F+∪{q"};
               For all unmarked w in S- do
                    If δ(q₀, w)=q" then mark (w);
                                          F-←F-∪{q"};
          else Tested(q, a)←Tested(q, a) ∪{q'};
     If |Tested(q, a)|=n+1 (*impossible to merge *)
          then (*creation of a new state*)
               n←n+1; Q←Q∪{qₙ}; δ(q, a)← qₙ;
               For all unmarked w in S+ do
                    If δ(q₀, w)=q" then mark(w);
                                          F+←F+∪{q"};
               For all unmarked w in S- do
                    If δ(q₀, w)=q" then mark(w);
                                          F-←F-∪{q"};
     ∀a∈Σ, Tested(qₙ, a)←∅;
End_while;
```

```
(* conversion into a consistent prefix dfa*)
Q←F+;
For all q∈F+ such that ∀a∈Σ δ(q, a)∉Q
        chose w minimal such that
                ({u: δ(q₀, u)=q}.Pref(w))∩S- = ∅;

        Q←Q∪{qᵢʷ: 0<i<|w|};

        F+←F+∪{qᵢʷ: 0<i<|w|};

        δ(q, w(0))←q₁ʷ;
        For all i from 0 to |w| do
                                    δ(qᵢ₋₁ʷ, w(i))←qᵢʷ;
            For all a in Σ do δ(q|w|ʷ, a)←q|w|ʷ;
End.
```

Function Chose_transition: returns a triplet $<q, a, q'>$ corresponding to the transition $\delta(q, a)=q'$ where $\delta(q, a)$ is undefined and $q'\notin$ Tested(q, a). Different functions can work. Typically EDSM type functions have been shown preferable [8].

Function Possible($\delta(q, a)=q'$): returns True if adding to δ rule (q, a, q') does not lead to an inconsistency, False otherwise.

Inconsistency is tested on the current automaton on which rule $\delta(q, a)=q'$ is added. It can have two causes:
- there exists two words uaw and vw such that $\delta(q_0, u)=q$ and $\delta(q_0, v)=q'$ and $uaw\in S+$, $vw\notin S-$, and $uaw\notin S-$, $vw\in S+$.
- a state is no more alive; a state q is alive if it can still lead to an accepting state: $\exists w\in\Sigma^\omega / (\{u: \delta(q_0, u)=q\}.Pref(w))\cap S-=\emptyset$. This insures that the current automaton (and thus by induction the last one) can be transformed into a prefix dfa.

The main elements of the proof of *RPNI*-prefixes2 are:
- The algorithm returns a prefix automaton (by construction).
- The possible test insures that all states are alive and that at any moment the automaton can be transformed into a consistent prefix automaton.
- In the case where a characteristic set (for *RPNI*) is included, no transformation will take place.
- Finally, the algorithm works in polynomial time.

We refer the reader to [6] for a complete proof (in the case of *dfa*s, but the proof can easily be adapted to the case of prefix automata).

Author Index

Lecture Notes in Artificial Intelligence (LNAI)

Lecture Notes in Computer Science